MYCENAE
AND THE MYCENAEAN AGE

MYCENAE AND THE MYCENAEAN AGE

BY GEORGE E. MYLONAS

PRINCETON, NEW JERSEY
PRINCETON UNIVERSITY PRESS
1966

GEORGE E. MYLONAS is the Rosa May Distinguished University Professor in the Humanities at Washington University in St. Louis. He also holds the honorary title of Professor of Archaeology at the University of Athens in Greece. Author of *Ancient Mycenae, The Capital City of Agamemnon* (1957), which this book supplants, he took an active part in the excavation of the second Grave Circle of Mycenae (1952-1954) and since 1958 has directed the current excavations at that site.

The vignette on the title page is from an engraving on a Mycenaean gem found at Mycenae in 1954. It represents the Mycenaean goddess riding through the ether on her mythical animal.

Printed in the United States of America
by Princeton University Press, Princeton, New Jersey
Illustrations printed by the Meriden Gravure Company
Meriden, Connecticut

To
LELLA

PREFACE AND ACKNOWLEDGMENTS

In 1893 Chrestos Tsountas published in Athens a book that gave for the first time a clear picture of what came to be known as Mycenaean civilization. Shortly afterwards in 1897, it was translated into English by J. Irving Manatt and published in New York under the title *The Mycenaean Age*. The work became a classic and for two generations served scholar and layman alike. Since that time a great amount of evidence bearing on the subject has been brought to light and published by scholars on both sides of the Atlantic. Excavations continue in the Mycenaean area and almost daily additional information is unearthed. At Mycenae itself the work of the late Professor Alan J. B. Wace and the Greek Archaeological Society of Athens revealed important remains, the existence of which was not even imagined in the early days of Schliemann. The purpose of the present volume is to attempt to bring up to date our knowledge of the Mycenaean Age. In the treatment of the material it follows the arrangement of Tsountas' book and a book of mine entitled *Ancient Mycenae, The Capital City of Agamemnon*. Since the latter, published in 1957, is out of print, the present volume aims to replace it.

A good deal of the material and most of the conclusions contained in this volume were presented in three lectures delivered at Brown University in November 1961, in its series of Charles K. Colver Lectures. For the invitation to participate in the series, I wish to express my thanks to President Barnaby C. Keeney of Brown University. To my late friend of long standing and associate in the cause of Archaeology and the Classics, Professor Charles Alexander Robinson, Jr., whose recent death is mourned by scholars the world over, I am also grateful for the invitation and for the Homeric hospitality extended to me.

The main problems facing the writer of such a volume as this is how much and what part of the material available should be included; how many and which of the theories advanced and known should be analyzed or refuted; which of the remains should be illustrated and how much scope should be allowed to fantasy in an attempt to reconstruct the life and culture of the Heroic Age; how many of the dry facts and statistics can be included without making the book too difficult for the general reader. I have tried to give the important facts without a mound of numbers, to go into detail only in the case of theories which have either become or are tending to become dogmas, to refute preconceived ideas which do not correspond to the evidence unearthed by the pick and shovel of the excavator. We believe that the Mycenaean Age, as well as any other, should not be viewed through the remains of a single site or section to which a writer has had access, but through the cumulative evidence amassed from all over the area by different scholars; that theories and varied explanations should not be created in the confines of libraries but that they should be based on excavations known at first hand, on knowledge derived from long association with the country and its remains. The Mycenaean Age should no longer be an exercise for the imagination, but the subject of serious study based on precise and clearly established evidence.

In the transliteration of Greek into English, I have followed the standard practice of the American School of Classical Studies in Athens.

The Mycenaean Age will often be referred to as the Late Helladic Period (=LH) and will be subdivided as usual into LH I, II, and III. There is no general agreement on the absolute chronology of the sub-periods of the Age and especially of the LH III B and C. For our purpose we shall adopt the general dates shown in the chronology on p. 237.

Perhaps the pleasantest task of a writer is the privilege of acknowledging his indebtedness

vii

to friends and institutions whose encouragement and help made his work possible. Sincere thanks are due to the American Philosophical Society, to the John Simon Guggenheim Foundation, and to the American Council of Learned Societies, for the grants and fellowships that made it possible for me to return to Greece and take an active part in excavating its soil. To Washington University of St. Louis and its Chancellors, Ethan A. H. Shepley and Thomas H. Eliot, I am grateful for their interest in my research and for leaves of absence granted for the purpose. To the many friends in St. Louis who make possible the continuation of my work in Greece, I wish to express my gratitude for their sustained help and encouragement.

To the Council of the Archaeological Society of Athens and to its General Secretary Professor Anastasios K. Orlandos, to the Archaeological Council of the Service and its late General Director John Papadimitriou, to Dr. John Kondis, Acting General Director of Antiquities, I am grateful for entrusting me with the direction of the excavations at Mycenae and for the privilege of continuing the work of Tsountas and Wace. To the Ephor of the district and my collaborator, Dr. N. Verdelis, to my collaborators and assistants, Dr. S. Iacovides, Dr. T. Leslie Shear, Jr., Mrs. Ione Mylonas Shear, Mrs. E. Papantoniou, Dr. Betty Grossman, Mrs. Lucia King O'Reilly, the Misses Elizabeth Brokaw, Nancy Bookides, Nike Skouphopoulou, Mary Koutroubakis, Arghyro Tataki, to Mr. Andrew Love, and to my architects and artists, Messrs. A. Papaeliopoulos, J. Bandekas, A. Petronotes, R. Rothman, G. Compton, W. Roudebush, G. L. Garvey, and J. H. Collins, I express my great indebtedness and thanks for their generous help and faithful work.

All photographs published here, with the exception of those acknowledged at the end of the Preface, are the work of Mr. N. Tombazis, the faithful collaborator and friend of Mycenae, to whom my thanks are offered. Thanks are also due to the colleagues who allowed me to use their photographs and drawings in this work and especially to Professor Carl W. Blegen, Dr. C. Karouzos, Professor A. Prokopiou, Dr. E. Stikas, Dr. N. Verdelis, Dr. S. Iacovides, Dr. S. Alexiou, Mrs. John Threpsiades, Miss Marion Rawson, and Miss Alison Frantz, and the Royal Hellenic Air Force.

To Mrs. Harvard Hecker I owe especial thanks for reading the manuscript and for many valuable suggestions and corrections. Last but not least in this long record are my faithful laborers headed by Panayiotes Vlachos, whose work brings our campaigns to a successful end; to them as well as to the guards of Mycenae I express again cordial thanks. To the friend of all archaeologists and mine, Mr. T. Karadondis, and to his personnel of the Tourists' Pavilion, I owe special thanks on behalf of the members of our excavations for unceasing and most successful efforts to make our stay at Mycenae a happy one.

The reading of this volume will make evident my indebtedness to the work and publications of Tsountas and Wace. Words will never convey the full measure of our indebtedness to those who have gone ahead, but who while with us blazed the trail which we follow. The memory of Schliemann, of Tsountas, of Wace, and of Papadimitriou will remain alive as long as the Lions guard the Gate of Mycenae. My indebtedness to the other scholars who labor in the field will also become evident from my numerous references to their excavations and publications; to them go my sincere thanks. Especially I wish to express my gratitude to Professor Carl W. Blegen for the many years of instruction, advice, and friendship, and for the privilege of working under him at the American School of Classical Studies in Athens and in the excavations of the Palace of Nestor. To the Director of the School, Professor Henry S. Robinson, I am also grateful for making available to us the facilities of the School.

Preface and Acknowledgments

To the Princeton University Press, its Director, Herbert S. Bailey, Jr., and especially its Fine Arts Editor, Miss Harriet Anderson, I am grateful for their advice, corrections, and care extended in the preparation and publication of this volume. I am grateful, likewise, to the Meriden Gravure Company, to its manager Harold Hugo and to John Peckham for excellent reproduction of my photographs and drawings.

This volume is gratefully and humbly dedicated to my wife Lella as a very small token of my deep appreciation of lifelong dedicated comradeship and help, of unselfish love and devotion with which she has blessed and strengthened my life:

Τῷ οἱ κλέος οὔ ποτ᾽ ὀλεῖται ἧς ἀρετῆς.
(Odyssey, xxiv, 196)

Washington University
St. Louis, Mo.

G.E.M.

Acknowledgment is made to the following for the use of photographs:

Alexiou, S., Fig. 134
Blegen, C. W., Figs. 52-55, 137
Frantz, A., Figs. 2, 3, 5, 46, 84, 85, 113, 120, 140, 141
Iacovides, S., Fig. 152
Kallipolites, V. G., Fig. 132
Karouzos, C., Figs. 129, 143
National Museum of Athens, Figs. 121, 131
Prokopiou, A., Fig. 43
Royal Hellenic Air Force, Figs. 8a, 9, 48, 69
Shear, T. L., Jr., Fig. 56
Stikas, E., Figs. 17, 18, 20, 116
Threpsiades, J. Mrs., 49, 50, 74-77
Verdelis, N., 6, 7, 145

CONTENTS

LIST OF ILLUSTRATIONS

TEXT FIGURES

MYCENAE
AND THE MYCENAEAN AGE

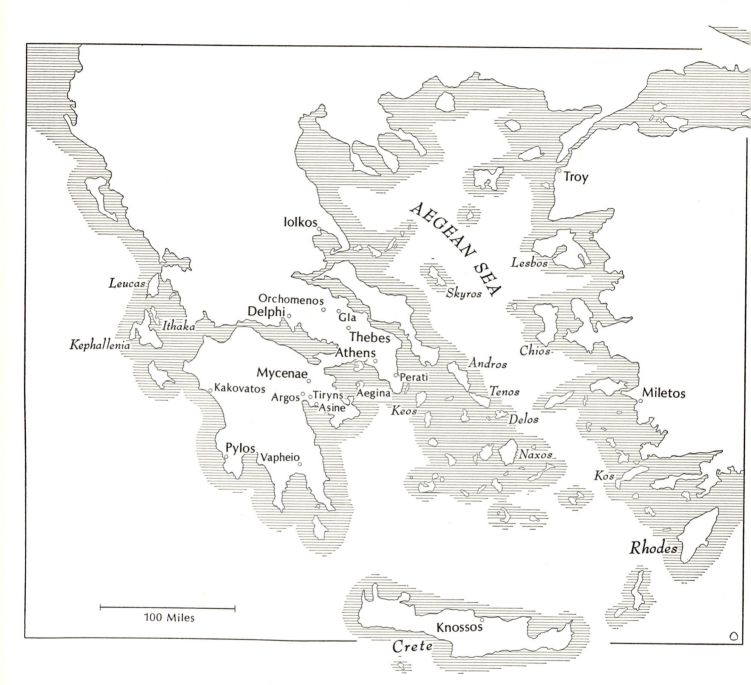

Troy

Iolkos

Aegean Sea

Lesbos

Skyros

Leucas

Orchomenos

Delphi

Gla

Ithaka

Thebes

Chios

Kephallenia

Athens

Andros

Mycenae

Perati

Miletos

Kakovatos

Aegina

Tenos

Argos Tiryns

Asine

Keos

Delos

Pylos

Vapheio

Naxos

Kos

Rhodes

Knossos

Crete

100 Miles

CENTERS OF MYCENAEAN CIVILIZATION

CHAPTER I

INTRODUCTION

The first Greek-speaking, Indo-European tribes appear to have come to the mainland of Greece about 1900 B.C., at the beginning of the Middle Bronze Age, as Carl Blegen was the first to maintain. For a long time it was believed that the Indo-Europeans came from the north along the Pindos Mountains, but now it is generally suggested that they came from the northwest corner of Asia Minor along the Southern coastline of Thrace and Macedonia to the area below Thessaly.[1] At any rate, they established themselves in the greatest numbers on the eastern half of the mainland, their chief domain being Boiotia, Attika, and the Argolis. They brought with them a rather unimpressive culture, characterized by a monochrome, wheelmade pottery, of good technical quality, gray in color and of smooth finish, almost soapy in texture. Their vases seem to imitate metallic prototypes, have a carinated profile, and high swinging handles. They became known as Minyan ware, a name suggested by Schliemann, who was among the first to find it at the Minyan Orchomenos in Boiotia. Along with the Minyan ware they developed a patterned ware known as matt-painted, because the designs, usually linear geometric, are often applied directly to the clay with a dull black paint.

The homes of these people were rather small, rectangular structures, often with one end terminating in an apsidal section and the other, the front, in an open portico. Their burial customs are very characteristic of their culture. They buried their dead in rectangular cist graves made of four slabs set vertically in the ground; the floor was covered with pebbles and the cover usually consisted of two slabs. Their small dimensions necessitated the contraction of the bodies laid in them. At first only one person was buried in each grave without any gifts or furnishings. Gradually the graves became family sepulchers. Timidly, gifts for the dead began to appear—a cup, perhaps, or a pitcher—placed alongside the body. Apparently the custom developed under Cretan influence. Very typical of the culture are intramural burials in which the burial, especially of children, was made under the floors or between walls of adjacent houses. Often the bodies of children, particularly of infants, were placed in pots before burial or were laid in a contracted position in small cist graves.[2]

In this manner began the cultural career of the earliest Indo-Europeans who came into the mainland of Greece; a plain beginning, rather coarse and without glamour. From the very start, however, these tribes exhibited the racial characteristic that distinguished the Greeks of the Classical period; they were ready to learn, eager to accept, adopt, and develop new ideas and cultural impulses. It was natural that these people, settled among inhabitants who were racially related to the Cretans, sooner or later would get in touch with the people of that island and would be exposed to the Minoan culture. Under that influence, these mainlanders late in the seventeenth century B.C. began to develop a new culture, the Mycenaean, which gradually and almost at the turn of the century, about 1600 B.C., reached great heights.

THE MYCENAEAN AGE

The Mycenaean Age was as brilliant in its way as the Periklean Age in historic times. This age was brought to light in a dramatic way by the marvelous discoveries of Schliemann, by the treasures preserved in the royal graves of Mycenae and disclosed in 1876. Gold cups, magnificent work in repoussé and inlay, carved semiprecious stones, royal swords, all indicated an affluence and an activity seldom found in the history of prehistoric man. And from the sixteenth century this activity and culture, known as Mycenaean because it was first revealed at Mycenae, developed steadily and spread in ever-widening circles. As early as the sixteenth century Mycenaean pottery appeared in Egypt.[3] Some scholars believe that by the middle of the fifteenth century, by 1450 B.C., the Mycenaeans were able to subdue the great king of Knossos and to establish their domain in the very city of Minos, which they ruled for some fifty years at least.[4]

[1] C. W. Blegen, "The Coming of the Greeks," *AJA*, 32 (1928), pp. 146-154. J. P. Harland, *Prehistoric Aegina*, pp. 111-112. For a recent review of the problem see G. E. Mylonas, "The Luvian Invasions of Greece," *Hesperia*, 31 (1962), pp. 284-309.

[2] C. W. Blegen, *Korakou*, pp. 15-35. Blegen and Wace, "Middle Helladic Tombs," *Symbolae Osloenses*, 9 (1930), pp. 28-37.

Mylonas, "The Cult of the Dead in Helladic Times," in *Studies Presented to David M. Robinson*, I, 1951, pp. 64-105.

[3] Blegen and Wace, *Klio*, 1939, p. 147.

[4] This was Wace's view, cf. J. D. S. Pendlebury, *The Archaeology of Crete*, p. 229. For the occupation of Knossos by the Mycenaeans cf. Sterling Dow, "The Greeks in the Bronze Age,"

From Mycenae and the mainland the influence, and perhaps their domain, spread to the Cyclades beyond the east coast, to the Dodekanese Islands—especially to Rhodes, to Cyprus—and even to Ras Shamra on the coast of Syria, where by 1300 B.C. we find a commercial settlement of Mycenaeans, an "emporion." They seem to have established another trading post in Tell Abu Hawan, near Haifa, in the thirteenth century B.C. From these posts and from along the coast at Askalon and Tell el-Ajjūl near Gaza, their pottery found its way to a number of inland sites in Palestine and Syria. Along the coast of Asia Minor the Mycenaeans must have been established; at Miletos, certainly, and near Halikarnassos and Kolophon, and probably elsewhere.[5] In the Hittite documents of the fourteenth and the thirteenth centuries B.C. we read of a domain called Ahhiyavā,[6] apparently the land of the Achaeans, or Mycenaean Greeks; in fact we seem to have two Ahhiyavās, one on the coast of Asia Minor and another beyond the sea, a greater Ahhiyavā—Achaia whose king was called "brother" by the mighty Hittite rulers.

To the west, also, they must have spread, since we find traces of their pottery in Sicily and South Italy.[7] The thirteenth century marks the period of their farthest expansion and cultural development. In the mainland of Greece we find remnants of their culture at every turn, from Iolkos in Thessaly, the site from which Jason's storied Argonautic expedition started, to Aulis, where the fleet of the Greeks gathered on their way to Troy; to Thebes, the city of fated Oidipous; to Athens, where Athena used to go and rest in the mighty house of Erechtheus; to Mycenae and Sparta, the capital cities where the sons of Atreus ruled; to sandy Pylos, where lived the old man Nestor, wisest of mortals; to Ithaka, the island of the crafty Odysseus. Many of the cities and islands mentioned in the *Iliad* and other legends of Greece are now proved to have been centers of Mycenaean culture.

The Mycenaean Age ended with one of the most publicized wars in the history of mankind even though it was fought centuries ago and between forces which would seem puny today. It was the war fought between the Achaeans and the Trojans—a comparatively small affair raised to heroic proportions and immortalized by gifted bards. For whatever reason that war was fought—whether for the sake of Fair Helen, or for securing a free passage through the Hellespont, or because the Achaeans attempted to fill the vacuum created on the coast of Asia Minor by the destruction of the Hittite Empire, or simply for booty[8]—the fact remains that such a war was fought, that it was a long war, and that it ended with the destruction of Troy. In the devastated remains of Troy VIIa, on the hill of Hissarlik, further excavated by Blegen and the members of his expeditions from the University of Cincinnati, we have the clear evidence of the historicity of that event.[9]

The date of the Fall of Troy is of paramount importance to the study of the Mycenaean Age for, according to the ancient testimony repeated by Thucydides, eighty years after the fall there occurred what is known as the "Descent of the Herakleidai" or "the Dorian Invasion," which is generally assumed to have brought about the collapse of Mycenaean power and the end of the age.[10] To the discussion of chronology we shall return later; here we may remark that the Dorian Invasion seems to have taken place in the course of the twelfth century B.C. It was after that event that the position of preëminence and the role of leadership exercised by Mycenae and the other great centers of the Mycenaean world passed to other centers, to the Dorian city of Argos, to Sparta, and to Corinth. The city of Athens alone escaped destruction, but even the culture and prosperity of Athens were influenced by the great catastrophe that overtook the other Mycenaean centers. At this time its population was apparently augmented by Achaean refugees who were forced by the invaders to abandon their own centers. As a result its culture was set back considerably and underwent a profound change. Here we may note the fact that the city of Athens, which was not destroyed by the Dorians but continued its life uninterrupted from the Mycenaean Age to the Protohistoric and Historic eras, has yielded comparatively few remains to illustrate the activity and culture of its people of the Mycenaean Age. The centers which were destroyed, Mycenae, Tiryns, and Pylos have con-

---

in *XIe Congres internat. des sciences historiques*, 1960, pp. 14-15.

[5] F. H. Stubbings, "The Expansion of Mycenaean Civilization," rev. ed. of *CAH*, I & II, pp. 18-22. A. Furumark, *Chronology of Mycenaean Pottery*, pp. 52 ff., 99 ff., 116 ff. F. H. Stubbings, *Mycenaean Pottery from the Levant*, pp. 8 and 23. A. v. Gerkan and C. Weickert, *Bericht über den VI. internationalen Kongress für Archäologie* (1940), pp. 325-332, pl. 24; and C. Weickert, "Die Ausgrabung bei Athena-Tempel im Milet," *Istanbuler Mitt.*, 7 (1957), pp. 102-132; 9/10 (1959-1960), pp. 1-96. A. Furumark, "The Settlement at Ialysos and Aegean History c. 1500-1400 B.C.," *Opuscula*, 6 (1950), pp. 150-271. G. Bass, *AJA*, 67

(1963), pp. 353 ff. H. Goldman, *AJA*, 27 (1923), pp. 67-68. M. Mellink, *AJA*, 63 (1959), pp. 81-82.

[6] For a recent discussion of Ahhiyavā, cf. D. L. Page, *History and the Homeric Iliad*, pp. 3 ff.

[7] Lord William Taylour, *Mycenaean Pottery in Italy and Adjacent Areas*, 1958. M. Cavalier, *BCH*, 84 (1960), pp. 319-346.

[8] Cf. D. L. Page, *op.cit.*, pp. 68-70, 109-110, and Dow, *op.cit.*, p. 22.

[9] *Infra*, pp. 215 ff. The settlement was revealed originally, of course, by Schliemann and Dörpfeld.

[10] *Infra*, pp. 218 ff.

tributed the most to our knowledge of that age. Speaking of Mycenae, Tsountas long ago remarked that "it was the good fortune of the old Achaean capital to perish in the height of its bloom and to rest almost undisturbed in its buried glory until Schliemann's spade uncovered it. By its fortunate catastrophe Mycenae remains the well-nigh perfect type of the ancient fortress city."[11] The same could be said for Tiryns and Pylos, in spite of the fact that the latter was not a fortified citadel.

TIRYNS

According to legends, Tiryns was the oldest of the three great centers of the Peloponnesos which were destroyed by the Dorians. Proitos, the son of Abas and Okaleia, is reported to have built the citadel after his return from Lykia and after the inconclusive battle against his twin brother Akrisios, the king of Argos.[12] Strabo (VIII, 372) has preserved the tradition that for the construction of the walls of Tiryns the legendary Cyclopes, imported from Lykia, were employed. The same legends tell us that, two or three generations later, Tiryns came under the domination of Sthenelos, the Perseid king of Mycenae, and the stories of the labors of the Tirynthian Herakles and the expulsion of his sons seem to indicate that it remained under the control of Mycenae.[13] Tiryns submitted to Argos during the Dorian Invasion, but, as was the case with Mycenae, some of its people survived the catastrophe and remained on the site among the ruins of the citadel until the Persian wars, when, along with Mycenae, Tiryns contributed a contingent to the army that fought the Persians of Mardonios at Plataiai (479 B.C.). Shortly afterwards, ca. 468 B.C., the people of Argos captured the citadel of Tiryns and forced its inhabitants to settle at Argos.[14] The result of its abandonment and destruction is given by Pausanias in a terse statement: "Nothing is left of the ruins of Tiryns except the wall, which is the work of the Cyclopes." This "wall" has been completely revealed, and in many parts restored in our own day. Schliemann, with the assistance of Dörpfeld, and then Karo and Müller are responsible for the revelation of the ruins of Tiryns.

MYCENAE

The building of Mycenae is attributed by the legends to the mythical Perseus, the son of Zeus and of Danaë, daughter of Akrisios, the king of Argos. Apollodoros tells us how the hero, distressed because of the accidental death of his grandfather Akrisios, "went to Megapenthes, son of Proitos, at Tiryns and effected an exchange with him, surrendering Argos into his hand. So Megapenthes reigned over the Argives, and Perseus reigned over Tiryns, after fortifying also Midea and Mycenae."[15]

Pausanias repeats the story and explains how the site was chosen and how it received its name. According to his version, Mycenae was founded on the site it occupies "because in that site the cap [*mykes*] of his [Perseus'] scabbard had fallen off and he regarded this as a sign to found a city." But he added: "I have also heard that being thirsty he chanced to take up a mushroom [*mykes*] and that water flowing from it he drank, and being pleased gave the place the name of Mycenae." A copious spring at a short distance to the east of the Citadel, known as Perseia, was pointed out in antiquity as the one revealed by the plucking of the mushroom. In our day it still provides the village of Mycenae with a good supply of excellent water. A third derivation of the name from that of a woman named Mykene was discarded by Pausanias.[16] However, even the other two possibilities are aetiological and resulted from the similarity of the first part of the name of the site to the word *mykes*. Perhaps the site was chosen for its dominant position over the Argive plain which gave it control over the passes that led to the north and Corinth, to the east to the plain of Berbati, and to the west to Arkadia. Whatever prompted the choice of the site and inspired its name, the fact remains that Perseus is the acknowledged founder of Mycenae and was venerated as such to the time of Pausanias.[17] For the construction of its walls, as noted above, Perseus is reported to have used the Cyclopes, the legendary builders of Tiryns, and to this tradition Euripides refers when he calls the walls of

---

[11] C. Tsountas and J. I. Manatt, *The Mycenaean Age*, p. 13. (Hereafter referred to as *Mycenaean Age*).

[12] Apollodoros, II, 2, 1. Pausanias, II, 25, 7.

[13] Apollodoros, II, 4, 12.

[14] Pausanias, II, 17, 5; 25, 8; VIII, 27, 1.

[15] Apollodoros, II, 4, 4. Ed. Heyne, tr. Sir J. G. Frazer.

[16] Pausanias, II, 16, cf. tr. Frazer. *Odyssey*, II, 120. Also the derivation from μυκάομαι was not popular in antiquity.

[17] Pausanias, II, 18, 1. Wace, *Mycenae*, p. 22, suggested that copper mines in the mountains of the Argolid provided an additional reason for the strength and wealth of Mycenae. However, as yet no copper mines have been found in the district.

Mycenae Cyclopean and Mycenae itself a Cyclopean city.[18]

The dynasty established at Mycenae by Perseus is known as the Perseid, the earliest known to tradition. It was followed by the Pelopid dynasty established by Atreus, the son of Pelops. Tradition has preserved the story of the change but says little about the length of time during which Perseus and his descendants ruled over Mycenae. We learn from Apollodoros that in Mycenae Perseus had five sons and a daughter by Andromeda: "Alkaios and Sthenelos and Heleus and Nestor and Elektryon and a daughter Gorgophone, whom Perieres married."[19] It is not recorded how many of these sons and their descendants ruled over Mycenae and for how long. We hear that Elektryon and Sthenelos ruled over Mycenae after the death of Perseus. Through Sthenelos the Pelopids came to the site, for he married Nikippe, the daughter of Pelops, and to her at Mycenae her brothers Atreus and Thyestes went when they found themselves in disagreement with their father Pelops. When Eurystheus, the son and successor of Sthenelos, known as the king for whom Herakles performed his exploits, was killed in Attika, the people of Mycenae elected Atreus to rule over them.[20] In this manner, according to tradition, occurred the change of dynasties, and in a peaceful way the Pelopids succeeded the Perseids.

In the *Iliad* we find the story of the succession of the Pelopid dynasty down to the days of Agamemnon.[21] Atreus was succeeded by his brother Thyestes, and he in turn by Agamemnon, the king who led the expedition of the Achaeans against Troy. In the days of the Perseid dynasty the rulers of Mycenae apparently controlled the Argolid and its cities of Argos, Tiryns, and Midea. Their power was increased during the reign of Eurystheus, as the exploits of Herakles indicate, and reached its zenith in the days of the Pelopids. An echo of this growth is preserved in the *Iliad*. There we find that Mycenae had grown to a state that dominated the southern section of Greece, an exalted position reflected in the role of leadership given its king. Agamemnon, the "*anax* of men," is not only the ruler of Mycenae, "the well-built citadel," but also of "wealthy Corinth and well-built Kleonai," of those who "dwelt in Orneiai and lovely Araithyrea and Sikyon . . . ," of those "who held Hyperesia and steep Gonoessa and Pellene," and of those "who dwelt about Aegion and throughout all Aegialos, and about broad

Helike." In other words, Agamemnon supposedly ruled over the northeastern corner of the Peloponnesos. Furthermore, he was the "lord of many isles and of Argos."[22] Apparently it was further believed that his domain included areas far to the southwest of Mycenae, because Agamemnon promised to give Achilles seven well-peopled cities, if only the hero would relent and again join the sorely pressed Achaeans. All seven cities were located in a district at a great distance from the Argive plain, the plain of Mycenae; they were located "by the sea, in the uttermost border of sandy Pylos," on the southwestern coast of the Peloponnesos.[23] Thus the epic tradition pictures Agamemnon as the suzerain of a large section of the Peloponnesos and of the islands by its northeastern coast. Because of his domain, he was the acknowledged leader of the expedition and was considered "the most kingly of all." That his power extended also over the sea is indicated by his contribution of one hundred ships to the expedition, the largest contingent mentioned, and by his lending sixty additional galleys to the Arkadians, who, being a landlocked people, did not possess ships.[24]

It is interesting to remark that the reputed reigns of the Perseid and Pelopid dynasties down to Agamemnon coincide with the greatest expansion of Mycenaean culture in the Mediterranean area as revealed by pottery found in a great number of sites. As a matter of fact, the Mycenaean pottery produced towards the end of the fourteenth and in the thirteenth century has come to be known as *koine*, and it is to be found from Troy to Ras Shamra and from Cyprus to Lipari.[25]

The tragic fate that overtook Agamemnon on his return from Troy, exploited by the great Athenian tragedians, has become one of the most famous stories of the ancient world. Seven years after the violent death of the "great king," his murderers, Klytemnestra his wife and her paramour Aigisthos, were killed by Orestes, who apparently ruled for a short time over Mycenae.[26] He was succeeded by his son Tisamenos, during whose reign the power of Mycenae collapsed under the impact of the latest incursion of the Dorian tribes. Then its citadel was finally stormed and its palace and houses of the officials within it were looted and burned for the last time. The destruction of Mycenae may have failed to extinguish life completely, but it succeeded in eliminating Mycenae from

---

[18] Euripides, *Elektra*, 1158; *Troades*, 1087-1088; *Iphig. Aul.*, 265, 534, 1501; *Iphig. Taur.*, 845.

[19] Apollodoros, II, 4, 5.

[20] Thucydides, I, 9; Hellanikos *apud schol. Iliad*, II, 105; Strabo, VIII, 6, 19 (377).

[21] *Iliad*, II, 102-108.

[22] *Iliad*, II, 569-575 and II, 108.

[23] *Iliad*, IX, 149-153.

[24] *Iliad*, II, 610-613. Cf. Thucydides, I, 9, 1.

[25] Cf. S. Marinatos, "The Minoan and Mycenaean Civilization and Its Influence on the Mediterranean and on Europe," *Atti del VI Congresso Internazionale delle Scienze Preistoriche e Protostoriche*, I, pp. 161-176. Also *supra*, n. 5.

[26] *Odyssey*, I, 28-43 and III, 303-308.

a role of importance and leadership. Its power and prestige, the suzerainty of the Argolid, passed over to the city of Argos, and Mycenae became a secluded village. The legends which have been preserved seem to indicate that the life history of Mycenae in the prehistoric age was rather short, limited to six or seven generations, three or four of which belonged to the Perseid dynasty and four to the Pelopid. Surveying the chronology of Mycenae from its destruction to its mythical founding, we find for the Pelopid dynasty Tisamenos-Orestes, Klytemnestra-Aigisthos-Agamemnon, Thyestes-Atreus; for the Perseid dynasty: Eurystheus, Sthenelos-Elektryon, Perseus. If we allow even forty years for each generation, we shall be forced to conclude that, according to the preserved tradition, at the most two hundred and eighty years are comprised in the life-span of prehistoric Mycenae, between its founding by Perseus and its final destruction by the so-called Dorians.

For centuries after that destruction, the fortunes of Mycenae remain unrecorded. We next hear of the city when another menace threatened Greece, when the Persian armies of Xerxes poured over Greece like the uncontrolled waters of a mountain torrent. A contingent of eighty Mycenaeans is recorded as having joined the small force of Leonidas at Thermopylai.[27] A year or so later Mycenae, along with Tiryns, contributed her men to the battle of Plataiai and had the privilege of inscribing her name on the bronze serpents supporting the trophy placed by the Greeks at Delphi.[28] That honor, their refusal to accept the supremacy of the Argives, and their demand for a leading role in the direction of the affairs of the temple of Hera and of the Nemean games, raised against the Mycenaeans the envy and the hatred of the people of Argos. Taking advantage of the preoccupation of the Spartans with the Helots and the Messenians, the Argives without provocation attacked Mycenae and succeeded, through a long siege, in destroying its citadel a second time, ca. 468 B.C.[29] This second destruction seems to have been so great that Diodoros states, "Mycenae remained uninhabited until our day," while Strabo wrote that "not a trace of the city was to be seen" in his time.[30]

However, we learn from inscriptions, coins, and the excavated remains that in the third century B.C. the people of Argos established on the hill of Mycenae a township (*koma*), the Cyclopean walls of the citadel were rehabilitated, within the citadel a good number of houses were constructed, and the temple on top of the hill was rebuilt on a larger scale. Part of the ridge to the west of the citadel was enclosed by walls and was transformed into a Lower City.[31] Of the public buildings in the Lower City, the remains of the Perseia fountain, not far from the Lion Gate and alongside the modern road which leads to it, were cleared by Wace in 1952 and the remains of a small theater were revealed, built obliquely across the dromos of the so-called Tomb of Klytemnestra, a *tholos* tomb which was completely buried and invisible in classical times. How long this township continued to be inhabited is not certain. But fragments of lamps, a fragment of a grave stele, and the discovery of a few graves seem to indicate that the site was still inhabited in Roman Imperial times.[32]

When Pausanias visited the site in the middle of the second century of our era, he saw parts of the circuit wall with the Lion Gate, the underground "treasuries of Atreus and his children," "the graves of Agamemnon and those who were murdered with him on their return from Troy within the walls," the graves of Aegisthos and Klytemnestra beyond the walls (for they were not considered worthy to be buried along with Agamemnon within the citadel), and "the Perseia fountain among the ruins of Mycenae."[33] Since there is a good reason to believe that the graves which Pausanias identified as those of Agamemnon and his followers were completely covered and invisible at the time of his visit, it seems possible from his statement to conclude that he obtained his information from people who lived on the site and who cherished its traditions; in other words, it seems likely that Mycenae in the days of Pausanias was still inhabited, though completely deprived of its importance and glory. A few shepherds may have been the only occupants, and the important role which Mycenae played in the heroic past had become tradition and myth.

Pausanias is the latest of the ancient authors to mention Mycenae. After him, the site passed into oblivion until late in the period of the Turkish occupation of Greece, late in the eighteenth and early in the nineteenth centuries. Then it was noted by a number

---

[27] Pausanias, II, 16, 5.

[28] Herodotos, IX, 28, states that 400 men were contributed by the two cities. The relative size of both cities can be surmised from the fact that the city of Corinth contributed 5,000 men; Orchomenos in Arkadia 600; Sikyon 3,000; Epidauros, 800; Phlious, 1,000, etc. Argos did not participate in the Greek effort against the Persians.

[29] Pausanias, II, 16, 5. The story is dramatically told by Diodoros, XI, 65.

[30] Strabo, VIII, 6, 10 (372). Evidently the geographer did not

visit the site.

[31] For the 3rd century township cf. *BSA*, 25 (1921-1923), pp. 408 ff. and 422 ff. Tsountas not only revealed the foundations of a number of 3rd century houses within the citadel but he also found, in 1895, a hoard of some 3,786 coins among the ruins of a Hellenistic structure belonging to the middle of the 3rd century. Cf. *Ephemeris*, 1896, pp. 137 ff.

[32] Wace in *BSA*, 48 (1953), p. 17.

[33] Pausanias, II, 16, 5-7.

of early travelers and became the object of pilfering by art collectors and purveyors. Lord Sligo, Lord Elgin, and Veli, the Pasha of Nauplia, are three of Mycenae's known despoilers.[34] Such open depredations came to an end shortly after 1837 when the site came under the protecting care of the Greek Archaeological Society of Athens. In 1840 the Society started the investigation of her antiquities by undertaking the clearing of the Lion Gate, whose lions throughout the ages stood guard over its entrance in full view of visitors. Mycenae was, however, forcibly brought to the attention of the world by Schliemann in 1876 when he discovered and explored the royal grave circle within the citadel. He was followed by Tsountas who, from 1880 to 1902, cleared most of the area of the citadel, and by Wace, 1920-1922, 1939, and 1950-1957. Work is being carried on now by Greek, American, and English scholars under the auspices of the Archaeological Society of Athens. The remains brought to light by excavations justify fully Mycenae's legendary reputation and achievement.

PYLOS

For Pylos we do not have as full and long a record as we have for Mycenae. In the known tradition, Pylos was the capital city of Nestor, the old counselor of the Greeks in the Trojan War. It was established by his father Neleus, who, starting from Iolkos in Thessaly, moved southward, establishing himself at Pylos and forcing its earlier rulers to move to Elis. Interestingly enough, tradition has not preserved any hint of the building of fortification walls by Neleus; and none has been found. We next hear that Herakles destroyed Pylos and killed all the sons of Neleus except Nestor, whose long rule, according to the Iliad, "through three generations of men," became famous. He took an active part in the Trojan War, although he was an old man, and contributed to the Greek expeditionary force ninety ships, a contingent exceeded only by Agamemnon's. The gods proved kind to the old king, and he returned to his home safely and without perilous adventures. Some years later, in the tenth year after his return, according to the *Odyssey*, he entertained Telemachos and provided him with chariot and escort to go to Sparta. Tradition has preserved no record of the time of his death but mentions that a son, a grandson, and possibly a great grandson, succeeded him. In the end, Pylos came under the domination of the Dorians. Some of the Neleids found refuge in Athens where they started at least two families, both aristocratic, one of which was the family of Peisistratos. Others continued to Asia Minor to settle Ionia. Apparently the site of Nestor's Pylos was abandoned and was never again reoccupied.[35]

Until the days of Strabo the majority of the Greeks believed that Pylos was in Messenia and that Nestor was a Messenian. The geographer, however, pointed out that in his day there were three sites bearing that name, one in Elis, another in Triphylia, and still another in Messenia. Excluding the site in Elis, since it lies too far inland, Strabo remarked that "the greater number of other writers, both historians and poets, say that Nestor was a Messenian . . . but those who adhere to Homer and follow his poems as guides," the *homerikoteroi*, "are correct in their contention that the Pylos of Nestor was in Triphylia near the Alpheios River."[36] The controversy over the site of Pylos gave rise to the statement: "There is a Pylos in front of Pylos, and still another Pylos."

Until the period from 1906 to 1908 topographers placed Pylos in Messenia. But in those years the eminent explorer of Troy and Tiryns, W. Dörpfeld, claimed that the site known today as Kakovatos was Nestor's capital. His claim was based upon three *tholos* tombs of LH II times which he explored and on some remains of a modest building possessing a small court, a large room with two stone bases, and storerooms in which were found still *in situ* large pithoi; some of these contained carbonized figs. Traces of fortifications were also found on the hill where the building was discovered.[37] It was natural that Dörpfeld's claims found many followers.

In 1912, however, and again in 1926, the late K. Kourouniotes found and explored two beehive tombs in the neighborhood of the Messenian Koryphasion. Traces of others could also be detected in the neighborhood.[38] Thus it was proved that elements similar to those which led Dörpfeld to champion Kakovatos' claims existed in the Messenian territory. Since then, Kakovatos has been almost eclipsed by greater discoveries in Messenia-Triphylia. In 1939 Kourouniotes and Blegen located a large Mycenaean palace on top of the hill now known as Ano Englianos, some four kilometers from the modern town of Chora. In that year the Archives Room of that palace was discov-

---

[34] For the early travelers cf. Wace, *BSA*, 25 (1921-1923), pp. 283 ff.
[35] Pausanias, IV, 2, 5; 3, 3 and 3, 6.
[36] Strabo, VIII, 3, 7; 3, 14; 3, 24-29.

[37] *AM*, 32 (1907), pp. vi ff.; 33 (1908), pp. 295 ff.; 38 (1913), pp. 101-139. For the pottery Müller, *AM* 34 (1909), pp. 269 ff.
[38] *Ephemeris*, 1912, p. 268; 1914, pp. 99 ff. *Praktika*, 1925-1926, pp. 140, 141.

ered, yielding over 600 inscribed tablets, which made possible Michael Ventris' great achievement in decoding the Linear B Script. The excavation of the palace, interrupted by World War II, was resumed by Blegen in 1952 and has continued to the present. Meanwhile, Professor S. Marinatos, who became, after Kourouniotes' death in 1944, the representative of the Greek Archaeological Service in the American-Hellenic project of the exploration of the territory, discovered and cleared a number of Mycenaean chamber and tholos tombs. It would be almost impossible to maintain that in this or the adjacent territory another palace existed; and the only royal family known from tradition was that of Nestor. Marinatos' explorations of the territory have certainly proved that no other similar palace does exist.[39] The conclusion that the palace at Englianos is that of Nestor seems to us inescapable. But whether or not one agrees with this conclusion, the fact remains that the palace at Ano Englianos, the Palace of Nestor as we believe, constitutes the third great center of Mycenaean power and art which has survived in the Peloponnesos; that its area was a most flourishing and important district comparable to that of Mycenae.

ATHENS

After the destruction of Pylos, the descendants of Nestor and their followers found refuge in Athens, another Mycenaean center with a long history, which seems to be better known because the Athenian legends were preserved in the writings of their many authors. According to those legends the Akropolis of Athens was the center of the Mycenaean city, and this has been verified by the archaeological exploration of the territory. That center, as we have seen, was not destroyed, as were the Peloponnesian centers, and its population remained in their ancestral homes and gradually advanced from the Late Mycenaean to the Proto-historic period without a violent upset. However, the many successive periods of occupation destroyed most of the remnants of the age. In legend we hear of the early kings of Athens who dwelt on the Akropolis: of King Erechtheus, for instance, in whose palace Athena was a frequent visitor, of Aigeus and Theseus of the many exploits, but we have no description worth consideration of their art and culture. Of their palace on the Akropolis the scantiest possible remains survive, "two column bases," and these are doubtful. They were brought to light in the course of the excavations conducted from 1885 to 1890 by the Greek Archaeological Society of Athens and described by P. Kavvadias and G. Kawerau.[40] During this period the remnants of the Cyclopean walls of the Akropolis were revealed. Details were added to the general account in later years, but a clear picture of that citadel was obtained only after 1930 with Professor Oscar Broneer's discoveries on the north slope, with the revelation by N. Balanos of the mighty tower below the temple of Nike in 1936, and the most recent investigations of Iacovides.[41] Chamber tombs found by the American excavators of the Agora add considerably to our knowledge of Mycenaean Athens,[42] which, however, cannot be considered as complete as that of the other three centers we have discussed.

THEBES, GLA, IOLKOS

In the dawn of history, Kadmos, the mythical leader of the Phoenicians of Herodotos, is reputed to have built a city in Boiotia which later became known as the Kadmeia. His descendants, Amphion and Zethos, added towers and walls, as Homer states (*Odyssey* XI, 263 ff.), and transformed it into the formidable citadel of Thebes. The fateful story of the kings of Thebes, immortalized by the great tragedians of the ancient world, ended with the quarrels among Oidipous' sons and the destruction of the citadel at the hands of the Epigonoi shortly before the Trojan War. The charred remains of the Palace of Kadmos, buried below modern structures, were revealed by the late Professor A. Keramopoullos in 1906.[43] In 1963 the exploration of that Palace was resumed by Dr. N. Platon and Mrs. E. Stasinopoulou Touloupa, with striking results,[44] but the walls and towers which Amphion and Zethos built have not yet been found. As a result our knowledge of the citadel of Kadmos is limited to the surmise that it occupied the hill on which the modern town of

---

[39] Blegen, *AJA* from 1953 to date. Marinatos, *Praktika*, from 1953 to date. Cf. *infra*, pp. 52 ff. See also Blegen in *Yearbook of the School of Philosophy, Univ. of Athens*, 1964, pp. 285-305.

[40] *Die Ausgrabungen zu Akropolis*, 1907.

[41] *Infra*, Chapter II, pp. 35 ff.

[42] T. L. Shear, *Hesperia*, 9 (1940), pp. 274-291. E. Townsend, *Hesperia*, 24 (1955), pp. 187-219 where bibliography.

[43] *Ephemeris*, 1909, pp. 57-122. *Praktika*, 1927, p. 32 ff.

[44] Cf. N. Platon and Mrs. E. S. Touloupa in *ILN*, Nov. 28 and Dec. 5, 1964. Also, Mrs. E. S. Touloupa in *Kadmos*, 3 (1964), pp. 25-27.

Thebes is standing and that at its summit stood the proud palace of the descendants of Kadmos.

Recent excavations at the Boiotian site of Gla were carried out by Threpsiades.[45] No legends or myths about its citadel are known to us and its identification as the Homeric Arne does not seem to be acceptable.

Neleus, the father of Nestor and founder of Myce-naean Pylos, started from Iolkos in Thessaly, and since this is where the Argonautic expedition originated in the heroic period of Greece, it is fitting that Theochares' revelation of the palace of Iolkos should close the list of discoveries of Mycenaean sites, although the excavation still is in its initial stage.

[45] *Infra*, pp. 43-44 and 84-85.

CHAPTER II

MYCENAEAN CITADELS

"When we are about to enter the polis (city) around which runs a lofty wall, a fair harbour lies on either side of the city and the entrance is narrow and curved ships are drawn up along the road, for they all have stations for their ships, each man one for himself. There, too, is their (*agora*) place of assembly about the fair temple of Poseidon, fitted with huge stones set deep in the earth. Here the men are busied with the tackle of their black ships with cables and sails, and here they shape the thin oar-blades. . . . And as Odysseus went through the city . . . he marvelled at the harbours and the stately ships, at the meeting-places where the heroes themselves gathered, and the walls, long and high and crowned with palisades, a wonder to behold." (*Odyssey*, VI, 260-269 and VII, 40-45. Tr. A. T. Murray)

This, the only description of a city (*polis* or *asty*) to be found in Homeric poetry has, with reason, been accepted as the description of a post-Mycenaean, possibly an Ionian, fortified settlement. For, as Tsountas suggested long ago, the common people did not live in a city as we know it today or as it was organized in the Historic Era, but in small, detached groups at a short distance from each other, in family units, separated by streets and the graves of their ancestors.[1] They lived κατὰ κώμας, in a system known to have been used in Sparta in the historic period, and perhaps also reflected in the ancient demes of Athens. Besides, in the major settlements there existed a fortified citadel within which lived the members of the ruling family and apparently some of the other leaders of the community. The vague description of the akropolis of Troy, to be found in the *Iliad*, seems to reflect the lingering recollection of the Mycenaean citadel, while the delineation of the palaces of Odysseus in Ithaka, of Nestor in Pylos, of Menelaos in Sparta, and of

Alkinoos in Phaeacia seem to indicate that some details of the palaces of the Mycenaean rulers were still remembered in the days of the composition of the *Iliad* and of the *Odyssey*.

The fortified citadel is the characteristic feature of the Late Helladic III period; and of the many examples that were constructed in the mainland, we have at least three formidable representatives in a good state of preservation—the citadels of Mycenae, of Tiryns, and of Gla. The outward aspect of the citadels of Mycenae, and Tiryns, which, it should be noted, supplement each other, has been greatly improved by the restoration work that is being carried on by the Greek Service for the Preservation and Restoration of Ancient Monuments. When we stand by the restored northwest corner of the citadel of Mycenae and look at its stony height, we can realize the tremendous impression these strongholds of powerful dynasties made on foe and friend and the sense of impregnability which they conveyed (Fig. 1).

THE CITADEL OF TIRYNS

We are indebted especially to Müller for the complete and final publication of the architectural remains of the fortification of Tiryns. His book contains a complete description and discussion of its remains.[2] Here I shall give but a brief, general account of that citadel, based upon his learned descriptions, reserving a fuller discussion for the citadel of Mycenae, to the study and exploration of which I have devoted the past ten years, and to the knowledge of which I may have added some important details.

The site of Tiryns is a low-lying hill, long and narrow, spreading from north to south, some three-

quarters of a mile from the sea. Its highest point rises but 18 m. above the plain and 22 m. above sea level. The area of the entire citadel amounts to some 20,000 square m.; each of the sides measures about 300 m. in length from north to south, while its circuit amounts to 725 m. Its width at the narrowest point is some 45 m. The hill of Tiryns is proved to have been inhabited prior to Mycenaean times. On its summit the German scholars, Dörpfeld, Karo, and Müller, who conducted the excavations of the site for almost half a century, disclosed fragments of the foundations of a large round structure some 14 m. in diameter

[1] *Mycenaean Age*, p. 33.
[2] Kurt Müller, *Tiryns*, III, 1930. Georg Karo, *Führer durch*

Tiryns, 1934. For earlier accounts cf. Schliemann and Dörpfeld, *Tiryns*, 1885.

belonging to the Early Helladic period.[3] These foundations and the pottery found on the hill prove that it was inhabited from the middle of the third millennium B.C. However, it was in the Mycenaean Age that the site reached its maximum development. A tholos tomb, located some years ago by Karo, remains unexcavated, but a hoard of precious objects accidentally found by peasants, preserved by the late Professor A. Arvanitopoulos and described by Karo, indicates the affluence of the people of Tiryns in that age.[4]

The fortification walls of Tiryns belong to the late Mycenaean period and are built of limestone, roughly blocked in the Cyclopean style of construction. The walls range in thickness from 4.50 to 17 m. and in many places they average 7.50 m. The total height of the walls, originally crowned with palisades of sun-dried brick, cannot be determined now; the best-preserved sections stand to a maximum height of 7.50 m. The large size of the stones, some of which weigh as much as twelve tons, must have given rise to the legend that Cyclopes were employed in the construction of the walls of the citadel. However, Pausanias exaggerated when he said, "The walls are made of unwrought stones, each stone so large that a pair of mules could not even stir the smallest of them."[5] Characteristically the walls have insets recalling the ribs of the walls of Troy VI.

In the development of the citadel of Tiryns and the construction of the fortification walls, Müller has distinguished three phases, each of which has two periods. To the first phase belong the walls which surround the very summit of the hill, the south plateau or upper citadel, as it is called (text fig. 1, Citadel I). The entrance to that citadel was located in the southeast corner (No. 1). The door was set in the inner line of the fortification walls, whose thickness at that point was increased on the outside to form bastion-like projections on either side of the doorway. A little later, in the interior of the akropolis, two massive towers were built on either side of the entrance (No. 2).

In the second phase, the area of the first citadel was augmented by additions to the north, south, and east. What is known as the middle citadel was now added on the north side (text fig. 1, Citadel II, 3). Perhaps it was then realized that the entrance to the original akropolis, in spite of its inner towers, was rather exposed, and an arrangement was devised to make the storming of the doorway almost impossible. The arrangement, recalling that of the projected gate to the

first *enceinte* of Mycenae, marks a great development in military tactics and consists of a *dipylon*, or a double doorway, opening into a southeast court (Citadel II, 4 and 5). Even this was improved and strengthened in period 2b when another doorway was constructed. It was approached through a long and narrow passage dominated by formidable walls and an elongated tower on the east side (Citadel II, 6, 7, and 8). This approach considerably reduced the number of assailants that could attack the gate and at the same time exposed them to the missiles of defenders standing on top of the walls that flanked the passage. It recalls the arrangement of the postern gate and even of the Lion Gate at Mycenae. As a matter of fact, long ago Dörpfeld pointed out that the outer gate (No. 6) has almost the same dimensions as the Lion Gate, and blocks of conglomerate were employed in its construction.[6]

To the third and last phase of the development of the citadel belongs the rest of the walls visible today. In this phase the following were added: the elongated extension to the north, which we may call the lower citadel (Citadel III, 9), the east entrance with its ramp (No. 10), the galleries and casemates on the southeast and south sides (Nos. 11 and 12), and the rounded bastion on the west side which protected a narrow stairway leading to a small postern gate (Nos. 13 and 14). The last phase is characterized by huge stones of varied shapes and even faces set so as to leave wide spaces between them. These spaces were filled with small stones. Thus, gradually in the course of the LH III period, the citadel of Tiryns was enlarged, its gates were arranged more strategically, and within its walls ample space was provided for the needs of the ruler and the people of the city during invasion.

On the east side of the citadel we find its main entrance, a wide opening 3 m. broad, apparently never closed by a door.[7] To this opening led a ramp, 4.70m. in width and some 20m. in preserved length, running along the northeast face of the Cyclopean wall (text fig. 1, Citadel III, 10; and Fig. 2). Thus, an enemy force had to advance in small numbers with undefended right sides exposed to the attacks of the defenders stationed on top of the wall. Even if they succeeded in getting through the opening, they would find themselves in a narrow corridor leading north and south. The north section led to the lower citadel (No. 9), to a large elliptical space still unexcavated, which might have served as an area where the common people of Tiryns and their animals could have found refuge in times of hostile attack or invasion. Three

---

[3] Müller, *Tiryns*, III, 1930, pp. 80 ff. and IV, 1938, for the pottery.

[4] G. Karo, "Schatz von Tiryns," *AM*, 55 (1930), pp. 121 ff.

[5] Pausanias, II, 25, 8.

[6] Dörpfeld, in *Tiryns*, p. 189. Müller, *Tiryns*, III, pp. 70 ff.

[7] The opening, originally as wide as the ramp, was at a later time reduced to its present width.

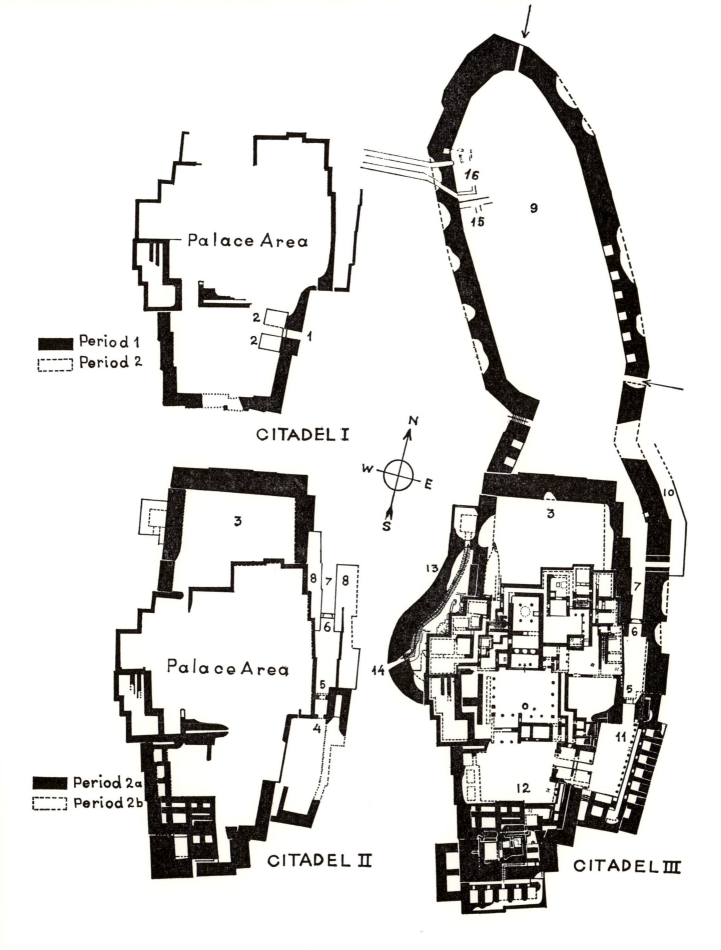

Period 1
Period 2

CITADEL I

Palace Area

Period 2a
Period 2b

CITADEL II

Palace Area

CITADEL III

N
W   E
S

10 5 0 5 10 15 20

1. Citadel of Tiryns (after Müller)

narrow openings, one on each side—east, north, and west—provided direct communication between the lower citadel and the outside. Since the level on the west side changed abruptly, a staircase was made in the southwestern opening, which apparently was closed by a door since pivot holes are to be seen on the threshold. In the thickness of the east and the west sections of the peribolos were made a number of rectangular niches. Perhaps they served as storage places for the more valuable belongings of the refugees in the lower citadel. A smaller niche, possibly serving as a small guard room or checking point is to be seen some 12 m. to the north of the east entranceway.

The south section of the corridor (text fig. 1, Citadel III, 6) led to a dipylon with a long, narrow court between two gates. What we may call the south gate, an almost duplicate in size, materials, and parts of the Lion Gate of Mycenae, is partially preserved; its doorposts with deep rebates and its large threshold are made of blocks of conglomerate, a stone which is not to be found in the neighborhood of Tiryns; apparently the stone was brought from the area of Mycenae and was worked in the same way as the blocks used for the construction of the Lion Gate. The opening of the doorway (3.16 m. on its inner side) almost equals its height (3.20 m.), and consequently its wooden two-leaf door formed almost a square. Pivot holes, 15 cm. in diameter, indicate the type of doors employed. On its doorposts, some 1.55 m. above the threshold, is seen a cylindrical cutting, about 17 cm. in diameter, which apparently served the wooden bolt that kept the doors securely shut. The cutting on the eastern doorpost is continued through the wall beyond it, so that the wooden bolt could be pushed back through the doorpost and into the wall to rest there when the door was opened. This is certainly a refinement and an improvement of the arrangement employed in the Lion Gate and indicates once more that the gate at Tiryns followed the construction of its sister gate at Mycenae.[8] Even after entering the gates, one had to pass a succession of courts closed by two propylaea, the greater propylon and the inner or lesser propylon, before he could reach the court beyond which stood the main unit of the palace.

On the west side of the citadel (Fig. 3) the circuit projects into a nearly semicircular bastion protecting a long flight of steps, 65 of which are still extant, connecting a postern gate (Citadel III, 13, 14 and Fig. 4) and the middle citadel. The postern gate apparently was not blocked by a door, since its defence, with a rising stairway behind it dominated on either side by heavy bastions, would have been very easy

indeed. No enemy would have dared to attempt to force an entry to the citadel through that veritable death trap. Furthermore, between the top of the stairway and the tower was a fissure in the rock some 7 m. wide, which would have interrupted any possible progress of an enemy to the Middle Citadel (No. 3). In peaceful times it could have been bridged by a removable wooden ramp.

The most characteristic features of the walls of Tiryns are its impressive galleries and casemates (Fig. 5). They are to be found on the southeast and south sections of the citadel, as developed in the third phase (text fig. 1, Citadel III, 11 and 12), and are corridors and storage rooms built within the thickness of the latest Cyclopean wall. The corridors or galleries average 1.65 m. in width and exhibit vertical walls to a height of 1.75 m. Above this the sides are inclined towards the interior to form an inverted V corbel vault, which gives to these corridors their characteristic aspect. The rooms, seven on the southeast side and five on the south side, averaging some 4.30 by 3.30 m., served most probably for storage. A stairway leading to the south gallery is pretty well preserved. The south gallery received light from a loophole at its eastern end that splayed internally almost to the full width of the corridor.

On the southwest end of the circuit projected a rectangular tower containing two rooms. Another rectangular tower was constructed during the second period of the second phase at the then northwest end of the middle citadel. In the third phase of the citadel this tower was incorporated in the construction of the bastion which protected the postern gate (text fig. 1, Citadel III, 13 and 14). That gate and bastion are believed to have been constructed to insure the water supply of the citadel in time of war; they could have been used for the defense of parties going to fetch water from the wells that existed outside the citadel and below the fortification walls. Archers placed along the bastion would have been able to protect the parties since the wells were within the distance covered by their bows and arrows. One wonders, however, how the wells themselves could be protected against the night raids of an enemy, who under cover of darkness could approach and fill them with stones. The problem connected with the water supply of the citadel was a most important one since there were no springs on the hill itself.

A recent lucky discovery has disclosed the way in which the Tirynthians tried to solve this problem in the closing years of the Mycenaean Age. Early in December 1962 the technicians restoring the walls

---

[8] Cf. Müller, *op.cit.*, pp. 72-73, where the door at Tiryns is accepted "nach dem Löwentor gebautist, ober jedenfalls nicht viel später."

noticed an opening on the outer face of the northwest end of the peribolos some 95 m. northwest of the southwestern door opening of the lower citadel (text fig. 1, Citadel III, 15 and 16). When this was cleared by Verdelis, it was found to lead to a built passage which passed at right angles under the fortification wall and continued underground to a distance of some 20 m. (Figs. 6-7). There it ended deep below the surface of the soil in what must have been originally a spring of water coming out of the rock. Almost parallel to this passage, only 9 m. from it, a second underground passage was disclosed, of about the same length; that also led to what originally was a spring. Apparently the people of Tiryns surmised the position of these deep springs by studying the direction from which water came to the wells existing beyond the walls and would have been able through these underground passages to secure water in times of war and siege.

The passages, averaging 1.40 by 3.50 m. in height (Figs. 6-7), are lined with strong walls built of large stones. These walls are vertical up to a certain height, then incline inwards to roof the passages with the well-known inverted V archways so characteristic of Tiryns. However, the roof is actually of the saddle type of the inverted V construction, that is, the sides do not come to the angular point, but are interrupted there by horizontal roofing slabs. The hard rock forms the sloping floor of the passages. Often enough the incline of the floor drops abruptly and then steps were cut in the rock; at other times steps must have been made of wood to facilitate the descent. Apparently by the entrance of the south passage at least there was a room, perhaps a guardroom, where soldiers could be stationed. Both passages were found filled with debris in which pottery abounds. The great quantity of LH III C ware they contained seems to indicate that the passages were in use to the very end of the Mycenaean era.[9]

The last phase of the citadel is a clear proof of the developed technical skill the Mycenaeans attained in the closing centuries of their age. Doorways are so constructed that they could not have been attacked by great numbers of an enemy army. The undefended right side of an attacker is as a rule exposed to the missiles of the defenders of the gates. Even if the enemy had succeeded in breaking through the gate they would have found themselves in narrow corridors dominated by heavy walls which provided battlements for the defenders. The enemy had to pass through successive corridors, doors, courts, and propylaea, before they could reach the palace of the ruler on the summit of the hill. The interior arrangements of the citadel of Tiryns recall the elaborate interiors of mediaeval castles. And one wonders how a citadel so well designed and so strongly fortified could have been stormed by an enemy equipped with the armor usual in the Heroic era.

THE CITADEL OF MYCENAE

Less complicated, but equally impressive, are the fortification walls of the citadel of Mycenae. A flat-topped, rocky hill, rising some 280 m. above sea level, was transformed into a formidable citadel in Late Helladic III times (Fig. 8a). The hill as well as the area of Mycenae is proved to have been occupied in Early and Middle Helladic times. From the Early Helladic period only pottery indicates the occupancy. Pottery, fragmentary walls, and graves represent the Middle Helladic period, and the older shaft graves of Grave Circles A and B belong to its closing years. The latter prove that by the end of the seventeenth century the people of Mycenae were very prosperous and had, under the influence of Minoan Crete, started to develop what came to be known as Mycenaean art and culture. The objects found in the earlier shaft graves suggest the existence of an affluent royal family which must have had an impressive home or palace.

Scanty remains of walls and a good deal of pottery suggest the existence of such a palace on the very summit of the hill. The question arises whether the top of that hill was fortified.

Wace, whose excavations and studies of Mycenae have laid solid foundations for our knowledge of the age, believed that in Middle Helladic times a wall was built around the top of the hill enclosing a little more than the area that was later occupied by the Mycenaean palace. That fortified area he called the "Original Citadel." He based his belief on the fragment of a Cyclopean wall which is preserved on the northwest slope of the hill (Figs. 8a, No. 6 and text fig. 18, MM). His more recent exploration, in 1953, did not yield concrete evidence to prove the age of that wall. In the summer of 1961 we investigated that wall thoroughly. We cleared the area behind its entire length and found that it was a retaining wall that

9 To Verdelis I am indebted for the information and the two photographs, which he kindly provided to be included here. For the views that prevailed before Verdelis' discovery regarding the water supply of Tiryns see Müller *Tiryns*, IV, p. 176 and Karo, *op.cit.*, p. 34.

supported the terrace in front of the Northwest Entrance to the Palace. The wall shows at least three different periods of construction; each time an additional piece of wall was added to the original segment to support the augmented area of the terrace. The fill that the wall supported was composed of small unworked stones and a small quantity of earth. Unfortunately the fill contained very few pieces of pottery and even fewer sherds with painted decoration. However, all the pottery belongs to the LH III period.[10]

In the undisturbed areas of earth above the rock level that did not form part of the terrace fill, we found Middle Helladic sherds. But these only prove that in Middle Helladic times, before the terrace and its retaining wall were built, the slope of the hill was inhabited. In its last phase the retaining wall extended from the north staircase, at its east end (text fig. 18, C, on p. 71) to the position of the modern stairway that today leads to the northwest entrance of the great palace (see Fig. 8a, No. 6). That modern stairway, in fact, lies over its west end. From there the wall and the terrace fill curved towards the west wall of the propylon of the northwest entrance, against which both terminated.

Of course, we cannot exclude the possibility that the top of the hill was fortified in Middle Helladic times, that it was a citadel; but thus far no remains of its fortifications have been found. No remains belonging to a Late Helladic I or Late Helladic II circuit wall have been discovered thus far, and as far as we can prove today, it seems that the hill of Mycenae was not fortified and thus transformed into a citadel until Late Helladic III times.

The area enclosed by walls has a roughly triangular shape of some 30,000 sq. m. The perimeter of the circuit amounts to some 900 m. This circuit wall is preserved in its entire length (Fig. 8a) except for a small part in the bulge of the west Cyclopean wall that goes around Grave Circle A, the part faced by the so-called polygonal tower, and a section on its south side, apparently swept down into the precipitous gorge, the Chavos, by landslides (Fig. 9). The greater part of the fortification walls of Mycenae is built in the well-known Cyclopean style. The walls, in other words, are built of large limestone blocks of different sizes, roughly dressed with the hammer or completely unwrought, and piled on top of one another with their interstices filled with clay and small stones (Fig. 10). These large stones, however, form but the inner and outer faces of the wall; the space between them,

the width or thickness of the wall, is filled in with smaller stones and earth.

A smaller part of the circuit is built in ashlar masonry. The conglomerate used is shaped by hammer and occasionally by saw into almost rectangular blocks which are placed in horizontal courses, more or less even, without regard for the lining of the joints (Figs. 11 and 13). Blocks used are as a rule smaller than those in the Cyclopean construction, although some are of great dimensions. One of the blocks, for instance, used in the construction of the bastion of the Lion Gate measures some 3 m. in length and 1.90 m. in height. This ashlar construction, however, in most cases formed but a facing, at the back of which the wall was constructed in the Cyclopean fashion. The ashlar system was used for the construction of the main gate of the citadel, the Lion Gate, its bastion, and the section of the original west wall which flanked the outer court of that gate. It was used for the postern gate and for the erection of a rectangular tower at the southeastern edge of the *enceinte* below the terrace of the "House of Columns."

There is a difference of opinion as to the date of the two types of construction. Some believe that the ashlar construction is later than the Cyclopean, while Tsountas and Wace believe that they could be contemporary. Pointing out that ashlar was used in the construction of the *dromos* and the façade of the "Treasury of Atreus," they conclude that it was used because it gave the feeling of greater strength to the wall, offered no foothold to an escalading foe, and contributed to the impressive appearance of the gates.[11] We shall see later that the Cyclopean system of construction is earlier than the ashlar, but that the former continued to be used concurrently with the latter in later times.

A third system of wall construction is apparent today. Small and well-cut stones of polygonal shapes were used to form a wall of solidity and good appearance. In the days of Schliemann this system caused a good deal of speculation, but we now know that the polygonal construction belongs to the Hellenistic period and that it was employed to fill the gaps in the Cyclopean walls caused by the destruction of ca. 468 B.C. The most conspicuous piece of polygonal construction is to be seen around the northwest corner of the bastion which protects the Lion Gate (Fig. 11, P). Part of the west Cyclopean wall forming the bulge to the south of that gate was also repaired in the polygonal style as well as the so-called "polygonal tower" farther to the south. The latter is built mainly of con-

---

[10] Wace, *Mycenae*, fig. 18 and pp. 69, 84, 86. K. R. Rowe, "A Possible Middle Helladic Fortification Wall," *BSA* 49 (1954), pp. 248-253, and Mylonas, *Ephemeris*, 1958 (circulated

1961), pp. 157-158.
[11] *Mycenaean Age*, p. 26. Wace, *BSA*, 25 (1921-1923), p. 13.

glomerate blocks and was actually erected to bridge a gap in the Cyclopean wall.

The fortification walls of Mycenae average 5 m. in thickness, although in places they reach a maximum of 8 m. It was once believed that the increased thickness concealed galleries like the ones found at Tiryns, but the complete investigation of the walls has proved that galleries of that type do not exist at Mycenae. Our work in the summer of 1962 proved that storage rooms were constructed in the thickness of the north Cyclopean wall, but in very late Mycenaean times, long after the fortification walls were constructed; those storage rooms were not part of the original Cyclopean construction. A small room covered by a saddle roof, halfway between the Lion Gate and the postern gate, was built alongside the wall, and not in it, about the time when the storage rooms were made (Fig. 12). Consequently this room should not be considered as "a gallery."[12]

The original height of the wall cannot be determined now, since nowhere is its summit preserved. Nor is it possible to know whether or not mud-brick palisades or other protective parapets were erected over the stone part. Usually the height of the Hellenistic "Polygonal Tower," some 18 m. above the rocky ground upon which it stands, is taken as an indication of the original height of the circuit wall, but we cannot be certain even of that. In the summer of 1961 we cleared the inner face of the west Cyclopean wall by the granary; there it is preserved to a height of 8.25 m. above the rock, which is the greatest preserved height of the Cyclopean walls at Mycenae. As is usual in Mycenaean times, the circuit wall follows the contour of the ground, is founded upon the rock, and often the rock formation is incorporated in its construction. A very good example of this method is to be seen on the stretch of the wall to the left as we approach the Lion Gate (Fig. 11), but other examples, especially on the north side, are also visible.

A wide passage was left in the interior of the citadel between the peribolos wall and the structures on the slope above it. Apparently this was customary in the construction of *enceintes* and we find it even in the citadel of Troy VI. The purpose of this passage, as Wace suggested, "was no doubt to prevent treachery and secret communication from without or from within the fortress. Rahab's help to the spies escaping from Jericho and St. Paul's escape from Damascus are illustrations of this danger."[13] In most places this passage seems now to be blocked by foundations of small structures, but these belong to the Hellenistic period when all free spaces were occupied. Only in the section immediately to the south of the Lion Gate, between it and Grave Circle A, the passage was blocked by a building shortly after the construction of the west Cyclopean wall; but that building, known as the granary, seems to have belonged to the state and could have served also as a guard room.

The *enceinte* was entered by two gates, a main and a postern; in later years two sally ports were also added at its northeastern end. The main entrance is the famous Lion Gate (Fig. 11). Here terminated one of the main roads of the lower city, transformed at its extreme end into a gradually ascending ramp, retained by a wall, remains of which are to be seen below the modern ramp to the entrance. The Lion Gate was defended by a long stretch of ashlar wall on the east side and on the west by a rectangular bastion 14.80 by 7.23 m. in width. Between them lay a comparatively narrow court, some 15 by 7.23 m., which served to reduce the numbers of an attacking army that could possibly maneuver in front of the gate. While the invading army's right or unprotected side was exposed to the defenders on the bastion, its entire force was exposed to the missiles—including perhaps huge rocks—which could be hurled from the top of the east line of the wall.

The Lion Gate itself is of massive and imposing construction (Fig. 13). Four huge monoliths of conglomerate, Schliemann's *breccia*, known to the inhabitants of the district as "almond stone," hammer-dressed in the main but also cut by saw, form the two door jambs, the threshold, and the lintel. The gate is almost as wide as it is high, and measures 3.10 m. high, 2.90 m. wide in the façade and 3.10 m. in the interior at the threshold. It narrows somewhat upwards, measuring 2.78 m. below the lintel. The opening was closed by a double door, as is proved by the pivot holes visible at either end of the threshold and the lintel.[14] The wooden doors were mortised to a vertical beam acting as a pivot around which they revolved; the ends of the beam projected above and below and were fitted into the pivot holes cut in the threshold and lintel. Sockets meant to receive a sliding bar or cross-beam securing the doors when closed—an arrangement we have already noted at the south gate of Tiryns—can be seen on the inner face of the sideposts; there are also oblong sockets into which apparently the door handles would sink when the doors were kept wide open (Fig. 14). The threshold has preserved equally eloquent traces of its life and use (Fig. 15). Along either end there is a rather broad and shallow depres-

---

[12] For the rooms in the fortification wall cf. *Ergon*, 1962, pp. 95-97 and figs. 113-114. *Mycenaean Age*, p. 330 and Wace-Rowe, *BSA*, 49 (1954), pp. 254-257, for the so-called "gallery."

[13] C. W. Blegen *et al.*, *Troy*, III, figs. 446-447. Wace, *Mycenae*, p. 57.
[14] The pivot holes in the threshold have been altered.

sion, assumed to have been made by chariot or cart wheels;[15] along its east end a deeper groove, some 26 cm. wide, served as a drain, while its surface was scored to provide a firm footing for man and animal. The rectangular cutting in the center, usually taken to be of a later date, perhaps served as a base for a short post or peg against which the wooden doors could rest when closed. The round hole in its middle could have been used for a short pole against which a rectangular block of wood could rest to back the door when it was securely closed. The huge threshold cracked towards its west end, perhaps not long after the construction.

The wall above the gate and its lintel is constructed so as to form an empty triangle, a feature characteristic of late Mycenaean construction and known as the "relieving triangle." This empty area is blocked by a slab of hard limestone. Its base line is worked in a curve to fit the top of the lintel which bulges upwards. Since there is a tight fitting at the corners, the weight of the slab in the main is borne by its extremities. The slab was furthermore secured in its position by a slight projection of the topmost stone now preserved of the wall on the east side. In 1950 Papadimitriou identified and restored to their original position the two blocks at the right side of the triangle, almost completing it, and so the composition, carved on the slab blocking the triangle, can now be seen in its original frame, gaining in clarity and vigor (Fig. 16). The relief, from which the gate receives its name, can be considered one of the earliest monumental pieces of sculpture of the Greek prehistoric world.[16] In spite of its exposure for so many centuries, it is excellently preserved. Its subject is well known: two lions stand on either side of a column which bears an entablature. To the discussion and possible meaning of this we shall return in the chapter dealing with the religion of the Mycenaeans. After passing through the entrance, we find a small, well-enclosed court, originally roofed, some 4 m. square, and in the eastern wall of this a small chamber known as the "Guard Room." Its position, 1.20 m. above the floor of the court, and its small size may indicate that it was used for a watch dog.[17]

The postern gate is located in the north line of the

circuit wall, some 250 m. east of the Lion Gate (Figs. 8a, No. 7; 17-18). It is placed in a set-back of the north Cyclopean wall, the east end of which is transformed into a bastion guarding the gate and so situated as to command the unprotected right side of anyone approaching from the north. Again a small court or passageway is formed in front of the gate, the length of the bastion.[18] The gate, much smaller than the Lion Gate, is constructed of conglomerate blocks worked and cut by hammer and saw in the same way as the blocks used in the construction of the more important entrance to the citadel. Four large blocks are used for the doorposts, the lintel, and the threshold, and serve to frame an opening on its façade. Two pivot holes in the lintel indicate that the gate was closed by a double door; when shut, this door was secured by a wooden beam that slid into well-cut sockets on the side of the doorposts in a manner similar to that known from the Lion Gate. No striations were cut on the threshold, but here too, off center, is a shallow rectangular cutting, the date and purpose of which remain uncertain. Instead of a relieving triangle over the lintel, two rectangular slabs were placed back to back, with an empty space between them. These slabs carried the wall construction across and were so fitted as to transfer the pressure to the sides.

On entering the postern gate we find a small court, open to the sky, from which begins Road B of the citadel (Figs. 17-18). On one's left is a small triangular room with three large blocks forming its roof. The room was accommodated under a staircase revealed in 1963, which connected the court with the northeast road of the citadel, the west end of which is some 3.50 m. above the threshold of the postern gate. While Road B from the postern gate led to the north staircase and thence to the northwest entrance of the palace, the northeast road, starting from the landing of the staircase just discovered, led to the northeast extension of the citadel and to its subterranean cistern.

What has thus far been known as the "sally port" was added to the latest extension of the circuit walls at the extreme southeast end of the citadel. It actually is a small narrow passage through the Cyclopean wall (Fig. 19). It is roofed over by a corbel vault of the inverted V type, similar to corbels used in the galleries

---

[15] In a recent study, (*Ephemeris* 1961, pp. 180-197, pl. 8) Iacovides has proved that the striations were not made in Mycenaean times and that the channels were made for drainage and are not the result of the wheeled traffic which crossed the threshold. Shear agrees with this conclusion, having studied the problem independently.

[16] Of course the reliefs on the stelai from the shaft graves are much older, but the workmanship is so primitive that one wonders whether they are entitled to be called monumental sculpture.

[17] We now have good examples of guard rooms behind gates

in the citadel of Gla disclosed by Threpsiades. Surely a guard room for a citadel such as that at Mycenae would have been at least as large as the smallest guard room at Gla. Recently Charitonides suggested that it may have served as a shrine, *AM*, 75 (1960), pp. 1-3. To his parallels we may add the relics found by Blegen in front and within the gate of Troy VI (*Troy*, III, pp. 96-100).

[18] For a fuller discussion of the postern gate see now Mylonas in the *Charisterion* (Festschrift for A. K. Orlandos), Vol. A, pp. 213-227.

of Tiryns. Our latest investigations have proved that it is a passage to a platform made along the southeast side of the extension that served as a lookout post over the ravine known as the Chavos. The passage was not closed by a door, and of course it could have been detected by enemy scouts and easily entered. However, because of its small size and perilous position, it could be defended successfully by a small force. On the north wall of the extension there is another passage (Fig. 20) usually referred to as a drain but proved to have been a real sally port that served for sorties of the garrison aimed at an enemy attacking the postern gate or the subterranean cistern.

Chronology of the Walls and Gates

Early in the study of Mycenaean remains Tsountas proved that the easternmost projection of the *enceinte* was a later addition, the latest extension to the citadel. He as well as Adler furthermore suggested that the Lion Gate and the now existing west Cyclopean wall were later additions to an original citadel to which belonged the North Cyclopean Wall.[19] Wace, who was actually the first to attempt to determine the chronology of the walls scientifically, maintained that, with the exception of the northeast extension, the fortification walls of Mycenae belonged to one period, and he placed their construction in the second half of the fourteenth century, around 1330 B.C.[20] Our investigations of the walls and gates of Mycenae, carried out from 1958 to 1963 prove, I believe, that here too, as in Tiryns, we have more than one period of construction; that at Mycenae also the area of the citadel was increased gradually.

The Cyclopean walls of the north and south sides, to the east of the existing gap in the peribolos, are proved to have formed part of the first and oldest circuit of the citadel of Mycenae. The north Cyclopean wall was the object of our investigations in the summer of 1958 and 1959. At that time we had an opportunity to make sections across the thickness of the wall at three places in its length between the postern gate and its western end;[21] these positions are indicated by the scaffoldings apparent in Fig. 21. While the technicians of the Service were restoring the outer face of the wall, we removed the fill from its core down to rock level. This made possible the thorough study of the method of construction as well as the collection of fragments of pottery. From the outset it became

apparent that the blocks employed in the construction of the outer face were set in an irregular system of headers and stretchers so that they would bind the façade securely to the fill of the core. Furthermore, we were able to determine that the lowest or foundation course of the wall was laid throughout its length directly on rock, somewhat leveled off to make an appropriate bedding. The small empty spaces left between the rock and the foundation blocks were filled with very small stones fitted like wedges (Fig. 22). Nowhere was the yellowish-white clay (ἀσπρόχωμα) employed as a layer between the rock and the foundation block, a detail which characterizes the construction of the west Cyclopean wall. Everywhere the north Cyclopean wall follows the line of the hard limestone outcrop, which forms the higher parts of the hill of Mycenae. Finally we noted that the entire length of the wall was built of hard limestone; we were able to find only two blocks of conglomerate, which seem to be due to repairs made at a later time.

The pottery collected found its way into the core of the wall in one of two ways. Some fragments penetrated into the small cavities between the stones of the fill with rain water and earth after the top of the wall was destroyed; others found their way into the wall at the time of its construction with the earth that was thrown in by its builders to fill in the small empty areas which naturally developed between the irregularly thrown stones of the core. Of course the former group is of no use as evidence for the date of the construction of the wall; the latter is most valuable and decisive. Great pains were taken to determine the location of the sherds found and the possibility of their being intrusive. Again a good many of the fragments belong to unpainted ware, are too small to give us structural characteristics that are dependable, and are of minor practical value if any. A good many bear a painted decoration but are so fragmentary that they could be placed only in very broad chronological limits; these are not very helpful for our purpose. But some painted sherds were found which are proved to have been contemporary with the construction and which can definitely be classified within well-defined chronological limits. The best group of sherds for our purpose was found in Section N. Only 85 cm. above the rock and some 1.08 m. from the face of the wall we found what can be considered as a sealed layer contemporary with the construction. It consisted of

---

[19] Tsountas, "Zur einigen mykenischen Streitfragen, *Jahrbuch*, 1895, pp. 143 ff. Adler in Schliemann's *Tiryns*, pp. xiv-xv.

[20] Wace, *BSA*, 25 (1921-1923), p. 13. Idem, *Mycenae*, pp. 133-134. For the dates suggested by Wace cf. Mylonas, *Ephemeris*, 1958, pp. 173 ff.

[21] These were made during the work of restoration of the walls and with the help of the technicians of the Greek Service

for the Restoration of Ancient Monuments under the direction of Dr. Eustathios Stikas, to whom I wish to express my thanks for help and cooperation. In this work I was ably helped by Dr. S. Iacovides, who had the responsibility of supervising the section. For a detailed account of the work see my forthcoming study in the *Ephemeris*, 1962 (1966).

the remnants of a fire (ashes and small pieces of charcoal covering a compact area), bones of animals, including the lower jaw of a goat, and fragments of pottery. This layer, lying above the stones and earth which formed the fill of the lowest section of the core, was in turn covered by loose stones and then earth, evidently the continuation of the fill. The remnants of fire, the bones, and the sherds could not have found their way from the top of the wall after its demolition. They were left there at the time of the construction and seem to be the remnants of a meal consumed by the ancient builders on the spot and in the course of their work. Hence the sherds found there constitute a group on which we can depend and they give us decisive evidence for the date of the construction of the north wall. The fragments, which bear a painted decoration (Fig. 23a), belong to the ceramic phase known as LH III A, possibly to its second half. To the years covered by that ceramic phase, about the middle of the fourteenth century B.C., belongs the north Cyclopean wall of the citadel. Thus the date suggested by Wace for the entire circuit wall is true for the north Cyclopean wall only.

The north Cyclopean wall at its extreme west end exhibits an outer face built of conglomerate in ashlar fashion. The ashlar masonry proceeds around the northwest corner of the citadel (Fig. 1) and continues to the south, until it reaches the Lion Gate. The gate itself and its bastion are constructed in the same style and in blocks of conglomerate. It should be noted again that the ashlar wall follows the configuration of the hard limestone formation of the hill and is based on the edge of that formation (Figs. 1 and 11). Thus the abruptly falling rock of the hill forms part of the rising wall. Here along the line of the wall the part of the hill that is made up of hard limestone terminates; below it the soft conglomerate composing the lower areas and the west slope of the hill comes to the surface. In this soft conglomerate were cut the shaft graves of Circle A as well as the cists of the Middle Helladic cemetery.

In *Ancient Mycenae* I maintained that the ashlar masonry of the wall from the northwest corner of the citadel to the Lion Gate was a curtain or a coating behind which a Cyclopean fill of limestone belongs to an older wall. It was apparent, before the restoration, when one looked at the wall from above, that the conglomerate curtain had a different direction from that of the inner limestone fill; that it ran obliquely to the body of the Cyclopean wall, and that its stones did not bind with those of the wall behind it, but were laid as stretchers the one on top of the other. Unfortunately, while I was in the States, the wall was

restored before I could make photographs and drawings, and the area between the ashlar masonry and the core was filled with concrete. The technicians who participated in the restoration assured me that the rectangular stones of the curtain which remain in their original position were all stretchers and did not penetrate into the core. Their statements were confirmed by the records of Stikas, the Director of the Service. I was happy to find corroboration of my observations in statements made almost at the beginning of the Mycenaean studies by a scholar who could not be accused of harboring ulterior motives. In his preface to the volume on *Tiryns* published by Schliemann, Adler wrote: The wall "consists of two separate parts separated vertically: first of a thick core of limestone piled up in Cyclopean fashion; and then, of a relatively thin coating of oblong blocks of *breccia*, in the lower strata of which no binding-stones are to be found, the southern wall of the same approach [i.e., the wall of the bastion] shows the same oblong ashlar masonry of *breccia*, not laid on, however, as a mere coating without binding-stones, but joined thoroughly with the core structure. From both observations it follows with absolute certainty that the oblong ashlar masonry must be more recent than the old Cyclopean limestone building and is only connected with the extension of the fortress towards the south and with the erection of the Lion Gate."[22]

The Lion Gate is one of the most impressive sections of the walls of Mycenae. Its date was based upon pottery found in 1921-1922, especially in the "staircase" by the granary and also upon the similarity of its material and workmanship to that of the so-called Treasury of Atreus.[23] At the time of the clearing of the "staircase," whose stratification was obtained and published in a most exemplary way, our knowledge of Mycenaean pottery was not as advanced as it is now, and in the course of the years the chronological evidence indicated by the sherds from the "staircase" was interpreted in various ways not only by different scholars, but by the excavator himself. Unfortunately, it is impossible to study the evidence again because the pottery then found was destroyed or mixed up with other specimens in the course of the Second World War, during the occupation of Nauplia by the German Army. This loss, and the indications gleaned from the curtain in ashlar masonry convinced me that an exploration of the area around the Lion Gate would prove fruitful.

In 1958, consequently, I started an investigation of the area of the gate and its threshold. For the first time in its long history the threshold was completely revealed and was found to rest on a fill of clean earth

---

[22] Schliemann, *Tiryns*, p. xiv.

[23] Wace, *BSA*, 25 (1921-1923), pp. 13, 20-23.

with its two ends supported by rather small stones placed in mortar of yellowish-white clay (Fig. 25), known to the villagers of today as ἀσπρόχωμα. This use of clay in Cyclopean construction is very interesting and should be carefully noted. One of the small stones which supported the west end of the threshold cracked under the pressure of the door jambs and the wall which stood on top, and this most probably caused the cracking of the threshold itself, which we have noted (Fig. 26). The placing of the threshold block on a layer of earth and not on the rock directly, although the rock below it is the soft conglomerate which is easily worked, apparently was the method followed in securing thresholds made up of large blocks and meant to support a great load, since we find it employed in the threshold of the postern gate, and also in that of the outer propylon of the citadel of Tiryns.[24] This method apparently enabled the builders to move the huge block easily until they obtained the level required. It also insured the block against an upward thrust to its center which could be generated by irregularities of its under surface and of the rock on which it would lie when pressure was placed at its extremities and by the momentum developed from the vertical pressure of the door jambs.

The placing of the threshold block on soft earth with its ends secured by small stones imbedded in yellowish clay was also demonstrated by the exploration of the south or inner side of the threshold (Fig. 27). Against that side stones were piled and then were covered with a thick layer of water-resisting, yellowish clay, known to the villagers as *plesia*; thus the threshold was insured against water and moisture. The area to the south of the gate was filled in with stones which formed the understructure of the road leading from the gate to the interior of the citadel. The fill of stones continued to the west below the wall of conglomerate which forms the west side of the small, inner, covered court of the gate (text fig. 19, No. 6, on p. 74), and beyond it to the granary. This stone fill was covered with a coat of clay, over which was found a layer of hard-packed earth, averaging 38 cm. in thickness, that formed the surface of the road. This layer of hard-packed earth was continuous around the south end of the conglomerate wall and formed the first level of the "staircase" as established by Wace.[25] In this hard-

packed earth we found, along with sherds, chips of conglomerate apparently produced when the door jambs were finally dressed by hammer and saw and were being prepared for placement in position. Some of the chips were what the laborers called "bitings" of the saw, discarded in the process of cutting. These chips definitely prove that the laying of the road, in the cover layer of which they were found, and Wace's Stratum 1 of the "staircase" are contemporary with the construction of the Lion Gate. The sherds, therefore, found in this fill and in Wace's Stratum 1, as well as those found on the side and below the threshold, give us the date of that construction. All these sherds belong to the period known as Late Helladic III B and to an advanced stage of it.[26] Among the pottery found by Wace in Stratum 1 of the "staircase" was one sherd which, according to the excavator himself, is "in the so-called 'close-style,' which close-style and the granary class are not only closely akin, but also contemporary." With this sherd in mind, Wace stated in his last study of the Mycenaean remains that in Stratum 1 pottery of "incipient close-style is present."[27] From that stratum he obtained many sherds with "small dots on the rim." We have seen that Stratum 1 is contemporary with the construction of the Lion Gate. Its contents therefore will place the gate in advanced years of Late Helladic III B.

The examination of the method employed in laying the blocks of the lowest course of the north and the west Cyclopean walls brought to light another important fact. The blocks of the north wall are laid directly on the hard rock, whose upper surface was somewhat worked to provide a more secure footing. The blocks of the west wall were often placed in a thick layer of mortar made up of yellowish clay which covered the top of the rock that remained unworked (Fig. 28).[28] We have seen this use of clay in the supports of the east end of the threshold of the Lion Gate. Apparently it forms a development in construction in Late Helladic III B times.

In 1962 we examined carefully the base of the inner face of the west Cyclopean wall from the area marked 20 to that marked 63 (text fig. 19). In this section the wall is preserved to a height of 8.25 m. above the rock. Between the rock and the lowest stones in two areas we managed to find spaces filled with small stones and

[24] Dörpfeld in Schliemann's *Tiryns*, p. 195. For the reasons underlying the arrangement see now Mylonas, in Orlandos' Festschrift, pp. 222 ff. The work around the Lion Gate was supervised by T. Leslie Shear, Jr.

[25] Wace, *BSA*, 25 (1921-1923), p. 20.

[26] For a full discussion of the finds cf. Mylonas, *Ephemeris*, 1962 (1966). Similar sherds were found in the deposit of the street of the House of the Oil Merchant: Mrs. David French, in "The Mycenae Tablets III," *TAPS*, 52, part 7, 1962, p. 32, fig. 61 no. 54.545.

[27] Wace, *BSA*, 25 (1921-1923), p. 20 and fig. 7, and p. 41; *The Aegean and the Near East*, pp. 129 and 130. Mrs. D. French has kindly informed me that the sherd belongs to the LH III B advanced period. Fortunately we do not have to depend on this sherd, which I know only from illustrations, for the date of the west Cyclopean wall.

[28] In the summer of 1959 J. Rubright, of Ohio State University, examined the foundations of the entire length of the north Cyclopean wall. Nowhere did he find this mortar used in their construction.

earth containing sherds. This fill was placed there at the time of the construction of the wall, and the sherds it contains date that construction. The painted sherds found in the wall itself (Fig. 23b) belong to the Late Helladic III B period and not to its very beginning; sherds with chevrons, which seem to be in the majority, would certainly indicate the middle of the period at the earliest. Sherd 1 is a specimen for which we find no parallel, but which seems to indicate the deterioration of a well-conceived original pattern; such deterioration characterizes the second half of the period. Among the sherds we found the cylindrical lower section of two Mycenaean terra-cotta figurines (Fig. 23b, lower left). They are hollow and most solid. It is generally believed that hollow cylindrical stands continue into later years, and Professor A. Furumark places them well into the LH III B period.[29] The sherds at any rate will place the construction of the west Cyclopean wall in later years of the Late Helladic III B period.

The study and exploration of the postern gate in 1958 led to interesting conclusions, corroborating those obtained from the area of the Lion Gate. The threshold is supported at its two ends, while most of its length rests on soft earth (Fig. 29). The sherds found in that soft earth as well as those from the layers in its passageway, contemporary with the construction of the gate, belong to an advanced stage of the Late Helladic III B ceramic phase. Furthermore, structural evidence was revealed proving that the postern gate is a later addition. The north Cyclopean wall, following the contour of the rock, approaches the area of the gate in a wide curve which is continued by at least three blocks of hard limestone and of irregular shapes that are to be seen below the lowest course of ashlar conglomerate blocks forming the east side of the bastion. The opening of the passage at its extreme east end is blocked by a huge limestone block, wedged in its original position on the rock, that continues the curve of the Cyclopean wall. On that block is based the northwest corner of the bastion. Behind it, filling the entire width of the passageway and for a length of 4 m., we revealed a fill of stones that evidently belonged to the packing of a Cyclopean wall. On that fill-packing is founded the lowermost course of the south side of the bastion built in conglomerate rectangular blocks. These remains definitely prove

that originally the north Cyclopean wall was continuous at this section; that at a later time an opening was cut through it to form the postern gate. This is also indicated by the pottery found: the north wall is characterized by sherds of the LH III A period, the postern gate and its fill by pottery belonging to an advanced stage of the LH III B period.[30]

The Cyclopean walls along the north and west sides of the citadel of Mycenae as they exist today are proved to belong to two different periods of construction. The difference is based on the pottery found in the walls themselves: LH III A-2 sherds characterize the north wall, advanced LH III B sherds the west Cyclopean wall. Laying of the lowermost course of the outer face in a thick layer of water-resisting yellow clay, a late element in the method of construction discovered in the west wall, was not employed in the building of the north wall. To the first period of construction belongs the north Cyclopean wall; to the second the west Cyclopean wall, the Lion Gate, and the postern gate.

The First Enceinte

The north Cyclopean wall must belong to an early peribolos, the first revealed thus far, which surrounded the hill of Mycenae and transformed it into a citadel. The question now arises: can we determine the course and the extent of the first *enceinte*? The east end of the north wall and its turn to the south, what could be called its exterior northeast corner, cleared again in 1958, can easily be seen (Fig. 30 N). From that turn begins the northeast wall, which was pulled down when the northeast extension was added to the first citadel in later years. Traces of the east wall we uncovered during the 1958 campaign, and these prove that its course did not follow a straight line, as it is commonly restored in the general plan of the citadel. It formed an angular projection toward the south (text fig. 2, Δ) before it reached the middle of its length and thence proceeded in a graceful curve to the southeast corner of the south wall, whose turn to the north is well preserved (Fig. 31 and text fig. 2, Δ-A). The south wall of the first *enceinte* is preserved to nearly below the southeast corner of the palace. To this wall in later years was added the so-called southeastern tower built in ashlar style and in conglomerate. A little beyond the tower to the west, the

---

[29] A. Furumark, *The Chronology of Mycenaean Pottery*, pp. 87-88. A late date for the wall of Mycenae was suggested by Mackeprang, *AJA*, 42 (1938), pp. 555-559 and Daniel, *AJA*, 52 (1948), p. 108.

[30] For a full discussion of the results of the excavation around the postern gate see now Mylonas, *Ephemeris*, 1962 (1966). The sherds found by Wace and Stubbings in the retaining wall of the peribolos of Grave Circle A in 1953 can be compared with those found by us around the Lion Gate. That

the postern gate was a later addition can also be proved by the study of the outer face of the north Cyclopean wall at the section where the ashlar construction of the bastion of the postern gate is joined to that wall and by the drains preserved in that section of the wall. We can still see a patch of small stones by means of which a later member was added to a pre-existing part. The work around the postern gate was supervised by Iacovides.

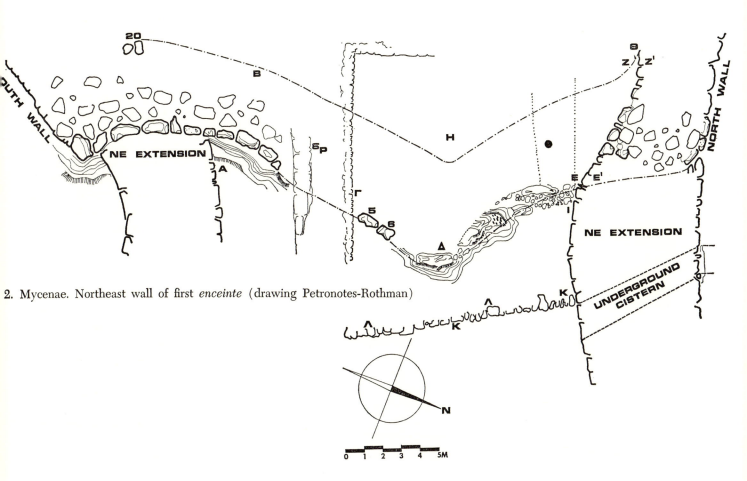

2. Mycenae. Northeast wall of first *enceinte* (drawing Petronotes-Rothman)

south wall is not preserved; it went down the Chavos ravine when that extreme end of the hill collapsed (cf. Fig. 9). Thus the north side, the east, and a section of the south of the first citadel can be definitely established. What of its west side?

The beginning of that side from the northwest corner of the citadel to the Lion Gate, to be called hereafter the north section of the west wall, is to be found behind the "curtain" of ashlar conglomerate masonry that flanks the outer court of the Lion Gate. Immediately to the southeast of that gate the section stops. Years ago Tsountas suggested that originally the wall continued to the west and extended all the way to the Chavos ravine. He noted that "a few traces of this work, indeed, are preserved on the left of the ascending roadway (E) as one goes up," and that "the earlier gate must have been about midway along this wall."[31]

That view was rejected by modern scholars, who, misinterpreting his words, equated the "few traces" mentioned by Tsountas with Wall 9 (text fig. 19, No. 9), which clearly is a terrace retaining wall. Furthermore, scholars questioned his suggestion that the original west wall from the Lion Gate to the Chavos was demolished when the *enceinte* was extended to the west and south and its stones used in the construction of the longer west wall, which has survived. That suggestion, however, and the secondary use of material do not seem impossible now that we can prove that the original northeast wall of the *enceinte* was also demolished and that its material was again used at the time the northeast extension was added. We can now prove that in the construction of the surviving Cyclopean walls on the north and west sides of the hill we have two periods of construction representing an earlier and a later *enceinte*. The surviving west Cyclopean wall beyond the Lion Gate could not have closed the west side of the earlier *enceinte* because it is proved to belong to the later construction period; it was built when additional space was desired and was added to the earlier enclosure. The west wall of the earlier *enceinte* would have been located farther to the east of the line followed by the later west wall since it limited a smaller area of the hill enclosed in the citadel.

An examination of the terrain will disclose another interesting fact: up to the Lion Gate, the builders of the north Cyclopean wall followed the contour of the hard limestone formation of the hill so exactly that shortly before reaching its northwest corner the north wall forms a deep rectangular recess which certainly has no meaning but which was imposed by the contour line of the rock. The northwest corner of the wall is

based upon a similar corner made by the hard limestone formation, and the north section of the west wall is based on the edge of that formation as it proceeds to the south. The north section of the west wall now stops by the area of the Lion Gate. At that gate its builders abandoned the hard limestone formation and followed the contour of the soft conglomerate for the construction of the wall to the south of it. It is reasonable to suggest that originally the builders, who followed the hard limestone formation on the north, east, and south sides, would have followed that same line on the west side also, especially since the west wall built over the edge of the soft conglomerate formation is proved to be of a later date. That line was suggested by Tsountas as possibly marking the course of the original west wall of the citadel. Thus all around, the hard limestone formation provided the foundation line for the fortification walls of the citadel and ample space for the needs of its ruler.

In 1958 we cleared the northeast area behind the Lion Gate and revealed the south end of the north section of the original west wall back of the ashlar conglomerate curtain of the gate (text fig. 19, No. 5). That end was found to present neither a finished face nor a turn, nor was bound with the inner row of blocks which form the screen wall of the gate. Instead, the wall ends abruptly and irregularly as if it had been carelessly broken, and the distance between its outer and inner faces was found filled with rather small, unworked stones. That fill is quite different from the one normally found in the north Cyclopean wall but is identical with that revealed in the artificial terrace supported by Wall 9 and with that of the terrace on which stands the megaron of the palace. It seems obvious to us that originally the Cyclopean wall behind the conglomerate curtain could not have ended in the manner in which we find it today; that what we have is the remnant of a later rearrangement. The date of the rearrangement is indicated by the sherds found among the stones of the fill, the painted examples of which belong to the later years of the LH III B period. What the original form of that Cyclopean wall was in that area cannot be determined now; but indications, such as cuttings on the hard limestone formation of the hillside, favor the view that originally it continued to the south at least for a short distance.

To verify this conception, we studied and cleared the area in front of the broken end of the north section of the west wall in 1958, 1961, and again in 1962. It proved to be an artificially made terrace, to be known as the east terrace, supported by Wall 9, through which access was obtained to the top of the walls and perhaps to the northwest slope of the hill.

---

[31] *Mycenaean Age*, pp. 109 and 113.

It seems to us that because of this terrace and this new approach to the wall, the so-called "staircase" to the southwest of the Lion Gate was abandoned in the second half of the LH III B period; to that phase of the period the east terrace also belongs. Beyond the east terrace to the south we found traces of leveling on the upper surface of rocks which form almost a chain leading across the modern path of ascent to the palace to the broken end of a Cyclopean retaining wall existing on the west slope of the hill. The wall has been marked in Drosinos' plan as "Remnants of interior enclosures of Cyclopean Masonry" (the remnants nearer the summit) and in Steffen's plan as "Kyklopische Stutzmauer" along the contour numbers 275.2 and 257.1 (Fig. 32, B). That wall, hereafter to be called *TW* in memory of Tsountas and Wace, was cleared to a good length by Tsountas, who revealed a number of Hellenistic structures built against its outer face. He originally suggested that the wall retained the road which led from the main ramp to the southwest staircase, the Grand Staircase, of the palace. Wace accepted that suggestion, but remarked that the road passed at a considerable distance from the staircase.[32] We cleared Wall *TW* again in 1962 and found that not only is Wace's observation correct but the wall continues to the Chavos ravine where originally the South Cyclopean Wall ended. Then we concluded that *TW* follows the line of the older west Cyclopean wall of the first *enceinte*, the fill as well as small parts of which it utilized.

We have proved the existence of the first *enceinte* belonging to the LH III A-2 period. We have seen that the north, east, and south sides of this *enceinte* can be accurately determined; that part of its west side also can be determined. The rest of its west side would have been closed as well. The line of the hard limestone formation of the hill, followed by the builders of the first LH III *enceinte*, indicates the course of the west wall that has to be restored. That line was followed exactly by the builders of the retaining Wall *TW*, whose extent and location can only be explained if we assume that it followed the line of a wall which antedated its construction. That wall would form the rest of the extent of the west wall of the first LH III *enceinte*. Text fig. 3 gives us the first proven citadel of Mycenae, which apparently belongs to the second half of the LH III A period.

The entrance way or the gate to that citadel has not been preserved. Tsountas, as we have seen, believed that it "must have been midway along the wall, and," he added "in fact, some 80 feet southeast of the

end of the ascent (E), at the point indicated by the letter C in the plan, some blocks were found, which are in all probability remains of this gate." I failed to find Tsountas' blocks, but in the area he mentions are still to be seen the rocks with their worked top surface which indicate the line of Wall *TW*. Before the earth that was piled against them was cleared away, they looked like Cyclopean blocks in position, and only the removal of the earth proved that they were natural rocks. Perhaps these are the blocks mentioned by Tsountas. He believed that they were the remnants of a gate because he also believed that the main ramp as it exists today formed the approach to the first citadel. "The approach," he wrote, "was . . . from the north . . . ; it was, in fact, the causeway with Cyclopean substructions [i.e., the ramp], which was not destroyed with the rest of the wall on this side on the enlargement of the fortress" [i.e., the original west wall] "but was left to serve as an avenue from the Lion Gate directly to the upper citadel."

The conception of the early date of the ramp was proved wrong by Wace, who concluded that the construction of "the ramp . . . like the Lion Gate and the fortifications, would fall at the beginning of the fourteenth century B.C.";[33] in other words, that these structures were contemporary. It became necessary to verify this conclusion when Papadimitriou in 1957 proved by excavation that the foundation blocks of the retaining wall of the ramp were laid on top of a layer of chips which resulted from the working of the slabs of the peribolos of Grave Circle A. This fact led him to conclude that the ramp was not contemporary with the circle but later in date.[34] On continuing his investigation, I found that the blocks of the foundation of the ramp were laid over the top of the broken part of the outer slabs of the circle which remained *in situ*, while the larger sections leaned inward (Fig. 34). Furthermore, the lack of any signs on the face of the slabs of an area of percussion and the clean break along the entire width of the slabs proved that they were not broken by the builders of the retaining wall, but that their breaking antedated the construction of that wall. This proved definitely that the surviving ramp (Fig. 33) was later in date than the rearrangement of Circle A and the building of its peribolos, and consequently later than the Lion Gate.

In 1959, with the help of the technicians of the Service for the Restoration of Ancient Monuments, we examined the ramp itself for further evidence. We opened up an area some 5.50 m. in length and 3.45 m. in width. Since the days of Tsountas, it has been well

---

[32] *BSA*, 25 (1921-1923), p. 148, and *Mycenae*, pp. 68-69. We have to bear in mind that it has not been proved conclusively that chariots did go through the Lion Gate and up the ramp. For details of the work and the indications see my study in the

Ephemeris, 1962 (1966).

[33] Wace, *BSA*, 25 (1921-1923), p. 67.

[34] *Ergon*, 1957, p. 65, and *Praktika*, 1957, p. 109. The work in the ramp area was supervised by Iacovides.

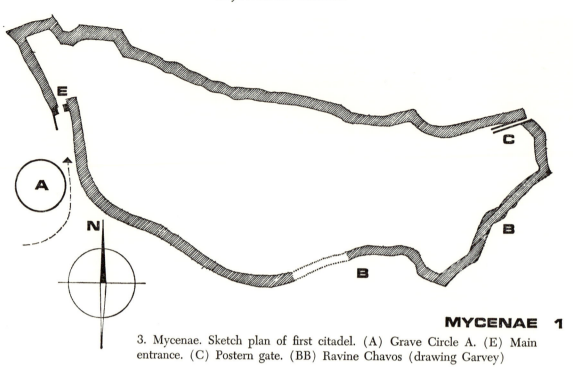

3. Mycenae. Sketch plan of first citadel. (A) Grave Circle A. (E) Main entrance. (C) Postern gate. (BB) Ravine Chavos (drawing Garvey)

known that the ramp is an artificial construction, whose fill is retained by the Cyclopean wall that towers over Grave Circle A. The main part of the fill is composed of large limestone blocks piled on each other with a little earth and tiny stones loosely filling the openings between them (Fig. 35, No. 1). In the area examined, the fill consisted of three superposed rows of blocks. Below them we found a layer of hard-packed earth and pebbles, the surface of which was well pressed. It was apparent that this formed the surface of an earlier ramp, which we may call No. 2 counting from the top, while the existing ramp we may call No. 1. The width of Ramp 2 was proved to be about 2.50 m. by the stone curbing that exists along its west side. The grade of its inclined surface was from north to south, like that of Ramp 1. Below Ramp 2, some 2.00-2.05 m. from the surface, we found a layer, averaging 15 cm. in thickness, of hard reddish earth with small pebbles. It evidently belonged to an even earlier ramp, No. 3, whose inclined surface, however, proceeded in a direction opposite to that of Ramps 1 and 2, i.e., it ascended from south to north. A still earlier ramp, No. 4, was revealed under the third; its grade also ascended from south to north. Below its surface we found a fill made of a single layer of stones and, below that, earth extending to the rock. The pottery found in the fill of Ramps 1 and 2 belongs to the LH III B period; the pottery that would characterize Ramp 3 is very limited; some of it apparently belongs to the LH III period—further definition in

sub-periods is impossible—and some is matt-painted and belongs to MH times. All the pottery from Ramp 4 is Middle Helladic. The sherds from the earth layer below Ramp 4 belong to the Middle Helladic period, and only those from the fill (which had an average thickness of 10 m.) immediately above the rock contained Early Helladic sherds.

The direction of the incline and the pottery will determine the date and the association of the four different ramps established by our work. It is evident that Ramp 1, the one surviving and in use today, led from the Lion Gate to the upper citadel; it belongs to the late years of the LH III B period. Ramp 2 preceded it, but it also belongs to the same time, LH III B period, and apparently also led from the Lion Gate to the upper citadel. We have already seen that Ramp 1 is proved to be later than the rearrangement of the Circle and consequently later than the construction of the Lion Gate. Ramp 2, therefore, must have been the ramp made when the Lion Gate was constructed. Ramp 3 cannot be associated with the Lion Gate, since the grade of its inclined surface proves that it could not have originated at that gate. It must be associated with the opening which preceded the construction of the Lion Gate; with the gate of the first LH III *enceinte*. Ramp 4 belongs to the Middle Helladic period and indicates the original and earliest path which people followed to climb to the top of the hill. We should perhaps note that Ramp 4 would have brought people along the north slope of the hill, which presents the most natural approach and ascent to its top. It was used from the beginning of the life history of Mycenae, and, to the later builders, indicated the position at which the gate to the first Late Helladic *enceinte* could be placed. The discovery of MH sherds along with LH III in Ramp 3 indicates definitely that until Late Helladic times Ramp 4 was used, i.e., the path established long before; that when the first *enceinte* known to us was built and the old path to the hill top was to be used, it was repaired and reinforced by a new hard surface to withstand increased use since the fortification walls made other paths of ascent to the top impossible. It is obvious, I believe, that the gate stood where the prolongation of Ramp 3 meets with the line of the West Wall of the first citadel. That position is in the area of the broken end of the north section of the west wall, the area over which was constructed in later times what we called the east terrace to the northeast of the Lion Gate. Unfortunately, that section has suffered considerably in later years and especially when a structure apparently of the LH III B or possibly C period was built on the area over which stood, we believe, the gate. I was unable to find traces of it, in spite of my efforts in the campaigns of 1959 and 1961. However, I would like to suggest the position of the gate and its area (as indicated in text fig. 4), repeating again that no remains have survived to prove or disprove the suggestion.

It seems to me that the existing end of the north section of the west wall proceeded for a short distance, forming a narrow bastion which may have ended some 4 m. from its present end. The main section of the west wall perhaps began some 4 or 5 m. further to the east and from a point some 5 or 6 m. to the north of the south end of the bastion. Thus the two walls were parallel for some distance, and a passage was left between them some 4 or 5 m. broad. That passage was blocked by the gate. In that passage terminated Ramp 3, ascending from south to north and proceeding for some distance along the main section of the west wall. Thus an enemy using the ramp would have his unprotected right side exposed to the defenders mounted on top of the main section of the west wall. The rather narrow passage in front of the gate, formed between the two sections of the west wall, would have forced the reduction of the number of possible enemies who could attack the gate at any one time. The arrangement of walls, ramp, and gate would parallel that employed in the second citadel of Tiryns (period a). Whether or not at Mycenae, too, a dipylon arrangement existed as it did at Tiryns, it is impossible to surmise. However, it seems to us that the builders of the two citadels learned from each other and used the

devices and developments achieved in the course of their building. We find that, at a later time, the builders of Tiryns copied the Lion Gate, and even used in its construction conglomerate that had to be imported. We should note that the entrance to the first citadel of Tiryns was an open passageway; that in the second citadel the builders used the arrangement of a doorway approached through a corridor domi-

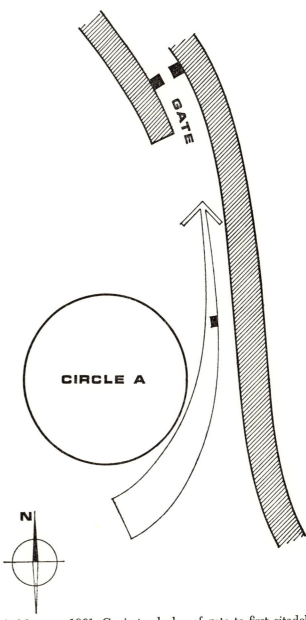

4. Mycenae 1961. Conjectural plan of gate to first citadel (drawing Compton)

nated by a projecting bastion and the wall of the citadel. This arrangement, actually attached to the side of the existing first citadel, seems to indicate that its builders copied it from somewhere else. Mycenae must have provided the prototype, which was developed in the building of its first citadel known to us.

At Mycenae, the position of the Gate and the arrangement of the approach to it was dictated by pre-existing conditions, by the existence of the Middle Helladic to Late Helladic III path employed for generations.

At the gate and its ramp the main road which led to the citadel from the west terminated. Towards its end that road must have skirted the south and the southeast sections of Grave Circle A, which at the time was outside the walls of the citadel (text fig. 4). As yet, remains of that road have not been found. But some 150 m. to the west of the southwest corner of the citadel and in the dry bed of Chavos we found evidence, in the summer of 1962, of the existence of a bridge that spanned the torrent and the remnants of the roads leading to the bridge from the west, and from the bridge to the citadel. In its construction limestone blocks of Cyclopean proportions were employed, some of which are still lying around, and none of which was found *in situ*. These blocks prove that its construction differed radically from that of the known "Mycenaean bridge" below the area of the cemetery of St. George. This difference is certainly due to a difference in age. Of the two, the newly located bridge is the older. Perhaps in it we have the indication of the direction of at least one of the roads which led to the first-known citadel from the area of Tiryns, the Heraeum, and Argos. Following the natural slope from the bridge, the road would have proceeded in a northeasterly direction until finally it reached the south and southeast section of Grave Circle A and Ramp 3 to the gate. It is hoped that in the near future the territory of the bridge and road will be fully studied and mapped. Meanwhile, this preliminary detail of its discovery may help to indicate one of the approaches to the citadel.

The Second Enceinte

If we compare the area of the first citadel (text fig. 3) with the sketch plan of the second citadel (text fig. 5), we shall see clearly the additions made that transformed the first into the second. The west wall of the earlier citadel was demolished and considerable area was added to the south and west. The Lion Gate was now constructed, and from its south side a new Cyclopean wall was erected which, swinging around Grave Circle A, enclosed a wide area and terminated in an addition to the south wall. Grave Circle A was rearranged, and its peribolos of vertical slabs was erected. We should note, however, the possibility that this rearrangement of the circle might have preceded the construction of the gate and of the west wall which

enclosed it. A ramp was made (Ramp 2) leading from the Lion Gate to the palace on top of the hill. At a later time this was replaced by a wider and more monumental ramp (Ramp 1), a section of which has survived. Sometime after the construction of the Lion Gate, the postern gate was built. The picture of the second citadel is almost complete. Now within its area not only a palace is to be found, but a number of houses and even a public granary. A good many of these are located in the additional area incorporated in the citadel in LH III B times. The most important house, however, is to be found on top of the hill to the east of the palace; it is known as the House of Columns. In what we may call the lower citadel, in the area of Grave Circle A, we find the granary, the House of the Warrior Vase, the South House, the Ramp House, the Citadel House,[35] and Tsountas' House (text fig. 19, Nos. 10-16, 40-56). These homes within the citadel belonged most probably to important citizens, perhaps even to members of the royal family or to military leaders.

A wide passage was left between the peribolos wall and the structure on the slope beyond it. In our 1962 campaign, we found out that a section of this passage along the north Cyclopean wall was used for a different purpose sometime in the course of the life of the citadel. In the upper part of the Cyclopean wall and in its thickness a number of storerooms were constructed. In the regular free passage, corridors and stairways were erected leading to these rooms. The construction seems to terminate at the east in the small vaulted chamber which was indicated in Steffen's plan as "Galerie" and which was cleared by Tsountas in 1888 (Fig. 12 and text fig. 6, T). He then noted that "what had long been taken for a gallery in the north wall proves to be nothing but a little chamber measuring less than 7 by 12 feet," that it is not a real gallery.[36] Wace cleared this chamber and measured it again; it may have been "formed by covering the passage with an inverted V roof resting on one side against the Cyclopean Wall and on the other against the rock which rises rather steeply southwards at this point within the walls. . . . This was probably done at a comparatively late stage in the history of the prehistoric citadel." Rowe, who supervised the clearing of the chamber, remarked, as Tsountas did before him, that "in fact this is not a 'gallery' at all, since it does not run within the wall, but it is a roughly built structure lying adjacent to the inner face of the wall."[37]

This chamber opens toward the west, into a series of four corridors (text fig. 6, A-D) and four stairways

[35] For the houses in the lower citadel, cf. Wace, *BSA*, 25 (1921-1923), pp. 38-95. For the House of Columns, *Mycenae*, pp. 91-97. For the Citadel House, cf. W. Taylour, in *Mycenae*

Tablet, III, pp. 35-46.
[36] *Mycenaean Age*, p. 331.
[37] *BSA*, 49 (1954), p. 254.

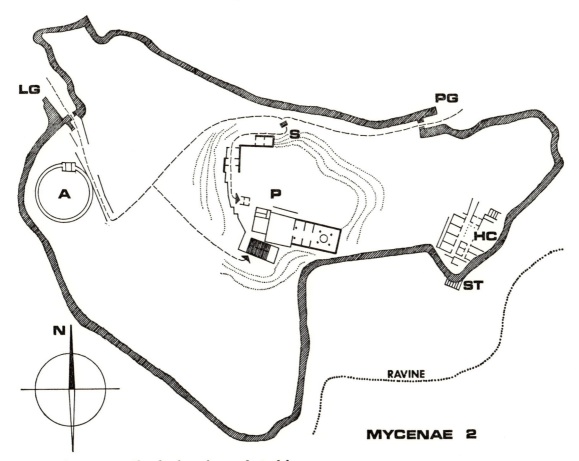

5. Mycenae. Sketch plan of second citadel
    (A) Grave Circle A. (LG) Lion Gate. (P) Palace. (S) North staircase
    (PG) Postern gate. (HC) House of Columns. (ST) Southeastern tower
    (drawing Garvey)

which run along the side of the Cyclopean wall lead-ing to the rooms constructed within the thickness of the wall. These rooms were in the upper section of the wall, and for their construction a number of stone courses apparently were removed to accommodate them. Unfortunately, these rooms are not well pre-served and their roofs, as well as part of their floors, were destroyed when the upper section of the Cyclo-pean wall rolled down the hillside. There can be no doubt of their existence, however, since sections of their side walls and floors and even the doorways lead-ing into them are preserved (Fig. 36). We have deter-mined the area of three rooms in the thickness of the wall and the threshold of a fourth. That threshold is made of conglomerate, and similar conglomerate blocks we found in what would have been the interior of the room, the fill below its floor. Room 2 is the best preserved.

There can be little doubt that the corridors and rooms are not part of the original design of the north Cyclopean wall (Fig. 37). They are later additions; the free passage along the wall was transformed into the corridors to the terminal small chamber, while the stones of the wall itself were removed in sections to make free space for the rooms. These rooms and cor-ridors recall the galleries and casemates of Tiryns. Those were designed and constructed along with the Cyclopean walls which enclose them. Their counter-parts at Mycenae seem to be the result of an after-thought—later additions which fit less well into the over-all design of the walls. It is evident, I think, that after the construction of the galleries and rooms at Tiryns, the people of Mycenae, realized their useful-ness and made the corridors and rooms in obvious imitation, adapting them as well as they could to the pre-existing old north Cyclopean wall. The galleries and casemates of Tiryns belong to the latest construc-tional period of that site; these imitations must belong to a comparable late period. In the case of the cham-ber with the inverted V roof structure, Wace con-cluded that it "was probably done at a comparatively late stage in the history of the prehistoric citadel." The exact date of the construction, however, cannot be definitely established at present. The pottery found

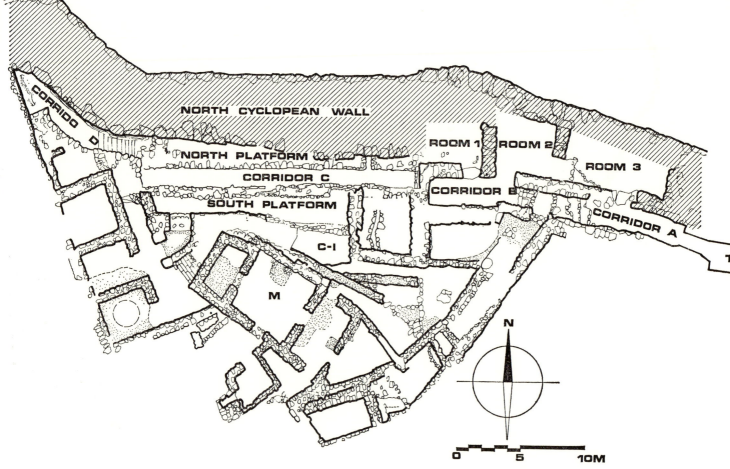

6. Mycenae 1963. Structures on northwest slope of citadel (drawing Rothman)

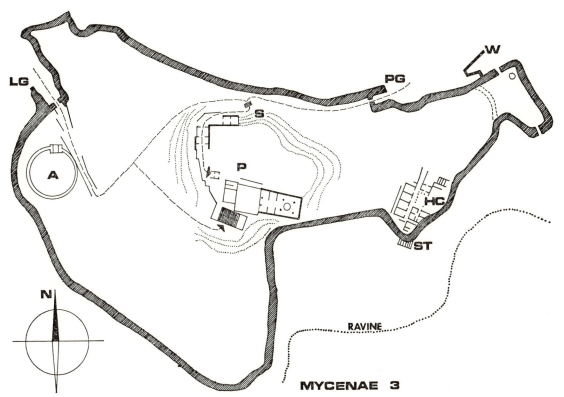

7. Mycenae. Sketch plan of third citadel. (A) Grave Circle A. (LG) Lion Gate. (PG) Postern gate. (W) Underground cistern in northeast extension. (S) North staircase. (P) Palace area. (HC) House of Columns. (ST) Southeastern tower. (drawing Garvey)

on the floor of Room 2 and in Stairway B proves that the corridors and rooms were still in use in LH III C times. Sherds of LH III C style, along with much of the B variety, were found by Wace on the floor of the small room he cleared. Among the sherds from Staircase B is the handle and rim of an open phiale typical of LH III C times (Fig. 38). It is possible to assume that corridors and rooms were added when the northeast extension was made, which constitutes the third building period of the citadel.

In 1963 we uncovered a substantial building (text fig. 6, M) to the south of Corridors B and C, belonging to LH III B times and possibly used by the military governor of the citadel.

The Third Enceinte (text fig. 7)

The northeast extension added very limited space to the *enceinte* but it remedied a serious shortcoming of the citadel. In time of a siege the people had to depend on rain for their water supply since there is no spring on the rocky hill of Mycenae. Numerous cisterns found on the hill, some of which at least must belong to the Mycenaean period, offer clear proof of a

concern over water. In addition, a few wells might have provided a limited supply. This supply, however, could not be depended upon, and if conditions were then as they are now, the situation must have been very precarious. The lack of water made the immense and almost impregnable citadel very vulnerable. To remedy this the rulers of Mycenae constructed a remarkable underground cistern and aqueduct accessible to the citadel through the northeast extension. Because the underground cistern had to be carved from living rock, and the area enclosed by the walls was hard limestone, the cistern was located immediately outside the wall where it could be dug in the soft conglomerate that forms the lower reaches of the slope. Since they did not consider it advisable to make a passage through the existing north Cyclopean wall, they built an extension and made a passage through it. The underground cistern was located below the northwestern course of the extension (text fig. 7, W).

It is the most striking construction in the citadel, a truly Cyclopean undertaking.[38] It is composed of three parts or sections. Part one is formed by a descending stepped passage cut obliquely through the north wall

[38] G. Karo, "Die Perseia von Mykenai," *AJA* (1934), pp. 123-127, pls. XII-XIII. Its opening could be seen in the days of

Schliemann, but the monument was cleared by Tsountas.

(Figs. 39, 40). Sixteen of the original steps are still preserved in the passage, which takes us, through a well-constructed doorway, outside the wall and onto an underground rectangular platform. Until recently the platform was open to the sky because its roof had collapsed. Its original arrangements, however, have been restored, and today the platform is underground and invisible from the outside, as it was in Mycenaean times. Thus it was safe from enemy attack. The approach to its covered roof was further defended by the north wall, under the shadow of which it had been placed. On the southwest side of the platform a door opens to the second section: an underground stepped passage, with twenty preserved steps, leading west and terminating in a landing some 2.80 m. below the level of the first. Three steps on the north side of the landing take us to the third section, which now turns at right angles to the platform and proceeds steeply toward the northeast (Fig. 41). Some fifty-four steps below, and about 12 m. deeper, the passage terminates at a well-like reservoir 1.60 by 0.70 m. and some 5 m. deep. The reservoir was kept filled with water through a large opening in its saddle roof, where an underground water conduit of terra-cotta pipes ended. The steps and the walls of the third section are covered with a thick coat of watertight plaster; evidently part of the stepped passage acted as an extension to the reservoir. The passages are roofed over by the typical inverted V corbel vault, or by its variation, the saddle roof, or by huge slabs placed horizontally across its walls. The first section exhibits corbel vaulting. The platform at the foot of this section was apparently roofed by horizontally placed slabs. The roof of the second section was made of slabs placed horizontally from side to side, while the third section presents both the corbel vault and the saddle type of roofing. Immediately over the reservoir the roof is of the saddle type. The steps are made mostly of limestone slabs. The construction is awe-inspiring, and the sight of anxious visitors descending into the dark depths of the earth holding lighted candles is unforgettable.

Some 2.50 m. from the opening of the cistern there is another opening in the wall, generally accepted as a drain (Fig. 42).[39] Its dimensions, however, and its careful construction are such that the opening must have served a different purpose. We are familiar with drains made in the Cyclopean wall, since at least six, belonging to two different periods of construction, have been cleared in the last four years. Drains built in the earlier period have very small openings, being mere holes in the wall; drains of the later period have well

constructed, almost rectangular, openings averaging 70 cm. in height. The so-called drain on the north wall of the extension has a channel, 7.50 m. in length, traversing the wall from outer to inner face. A person of average height can walk in it comfortably. Its opening, as we have it now, is high enough to be taken as a small doorway (Fig. 20). Even if some of its height be attributed to restoration, still it is more than the builders of the walls allowed for drains. Our excavation in July 1964 revealed a ramp leading to the opening (Fig. 43) and a substantial building occupying half of the area of the extension. The construction of the passage and the newly revealed remains prove that this opening actually is a sally port to be used especially for the protection of the underground cistern. An enemy trying secretly and at night to dig down to the roof of its underground platform could be attacked by a few men sallying forth through this opening, which could be defended easily because of its narrowness and its course.

To protect the opening of the underground cistern from the earth and stones washed down the sharp slope of the hill by rain, a retaining wall was constructed beside the opening and against the north wall (Fig. 42, R). Steffen's plan shows this retaining wall, and also marks a second wall, farther to the south. All subsequent plans of the citadel of Mycenae have followed Steffen, and until recently these were taken to be the remnants of the northeast Cyclopean wall of the first and second *enceintes*. Our discovery of the remains of that wall, however, proved the true character of the surviving walls and its purpose. Furthermore, our work in the summer of 1963 proved that what was taken to be a second retaining wall by Steffen was not a wall at all but an accumulation of stones fallen from the fortifications lying on top of a fill of earth some 1.80 m. deep. The removal of that earth-fill in 1964 revealed a storage room containing seven large pithoi and an anteroom in which the greater part of a terra-cotta bathtub was found *in situ* (Fig. 44). These rooms apparently belonged to a structure (Building A) built against the south Cyclopean wall and occupying a good section of the extension. The northern half of the area enclosed by the extended peribolos was occupied by another structure (Building B), apparently connected with the underground cistern and the north sally port (Fig. 45). These structures prove that the extension was made for the sole purpose of securing an adequate supply of water in times of war and invasion.[40]

Our excavations of 1964 also proved that the north-

---

[39] See text fig. 7. For a full discussion of the passage as revealed in 1964 cf. Mylonas, *Ephemeris*, 1962 (1966).

[40] *Supra*, p. 31. For a full discussion of the discoveries of

1964 in the northeast extension see Mylonas, in *Ephemeris*, 1962 (1966).

east extension was added at the very end of the Late Helladic III B period and constituted the latest project in the development of the citadel of Mycenae.

Summary

It may perhaps be useful to summarize the results of our study and list the building activities connected with the citadel of Mycenae, insofar as we can now detect them from existing remains.

1) Building began with the construction of the first citadel to which belong the north Cyclopean wall, the north section of the original west wall, the east section of the south Cyclopean wall, and the traces of the northeast wall found in 1958. The pottery connected with this construction belongs to the advanced years of the ceramic phase known as LH III A (*ca.* 1340 B.C.).

2) The second construction period follows, during which were built the Lion Gate and its bastion, the curtain of ashlar conglomerate which masks the north section of the west wall of the first period, the existing west Cyclopean wall, and the west section of the south wall. The original south section of the west wall of the first period was demolished. The pottery associated with these constructions belongs to the advanced years of the ceramic phase known as Late Helladic III B (*ca.* 1250 B.C.).

3) Either shortly before or along with the construction of the Lion Gate and the west Cyclopean wall of the second period, Grave Circle A was rearranged and its peribolos of slabs was erected. The pottery associated with this work belongs to the LH III B period.

4) A ramp was constructed (No. 2) leading from the Lion Gate to the top of the hill. It was 2.50 m. wide and ran from north to south. It must be considered as contemporary with the Lion Gate.

5) The postern gate (Figs. 17, 18) was constructed in a breach made in the north Cyclopean wall.

6) Some of the outer slabs of the peribolos wall of Grave Circle A were broken and left in the inclined position they assumed. The cause and date of the event are unknown.

7) A broader and more monumental ramp (No. 1) (Fig. 33) was constructed to replace Ramp 2; it was retained by the Cyclopean wall rising above the grave circle. Some of the stones of the foundations of that wall rest on the broken pieces of the circle's slabs (Fig. 34). Thus it is proved that Ramp 1, a section of which has survived, is later in construction than the re-

arrangement of the circle and the erection of the Lion Gate. It seems to be contemporary with the east terrace and its retaining wall (No. 9). The pottery associated with this building activity cannot be precisely attributed to sub-periods. The sequence of construction seems to indicate that Ramp 1 belongs to the second half of LH III B.

8) The northeast extension with the underground cistern and Buildings A and B was constructed in the closing years of the LH III B period.

9) Finally, the corridors and storerooms in the north Cyclopean wall were constructed. The date of their construction is not defined, but they must be somewhat later than the galleries of Tiryns. They were still in use at the beginning of the LH III C period since pottery of that period was found on their floors.

Perhaps more definite information will be obtained through future excavations. The summary, however, gives the sequence of the construction of the various parts of the citadel, as can be detected and proved at present.

Relationship of the Citadels of Mycenae and Tiryns

It is rather difficult to understand how a citadel so formidable, so amazingly constructed in a rugged terrain, could have been stormed by an enemy with spear, bow, and sword. Pausanias has recorded another experience of the people of Mycenae of a later period, the fifth century B.C., which may clarify the situation. About 468 B.C. the Argives attacked the Mycenaeans, who enclosed themselves in the citadel. "It was impossible," he adds, "for the Argives to storm the fort of the Mycenaeans since it was so very strong (being like Tiryns the work of the Cyclopes). Forced by necessity, however, the Mycenaeans surrendered their citadel because their food supplies were finished."[41] Perhaps their ancestors also were finally forced by necessity to surrender to the Dorian invaders, although internal dissension and treachery may have contributed to the downfall. At any rate the looting, burning conquerors destroyed the proud house of the Perseids and the Pelopids so thoroughly that it never recovered from the blow.[42]

Mycenae and Tiryns, two mighty fortresses standing at a comparatively short distance from each other and built at about the same period in the life history of the Argive plain, pose a problem of relationship which has long been under discussion.[43] It seems logical to assume that the one or the other was built

---

[41] Pausanias, VII, 25, 5, tr. J. G. Frazer.
[42] Eloquent testimony of the destruction by enemy attack of the citadel we find not only in the calcined remains of the palace but also in the hoards of bronze objects found hidden between the stone work of foundations. Tsountas, *Ephemeris*,

1891, pp. 25 ff. and Mylonas, *Ergon*, 1959, p. 99.
[43] For a full discussion of the problem cf. F. Schachermeyr, *Hethiter und Achaeer*, 1935, pp. 156 ff. D. L. Page, *History and the Homeric Iliad*, pp. 129 ff. But see S. Dow, "The Greeks in the Bronze Age," p. 21. In this discussion we do not mention

first, since building them concurrently would have been a very difficult task for the times. The construction of citadels as strong and extensive as those of Mycenae and Tiryns would have required many years of continuous effort. One look at these mighty walls would prove sufficient to convince any skeptic of the fact. The quarrying, the transportation, even the rudimentary dressing of the hard limestone with bronze tools, the erection of the huge walls could not have been done within a few years. The immense task also indicates the considerable strength and importance of the ruler who undertook it. It follows, therefore, that the mighty ruler of the citadel that was constructed first would not have allowed the erection of another fortress so near his own—a construction which could have been interrupted so easily and often if necessary—unless it was related in some way to his own; he could not permit another great fortress to be built which might develop into the seat of a rival for mastery of the Argive plain.

Again, it has been pointed out that the mode of living of the people of the two sites was such that it could not have existed long if a threat of a raid mounted from the one or the other citadel was ever present. We may recall that the population of each site actually lived beyond the citadel in the open country around it. It seems reasonable to assume that a close relationship existed between the two.

A close relationship is also indicated by their architectural remains. Certain elements appear first in the one and are then repeated in the other. The gradual expansions of the two citadels parallel each other. We noted how the gate of the first citadel of Tiryns was in the middle of its east wall, and how it stood unprotected by side bastions. The second citadel resulted when new gates were added defended by bastions and reached through an easily defended passage. Such a development, proving a consciousness of the vulnerability of an unprotected gate and the value of bastions limiting the space in front of it and exposing an approaching enemy to attacks from three sides, was not reached in a drafting room but through experience gained from actual construction. This experience perhaps was obtained when the gate of the first citadel of Mycenae was built. If our restoration of its ground plan is correct, in that gate we find used for the first time a valuable principle of military tactics; that of forcing a reduction in the numbers of an enemy attacking the gate and at the same time exposing him to

the fire of defenders from three sides. That is, we find for the first time a gate approached by means of a narrow passageway placed along the length of a fortification wall and ending in a narrow court between that wall and a projecting bastion. This element by itself cannot prove relationship or dependence, since the people of Tiryns could have repeated the arrangement after seeing it, but then the Lion Gate was built at Mycenae. Shortly afterwards an almost identical gate was constructed at Tiryns and the conglomerate blocks used in its construction were most probably carried there from Mycenae. The galleries and casemates of Tiryns are reflected in the corridors and rooms constructed along and within the thickness of the north Cyclopean wall of Mycenae. The underground cistern in the Northeast Extension of Mycenae, reached from the interior by an underground passage cut under the fortification wall, apparently is reflected by the underground vaulted passages just disclosed by Verdelis at Tiryns. It seems to us that these architectural parallels indicate a close relationship between the two citadels and their masters.

If we now turn to the legends of the district we shall find echoes of similar relationships. Certainly legends should not be treated as historic facts, but their consideration should not be excluded entirely. They form the only pointers and guides we have to the Heroic Age of Greece and were built around a kernel of fact which is most important to consider. These legends relate that first Proitos built Tiryns, using the Cyclopes whom he brought from Asia Minor for the purpose.[44] The citadel of Mycenae was built later by Perseus, a contemporary of Megapenthes, son of Proitos, and he too used the Cyclopes for the construction. Apollodoros has preserved the tradition according to which Sthenelos, the son of Perseus, brought Argos and Tiryns under his domain;[45] and the exploits of Herakles the Tirynthian at the order of Eurystheus, the king of Mycenae, seem to indicate that Tiryns was still subject to Mycenae in the closing years of the Perseid dynasty. We have no legends indicating the relationship of these citadels after that. But the second book of the *Iliad* seems to indicate that Mycenae must have had not only access to the sea but a stronghold there, since its king was also the ruler of many islands and since he possessed so many ships.[46]

The survey of all possible information seems to indicate that a close relationship must have existed between the two citadels; that perhaps Tiryns was a

---

Argos since its Mycenaean citadel is not preserved, but the same reasoning holds true for that site also.

[44] Strabo, VIII, 372. Proitos imported from Lykia seven Cyclopes.

[45] Apollodoros, II, 4, 6.

[46] *Iliad*, II, 569-575, and 108. Agamemnon contributed to the

expedition 100 ships and besides lent 60 additional galleys to the Arkadians. In the Catalogue, however, Tiryns is ruled over by Diomedes and this does not agree with the rest of the tradition unless we assume that Diomedes was under the sovereignty of Agamemnon.

dependent of Mycenae. The two citadels dominated the two ends of the plain, while a third, Argos, was located at the third point of entry and exit. Furthermore, Tiryns would have guarded the approach from the sea and the area where the ships of the Mycenaeans must have docked.

We may note in this connection that perhaps the builders of these mighty fortresses formed a guild or an association of artisans who carried from one job to another the experience gained. From the tablets of Pylos we learn of the existence of associations of carpenters, of bronze workers, of masons who carried out the wishes of the *wanax* and filled the need of his state.[47] To such families and guilds of masons we may attribute the construction of the great citadels of the Argolid, even that of palaces so far apart as those of Mycenae and Pylos. That these associations were controlled by the ruler of the state seems to be indicated by the contents of the tablets. As Professor Page put it so graphically, "one would suppose," from the intimate detail contained in the palace archives, "that not a seed could be sown, not a gram of bronze worked, not a cloth woven, not a goat reared or a hog fattened, without the filing of a form in the Royal Palace."[48] The system of government revealed by the palace

archives would also indicate that the mighty citadels of Mycenae and Tiryns, so near each other, were related administratively. It seems to us that Tiryns was the dependent and Mycenae the ruling center, that Tiryns provided Mycenae with the safe approach to and control of the sea lane which connected the Argive plain with the outside world. That sea lane was of the utmost importance to the commercial activities of Mycenae, which in LH III times are proved to have been considerable.

Pylos presents a different situation and a mystery. The palace of the king covers the top of a hill with a breath-taking view and with beautiful olive trees, but thus far no protecting fortification walls have been found. The palace does not seem to be the center of a citadel. The sides of the hill may be steep and the location might have been easy to defend, but the hill of Mycenae is more easily defended, and yet it was strongly fortified. Why was the palace of Nestor open when all other Mycenaean palaces known to date were so elaborately protected by formidable walls? Here we have a problem which awaits solution. The evidence found thus far yields no explanation. The palace of Nestor remains unique.

THE CITADEL OF ATHENS

The Akropolis of Athens is also easy to defend, and yet in late Mycenaean times its summit was surrounded by mighty fortification walls. Like Mycenae, the Akropolis and its slopes were inhabited from Neolithic times through the Bronze Age. Remains of the Early, Middle, and Late Helladic I and II periods are limited to pottery, graves, and fragmentary walls. The sacred rock was used so much in the Historic era that the remains of its prehistoric structures in later years had to yield to more important monuments. It seems, however, that the Akropolis remained unfortified until late Mycenaean times. A number of structures which stood on its summit even in the early years of the LH III B period were constructed on terraces, and the terrace walls of considerable height apparently served for defense although they were not primarily built as fortifications.[49] A stepped pathway built in a natural cleft with steep rocky formations on either side led to the northeast corner of the summit (text fig. 8, No. 6).

This was cut in two by the mediaeval wall of the Akropolis. The part within the summit, its west end, was cleared between 1880 and 1885 by Kavvadias,[50] who found it covered with a fill, which was piled over it after the Persian withdrawal from Athens in 480 B.C. Its eastern section was cleared by Broneer in 1931-1932 and in 1933-1934.[51] A good section of the pathway to the east of the mediaeval wall was found covered with undisturbed deposits of the LH III B late period; for instance, its four steps by the wall were so covered, as well as the first ramp farther east, and the lower steps of the passage revealed in 1931-1932; in the last case the deposit had a depth of 65 cm. It is evident therefore that the construction of the stepped path antedates the late years of the LH III B period. How far back it goes, however, cannot be ascertained. Perhaps it is reasonable to assume that it existed at a very early period and that, repaired and modified, it was used through a number of centuries, perhaps afford-

[47] M. Ventris and J. Chadwick, *Mycenaean Documents*, pp. 123, 133-136 and L. Palmer, *Minoans and Mycenaeans*, p. 153. It may be added that perhaps the control exercised by the *wanax* over these associations of technicians is reflected in the myth of Daidalos who was retained by Minos after the construction of the palace at Knossos.

[48] Page, *op.cit.*, p. 182.

[49] For a complete description of the prehistoric remains of

the Akropolis of Athens together with the bibliography see now the excellent monograph of Spyros Iacovides, Ἡ μυκηναϊκὴ ἀκρόπολις τῶν Ἀθηνῶν, 1962; for the terraces see his fig. 16 and pp. 104-105.

[50] Kavvadias and Kawerau, *Die Ausgrabugen zu Akropolis*, 1907, pls. Γ and Δ.

[51] *Hesperia*, 2 (1933), pp. 351-355, and 4 (1935), pp. 109-113. Iacovides, *loc.cit.*

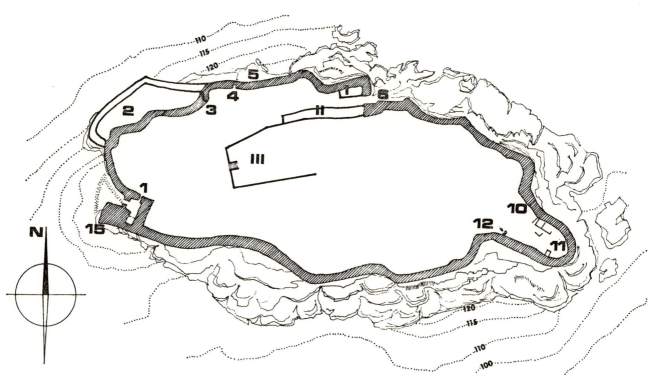

8. Athens. Sketch of citadel (after Iacovides and Mylonas)

ing, in spite of its steep grade, an ascent to the summit from the very beginning of its use for habitation.[52]

At least in two sections of the stepped passage it was found that below the Mycenaean accumulation that covered it there existed a fill characterized by sherds belonging to pre-Mycenaean periods. Perhaps this earlier fill indicates the period in which it was originally made. Whatever the date of its construction may be, it can be assumed that in the late Mycenaean era, most probably in the early years of the LH III B period, a gate was constructed to which the stepped passage led. Holland maintained that to the north of that gate was added a tower or bastion protecting it; he figured out its position and drew an impressive restoration.[53] Whether or not his suggestion and restoration is accepted (and Iacovides has proved that the walls on which Holland based his conclusion are not Mycenaean), the fact remains that an arrangement of a formal gate-opening did precede the construction of the Cyclopean peribolos wall of the Akropolis, because that wall on the northeast corner of the hill was constructed upon the upper edge of the cleft. This left the stepped passageway outside the wall but under its shadow, and it was continued to the retaining wall of the terrace, which apparently formed the south side of the opening. Traces of the Cyclopean peribolos we

find again farther north and beyond the foundations which Holland attributed to a tower complex. The gap in the Cyclopean wall may indicate that here the continuous course of the peribolos was interrupted and it was interrupted because the opening existed. If this reasoning is correct, then the stepped passageway and its gate were still in use when the Cyclopean wall was constructed and even after its construction.

It may be objected that Holland states that the gate-opening to which the ascent led was blocked during the construction of the Cyclopean wall, since three walls parallel to each other are found across its opening.[54] The existence of these walls is certain. They were uncovered in the early years of the excavation of the Akropolis and they are to be seen in the original plans. No concrete evidence, however, has been brought forth to indicate, let alone prove, the date of these walls. They were assumed by Holland to be Mycenaean, because their position agreed with his hypothesis. Later on they were assumed to be Mycenaean because they block the northeast Late Helladic III ascent to the summit. But they could have been built long after the construction of the Mycenaean fortification wall, in fact at any time between the Prehistoric era and the Persian Wars. It has been suggested also that the walls blocking the passage

[52] It is interesting to note that the approach to the main gate of the citadel of Gla was also stepped. *Infra*, p. 44.

[53] L. Holland, *AJA*, 28 (1924), pp. 146-147, fig. 3.

[54] Holland's conclusion of the Mycenaean date of the cross-walls was accepted by Broneer, *Hesperia*, 2 (1933), p. 352, and with modifications by Iacovides, *op.cit.*, pp. 74-77 and 97-98.

served a staircase built, at the time of its construction, within the width of the Mycenaean fortification wall. This of course is a hypothesis that cannot be proved. Against it is the fact that such an arrangement is unparalleled in the history of Late Helladic construction. Both the staircase by the Lion Gate of Mycenae and the ramps to the top of the walls of Gla were built outside the wall itself and not within its width. We would expect an outside staircase, if such did exist at that point of the fortification wall of Athens, to be a staircase built in accordance with the pattern exhibited at Mycenae and Gla.

One, perhaps, may wonder how in the pre-citadel days of the Akropolis of Athens there could be a gate when there was no fortification wall enclosing the summit. To this can be countered that the existence of the stepped passage is certain and it led to the top of the Akropolis. We have already noted that the structures on the Akropolis in its pre-citadel period were built on high terraces or platforms whose retaining walls acted as fortifications. Two of those terraces were actually built at the edge of the rocky formation of the Akropolis on either side of the west section of the stepped passage.[55] They certainly acted as bastions defending that access and between them a gate could have been constructed. Whether or not that access and gate were the only ones leading to the summit of the Akropolis in this earlier period cannot be ascertained now. Another approach and passage, even the principal approach, may have existed on the west side, where we find the later ascents to the Akropolis. However, no traces of it have been reported thus far.

Late in the Mycenaean period a Cyclopean peribolos wall was finally built around the summit of the Akropolis transforming it into a real citadel. Remains of this peribolos were revealed especially during the great excavations conducted by Kavvadias between 1880 and 1885 and some can be seen even today. The best-preserved sections are to be seen to the south of the southwest corner of Mnesikles' Propylaia (Fig. 46), deep down below the present surface at the southwest corner of the Parthenon, and behind the Akropolis Museum at the southeast corner of the hill, where, following the rocky configuration of the ground, the wall forms a long loop (text fig. 8, No. 11); smaller sections can be traced here and there;[56] thus its perimeter on the summit can be established with a great degree of certainty. The peribolos is of typical Cyclopean construction. Its width ranges from 3 to 6 m. and its best-preserved height, by the southwest corner of the Propylaia, amounts to 4 m. Perhaps its original

height reached 9 to 10 m. Its perimeter approaches the total of 700 m. and the enclosed area amounts to 25,000 square meters. In the course of the restoration in 1936 of the bastion on which stands the temple of Nike, Balanos found the remains of a massive tower below the floor area of that bastion. It is long and narrow, 9.50 m. in maximum width by at least 19.50 m. in length, and its axis, somewhat different from that of the later bastion, runs approximately from east to west (text fig. 8, No. 15, and text fig. 9). The south side of the tower is almost completely preserved, and so is the greater part of its west side. Only a fraction of its north wall survives and seven blocks in a single row, discovered in the early years of the excavation of the Akropolis, are taken to be part of its east side. Some 4.50 m. from its west side and within the width of the tower was found a solid wall built from the north to the south side, while the rest of its body was filled with small stones loosely piled. We should note especially that no wall was revealed connecting the tower to the section of the peribolos wall, which we shall call the west Cyclopean wall, preserved farther to its east; nor are there any signs on the face of that wall indicating such an attachment.

This tower definitely proves the existence of a gate, a main gate, at this the west side of the Akropolis. Unfortunately, no traces of this gate are preserved and its exact position and plan become problematical, especially since paucity of remains makes uncertain the actual course of the peribolos from the point where it is interrupted by the south wall of the Propylaia. The late Professor Gorham Stevens in 1946 revealed a fragment of the Cyclopean wall to the north of the northwest corner of the tower and almost due west of the central passage of Mnesikles' Propylaia. It consists of a number of large limestone blocks that originally formed the outer face of the Cyclopean wall, which we shall call the southwest wall. The size of these blocks, some 5 m. in length, and the formation of the rock, enabled him to suggest the course of the wall to the northeast and across from the tower. He also noted a stepped approach ascending the west side and located along the west and north side of the tower. On the basis of these observations he restored the west gate of the Mycenaean citadel of Athens (see text fig. 8) leaving the tower unattached to the main body of the Mycenaean west wall which has survived (text fig. 9, No. 3).[57] The arrangement offers striking strategic advantages. Enemies ascending the slope would find themselves in a court-like area some 14 by 20 m.; they would be exposed to the missiles of defenders mounted on top of the tower and the wall

---

[55] Iacovides, *op.cit.*, drawing 16, I-II.

[56] They were studied again and are completely described by Iacovides, *op.cit.*, drawings 17, 19, 20-23, 25-33. For the latest

description of the Mycenaean tower below the Nike temple see now Iacovides, pp. 106 ff., where the pertinent bibliography.

[57] G. Stevens, *Hesperia*, 15 (1946), pp. 73-77 and plan 2.

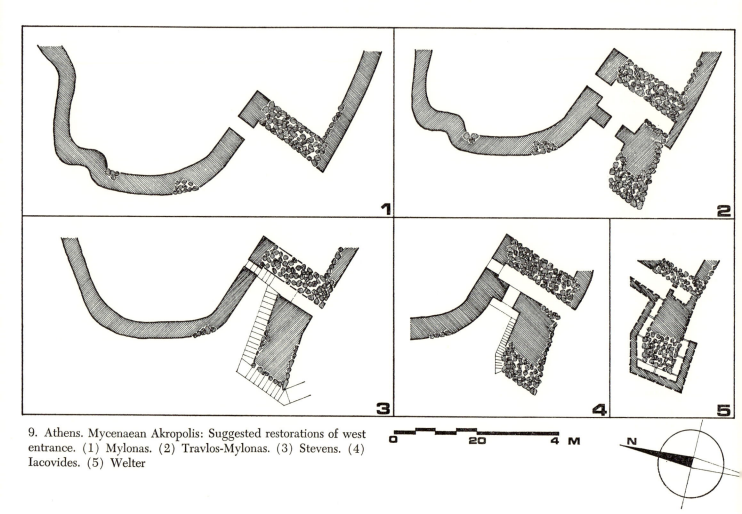

9. Athens. Mycenaean Akropolis: Suggested restorations of west entrance. (1) Mylonas. (2) Travlos-Mylonas. (3) Stevens. (4) Iacovides. (5) Welter

0   20   4 M

N

across it to the north. As they reached the top of the slope, they would have to turn at right angles and thus again expose their undefended right sides to the defenders on top of the west wall. Thus harassed they would have to attack the comparatively narrow gate. However, the tower standing isolated from the rest of the peribolos would not offer great protection. Of course, one could suppose that it was connected by a wooden bridge with the wall. But the technicians who planned and carried out the construction of the peribolos and gate appear to have been more ingenious and better versed in arranging fortification walls than to have accepted this rather awkward solution.

Welter, who was among the first to study the remains of the tower at the time of its revelation by Balanos, attaches the tower to the surviving Cyclopean west wall and suggests the existence of a guard room between it and the wall (text fig. 9, No. 5).[58] Similarly Travlos in his first restoration of the course of the peribolos attached the tower to the existing wall.[59] However, Iacovides rightly remarked that no traces of an attachment of the tower to the wall are to be seen, especially on the face of the west wall, which has been perfectly preserved.[60] Proceeding on the basis of Stevens' solutions, he suggests a most ingenious arrangement of tower and gate (text fig. 9, No. 4). However, his restoration leaves an empty space between tower and west wall open to the southwest and accessible from that point where the rock formation is not prohibitive to climbing. This forms a disadvantage that is difficult to justify.

Perhaps the situation could be satisfactorily explained if we assumed that the tower was a later addition; that at first the entrance was arranged as indicated in text fig. 9, No. 1. Later a tower was built on top of the projecting boulders to the west of the west Cyclopean wall. The tower was attached to that wall by a spur whose width was less than that of the west side of the tower. Since the attachment was not contemporary with the west wall, its stones, in accordance with Mycenaean construction methods, would not have been bound with those of that wall, but would have merely been placed against its face so that when they were removed they left no trace on that face. And the connecting wall was removed in the Historic era when that section of the hill was rearranged for an early shrine, perhaps of Nike.[61] The fragment of the east wall of the tower, if it actually goes back to the Mycenaean era, becomes meaningful if we placed a small guardroom between it and the

west Cyclopean wall. I had reached that conclusion when Travlos showed me his revised plan of the citadel of Athens in which the same solution, independently reached, is given. A guard room placed in a dipylon arrangement, added at a later period, will adequately explain all the disclosed remains to date (text fig. 9, No. 2). It seems to us that our solution is in agreement with the ability of the Mycenaean wall builders and with other parallels of a gradual expansion of defenses.

Whatever the form of the west gate may have been, the fact remains that an entrance to the Mycenaean citadel did exist on the west slope of the Akropolis and that it was its principal gate. The question arises whether or not the northeast approach to the summit used in the pre-citadel period was also in use at this time; whether it led to a postern gate. The consensus of those who studied and worked in the Akropolis area is that the northeast passageway was blocked and abandoned when the Cyclopean fortification was constructed.[62] The opinion is based on two points: 1) Across the passage and between the two platforms that formed the sides of its gate three parallel walls are to be found. It is assumed that they were built when the Cyclopean wall was constructed. Thus, it is reasoned, the passage was blocked in LH III B times; 2) Broneer found over some of the steps of the passage a fill dating from the late Mycenaean period. Also he found a paving (*strosis*) which he attributes to a house, and foundations of two structures built across the passageway. He attributes all these remains to humble homes which were abruptly abandoned—so suddenly indeed that their owners left their pots and pans on the floor of the houses. Since the "debris from these houses extended over a part of the stepped passage, it seemed reasonable to conclude that the postern gate was no longer used at the time when the houses were built."[63] The abandonment of the houses is placed at the end of LH III B and the beginning of LH III C period by the pottery found.

There are a number of questions which the logical conclusions based on Broneer's discovery will leave unanswered. First of all, the date of the walls blocking the passage (the first point above), as we have seen above, is not established by concrete evidence but is assumed on an architectural hypothesis. The second point also raises difficult questions. If the people who abandoned their "homes" across the passageway so abruptly were poor, one wonders why they did not go after their belongings when the danger

---

[58] G. Welter, *AA*, 54 (1939), fig. 4.
[59] J. Travlos, Πολεοδομικὴ ἐξέλιξις τῶν Ἀθηνῶν, 1960, fig. 7.
[60] Iacovides, *op.cit.*, p. 167.
[61] G. Oikonomos, *Ephemeris*, 1939-41, pp. 97 ff. G. Welter, *AA*, 1939, pp. 1 ff. I am indebted to Travlos for permission to

use his unpublished revised plan.
[62] Holland, Broneer, and Iacovides agree that the passage was abandoned in Mycenaean times.
[63] Broneer, *Hesperia*, 4 (1935), pp. 109-111.

had passed. Since their vases were found broken but not scattered the breakage could not be attributed to enemy action. Intruders and destroyers do not break vases without hurling or kicking them out of the house.[64] The remains found by Broneer, except for those in one area, are hard-packed pavements. No walls limiting them are preserved. The walls found across the stepped passage in one area are so flimsy that they are said to belong to a shelter rather than to a house. The Mycenaean fill found over the steps of the passage is taken to indicate the abandonment of that passage in Mycenaean times. The fill seems to belong to one phase of the late LH III B period, and in one section is 65 cm. deep. This seems to indicate that it did not accumulate gradually over the years, but that perhaps it is an artificial fill. One wonders whether the covering of the stepped passage in sections was not due to an effort to resurface it for continued use. This might hold true especially if the date of the construction of the stepped passage, which remains undefined, is placed in an era older than LH III. Again one may wonder whether some of the people of Athens did not build temporary shelters under the protecting fortification wall of the citadel and right in front of its gate in time of danger; they could have rushed through that gate to the protection of the *enceinte* in case the enemy below the hill tried to reach their shelters, which could actually be protected by defenders on the wall rising above the south side of the passageway. When the enemy withdrew, the walls of the shelters near the gate were removed leaving only a pavement. The wall of shelter E, across the passageway, may have been left to act as a retaining wall for a raised level of the passageway. Finally, since at two well-preserved Mycenaean citadels, at Mycenae and Tiryns, a postern gate was added to the existing old entranceways, it is difficult to accept the abandonment on the Akropolis of an existing ascent which was in long use and which was of value since it was located at the other end of the hill. Perhaps the problem needs further study, but to us it seems reasonable to assume that the old northeast ascent to the summit of the Akropolis was still in use and led to a small postern gate after the construction of the Cyclopean wall.

Farther west on the north side of the citadel is another stepped descent, the northwest descent, which was investigated by Kavvadias in 1897 and again by Keramopoullos in 1929.[65] It goes through the Classical wall of the Akropolis to the rocky slope below, where it continues with 31 steps to the edge of the rocky plateau that spreads before the openings of the caves of Pan and Apollo (text fig. 8, No. 3). Iacovides suggests that it was originally made in Mycenaean times to provide communication between the summit and the caves that form an intermediate plateau between it and the foot of the hill. His investigations of the area revealed along the edge of the plateau fragments of a wall and traces on the rock where once a wall stood and these enabled him to trace a Cyclopean lower peribolos enclosing this intermediate plateau (text fig. 8, No. 2). It starts from a point immediately east of the top of the northwest descent and terminates above the original small cave of the Klepsydra under the northeast corner of the Pinakotheke. The area enclosed is that of the caves of Pan, Apollo, and the Pythion. This small enclosed space he identifies as the Pelargikon of tradition. It could have been used as a lower citadel to which people repaired in time of war, though the area it encloses is very small. Its only communication seems to have been with the summit through the stepped northwest descent.[66]

Some 45 m. west of the Erechtheum a natural crack in the north rocky slope of the Akropolis developed into a deep, almost vertical fissure when the outer piece of the rock broke away and slid a little down the slope. The top of this outer piece, however, rests against the main mass of the hill; thus the fissure is almost closed at the top. Over that top passes the Akropolis wall, leaving in one point, inside the fortified area, an opening leading to the fissure. This opening is to be found at the northwest corner of the small square building generally referred to as the House of the Arrephoroi (text fig. 8, No. 4). The top of the fissure was investigated in 1897 by Kavvadias, who found in it two flights of stairs terminating in the cave of Aglauros. He placed their construction in Frankish or Turkish times, but it was evident that the fissure was used as a descent in the Classical era. His suggestion that it was used by the Arrephoroi in their nightly mission to the Peribolos of Aphrodite met with wide acceptance.[67] In our times, however, it has been discovered that the stairway continued below the floor of the cave. Broneer, who made the discovery, cleared the fissure with great ingenuity and success in two exciting campaigns in 1937 and 1938. He cleared it to its very bottom and proved that in Mycenaean times it was made into a fountain and reservoir

---

[64] At the time of the abandonment and evacuation of Smyrna by its Greek population, I was able to see what happens to the possessions of people who suddenly abandon their homes at the approach of an enemy. Whatever the Turkish soldiers could not carry to their homes, they tossed into the streets.

[65] Kavvadias, *Ephemeris*, 1897, pp. 1-32, pl. 4. Keramopoullos, *Deltion*, 1929, pp. 86-88.

[66] Iacovides, *op.cit.*, pp. 188-199.

[67] Kavvadias, *Ephemeris*, 1897, pp. 26-32; *Praktika*, 1896, pp. 17 ff. Kavvadias and Kawerau, *op.cit.*, pp. 45 ff.

reached by long flights of stairs secured against the sides of the fissure.[68] The total depth of the chasm amounts to 34.50 m.; its width of about 1.35 m. at the top increases to about 2 m. in its lower portion. The descent was made by eight flights of stairs; the first two were revealed by Kavvadias, the rest by Broneer. The steps of Flights III and IV were supported by loose rubble secured by a timber framework (text fig. 10) similar to that employed by the Mycenaeans in the construction of their houses. The last three flights, VI-VIII, had stone steps well secured in cuttings in the rock and supported by an understructure of rubble walls. Below the last step of Flight VIII to the level of the water, a sheer drop of about 8 m. was made into a circular well-shaft, about 2 m. in diameter at the top, whose sides were shored up by wooden beams and planks, since the clayish rock into which the well was cut is soft and crumbles easily. A small reservoir some 4 m. in diameter, shaped perhaps like a beehive, was cut at the bottom of the well-shaft with a deep settling-pit at its center. The water that drained out of the rocky formation of the slope collected in the reservoir, providing a copious supply for the people of the citadel. The water could be drawn with the use of a rope from a platform below Flight VIII (text fig. 10). This amazing and most ingenious construction was completely underground and hidden from the view of the outsiders. And when the opening to the cave of Aglauros was walled up, it could not be detected and was completely secured from outside attack.

The pottery found in the reservoir and in the passage enabled Broneer to conclude that the life of the fountain was comparatively brief. Apparently the wooden supports deteriorated quickly from exposure to so much moisture, and when they broke loose the whole structure collapsed. No attempt was made to restore it; the fountain was abandoned and the fissure was used as a dumping place thereafter. Again the pottery indicates that the fountain was constructed in the closing years of the ceramic phase known as LH III B and continued in use in the early years of LH III C. Perhaps it served the people of the citadel for a quarter of a century, the twenty-five years around the turn of the thirteenth into the twelfth century.

The Mycenaean remains of the Akropolis are neither extensive nor spectacular, yet they are sufficient to give us a clear picture of a citadel fortified comparatively late in the history of the building of citadels. It seems certain that the hill of Athens was fortified later than the hills of Mycenae and Tiryns. The questions arise: what is the date of its fortifica-tions, and was the citadel of Athens gradually enlarged, as were the other two. Iacovides has aptly pointed out that the formation of the Akropolis is such that its entire area from the very beginning had to be enclosed by its peribolos which, in accordance with the Mycenaean custom, had to be erected on the brow of its rocky formation. This fact and the pottery found by Kolbe in the wall itself below the northwest corner of the Parthenon, the sherds found in the tower, as well as those from the shelters of the "squatters" and in the fountain by Broneer, led him to conclude that the walls of the citadel were constructed at one time after the third quarter of the thirteenth century B.C.[69] Unfortunately, the sherds found in the tower and those in the fragments of the wall of the Pelargikon are too few and too uncertain to serve as a determining factor. They would not exclude the suggestion, already made, that perhaps the tower was a later addition to the peribolos. It would be equally possible to maintain that what Iacovides calls the Pelargikon was added later, and of course the fountain is a later development since its construction is placed in the closing years of LH III B period. The difference in date suggested would not be great; it indicates only a gradual development of the *enceinte* to fill needs felt in the course of its usefulness.

The construction of the fountain finds striking parallels in the building of the underground cistern at Mycenae and especially in the underground passages from the lower citadel of Tiryns to a water supply outside the walls. All these attempts to remedy an outstanding weakness of the fortified citadel seem to have been almost contemporary. It would be perhaps nearer the truth to maintain that they followed each other in close succession. Perhaps the effort to provide the citadel with its own water supply, independent of weather conditions and immune to enemy attacks, was spurred not only by impending enemy actions but also by the construction, as an example, of the first solution to the problem. That example we think must have been the underground cistern of Mycenae. Its success inspired the other attempts.

Perhaps next the passages of Tiryns were made, that citadel being so closely connected with Mycenae. There we find the attempt to solve the problem without changing the existing arrangement of fortifications. After all, in Tiryns there did not exist the factor of the hard rock which had forced the people of Mycenae to build an addition to their *enceinte*— an addition for which they fortunately had the space. Finally, using the existing arrangement, the people of Athens developed the fissure into a fountain in a simi-

[68] Broneer, *Hesperia*, 7 (1938), pp. 168-170; 8 (1939), pp. 317-433, and *AJA*, 42 (1938), pp. 445-450.

[69] Iacovides, *op.cit.*, pp. 205-208, where the pertinent bibliography.

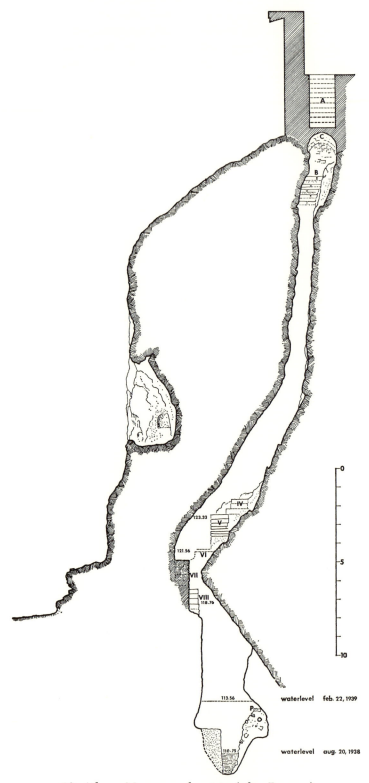

10. Athens. Mycenaean fountain (after Broneer)

lar manner. Instead of an underground stepped passage, they developed a vertical, stepped passage in the fissure, which in a way was underground since it was enveloped by the rocky formation. It is possible, as Iacovides suggests, that the opening to the fissure was detected when the Cyclopean wall was being constructed over its top. Someone, perhaps, realized that water would accumulate at the bottom of the fissure, just as someone figured out at Tiryns that water would be found in the rocky formation beyond the walls. When the building activity for fountains occurred, then the possibilities of the fissure were recalled and this resulted in the creation of that ingenious arrangement. When it collapsed, it was felt that its short-lived function did not justify the effort needed to restore it and so the fountain was abandoned. One may wonder whether the same ingenious artisans were not responsible for all three of the surviving solutions to a water supply.

The Mycenaean citadel of Athens was neither destroyed by the enemy action that laid low the citadels of Mycenae and Tiryns nor was it abandoned. It survived into the Historic era and served the people of Athens for centuries. Gradually, however, it was transformed into a great religious and monumental center and its remains were buried below the expanding area of the Akropolis or were demolished to yield to newer structures imposed by the changing needs and ambitious development of the community. Its ruins, however, help to point out the fact that in late Mycenaean times, perhaps in the legendary days of Theseus, the Akropolis was the center of a thriving and powerful state.

THE CITADEL OF GLA

A Mycenaean stronghold that cannot be compared to any other known citadel is to be found in the eastern end of Lake Kopais in Boiotia, on a rocky eminence known today as Goulas or Gla. We find no reference to it in ancient literature and its name has remained unknown. Noack, years ago, maintained that it is the Homeric Arne, but his identification has not found favor with scholars.[70] Its ruins were excavated by de Ridder, but they were more fully investigated and cleared between 1955 and 1961 by Threpsiades.[71] Owing to his efforts, we now have an excellent survey map of the site made by the Geographic Service of the Greek Army (Fig. 47) and striking air photographs made by the Royal Hellenic Airforce (Fig. 48).

The site is an isolated rocky island, shaped like a pear, rising at its northwest section to a maximum height of 70 m. above the level of the plain. Its fortification wall, closely following the edge of the rocky plateau as was customary in Mycenaean times, has a perimeter of some 3,000 m., and encloses an area of some 200,000 sq. m. The citadel of Gla is the largest known, encompassing nearly seven times as much space as that enclosed by the walls of Mycenae and ten times as much as that of Tiryns. Apparently its circuit was constructed at one time. Its walls nowhere rise more than 3 m. above the rock on which they stand, but their foundation courses are everywhere preserved and exhibit an average thickness of 5.50 m. They present an interesting indented outline, a series of retreating angles set at intervals of about 6 to 11 m., ranging from 30 to 60 cm. in depth; in very few cases the depth is less.[72] Most of the stones used in its construction are rectangular in shape and are laid in horizontal courses (Figs. 49 and 50). Thus the walls differ in appearance from the Cyclopean walls of Mycenae, Tiryns, and Athens.

Four gates gave access to the *enceinte*. One of these is on the north side (Fig. 47, Gate Γ), another about the center of the west side (Gate Δ), and two in the indentation of the south side (Gates A and B). The easterly gate of the south side, Gate B, is a double gateway, while what we may call the southwest gate (Gate A) seems to have been the main gate of the *enceinte*. There the ends of the two walls, forming a

---

[70] Noack, *AM.*, 19 (1894), pp. 405-485, and especially 461-480. De Ridder, *BCH*, 18 (1894), pp. 271-310 and 446-452. J. G. Frazer, in Pausanias, v, pp. 120-130. T. W. Allen, in *CR*, 17 (1903), p. 239, equated Gla with Glechon, known from fragment 38 of Hesiod (ed. Rzach 1902), while A. W. Gomme, in *Essays and Studies Presented to William Ridgeway*, 1914, p. 123, suggests that "either Phlegya or Gyrton might be the ancient name of Gla." Villagers today call it *Kastraki* (castle). The site is two and a quarter miles from the east shore of the lake and some three miles from the natural outlets (*katabothrai*), to which the people of the Mycenaean period dug three drainage canals and other dikes by means of which they controlled the waters of the lake. N. Kambanis, "Le dessèchement du lac Copaïs par les anciens," *BCH*, 16 (1892),

pp. 121-137; 17 (1893), pp. 322-342. E. Kenney, "The Ancient Drainage of the Copais," *Liverpool Annals of Art and Archaeology*, 22 (1935), pp. 189 ff. The height of the site at the north gate is only 12 m. above the plain.

[71] Threpsiades, *Praktika*, 1957, p. 49. The results of his work appear in this and subsequent volumes of the *Praktika* and in the *Ergon* for the years 1957-1961. To Mrs. J. Threpsiades I am indebted for the illustrations of the site published here (Figs. 47-50). Fig. 47 has intentionally been placed with South to the top of the page to correspond to the airview of fig. 48; the arrangement permits an instructive comparison of the two.

[72] Thus they differ from the offsets known from Troy VI and Tiryns.

re-entering angle, terminate in two large towers, the eastern almost twice as long as the western (11.50 m. to the door post as against 6 m.), between which a gate is formed 4.15 m. in width.[73] To the gate a stepped, paved approach led from the plain. A guard room, measuring 4.25 by 2.90 m. with a door 1.80 m. wide, was made in the thickness of the west tower; it opens to a roofed court which to the east is flanked by a long and narrow room. Similar guard rooms and courts are to be found behind all the other gates. Fragments of bronze plates and nails discovered in the fill of the passage indicate that the wooden doors were covered or decorated with bronze plate. Ramps led to the top of towers and palisades. Perhaps we should note that between the towers of the southwest gate, gate A, and in front of it a court is formed with a longer east side along the greater tower. This recalls the arrangement of the postern gate of Mycenae. Thus the number of an enemy attacking the gate could have been reduced by the narrowness of the court, and at the same time the attackers' unprotected right sides would have been exposed to the missiles of the defenders stationed on top of the eastern tower. Threpsiades' clearing of the gates proved that only the southwest gate, the main

gate A, was provided with towers. In the other cases the thickness of the wall was increased on either side of the gate, forming narrow projecting buttresses of a small width suggesting bastions. In these gates it appears that the actual wooden door was placed at the interior line of the wall, thus forming a narrow passage in front of it which corresponds to the thickness of the wall. It is interesting to note that the guard room by the right hand entrance of the south gate, the smallest of these guard rooms, measures 2.40 x 3 m., and its walls are preserved to a height of 1.10 m.

The large area enclosed by the walls of Gla and the lack of remains of a settlement in the neighborhood have led scholars to suggest that the citadel was built by the people of many small settlements scattered along the shores of the Kopaic Lake to serve as a common refuge in times of war or invasion. If that suggestion is true, then in Gla we have a unique example of a Mycenaean citadel serving a large area and apparently under the rule of a number of princes. The date of the construction of the walls has not been determined, but Threpsiades' work has proved that the citadel and its gates were still in use in the closing years of the LH III B period.[74]

OTHER LATE HELLADIC CITADELS

At Eutresis Miss Hetty Goldman revealed traces of a Late Helladic III citadel perhaps as extensive as that of Gla, built in the same type of masonry.[75] Remains of citadels are known from a number of other sites, Asine, Midea, Malthi-Dorion, Brauron, Thorikos, etc., but the examples described are the best preserved and are sufficient to give us a complete picture of the strongholds of the Mycenaean world. To these, however, we should add the Cyclopean wall, found by Broneer, erected on the Corinthian Isthmos, because it is an impressive example of fortification apparently built to block the passage to the Peloponnesos or to defend a section of the coast in the district of Kenchreai.[76] A heavy Cyclopean wall was erected "in the early years of the Late Bronze Age" to protect the settlement of Keos on the landward side.[77] Not only important centers were surrounded by walls in the fourteenth and thirteenth centuries B.C., but even small settlements, whose inhabitants felt the danger of exposure to sudden piratical assaults. Thus the small site of Aghios Kosmas was surrounded by a wall in the

thirteenth century and the site of Mouriatada in Triphylia, discovered and explored by Marinatos, possesses a well-built Cyclopean wall surrounding the "palace" of its chieftain and the houses of the citizens, all located on top of the hill.[78] The wall of Mouriatada recalls the peribolos of Gla and even the main building seems to reflect the palace of that Kopaic site. The small fortified sites perhaps serve to point out that the reason underlying the construction of the Mycenaean citadels was not only the desire to protect the treasures of the rulers but also to provide a safe shelter both to the ruling class and to the citizens in times of war and peril.

The earliest remains of Mycenaean citadels seem to belong to the Late Helladic III A period, i.e. to the fourteenth century B.C. They already exhibit an advanced technique in masonry work and a good knowledge of military tactics. We may wonder whether on the mainland of Greece we find earlier attempts at fortifications which could illustrate the successive stages followed in the course of development. The

[73] Threpsiades, *Praktika*, 1957, p. 52, fig. 4. *Ergon*, 1958, pp. 43-44.
[74] *Ergon*, 1960, p. 47.
[75] H. Goldman, *Excavations at Eutresis in Boeotia*, pp. 68-69, 70-75 and plan I.
[76] Broneer, *Antiquity*, 32 (1958), p. 80. Wiseman, *Hesperia*,

32 (1963), pp. 248-278.
[77] Caskey, *Hesperia*, 33 (1964), pp. 320-321.
[78] Mylonas, *Aghios Kosmas*, p. 58. Marinatos, in *Ergon*, 1960, pp. 149-152. The site may be equated with Amphigeneia according to its excavator.

oldest fortified settlement revealed by Tsountas at Dimini belongs to the last phase of the Neolithic period and it is the only example of its age.[79] It may, however, be contemporary with the fortification wall that was built in the first Early Helladic period around the settlement of Lerna. John Caskey, the excavator of Lerna, has proved that over the first fortification wall was later built a massive second one with towers projecting from the angles.[80] The type recalls the circuit wall revealed by Tsountas at Chalandriani in the Island of Syros.[81]

From the Middle Helladic period we have the fortified town of Malthi-Dorion revealed by Valmin, the walls of Aigina,[82] barely mentioned in the official publication of the site, the walls of Brauron noted by Papadimitriou, and the concentric walls of the Aspis of Argos.

These examples in the mainland and adjacent islands, known to date, do not seem sufficient to establish the antecedents from which stemmed the works of Mycenae and Tiryns. Like the ancient Greeks, who supposed that the Cyclopes imported from Lykia accounted for their construction, today we may assume that the craft of erecting stone fortification walls was imported fully developed from elsewhere, from Asia Minor, Troy, and the Hittite area for example, or we may maintain that we have to await a more complete investigation of Greece before we decide the issue. Perhaps the latter attitude may prove

the wiser. Whatever the answer to our riddle, the fact remains that the citadels of the Mycenaean world are among the best devised by men for the protection of their homes.

When we stand before the walls of Mycenae or Tiryns and recall that the attackers would have been armed with bows and arrows, with spears and swords, with slings and stones, we can well understand the enormous task facing them; then we can appreciate why it took the Achaean army so long to capture and destroy Troy, since Priam's city also was a citadel protected by great walls similar to the Mycenaean. These citadels were well nigh impregnable, and probably could have been reduced only by a long siege and by depriving their defenders of their food and water supplies. Perhaps internal dissension and the greed of a few also played a significant part in their destruction. For whatever reason, the fact remains that in spite of the formidable nature of the Mycenaean citadels, they were stormed in the course of the twelfth century B.C., with the exception of Athens, and their destruction brought to an end a brilliant period whose achievement excites admiration. Agamemnon's prophetic words seem to have been valid not only for Troy, but for the entire Mycenaean area and its states: "The day shall come when the sacred Ilios shall be laid low, and Priam and the people of Priam with good spear of ash."[83]

---

[79] C. Tsountas, Αἱ προϊστορικαὶ ἀκροπόλεις Διμηνίου καὶ Σέσκλου, pl. 2. Dimini's fortifications consist of six successive walls not very high; in reality they are breastworks behind which the villagers could stand and fight. Sesklo seems to have been surrounded by a wall, Tsountas, *op.cit.*, pl. 3. Mylonas, Ἡ νεολιθικὴ ἐποχὴ ἐν Ἑλλάδι, p. 18. Sterling Dow, *op.cit.*, p. 5.

[80] Caskey, *Hesperia*, 27 (1958), p. 128, fig. 1 and pl. 33. For the walls at the site of Asketario, cf. Theochares, *Ephemeris*, 1953-54, pp. 59-73; *Ergon*, 1954, p. 12, 1955, p. 131. *Praktika*, 1953, pp. 105-107; 1954, p. 106. For the walls of Rafina, cf.

Theochares, *Praktika*, 1953, pp. 105 ff.

[81] Tsountas, *Ephemeris*, 1899, p. 118, fig. 32.

[82] M. N. Valmin, *The Swedish Messenia Expedition*, plans I and II. For Aigina see G. Welter, *Aigina*, pp. 8-9, fig. 9 on p. 11. St. Dow, *op.cit.*, pp. 7-8. Perhaps the walls of Aghios Andreas on the island of Siphnos should be added here, Tsountas, *Ephemeris*, 1899, p. 130. For the Aspis cf. *BCH*, 31 (1907), p. 141, fig. 1, plan v.

[83] *Iliad*, IV, 164-165.

CHAPTER III

MYCENAEAN PALACES AND HOUSES

"Son of Nestor, dear to this heart of mine, mark the flashing of bronze throughout the echoing halls, and the flashing of gold, of electrum, of silver, and of ivory. Of such sort, methinks, is the court of Olympian Zeus within, such untold wealth is here; amazement holds me as I look." (*Odyssey*, IV, 71-75. Tr. A. T. Murray)

The palaces of the ruling families were the principal buildings within the citadels. Only broken foundations remain to indicate their extent and nature, for all the known palaces were destroyed by fire when, presumably, the last wave of the Indo-Europeans we know as the Dorians marched southward to establish themselves in the fertile plains of the Peloponnesos, sometime before the end of the twelfth century B.C. What survives, however, can testify to the fact of the original brilliance and grandeur of the palaces. For centuries they remained buried under their own debris until the excavator's pick and shovel uncovered them. From the very beginning of the Mycenaean excavations, it became apparent that these palaces and their citadels commanded settings of great, almost heroic, impressiveness and great beauty. One could find no better location than the rugged hill of Mycenae for the palace of Agamemnon where so many violent

deeds were to be committed, no better setting than the idyllic hill of Ano Englianos for the palace of wise Nestor.

The palace of Tiryns was the first to be revealed by Schliemann and Dörpfeld in 1884 and 1885. The palace of Agamemnon at Mycenae was cleared by Tsountas shortly after 1884. Little remains of the palace of Erechtheus on the Akropolis of Athens where a doubtful base or two are its supposed remnants, and the palace of Kadmos in Thebes can scarcely be made out in the midst of modern structures. The palace on Gla has been recently reinvestigated, and also in our day, especially since 1951, Blegen has cleared the palace of Nestor at Ano Englianos. The palace of Tiryns, the first to be revealed, in some respects is most instructive, not only because its parts are well defined, but because its setting within a citadel is clear and well established.

THE PALACE OF TIRYNS

The palace of Tiryns is the main building on its citadel, occupying the highest, southern terrace of the hill.[1] To reach it the visitor had to pass through a series of well-protected courts and two propylons (text fig. 1 on p. 13, and Fig. 51). Its outer propylon already possesses the classical plan associated with such structures: an H-shaped ground plan with distyle outer and inner porticoes (Fig. 51, No. 11). The inner propylon (No. 12) is smaller in proportions, but of the same H-shaped plan and arrangement. It gives access to the main open court (No. 13), a rectangular area paved with the typical Mycenaean "lime-cement" plaster.[2] The court is flanked on three sides by colonnades. Opposite the northeast anta of the inner propylon there was a round subterranean altar, of undetermined date, measuring 1.50 m. in diameter and rising some 25 cm. above the floor of the court. At a later time, the round altar was surrounded by a rectangular pavement. Attached to the east side of the inner propylon are two rooms, which served perhaps as guard rooms or even as archive rooms.

On the north side of the court stood the main unit of the palace, the megaron, an oblong roofed structure open on its south side (No. 14). The unit is the most typical mainland architectural feature to distinguish the Helladic palaces from the Minoan. The open side, facing the court, is a distyle portico in antis entered by two steps. The limestone bases of the columns exhibit a raised circle 75 cm. in diameter and their intercolumniation amounts to 3.80 m. The portico, which hereafter we shall call by its Homeric name *aithousa* ("the section of brightness"), had three doorways, closed by wooden doors, as the pivots on their thresholds indicate, to connect it with a rectangular vestibule or *prodomos*. A door on the west side of the *prodomos*, closed by a single-leafed door, opens into a corridor which gives access to apartments in the northwest section of the palace, including a bathroom (No. 15). A single doorway, apparently not

[1] *Supra*, Chapter II n. 2.
[2] By "lime-cement" we mean a mixture of lime and thin sand which becomes almost as strong as modern cement. In

Mycenaean times as well as in Classical times what we now understand by cement was unknown.

closed by a door, leads from the vestibule to the main room of the megaron, to the *domos*, a large almost square room (11.80 by 9.70 m.), originally richly decorated with wall frescoes and with a plastered pavement divided in squares and ornamented in color. A round, low hearth (ca. 3.30 m. in diameter) was placed in the middle of the *domos*, surrounded by four wooden columns, the stone bases of which have survived. No evidence was found of an arrangement for the escape of smoke, but it is believed that an opening through the roof was left for the purpose, a clerestory arrangement or merely a small vent. A throne once stood about the middle of east wall, to the right of a person entering the *domos*. It is also generally believed that this megaron was one story high.

To the east of this main unit, separated from it by a winding corridor, is a second, simpler megaron, which is known as the "Women's Megaron" or the "Little Megaron" (Fig. 51, No. 16), with another smaller one to the east of it. The women's megaron also opens into a rectangular court (No. 17) but has only two parts: an open, nearly square *aithousa* and a *domos*. In the center of the *domos*, indicated by a depression in the pavement, was a rectangular hearth about 1.24 m. in length. The pavement, like that of the first unit, was divided by incised lines into squares, decorated in color with two dolphins alternating with a single octopus. Access to the court of the women's megaron was obtained from the outer propylon by means of a corridor (No. 18). Doors on both sides of the *aithousa* lead to side corridors. Along the east side of the court (No. 17) is a portico of three columns, and along its north side a smaller portico with two columns in antis.

Arranged around the two main units are a number of corridors and smaller rooms. Of these, most interesting is a small room to the southwest of the *prodomos* of the main megaron that is believed to have been a bathroom (Fig. 51, No. 15). The floor is a single limestone block. Along the edges and at specified distances are small holes about 3 cm. in diameter, apparently meant to receive wooden dowels by means of which wooden paneling was secured to the floor. On the north wall about 25 cm. above the floor were found two round receptacles some 48 cm. in diameter, the inner side of which was well-smoothed with plaster. Perhaps they held water or even oil for use in bathing. At the northeast corner of the room a square drainage outlet cut in the floor block leads through the partition wall to a paved court in which originates a well-built drain.

To the west of the bathroom were a series of substantial rooms, which unfortunately are not well preserved. Dörpfeld reported that fragments of frescoes "were found in the debris of the various rooms, most of them in the room that borders the bathroom on the northeast side" and that "corridors XII and XIII had a painted pavement." He also noted that "the floor of corridor XII was covered with painted geometric ornaments in red on the yellow and white concrete."[3] This suggests, therefore, that near the bathroom were important rooms and corridors gaily decorated.

Murals painted in fresco technique covered the walls, and painted designs in the same technique covered the pavement of the important rooms and corridors of the palace. Fragments of these paintings have survived. From the women's megaron were recovered fragments of the well-known dado with stylized plant and geometric patterns in combination, painted in red, blue, green, and yellow. From the flat area of the walls came fragments of figure compositions: the boar hunt, women on a chariot going to a hunt, a woman holding a pyxis from a processional composition, etc.[4] In technique, color scheme, and conventions, these murals follow Minoan painting closely, but lack the brilliancy and vigor of the prototype. Often they are referred to as products of a provincial art. Nevertheless, they provided the interiors with color and decoration. Perhaps we should note that occasionally slabs of alabaster or other stone also were used in dadoes and were decorated with geometric patterns in relief. The best known are the seven slabs found in the *aithousa* of the larger megaron.[5] They bear the typical Mycenaean rosette with eyes emphasized by a glass-paste, blue in color.

In summary, we may note that there is very little evidence to indicate with certainty the exact function of each part of the palace. We may feel sure that the megaron was the unit where the king received his visitors, held public audiences, and perhaps public affairs like state banquets, etc. The memory of such a use is mirrored in epic poetry.[6] The single slab of the small room with a drain at the corner and the receptacles in the wall will indicate its use as a bathroom. Rooms in which pithoi are found could be considered as storerooms. But there is no evidence whatever to indicate, for instance, that the little megaron was actually a women's hall, nor can we identify a shrine in the many small rooms surrounding the megaron. We have, therefore, to bear in mind that often enough the identification of a room rests on personal impressions and predilections.

---

3 Schliemann, *Tiryns*, pp. 234-235 and 297.
4 *Ibid.*, pls. V-XIII.
5 *Ibid.*, pp. 284 ff. and pl. IV.

6 For example, in the description of Odysseus' arrival at the palace of Alkinoos, *Odyssey*, VII, 135 ff., or the descriptions of the banquets of the suitors in the palace of Odysseus.

According to the latest excavation results, the little megaron was built at an earlier period than the greater megaron; however, when the latter was erected and became the hall of the king, the former was preserved and used until both were finally destroyed by fire. The use of conglomerate blocks, Schliemann's *breccia,* in the greater megaron, and the lack of this material in the little megaron certainly indicates an earlier period of construction for the smaller apartment.

Secondly, we should note the way the walls of the palace were built. Certainly they do not exhibit the monumentality associated with edifices of their nature. As a rule walls exhibit a low foundation, rising about a meter above the floor level, made of stones laid in mortar. On this foundation was placed a superstructure sometimes constructed of sun-dried brick, more often of small stones set in mortar. For the superstructure the Mycenaeans used a system of wood-framing or chasing, apparently developed when sun-dried brick was universal and maintained in use after brick gave way to stone-rubble construction. Wooden beams set horizontally and vertically divided the wall area into rectangles, and then these beams were connected through the thickness of the wall by closely aligned shorter pieces of timber (text fig. 11). The

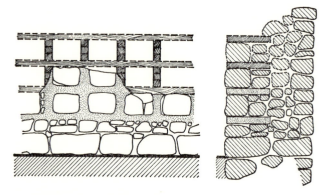

11. Mycenaean rubble-wall construction showing placement of timber (after Müller)

exterior walls often were built with an outer facing of ashlar masonry, squared blocks of poros, with rubble for the inner facing and for the cross walls. Thus, though the walls were solid brick or rubble creations, they were supplied with massive wooden framework. Wood also was used for the making of columns, which apparently tapered downwards in the Minoan fashion, of door-casings, ceilings, and roofs. To the extensive use of wood in wall construction must be attributed the transformation of the rubble walls when the palaces were burned down; they were fused into a solid mass that looks like concrete covered with lime.

Closely associated with this transformation of the

walls by fire into a mass of calcined ruins is the story of the destruction and the subsequent use of parts of the palace. There can be no doubt that the Palace of Tiryns was completely destroyed by fire. Other structures in the citadel which were liable to destruction by fire, such as the propylaea and rooms in the corner towers, were also devastated in a similar fashion. The exact date of this final destruction by fire was not fixed by the evidence obtained in the excavations. Some scholars believe that the final destruction of the Palace occurred at the end of the LH III B period; others, including Müller, place it in the eighth century B.C. Over the ruins of the greater megaron a structure was built, known as Structure T, the foundations of which survive (text fig. 12). Again, no evidence was obtained

12. Tiryns. Megaron and Structure T (after Frickenhaus)

to prove definitely the date of that later structure. The foundations indicate that Structure T was a long and narrow building measuring some 6 by 20 m. Its orientation is identical with that of the megaron (approximately from north to south). Its west wall rests on the paved floor of the megaron, while its east wall is superposed on the corresponding wall of the megaron along the inner half of that wall. Structure T is divided by an inner crosswall into a deep front portico, opening to the south, and a long narrow room.

Frickenhaus, who published a detailed description of Structure T,[7] maintained that it was a Greek temple built after the megaron was destroyed by fire, perhaps toward the middle of the seventh century B.C. Rejecting this view, Blegen concluded that "the later building within the megaron at Tiryns is not a Greek temple; it is simply a modest reconstruction of the earlier megaron—a reconstruction carried out toward the end of the Mycenaean period after the destruction of the palace by fire."[8] Müller, after his excavations of 1926 undertaken to clarify the architectural history of the site, maintained that the palace decayed gradually and was destroyed by fire probably in the middle of the eighth century B.C.; that until then it was inhabited and that only after its destruction was Structure T, a temple, constructed.[9] In his excavations Müller found a refuse pit filled with objects of ritualistic nature evidently discarded from a shrine; these cover the period from the middle of the eighth to the middle of the seventh century B.C. and prove the existence on the hill of Tiryns of a temple antedating the middle of the eighth century. Nilsson seems to accept Müller's conclusions, and sees in Structure T an early Greek temple.[10] Lorimer, confessing that at "Tiryns the circumstances are obscure," nevertheless concludes that "it appears certain that while a Geometric population squatted in the secondary apartments, the megaron remained intact and uninhabited until it perished in a conflagration probably c. 750."[11]

The lack of definite evidence obtained by excavations thus brought about a divergence in the conclusions of scholars regarding the remains found. I join Blegen in doubting the possibility of the survival to the middle of the eighth century B.C. of the megaron, whose structural parts were principally of wood. It has been argued that other structures have survived for a long period in spite of the fact that they were made of wood. The Temple of Hera at Olympia is cited as a proof. But in that temple the wooden members were replaced, often by stone, as soon as they decayed and it is impossible to establish when this replacement

occurred. Pausanias, indeed, mentions a column of oak in the *opisthodomos*, but there again one cannot be absolutely sure that it was the original column. Certain parts in the megaron could be replaced: the wooden columns, architraves, and even members of the roof structure. But others could not be replaced: the wooden beams built into the walls and covered by the plastering; especially the closely placed crossbeams, which could not be replaced without destroying the wall. We have also to remember the strong firing of the walls which fused together their materials and turned them into a mass as hard as concrete. Excavators of Mycenaean sites are familiar with the toughness of these calcined walls, and even Schliemann observed this fact when he remarked that the heat of the fire "was such, whenever beams of timber fed the flames, that the stones were calcined, the binding clay turned into red brick, and the whole reduced to so hard a mass, that our strongest men had the greatest difficulty in breaking it with pickaxes."[12] The timber that could transform the walls and their debris into this strong mass was not that of the roof, which would have collapsed and burned on the floor level to be covered by the fallen walls, but the wood used in the construction of the walls and especially the closely placed crossbeams and the heavy door-casings. The wood experts whom I consulted were unanimous in their opinion that the type of wood most probably used in the construction of the walls of the palace— that is, wood that could not have been replaced periodically without destroying the wall itself—would have decayed completely long before the eighth century B.C. They furthermore agreed that decayed and powdered wood could not have produced the strong and sustained fire required to transform a rubble wall into a fused mass of almost concrete hardness. It seems to us that the type of construction used and the calcined remains prove that the palace was destroyed by fire at the end of the Mycenaean age. Can we conclude that it was destroyed at the end of the LH III B period? A recent find seems to strengthen this conception.

In 1956 on the west slope of the hill, between the postern gate and Schliemann's great dump, Verdelis explored a fill found by the technicians engaged in the restoration of the fortification wall. It averaged 2.50 m. in depth and it was made up of four strata, the uppermost of which, 80 cm. in depth, contained LH III B sherds, fragments of wall paintings, and remnants of burnt wooden beams. Under this stratum he discovered two human skeletons, evidently not

---

[7] In *Tiryns*, I, pp. 2-46 ff.
[8] Blegen, *Korakou*, p. 133.
[9] Müller, *Tiryns*, III, pp. 214 ff.
[10] M. P. Nilsson, *The Minoan-Mycenaean Religion and Its Survival in Greek Religion*, 2nd ed., 1950, p. 477.
[11] H. Lorimer, *Homer and the Monuments*, 1950, p. 435.
[12] Schliemann, *Tiryns*, p. 8.

buried but killed and covered by the fallen debris. The other three strata, ranging in depth from 40 cm. to 1 m., contained sherds and fragments of frescoes; the earth of stratum III was ashy-dark in color. Some of the sherds of the lowermost stratum "seem to go beyond the LH III B period," the rest belong to LH III B times.[13]

Of course, we shall have to await the final publication of this important discovery before we can draw definite conclusions from its evidence. But it is possible now to ask whether the finds from the fill justify the conclusion that the entire palace was destroyed by fire at the end of the LH III B period. Let us recall first of all that discarded fragments of wall paintings and sherds of a late phase of the LH III B ceramic period were also found in the palace itself. Dörpfeld reported that in "Room x . . . were found the largest and best fragments of pottery and the best remains of the painted wall-plaster." He furthermore stated that "this room must have been used in ancient times as a lumber-room for broken vessels and all kinds of debris, for the many objects here found were mixed with perfectly black earth, such as is not found anywhere in the palace."[14] The black earth, corresponding to the "ashy-dark" earth of Verdelis' stratum III, was not burned and its color was not due to firing for otherwise Dörpfeld, who had seen a great many remains of fires, would have pointed out that fact. We learn from Müller that in the fill of the "lumber-room," Room x, were found the fragments of the "Stierspringerin" fresco that belongs to a late period and the large krater with the chariot and warriors which also belongs to a late phase of Mycenaean ceramics.[15] Müller also states that the fill of Room x is earlier than the great fire which finally destroyed the palace. The debris it contained must have resulted from repairs or redecoration of the walls of sections of the Palace, and these belonged to a very late period. To the same cause could be attributed the contents of strata II, III, and IV of the fill below the wall investigated by Verdelis.

That repairs and the throwing away of replaced frescoes was not an unusual practice in Mycenaean palaces is indicated by the fragments found by Tsountas and Wace in the "Hellenistic pithos area" of the palace at Mycenae, and by Blegen in the palace at Ano Englianos. In the case of the latter, Blegen states that the material he uncovered in 1961 was considerable, comprising some 3,000 fragments, and that it

"had been thrown over the bank of the hilltop presumably at some time when the palace was being redecorated."[16] The same could have happened at Tiryns and the replaced frescoes could have been thrown over the walls.

We cannot state the same for the contents of the uppermost stratum, nor can we maintain that it was formed by the debris of the destroyed palace, thrown over the walls sometime after the final catastrophe when new building activities were undertaken because, as Verdelis aptly remarked, the stratum was formed by debris that fell over the wall while still burning, since the rock which came into contact with them was transformed into lime by the heat. That, I think, proves only that the unit of the palace adjacent to the wall that stretches above the area of the fill was damaged by fire at a time when LH III B pottery was still in existence. It does not prove that the entire palace was then destroyed by fire, as would have been the case had enemies stormed the citadel of Tiryns. That a fire did occur on that side of the palace was known before Verdelis' investigations. Müller in his fundamental book pointed out that a number of rooms in the west section of the palace were damaged by fire,[17] that their wooden beams fell burning over the walls, and that the west stairway of the "postern gate" became useless when a great part of its eastern wall collapsed because of that fire. Verdelis suggested that some of the fresco fragments he found may join with others discovered in the west stairway, thus indicating that the contents of both areas may have resulted from the same cause. And that cause, the fire, according to Müller, does not indicate the destruction of the entire palace at that time. The skeletons found under the debris of stratum I could as well indicate an accident as an act of war. Thus the recent discovery of Verdelis is not sufficient to prove the general destruction of the entire Palace at the end of the LH III B period.

Damage by fire of a palace before its final destruction was not a unique experience in the life of a Mycenaean royal dwelling. The palaces of Mycenae and of Pylos seem to have suffered periodic destructions. Wace, long since, proved that the "Pillar Basement" together with sections near it were damaged by fire before the construction of the existing "Megaron unit."[18] In the summer of 1963 Shear and I found that the floor of the so-called "pithos room" on the uppermost terrace of the palace at Mycenae was laid over an older floor of gypsum slabs, cracked and almost

---

[13] N. Verdelis, *Ephemeris*, 1956, Χρονικά, pp. 5-8. Cf. also P. Ålin, *Das Ende der mykenischen Fundstätten auf dem griechischen Festland*, 1962, pp. 25 ff.

[14] Schliemann, *Tiryns*, p. 234.

[15] K. Müller, *Tiryns*, III, p. 211. Cf. also Schliemann, *Tiryns*, pl. 14.

[16] Tsountas, *Praktika*, 1886, pp. 72-73. Wace, *BSA*, 25 (1921-1923), pp. 161 ff. Blegen, *AJA*, 65 (1961), p. 157 and especially *AJA*, 66 (1962), pp. 146-147.

[17] Müller, *Tiryns*, III, pp. 209 and 211.

[18] Wace, *BSA*, 25 (1921-1923), pp. 182-185.

pulverized by fire. Evidently the section to which the floor of gypsum slabs belonged was damaged severely by fire and over it was built the "pithos room" which remained in use until the final destruction of the palace. Blegen has recently reported that "several phases of construction are represented" in the palace at Ano Englianos, and "each seems to have ended in a catastrophe; the last was surely of incendiary origin, and some of the preceding disasters were probably also accompanied by fire."[19]

The opinion that the later long and narrow Structure T at Tiryns is a house built over the burned remains of the megaron in the closing years of the Mycenaean Age is based on two considerations: on the construction of its surviving walls and on the assumed floor level of the structure. Frickenhaus in his study assumed that for Structure T the floor of the megaron was employed. No evidence was found to support this assumption. Nilsson has already remarked that the floor level of the later structure may have been laid considerably above the pavement of the megaron.[20] Two factors favor that suggestion.

First. If we assumed that the floor level of Structure T had been lowered to the pavement of the megaron, we would have to maintain that its builders cleared the debris accumulated over that pavement after the destruction of the palace. Consequently we would have to assume that the debris found in the area of the megaron over which Structure T was built belongs to that building. That debris seems to have had the same thickness as that covering the area of the megaron not used in the construction of the later building, for if it formed a much thinner layer, it would have been noticed by Schliemann and Dörpfeld. It is impossible to assume that the debris of the modest Structure T would have formed an accumulation equal in thickness to that produced by the destruction of the megaron.

Second. To reach the pavement of the megaron the builders of Structure T would have had to remove the burned debris which covered it. We have noted Schliemann's comment that this is not an easy task. I do not think it is possible to maintain that people who constructed the rather flimsy later structure would have undertaken such a hard job. It would have been more natural and far easier for them to level off the debris and use the leveled layer as their top floor. But this conception may seem to create another problem.

The west wall of Structure T rests on the pavement of the megaron. If the debris covering the pavement was so hard, why did they not base both their walls on it? The answer to this question is perhaps indicated by a lesson learned in the excavations of Ano Englianos.

In 1952 I was privileged to assist Blegen in his excavations there, and I was entrusted with the direction of the work that revealed the megaron of the Palace, and especially its *domos*. I noted that the fill along its northeast wall was as hard as concrete; it was made up of the remains of the collapsed wall, which had been strongly fired. This calcined hard fill extended from the wall to a little more than half the width of the hall, to a line reaching a little beyond the center of the hearth. The fill of the hall beyond that line toward the southwest wall was of the regular packed variety, soft compared to the fill along the northeast wall. This, I guess, is to be expected; for the upper reaches of the wall, when it collapsed, would not have completely covered the extent of the room unless its height was more than the width of the room; in the case of Pylos it would have amounted to over 12 m., since the width of the *domos* is 11.20 m. Professor Blegen has figured out that "the level of the upper story of that palace was approximately 3.25 m. higher than that of the ground floor." If we assume that the second story had a similar height, we shall have to conclude that the total height of the palace was 6.50 to 7 m. above the floor level of its court. In the megaron of Tiryns, too, the collapsed east wall would have covered but a section of the floor of its *domos* along the length of that wall. The builders of Structure T planned to erect a building not as wide as the megaron, and consequently they could only use one of its long walls, as much of it as had survived. The east wall of the megaron was used and formed the east side of Structure T. The other long wall of that structure apparently had to be built beyond the line reached by the calcined hard debris of the taller east wall of the megaron. Since the fill over which the west wall of Structure T was to be built was rather soft, its builders lowered it to the hard pavement of the megaron. The floor level of Structure T remained above the calcined debris; it was laid perhaps slightly over a meter above the Mycenaean pavement. Thus the lowering of the west wall of Structure T can be explained. The position of the column bases of the megaron on the axis of Structure T can be attributed to an accidental coincidence. They were not used to support the columns of the later structure. Nor is there any evidence or necessity to prove or to assume that Structure T had columns. Its width, only 6 m., could have been spanned by a light thatched roof stretched from wall to wall. But even if supports were needed, these would have been of a simple nature and not monumental enough to leave traces behind.

The width of the walls of Structure T, comparable to that of the poor Mycenaean houses, and its nature,

---

[19] Blegen, *AJA*, 65 (1961), p. 154.

[20] Nilsson, *Minoan-Mycenaean Religion*, 2nd ed., pp. 475-477.

which does not agree with that of the stone Greek temples, will parallel perfectly the walls of the "humble houses" of the Geometric period found in the area of the palace east of the megaron. One could maintain with a greater degree of probability that the builders of those humble houses were responsible for the construction of an equally humble temple, compared to later edifices, over the leveled remains of the megaron. That temple would have been monumental compared to the humble house remains of the Geometric period. We have already noted the relics of ritualistic significance which were discovered in a pit by Müller; the earliest of these relics seem to be dated in the eighth century B.C., proving the existence of a temple in that century. At Mycenae we have the parallel of humble houses of the Geometric period built over the ruins of the palace and of a temple built in the Historic era over those ruins. Unfortunately, the houses at Mycenae were removed when the palace was being excavated, and any temple of the period which might have existed was completely cleared when in archaic times a more ambitious temple was constructed. But in the summer of 1962 Verdelis uncovered the remains of a small structure of the Geometric period beyond the south side of the so-called House of the Oil Merchant, whose walls recall those of the structure in Tiryns. A similarly built wall of the Geometric period was revealed by Papadimitriou below the south segment of Grave Circle B.[21] We could maintain with a degree of probability that the later structure of Tiryns belongs to the

Geometric period and should be considered as contemporary with the humble houses uncovered in the east section of the palace. It will then be possible to conclude that it is a temple, the earliest temple erected in Tiryns to which belong the discarded ritualistic relics found in the refuse pit. Its orientation from south to north, rather unusual for a Greek temple of the Classical era but not unique, was imposed by that of the Mycenaean megaron, one of the walls of which was used in its construction. It finds a parallel in the Greek temple on top of the citadel of Mycenae, which also faces the south.

Ever since the uncovering of the palace at Tiryns by Schliemann, scholars have pointed out its similarities to and differences from the palace of Odysseus in the *Odyssey*. It is not our purpose to go into this intriguing but controversial subject,[22] but we must emphasize the fact that a great many similarities do exist, and these add interest and a touch of real life to the Homeric stories. Exactly when the Mycenaean palace of Tiryns was destroyed by fire cannot be determined from the evidence obtained in its excavation. Müller suggests the beginning of the eighth century; Blegen, the end of the Late Helladic III B period or around 1200 B.C. It seems to us that the Palace did not outlive the Mycenaean Age, that perhaps it was destroyed finally at its very end, in the course of the twelfth century B.C. Over its ruins in the Geometric period was erected a temple, Structure T, whose walls have survived.

THE PALACE OF NESTOR

The Palace of Nestor at Pylos occupies the southeastern half of the hill of Ano Englianos, some 4 km. south of the modern town of Chora in Triphylia and 17 km. north of the modern city of Pylos in western Messenia. The site commands a magnificent view of the Bay of Navarino on the south, a wide expanse of hills and sea to the southwest, and the range of Mount Aigalion toward the north and the northeast. The story of its discovery and excavation is another instance of successful modern exploration. In 1912 and 1926 Kourouniotes excavated in its neighborhood two tholos tombs and noted surface indications of several other sepulchers of the same type.[23] These royal tombs suggested the existence of a Mycenaean settlement and palace in the territory. Kourouniotes and Blegen located important remains in 1938 on the hill of Ano Englianos and began their excavation in 1939.

Then they proved by means of definite evidence, in the form of walls, fragments of frescoes, stuccoed floors, and above all by a tremendously impressive number of tablets, that on the hill were preserved the remains of a great Mycenaean palace which had been destroyed by fire.[24]

The excavation of that palace, interrupted by World War II and by the death of Kourouniotes, was resumed by Blegen in 1952. To date work has continued annually; the revelation and clearing of the Palace are completed, and the final report of the excavation is in the process of publication. Until it appears, no detailed study of the palace can be made. However, at the close of every campaign general reports of the work were published in the *American Journal of Archaeology*,[25] and these, as well as the *Guide to the Palace of Nestor*, published in 1962, enable us to draw a good prelim-

[21] Papadimitriou, *Praktika*, 1952, p. 467. To Dr. Verdelis I am indebted for permission to mention his find, cf. *Ergon*, 1962, pp. 106-107.

[22] See Lorimer, *op.cit.*, ch. VII, "The Homeric House," pp. 406 ff.

[23] *Ephemeris*, 1912, p. 268; 1914, pp. 99 ff. *Praktika*, 1925-1926, pp. 140, 141.

[24] Blegen, *AJA*, 43 (1939), pp. 557-576, and E. L. Bennett, Jr., *The Pylos Tablets. A Preliminary Transcription*, 1951.

[25] Blegen, *AJA* from 57 (1953) to date. From his preliminary

inary picture of the Palace. Before we repeat Blegen's accounts of his excavation, it may be profitable to emphasize the importance of the exploration of a Mycenaean palace at the present time when the methods of excavating make possible the preservation of all relics and of the evidence disclosed. The conclusions reached at Pylos, therefore, will add considerably to our knowledge of the Mycenaean Age. It will also be profitable to remember that the determination of the function served by many of the parts of a palace has to be adduced from circumstantial indications which often are liable to varied interpretations. But the archaeological facts as established by excavation remain constant.

The palace at Ano Englianos does not occupy the height of a citadel but lies unprotected by fortification walls on top of the hill, the two sides of which are indeed precipitous. It occupies an area approximately 85 m. from southwest to northeast and 70 m. from southeast to northwest. It is divided into three separate complexes or *insulae*. The central complex, measuring some 50 by 32 m., is the most important section of the palace. It, as well as the rest of the palace, is oriented from northwest to southeast, with its entrance on its southeast side. Opening onto an outside paved court is an H-shaped propylon with an inner portico and an outer portico, somewhat more shallow, on either side of the entrance (text fig. 13; Fig. 52, Nos. 1 and 2). In each portico stood a single column on the logitudinal axis. The columns of wood were destroyed by fire, but their stone bases are still *in situ*, as well as the stucco ring that protected the lower end of their shaft. The impressions on the ring prove that the columns had some 64 narrow flutings. Next to the propylon on the right are two compartments considered by Blegen to be a tower and a guard room (text fig. 13; Fig. 52, Nos. 55-57), while on the left two connected rooms are proved to have been the palace archives by the hundreds of tablets found in them (text fig. 13; Fig. 52, Nos. 7-8). Perhaps in these rooms the tax collectors had their offices. In the outer portico and at the left of the door opening was revealed a raised platform of plaster.

Through the propylon access was obtained to an interior paved court, open to the sky (text fig. 13; Fig. 52, No. 3). Onto this comparatively shallow court opened the megaron, the chief state unit of the palace. To right and left, openings were provided through which access was obtained to other sections of the complex. An opening by the southwest anta of the megaron led to a corridor through which were reached a series of rooms parallel to the length of the megaron, and at the same time to a suite of two rooms. One of these (text fig. 13; Fig. 52, No. 9) was apparently provided with wooden shelves on which stood hundreds of kylikes, and is known as the pantry. The second room (No. 10) was provided with a low bench, about 32.5 cm. high and 40 to 45 cm. deep, coated with stucco, decorated in color with geometric patterns. Evidently it was a waiting room where "guests could sit until summoned." A clay stand found in the corner contained "two large jars, no doubt for wine. . . . The guests thus seem to have been offered refreshments while waiting." Right across the portico from these rooms was a small loggia with two columns on its façade (No. 44) opening into a series of corridors and rooms that flank the megaron and the court on the northeast. The columns stood on stone bases which remain *in situ*, and each had a stucco ring around its lower end with impressions of 60 flutings. Traces of red color with which the outer face of the stucco ring originally was painted still survive. According to Blegen "the columns must have supported a balcony from which the women and children and other spectators could look out over the court, with a good view of the ceremonies that no doubt often took place there on occasions of state."

The megaron, like those of Tiryns and Mycenae, has an *aithousa*, a *prodomos*, and the *domos* (text fig. 13). The *aithousa* faces the court and is distyle in antis. Its evidently unfluted wooden columns were destroyed, but their stone bases are still *in situ*. Its "walls seem to have been elaborately decorated with wooden wainscotting and panels. Its floor was covered with stucco, which was apparently renewed several times, but the final original finished surface is entirely destroyed." Another raised platform was revealed to the right of the doorway leading to the *prodomos*.

The *prodomos* had a painted stuccoed floor, and its walls, preserved to a height of one meter or more, still retain much of their finished coat of plaster once covered with gay frescoes. A third raised platform was revealed to the right of the doorway leading to the *domos*. Blegen suggests that these raised platforms were stands for a servant or a soldier on sentry duty. I believe they held stands to support torches lighting

reports and his *Guide to the Palace of Nestor* issued by the University of Cincinnati we have drawn the details of our description. His *Palace of Nestor at Pylos in Western Messenia, I: The Buildings and Their Contents* will be published by Princeton University Press in 1966. It should be noted that

after the death of Kourouniotes in 1945, Marinatos became the representative of the Greek Archaeological Society and he undertook the exploration of the cemeteries and settlements of Western Messenia and Western Triphylia. For a very interesting description of the Palace of Nestor and its excavator cf. Joseph Alsop, *From the Silent Earth*, 1962.

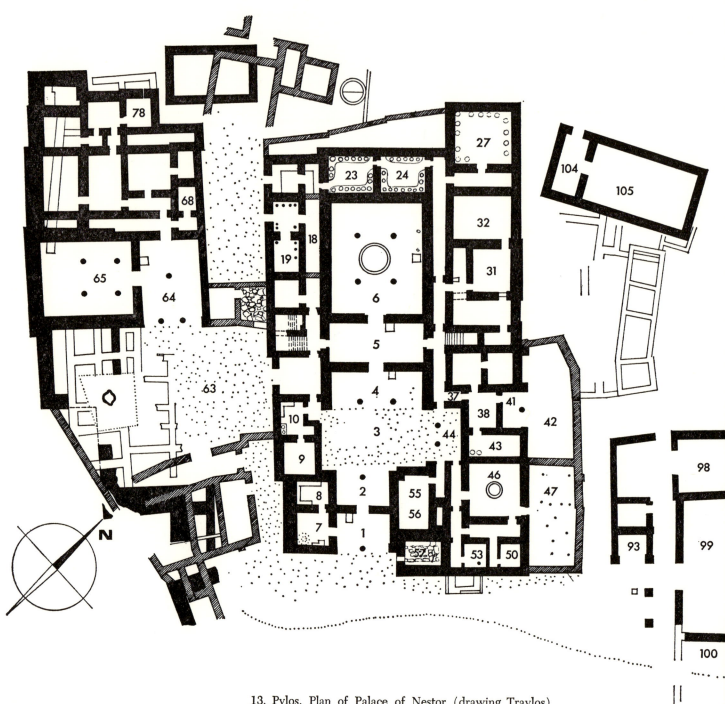

13. Pylos. Plan of Palace of Nestor (drawing Travlos)

the entrances during the night.[26] The entrance was not furnished with a door.

The main room or *domos* is a spacious hall, measuring 12.90 by 11.00 m. In the center is a round hearth, some 4.00 m. in diameter, made of clay coated with stucco and rising some 15 or 20 cm. from the stuccoed floor. It has a two-stepped modeled edge and a broad flat rim, encircling a depressed area, 3 m. in diameter, where a fire was kept burning. The hearth was found covered with three successive layers of plaster, each bearing painted decoration. On the latest plaster of the vertical face was painted a notched plume or flame pattern in black edged with red; on the horizontal edge above it were painted a series of triangles, while the broad rim was covered with a design of running spirals, outlined in black and filled with yellow, with large white eyes and red angle motives between spirals. Around the hearth were placed four wooden, fluted columns (32 flutings), not in a strictly symmetrical arrangement, resting on stone bases; these columns supported a lantern through which the smoke of the fireplace could escape. A chimney made of two sections of terra-cotta pipe carried through the roof completed the arrangement. Against the northeast wall of the hall and towards its center stood the throne of the king, facing the hearth (text fig. 13, No. 6; Fig. 53, th). It was apparently of wood and was destroyed by fire, but its existence is proved by a rectangular depression still to be seen on the stuccoed floor in which were found charred remains of wood. On the right-hand side of the throne were found two shallow basin-like depressions in the floor connected by a narrow channel, some 2 m. in length; the arrangement is curious, but Blegen suggests that perhaps it permitted "the king, without getting down from his throne, to pour out libations to one or another of the gods." The position of the throne corresponds to that of the throne at Tiryns and is to be found to the right of a person entering the *domos*.

The walls of the *domos* were covered with gay frescoes, fragments of which were recovered.[27] Those found near the eastern corner seem to represent a scene showing a seated man playing a five-stringed lyre, and a bird, possibly a partridge, in flight. Other fragments seem to indicate that on the wall behind the throne and on either side of it were painted griffins backed by lions in a heraldic arrangement. The stuccoed floor was laid out in squares separated by double incised lines, the entire grid being somewhat irregularly accommodated. Each square was filled with painted linear designs, wavy lines, chevrons, arcs, zigzags, net patterns, etc., in red, yellow, blue, white, and black. The second square directly in front of the throne was decorated with an octopus, the only realistic representation to be seen on the entire floor. By the west column base, near the hearth, was found a table of offerings made of clay coated with stucco.

Evidence was recovered along the southwest corner to indicate the existence of a mezzanine or balcony in that section of the hall. Whether or not this balcony went around the hall is not certain since no evidence of its existence was found along the northeast wall, the southeast corner, or the northeast corner. In any case, the hall with its fluted columns, frescoed walls, painted hearth and floor, its throne and other richly decorated furniture must have presented a magnificent sight to the visitor.

Beyond the rear wall of the *domos* two storerooms were unearthed (text fig. 13; Fig. 53, Nos. 23 and 24), where 17 pithoi and 16 pithoi, respectively, were found deeply set into plastered stands. A number of tablets discovered in these rooms deal with various scents used in the preparation of perfumed oil and the word for oil is to be read on at least five of them.[28] Apparently the pithoi were used for the storage of oil.

On either side of the Megaron two long corridors opened into a number of rooms, evidently storerooms. At some later time the southwest corridor was transformed by crosswalls into additional storerooms which, along with the other rooms, perhaps served as pantries since they were found filled with crushed ordinary household pots. In one of those corridor-rooms (in No. 18) with many large pots were found numerous diminutive votive vessels and parts of a table of offerings. Room 19, one of the original compartments, yielded 2,853 tall-stemmed kylikes which once stood on wooden shelves. Pots of a variety of shapes, some 23 different shapes, were found in the other pantries. The total number of vases found in these pantries exceeds 6,000. It is interesting to note that there was no direct communication between the *domos* of the megaron and the corridors on either side of it; doors in the *prodomos* led to these corridors from the megaron. As we have seen, doors in the inner court also gave access to these corridors and storage rooms.

The northeast corridor was left in its original state and through it access was obtained to a number of rooms and a magazine, No. 27, that occupies the extreme northeast corner of the complex. In this magazine were found *in situ* remains of 16 large pithoi. In

[26] It would parallel the arrangement in the palace of Alkinoos described in the *Odyssey*, VII, 100-102.

[27] *Guide to the Palace of Nestor*, figs. 7 and 9. *AJA*, 60 (1956), p. 95, and pls. 40 fig. 2, and 41 fig. 3.

[28] For the Pylos tablets see: E. Bennett, *The Pylos Tablets,*

A Preliminary Transcription, 1951; *The Pylos Tablets; Texts of the Inscriptions Found in 1934-54*, 1955; *The Olive Oil Tablets of Pylos: Texts of Inscriptions Found in 1955, Suppl. Minos*, 2, 1958. For the fragments found after 1955 cf. M. Lang, *AJA*, 62 (1958) - 67 (1963).

the other rooms were found pots that once contained olive oil. In Room 31 were found fragments of badly broken ivory burned and blackened by fire, which obviously had fallen from the room above. In rooms of the second story were also kept pithoi and smaller jars containing oil, fragments of which were found especially in Room 38. Apparently their contents contributed to the intensity and the destructive fury of the flames. In the burned debris were also found fragments of inscribed tablets, many of which deal with oil. Stairways led to the second story over these rooms as well as over the pantries; a number of steps were found *in situ* opposite the doors of the *prodomos* of the megaron. Thus existence of a second story over certain sections of the palace is established. The remains of the stairways enabled Blegen to figure out that the level of the second story was approximately 3.25 m. above that of the ground floor.

The main complex or *insula* of the palace on the ground floor contains 46 halls, rooms, porticoes, stairways, passages, and courts. Of these, after the megaron, the most important rooms are to be found in the southeast section of the *insula*. That was accessible from the inner court through the distyle loggia (text fig. 13; Fig. 54, No. 44) which we have already noticed. A corridor from its southwest corner led to a stairway that gives access to the suggested guard room and tower beside the propylon, to "the headquarters perhaps of the palace guard" (text fig. 13; Fig. 54, Nos. 55-57). Another corridor gave access to a rather large and elegant room, called the "Queen's Hall" (text fig. 13; Fig. 54, No. 46). Nearly square in shape it is almost half as large as the *domos* of the megaron. In the center of its stuccoed floor a circular hearth rises, with a narrow intermediate step, to a height of some 10 cm. above the floor (again in proportion almost 1:2 to the hearth of the megaron). It is made of clay coated with stucco, decorated with flame patterns, zigzags, and spirals in a most delicate manner. The intensity of the fire that destroyed the palace ruined the surface of the stuccoed floor so that its presumed decoration has vanished. Broken and pulverized also is the plaster that once covered its walls, but from fragments that survive it is proved that it was covered with frescoes. Apparently life-sized couchant griffins and lions or leopards were among the subjects represented. The smoke of the hearth escaped through an opening in the roof where two chimney pipes were placed. The room, even in its ruinous state, today conveys the impression of grandeur and opulence. A door in its east corner led to an open court surrounded by walls (text fig. 13; Fig. 54, No. 47).

Less impressive but equally interesting are two corridors and two small rooms connected with the hall. The walls and floor of Room 50 (text fig. 13; Fig. 54) were covered with frescoes and painted squares. Unfortunately the frescoes on the walls were badly damaged by fire, but the decoration on its stuccoed floor as well as that on the floor of the narrow corridor separating the two rooms, has survived. The floors were divided, in regular Mycenaean fashion, into squares about 35 cm. on a side, and the squares were decorated with painted abstract linear motives as well as semi-realistic octopi, dolphins, and other fish in alternating squares. The second room, No. 53, was possibly a lavatory. Seventeen false-necked amphorae stood on its floor to the left of the door, and near the east corner is an opening in a large stone slab placed over an underground drain; through the opening water could escape to the drain. Because of the lavish decoration of the small room with the hearth, the excavators identified this suite as the "Queen's Hall." But I would see in the compartment the section of the palace in which visiting dignitaries could be housed. Its position by the court, by the guard room, and by the bathroom and its distance from the rooms where house utensils were stored would accord better with such a function.

Against the northwest wall of the room with the hearth another suite of rooms of great interest was found (text fig. 13; Fig. 54, Nos. 38, 41, 43). To this suite access was obtained from the inner court by means of a door opening in the northwest corner of the distyle loggia (No. 44). A small vestibule, No. 38, gave access to a long and narrow room (No. 43), a bathroom, "the only one of its kind yet found in a Mycenaean palace on the Greek mainland with its equipment still fairly well preserved." (Fig. 55) It measures 6.20 by 2.50 m. Against the southeast wall stands a built-in larnax set into a clay container coated with stucco. The container is made of clay and perhaps of crude brick. The terra-cotta larnax set in it is of the pinched-in-waist type and of somewhat smaller dimensions. Spiraliform patterns painted in whitish color against the dark ground of the terra-cotta decorate the interior of the larnax.[29] A step made of clay and coated with stucco was placed in front of the container to facilitate stepping from the floor into the tub. In the south corner of the room was disclosed a fairly high clay stand containing two large pithoi, apparently for storing water to be used by the bathers.[30] Plain kylikes, seven and nine respectively, were found in the bottom of these pithoi, while one kylix was found in the larnax. Apparently these vessels

---

[29] A fragment of a tub similarly decorated was found by Schliemann at Tiryns, but unfortunately the exact place of discovery is not recorded (*Tiryns*, pl. XXIV, d-e). Perhaps it was

found in or near the bathroom of that palace.

[30] The pithoi in the stand prove that the two round receptacles found by Schliemann in the north wall of the bath-

were used for pouring water. A small channel through the northeast wall served to carry waste water to an underground drain outside the room. From the vestibule or lobby (No. 38) of the bathroom a monostyle loggia was reached which opened to a fairly large walled court paved with stucco (text fig. 13, No. 42) adjacent to the court (No. 47) of the so-called "Queen's Hall" and separated from it by a wall. Blegen suggests that "this might have been the king's private court to which he could retire when he wished solitude or freedom from disturbance." It might, however, also have been associated with the bathroom for use by the bathers after their bath.

Beyond the central *insula* to the northeast, and separated from it by a broad ramp paved with stucco, is the second palace complex known as the northeast *insula* or wing. It contains six rooms and a passage, of which Room 93 is of especial interest (text fig. 13; Fig. 54). It is a small, almost square room (3.10 by 3.40 m.) open across the front, between two massive anta blocks. The floor, mostly plowed away, is at a much higher level than that of the court onto which it opens. In front of its façade and set in the stuccoed floor of the court is a rectangular limestone block coated on all four sides and on top with plaster bearing painted patterns. This block may have been an altar, and it is suggested that the small room in front of which it stands may have been a shrine. It is interesting to note that on one of the fragments of inscribed tablets discovered in the building is to be found "the name of a goddess," Potnia Hippeia, a "horse-goddess."[31]

Facing the same court of the shrine and forming the southeast limit of the palace are three contiguous rooms nearly 15.50 m. in total length and 6.40 m. average width (text fig. 13; Fig. 54, Nos. 98-100). A few scattered potsherds and objects of terra cotta were found in these rooms but also "56 completed, inscribed tablets, many of which deal with repairs in leather or in metal; others are records of parts of chariots, yet others refer to supplies of leather or bronze expected or received." According to Blegen "this inscriptional evidence is sufficient to establish the character of the building as a Workshop." At the extreme northeast corner of the palace area is a large structure (Nos. 104-105) divided internally into a narrow vestibule and a large room, in which was found an impressive array of pithoi firmly set into hollows cut in the clay floor in regular rows. Blegen states that "at least 35 still stood in place on the day the palace was reduced to ruins." Some 40 sealings, complete or frag-

mentary, were found in the room; on the obverse of four of these was inscribed the ideogram indicating wine. Apparently, this large room was the wine cellar of the palace.

The third *insula* or complex of the palace comprises its southwest wing. Unfortunately, a good part of the southwest slope of the hill was used by modern builders as a quarry for a long period and consequently remains it once held are not as well preserved as those in the other sections. Perhaps the most important remains belong to a unit composed of a large room fronted by a vestibule facing an open court with stuccoed floor (text fig. 13, Nos. 64, 65). The vestibule (No. 64), of considerable size, had a stuccoed floor, which may have borne painted decoration that is not preserved, and two wooden fluted columns (with perhaps 44 flutings) in its façade on the court. Its walls were decorated with frescoes, fragments of which have survived, indicating that a frieze of pink griffins was among its many compositions. On the lower part of its walls fragments of a dado course were found in their original position. Fragments, possibly fallen from the room above, exhibit a warrior wearing a helmet decorated with boars' tusks, surrounded by human bodies in contorted attitudes. A single column stood in the middle of the vestibule, opposite the middle of the broad entrance to the main room. To the right of that entrance is a raised platform accepted by Blegen as a platform for a sentry.

The large room, No. 65, is not preserved in its entirety, but it apparently had a stuccoed floor and frescoed walls. One stone column base and three circular foundations which once supported column bases, found *in situ*, prove that the hall originally had at least four columns, but it is stated that "it is not impossible that two additional columns stood farther to the southward; they would make this a hypostyle hall with six interior columns in two rows of three." No traces of a hearth were found, but it should be remembered that only part of the room is preserved. Certain facts concerning this unit seem to be established: it is the principal unit of the southwest wing and it belongs to an older architectural phase. I would like to suggest that in the final period of the palace these quarters served as the queen's hall, situated as they are near the compartments where vessels to be used for daily needs were stored and where a good many women workers, possibly slaves, could be housed.

A number of rooms, small and large corridors, were cleared beyond the unit. Of these Room 68 (text fig. 13) has been identified as a "kitchen-pantry" in which

---

room at Tiryns served the same purpose; they too must have contained water for use of bathers, cf. *supra*, p. 47.

[31] L. R. Palmer, *The Interpretation of Mycenaean Greek*

Texts, p. 226, and glossary, p. 422; to be referred to as *Interpretation* hereafter.

were recovered some 300 vessels, for the most part cooking pots, "some standing on three legs; . . . two large circular pans, braziers, and many deep two-handled jars," and Room 78 "may have been a bathroom."[32]

The palace of Ano Englianos, like the other known Mycenaean palaces, was violently destroyed by fire, but unlike the others its ruins and site were abandoned and never again utilized by possible survivors or their descendants. Blegen believes that the destruction occurred when the ceramic phase known as LH III B had not yet been overtaken by that of LH III C. Pottery of the latter style was found on the floors of the palace, but the great bulk of the ware found belongs to the closing years of the LH III B period.

Before we move on to the discussion of the palace of Mycenae, it may prove interesting to compare the palace of Pylos with that of Tiryns and to consider more carefully the identification of some of its parts. Both palaces were destroyed by fire. Both exhibit at least two architectural phases. The structure belonging to the earlier phase was incorporated in the later palace and it seems to have been an important unit. In the case of Tiryns it is the so-called women's megaron, in that of Pylos the so-called second Throne Room (Room 65). Both have doors in the *prodomos* of their megara through which various rooms and corridors of the palace could be reached. Each has a bathroom to the side of the megaron and its open court, and in each case there were some very elaborately decorated rooms near the bathroom. Each has a series of rooms by the propylon which have been identified as guard rooms. Both have evident resemblances to the palaces delineated in epic poetry, and both seem to belong to the same period. Their difference is one of setting: the Palace of Tiryns is surrounded by heavy fortification walls, while that of Pylos is not the focal area of a citadel. The use of many sections in both palaces cannot be definitely determined and can be interpreted variously, but there can be little doubt that their megara served as the

state units where official receptions were held and audiences were given.

In the *Odyssey* Telemachos was received and entertained in the megaron of the Palace of Nestor. It is interesting to see how Telemachos' visit fits into the setting of the palace of Ano Englianos. The pertinent passage in epic poetry is in the third book of the *Odyssey*. While the preparations for a sacrifice were readied, Telemachos, who had spent the night in the "guest room" by the court, in the room with the round hearth, was conducted to the bathroom next door and was bathed by the younger daughter of Nestor, Polykaste. He was then anointed richly with oil and "casting about him a fair cloak and a tunic, went forth from the bath like unto the immortals; and sat down by Nestor, the shepherd of the people." We can picture Telemachos in the palace at Ano Englianos proceeding after his bath in Room 43 (text fig. 13) through the lobby 38, the passage 37, and the loggia 44 to the inner court of the central unit, No. 3, and hence to Room 10 with the low bench covered with stucco, located by the great southwest anta of the *aithousa* of the Megaron to place himself by Nestor who "sat down on the polished stones which were before his lofty doors white and glistening with oil."[33] Shortly afterwards the sacrifice was offered to the gods in the open court in front of the Megaron.

The difference in interpretation of certain compartments of the Palace of Nestor at Pylos does not obscure the most important fact: that in it we have one of the best-preserved Mycenaean palaces, whose remains have added much to our knowledge of the houses of the great kings of the heroic age. Its contents, and especially its tablets, have shed a great deal of light on the type of community which gave birth to the palace era of Greece. The final publication of these remains will give us a new and documented basis for the fuller evaluation of the Mycenaean Age. Meanwhile, we may repeat the conclusion of Blegen, its excavator, that the Palace at Ano Englianos was destroyed by fire about 1200 B.C.

THE PALACE OF MYCENAE

The legendary Palace of Agamemnon in the citadel of Mycenae was revealed by Tsountas in the years from 1885 to 1887 on the very top of the precipitous hill which Cyclopean walls transformed into a formidable stronghold (text figs. 5 and 7 + 29, 31).[34] Tsountas published a careful preliminary report of his

discoveries accompanied by a plan drawn by Dörpfeld, but was not destined to give us a final publication. This was done, after a good deal of supplementary excavation, by Wace, whose excellent description and plans of the palace are universally accepted.[35] The extent of the palace to the north, west, and south is

---

[32] After the final publication of the palace, it may perhaps prove possible to determine the function of its parts with greater precision. For the fresco fragments found in Room 64 cf. *AJA*, 60 (1956), p. 95. Room 65 is called by Blegen "Second

Throne Room."

[33] *Odyssey*, III, 464-469, and 406-408.
[34] *Praktika*, 1886, pp. 59-79.
[35] Wace, *BSA*, 25 (1921-1923), pp. 147-282, and *Mycenae*, pp.

clearly defined. The east side alone is undetermined and, according to Tsountas, it was in the eastern area of the palace that the domestic quarters seem to have been located. Constructed on uneven ground and on different levels, on top of the hill and along its sloping sides to the west and south, the palace must have presented a stepped or terraced appearance. Most of the foundations now visible belong to the last period of the life of the palace—to the years that preceded its final destruction by fire. However, fragments of walls found below the surface, discarded frescoes, a filled-in room, sherds of different periods, and reused blocks enabled Wace to work out convincingly the architectural phases represented by the remains discovered. His general conclusion that an early palace, built perhaps in LH I or II times on the natural terrace of the summit and adapted to the site, was followed by a later palace for which the site was adapted to a preconceived plan, is based on fact and should be accepted with confidence. Leveling and bold terracing extended the area over which the later palace was erected, especially to the southwest. The design of the later palace is simple but harmonious; it exhibits the great skill of the architect, who took advantage of the natural setting and modified it to fit his preconceived design. This later palace underwent alterations, and part of it at least seems to have been reconstructed after a devastating fire. The remains we see today on top of the hill belong to the later palace after its reconstruction. Wace has pointed out that the later palace could not have been built before the construction of the south section of the Cyclopean fortification wall, since apparently that acted as a retaining wall for its Megaron unit. We have therefore a *terminus post quem*, for the erection of that palace. It is impossible to determine with any degree of certainty the date of the fire that necessitated its reconstruction and the date of the grand staircase on its southwest side, which we can accept with a good degree of certainty as the latest addition; but there can be no doubt that the palace as reconstructed, altered, and added to was finally destroyed by fire when the citadel was captured and sacked by the enemy.

We can have no conception of the plan of the earlier palace at the moment. It is natural to believe that it occupied the top of the hill, that it possessed a megaron as its main unit, that the megaron was oriented from south to north, with its open, front portico facing the south. This orientation was imposed by the natural climate of the territory; the strong north winds, which plague the site even now, would

have made any other orientation impossible. It seems probable that in spite of destruction, additions, and alterations part of the earlier palace, perhaps its megaron as repaired was incorporated in the later. This was the case both at Tiryns and at Pylos, as we have seen. Of course, around that first megaron other rooms and corridors must have been grouped. Of these and of what replaced them when the later palace was built very little survives. Over their burnt ruins in the Historic era other structures were erected, and in Hellenistic times a temple of considerable extent was built, apparently dedicated to Athena. Perhaps the early palace extended to the line where the south corridor of the second palace was later made. The area of that corridor could have formed a ramp supported by the earlier north wall revealed by Wace, which led to a main entrance located in the area that later formed its southeast end (text fig. 14, No. 5). The earlier palace stood on top of the hill when the first *enceinte* had been completed. From the gate of the *enceinte* which, as we have seen, was beyond the southeast corner of the Lion Gate, a road must have led to the palace. That road presumably followed the gentler north slope of the hill, reached the area where in later Mycenaean times were built the north staircase and the northwest entrance (text fig. 14, Nos. 2-3), and terminated in the area of the west portal (No. 4); from there a ramp commenced, leading to the megaron and other apartments built on top of the hill (No. 6).

The Later Palace

For our knowledge of the later palace we do not need to depend on conjecture and imagination. The surviving remains give us a definite picture of its extent and plan. One of its main features was the excellently designed unit of a new "megaron," "court," and apartment to be known as the "guest room" or "hostel," a unit constructed in an artificially leveled and terraced area on the south and southwest slope of the hill (text fig. 15, Nos. 51-57). The presumed ramp of the earlier palace was developed into a long paved corridor, the south corridor (text fig. 15, No. 37), its old entrance, was transformed into the west portal (No. 45), an inner main entranceway, and the old path leading to it was made into the west passage (No. 44).

The plan of the later palace is admirable in its simplicity (text fig. 15). Two corridors, the north (Nos. 18-20) and the south (No. 37), running nearly from west to east, placed at different levels, separate the state and public units of the palace, the magnifi-

---

69-90. To avoid confusion we are using the numbers given to the various sections of the palace by Wace as shown in L.

Holland's plan. See also Mylonas, *Ancient Mycenae*, pp. 42-67.

59

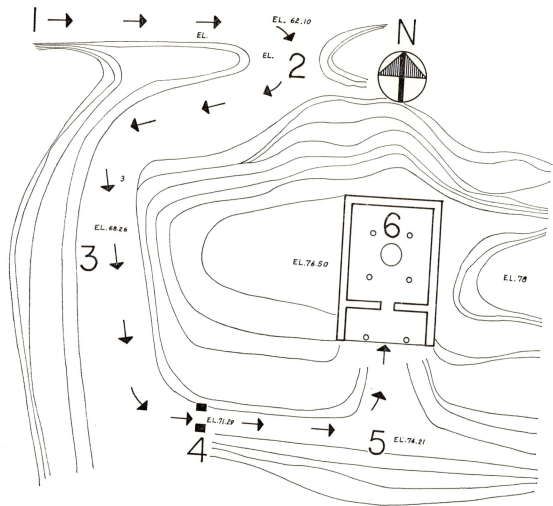

14. Mycenae. Conjectured sketch plan of ascent to first palace (2-5) Ascent (6) Megaron (drawing Compton)

cent "megaron unit" (Nos. 53-57), from its more private apartments (Nos. 12-14, 30-33). They also provide an easy access to these apartments from the main, the west passage (No. 44), which begins at the main entrance to the palace (No. 9) and terminates either before the west portal (No. 45) or, skirting the southwest corner of the "guest room" (Nos. 51-52), ends in the small court in front of it. The best preserved section of the palace is its south wing, and by chance this was not only the part that was added to the earlier palace, but also the state unit of the later. It comprises its great megaron (text fig. 15, Nos. 55-57), its court (No. 53), a square room beyond the court to the west (No. 52) with its court and perhaps a small adjacent room (No. 51). The south side of the megaron and of the court rolled down the abrupt slope of the hill to the Chavos when the south Cyclopean wall, which had acted as its retaining wall, collapsed and crumbled into the ravine. In the last few years the foundations of that side have been restored, under

Stikas' direction, by the Greek Service for the Restoration of Ancient Monuments. As a result the plan of the wing is easily appreciated by the visitor.

The megaron (text fig. 15; Fig. 57, Nos. 55-57), comparable to that of Tiryns and especially to that of Pylos, is a long rectangular structure measuring some 23 by 11.50 m. (inner dimensions). It is oriented approximately from west to east with its entrance facing the west, the main court. By crosswalls the structure is divided into three sections, the westernmost of which forms the *aithousa*. It is an open portico with two columns *in antis*. The wooden columns were destroyed in the fire that devastated the palace, but the stone bases are still *in situ* (Fig. 58, b). Large gypsum slabs, usually assumed to have been imported from Crete, were used to pave the floor, and the walls were covered with painted plaster. A small sample of it has been preserved at the bottom of its northeast corner. It is part of the well-known Mycenaean "rosette and triglyph" pattern and seems to have

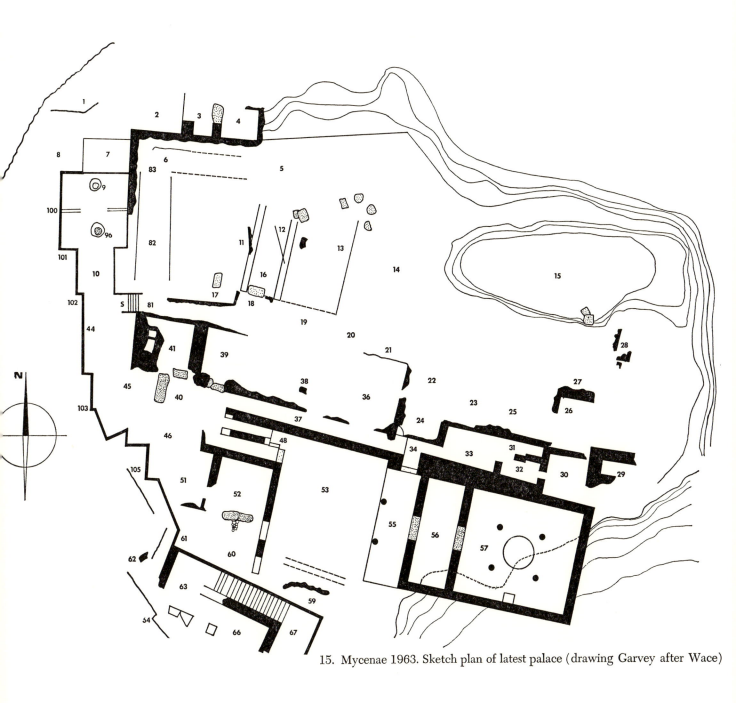

15. Mycenae 1963. Sketch plan of latest palace (drawing Garvey after Wace)

belonged to a dado going around the lower part of the walls. A threshold block at the north side of the *aithousa* (Fig. 58, a) proves that a doorway existed there. Fragments of charred wood discovered nearby indicate that a wooden stairway was originally located beyond the door by means of which the megaron communicated with the so-called domestic quarters to be found in the higher slope of the hill (Fig. 56, No. 14). By the south column base of the *aithousa* Papadimitriou discovered in 1954 the foundations of an altar (Fig. 58, d) and the remains of a table of offerings of deep red *rosso antico* with a beautifully carved running spiral on its sides. Near these he found, in the gypsum slabs of the flooring, a shallow basin-like depression, divided into two compartments (Fig. 58, e), recalling the depressions found near the throne in the *domos* of Pylos. Below the floor slabs he also found fragments of painted plaster belonging to tables of offering.[36]

A single large doorway connected the *aithousa* with the second division of the megaron, the *prodomos* (Fig. 58, c). Details of the doorway are clear. Its threshold, still *in situ*, is made up of a single block of conglomerate cut to size by means of a saw. The actual width of the doorway, however, was smaller; the balance was taken up by the heavy wooden frames of the door. On the south side of the threshold, to the right as we enter, a pivot hole is partially preserved; in it Tsountas found fragments of bronze which enclosed the end of the pole around which the door revolved. Along the inner side of the threshold is a cut ledge against which the door would rest.

The *prodomos* is deeper than the *aithousa*. With the exception of the south wall, its sides stand to a considerable height, and they demonstrate not only the construction of the walls, in rubble with wooden framework, but also the plastering, with the outer layer originally ornamented with frescoes. Both plaster and the rubble masonry were so badly damaged by the fire that destroyed the palace that nothing can be made out of the murals. The floor has a border of gypsum slabs laid along the walls and its central area is covered with painted stucco. Dark red lines divide this central area into squares decorated with motives reminiscent of those on the columns of the Treasury of Atreus, that is, zigzag patterns painted in blue, red, and yellow. The floor slab to the right of the doorway leading to the *domos* is higher than the rest of the floor, forming a raised platform comparable in size and height to those of the Palace of Nestor in Pylos.

A single doorway led from the *prodomos* to the *domos* or main room of the megaron (Fig. 56, No.

57). The threshold, again of conglomerate stone, is still *in situ* although badly damaged by fire. The heavy wooden frame of the doorway covering the rest of the length of the threshold is indicated by the cuttings on either end of the sill block. The lack of pivot holes seems to indicate that the opening was not blocked by a door. This is the case also at Tiryns and Pylos. Perhaps the opening was curtained.

The main room of the megaron, the *domos*, apparently measuring 12.96 by 11.50 inner dimensions, is very imposing. Unfortunately, the south wall, most of the eastern wall, and a good portion of the adjacent floor, including the corner between the two walls, have gone down the precipitous slope. Apparently the *domos* was paved in the same manner as the *prodomos*, with a border of gypsum slabs laid along the walls; the rest of the floor within the border was covered with painted stucco. Again, the stuccoed floor was divided by painted double lines into square panels. The patterns that originally decorated these panels have not survived. At least four superposed coats of stucco have been distinguished, indicating the custom of renovating the floor from time to time.

The surviving walls of the *domos* are of rubble masonry and originally were covered with plaster decorated in fresco. Though badly damaged by fire, fragments of these frescoes were recovered. Tsountas recognized in them horsemen and soldiers, and later Rodenwaldt and Miss Lamb were able to reconstruct parts of the compositions showing warriors and horses as well as women in front of a palace standing on a rocky ground. Another sector seems to have represented a battle fought in front of a fortified citadel with women watching it from the walls, a composition reminiscent of the battles before the walls of Troy.[37]

The main features of the *domos* were the throne of the king, the central hearth, and the lofty columns placed around it. Unfortunately no trace of the throne survives. Judging from the position of the throne in the *domoi* of Tiryns and Pylos, we may conclude that it was to be seen to the right of a person entering the *domos*; that it stood against the south wall of that room (text fig. 16). When that wall collapsed into the ravine, it carried with it the remnants of the throne as well as a good part of the floor in front of it. Of the central hearth only a third has survived, sufficient not only to prove its existence and location but also its nature and decoration. It was circular in shape and was built with a ring of poros stone enclosing a center of clay; both were covered with stucco. At least ten layers of stucco were distinguished by Tsountas and Wace, and apparently most of them were covered

---

[36] Papadimitriou, *Praktika*, 1955, p. 230 ff. and pls. 78-79.

[37] Tsountas, *Ephemeris*, 1887, pls. 11-12. G. Rodenwaldt, *Der Fries des Megarons von Mykenai*, 1921. W. Lamb, "Palace Frescoes," *BSA*, 25 (1921-1923), pp. 163-171 and 249-255.

with painted patterns; a "plume" or "flame" pattern was painted on the sides in deep red, while a spiral motive covered the flat rim of the hearth.[38]

The position of the four columns around the hearth can be accurately determined since two of the stone bases and the block on which the third was placed were found in their original positions. By the northwestern base Tsountas found fragments of bronze plates bearing nails, and it seems reasonable to suppose that the columns, which were made of wood, were covered, at least in their lower sections, with bronze plate and ornaments. Whether or not the shafts of the columns were fluted, as is the case in Pylos, cannot be determined, since no evidence relative to this detail was found; but no protecting stucco rings, so common in Pylos, were found at Mycenae. It may perhaps be interesting to note that the measurements of the megara of Mycenae and Pylos are almost the same, that their plan is identical, differing from that of the great megaron of Tiryns not only in dimensions but also in that each has one doorway from the *aithousa* to the *prodomos* instead of three (text fig. 16).

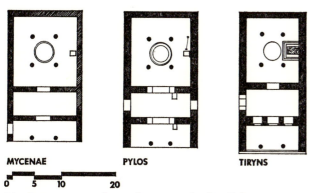

MYCENAE   PYLOS   TIRYNS

0 5 10   20

16. Comparative plans of megara in the Peloponnesos (drawing Garvey)

No evidence is preserved to prove whether or not the megaron or any part of it was two stories high or had balconies in the *domos*, as seems to have been the case at Pylos. I believe that it was only one story high and had a flat roof. Nor is there any evidence indicating what arrangement was made for the smoke of the hearth to escape. In Pylos, as we have seen, a lantern surmounted by "chimney pipes" seems to have been employed for the purpose. It seems to me that the same system was employed at Mycenae. The "chimney pipe" found in the house Mrs. Shear excavated in 1962 in the neighborhood of the Treasury of

Atreus corroborates this. As at Pylos, the fragments were discovered around a circular hearth located in the center of the room. This proves that the people of Mycenae were familiar with the arrangement and used it; they must have employed it in their megara. In some mountain villages of Greece the use of pots and pithoi as chimney pipes is still in evidence, and an excellent example of the arrangement is still to be seen in the Monastery of Kaisariani, near Athens.

It has been stated that too much faith is placed in parallels to be found in the *Iliad* and the *Odyssey*, but certainly in those poems we have a good recollection of the Mycenaean palace and some coincidences are striking. I want to draw attention, at the risk of drawing criticism also, to the border of gypsum slabs placed along the walls of the *prodomos* and *domos*, while the rest of the floor is in stucco. Interestingly enough, in the description of the megaron of Alkinoos we find that the thrones of the Phaeacian leaders were placed along the walls: "within, seats were fixed along the wall on either hand . . . and on them the leaders of the Phaeacians were wont to sit drinking and eating."[39] Was the border of slabs intended to give a solid base for the placing of seats for guests, and to spare the stuccoed floor unnecessary wear?

The megaron opens onto the main court of the palace to the west (text fig. 15, No. 53). Compared to the courts of Minoan palaces it is a small but well-proportioned area; its length is almost equal to the width of the megaron. This court is larger than that of the Palace of Nestor, but resembled it in having a floor paved with a thick layer of Mycenaean lime-concrete covered with a thick coat of smooth, painted stucco. By double-impressed lines its area was divided into squares which were filled with alternating colors, yellow, blue, and red; on these colors were painted linear patterns in black. Because of this decorated floor and the painted walls, Rodenwaldt suggested that the court was roofed.[40] The court, however, is so large that a roof over it would have required interior supports. No traces of supports, such as bases of columns, have been found in spite of the fact that a good deal of the original floor is preserved. It seems very probable that the court was open to the sky. Very scanty remains of a wall were found along its south side and these cannot indicate definitely whether at that side a high wall closed the court or a mere balustrade.[41] I believe that a balustrade should

[38] Wace, *BSA*, 25 (1921-1923), pp. 241-244, and *Mycenae*, p. 77. The diameter of the hearth is calculated to have been about 3.70 m.

[39] *Odyssey*, VII, 95 ff. A comparable arrangement of large gypsum slabs surrounding a central rectangular area paved in mosaic, which, according to Evans, originally was covered with painted plaster, is to be seen in the entrance hall, the hall of the

peristyle, and the great megaron of the little palace at Knossos. Evans, *Palace of Minos*, II, p. 517 and fig. 318.

[40] Rodenwaldt, *Jahrbuch*, 34 (1919), p. 95. The court is 11 m. from east to west and more than 15 m. from north to south.

[41] Cf. Wace, *BSA*, 25 (1921-1923), p. 189, and *Mycenae*, p. 75. Contra, see Mylonas, *Ancient Mycenae*, pp. 50-51.

be postulated on that side. A high wall would have blocked the magnificent view of the Argive plain which unfolds below the corner of the citadel. It would also have blocked the south winds which bring so much freshness in the summer months. Why would the builders and occupants of the palace have gone to so much trouble to create an artificial terrace at this particular spot if they were not to enjoy the benefits of the site? Wace rightly observed that, when the court and the apartments around it were designed, the site was adapted to the plan and that plan evidently took cognizance of the view.

The north wall of the court is preserved to its entire length and stands to a height of 2.50 m. and in six tiers. It is built of rubble, but it was faced with poros blocks laid in the Mycenaean ashlar fashion. Between the two lower courses was originally laid a horizontal wooden beam, example of the well-known wooden tie system employed in their construction. The entire surface of the wall originally was covered with painted stucco. Behind this north wall there was another, faced with plaster; it apparently belonged to a structure earlier than that represented by the court. Beyond the north wall we find the ascending ramp of the South Corridor.

The west side of the court is also well preserved. At its northwest corner an opening, with a threshold *in situ*, gave access to the southwest corridor, which apparently started in the area within the western portal. Its floor is covered with lime-cement. To the right as one enters this corridor from the court, two steps of stone, originally covered with stucco (text fig. 15, No. 48), lead to a landing from which a wooden stairway led first westward to an upper level or story, perhaps to a story over Room No. 52.

The west wall of the court also had a facing of poros stones laid in ashlar fashion; of this only one course is preserved for a distance of 6 m. Behind this wall is a compartment that has caused a good deal of discussion (text fig. 15, No. 52). It is an almost square room, measuring 5.50 by 6.20 m. The floor was covered with painted stucco, surviving only along the edges of its walls. Against the north wall Tsountas found and excavated a rectangular area 80 cm. by 1.07 m. rising from the floor about 5 cm. When Wace again cleared the rectangular area, he found that a rim made of plaster rose 2 to 3 cm. above the floor level while the oblong was actually sunk 1.5 cm. below it. Its surface was found covered with plaster, only small parts of which were missing. A painted border, com-

posed of a blue stripe between red lines, offset the oblong from the rest of the painted floor, while red color covered the wall behind it. Elsewhere, the wall seems to have been white with a dark stripe below.[42]

Tsountas accepted this rectangular pit as a hearth; Wace considered it the placement of a throne and on this based his identification of the chamber as a throne room, where audiences were granted and visitors were received. I have already pointed out that in the palaces of both Tiryns and Pylos the throne of the ruler was located in the *domos* of the megaron to the right of a person entering. In neither of these was there a special room for the throne. The example at Knossos perhaps influenced Wace's conclusion, which was reached before the second example of a throne in a *domos* was found at Pylos. It differs in arrangement and in character from the square room; in fact it is not certain whether the "throne room" of Knossos was not used solely for religious rites indicated by the "sunken area" disclosed across from its throne. We have neither the sunken area nor the bench along the wall in the square room of Mycenae. The surface of the rectangular space covered with plaster indicates that a chair or throne was not placed over it, for it does not show any imprints of the legs of a throne or scratches which would have normally resulted. The area under the throne at Pylos was not covered with plaster, but generally the surface of hearths was covered with plaster and was edged by a raised border, like the border found around the square hearth in our room. Rectangular hearths are not unusual in Mycenaean architecture. The hearth of the "little megaron" at Tiryns was rectangular in form, as was that of the so-called house of Tsountas at Mycenae. The dimensions of the latter, 1.10 by 0.88 by 0.09 m., almost repeat those of the hearth in the square room. The hearths mentioned are in the middle of the rooms; however, a rectangular hearth placed against the wall was found in the Gallery of the Curtains of the palace itself at Mycenae.[43]

Furthermore, Holland years ago pointed out that the square room is so broad that interior supports, columns, were necessary for its ceiling and the second story over it. And, although he believed that "a single column in the centre would be excellent from the structural point of view," he rejected the preferable solution in favor of two columns because a single column "would come directly in front of the throne—rather a preposterous arrangement."[44] It would indeed

---

[42] Tsountas, *Praktika*, 1886, p. 68. Wace, *BSA*, 25 (1921-1923), pp. 187 ff. and *Mycenae*, p. 75.

[43] It was disclosed again by Papadimitriou, to whom I owe the information.

[44] Holland in *BSA*, 25 (1921-1923), p. 276. In my *Ancient Mycenae* I used the term hostel for Room 52. Perhaps the term guest room is preferable.

have been a preposterous arrangement in a throne room, but quite acceptable otherwise; if the rectangular area was a hearth and not the setting for a throne, a column placed in front of it would not have interfered with its use. That a single column could be used in those days as an interior support in a roofed structure even at Mycenae is indicated by the single column of the porticoes of the northwestern propylon.[45] We find a monostyle arrangement in the propylon of the palace of Pylos and in the vestibule of its women's hall (Fig. 13, No. 64).[46]

Both Tsountas and Wace have pointed out that to the northwest of the square room only a small area of the palace remained, held up by the western retaining wall (text fig. 15, No. 51). Unfortunately, whatever stood on that area has been completely destroyed, leaving no traces behind. We may suppose that another very small room stood next to the square room, and shared a common wall with it; this seems to be indicated by the well-constructed corner which survived beyond the northwest corner of the square room. We may now note that Tsountas found a drain built of terra-cotta, pi-shaped tiles immediately below the floor of the square room. The entire length of that drain has not been investigated, but its direction, verified before the floor was cemented again, indicates that possibly it continued to the room we are postulating. This tile drain may indicate that the small chamber was a bathroom. If this hypothesis is correct, then in the square room with the attached bathroom we find a parallel to the bath and room with the round hearth of Pylos.

In my earlier book, *Ancient Mycenae*, I suggested that the square room served as the place where honored guests were housed during their visits. It is paralleled by Room 46, with the round hearth, of the palace at Pylos. Both apartments are immediately off the main court of the palace; both exhibit dimensions nearly half as large as those of their *domoi*; each has a hearth, although in different positions and of different shapes; and, if our assumption made before the discoveries in Pylos is correct, that there was a bathroom next to the square room, then each has a bathroom attached to the main room with no direct communication with it. The room at Pylos is perhaps later in date and probably was fashioned after the square room at Mycenae since it presents an elaboration and an improvement of the plan: a central hearth surrounded by columns, rather than a hearth against the wall and a single column in the middle of

the room. Their similarities perhaps indicate a similar function; neither was a throne room.

Two doorways on its south side, separated by a pier of rubble masonry, led from the square room, from the "guest room," to a forecourt of an irregular quadrilateral form exhibiting a "well-cemented" floor (text fig. 15, No. 60). The existence of a small drain running through its east wall seems to indicate that the forecourt was open to the sky. The west wall of the main court of the palace separates it from the forecourt. A red sandstone sill, *in situ* at the north section of this wall, may have served as a threshold to a doorway. It seems, however, that the main opening between the two courts was at the south end of the wall, because to such an opening belongs a threshold block of conglomerate, partly preserved. It was found by Tsountas projecting beyond the end of the west wall and over the top of the existing flight of steps of the grand staircase.[47] For safety he removed it from its position. The Service for the Preservation of Ancient Monuments has recently placed it at the southeast end of the forecourt, thus creating the possibility of a doorway between the upper landing of the grand staircase and the forecourt. I believe that this restoration is wrong and does not correspond to actuality. The area over which it was placed had collapsed in antiquity, and if the threshold was originally there it would have fallen along with the wall to the bottom of the stairway. Secondly, it is very improbable that a block of such dimensions would have been pulled away from its original position, or that it would have been transported some meters and left where it was found by Tsountas. It may be argued that two doorways or openings from the forecourt to the main court were unnecessary; one would have been sufficient. The argument perhaps is valid. But it should be pointed out that the threshold of the smaller, more northerly opening is not of conglomerate, but of sandstone; that all thresholds, found thus far, that belong to the last period of construction of the palace are of conglomerate. It is therefore possible to assume that the red sandstone sill is the remnant of an older opening, which belongs perhaps to the first phase of the later palace, that in the second phase it was replaced by the larger opening further south with a threshold of conglomerate. Actually it cannot be proved that the wall, in the last phase of the palace, was not continued over the red sandstone sill, blocking that entrance; in the second phase thus we would have but one opening, the larger one with the conglomerate sill at the southeast end of the forecourt.

---

[45] *Infra*, p. 67 and text fig. 17.
[46] Blegen, *AJA*, 58 (1954), p. 29, pl. 4 fig. 2, and *AJA*, 59 (1955), p. 32, pl. 24. *Supra*, p. 54.

[47] Tsountas, *Praktika*, 1886, pp. 63, 64. See also Wace, *BSA*, 25 (1921-1923), p. 180 and Steffen, *Karten von Mykenai*, pl. II.

Immediately below the southeast side of the forecourt is the southwest or grand staircase with its preserved· lower flight of twenty-two steps, with its vestibule, lobby, and storeroom (text fig. 15, Nos. 63-67). It was revealed by Tsountas, and studied and published finally by Wace.[48] The latter, furthermore, proved that this grand staircase is the latest addition to the later palace, made after its second phase. The "guest room" (No. 52) and its forecourt, the main court (No. 53) and its megaron (Nos. 55-57), were conceived and designed as one unit. This becomes evident from the study of the plan and of the remains. The unit stood on an artificially made terrace, the filling of which consisted of loose stones ultimately retained by the south line of the Cyclopean wall. The grand staircase does not fit into the unit; it is placed obliquely to it and it is an apparent later addition.

Below the forecourt (text fig. 15, No. 60), Wace revealed a basement room which was destroyed by fire and then filled in to form part of the terrace on which stood the forecourt and its square room. This basement, known as the pillar room, therefore belongs to a phase of the palace construction older than that represented by the remains of the forecourt and of the square room.

A heavy retaining wall supports the terrace to the west and northwest of the square room and its forecourt. It proceeds with setbacks to the north and supports the well-known text west passage (fig. 15, No. 44). This retaining wall is not contemporaneous in its entire length, but it represents at least two building periods. Its north end terminates near a paved area, apparently the outer court of the palace (text fig. 15, No. 7). It is in front of what Wace considered the original and main entrance to the palace, the northwest entrance (No. 9). Unfortunately that entrance was badly damaged and its plan was obscured by later constructions and especially by a Hellenistic building which came to be known as the oil press. Wace cleared the northwest entrance partially in 1921-1922 and concluded that it consisted of a propylon with a monostyle outer portico and a distyle inner portico.[49] In 1955 he reexamined the northwest entrance area and finally concluded that it was not in the form of a propylon but of a long hall with three columns in single file on its long axis.[50] In 1962 we cleared the entire

area of the entrance to the rock level and found a few sections that had not been excavated before. It was the first time in the history of the excavations that the entire area was cleared and exposed to view at the same time (Fig. 59). Then it was found that of the two conglomerate bases in the south section of the entrance the northernmost (Fig. 60) was in its original position and the second (base c) was originally placed on top of the first.[51] This and other observations made possible the establishment of the ground plan of the structure which formed the northwest entrance of the palace (text fig. 17). It was in the form of a rectangular propylon with a monostyle outer portico and another monostyle inner portico. The level of the outer or north portico apparently reaches almost the top of the base, some 90 cm. above the level of the cobblestone court. We shall, therefore, have to place in front of the outer portico a number of steps to reach its level. From there southward apparently a ramp ascended gently to the south.

Below the floor level of the propylon and parallel to its west wall we uncovered the remains of an older structure, evidently the foundation of an older propylon. Unfortunately, the sherds found in the small unexcavated band of earth along its side are so few and indefinite that they offer no basis for chronology. They help us only to conclude that we have two periods in the construction of the northwest entrance, the later one reaching down to the years of the final destruction of the palace. Two periods also were indicated by the retaining walls of the artificial terrace in front of the northwest entrance. In the south portico and by the base *in situ*, but below the floor level and in its fill of stone, we found a column base of limestone, finished by means of a saw, whose marks are apparent on its side (Fig. 59, d). The base was placed in the fill of the floor when the last propylon was constructed, and of course it was not in its original position. Perhaps it belonged to the earlier propylon which may have had a plan similar to that exhibited by its successor. Wace had suggested the existence in this corner of an earlier and a later entrance, even an entrance that belonged to the earlier palace.[52] He based his suggestion on the difference in style between the propylon terrace wall forming its west side and the main west terrace wall, and on the conglomerate

---

[48] *BSA*, 25 (1921-1923), pp. 149-160.

[49] *Ibid.*, pp. 210-213.

[50] *BSA*, 51 (1956), p. 106. It is interesting to note that L. Holland, *BSA*, 25 (1921-1923), p. 272 n. 2, ascribed the two thicker column bases to a later period than those of the megaron because they are larger and more skillfully dressed. He maintained that they are contemporary with the conglomerate bases on the summit and found them closely related to the "masonry of the Treasury of Atreus probably not far apart in date." Thus he suggested that the Treasury

belonged to the advanced years of LH III B.

[51] Stepped bases are not unusual in Mycenaean architecture, and on a glass cylinder on which columns are represented some stand on two round bases. *JHS*, 21 (1901), p. 141 and fig. 24. The bases for the engaged column in the façade of the Treasury of Atreus are stepped.

[52] *BSA*, 25 (1921-1923), p. 213. And we noted above that through this area was obtained the ascent to the top of the hill where a first palace may have stood.

bases. His suggestion is proved correct by our discoveries of the earlier wall.

To the south of the propylon there was evidently a small inner court (text fig. 17, d), the east wall of which was a continuation of the east wall of the propylon. Its west wall was based on the second length of the west retaining wall, between its first and second setback counting from the north end (text fig. 15, No. 101). Remnants of its east wall determine its east side and the end of the court. Within this court is the limestone block (near No. 10 in Wace's plan) that was considered in position. The clearing of the area proved that it was not in position. Perhaps the floor of the inner court was a ramp ascending from north

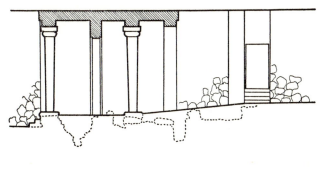

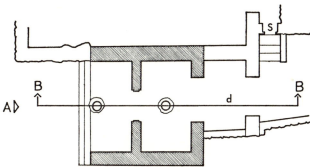

17. Mycenae 1962. Restored plan and section of northwest propylon (drawings Rothman and Compton)

to south, reaching the beginning of the west passage at an elevation of 68.94.

The west passage (No. 44) begins between Room 41 and the west retaining wall (No. 102) after its second setback (text fig. 15). It is noticeable that the passage gradually becomes narrower as it proceeds to the south. At the north end, the widest part, between the southeast corner of the inner court of the northwestern entrance and the northwest corner of Room 41 (at the area marked as elevation 70.68 in Wace's plan) we found, in 1962, a stairway oriented east and west (Fig. 61; text fig. 17, S) . This we shall call hereafter Stairway

S. The foundations of three broad steps, with an average rise of 19 cm. have in part survived. Along their south side a parapet of clay covered with stucco separated the staircase from the passage (text fig. 17, S). Perhaps this stucco-covered surface was what Wace noted as "a small fragment of . . . cement floor just at the northwest angle outside the room (41) north of the Western Portal." This cement floor has a level of 70.68.[53]

The three broad steps led to a threshold, a great part of which is still *in situ* (Fig. 61). Its central part is missing, but the corner of the other end can still be seen below the masonry of the wall of Room 41.[54] A pivot hole at the northwest corner indicates the position of a door. Whether it was a single or a double-leaf door, as in the case of the doorway at the north end of the *aithousa* of the megaron, cannot now be determined, since the part of the threshold where a second pivot hole would have existed is not preserved. The door opening seems to have been about 1 m. in width. In the substructure of the missing part of the threshold we found a few pieces of pottery which seem to belong to the LH III A ceramic phase, indicating that the stairway perhaps was originally designed in the days of the earlier palace.

Beyond the threshold to the east we uncovered a landing-corridor with lime-cement pavement preserved almost in its entirety (text fig. 15, No. 81; Fig. 61). This landing gave access on the one hand to a broad gallery (No. 82) along the east side of the propylon at an intermediate height between its floor and the level of the northwest section of the hill and on the other to the north corridor (Nos. 18-20). Thus direct communication was obtained between the beginning of the West Passage (No. 44) and the summit of the hill where important apartments were located. Wace suggested the existence of such a communication in 1923, but failed to find it.[55]

The west passage, starting from the inner court (text fig. 15, No. 10) led southwards in an ascending grade to end at what has been called the west portal (No. 45). The grade, determined from its beginning to the top of the threshold of the west portal, seems to have amounted to a rather steep grade, about 2 m. for a distance of some 10 to 11 m. The west portal actually formed the main entrance to the palace. Whether or not the west passage continued, in a southeasterly direction, greatly diminished in width, around the guest room and its adjunct to reach their forecourt (No. 61) and thus connect the northwest entrance with the southwest grand staircase, cannot be deter-

---

[53] *Ibid.*, p. 210.
[54] This of course proves that the stairway antedates Room 41. A full account of the area of the Northwest entrance will

be published by T. Leslie Shear, Jr.
[55] *BSA*, 25 (1921-1923), p. 216.

mined from the surviving remains. I rather favor this conception, although greater security would have resulted from a termination of the west passage at the west portal and the area in front of it.

All that survives of the west portal is its huge threshold block of conglomerate, still *in situ*. At its south end is a pivot-hole and a sawn ledge against which a door would rest. Both these elements prove that the opening was closed by a massive door. Some poros blocks laid in ashlar style, a few of which are still *in situ* lying directly outside the threshold, enabled Wace to conclude that in front of the doorway (to the west of it) a porch originally stood, perhaps roofed, extending probably as far as the west wall of Room 41. This porch, together with the doorway forms the west portal. On entering that portal we find ourselves in an area where there may have been a small inner court (No. 40) through which access was obtained to two important corridors. The section of the palace to the southeast of the small court is completely destroyed; thus no conclusions are possible as to the arrangement of rooms and passages that may have existed there. However, it is reasonable to assume that some access was provided to the southwest corridor which led to the main court and through it to the megaron. To the inner court (No. 40) opened Room 41 and a compartment (No. 39) of unknown use.

It is clear that from the inner small court of the west portal direct access was obtained to the south corridor (No. 37). It was perhaps originally made as an approach to the earlier palace built on the summit of the hill; then it was transformed into a corridor running approximately from west to east to serve the later palace. Its floor was covered with lime-cement, surviving for quite a distance, and this makes possible the determination of its grade. In a distance of 10 m. the grading seems to correspond to that of the west passage. Beyond the 10 m. of length the floor of the passage was destroyed by one of Schliemann's pits. It seems that in the first phase of the later palace the south corridor led to the apartments which formed, according to Tsountas, the domestic quarters. At a later time, perhaps in the rebuilding which marks the second phase, its east end was blocked, and this terminated its use as a passage to those quarters. It was then that in the north wall of the *aithousa* of the megaron a door was opened, beyond which a wooden stairway (No. 34) led to the domestic quarters through the room I call the Gallery of the Curtains, to the Vestibule to the Domestic Quarters of Wace (No. 33).

The blocking of the south corridor poses a difficult and thus far unsolved problem. What could have been the function of this passage in the second phase of the

life of the later palace? It seems to have been a passage leading nowhere, a dead-end passage. On its south side a straight wall separates it from the main court of the palace. At the existing west end of the corridor on its north side there is a conglomerate threshold *in situ*. This gave access to an area (No. 39) in which the rising rock leaves very little free space. Nothing was found in that area to lead to the belief that it was used as a storeroom, and Tsountas suggested that a wooden stairway must have existed there through which access to the north corridor was obtained. No charred remains were found, as was true in the case of the wooden stairway of the *aithousa*, to justify this suggestion, which, however, in the days of Tsountas seemed reasonable since no other access to the north corridor had been found. But now that we have Stairway S, which provides direct communication from the west passage to the north corridor, the suggestion of Tsountas becomes untenable. Why would people come all the way up the west passage, through the west portal and its inner court, through the beginning of the south corridor and Room 39 to a stairway which would take them to the north corridor when they could have reached it directly through Stairway S?

To solve the problem of the dead-end corridor, Holland suggested that at its blocked east end a stairway was built leading to a higher level of the domestic quarters, above the Gallery of the Curtains (No. 33).[56] Since there was a stairway (No. 31) immediately beyond that gallery which led to higher levels, such a duplication seems to me completely unnecessary; Holland's suggestion does not seem to provide the solution needed. Wace, realizing the difficulties involved, concluded that "the South Corridor ceased to have any purpose except to give access to the basement rooms which lay on its north side."[57] However, the question arises: were there basement rooms beyond that side?

Our investigation of the section between the north and south corridors in 1963 and again in 1965 revealed no traces of partition walls and no other evidence indicating the existence of basement rooms. In the entire area, measuring some 23.50 m. in length and some 7 m. in width, the rock was not cut away but was allowed to rise to its original height. Here and there projecting tops were hammered down to a uniform level over which apparently a floor was laid. Along the south edge of the rocky formation and between it and the north wall of the south corridor there exists a narrow strip of earth, averaging 1 m. in width. This was artificially filled and brought up to the level of the rocky formation. The north wall of the corridor retained that fill thus serving a necessary function. No remains of partition walls were found in this strip and

[56] *Ibid.*, p. 281.

[57] *Ibid.*, p. 208.

no traces of abutting or bonding walls on the north face of the retaining wall. It seems to me that this area between the two corridors can only be conceived as a broad balcony-court placed in front of the rooms which occupied the uppermost terrace of the hill. Access to this balcony-court was obtained through the northeast end of the blocked south corridor, which thus continued to perform a necessary function. Unfortunately the northeast end of the corridor was destroyed completely by one of Schliemann's pits and no evidence survives to prove or to disprove the suggestion.

To the east of the blocked end of the south corridor, and some 50 cm. below its level, there is a landing (No. 34) to which access was obtained by the wooden stairway entered from the north end of the *aithousa* of the megaron. The landing opens on its east side to a narrow corridor, with a floor sloping upwards from west to east, that leads to a long and narrow room or gallery some 6 by 3.50 m. (No. 33). Wace suggested that it served as an antechamber to the domestic quarters. Stone benches, covered with white stucco, were arranged along its west and south sides, while a rectangular hearth was found by Papadimitriou in the middle of its north wall. The walls of the gallery were covered with frescoes, many fragments of which were recovered by Tsountas.[58] A number of them bear a representation that suggests embroidered curtains, or as Rodenwaldt explained, "hanging rugs." Because of these unparalleled fresco compositions we have called this long and narrow room the Gallery of the Curtains. At the east end of the gallery was a staircase (No. 31), now restored, which, in two flights at right angles to each other, led up to the higher level of the hill, to the domestic quarters. Below the second flight a basement was formed (No. 32) in which Tsountas found a handleless vessel and a double axe, both of bronze.[59] Beyond this basement is another (No. 30) of uncertain use to the east, and still farther east a narrow compartment with heavy walls and a lime-cement floor (No. 29). Holland suggested that it may have served as a cistern or tank, its walls intentionally made thick to resist the pressure of the water.[60]

Of the domestic quarters, reached by the stairway at the end of the gallery, practically nothing survives. At the level 77.06 are the remnants of a room that has caused a good deal of excitement (No. 26). Only its northwest corner is preserved and indicates that the room had a stepped floor covered with red stucco. A drain on the preserved east end of its north wall suggested the possibility of its having served as a bath.

This identification is enthusiastically accepted by the modern Mycenaeans and is repeated by the guides, who see in the red of the stucco the proof that the little room is no other than the bath in which Agamemnon was murdered! However, the drain does not originate in the room but in an area above it to the north and the steps seem to go around the walls with only one step going along the north side. One would expect to find a drain opening on the south side of the room, the side towards the slope, if the area served as a bath, and a stairway on one of its sides, if the room was something like the "sunken areas" of Knossos. Perhaps the single step along the north side is one of those benches usual in Mycenaean chambers and the room may have been an antechamber and waiting room to some important, but not preserved, hall of the palace. The bathroom of the palace at Pylos, and its counterpart at Tiryns, indicate the impossibility of accepting the room with the red stuccoed floor and benches as a bathroom in spite of the local tradition.

Almost parallel to the south corridor but some two m. higher than the level of its existing east end and some 7 m. further north from it, another corridor, the North Corridor, is roughly set from west to east (text fig. 15, Nos. 18-20). Scanty remains of this corridor survive, and beyond it to the north stretches the uppermost area of the hill on which stood the section of the palace on the highest level. Unfortunately very little of that section survives; Wace has noted the remnants of two long and narrow rooms (Nos. 11 and 12), three large conglomerate bases built in the foundations of the Hellenistic temple, and small patches of lime-cement floor here and there. It has been suggested that the bases belonged to a colonnaded hall, occupying most of the summit of the hill, built when the later palace was constructed to replace the section of the earlier palace that stood there. In 1962, in the course of our study of the remnants on the summit of the hill, Shear and I noted cuttings in the rock of the hill which must belong to the Mycenaean Age. These seem to indicate the existence there of a number of rooms and to exclude a colonnaded hall. Alongside Room 12 rock cuttings and preserved remains of walls and floor indicate a room (Room 13) on the long median axis of which the foundations of a column were found. There are indications that another was placed beyond the first on the same axis. Thus two columns in single file supported its ceiling. The foundations are too small to accommodate one of the large bases embedded in the Hellenistic wall. Cuttings on the rock seem to indicate the existence of a large room,

[58] *Ephemeris*, 1887, pl. XII. Rodenwaldt, *Tiryns*, II, p. 232. Lamb, *BSA*, 25 (1921-1923), p. 258.

[59] *Praktika*, 1886, p. 70. The double axe was a tool with its

edges somewhat blunted and had no votive significance.

[60] *BSA*, 25 (1921-1923), p. 262.

adjacent to Room 13 and to the east of it, in the area marked 14 in Holland's plan. The large conglomerate bases used in the foundations of the Hellenistic temple may belong to this room whose roof was supported by four columns placed in the usual manner in its center and perhaps around a circular hearth. The room corresponds to the *domos* of the megaron in size and this, as well as its position on the summit, makes it possible to suggest that perhaps Room 14 occupies the area of the megaron of the first palace which was erected on the hill; that it may have been the section of the earlier palace which was incorporated in the later in the way followed by the builders of the palaces of Tiryns and Pylos.

Of the two long and narrow rooms noted by Wace, the westernmost (No. 11) was identified as a storeroom since a number of pithoi were found sunk into its cemented floor. The threshold of that room, removed from its original position, lies nearby. So few traces have survived of the second (No. 16) that one wonders whether it was a room at all. At any rate its threshold, adjacent to the storeroom, is still *in situ*, and its size, determined by Shear, in 1963, amounts to 7.50 by 3 m. It was first suggested tentatively, and then definitely identified by Wace, as the shrine of the palace. In the room, partially explored by Tsountas, Wace found two movable "altars or hearths or tables of offerings of painted stucco on a clay backing."[61] These fragmentary "tables of offerings or portable altars" provided the only evidence on which the identification was based. We feel that the evidence does not justify the identification. Fragments of "altars" were found in other parts of the palace by Tsountas and Papadimitriou, and Wace himself reported a fragment from the central lobby of the southwest grand staircase.[62] All the places where "altars" were found could not have served as shrines. Furthermore, in Room 11 was found pottery similar to that discovered in other rooms of the palace, "two spindle whorls, of the ordinary Mycenaean (Late Helladic III) type, two terra-cotta spindle whorls of a conical shape, a small triangular piece of stone possibly from some inlay, two or three scraps of gold foil, a small carnelian bead, an amygdaloid bead of glass paste, another glass paste bead shaped like a grain of wheat, part of a small plaque of glass paste, a lead disc, a rolled bronze band, an obsidian and a flint arrowhead." Of course the original contents of the room did not remain until the time of

the excavation, but what survived does not seem to characterize the room as a shrine. The spindle whorls and the arrowheads seem especially out of place, and we look in vain for fragments of small votive vessels, of figurines, and even of ledges on which they might originally have stood. In his general discussion of the Mycenaean palace, Wace states "the palace was divided by long corridors and off them on the ground floor were storerooms."[63] A shrine would indeed be out of place among them. Its proximity to a defined storeroom and the coarse plaster which is proved to have covered its walls seem also to indicate that it was not used as a shrine. Its plan differs from that exhibited by the "shrine" of the palace at Pylos and its façade does not agree with that on the fragment of fresco recovered by Professor Mabel Lang. That "tables of offerings" or "portable altars" were stored with other objects in magazines, was proved long ago by their discovery in the magazines of the villa at Nirou Chani.[64] Lately Blegen found in Room 18, clearly a storeroom, of the palace at Pylos, "many large pots of various shapes, numerous diminutive vessels, as well as part of a table of offering." The discovery, therefore, of two "tables of offering" would not define the room as a shrine.

In his excavations of 1939 Wace discovered a lovely ivory group representing "two women squatting with a boy standing by the knees of one of them" in the fill of a room lying against and below the great north terrace of the Hellenistic temple (text fig. 18, No. 5).[65] In the group the discoverer recognized Demeter, Persephone, and the boy Iakchos and suggested that they might have belonged to the so-called shrine. At the same time the existence of this group was used to support and strengthen the theory that the storeroom was a shrine. We shall come back to the identification of the members of the group later; at present we may state that before we can use it as evidence bearing on the function of the room under consideration, we first have to prove that the group actually came from that room. This, of course, is impossible.

The orientation of the Hellenistic temple, from north to south instead of the conventional east-west direction, is also used in defense of the identification of Room 16 as a shrine. But there is a great lapse of time here. We must always bear in mind that the palace was finally destroyed at the end of the Bronze Age; that its site apparently was not occupied in Proto-

---

[61] *Ibid.*, pp. 223-229.
[62] *Ibid.*, p. 154. We found fragments among the debris of the north slope. Shear noticed that the threshold has no pivot holes and thus the so-called room might even have been a corridor. In addition, our investigations of the area in 1963 proved that it had a sloping floor, and a stairway in its southeastern corner.

[63] *Mycenae*, p. 104.
[64] Excavated by Xanthoudides, *Ephemeris*, 1922, pp. 15-16. Professor Nilsson also rejected the identification of the room as a shrine, *Minoan-Mycenaean Religion*, 2nd ed., p. 110. For the fragment of fresco from Pylos see *AJA*, 65 (1961), pl. 60 fig. 16a and *AJA*, 66 (1962), pl. 40 fig. 12.
[65] *JHS*, 59 (1939), p. 210. *Mycenae*, pp. 83-84. Figs. 101-102.

18. Mycenae 1961. Ascent to palace (drawing Bandekas, Iacovides)

Geometric times; that the earliest remnants of the Historic era belong to the Geometric period; that the earliest possible temple whose traces we have belongs to even later times, to the Archaic period. Besides, the so-called shrine was not an individual building whose orientation was known or remembered, but a small unit among others whose remains would not be distinguished in the piles of burned debris. Its orientation could hardly have been remembered even by the sons of the survivors of the destroyed Mycenaean citadel, let alone by those who lived at the site so many generations later. It should also be remembered that no rule for the orientation of temples and buildings seems to have existed in Mycenaean times. We have to find another reason to account for the orientation of the Hellenistic temple, if we actually have to account for it. In my *Ancient Mycenae*, I suggested that perhaps the rise of the rock from west to east, and the necessity of cutting away a good deal of hard rock, forced its builders to orient the temple from north to south.[66] Our investigations of the hilltop in 1963 indicate that the orientation of the Hellenistic temple was influenced by that of a smaller and earlier Archaic temple, which was constructed along the lines of the Mycenaean rooms that in the period of the later palace occupied the summit of the hill and must have been its most conspicuous remnants. These rooms were oriented from north to south to provide shelter against the bitter north winds that plague the site winter and summer. That orientation, first established by the builders of the archaic temple and repeated in the Hellenistic period, parallels in a way the history of the post-Mycenaean temple at Tiryns.

The area immediately around the palace has been partially investigated. A small section to the southwest of the square room—the guest room—by the west wall, known as the pithos area from some Hellenistic storage jars found there, was explored by Tsountas (text fig. 15, No. 105). Among other things contained in the fill, he found a copper ingot in the shape of an ox hide, a talent, the only remnant of the treasures kept in the palace, and fragments of frescoes. Some of the fragments seem to be burned and apparently were thrown away in a period of reconstruction. On some we find representations of women carrying small cylindrical vases, *pyxides*, on others geometric patterns in which the spiral predominates, and on still others decorative plant motives such as lotus patterns and the like.

To the east of the cobbled courtyard (text fig. 15, No. 7), Wace discovered two rooms (Nos. 3 and 4), one of which perhaps acted as a vestibule to the other.

They are quite small, the main room measuring 4.50 by 3 m., have floors of clay, and walls coated with clay plaster. A large conglomerate block, still *in situ*, served as threshold to the main room. Wace remarked that these two rooms could "have had no communication with the rest of the Palace except through the Propylon. . . . As they are placed so conveniently to the Propylon and by the side of the cobbled area before it, it is possible that they formed a kind of guardroom, housing the detachment of the royal bodyguard which provided the sentries to guard the Propylon."[67] Farther east of the guard room Wace explored two little rooms in the fill of one of which he found the ivory group of the two women and a boy.

The extent of the palace to the north, west, and south is clearly defined. There can be little doubt that the south Cyclopean wall of the *enceinte* acted as a retaining wall for the terrace of the later palace in that direction; a retaining wall, of a later date, marks its northern limit, while a well-preserved retaining wall with frequent setbacks can be seen along the entire length of its west side. The east side remained undetermined until 1965 and, according to Tsountas, it is in the eastern area of the palace that the domestic quarters seem to have been located. Indeed, the east slope of the hill is less abrupt than any of the other three and more appropriate for building. If the palace was to be extended beyond the summit to provide for the needs of the ruling family and their retinue, it could only be extended to the east. Fragments of walls, the evidence of careful terracing of the slope along lines indicated by the rocky formation of the hill, a broad corridor with lime-cement floor skirting a circular terrace, revealed in our excavations of 1965, seem to indicate that the palace extended to the east beyond the area of the so-called red bath.

The most important remains on the east slope, evidently belonging to the palace and partially excavated by Tsountas in 1892, were revealed again on the third terrace from the summit located directly above and to the west of the "House of Columns." They comprise a large Mycenaean building over which was constructed an even larger Hellenistic structure in the third century B.C. The Mycenaean building contains on the ground level at least 8 rooms, a court open to the sky, and 2 long and narrow corridors which in the ground level could have served as magazines for storage. The east section of the building rose to at least two stories, served by a stairway three steps of which are still preserved. To this building belong the rooms excavated by Tsountas and Wace and included

<hr>

[66] *Ancient Mycenae*, p. 64.
[67] *BSA*, 25 (1921-1923), pp. 213-216. For the finds of Tsountas

in the Hellenistic pithos area see *Praktika*, 1886, p. 73 and Wace, *BSA*, 25 (1921-1923), pp. 161-162.

in the latter's plan of the House of Columns (Nos. W-1 to W-4).

The building was destroyed by fire, most probably at the same time as the rest of the palace. Among its debris and in undisturbed fill were found hundreds of ivory chips evidently discarded in the process of making various articles in this precious material, tiny pieces of gold leaf, discarded cores of opal from which sections had been removed to be transformed into articles for adornment, pieces of a substance which when heated is transformed into a brownish sticky matter that could have been used for inlaying, remnants of copper ore from which the metal had been extracted by firing, and many fragments of brilliantly painted tables of offering. All these articles seem to prove that the building served as the workshop, storage place, and residence of the royal artists and technicians. That its second story rooms were elaborately appointed is indicated by the many fragments of painted plaster found everywhere. There can be little doubt that the building formed the east wing of the palace. Its relation to the House of Columns has yet to be established; but it seems possible to believe that both these buildings belong to the extreme east wing of the palace. Thus the area covered by the palace as now defined is considerable. It measures some 130 m. in length from east to west and, at its broadest section, some 80 m. in width from north to south. A great palace indeed, worthy of the most important *wanax* of the Mycenaean world.

The description of the surviving parts of the palace of Mycenae, I hope, made evident its general ground plan, which is as simple as it is harmonious (Fig. 56). The palace was constructed on two main levels (the modern system of split-level architecture is well represented here), separated by two main corridors, the north and south corridors, dividing it into two parts. One part was located on the very summit of the hill, and in it were incorporated sections of the older or earlier palace; one of these perhaps was a megaron. The second part of the palace was built on an artificially leveled and retained terrace along the south slope of the hill. There we find the state unit of the palace, its main megaron, the guest room, and the later southwest grand staircase. A main passage, the west passage, on the terraced west slope supported by the massive west retaining wall with its conspicuous offsets, led from a propylon, which formed the original main entrance to the palace, to the west portal from which one could go through the southwest corridor to the megaron, or through the south corridor to the so-called domestic quarters and to its higher level. That level could also be reached through Stairway S and the north corridor. When the east end of the south

corridor was blocked, access to the domestic quarters was obtained from the *aithousa* of the megaron. In the closing years of the life of the palace its visitors could also enter it through the southwest grand staircase which led directly to the guest room.

The later palace of Mycenae in its last phase, with its simple and harmonious plan, its difference in levels, its artificial terracing cut in the rocky slopes of the hill, with its splendidly designed megaron unit perched on the edge of a ravine of rugged impressiveness, with its command of a magnificent view of the Argive plain hemmed in by a continuous chain of crystalline mountains, must have been one of the most impressive palaces built in Mycenaean times. Standing aloft on the summit of a high hill, surrounded by giant mountains and Cyclopean walls, it must have looked to the approaching friend or foe as the very embodiment of the power and majesty of the most influential *wanax* of the Mycenaean world.

The Ascent to the Summit

The summit of the hill is some 280 m. (912 feet) above sea level or some 38 m. above the Lion Gate. The question of how people ascended from the Lion Gate to that summit and to the palace has not been definitely and satisfactorily answered to date: Not even a good section of the road which led from the Lion Gate to the palace is preserved. Today on passing through that gate we find ourselves in a small wall-enclosed court, evidently once roofed (text fig. 19, No. 6). From this court once started a well-constructed road, some 4.50 m. broad at its beginning, artificially graded to lead to the main ramp. Unfortunately the area between the court and the ramp was dug away by Schliemann in his excavations of 1876, so that practically nothing survives to show how the ramp started. A heavy Cyclopean wall built along the west side of the ramp and towering over Grave Circle A, retains it to the length that is preserved. At its south end the ramp breaks abruptly; apparently the break was caused by later construction. It is generally assumed that at that point the ramp turned at right angles to the east, proceeded for some distance up the western slope, and finally forked in two directions. One of the branches proceeded in a southeasterly direction to terminate at the grand staircase in the southwestern corner of the palace, while the other gradually ascended the slope in a northeasterly direction and led to the northwestern entrance of the palace. We have already seen how retaining wall *TW* perhaps supported the road to the grand staircase. Since that staircase was a very late addition to the palace its road must of necessity be considered as a very late approach to it. The south slope of the hill is indeed very abrupt and did not

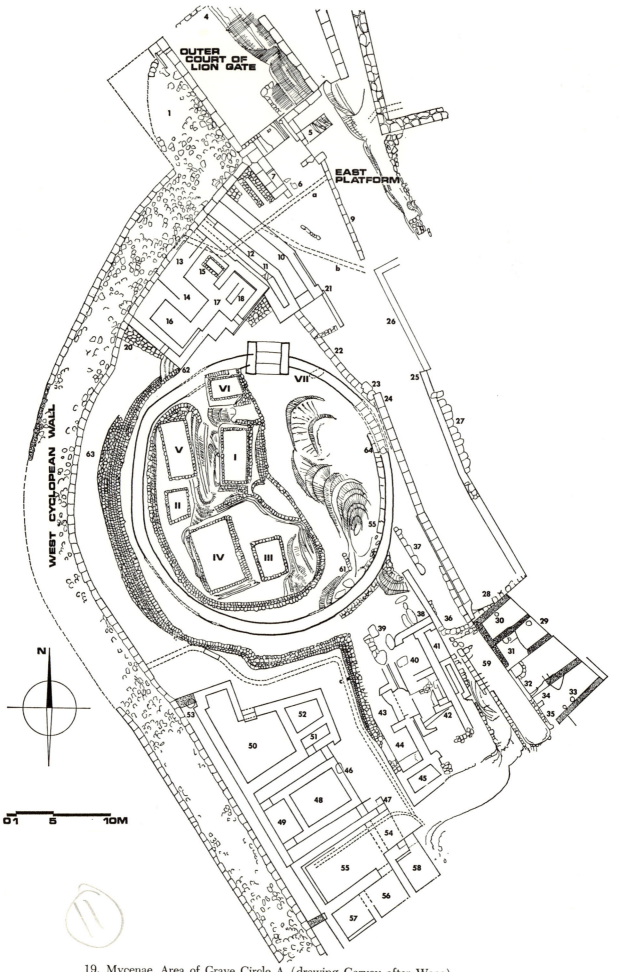

OUTER
COURT OF
LION GATE

EAST
PLATFORM

WEST CYCLOPEAN WALL

N

0 1   5   10M

19. Mycenae. Area of Grave Circle A (drawing Garvey after Wace)

offer a natural way of ascending to the summit. The original and main path that led to the top of the hill could only have been located on the northwest slope. That is why the original and main entrance to the palace was located on its northwest corner. The road from the Lion Gate terminated at the paved court (text fig. 15, No. 7) in front of the propylon of that entrance. But exactly how the court and the propylon was reached was not clear. Wace was the first to realize that the north slope presented the natural possibilities of an ascent to the top, "after all the easiest and most natural ascent of the acropolis from the north, south or west is by way of this northwest angle."[68] He, however, suggested that the road from the Lion Gate reached its final bend in Area 8 (text fig. 15), immediately below the west side of the cobbled courtyard, from which one ascended directly to that court. In other words, he suggested that the road in its final stage was laid in a course almost identical to that followed by the modern path and stairway made for the convenience of the visitors. However, that path was originally blocked by the Cyclopean retaining wall which supported the terrace of the court and of the propylon. Furthermore, the room and its vestibule (Nos. 3, 4) which he uncovered, and which he rightly characterized as a guardroom, is so far to the east of Area 8 that it is not exactly in proper relation to the direct ascent he postulated.

The question remained without definitive answer until the summer of 1959 when we undertook the clearing of the north slope of the hill, which had been only partially explored. In the course of that excavation and immediately below Room 5 (text fig. 18) lying against and below the Hellenistic temple cleared by Wace in which the ivory group was found, and as a matter of fact under the earth dumped in 1939 over the lower reaches of the slope, we found the remnants of an impressive staircase. We shall call it hereafter the north staircase. It is placed in a triangular fissure left between two jagged ledges of rock which descend sharply from the heights and almost bar passage farther east. Six steps are well preserved, giving us the width of the staircase and the average rise of its steps (Figs. 62, 64; text fig. 18, C). They are made up of well-fitted, flat stones of average size, forming wide treads with a rise of some 15 cm. The width of the stairway (2.50 m.) is wider than the grand staircase. The topmost of the preserved steps apparently led to a broad landing (text fig. 18, C), beyond which the staircase is not preserved and even the finished surface of the landing has gone. On it were found two plain small pots, one of which was a kylix. Probably at the

landing the staircase, turning at right angles in typical Mycenaean fashion, proceeded westward along the face of the rock and was carried to its summit by means of artificial terracing. At its top another landing (text fig. 18, D) gave access to the beginning of a ramp, D-E, indicated by a row of three stones *in situ* which perhaps formed a step. If we estimate an average rise of 15 cm. for each step, the flight across the face of the rock, which has not been preserved, must have been made up of twenty steps. The retaining walls which supported the terrace on which the second flight of steps was based have not been preserved, but cuttings on the rock on which the walls were based give us the proof of their existence (Fig. 62, C).

Ramp E started at the top of the stairway and was artificially constructed and supported by a retaining wall, the east end of which, by the staircase, has survived (Fig. 63). The fill of the ramp is composed of loose stones and earth, while the retaining wall is constructed in Cyclopean fashion. Its westward course is along the north side of the guard room (text fig. 18, Nos. 3 and 4), which thus is proved to have been placed in a controlling position. At the northwest corner of the guard room the width of the path was reduced, but from there on it broadens until it reaches the cobbled courtyard (text fig. 18, No. 7) in front of the propylon. The grade of the ramp is gentle. Below its entire length was a lower terrace supported by a Cyclopean retaining wall (text fig. 18, MM), whose east end terminated at the north staircase and whose southwest end joined with the Cyclopean retaining wall that supported the terrace of the cobbled court and of the propylon. Only the beginning of the retaining wall of Ramp E, its eastern end, has survived; its continuation to the area of the court was destroyed, altered, or rebuilt in Hellenistic times when a series of rooms were constructed against its face and on the lower terrace supported by the Cyclopean wall MM. However, the course of the ramp and its extent is clearly defined by the fill which formed its understructure.

Not only the upper flight of steps of the north staircase is gone, but also the lowest section of it below the steps that survived. That section was apparently destroyed in Hellenistic times, long after the staircase was abandoned, when a retaining wall was built across its width and the level was raised to form a path leading eastward. Actually the date of that retaining wall could not be established since no pottery was found in it or in its immediate fill; but the pavement of the path it supported was found to contain a good many black-glazed sherds, fragments of Hellenistic

[68] *Ibid.*, pp. 213 and 216.

pithoi, and a very badly corroded bronze coin.[69] Below the level of that pavement, and consequently below the top of the retaining wall, we found *in situ* half a length of a step as well as the substructure for another step below it. Thus it is proved that the staircase continued below the top of the wall and that the lower section of the staircase was destroyed and some of its area was filled in when the retaining wall was constructed. As a matter of fact, a close examination of the retaining wall will prove definitely that it was built across the width of the staircase and between its flanking walls, with which the wall is nowhere bound (Fig. 64, F). The staircase was lowered to the rock, the top of which was worked almost smooth (Fig. 64, G), in a graceful curve that ends in the direction of the Lion Gate.

The point at which the staircase began became evident as early as 1959; but the discovery, in 1961, of the road which led from the Lion Gate to the staircase proved the point decisively. The road, to be known as Main Road A, is an artificially constructed ramp, the fill of which, made of loose stone and earth, is supported by a well-built retaining wall in some parts in Cyclopean style. A length of 17 m. of this road has been revealed (Figs. 64-66; text fig. 18, A) under the fallen debris of the retaining walls and parapets of terraces which formed part of the main approach to the northwest entrance. The road, which averages 2 m. in width, is laid along the slope following the configuration and going around the sharply falling rock formations. Its inner side, facing south, was flanked by a high retaining wall that apparently supported a terrace extending above and along the length of the road. In contrast to its north retaining wall which was excellently built in a solid and compact fashion (Fig. 66), the south retaining wall was not so carefully or compactly constructed. Some evidence was found, impressions of poles on plaster lying across the width of the road, to justify the suggestion that the south wall was faced with a plastered revetment supported by upright poles set at a distance of 6 cm. from each other. The area above the south retaining wall was unfortunately disturbed in Hellenistic times when any structures that may have stood over it were destroyed. The fused and calcined remains of a rubble wall found on the pavement, however, seem to indicate that along the edge of the terrace supported by the south retaining wall stood a rubble wall, acting perhaps as a parapet or balustrade for the terrace. In a similar manner a rubble wall seems to have stood along the east side of the great ramp by the Lion Gate.

At a point 17 m. west of the staircase, Main Road A

meets with an outcrop of rock rising some 50 cm. above its pavement. At that point we lose its continuation to the west. It has not become apparent to date whether the road went around this rocky formation or over it and how it proceeded farther west. Perhaps the complete clearing of the area to be undertaken in later campaigns will elucidate the point. However, there can be little doubt that the road continued westward and perhaps to a point where the lane from the great ramp forked to right and left, to the two sides of the hill where the two staircases of the palace have been revealed. The way people ascended to the palace is now clear. Following Main Road A they would reach the north staircase, through which they would mount to Ramp E that led them around the guard room, Nos. 3 and 4, to the northwest entrance of the palace (text fig. 18, No. 9). In the last period of the life of the palace important people perhaps would reach the state units of the palace through the grand staircase. But since that staircase was a later addition, it seems proper to maintain that the approach through the north staircase was the original and older way used even for the earlier palace although the construction of the staircase itself may date from the period of the later palace.

The clearing of the area at the foot of the staircase proved that its original arrangement was changed somewhat in later, but still Mycenaean, times. From the beginning of the exploration of the remnants of the staircase, it became evident that it did not open in the direction of the postern gate; that it was not designed in relation to that gate since, as a matter of fact, it turns its back to that entrance. But when the postern gate was built it became imperative that some means of communication be established between it and the northwest entrance to the palace through the north staircase. Then a road was constructed going westward from the postern gate and along the north Cyclopean wall, over the free passage which originally must have existed in accordance with Mycenaean custom. This we call Road B. A strong retaining wall was built along the slope of the hillside to flank the inner or south side of the road. Fragments only of this retaining wall survive here and there, sufficient, however, to prove the arrangement. Road B terminates at level 58.59, some 30 cm. below the level of Main Road A (Fig. 64, B). A change had to be made to bring the lower level of the Road B into relationship both with the level of the Main Road A and with the foot of the staircase. An old block, which might have served originally as the base of a column, was used to form the landing at which Road B terminated.

---

[69] Mrs. Eirene Varoucha Christodoulopoullou kindly cleaned and identified the coin for me. It is a Corinthian coin dating

from ca. 286-260 B.C.

At right angles to this landing, apparently two or three steps, not preserved, were built; thus the level of the first step of the staircase was reached, and connection was obtained between the postern gate and the staircase.

At the same time, apparently, the area between the west section of Main Road A and the north Cyclopean wall was transformed into a court. The floor level of this court, though not preserved since the area was rebuilt in Hellenistic times, can be determined with some degree of accuracy. It must have reached the base of the retaining wall of Main Road A, the line of the landing where Road B came to its end. This is indicated not only by the foundation of flat stones which projects from the base of the retaining wall of Road A as it reaches its west end (Fig. 64, K, L), but also by a lucky find made in 1959. Between two of the large stones of the retaining wall a small cavity is formed just above the footing of the wall. In it we found a bronze hoard, the possessions of a Mycenaean, hidden there by its owner at a time of impending enemy attack (Fig. 67). Apparently its hopeful owner did not survive that attack and his treasure remained hidden over the centuries for us to find. It is evident that the place used for hiding the objects in bronze must have been at the level of the floor of the court that stretches before the retaining wall. Perhaps we should note that Tsountas found at least two other hoards of bronze objects, of a nature identical to ours, hidden in the walls of Mycenaean structures to the southeast of the area of the Lion Gate.[70] Those, too, were concealed in their hiding place before the destruction of the citadel and were dated by Tsountas to the very end of the Mycenaean Age. In the Akropolis of Athens Kavvadias found a similar treasure in the area between the Museum and the south Cyclopean wall.[71] A curving bronze blade, five examples of which are included in our hoard (Fig. 144), seems to be common in all these hoards and perhaps is characteristic of the closing years of the age.

Our discussion and description of the remains we uncovered on the north slope of the hill between 1959 and 1962 reveal fully the nature of the approach to the palace and the roads that led to it. From the Lion Gate the roadway followed the original ascent to the top of the hill, employed apparently from the Middle Helladic period at least. That was the only path which led to the earlier palace. When the later palace was constructed, the north staircase, the roads, and the

terracing perhaps were given the form that we can trace today from their remains. It was then perhaps that the Lion Gate and the west extension were added to the citadel. A person entering the Lion Gate found himself at the foot of the great ramp that led to the summit of the citadel. Following the extension of it, which is not preserved, he would reach Main Road A which brought him to the foot of the north staircase. As he approached that staircase he would see and admire the stepped terraces, three at least in number, that rose to his right while a view of rolling green hills, seen over the top of the north Cyclopean wall, spread before him at the left. The north staircase provided a beautiful approach to the palace outer ramp which, with an easy grade, led to the outer court and the propylon of the northwest entrance. It is possible to assume that on the lower terraces were standing loggias or pavilions where the visitor could rest. A column base of conglomerate, found among the fallen debris above the west section of Main Road A may indicate the possibility of the existence on the lower terraces of such structures. Again the visitor could reach the state unit of the palace and its guest room by using the grand staircase. That approach, in spite of the imposing structure of the staircase, did not offer the monumentality of the terraced approach afforded by the north slope.

The palace was finally destroyed by fire toward the end of the Mycenaean Age. The specific date of that destruction remains unsettled. Wace believed that it occurred in LH III C times.[72] There is a tendency at present to maintain that the palace was finally destroyed at the end of the LH III B period.[73] Unfortunately our excavations thus far have provided no evidence to strengthen either position. Since the palace areas that we investigated had already been cleared of most of their fill, I am not justified in formulating, on the basis of the few, uncertain sherds found in key areas, such important conclusions as those dealing with the absolute chronology of the final destruction. Furthermore, it is becoming increasingly difficult to establish, with any degree of unanimity, what actually constitutes the characteristic types of pottery of the various sub-periods of the Late Mycenaean era. One of the great needs in the field is the discovery and careful excavation of an undisturbed fill of considerable depth which will enable the establishment of a definite sequence based on stratigraphy and not on stylistic analysis alone. Until then, it may prove difficult, if

[70] *Ephemeris*, 1891, pp. 25 and 26. For a brief summary of the work around the foot of the staircase see now Mylonas, *Praktika*, 1961 (1965), pp. 155 ff.

[71] P. Kavvadias, *Deltion*, 1888, p. 83. O. Montelius, *La Grèce préclassique*, 1, pl. 16.

[72] *BSA*, 51 (1956), p. 105 and *Aegean and the Near East*,

"Last Days of Mycenae," pp. 126 ff.

[73] This is the tendency now, based on the evidence obtained in the so-called Citadel House, but see *infra*, pp. 221 ff. Cf. also Ålin, *op.cit.*, pp. 10-25, for an excellent summary of evidence and opinions.

not impossible, to establish absolute dates acceptable to all. What, however, can be agreed upon is that in the closing years of the LH III B period the palace was still standing in all its glory.

Before we consider briefly the houses of the citadel we may once more draw attention to the similarities existing between the Palace of Nestor at Pylos and the Palace of Agamemnon at Mycenae. There are striking similarities in the dimensions, arrangement, and furnishings of their megara (text fig. 16, p. 63) and in the size of their guest rooms, which are almost half the size of the *domoi*. One wonders whether these and other measurements the two palaces had in common do not justify the belief that the builders of the one palace were influenced by those of the other if they did not belong to the same association of builders; and since the palace at Pylos shows a more elaborate and regular form, whether we could not assume that its construction followed that of the palace at Mycenae. The opening of a side door in the *aithousa* of the megaron of Mycenae and the consequent abandonment of the end of the south corridor may be considered an innovation introduced after the building of the palace at Pylos, which demonstrated the advantage of direct communication of the megaron with the domestic and other quarters of the palace. Of course the different arrangement of these quarters was imposed by the terrain over which those palaces were built. We have noted before how the builders who constructed the fortifications of the citadels adopted new developments readily and apparently the builders of the palaces learned from each other with equal readiness if indeed they were not the same men.

Houses within the Citadel

Within the citadel of Mycenae were found a number of other buildings considered as houses. One of the most important, and perhaps one of the largest, was found at a short distance to the southeast of the palace, on a terrace supported by the south Cyclopean wall at the point of the so-called southeast tower. It was excavated by Tsountas in the main and was further explored, cleared, and drawn by Wace.[74] It is now known as the House of Columns from the numerous columns which once stood in its court (text fig. 5, HC). A threshold block, still *in situ*, indicates the position of its doorway. From that doorway a long corridor leads to the court, which was open to the sky

and around which are arranged the rooms and compartments of the house. Beyond the north side of the court is the megaron, divided into three sections, a stairway leading to an upper story, and an inner room. Rooms and a basement with four magazines flank the west side of the court, while more basement rooms may be seen beyond its south side. In the east basement room, across the corridor, a number of stirrup vases were found, one bearing an inscription in Linear B Script. The vase and the inscription are similar to those found at Tiryns, Eleusis, Thebes, and Orchomenos.[75] On the south side of the court, the house rose to three stories, counting the basement as one. Corridors and one room flank the court on the east side. The proximity of the house to the palace, its extent and impressiveness, would justify the belief that it belonged to an important personage, even to a member of the royal family. One may wonder whether it could not be considered as an annex to the palace. Wace has pointed out how closely this House of Columns parallels the house of Odysseus in Homeric Ithaka.

The south wing of the House of Columns is built on a terrace supported by the so-called southeast tower (text fig. 5, ST). We noted before that this tower is constructed of conglomerate blocks in ashlar style, one of the three sections of the *enceinte* so built. It has been suggested that the ashlar style was employed when additional strength was needed for the wall and that in addition the tower was built as a lookout post since it commands a grand view of the Argive plain. Such a view, however, can be enjoyed from many a point along the south side of the citadel; an approaching enemy could have been detected from a multitude of points along that side. The special construction of a tower to keep watch over the plain seems altogether superfluous. Again, no defensive purpose could have been served by the tower since the terrain on the south and southeast sides is so rugged and precipitous that no enemy would have attempted to scale the walls on that side. Usually towers flank openings or strengthen corners. This so-called tower fulfills neither of these functions. But the tower covers a large drain, whose construction and opening correspond closely to those of the drains of the postern gate which were cut through the north Cyclopean wall at the time of the construction of that gate. This would suggest a late date for the drain and the tower, indicated also by the

74 Wace, *Mycenae*, pp. 91-97 and fig. 33. Over its ruins was constructed in Hellenistic times a large building whose remains, still standing, make it impossible for the visitor to see clearly the Mycenaean structure.

75 For the Mycenaean inscribed vases see *Archaeology*, 1 (1948), pp. 217 ff. Evans, *Palace of Minos*, IV, pp. 739-746. Caratelli, "Le iscrizioni preeleniche di Haghia Triada in Creta e

della Grecia peninsulare," *Mon. Ant.* 40 (1945), pp. 603-610 and pls. XXX-XL. Palmer, *Mycenaeans and Minoans*, pp. 167-170. Mylonas, "The Luvian Invasions of Greece," *Hesperia*, 31 (1962), pp. 305-307. For the fragment from the House of Columns, see Wace, *Mycenae*, fig. 110 f. For other fragments from Mycenae, E. Bennett, Jr., *The Mycenae Tablets*, II, pp. 76-77.

style of masonry and the conglomerate blocks employed in its construction. As a matter of fact, what has been called a tower is not built completely of conglomerate blocks. Our investigations of 1965 proved that this material was used only in the construction of its southwest corner, in the building of the section around the drain. This, I believe, reveals the purpose of the ashlar masonry. It is a repair made at the time of the construction of the existing drain. For this repair they used conglomerate blocks, set in horizontal courses, to give additional strength to the corner of the wall from which the drain issued, to strengthen it against any possible flows and pressures caused by a downpour.

Six additional houses or structures have been or are being explored on the west and lowest section of the citadel, around Grave Circle A.[76] One of these structures was built right against the west Cyclopean wall and between it and the northeast section of the grave circle, immediately to the south of the Lion Gate. It is known as the granary because of the carbonized barley, wheat, and vetches found by Wace stored in its basement. It could also have served as a guard room (text fig. 19, Nos. 10-20). Two basement rooms and two long adjacent and parallel corridors are the characteristic features of this building, which perhaps was three stories high including the basement. The granary was evidently erected after the construction of the west Cyclopean wall and the rearrangement of Grave Circle A in Late Helladic III B times; it was reconstructed and its corridors were extended later; and finally it was destroyed by fire in the course of the LH III C period. Among its ruins was found a type of pottery produced in the closing period of the Mycenaean era, named by Wace "the Granary style."

To the south of the grave circle the remains of five houses have been or are being cleared (text fig. 19, No. 40-57). Three of them were either fully or partially excavated in 1876 by Schliemann, who recognized in their ruins what he believed to be the Palace of Atreus. Later exploration of the area and the complete excavation of these houses by Wace proved that the ruins belonged to houses of the latter half of the LH III B period. These are now known as the Ramp House (text fig. 19, Nos. 40-42), the House of the Warrior Vase (Nos. 48-52), and the South House (Nos. 54-57). A building excavated in 1885 is now known as the House of Tsountas. Wace began the exploration of another building placed between these houses; this is now being fully cleared under the

direction, until 1962 of Papadimitriou and Lord William Taylour. Wace called this building the Citadel House, a name used by its present explorers. Since all the houses in the citadel can claim this name, I believe that a more appropriate name for it, "Wace House," is desirable, in honor of the excavator who dedicated his life to the study and clearing of Mycenae.

On the north slope of the hill a seventh building was disclosed by us in the summer of 1963 (text fig. 6, M). It is hoped that its excavation will be completed in 1966.

The houses were designed to fit the area they occupy, but in the main they exhibit similar features: a court, a megaron-like main apartment with rooms adjacent, and especially basement magazines. To date the most important of these houses is that known as the House of Tsountas, built on an area immediately to the northeast of the so-called "polygonal Hellenistic tower."[77] The court, the megaron, with a square fireplace in the middle of its *domos*, side rooms, and basement magazines, above which once stood other rooms, are clearly defined. Its walls seem to have been coated with fine plaster painted in fresco technique. To such a fresco band must belong a fragment with the well-known three figures with "asses' heads" bearing a pole (Fig. 124, No. 50).[78] On another fragment we find the motive of the nautiluses already noted at Pylos.

Each of these houses has contributed to our knowledge through the discovery of elements other than its architectural plan. Among the ruins of the Ramp House, for example, Drosinos, Schliemann's architect, found a treasure of gold objects which may have belonged to a destroyed shaft grave of the early years of the LH II period. Among its ruins also were found fragments of frescoes with representations of sports, bull grappling, and acrobatic displays. The House of the Warrior Vase, as the name implies, has yielded the well-known crater and also proof of the use of wooden thresholds recalling the oaken and ashen thresholds of Homer. All these houses illustrate the structural system of the Mycenaean rubble walls: a wall construction of rubble masonry in a wooden framework; timbers set horizontally and vertically so as to form quadrangular panels and further connected by poles set through the thickness of the wall. By means of this timber-framing a superstructure of adobe was supported and tied to the rubble masonry. However, this timber-framing, as we have seen, was used in the construction of walls in rubble masonry and in parts where ashlar masonry was employed, even in palace walls.

---

[76] For a discussion of these buildings see Wace, *BSA*, 25 (1921-1923), pp. 38-96 and *Mycenae*, pp. 54-58, 64-68, and figs. 3 and 25. For the so-called Citadel House see now Lord William Taylour, *The Mycenae Tablets*, III, pp. 35-46.

[77] The House of Tsountas will be published in full shortly by

Mrs. Ione Mylonas Shear. Above it Wace cleared a room which may have been a house shrine. Cf. *infra*.

[78] *The Mycenaean Age*, fig. 156. Tsountas, *Ephemeris*, 1887, p. 160 and pl. 10 no. 1. Marinatos-Hirmer, *op.cit.*, pl. XLIII, lower half.

It is rather difficult to see today how access was obtained to these houses from the Lion Gate, especially after the construction of the great ramp. The original ramp from the Lion Gate, Ramp 2, was only 2.50 m. wide, with a passage between it and the southeast section of Grave Circle A through which people could get to the houses from the Lion Gate. That passage, however, was blocked when the great ramp was constructed, when its retaining west wall was built immediately above the parapet of the circle. On the other hand, scarcely sufficient room for a passage was left between the northeast section of the circle and the southeast corner of the granary (text fig. 19, No. 62). How, then, did people reach their houses from the Lion Gate? The problem must await the completion of the excavation of the Citadel House. Meanwhile, it could be suggested that access was obtained through the so-called "little ramp," which must have been built for the purpose. People would go up the great ramp to the area now preserved, then would turn to the west and descend the little ramp which was built alongside the great ramp (text fig. 19, No. 59). Although circuitous, it seems to have been the only means of approach to the houses. The existence of an open drain in the retaining wall of the ramp adds further complications. Perhaps these will be explained when the Citadel House is published fully.

The houses within the citadel shared the fate of the palace on the summit of the hill and their ruins bear witness to the great destruction that finally befell the citadel sometime in the course of the twelfth century —a destruction which brought to an end the supremacy and cultural activity of Mycenae.

Houses beyond the Walls

The rulers of Mycenae, their relatives, and perhaps their military and administrative leaders, had their dwellings in the citadel. The people at large lived beyond the walls and in small detached groups surrounded by the graves of their ancestors.[79] Although a great number of these tombs were systematically cleared even in the early phase of the exploration of Mycenae, only recently has attention been concentrated on the houses of the living. Yet to date, very few houses have been brought to light beyond the walls of the citadel.

In 1923 Wace discovered and cleared the first remnants of a house on the north slope of the ridge of the Lion Tomb, even outside the Hellenistic wall of the lower city. These remnants include a heavy wall built in the Cyclopean style (and therefore known as the "Cyclopean terrace wall") and parts of two rooms which it supports. The nature of the building has not been determined, although its ruins were further investigated in 1951. The building seems to date from the LH III B period and it appears to have been no longer inhabited in LH III C times since burials of those times were disclosed on the top of its fill. To the southwest of these remnants a second terrace wall was found and at its western end a "ruined storeroom which seems to have been wantonly destroyed." In it were discovered at least eight pithoi and some fifty stirrup vases. Among them, in 1952, was found a superb rhyton, 55 cm. in height, decorated with an octopus pattern brilliantly painted in red-brown color picked out with white. There is no doubt in the minds of the excavators that the storeroom belonged to the house of a wine merchant (Fig. 68, F).[80]

To the east of the House of the Wine Merchant, Papadimitriou and the Ephor Photios Petsas, in their exploratory campaign of 1950, revealed the foundations of at least four different storerooms. In one of them, more than five hundred unused vases of the latest years of the LH III B period were found, neatly packed. As yet the house or houses to which these rooms belong have not been cleared, but from the evidence obtained here and elsewhere it is clear that the Mycenaean houses had magazines, often in their basement, where vases and other possessions were stored. Some 20 m. to the south of these storerooms and on the surface of the field was found a clay tablet bearing an inscription in Linear B Script. It was the first inscribed tablet to be found at Mycenae although objects bearing signs of that script were known since the days of Tsountas.[81] As yet the history of the houses in this area is not clear, but it seems that all of them were destroyed by fire in LH III B times.

To the south of the Tomb of Klytemnestra and close to the east side of the modern road that leads from the modern village to the citadel, Wace and his associates brought to light the remains of three adjacent buildings while immediately to the west of these a fourth was revealed by Verdelis. The middle structure has been cleared completely and because of its contents it has been called the House of the Oil Merchant (text fig. 20). Only its basement survived and it consists of one long corridor, running from north to south, and some eight rooms or compartments opening to the east of it. At the north end of the corridor some thirty stirrup jars of LH III B date were found. Most

---

[79] A false impression of the late Mycenaean town is conveyed by Professor Vermeule's statement in *Greece in the Bronze Age*, p. 160.

[80] Wace, *BSA*, 25 (1921-1923), pp. 403-407 and *BSA*, 48 (1953), pp. 15-16. *JHS*, 73 (1952), pp. 97 ff. Mrs. D. French, *BSA*, 56

(1961), pp. 81-87. Wace, *BSA*, 48 (1953), pp. 16-17.

[81] Papadimitriou, *Praktika*, 1950, pp. 203-233. E. L. Bennett, *The Mycenae Tablets*, II, pp. 48-49 and 87. Tablet X₁; *A]-ta-na a-ti-ja-[e* V.

of them still had stoppers in their spouts, with the original seals over them. Apparently they once contained olive oil with which their clay is impregnated, and that oil added fuel to the flames which destroyed the house.

The northernmost room, No. 1, proved very interesting. Around the wall were found, set in small bases and in alcoves with low clay side-walls, eleven large storage jars or pithoi, apparently used for storing oil. Under one of them an arrangement for heating was provided, another proof that oil was stored in the pithoi. Behind another and in the northeastern corner of the room was found an inscribed clay tablet broken in three pieces. It seemed "analogous," wrote Wace, "to an old piece of paper torn up and thrown in a corner." Thirty-seven additional tablets were found in Room 2; apparently they had fallen from the floor above. They are also covered with signs of Linear B, and all are business records. In the corridor as well as in some of the rooms, fragments of frescoes were found, apparently fallen from the rooms above and these prove the importance of the structure.[82] The tablets from this building are accounts dealing with oil (1 tablet, Fo 101), with wool or linseed (18 tablets, Oc 103-130), with spices (Ge 602-608), and two contain a list apparently of bakers.

In the summer of 1962 Verdelis uncovered along the east terrace wall of the house an imposing approach to its higher level (text fig. 20, V). It consists of a stairway cut partially in the rock that led to the main entrance to the house.[83]

To the north of the House of the Oil Merchant another house has been excavated by Wace (text fig. 20). It has yielded a unique collection of carved ivories of exquisite workmanship and detail. Among these are plaques bearing the carved figures of lions and a great number of model figure-eight Mycenaean shields, from which the building was named the House of Shields. One represents the helmeted head of a Mycenaean warrior. Some of the ivories were probably used as inlays for furniture, in a manner described in the Homeric poems. That such ivory inlays of furniture were usual is indicated by the *Ta* series of tablets from Pylos.[84] Some fine stone vases were also found in the rooms, as well as part of an Egyptian alabaster vase of the XVIIIth Dynasty.[85]

To the south of the House of the Oil Merchant remains of another structure were unearthed built on the rock and not on an artificial terrace (text fig. 20).

They are known as the House of the Sphinxes from a carved ivory plaque bearing two sphinxes facing each other heraldically, with their forepaws resting on the capital of a fluted column. Again, a quantity of carved ivory was found, among which are models of Mycenaean columns and four plaques with sphinxes. The structure is composed of a central corridor running almost from south to north. Three large and a small room open onto it on its west side, while along its east side extends a long room and an open narrow area. This east section is comparable to Rooms 98-100 of the palace at Pylos and perhaps, like the latter, served as a workshop. The unearthed rooms and corridor seem to have formed the basement of the house. In them was found a great deal of debris fallen from the upper story at the time of the destruction of the house by fire. In the doorway of Room 1, in 1953, were found seven seal impressions, all from the same signet. On the front of each impression we have the representation of a man standing between two wild goats. On the back of the impressions besides fingerprints are to be seen inscribed signs of Linear B, again illustrating the use of the script for common purposes, such as sealing the mouth of a pot.[86] In 1954, 9 tablets were found in the debris filling Room 6. One of them contains a list of men; another suggests that the owner of the structure was dealing also in pottery; the rest indicate that his main concern was with herbs, spices, and condiments.

Along the west side of this complex of buildings Verdelis cleared, between the years 1958 and 1961, a large structure, West House, which unfortunately was seriously damaged by Hellenistic constructions (text fig. 20). Of its remains he was able to distinguish a central megaron opening on a large court open to the sky. In one of its rooms against the wall he revealed a large installation of a fireplace with a low, mud-brick parapet on its back, perhaps to be used for heating the contents of large cauldrons. Besides numerous vases of the LH III B period, he found some 19 tablets the contents of which had to do with olive oil and various herbs used in the manufacture of perfumed oil. These and the large establishment of pithoi that apparently were used for storing oil, the many sealed stirrup vases found in the House of the Oil Merchant, and the fact disclosed by the inscribed tablets that the commercial activities of a state were controlled by its *wanax* or ruler, strengthened the view that this compound of buildings was not composed of

[82] Wace, *JHS*, 71 (1951), pp. 254 ff. and figs. 1 and 2. *BSA*, 48 (1953), pp. 9-15. *The Mycenae Tablets*, II, pp. 6-14 and figs. 1-5. E. L. Bennett, Jr., *The Mycenae Tablets*, II, pp 106 ff. See also Mrs. French, in *The Mycenae Tablets*, III, pp. 30-34.

[83] N. Verdelis, in *Ergon*, 1962, pp. 104-106.

[84] *Infra*, p. 195. M. Ventris and J. Chadwick, *Documents in Mycenaean Greek*, pp. 332 ff. Ventris, "Mycenaean Furniture

on the Pylos Tablets," *Eranos*, 53 (1955), pp. 109-124. L. Palmer, *Interpretation*, pp. 338 ff., especially pp. 345 ff.

[85] Wace in *The Mycenae Tablets*, II, pp. 5-6, fig. 3 on p. 16.

[86] *JHS*, 74 (1954), pp. 170-171 and pl. x. Wace in *The Mycenae Tablets*, II, pp. 9-13, and fig. 5 on p. 17. For the tablets see Bennett, in *Mycenae Tablets*, II, pp. 99 ff.

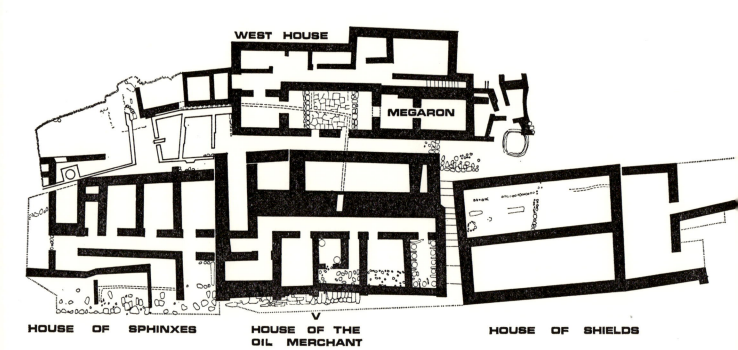

ROAD TO THE CITADEL

WEST HOUSE

MEGARON

HOUSE OF SPHINXES

HOUSE OF THE OIL MERCHANT

HOUSE OF SHIELDS

N

0   5   10   15M

20. Mycenae. Plan of structures to south of Grave Circle B (after Verdelis)

mere houses of merchants but was an adjunct to the palace of the ruler, where perfumed oil was manufactured.[87] Whatever the real function of these buildings, they indicate that security and great prosperity prevailed in the Mycenaean state in the second half of the LH III B period, for otherwise important manufacturing centers would not have been established beyond the safety of the Cyclopean walls and valuable objects, like ivory, would not have been found in such abundance.[88] Then suddenly, before the end of the LH III B period, according to the latest calculations of Verdelis and Mrs. David French, these structures were destroyed by fire; the discovery of so many ivory objects among the debris seems to indicate that the inhabitants or administrators did not have the chance to transfer their valuables to the safety of the walls when the catastrophe came upon them.

On the very top of the hill above the Treasury of Atreus Wace discovered remains of a building that he called the House of Lead because of the many fragments originally belonging to lead vessels.[89] In 1962 we cleared three rooms of a house some 50 m. north of the Treasury of Atreus (Fig. 70). The building (House I) must have belonged to a common citizen, and when fully excavated will perhaps give us a good example of the type. The central room of the three is the most interesting. It measures 5.25 by 4.40 m. and its floor was found covered with solid lime-cement. A round hearth, 70 cm. in diameter, was cleared at the center of the room rising only 20 cm. above the floor (Figs. 71, 73). Around it were a number of common

kitchen vases smashed to fragments; among them were parts of a cylindrical terra-cotta object resembling pipe. The patient piecing together of these parts by Mrs. Shear, who supervised the excavation of the house, resulted in the restoration of a chimney flue similar to those found at Pylos, which evidently was placed over a hole in the roof through which the smoke of the fireplace could escape. Along the northwest section of the room were found piles of stone and disintegrated mud brick and over the threshold of the doorway from the central to the west room a skeleton of a woman lying supine covered with stones (Fig. 71). The skull of the woman had been crushed by fallen stones. It seems to us that the house was destroyed violently and perhaps by an earthquake. The woman of the house, perhaps the wife of the owner or even a slave, rushing out of the room when the earth tremor started, was crushed by the falling superstructure as she was crossing the threshold. The pottery found in the rooms seems to indicate that the catastrophe occurred shortly before the middle of the LH III B period. Most interesting among the pots found is a large single-handled mug of yellowish-buff clay bearing a decoration in red of spirals with tangents painted in two superposed registers; another a two-handled deep bowl of a shape typical for the period bearing a vertical, metopic decoration; a third, a completely preserved stirrup jar (Fig. 72). Perhaps the destruction of some of the other buildings of Mycenae should be attributed to the same earthquake.

PALACES OF ATHENS, THEBES, GLA, AND IOLKOS

Beyond Mycenae and the Peloponnesos, we hear of Mycenaean palaces at Athens, Thebes, and Iolkos. The location of the first of these, tradition's "strong house of Erechtheus," is assumed to be in the area over which the "Old Temple of Athena" was built in historic times to the southwest of the Erechtheion. Practically nothing survives of this palace, and it is impossible even to conjure up its plan. Two stone bases of wooden columns, only one of which seems to be of Mycenaean date, are often attributed to the palace and scanty remains of foundation walls here and there. For all practical purposes the Mycenaean palace of

Athens is no longer in existence, nor can its plan be traced even in general lines.[90]

The ruins of the Palace of Kadmos on the akropolis of Thebes, destroyed by fire in the Mycenaean Age, may be lying under modern buildings which cover the Kadmeia today. Keramopoullos found but scanty remains of one of its corridors and a few storerooms that are inadequate to suggest its plan. More remains are now being uncovered, by Dr. N. Platon and Mrs. E. Stasinopoulou Touloupa, keeping alive the hope that further excavation will make possible the delineation of this important palace.[91]

---

[87] For the latest description of the house see N. Verdelis in *The Mycenae Tablets*, III, pp. 13-29. For its use as a perfume factory see Marinatos, *Praktika of the Academy of Athens*, 33 (1958), pp. 161-173. L. Palmer, *Minoans and Mycenaeans*, p. 108. J. Chadwick, in *The Mycenae Tablets*, III, p. 54. For the end of this compound of houses or building see Mrs. David French in *BSA*, 58 (1963), pp. 48-50 and especially p. 50. It

should be noted that Wace's opinion that the complex was composed of houses of merchants has many adherents.

[88] *Infra*, pp. 224 ff.

[89] Wace, *BSA*, 51 (1956), pp. 119-122 and Mrs. David French, *BSA*, 58 (1963), pp. 47-48.

[90] Cf. S. Iacovides, *op.cit.*, pp. 178 and 220.

[91] *Ephemeris*, 1909, pp. 105 ff., 57 ff. *Deltion*, 1917, p. 338.

In northern Greece in the mythical city of Jason and his Argonauts, in legendary Iolkos, Theochares has located and begun the exploration of a large building, perhaps of the palace of the ancestors of Nestor. We shall have to await the further development of his work before we know enough about that palace to describe it in its general lines, but it seems to belong to the LH III B period, to the great period of palace construction and to have been destroyed by fire in the course of LH III C.[92]

The akropolis that is not mentioned in our traditional literature, the citadel of Gla, has yielded a palace of unusual plan and function. It is located, along the northwest side of the citadel, and the rear wall of one of its wings is directly placed on the Cyclopean wall (Figs. 47, 74, and 76). Some remains of the palace were noted by Noack and cleared and described by De Ridder.[93] However, the clearing of the structure by Threpsiades has given us a more complete and detailed picture of its plan.[94] It forms a right angle with its two wings, north and east, enclosing to the northwest one part of a large court (Figs. 74, 76, and 77). The court is surrounded by a peribolos wall and was entered from two gates, one on the east, the other on the south section (Fig. 74, E and F). A road from each of the two entrances led to one extremity of the triangular palace complex. The one starting from the east entrance led to a door opening at the southwest corner of the east wing (Figs. 74 and 76, G), while the other from the south entrance led to the southwest corner of the north wing (Figs. 74 and 76, H). At these extremities are to be found two large suites which could be called the west unit and the south unit, respectively (Fig. 76, I and J). Through a doorway of the west unit one could go to a walled terrace, or, turning in the opposite direction, into a long corridor, the south corridor. From the terrace through a single door one enters a *prodomos* and through a triple door arrangement to the *domos*. The south unit (J), is composed of a *domos* and a walled *prodomos*. Entrance was obtained through a single doorway at the northwest corner of the *prodomos* from the west corridor to which opened the south doorway of the palace. Between these terminal units is a series of double corridors and rooms, whose purpose is not determined. A good many of the rooms have stuccoed floors and walls covered with plaster, three successive replacements of which were disclosed by the latest excavations. The foundations are characterized by

walls about 1.30 m. thick, indicating perhaps that the superstructure was of unbaked brick. Noticeable in this palace is the absence of columns and of hearths. The open porticoes fronting the megara in the Peloponnesos are replaced by vestibules completely surrounded by walls. By the west end of the north wing were found the foundations of guard rooms (Fig. 76, K), which were taken by De Ridder to have formed a tower. Equally unfounded proved De Ridder's conception of another tower at the south end of the east wing. There is instead of a tower a regular entrance to that wing and the south unit. The pottery found, according to its discoverer Threpsiades, belongs to the "last years of the LH III period." A segment, almost half, of horns of consecration in poros stone is included among his finds. The multiple doors of the west unit, the labyrinthine arrangement of rooms and corridors, the deviation from the typical megaron unit, the absence of hearths, may indicate strong Minoan influence. Again the two important apartments, which we have called the west and the south units, may indicate an arrangement for the use of two equally important occupants.

The unusual plan of the palace complex of Gla is not its only feature. Beyond the south segment of its peribolos and court lies a large enclosed area which came to be known as the agora (Fig. 74, L). Its maximum length from south to north amounts to 160 m. On its north wall we find a gate (F) equipped with a guard room, opening onto the court of the palace. On the south wall of its peribolos is a second gate (M), to which led a roadway from the main gate of the citadel (Fig. 74, A). The south gate has an opening of 5.60 m. and on either side a small guard room. Sherds found around this gate belong, according to Threpsiades, to "the last years of LH III." Within this "agora," surrounded by peribolos walls, we find a large central area which to date seems to be free of any structures; it should be admitted, however, that this area has not been excavated completely. This free space is flanked on either side by two long and narrow buildings that recall the stoas of the historic period. The west building seems to have been divided into five sections, three of which, at its south end, had columns along their longitudinal axis, 4, 2, and 4, respectively. The columns, perhaps of wood, have disappeared, but their stone bases are still *in situ* (Figs. 74 and 75). The east long building is narrower than the west, and it seems to have been divided into

N. Platon and Mrs. Touloupa, *ILN*, Nov. 28 and December 5, 1964 and *Kadmos*, 3 (1964), pp. 25-27.

[92] For his latest published report see now *Praktika*, 1957, pp. 54-69.

[93] De Ridder, *BCH*, 18 (1894), pp. 271 ff. Noack, *Ath. Mitt.*,

19 (1894), pp. 405 ff. Tsountas and Manatt, *The Mycenaean Age*, pp. 375 ff.

[94] *Ergon*, 1957, pp. 25-30; 1958, pp. 42-48; 1959, pp. 20-23; 1961, pp. 39-48. *Praktika*, 1957, pp. 48 ff. Other reports, prepared by Mrs. Threpsiades, will appear in the forthcoming issues of the *Praktika*.

smaller sections. At its extreme north end were attached two long and narrow rooms. The south ends of both the east and west long structures faced rectangular buildings containing four long and narrow rooms symmetrically placed on either side of a corridor.

The use of this so-called agora remains problematical. Threpsiades suggested that the free space between the long and narrow rooms served for assemblies, while the long, stoa-like structures perhaps stood in front of rooms that served as workshops.[95] Marinatos has recognized in the so-called agora "stables, rooms for the housing of chariots, and their personnel."[96]

Perhaps we may note that the citadel itself presents one deviation from what seems a principle followed by the Mycenaeans. At Mycenae, at Tiryns, and perhaps at Athens we have but one main gate and one smaller postern gate. In the citadel of Gla are four large gates, opening to different aspects of the plain. This was perhaps due to the desire of their builders to provide an easy entry into the citadel of people and their flocks, who in time of stress and invasion wanted to take refuge in that stronghold. If to this we add the fact that around Gla no remnants of habitations and graves were found and the peculiar arrangement of its palace, we may reach the conclusion, projected long ago, that Gla is not the citadel of a single king and community, but the project undertaken in common by a number of communities scattered along the shores of the Kopaic Lake to serve as a refuge to them all in time of need. The palace could serve the leaders of the communities in times of danger and perhaps that of the military leader entrusted with its safe-keeping in times of peace and quiet. Why this citadel was abandoned is still to be explained.

HOUSES IN OTHER AREAS

Remains of houses of the late Mycenaean Age, outside of Mycenae, are rather few. The best examples come from the site of Korakou excavated by Blegen in 1915 and 1916, and of these House L is perhaps the most typical of the age (text fig. 21).[97] It is in the form of a megaron with an open portico on the south narrow side, bounded on either side by the projection of the side walls. A flat stone midway between the projecting lateral walls apparently served as the base for a wooden column. A doorway with a threshold of small stones, made in the last phase of the house, led into a small vestibule, roughly paved with loose stones. A single door opening, rather irregularly formed, led into the main room or *domos*.[98] It is a large room and a stone column base and a flat stone which might have served as a column base suggest that two columns stood along the longitudinal axis of the *domos*. In the center of the room was a hearth of an irregular circular shape made of clay and paved with sherds and pebbles. Beyond the *domos*, the house possessed a small rectangular chamber of which little remains.

A similar arrangement of supports on the longitudinal axis of the *domos* we find in the remains of two LH III B-C houses excavated at the site of Aghios Kosmas in Attika (text fig. 21).[99]

The houses discovered by Valmin at Malthi Dorion in Messenia do not exhibit a regular type but seem to be composed of a number of rooms without a set

21. Houses of LH III B-C period: (left) Blegen (right) Mylonas

[95] In *Ergon*, 1961, pp. 39-48.
[96] In Iacovides, *op.cit.*, Preface, p. 14.
[97] Blegen, *Korakou*, pp. 80-83 and fig. 112.
[98] The two doorways are not on the same axis, a detail existing also in House I of Mycenae by the Treasury of Atreus excavated by Mrs. Shear. This arrangement has been attributed to the efforts of the builders to prevent a direct draught from reaching the central hearth.
[99] Mylonas, *Aghios Kosmas*, pp. 52 ff. Drawings 14 and 15.

relationship to a court; for example, Houses B52-B57 and B33-B38.[100] Perhaps in most cases the plan was dictated by the structure displaced in order to incorpo-rate existing walls. The final clearing of the settle-ments of Keos may yield other well-preserved exam-ples of Late Helladic houses.

MYCENAEAN ROADS AND AQUEDUCTS

Mycenaean towns were connected by roads con-structed with great skill and well maintained. Rem-nants of such roads have been known for a long time and indicate that Mycenae especially was the center of a net of roads spreading out in all directions. Steffen, in his famous survey of Mycenae, noted at least four roads starting from the Lion Gate: one lead-ing in the direction of Prosymna and Tiryns and the other three in the direction of Corinth.[101] We had a chance to investigate these roads once more in 1961 and 1962. Unfortunately, Steffen's Road 2, which went along the west slopes of Mount Elias, was almost totally destroyed just a few years ago by the villagers of Stephani who attempted to build a road connecting their village with that of Mycenae. However, its traces can still be seen in places along the slope of Mount Elias where the wheel traffic had cut deep ruts in the rock.

Steffen's Road 1 is still preserved for a long distance and can be considered one of the most extraordinary achievements of the Mycenaean Age. Roads 1 and 2 both started as one from the Lion Gate and went along the north side of the citadel. In the area below the postern gate we can still see the ruts made by wheel traffic on the rock that rose to the pavement of the road (Fig. 78). They are some 1.03 m. apart, indicating perhaps the width of a Mycenaean char-iot.[102] Near the northeast corner of the citadel the road divided into two branches, one leading north along the west slopes of Mount Elias, becoming Steffen's Road 2, and the other, Road 1, eastward. Road 1 passes by the Perseia spring and then proceeds to the area where the Chavos ravine originates. There the remains of a viaduct known as Dragonera indicate that the road proceeded southward along the west slopes of Mount Agrilovounaki and in the direction of the modern path leading to Berbati. Perhaps a branch of it followed the same direction as the modern path and descended to the valley of the Mastos and to Berbati. This has not been found as yet and no traces of it are evident. However, we find the retaining walls of our road on the southeast slope of the Agrilovou-naki, and these proceed northwards skirting the slopes of the high hills which limit the plain of Berbati to the north.

We followed the road beyond the point indicated by Steffen to a ravine known as the "Kalogherikos Mylos," where the road's course is still clear. It finally seems to reach the level of the watershed of the ravine at a place known as the Mill of Rijoyannis, where its traces are lost under heavy vegetation. Beyond this area we were unable to follow it. It seems probable that it continued to a pass and spring known today as Mavroneri, a divide that connects the Argolid with the plain of Aghios Vasileios in Corinthia. Through that pass of Mavroneri also went Steffen's Road 2, which our Road 1 may have joined. Near the pass, and a little to the south of it, a Hellenistic guard house or fort, known as Kastraki, proves that the pass was still used in the third century B.C. and later. Not far from the pass on a hilltop, we found a Mycenaean guard house or fort which had remained undetected under deep growth of wild vegetation. We hope to be able to clear it and draw a plan of it in the near future. Evidently it was there to protect the roads as they approached the Mavroneri pass. Roads 1 and 2 must have passed along its west side.

Throughout its course Road 1 is graded in an astonishing manner. It is made to go around ravines and gullies so that sharp drops and abrupt rises are avoided and its grade is kept even, although this process necessitated a longer road and resulted in a meandering course. Since the road is laid mostly along the slope of high hills, it had to be supported on its exposed side with heavy retaining walls, and these have survived for long distances, indicating the exist-ence of the road and course. The retaining walls are built in the Cyclopean fashion and have culverts at short distances and even small bridges to take care of the flow of rain water descending from the higher reaches of the hills; sometimes the retaining walls reach a height of 4 m. (Figs. 79, 80). The road, aver-aging 3.50 m. in width, is an immense job and its survival over a wild terrain is a testimony to the ability and thoroughness of its builders. Its understructure is made up of a fill of stones and earth of a depth vary-ing in accordance with the slope. On it was laid a layer of earth with small stones averaging 25 cm. in thickness and this supported the pavement, appar-ently of well-packed earth, clay, pebbles, and sand.

[100] M. Natan Valmin, *The Swedish Messenian Expedition*, pp. 173-182.

[101] Steffen, *Karten von Mykenai*, pp. 8 ff.

[102] See now Iacovides' study in *Ephemeris*, 1961 (1964), pp. 180-196.

No traces of wheel traffic were found on the few patches of the original pavement we were able to detect, but the greater extent of that pavement is now covered with a fill of earth and wild vegetation. In actuality it is uncertain that a pavement of earth would retain ruts of wheel traffic and only where the rock rises to the level of the pavement we may expect to find its traces.

What purpose did Road 1 serve? Along its course between Mycenae and Mavroneri no Mycenaean settlement exists, outside those in the plain of Berbati to which perhaps one of its branches may have led. There does not exist even an agricultural area that Road 1 could have served. Since a more direct communication between Mycenae and the pass of Mavroneri was served by Road 2, why was Road 1 constructed beyond the area where it branched off, possibly to the plain of Berbati, and why was it continued to the Mavroneri pass over a wild terrain that must have required great effort and expenditure? The Mycenaeans could not have believed that Road 2 was exposed to enemy attack because it faced the Argive plain; it was laid so high up in the slopes of Mount Elias that a successful enemy attack was problematical. To build a second road leading to Mavroneri on the east side of high hills was a luxury made possible only by great prosperity and strength. When could such a period have been experienced by the people of Mycenae? All indications would point to the period that saw the construction of the Lion Gate, of the last phase of the later palace, of the southwest extension of the citadel, of the great ramp, of the tomb of Atreus and the so-called Tomb of Klytemnestra, namely the second half of the LH III B period. The construction of the more monumental parts of the retaining wall, such as the culvert-bridge at Lykotroupi (Fig. 79), seems to indicate that part of the period. As yet we have tested only two spots on the length of Road 1 to determine its construction. Very few sherds, of which only two were painted, were found in these two trial trenches. Both of these sherds belong to late LH III B times. We hope to be able in the future to test the road further and perhaps obtain more material that would make possible a definitive chronological conclusion for the construction of the road. Tentatively the construction of this road can be placed in the second half of the thirteenth century B.C.

In the neighborhood of Mycenae and, as we approach from the modern village, the hill in which the Treasury of Atreus is to be seen, to the right of the junction of the road that leads to the Tourist Pavilion and the modern cemetery of St. George, the remains of a viaduct are clearly visible. It is usually called St. George's viaduct or bridge; it is believed to be of late Mycenaean date, and was included by Steffen in his survey. To it apparently came a Mycenaean road from Prosymna, now known as the site of the Argive Heraeum. In 1962 we found traces of another viaduct or bridge below the southwest corner of the citadel. We detected the remnants of a road on either side of the bridge; the north road led to the citadel approaching it from its southwest side, the south end perhaps led to Prosymna and Tiryns. The bridge is not preserved, but its structure is clear; unlike the St. George bridge which is built of comparatively small, rectangular, flat stones in almost horizontal courses, the new bridge was built of large limestone boulders roughly cut in the Cyclopean style. A good number of these blocks are now lying in the bed of the torrent they once spanned. The style of masonry indicates that this newly found bridge is older than the St. George bridge and perhaps it marks one of the older roads which connected the citadel of Mycenae with Prosymna and Tiryns. Along the roads were built guard houses and a lookout post was established on the summit of Mt. Elias dominating the territory of Mycenae.

Mycenaean roads have been lately reported by Professor William McDonald and R. Hope Simpson in the territory of western Messenia and Triphylia.[103] We shall have to await the final publication of the results of their explorations before we can determine their extent and compare them to the roads originating at Mycenae.

The memory of chariot travel over well-made roads is preserved in Homeric poetry. Readers of the *Odyssey* are familiar with the chariot trip of Telemachos, son of Odysseus, and of Peisistratos, son of Nestor, from Pylos to Sparta. The road system disclosed in the territory of Mycenae seems to prove that the memory is based on fact, that the Mycenaeans were great road builders and that wheeled traffic over well-constructed roads was common in the late Mycenaean Age.

In later historic times roads were intimately connected with aqueducts and we may ask whether the Mycenaeans, who are known to have used wells, cisterns, and natural springs, attempted the construction of aqueducts. Since the days when Tsountas cleared the underground cistern in the citadel of Mycenae it has been known that in the closing years of LH III period the Mycenaeans built an aqueduct that brought water to that cistern from neighboring springs. It seems, however, that the people of Mycenae succeeded in adding to the supply at least of the Perseia spring, located in the hills to the east of the citadel, by a built aqueduct whose remains we have detected some

---

[103] W. McDonald, in *Mycenaean Studies* (1964), pp. 217-240. Also *AJA*, 65 (1961), pp. 221 ff.; 68 (1964), pp. 229 ff.

400 m. to the east of that spring and between it and the Dragonera viaduct. Its conduit can be seen on the present surface of the soil; it was built carefully of stone and exhibits a channel 56 cm. in width and 50 cm. in depth. Its bottom is covered with the Mycenaean "lime-concrete." We hope to trace its entire course in the future.

An aqueduct also brought fresh water to the palace of Nestor from a spring almost a mile away. Part of it is made of pi-shaped terra-cotta pipes; a great section of it was cut in the rock in which the actual conduit, perhaps made of wood and consequently not preserved, must have been placed. Blegen was able to trace its course to a length of some 140 m.[104] It seems therefore that the Mycenaeans were not only expert road builders but also skilled in the laying of aqueducts and in marshaling the water supplies of their districts for the use of their people.

Surviving remains—citadels, palaces, fountains, and roads—indicate that the Mycenaean Age almost to its very end was a period of creative activity which deserves the admiration it has so richly received.

[104] *AJA*, 63 (1959), pp. 123-124.

CHAPTER IV

THE GRAVE CIRCLES OF MYCENAE

Hermes "... look over there to your right, and you will see Hyakinthos, Narkissos, Nereus, Achilles, Tyro, Helen, Leda,—all the beauties of old."
Menippos "I can see only bones, and bare skulls; most of them are exactly alike."
Hermes "Those bones, of which you seem to think so lightly, have been the themes of admiring poets." (Lucian, *Dialogues of the Dead*, XIX; Tr. F. G. Fowler)

The types of graves developed by the Mycenaeans and their burial customs are well known, thanks especially to the explorations and publications of Tsountas, Wace, and Blegen. The period is ushered in by the famous shaft graves of Mycenae, which actually give us the transition from the Middle to the Late Helladic periods. Until recently it was believed that the shaft graves with their unusually rich furnishings formed a marked innovation in the burial habits of the people of the mainland. It has been proved, however, that the shaft graves actually continue the habits of the earlier period although the increased interest in furnishings indicates a strengthening of outside influences.

It is a well-established fact that in the early years of the Middle Helladic period each grave had a single occupant; that no furnishings were laid by the body; that the graves were cists of small size made up of four slabs set vertically in the ground and were covered by a single roof slab.[1] However, with the passage of time the graves were gradually enlarged, each contained more than one burial, and furnishings were laid beside the body (text fig. 22). With the enlargement of the tomb more space was available in it for burial and bodies were laid in a more or less extended position instead of the contracted attitude characteristic of the earlier years. These developments are clearly illustrated by the Middle Helladic graves of the west cemetery of Eleusis.[2] There we find that the cist grave was gradually increased in size, that its sides, originally made of a single vertical slab, towards the end of the period were formed by slabs in association with built walls, that its roof was made of two or three large slabs instead of one. These enlarged cist graves contained more than one burial, and we find developing now the custom of brushing into the corner the bones of previous burials to make room for later interments in the same grave. Apparently at this stage graves were transformed from individual

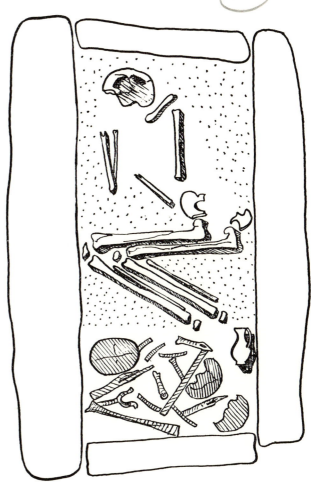

22. Eleusis. Cist grave in west cemetery (drawing Travlos)

into family sepulchers. Also, evidently under external influence, furnishings begin to appear in graves, very few at first—a cup or a clay jug—but gradually they increase in number and intrinsic value. In a grave belonging to the late years of the Middle Helladic period of the west cemetery at Eleusis we found a

---

[1] C. W. Blegen and A. J. B. Wace, "Middle Helladic Tombs," *Symbolae Osloenses*, 9 (1930), pp. 28-37. G. E. Mylonas, "The Cult of the Dead in Helladic Times," *Studies Presented to David M. Robinson I*, pp. 68 ff., to be referred to hereafter as "Cult of the Dead."

[2] For the west cemetery of Eleusis and its graves see Mylonas, *Praktika* 1952, pp. 58-72; 1953, pp. 77-87; 1954, pp. 50-65; 1955, pp. 67-77; 1956, pp. 57-62.

number of bronze circles covered with gold foil, which apparently served to keep the curls of a coiffure in place. The grave, it must be noted, had been emptied in antiquity and the gold circles, lying among the pebbles with which the floor of the grave was customarily covered, evidently were overlooked. One may be justified in assuming that the grave originally contained other valuable objects. Moreover the circles are sufficient to indicate that objects of value were now laid in the graves; and if this was done in a small, provincial village like Eleusis, it must have been done on a greater scale in capital cities. Perhaps we should note another development in the form of the graves illustrated at Eleusis. When a grave was re-used, it became necessary to lift the slabs forming the roof before subsequent burials could be made. This was a rather difficult task since these slabs were large and heavy. To facilitate the matter, side openings were substituted. These side openings, blocked by slabs, were gradually developed into well-defined passages projecting from the side of the grave; they correspond to what came to be known as the *stomion* of a grave.

At Mycenae cist graves cut in the soft rock continued to be used throughout the Middle Helladic period, and even into the early Mycenaean period, for the burial of the common people. There the shaft grave was developed for the burial of royalty. As Wace put it long ago, "the shaft graves are elaborate or royal versions of ordinary MH graves."[3] Their contents illustrate further the customs current in the closing years of the earlier period with one exception: the staggering number and the great value of the objects interred with the dead.[4] The increase in burial gifts can be attributed to external influences, which this time, I believe, stemmed from Egypt. The Mycenaean rulers seem to have become acquainted with the elaborate and magnificent burials of the Pharaohs and their nobles and, in a new-found prosperity, tried to imitate them. On the one hand the apparently embalmed body found in Grave v, the ostrich eggs, the masks of gold, the inlaid dagger with a Nilotic scene, and on the other, LH I vases found in Egypt seem to prove definite relations between the peoples of the two areas. The gold used in the making of the articles found in the shaft graves is now taken to have been imported from Egypt.[5]

Schliemann's discovery of the shaft graves of Mycenae in 1876 is a brilliant landmark in the history of excavation in Hellenic lands. Believing firmly in the historicity of Pausanias' passage about Mycenae, he identified the five shaft graves he explored as the graves of Agamemnon and the associates who were murdered with him on his return from Troy. Later excavations proved that the graves had nothing to do with the mighty king, but this did not detract from the great importance of Schliemann's achievement, for his work at Mycenae opened up a new field of research and brought mythical Greece within the orbit of early history. The story of the discovery has been told and the fabulous contents of the shaft graves have been described in a number of monographs by the most distinguished students of antiquity, beginning with Schliemann himself.[6] It will, therefore, be necessary to mention only the outstanding basic facts regarding them and to elaborate only certain controversial points.

GRAVE CIRCLE A

Grave Circle A is located to the south of the Lion Gate (text fig. 19; Fig. 81), surrounded by a parapet made largely of slabs of shelly sandstone set vertically and placed in a double row. The space between rows was filled with earth and small stones and was roofed over by slabs of the same shelly sandstone, under which were placed wooden beams resting in almost rectangular sockets. The purpose of the beams was perhaps to help keep the vertical slabs in position, rather than to support the horizontal roof slabs. Thus was formed a solid circular wall, 0.92 to 1.52 m. high and 1.35 m. thick, enclosing an area 27.50 m. in diameter. Along the east side of that enclosed area a nar-row pavement of slabs was disclosed forming a margin at the foot of the parapet wall. In the north section of the enclosure, at a short distance from the Lion Gate is a well-constructed entranceway 2.50 by 3.63 m., with long rectangular enclosures of upright parallel slabs standing for the door jambs on either side of the threshold, which was made of three large blocks of shelly sandstone. No door closed the opening.

The slabs employed for the construction of the eastern section of the parapet average 1.05 m. in height and were secured in a channel-like cutting in the rock, while those of the western section are taller, measuring 1.69 m. in height, and are set on a support-

[3] Wace, *BSA*, 25 (1921-1923), pp. 120-121.

[4] G. Karo, *Die Schachtgräber von Mykenai*, 1930.

[5] A. Persson, *New Tombs at Dendra*, pp. 146, 195, and 164-175. Mylonas, "The Cult of the Dead," pp. 100-102. S. Marinatos-Hirmer, *Crete and Mycenaean Greece*, p. 82. Mylonas, *Ephemeris*, 1958, p. 162 n. 1. Cf. Herodotos, III, 23. Excellent illustrations and descriptions of the most important finds from the shaft graves are to be found in convenient form in Marinatos and Hirmer, *loc.cit.*

[6] H. Schliemann, *Mycenae*, 1880. C. Schuchhardt, *Schliemann's Excavations*, 1891. Tsountas and Manatt, *Mycenaean Age*, 1897. G. Karo, *loc.cit.*

ing wall which, because of the abrupt falling off of the rocky ground, attains a maximum height of some 5.50 m. This supporting wall also served to retain the artificial terrace enclosed by the parapet, and exhibits a batter of about 75 degrees. At its base on the west side a foundation was revealed by Tsountas and studied by Wace, but its function remained uncertain until our excavations of 1961, when the entire length of the foundation was again brought to light. It was demonstrated that the fragment belongs to the original circular wall, to the original circle, surrounding the area within which the shaft graves were constructed (Fig. 82). The sherds Wace found in the retaining wall in 1922 and in 1953 belong to the LH III B period.[7] The sherds we found in the older foundation belong to the closing years of the Middle Helladic period and contain gray and yellow Minyan and matt-painted fragments, one of which has a decoration painted in dull white on a dark ground. This difference in the age of the walls indicates that the retaining wall replaced the older circular wall at a later period. Within the circular area Schliemann discovered and cleared five shaft graves and after his departure Stamatakes found and cleared a sixth. In addition, both found some cists cut in the soft rock apparently on the south section of the circle. Below the inner row of slabs of the parapet wall by the entrance of the circle, Papadimitriou in 1957 discovered and cleared another grave cut in the rock, containing a single skeleton and fragments of two pots of Middle Helladic times (Fig. 83).[8] Schliemann also found a good many human bones in the fill of the circular area, which Tsountas originally considered to be the remnants of human sacrifices.[9]

The shaft graves of Mycenae have no architectural character and can be defined as rectangular trenches or shafts, more or less oblong, cut vertically and deeply into the earth and the soft rock under it. The smallest measures 3.00 by 3.50 m.; the largest 4.50 by 6.40 m., while their depth varies from 1 to 3 or 4 m. Their sides, ranging to a given height of 0.75 to 1.50 m. above the floor, are lined with rubble walls, which reduce the floor space of the grave and which were apparently built to help support the roof. Dörpfeld was the first to understand their function. He suggested

that wooden beams were placed from rubble wall to rubble wall to support stone slabs which formed the roof. A number of shelly sandstone blocks found by Schliemann over some graves were regarded as roof slabs; however, these are too heavy to have been used in that capacity, and I should prefer to believe that small and thin slabs of slate were employed for that purpose, similar to those found in the newly excavated shaft graves of Circle B, or a simple thatch of twigs and dried leaves.[10] The roof, therefore, stood at a small elevation from the floor of the grave, and thus the bodies were placed in an empty area and were not covered with earth. The comparative disturbance of the skeletons and of their funeral offerings, noticed by Schliemann and attributed to a hasty and careless burial, was apparently caused by the collapse of the roof when the wooden beams had decayed. Over the roof, earth was poured to fill the shaft; and over the slightly mounded earth, stelai or other grave markers were placed.

The floor of the graves was covered with a layer of pebbles and on them the bodies were placed, sometimes in a contracted attitude. Around them their funeral furnishings were arranged.[11] No real evidence indicating cremation was obtained and, in spite of Schliemann's statements and Dörpfeld's ingenious explanations, the bodies were certainly inhumed and not "burned" or "toasted."[12] In one instance, in Grave v, as has been noted, a body seems to have been preserved by embalming. In the six shaft graves the skeletal remains of nineteen persons were found, apparently eight men, nine women, and two children.[13] With the exception of Grave ii, in which only one skeleton was found, the shafts contained from two to five bodies. Grave iii contained the skeletons of three women and two children, but those of three women were found in Grave iv along with the skeletons of two men; consequently we cannot conclude that women were buried separately. From the evidence obtained, it is clear that no fixed orientation for the bodies was observed and that none was required. In Grave vi, at least, the bones of the earlier occupant of the grave were brushed aside to make room for the final burial.[14]

Rich funeral furnishings were found in the graves.

[7] *BSA*, 25 (1921-1923), pp. 108-109 and *BSA*, 49 (1954), p. 246.
[8] Papadimitriou, *Praktika*, 1957, pp. 105-109 and pl. 46, a-b.
[9] *Mycenaean Age*, p. 97.
[10] Schuchhardt, *op.cit.*, p. 160.
[11] The objects laid with the dead we shall call furnishings, translating a Homeric term *kterismata*; we shall avoid the term offerings usually employed, as inferring an act of worship.
[12] W. Dörpfeld, "Verbrennung und Bestattung der Toten im alten Griechenland," *Mélanges Nicole*, 1905, pp. 95 ff. and idem, "Verbrennung und Beerdigung der Toten im alten Griechenland," *Comptes rendus du Congrès intern. d'archéologie*, 1905, pp. 161 ff.
[13] The numbers given by Schliemann to the graves were later

changed, so that today roman numerals are given to them differing from the original. Grave i (Schliemann's No. 2) contained three skeletons of women; Grave ii (Schliemann's No. 5) one man; Grave iii (Schliemann's No. 3) 3 women and 2 children; Grave iv (Schliemann's No. 4) 2 men and 3 women; Grave v (Schliemann's No. 1) three men; and Grave vi (excavated by Stamatakes) two men.
[14] In view of the evidence obtained in the graves of Circle B, one wonders whether the bones of previous burials brushed against the walls were not contained also in the other graves of Circle A. Such bones are usually so decayed that their existence could have been overlooked very easily.

Comparatively few vases were reported among these, but a goodly number of bronze swords and daggers.[15] Of the swords, most interesting are those with engraved decorations on their ribbed blades; of the daggers, those from Graves IV and V, on whose bronze blades inlaid designs in gold, silver, and niello were added (Fig. 140). Some of these weapons may have been wrapped in linen or may have had a scabbard of linen decked with gold buttons, since Schliemann often mentions the discovery of linen shreds associated with swords. The handles of the swords were apparently made of perishable materials and consequently did not survive, but in one instance the gold sheathing of a handle is preserved; it comes from Grave IV and exhibits a cylindrical gold hilt of cut work ending in dragons' heads below the top of the blade. Originally this was thought to have been the top of a scepter, but its use as a cover for a hilt is now established by a lucky discovery from Grave Delta of Grave Circle B.[16] Spearheads, arrowheads, and broad blades, which must have served as knives, were among the objects found by the skeletons of men. No remnants of defensive armor, such as shields or corselets, were discovered, although what seem to be breastplates made of gold foil are among the finds, and the so-called *Gamaschenhälter*, taken to indicate the existence of greaves or leather leggings.[17] In Grave IV were flakes of boar tusks, which apparently covered the surface of helmets of leather or felt, reminiscent of Meriones' helmet described in the *Iliad* (X, 261-265) and illustrated by a number of late ivory carvings.[18] Gold masks were laid in graves of men (a total of five were found in Graves IV and V) and, according to Schliemann, over the faces of the deceased. One of these he mistakenly identified as belonging to Agamemnon (Fig. 84). Thinner and summarily rendered masks covered the faces of the two children in Grave III, whose bodies were wrapped in gold foil. Women apparently were not given masks, but elaborate diadems and bands decorated their heads. A variety of hairpins kept the bands in position, while other pins, some of which possess heads in rock crystal, originally thought by Schliemann to have been scepters, were used to fasten their clothes. Of the pins that might

have been worn as jewelry, the silver pin with the gold pendant from Grave III Marinatos explains as "an elaborate symbol, which expresses the wish for happiness and long years for kingdoms and kings."[19]

Discs of gold-leaf bearing elaborate designs in repoussé work seem to have belonged mostly to women since some 700 pieces were found in Grave III where women and children were buried. Thirty-seven discs and twenty-one fragments come from Grave V, which was used for the burial of three men. Some of these discs, only 6 cm. in diameter, have holes for attachment; others bear traces of some sticky material by means of which they were glued onto the article they adorned. All are covered with delicately executed designs that include spirals, leaves, bees, cuttlefish, etc. Originally it was believed that they were applied to the garments of women or to the shrouds in which they were enveloped, a practice indicated even by Biblical references. "Ye daughters of Israel, weep over Saul, who clothed you in scarlet, who put ornaments of gold upon your apparel," exhorts the writer of II Samuel 1. 24. In an interesting study, Staes has tried to prove that these discs, as well as the masks and some of the diadems, were used to decorate wooden coffins in which the bodies were laid.[20] He further pointed out that a good many bronze nails were found in the graves and that in the cross-shaped rosettes we have a central nail, which in one instance measures 5 cm. Staes's theory found no followers, but it has been revived and vigorously supported lately by Persson.[21] Karo's examination of the evidence, however, has proved conclusively that no wooden coffins were employed in the shaft graves explored by Schliemann and Stamatakes. That conclusion is now strengthened by the results obtained in the excavation of Circle B; a total of twenty-four graves were found in that circle, of which at least fourteen are typical shafts. No traces of coffins were found in those graves, although special attention was given to the possibility of their existence. Furthermore, Schliemann observed that some of the gold discs were found *under* the skeletons, an impossible position if the discs decorated a coffin. Also, if the masks as well as the discs were used to adorn coffins, we ought to find them both wherever the one

---

[15] The swords have been divided by Karo (*op.cit.*, p. 201 and pls. 73, 81, etc.) into two types. Type A has a long blade, rounded shoulders, and a short tang. Type B has a shorter but broader blade, slightly horned shoulders, and a long tang with flanged sides for the handles. Both have a raised central rib along the length of the blade. Both types could be used only for thrusting and not slashing.

[16] Karo, *op.cit.*, pl. 87 no. 294. Cf. our Fig. 96.

[17] Cf. Karo, *op.cit.*, p. 221. H. L. Lorimer, *Homer and the Monuments*, pp. 253-254. A LH III A-1 corselet was found by Verdelis and Dr. P. Åstrom in a grave at Dendra (Verdelis in *Ephemeris* 1957—circulated in 1961—Parartema, pp. 15-18) and a pair of greaves were discovered by Dr. N. Ghialouris in a grave

at Kallithea in Achaia, belonging to very late LH III times; cf. *Ath.Mitt.*, 75 (1960), Beilage 28.

[18] Wace, *Chamber Tombs at Mycenae*, pp. 212-214 and pl. XXXVIII; *Mycenae*, p. 60. Karo, *op.cit.*, pp. 218-219. At Dendra, Persson found examples in glass paste, *The Royal Tombs at Dendra*, p. 36, pl. 25.1. For the gold masks see Karo, *op.cit.*, pls. 47-52 and pp. 76, 121, 180; and especially Fischer's study, pp. 320 ff. For the child's mask, *ibid.*, pl. 53.

[19] "Numerous Years of Joyful Life from Mycenae," *BSA* 46 (1951), pp. 102-116.

[20] *Ephemeris*, 1907, pp. 31-60.

[21] Persson, *New Tombs at Dendra*, pp. 113 ff. See also M. Meurer, *Jahrbuch*, 1912, p. 208 ff.

or the other is found. Yet, in Grave IV, where three masks were discovered, no discs or cross-rosettes with nails were found. It seems reasonable to conclude that the gold discs were applied to garments, as a rule to women's apparel, and occasionally to men's clothing. In this connection we may recall the representation of a clothed woman in gold leaf from Grave III.[22] Between the pleats of her skirt we find as additional ornaments small circles that may perhaps stand for gold discs, representations of the ones actually discovered in the graves. That gold ornaments were attached to men's clothing is proved by the last burial in Grave Nu of Grave Circle B. Under the jaw of the skeleton a gold band was found, which evidently decorated the upper end of the garment in which that person was buried. Around the wrists of the man's skeleton in Grave Iota were gold bands that had originally been sewn to his garment. And in Grave Omikron, among the funeral furnishings of the last burial, we found a cross-rosette of gold leaf reminiscent of the crosses from the shaft graves within the Citadel; originally it was attached to the woman's garment by a bronze pin preserved now to a length of 8 cm.[23] Apparently it was worn over the right shoulder. No trace of a wooden coffin was found in that grave. We believe that the available evidence proves that all these objects of gold foil were used to decorate the clothes of the deceased. Among the objects buried with women were wooden boxes, apparently their toilet boxes, covered with richly decorated gold plate (Fig. 139).

Gold and silver cups were laid by the sides of both men and women. Of these the most interesting is a gold cup with doves on top of its twin handles reminiscent of Nestor's "beauteous cup" (*Iliad*, XI, 632-635) (Fig. 85), and a silver goblet with plant motives inlaid in gold. With the cups should be mentioned three rhytons from Grave IV: the gold mask of a lion head, the silver rhyton trimmed with gold in the form of a bull's head, and the fragment of a funnel-shaped silver rhyton with a siege scene.[24] Gold rings with carved bezels, beads of agate, sardonyx, amethyst, amber, gold foil cut in the shape of a triple shrine (Fig. 122, e), a garmented lady, earrings and bracelets, gold plaques decorated in repoussé which once covered wooden boxes, a great number of gold buttons, and gold bands of various sizes, are among the rich

funeral furnishings of the graves. In addition we have a number of vessels of almost pure copper (98½ percent copper), while the swords are of bronze (86 percent copper and 13 percent tin). We may note that engraved on the handle of one of the copper vessels Dr. Chrestos Karouzos, Director of the National Archaeological Museum of Greece, recently detected a sign of Linear A script.[25] Even a casual view of the objects yielded by the shaft graves of Circle A, as they are displayed in the National Museum of Greece in Athens, will carry the conviction that no richer graves have been explored in Greece, and that Schliemann's finds have remained to date the outstanding single discovery in Greek archaeological research.

At different levels above the shaft graves, Schliemann found a number of stelai, some plain and some decorated. Heurtley maintained that at the time of the leveling of the terrace of the circle the plain stelai were erected to take the place of sculptured stelai which had been destroyed.[26] The discovery of unsculptured stelai over the shaft graves of Grave Circle B, where no leveling or replacing of stelai occurred, seems to make Heurtley's suggestion untenable. According to Schuchhardt, the plain stelai were placed over the graves of women, while the sculptured ones were used for men. Unsculptured stelai were discovered over Graves Gamma and Omicron; in the former the skeleton of a woman was found with three others belonging to men; in the latter, remains of women only were revealed. The new discoveries seem to strengthen Schuchhardt's theory, which, however, still cannot be proved completely.

Some of the unsculptured stelai could have been covered with painted stucco in a manner similar to that found on a later stele discovered by Tsountas in one of the chamber tombs he excavated. The stucco and color could have disappeared during their long years of exposure, but this, too, is a hypothesis that cannot be proved. Perhaps it should be added that the custom of erecting stelai over graves appears in the mainland of Greece in Middle Helladic times. Certain examples of stelai erected in those times have been discovered in the West Cemetery of Eleusis and at Lerna.[27]

The sculptured stelai are naturally the most interesting. Of these, three representing chariot scenes are the most important. These scenes have been taken to

---

22 *Schachtgräber*, pl. XXVII, no. 36. Our Fig. 122.

23 Mylonas, *Ancient Mycenae*, figs. 56, 67, 72. Other bronze pins with heads of rock crystal are preserved to a length of 16 cm.

24 Karo, *op.cit.*, pls. CXVIII-CXXII. For the gold and electrum cups see pls. CIII-CXIII.

25 Mylonas, *Archaeology*, 9 (1956), p. 278 and Grumach, *Kadmos*, 1962, pp. 85-86.

26 Schuchhardt, *op.cit.*, pp. 168-169. Heurtley, *BSA*, 25 (1921-

1923), p. 143. The possibility that the plain stelai were originally painted cannot be dismissed lightly. The stelai from Grave Circle A are now in the National Museum at Athens. Heurtley, *loc.cit.*, gave the first scientific description of these stelai. See also Karo, *op.cit.*, pp. 29-35.

27 Tsountas, *Ephemeris*, 1896, pp. 1-22 and pl. 1. Mylonas, *Ancient Mycenae*, p. 84 n. 32. Caskey, *Hesperia* 23 (1954), p. 14 and pl. 3, C.

depict actions of war or hunting. However, the charioteers are not equipped with the appropriate weapons for either war or the chase as they are in an illustration engraved on the bezel of a gold ring from Grave IV in which the charioteer and the hunter mount the chariot. The hunter is equipped with bow and arrows with which he attacks a deer.[28] It is hard to see how a single man could control the chariot and at the same time fight or hunt, especially when he is not equipped with weapons that could be used from a chariot. The impossibility of such a task was recognized even in the days of Homer, as we can see from the *Iliad*, where Automedon on the chariot of Achilles could not kill the fleeing Trojans

> "for in no wise was it possible for him, being alone in the sacred car, to assail them with spear, and withal to hold the swift horses."[29]

Thus it seems that on these stelai we have representations of chariot races,[30] perhaps held in honor of the dead. The sculptured work on these stelai seems primitive and much inferior to that presented by carved gems and objects decorated in repoussé, and because of this it has been suggested that the sculptured stelai were covered with stucco and color. As we noted already, there is no evidence that will prove the validity of this suggestion.

The stelai originally stood on rectangular blocks with a rectangular cutting on their surface in which the upright slabs were secured. Since no definite rule of orientation was observed in the disposition of the dead, the fact that the sculptured face of the stelai seems to have been set towards the west cannot have any religious or ritualistic significance. Most probably they were set to face the road, which skirted the circle and led to the gate of the first citadel outside of which the circle originally stood.

Over Grave IV, Schliemann brought to light a circular, well-like construction which is usually known as the "altar" of the shaft graves. The occurrence of this structure has been taken to prove that a cult was practiced in honor of the buried kings in the circle itself. However, a careful examination of the recorded evidence and a study of the formation of the ground will prove that the so-called "altar" had nothing to do with a cult of the dead. The structure must have been connected only with Grave IV and not with all the graves.[31] The "altar" was covered by a deep layer of earth at the time of the construction of the parapet; consequently it could not have been used for cult purposes when the grave circle was given the form and aspect known to us. Lately it has been suggested with reason that the "altar" served the burial ritual. Perhaps it was used to pour final libations into the grave after its roof was sealed in a manner similar to that practiced by the Sumerians.[32]

Between Graves IV and I, Keramopoullos found a cavity in the rock, a small cave. Since it is almost in the middle of the circle, and since traces of fire and ashes were found in it, he suggested that it formed the center of a cult. However, this cave also was filled and covered in Late Helladic III times when the grave circle was rearranged and consequently could not have served a cult purpose in late Mycenaean times.[33]

No stratified fill was observed over the shaft graves, but pottery of all periods, from the Middle Helladic to the closing era of the Late Helladic period; dark, red, and loose earth; animal bones; and a quantity of human bones, stones, and slabs, were found indiscriminately piled over the shafts. The animal bones are certainly the remnants of funeral feasts held after interments. The human bones, which gave rise to the theory of the practice of human sacrifices, apparently belonged to other disturbed graves.[34] The mixture of pottery of all periods, the earth and the stones are no longer a mystery but can be convincingly explained, and in fact they help to decipher the history of the circular area.

Wace, after a careful investigation and study of the area, concluded that the double ring parapet is not contemporary with the shaft graves. When the Lion Gate and the Cyclopean wall to the south of it were constructed, the area of the shaft graves was rearranged, its level was raised, and it was enclosed by the ring wall made of two parallel rows of vertical slabs. Then its eastern section was cleared and leveled off, and the earth from it and other earth brought from the outside were used to fill the western half, whose level was brought almost to the height of that of the eastern; the retaining west wall was constructed, a good number of stelai were raised to the new level, and the entrance to the enclosure was placed on the

---

[28] Karo, *op.cit.*, pl. XXIV, No. 240.

[29] *Iliad*, XVII, 463-465. Tr. Murray.

[30] Mylonas, "The Figured Mycenaean Stelai," *AJA*, 55 (1951), pp. 134-147.

[31] Keramopoullos' suggestion (*Ephemeris*, 1918, pp. 56-57), that originally it was placed over the rocky top of the small cave he explored in the center of the circle, is conjectural and does not correspond to the facts as recorded by Schliemann.

[32] Marinatos in *Geras*, p. 65 n. 1. Sir L. Woolley, *Ur und die*

Sintflut, pp. 46-47. Papadimitriou told me that the structure found over Grave IV was not an altar at all. For the proof that the "altar" was buried cf. Mylonas, *Ancient Mycenae*, p. 112.

[33] Keramopoullos, *Ephemeris*, 1918, pp. 56-57.

[34] *The Mycenaean Age*, p. 97. Schliemann found a cist grave containing 3 skeletons, Stamatakes cleared at least 4 additional graves cut in the rock in the eastern section (Report to the Archaeological Society of Athens, December 4, 1877), and recently Papadimitriou cleared another.

north section, towards the Lion Gate.[35] This rearrangement and artificial leveling would explain the juxtaposition of sherds belonging to different periods found in the fill of the area. It should be noted that the so-called "altar" was not raised to the new level, as was done for the stelai, and that the cave was filled and abandoned.[36] Wace's conclusions regarding the history of the Grave Circle A met with wide acceptance and were further confirmed by recent investigations. His own work proved that the west wall, which retains the fill and supports a section of the parapet wall, was built in LH III B times, long after the shaft graves were sealed and the area had fallen into disuse.[37] Papadimitriou's discovery of a cist grave under the inner slabs of the parapet proved that the builders of that parapet did not know how far the burial ground extended, a thing which would have been known to them or their employers if the shaft graves and the parapet were contemporary.[38] Grave Circle B proved the steps taken in the making of these circular areas and the shaft graves within them. First an area of a given dimension was surrounded by a wall; then within that area shaft graves and cist graves were dug as the need arose; apparently the construction of the circular wall preceded that of the graves. In this respect the almost identical extent of the area enclosed in both circles is significant. If the parapet wall were contemporary with the graves, it would be difficult to explain why it cuts across the corner of Grave VI and was built over the cist grave cleared by Papadimitriou. Furthermore, we now have a segment of the wall that originally enclosed the circular area of the shaft graves. The wall is proved to belong to the closing years of the Middle Helladic period—to the years, in other words, to which belongs the earliest of the shaft graves. It is interesting to note that the earliest wall, at its eastern preserved end, follows a course further to the northeast than that of the later retaining wall, indicating that it did not cross the corner of Grave VI and that it contained an area wide enough on the east side to enclose the newly found cist grave without encroaching on it. The graves within the circular area were covered with small conical mounds of earth which would indicate only in a general way the extent of the graves. The builders of the parapet wall could not have constructed a wall around these graves that infringe so little on their areas unless they followed the course of a pre-existing wall which de-

termined that area. Perhaps they deviated from the course of that earlier wall at the northeast section so as to allow more room for the construction of the granary which was to be located between it and the west Cyclopean wall. To the evidence outlined above we may add the indications offered by the construction of the parapet. Its wall made of slabs set vertically in parallel rows exhibits a technical knowledge that seems impossible for the closing years of the Middle Helladic period. This becomes especially evident if we compare the parapet with the wall which was built at that time around Grave Circle B (Fig. 86). The latter was constructed with large stones irregularly placed in a style that could be termed "primitive Cyclopean." It seems to illustrate the type of construction characteristic of those years. The double slab-roofed construction of the parapet of Circle A in comparison is a very much more advanced type of work that finds no place in the work of the earlier period. The elaborate entrance with its rectangular sideposts would also be out of place in the architecture of the Middle Helladic period; it can be compared to the deep entrances, to the *stomia*, of the tholos tombs in which it finds its counterpart. For all these reasons I believe that Wace's conclusion that the Grave Circle A was rearranged in LH III B times and that the parapet wall was part of this rearrangement is correct and has been verified by the latest discoveries at the site.

The date of the rearrangement and of the building of the parapet can be determined with a degree of confidence. We have already seen that the retaining wall of the parapet has yielded sherds belonging to LH III B times, indicating that the parapet it supports was made in those times. In the fill over the graves Schliemann found a quantity of sherds and figurines; these are not available now for study and were not fully described by their discoverer. However, among the furnishings of Grave I, Schliemann includes two figurines of which drawings were given.[39] Both belong to the crescent or Ψ type; the one seems to have a solid cylindrical stem, while the other has a hollow and broader stem. Furumark places the type in Late Helladic III B times and suggests that the specimens with hollow foot are later than those with the solid.[40] But how could these late objects be among the furnishings of Grave I? Karo, apparently in an effort to explain the appearance of objects now known to belong to

[35] Wace, *BSA*, 25 (1921-1923), pp. 103-126. It is interesting to note that Adler suggested a similar development of Grave Circle A in the preface of Schliemann's *Tiryns*, p. xxvii.

[36] Nilsson, *Minoan-Mycenaean Religion*, 2nd ed., p. 607, is wrong in stating that "over the tombs stelai and a circular pit-altar were erected." See Wace's restoration of the circle in *BSA*, 25 (1921-1923), pl. 18.

[37] Wace-Stubbings, *BSA*, 49 (1954), pp. 244-247.

[38] Papadimitriou, *Praktika*, 1957, pp. 105-109. It is interesting to note that LH III B sherds are reported to have been found below the layer of stone chips formed at the time of the erection of the peribolos slabs.

[39] Schuchhardt, *Schliemann's Excavations*, pp. 185-186, figs. 159-160. Karo, *op.cit.*, pl. 150 nos. 204-205.

[40] Furumark, *Chronology of Mycenaean Pottery*, pp. 87-88.

Late Helladic III B times in a grave the contents of which should belong to Late Helladic I times, states that they were found in the fill of the graves.[41] Schliemann, however, is definite in recording their provenience; he found them in Grave I with its other furnishings. I suggested, in explanation, that they fell into the grave when the cave was being filled at the time of the rearrangement. That cave is located between Graves I and IV. The north side of the cave, the side towards Grave I, "had an irregular small opening, some 50 cm. in diameter, which perhaps was made when Grave I was dug and which was closed by mud brick." In 1955, at my request, Keramopoullos went over his records and found that in actuality only the lower section of the opening was closed by mud brick, that the upper part was still open at the time of his investigation. Through that opening the figurines must have found their way to the floor of the grave at the time of the rearrangement of the circle when the cave was filled with earth. Since a hollow space or an irregularly filled space always exists between the sides of the walls lining the grave and its fallen roof, such an accidental intrusion is understandable. These figurines, dating from LH III B times, would indicate that the rearrangement took place in those times.

Keramopoullos' cave in the center of the circle was filled in at the time of the rearrangement. In discussing the sherds he found in the fill of the cave, he stated that "they were found mixed (φύρδην μείγδην in his expression) in the entire depth of the cave; some of them belong to the early Mycenaean times, to which belong the older of the Mycenaean graves, others to the end of the Mycenaean period; the last, I repeat, were scattered (κατεσπαρμένα) in all the layers of the cave even in the deepest."[42] This observation proves that the cave was filled in when the leveling and the rearrangement of the circle took place. The latest of the sherds found in the fill of the cave will give its date and that of the rearrangement. Those illustrated in the report belong to Late Helladic III B times.

The ceramic evidence, therefore, would place the rearrangement of the circle and the building of its parapet in LH III B times. The same date is indicated by the sherds found by Wace in the fill between the vertical slabs of the parapet. It has often been pointed out that the west Cyclopean wall to the south of the Lion Gate develops a curve concentric to the circle. This is taken to prove that the wall and the circle as rearranged are contemporary. We have seen

that the Lion Gate and the west Cyclopean wall were built in Late Helladic III B times, rather advanced than early. All evidence, therefore, seems to point to Late Helladic III B, or the middle of the thirteenth century, as the period of the building of the parapet wall and the rearrangement of Grave Circle A.

There can be no doubt that the ruling family whose remains we have in the shaft graves was not that of Agamemnon, for the graves antedate that ruler by three or four centuries. The graves belong to the sixteenth century B.C. and are usually dated from 1600 to 1510 B.C. Grave VI seems to be the earliest, and almost contemporary with it is Grave II. Then come Graves IV and V, Graves III and I being the latest. We may finally note that the shaft graves of Circle A formed part of an extensive cemetery of the Middle to Late Helladic I period. A good section of that cemetery was left outside the citadel when the western extension of the Cyclopean wall was erected. Within the citadel Late Middle Helladic graves were found beneath the Ramp House (four certain and two possible), under the South House (one), and Tsountas mentions a number of cuttings under the House of the Warrior Vase which may have been graves. The "golden treasure," found by Drosinos, Schliemann's architect, at the northwest angle of the Ramp House, could have formed part of the contents of a plundered shaft grave, and there can be no doubt about the plundered shaft grave under the granary.[43]

When Schliemann dug Grave Circle A, in 1876, excavation methods were in their infancy. It was natural, therefore, that a great many observations which could have been made were not made and that many things were not done in the way a modern excavation requires. As a result many problems developed which remained unsolved to date. To illustrate the point we may recall that one of the most successful excavators and scholars of the past few years, Sir Arthur Evans, tried to prove in a learned treatise that what Schliemann found in Grave Circle A were not graves at all but depositories where the contents of graves situated outside the walls of the citadel were transferred for safe-keeping in a period of danger and enemy incursions.[44] For years scholars were hopeful that other shaft graves would be discovered and excavated by modern methods, so that solutions might be provided for at least some of the problems raised by Schliemann's great discovery. That hope was realized in 1952, when the excavation of a

---

[41] Karo, *op.cit.*, p. 68. Even if they were discovered in the fill, they must have found their way in there during the rearrangement of the circle.

[42] *Ephemeris*, 1918, p. 53.

[43] *Mycenaean Age*, p. 111. Wace, *BSA*, 25 (1921-1923), pp. 118 ff.; 48 (1953), pp. 7 ff.; 49 (1954), pp. 232 ff. *Mycenae*, pp.

51 and 61. H. Thomas, *BSA*, 39 (1938-1939), pp. 65-87.

[44] This was advanced for the first time by Percy Gardner in *New Chapters in Greek History*, pp. 76, 78. Sir Arthur Evans, *Palace of Minos*, IV, pp. 237 ff. and *The Shaft Graves and Bee-Hive Tombs of Mycenae*, 1929.

second grave circle was begun. The account of the discovery and exploration of that circle, known now as Grave Circle B, is a story filled with excitement, suspense, and the benevolent intervention of Ἀγαθή Τύχη in the affairs and fortunes of the archaeologist.

GRAVE CIRCLE B

In the spring of 1951, during the restoration of the so-called Tomb of Klytemnestra, a broken stele was found a few meters to the west of the apex of the vault; some of its fragments were still standing on the original base which supported it (Fig. 87). Excavations below the area of the stele revealed the expected sepulcher, which turned out to be a shaft grave similar to those found by Schliemann in Grave Circle A. The grave was cleared and its contents were removed by the Epimeletes of the district, Seraphim Charitonides.[45] It became clear at the outset that not only the type of grave but also its contents corresponded to the remains of Circle A, and this caused great excitement and raised high expectations.

In November 1951 Papadimitriou and I visited the site and examined the area of the new shaft grave. A little to the south of it we detected three stones jutting from the surface which seemed to belong to a curving wall. That observation made us wonder whether they might not be a part of a circular wall enclosing the area within which the new grave was found. In January 1952 we conducted a preliminary investigation which proved that the stones actually did belong to a circular enclosing wall, a good section of which was then detected to the northwest of the excavated shaft grave. From that section we could roughly figure the diameter of the circle, which almost equaled the diameter of Grave Circle A (Fig. 86). Since the shaft grave cleared by Charitonides was not in the center of the indicated new circle but near its circumference, it became evident that within its area more graves were likely to be found.

The importance of the discovery was immediately realized by the Greek Archaeological Society of Athens, and its Council decided to assign the funds required for the excavation from the Pharmakopoulos bequest and entrusted the direction of the project to Papadimitriou, then Ephor of the district, and to an advisory committee composed of Keramopoullos and Marinatos and myself. I had the privilege of collaborating with Papadimitriou in the direction of the work of excavation that lasted from 1952 to September of 1954 when the last grave within the circle was cleared and its contents removed. Some of the objects uncovered are now exhibited in the Mycenaean room of the National Museum of Athens; others, especially vases, are exhibited in the Museum at Nauplion. Only preliminary reports have been published thus far by Papadimitriou in *Praktika* and a general account by me in *Ancient Mycenae*.[46] The final publication, in preparation now, will require some time. Meanwhile the preliminary reports and the account to be given below will help the scholar as well as the layman to obtain a good picture of the discovery.

At the very beginning of the exploration it became evident that some system of naming the graves of the new circle had to be devised to differentiate them from the shaft graves cleared by Schliemann. Since the latter are usually given Latin numerals, we decided to call the new shaft graves by the letters of the Greek alphabet. So the grave accidentally found was called Grave Alpha.

Grave Circle B is located by the side of the modern road to the citadel, some 130 m. to the west of the Lion Gate and only 10 m. west of the apex of the vault of Klytemnestra's tholos (Figs. 68, 69). Of its circular wall only a small segment and a few stones remain today (Fig. 86). A good deal of the eastern side was destroyed in Late Helladic III B times when the so-called Tomb of Klytemnestra was constructed. A glance at the plan (Fig. 88) will show how the circle of the tholos encroached upon the enclosing circular wall, and how by mere chance the excavators of the former missed Graves Alpha and Rho. Apparently a good part of the western section of the circular wall was destroyed when the modern road to the citadel was constructed, but there can be no proof that the wall on that side was still preserved at the time of the modern construction. The southern half of the circular wall, standing on the slope, apparently collapsed at an early period and only very few of its stones can be detected below the slope to the south. As a matter of fact, its southwestern arc must have been ruined before the Historic Era had set in since a Geometric round structure was found built over that area. At the southeast section we have only the three blocks that revealed the existence of a circle. They measure

45 Papadimitriou, *Praktika*, 1951, pp. 197-203.

46 *Praktika*, 1952, pp. 427-472; 1953, pp. 205-237; 1954, pp. 242-269. Mylonas, *Ancient Mycenae*, pp. 128-175 and figs. 40-87. Mylonas, Papadimitriou, *Archaeology*, 5 (1952), pp. 194-200;

and 8 (1955), pp. 43-50. Marinatos, *Geras Keramopoullou*, pp. 54-86. In 1963 the task of the final publication of Circle B and its contents was assigned to me by the Greek Archaeological Society.

only 1.10 m. in length, while the preserved north arc has a length of some 16 m. From that length, the diameter of Circle B can be figured as close to 28 m., almost the same as that of Circle A. The preserved north arc was somewhat damaged when the aqueduct of the village was carried across its width; however, it still suffices to offer a good account of its construction.

Large, unworked stones roughly cut and of uneven size and height, set erect by each other, form the inner and outer faces of the wall and are laid on a prepared layer of thin and small flat stones which project a little beyond their base. On top of this first course smaller stones were piled and all interstices were filled with even smaller stones and clay. The area, between the inner and outer face of the wall, was filled with small stones and earth rather carefully piled. The construction could be termed "primitive Cyclopean." The wall has a thickness of some 1.55 m. and attains a maximum height of 1.20 m. The northern section seems to be preserved to its original height since its top is level; the wall therefore can be considered a parapet. In many parts, its top was found covered by a thin layer of dust and chips that resulted from the final working of poros or of fine conglomerate. The layer extended into the circular area for more than 2.50 m. in the neighborhood of Grave Nu. The pottery found around and in the wall is Middle Helladic—gray, black, yellow Minyan, and matt-painted—and proves that the circular wall, and consequently Circle B, was built in late Middle Helladic times.

Within the circular enclosure 24 graves were found, of which only 14 can be considered shaft graves. The others were cists cut in the soft rock and trench-like graves dug in the earth. These less important graves, illustrate the manner in which the cist graves in Circle A reported by Schliemann and Stamatakes were found. Some of them certainly antedate the shaft graves at the side of which they were found, others seem to be contemporary. Two examples of earlier sepulchers infringed upon by shaft graves will be sufficient to prove the point. The east side of Grave Alpha[1] was cut away when Grave Alpha was being constructed. In it we found a well-preserved skeleton, laid in a contracted position on its left side, minus the skull. Apparently the skull was destroyed during the construction and any furnishings the grave might have contained were then removed. Grave Tau was revealed to the builders of Grave Lambda during the construction of the latter. Its contents, skeletal remains, and possible furnishings, were cleared out completely and its shaft was filled with stones and earth. On the other hand, Graves Zeta, Eta, and Theta seem to be contemporary with the early burials in the shaft graves and to belong to people of lesser importance.

All three are regular cist graves cut in the soft rock. The contents of Grave Theta were destroyed in 1946 when the aqueduct of the village was accidentally made to pass over it. A bronze sword is reported to have been found in it, but it was badly smashed by the laborers constructing the channel and its fragments have disappeared.

Grave Zeta measures at its floor only 1.90 m. by 1.10 m., and has an average depth of 60 cm. A single skeleton in a strongly contracted position was found in it, lying on its right side and facing north. Seven clay vessels and a bronze knife with an ivory pommel were found in front of the torso. Three of the vases were goblets and cups of Middle Helladic shapes, one a spouted jug, and the last one a prochous.

Grave Eta is another cist cut in the rock, measuring 1.10 m. in length, 75 cm. in width, and 62 to 65 cm. in depth (Fig. 89). It contained a single skeleton in a strongly contracted position, on its right side. A bronze knife was found in front of the torso, and with it five vases; two of these were stemmed goblets of Middle Helladic type, the third a spouted jug, the fourth a smaller jug, and the fifth a bowl.

In contrast to the cists, the shaft graves found in Grave Circle B are more numerous and somewhat more complex in construction. The greater number, fourteen, has yielded information sufficient to explain the details of their construction, thus providing answers to a number of questions raised by Schliemann's work. In size they range from 3.80 m. in length, 2.80 m. in width, and 3.50 m. in depth (Grave Gamma dimensions at the top) to 2.75 m. in length, 1.80 m. in width, and 2 m. in depth (Grave Xi dimensions at the top). They consist of a vertical shaft, more or less rectangular in form, cut through the earth and the rock below it. The sides of the shaft from the floor to a point 70 cm. to 1.25 m. above it were often lined with thin walls ranging in thickness from 30 cm. to 40 cm. The walls along the short sides of Graves Beta, Gamma, and others were made of sundried mud brick, while those of the long sides are in rubble masonry. Sometimes (Graves Delta, Sigma) instead of a wall a ledge was left in the rock, by cutting the rock farther back in the upper section of the shaft. Shelf or lining walls were used to support wooden beams placed near each other across the width of the grave. These formed the frame of the roof, which was completed in one of two ways. Sometimes flagstones were placed horizontally on the beams to close the opening completely. These were covered with a thick layer of water-resisting clay of yellowish hue, now known to the villagers as *plesia*. The best example of this method was found in Grave Lambda where the coat of clay averaged 15 cm. in thickness.[47] At other times instead of flagstones they placed over the beams a matting of dry branches, leaves, and twigs and this was covered with a layer of *plesia*, averaging 30 cm. in thickness. Grave Gamma provided the best example of this type. I believe that the roofs of most of the shaft graves of Circle A were composed of matting covered with *plesia*; this will explain the absence of flagstones in the remains of those sepulchers. The remains of clay found in the graves by Schliemann caused him a good deal of anxiety and wonder; now they can be explained as remnants of the roof structure. Thus the roof of the shaft graves stood at least 70 to 80 cm. above their floors and formed a cavity or burial chamber.

The lower part of the shaft used for the burial was securely sealed and protected from seeping water by its roof covered with *plesia*. The upper part of the shaft was filled with earth. At the line of the surface of the soil the perimeter of the grave was outlined with stones loosely placed and in the area thus outlined earth was poured to form a small mound, rising to a height of perhaps 40 to 50 cm. On the top of the mound a marker was placed. Sometimes, as is the case with the Graves Alpha, Gamma, Omikron and Nu, stelai were so placed. Other times, as is the case with Graves Xi and Upsilon, a pile of small stones was placed on the top of the mound. Before the mound was completed or the stele set, a funeral meal was eaten at the grave. The sea-shells and the bones of the animals consumed were placed in a layer over which the top of the mound was poured and the stele was erected.

In Graves Beta, Pi, Kappa[1], and Upsilon, there was only one burial. In others the number ranged from two (Graves Iota, Nu, Xi, etc.) to four (Grave Gamma). The order of burial is evident. For a single burial the roof was sealed, the upper section of the shaft was filled, quite often with the crushed rock obtained from excavating the shaft, the mound was formed and the stele was erected after the funeral meal. The shaft and its fill were no longer disturbed. In that fill, as a rule in its uppermost layers, were found only the remnants of the funeral meal, i.e., bones of animals and sea-shells. When the grave was to be used for a second burial, the stele or marker was removed together with the mound and the earth over the roof; the layer of *plesia*, the flagstones or the matting of the roof, and the beams supporting them were removed, and the second body was lowered to the floor of the grave. If there was insufficient room for it on the floor, the bones of the person buried previously were swept against the sides or pushed to one of the corners of the grave. Some of the furnishings were piled over the swept bones, others were placed outside the grave proper over the roof,[48] or were scattered in the earth that was used to fill its shaft; some were even carried away by living relatives. Thus room was made for the second occupant and his furnishings. Then the roof was rebuilt, the shaft over it was again filled with earth, the funeral meal was held, the mound of earth over the grave was completed, and the marker or stele was again set over the top of the mound. This process was repeated every time other members of the family had to be interred in the same grave. It is interesting to note that the fill over the roof of graves used for one burial is almost free of potsherds or other articles; the fill of graves in which more than one person was buried contained many potsherds and broken pots, and even fragments of other articles proving that furnishings of the earlier burials were thrown out of the grave. In the fill of Grave Gamma which contained four skeletons, for instance, were found not only the bones of animals consumed in the funeral meals but also a great quantity of sherds, from which some forty vases were pieced together. Along the edge of the roof of Grave Nu on the west side, a group of eight vases were disclosed arranged in two rows, while in its fill more sherds were found and with them some pieces of boar's tusks known to have been used to cover or adorn helmets. More pieces of boar's tusks were found among the bones that were swept to the side of the grave when the last burial was made. It seems possible to assume that one of the relatives participating in the last burial carried away a helmet perhaps of leather, decorated with boar's tusks, belonging to the person buried previously. Perhaps some of these tusks broke away when he lifted the helmet, while others came apart as he was perhaps participating in the funeral meal or was helping to fill in the shaft with earth. The sherds and vases found in the fill formed part of the furnishings of the first burial. Large pots belonging to the last burial were found embedded in a clay ledge beyond the feet of the skeleton.

The floor of the graves was covered with a layer of pebbles. These were assumed by Schliemann to have been placed to help the cremation of bodies. Actually they were placed in accordance with an old Middle Helladic custom and their function was to provide drainage. We may note that no trace of cremation was found in the numerous graves of Circle B and none was held. On the pebbly floor the bodies were placed supine and usually in an extended position. In very few cases, as in Grave Epsilon, the bodies were laid in a contracted attitude. In at least three

---

[47] Mylonas, *Ancient Mycenae*, fig. 77.

[48] *Ancient Mycenae*, fig. 65, Grave Nu.

cases, Graves Gamma, Mu and Nu, the body was laid in an extended position supine but with feet together and knees apart (Figs. 90, 91). This posture caused a great deal of excitement and various complicated and ingenious theories were advanced in explanation. Finally a simple interpretation perhaps approaches the truth. Apparently in this case the body was laid supine but with knees bent so that the heels rested on the floor. When advanced decay loosened the tendons and the flesh, the legs gradually slid to the side, giving the bow-legged appearance to the lower limbs.[49] No trace of wooden coffins was found in any of the graves, but apparently the body was lowered on an animal pelt which was spread out over the pebbly floor. The decomposed remains of such a pelt were found under and on either side of the skeleton of Grave Nu. Occasionally the head was somewhat raised, a pile of pebbles under the head forming a low pillow. This was the case in Graves Iota and perhaps Nu. Sometimes men and women were buried in the same grave; Grave Gamma contained the skeletons of three men and one woman. At other times women were buried in separate graves as in Graves Mu, Omikron, and Upsilon. Over graves Omikron and Gamma unsculptured stelai were found, perhaps confirming Schuchhardt's hypothesis that the unsculptured stelai found by Schliemann in Grave Circle A were originally erected over graves of women. Over Grave Gamma besides the unsculptured stele, one bearing a sculptured representation was found; but that grave contained the skeletal remains of three men as well. Grave Xi contained the skeleton of a very small girl who was buried last in it. We should note, however, that possibly some of the bones swept aside and found piled in corners and along the sides of graves may belong to women; their state of decomposition did not permit definite identification of sex.

Apparently the bodies were laid in the graves dressed in their fineries. We have already noted that a thin band of gold was found under the fallen lower jaw of the skeleton in Grave Nu (Fig. 91) and that gold ornaments were found around the wrists of the body in Grave Iota. Evidently they were gold trimmings decorating the edges of the garments in which the men were buried. In Grave Omikron a number of bronze and silver pins with elaborate rock crystal heads were found evidently used to fasten a woman's garment. The women especially were decked with ornaments such as earrings, necklaces, rosettes worn like a modern corsage; bands of gold and gold foil in the form of leaves or cruciform rosettes all decorated in repoussé were worn as diadems (Fig. 93). Graves Epsi-

lon, Mu, Omikron, Xi, and Upsilon provided good examples of such ornaments. In the graves of Circle B there were none of the gold discs decorated in repoussé that were found in such abundance in Grave III of Circle A. Comparatively few gold ornaments were found worn by men. In Grave Beta, perhaps one of the older graves of the circle, an armband of electrum was found still in its original position, and two other gold bands near the pelvic area which may have belonged to a shroud or the garment in which the man was buried.

Around the bodies were arranged carefully their belongings and grave furnishings (Figs. 90, 92). Vases constitute the most numerous class of objects found in the graves of Circle B. This contrasts sharply with the few vases reported by Schliemann from the graves of Circle A; but perhaps the lowly pots viewed in comparison with the gold treasures he found, did not impress him as being worthy of record or preservation. Large vases, often decorated, were placed along the short sides of the grave, as a rule, above the head and below the feet of the bodies (Fig. 92). They seem to have contained supplies; oil certainly—as is proved by the impregnation with oil of the biscuit—possibly wine and honey. One of the large pots found in Grave Iota contained a powdered substance that seemed to be flour made of millet. Jugs, that may have contained liquids, goblets, and cups are very common. We have already noted the stemmed goblets of a Middle Helladic type found in the cists Zeta and Eta. Similar stemmed goblets were found in Graves Beta, Nu, Iota, etc. Gold and silver cups, although not very common, were found in Graves Gamma, Iota, and Nu. The gold cup from Grave Nu is especially interesting for the grooved decoration in two registers to be seen on its sides and the dotted pattern pressed on the bottom and around the rim (Fig. 94). The resulting arrangement is very beautiful and brings out the decorative possibilities of the metal. A silver cup found in Grave Iota also presents a delicate, vertically grooved face. It is worth noting that clay cups were the only objects found in the earlier graves of Eleusis that belong to the latter half of the Middle Helladic period. They seem to be the first type of funeral gear placed in the grave when, perhaps under Minoan influence, the custom of placing objects in the sepulchers was adopted. They bring to mind the fact that drinking cups are the indispensable and often the only equipment of pilgrims, mendicants, and traveling monks even today. Were the cups and liquids placed in the graves to be used in the long and dreary trip to the lower world? Were these clay vases discarded

---

[49] For a similar attitude of a skeleton see the contents of a grave at Ras Shamra of the "Ugarit Moyen I" period; C. Schaeffer, *Ugaritika*, II, p. 54 and fig. 20. Professor E. Vanderpool kindly informed me that some of the skeletons he uncovered in the chamber tombs of the Agora were in a similar attitude.

and broken when the bones were swept aside, because it was assumed that the trip was completed and the vessels were no longer needed?

The absolute date of the gold and silver cups cannot be determined from their form and decoration but the vases of clay fall definitely into established categories whose chronological limits are determined. A good many of the vases, as we have seen, are high-stemmed goblets of a type usual in the latter half of the Middle Helladic period, and their yellowish clay indicates the closing years of that period. A number of vases are decorated with geometric patterns painted in matt color. They are characteristic of the latter half of the Middle Helladic period. Others make use of motives of birds and plants known from Phylakope of Melos. A jar found in Grave Alpha bears a decoration of a wavy band in creamy white color on a dark gray, almost black, ground reminiscent of the light-on-dark technique of the Middle Minoan IIIβ period. In the same grave a cup of the same period is made of faïence, the rim decorated with a spray of flowers. Some vases have a decoration in brilliant black to reddish brown color applied on the buff surface, characteristic of the transitional period of the Middle to the Late Helladic period and of the early years of the Late Helladic I. The vases found in the graves and their fill, therefore, are very important not only because of the customs they illustrate but because of the chronological evidence they provide and also for the picture they give us of the artistic activity of the people.

Swords and daggers are the special furnishings of men. We find them in numbers laid beside the bodies and within easy reach of the deceased (Figs. 90-92). They are made of strong bronze and could have been used in real life. Perhaps they were weapons used by the deceased during his lifetime and placed in the graves because of the primitive belief that the departed wanted to take with him personal objects that he valued in life. The swords are of the two types distinguished by Karo in his study of the weapons from the graves explored by Schliemann.[50] The type with rounded shoulder (Fig. 95) is the longer, averaging some 94 cm. in its blade. The type with the horned shoulder has a shorter blade not exceeding 70 cm. Each has a central rib, which is sometimes toothed; in very few cases a design was chased on the blade or the shoulder of the sword (Fig. 95). The handles were of perishable materials and were sometimes covered with gold sheathing, but they always seemed to be topped by pommels of ivory or alabaster (Fig. 96). It is instructive to note that a good knife or dagger is

always found with the sword and to recall that sometimes Homeric warriors carried a knife in addition to their trusted swords.[51] The blade of the example found in Grave A was silver-plated and had on a central band a design of connected spirals. Was it a Mycenaean custom to carry the two together, a habit still remembered in Homeric times?

Handles of both swords and knives, were secured to the blades by means of rivets, which often survive (Fig. 95). From Grave Delta we have a striking example of a sword whose sheathing over a wooden handle is preserved (Fig. 96). Its ribbed blade of bronze measures 94.5 cm. in length and is decorated on both sides with a series of engraved griffins. Its shoulders are rounded and possess a small central tang over which was placed the haft, apparently of wood. This was covered by a sheathing of gold, made of two plates front and rear, similarly decorated. The sheathing of very thin gold leaf was so worked around the shoulder of the blade as to give the impression of horns, and it was attached to the haft by small gold nails, a few of which can still be seen. Its repoussé decoration is of great delicacy: the cylindrical part is covered with connected triple spirals, while the ends, on either side of the blade, are terminated by two snub-nosed heads of lions. Their manes are graphically rendered by means of triangular incisions, while a pellet bears the triangular eye with a central dot. On each of the two horn-like projections of the sides, we find engraved the head of a smaller animal, having lozenge-shaped eyes with a dot in the center. Could this be the head of a goat and the entire composition a harbinger of the chimaera notion? Above a gold ring we have the regular ivory pommel of Mycenaean times, badly decomposed but still keeping its original shape and dimensions; the pommel measures 10 cm. in maximum diameter, while the length of the gold sheath is 12.5 cm. and its maximum width between the horned edges is 8.5 cm. The sheathing can be compared to that found by Schliemann in Grave IV,[52] which for a time was considered as the top of a scepter, but now is rightly known as belonging to the hilt of a sword.

No daggers with inlaid decoration were found in Circle B, but on a dagger from Grave Alpha we find on its bronze blade a central narrow band which originally was filled with a different material, perhaps by a silver strip that has perished. A broad knife from Grave Iota possesses a rather long tang above its broad shoulder, in which was fitted and glued a tiny, cylindrical handle of rock crystal (3 cm. in length). The

50 Karo, *Schachtgräber*, pp. 201 ff.
51 So did the Mycenaean Agamemnon in *Iliad*, III, 271-272; XIX, 252-253.

52 Schliemann, *Mycenae*, nos. 451, 452, p. 28. Schuchhardt, *op.cit.*, p. 250. Tsountas and Manatt, *Mycenaean Age*, p. 168, fig. 63. Karo, *op.cit.*, pl. 87 no. 294.

swords and daggers were often wrapped in linen cloth. The best examples of this came from Grave Nu. But scabbards of wood covered with linen and of leather seem to have been common. Naturally the leather has decomposed completely but its presence was indicated by the brownish matter that resulted. Clear remnants of such scabbards were found in Graves Nu and Lambda. The leather scabbard in the latter apparently was decked with gold trimmings.[53]

Other weapons found in the graves of men comprise spearheads and arrowheads. The best spearhead found comes from the first burial of Grave Nu. It was wrapped in linen and is perfectly preserved.[54] Apparently its blade was first covered with oil or fat and then wrapped in linen and to this treatment its excellent preservation evidently is due. It has a long cylindrical socket the opening of which is rolled and has the appearance of a thick ring. Around this long socket were preserved remains of cord, ending below in a primitive tassel. Apparently the cord was used to tie and decorate the wooden shaft of the spear, traces of which were found in the socket. The wooden shaft was further decorated by a narrow gold band, part of which was found coiled in a gold cup near the point. A similar gold band was found coiled around the remnants of the wooden shaft projecting from the socket of another spear point found in Grave Lambda. Fourteen stone arrowheads were found bundled together in Grave Delta. In Grave Lambda were revealed twenty-four arrowheads, twenty of which are of obsidian, grouped together. Apparently in both instances they were held in a bag. No defensive weapons were found in the graves, but perhaps the boar's tusks discovered in Grave Nu and its fill may indicate that the weapons supplied to the person who was first in that grave included a helmet, made of felt or leather, decorated with tusks. As we assumed above, that helmet, if it existed, seems to have been removed later by relatives.

Among the various objects found in the graves the following are the most interesting. A mask made of electrum was found in Grave Gamma, but not in its original position (Fig. 97). It seems more primitive in form than those found by Schliemann in Graves IV and V. Holes of attachments are evident beyond the ears and they were made by nails driven through the electrum plate. Further study of the mask will be required before any final conclusions are reached, but it is clear that it was not attached to a wooden coffin.

Also in Grave Gamma, among the piled furnishings was found a perforated bead of amethyst, 9 mm. in extreme length, on which a vivid portrait is carved in intaglio.[55] It is a bearded head, but without moustache, with long hair, reminiscent of the long-haired Achaeans, a rather broad skull, and an almost Grecian nose with both nostrils showing in a manner so beloved by our contemporary painters (Fig. 98). The eye in full front is vivid, and the modeling of the high cheekbones extraordinary. The ear, large for the head, is high but effectively placed. One wonders whether this portrait is an effort to represent one of the chieftains buried in the grave. That would be difficult to maintain, but it is possible to suggest that in general it does give the appearance of the Mycenaean rulers. Perhaps it will be instructive to compare the head on the gem with the archer represented on a steatite vase from Knossos of Late Minoan II times illustrated by Evans.[56] The trunks worn by that figure, resembling those we find worn by the hunters in the lion-hunt composition on the dagger blade from Grave V, may indicate that the man on the steatite vase is also a Mycenaean. Perhaps it will be more interesting to stress the ability of the artist who was able to produce such a vivid portrait in miniature without the help of a magnifying glass or diamond points. Of course, Evans maintained that the Minoans used discs of clear rock crystal as magnifying glasses, but such have not been found in the mainland of Greece.

Another engraved gem comes from Grave Mu, in which the skeleton of a young girl was found. It is horizontally perforated and formed part of a small necklace made up of semiprecious stones. It is of carnelian and biconical in shape, perforated on its long axis. Its design, carved in intaglio, represents a large tree with spreading branches, perhaps a palm.[57] It grows out of a spherical form which looks almost like a large vessel with two handles on either side of its neck. At a little distance to the right and to the left branches frame the central element. The spherical object could be taken to be a "flower-pot," but it will be nearer the truth to interpret it as a boulder, symbolic of the earth from which the tree grows. Rendering of boulders in this fashion is common in Minoan-Mycenaean art; it was used extensively by gem carvers.[58] What seem to be handles are the lower two branches of the tree whose tips touch the boulder. One might perhaps see here the "returning to earth" branches of the Anatolian "Tree of Life." Beads of

---

[53] Mylonas, *Ancient Mycenae*, fig. 79a and b. These gold ornaments find exact parallels in the gold articles pictured by Schliemann, *op.cit.*, p. 253. nos. 367-370; Karo, *op.cit.*, pl. 83.

[54] Mylonas, *Ancient Mycenae*, fig. 68.

[55] Cf. Papadimitriou, *Praktika*, 1952, p. 446. Biesantz: *Marburger Winckelmanns-Programm*, 1958, p. 13 ff., Blegen, in *AJA*,

66 (1962), p. 247.

[56] Evans, *Palace of Minos*, III, p. 106. Cf. also IV, part 1, p. 218.

[57] Mylonas, *Ancient Mycenae*, fig. 80.

[58] See among others, Evans, *Palace of Minos*, IV-2, p. 488, fig. 417a, b, etc.

semiprecious stones, but without carvings, were used to make necklaces as we have seen. Examples were found in all the graves of women, Graves Mu, Omikron, and Upsilon. A third engraved gem was found among the beads of semiprecious stones which formed one of the necklaces deposited with the body of the woman of Grave Omikron.

The object most worthy of description is a bowl made of rock crystal in the form of a duck that was found in Grave Omikron (Fig. 99). The body of the duck forms the bowl, its tail a flat spout at one end, while the neck and the head, which is turned backward in a most elegant manner, is used for a handle. The mastery with which the shape of the bird was adapted to the design of the bowl, the exquisite workmanship, the definite and graceful contour lines, and the thinness of its translucent walls, make this bowl the outstanding find from Circle B and an excellent sample of the advanced art of the lapidary. Although bowls in the form of birds are known, especially from Egypt, ours is the first example of its type unearthed in Greece.[59]

The furnishings found in the graves of Circle B, may be neither as numerous nor as glittering as those found in Circle A, but they are as important and impressive. Of greater value is the fact that we can now see exactly how they were arranged in the graves in relation to the body and what function they performed. This could not be pictured fully from Schliemann's descriptions, most of which are vague and somewhat influenced by afterthoughts. When the remains of Grave Beta were revealed, it was the first time that scholars were able to look into a shaft grave and see and study its contents as they were left at the time of burial so many centuries ago. Although it was one of the poorest shaft graves of Circle B, it was very impressive and it caused great excitement among scholars. Similar and greater excitement and enthusiasm were created every time the contents of another grave were revealed and cleared. The impression made by some of the finds of Grave Epsilon will remain vivid in the minds of those present. The roof had caved in before any earth found its way into the cavity of that grave to cover its floor. Consequently the flagstones used in the construction of that roof were found covering its contents. When two of the slabs were lifted a mass of gold ornaments was disclosed in the area covered by them. The impression created by the sudden appearance of these crushed gold ornaments can hardly be described; certainly it will never be forgotten. As we looked down on them, we were car-

ried back in one instant beyond the mythological era of Greece to the days when the greatness of Mycenae was being fashioned by the people whose ornaments were shining brightly once more beneath the rays of a Greek sun.

The importance of finding and studying the furnishings laid in the shaft graves justifies, I believe, the full description of a few burials.

Grave Iota contained a clearly defined arrangement of furnishings around the body (Fig. 92). The bones of the legs were disturbed by the fallen roof and consequently their position will remain undetermined, but it is evident that the body was laid supine with a slight turn toward the right side. The head, originally elevated by an arrangement of pebbles below it, finally rolled over the right shoulder. The arms were stretched alongside of the body with elbows slightly bent and hands directed toward the pelvic area. Along the right side were laid a bronze sword with an ivory pommel, a pair of bronze tweezers, and the bronze knife with the cylindrical handle of rock crystal. Around each wrist were found two triangular gold bands decorated in repoussé. Tiny attachment holes are evident. Two other narrower gold bands ending in circular pendants, reminiscent of the vertical bar of the "garter type" ornament (the *Gamaschenhälter*), were found in the abdominal section. Could they have decorated a belt?

Beyond the sword, in a line almost parallel to it, were found a number of vases, stemmed goblets of the Middle Helladic type and matt-painted pots, while beyond the feet were found four large matt-painted jars and three smaller vases. Of these at least one, decorated in black matt paint with a band around the neck and solid triangles suspended from it, seems to have contained oil. Nothing of its contents of course survived, and only at the bottom did the earth found in it have an oily feel, but its clay biscuit was so impregnated with oil that when its fragments were being put together and their joins were heated before gluing, the odor of oil filled the small laboratory. The second jar seemed to have contained flour. By the southwest corner of the grave the heaped bones of an earlier burial were found and among them a well-preserved, fluted, single-handled cup of silver.[60] Of course that could not have been the only furnishing of the earlier burial. It is evident that the balance was thrown out of the grave and the most useful and precious were carried away by those who participated in the second burial.

[59] For a fragment of a duck vase in ivory from Asine, see Frödin-Persson, *Asine*, pp. 388 and 391, fig. 254. For two ivory pyxides with a duck lid from Ras Shamra, see *Syria*, 1932, p. 6 and pl. VIII, 2. Cf. also Furtwaengler and Loeschcke, *Mykeni-*

sche Vasen, p. 14, fig. 3 for a find from tomb 31 of Ialysos, Rhodes.

[60] Mylonas, *Ancient Mycenae*, fig. 71.

A number of articles were as a rule placed around the bodies of men. In one case three vases only were found with the skeleton. This was in Grave Gamma where four skeletons were found, three of which were well equipped (Fig. 90). The skeleton of the fourth was found placed obliquely along the width of the grave and beyond the feet of the others, stretched from east to west with the head at the east. The hands were apparently held locked over the pelvic area. The head seems to have been turned to the right side and faced north. The three vases, two cups and a hydria with matt decoration of concentric circles, were a little beyond the face. At the time of the excavation it was believed that the skeleton was that of a woman, but Dr. Angel's careful examination proved that it belongs to a young man, about twenty-eight years of age. The skull showed evidence of a fracture and an extremely clean-cut trepanation done just before death.[61] Was death precipitated by the operation? This is the first and oldest instance on record of such an operation in Greek territory, antedating, as a matter of fact, the examples known from Egypt. Apparently the skeleton belongs to the third person buried in the grave, and the vases that belonged to the two persons previously buried were thrown out of the sepulcher to make room for him. We perhaps recall that the fill of the grave contained a great quantity of potsherds from which some forty vases were put together. This quantity of vases and the furnishings of the other occupants of the grave are in sharp contrast to the paucity of objects found near the head of the last skeleton—not a single weapon and only three rather small vases. Could this fact indicate that the young man was an unimportant member of the family, or that he died before he had a chance to amass wealth and fame which would entitle him to a more elaborate funeral gear? His case will bring to mind the middle skeleton of Grave V, whose lack of funeral furnishings, in contrast to the rich gear of the other two occupants of the grave, caused Schliemann to assume that he was despoiled in antiquity. That such spoliation was practiced will be illustrated a little later. However it is doubtful that only one out of three skeletons, and that the middle one, was despoiled; the lack of rich furnishings should perhaps be attributed to the fact that he was not a favored member of the family.

The most completely preserved example of a burial of a woman was revealed in Grave Upsilon (Fig. 100). It is a rather small and shallow grave, its perimeter indicated by the usual row of stones marking the edges of the mound which covered it. A pile of stones at the top of the mound formed its marker. On the floor, paved with pebbles, lay the well-preserved and fully extended skeleton of a woman. Around it, nine vases were found, of which at least four were typical Middle Helladic stemmed goblets; one is a matt-painted jug or prochous, and one a small matt-painted askos. The skull had rolled over the left shoulder, but over the right temple were still to be seen, at the time of the excavation, three leaves of gold decorated in repoussé, that once formed a head ornament. They were supported by a narrow bronze band which went around the skull and were held in place by three bronze pins found in their original position. Over the left shoulder another decorated gold band was found; originally it seems to have held a braid over that shoulder. The lady wore a large double necklace made of small beads of semiprecious stones, of gold, and of silver, and some amulets of faïence. Under each temple a circle of silver was found, apparently her earrings, while to the right of the skull, and between it and the matt-painted jug three bronze rings and five pins, two of silver and three of bronze came to light. One of the bronze pins had a beautifully grooved head of rock-crystal. This grave, the last of the series to be excavated in the closing days of the 1954 campaign, although not so rich as others, yielded not only invaluable evidence for the burial customs of the closing years of the Middle Helladic period but a complete female skeleton.

Grave Omikron, the sepulcher of a woman, contained more valuable furnishings,[62] among which were the rock crystal duck-bowl (Fig. 99), pins with rock crystal heads, once believed to have been scepters,[63] but now proved to have been used for garments, a ten-petaled rosette made of thin gold leaf kept in place by a central pin (Fig. 111), gold bands decorated in repoussé (Fig. 93), a gold necklace of beads in the form of stylized flying birds, and a long and most impressive necklace made up of 119 beads of amber and three rectangular spacer-beads with complex borings (Fig. 102). The specialist who examined these beads concluded that they are of Baltic amber.

The skeleton of the woman was found completely decomposed. In this connection it is interesting to note that skeletal remains found directly below the fallen flagstones of the roof were badly decomposed. Apparently the moisture that seeped under the unprotected flagstones brought about almost complete decay. This was true of Grave Omikron. In graves with roofs of matting, as in Grave Upsilon, or in which the skeletal remains were covered with earth that seeped

---

[61] I am indebted to Dr. L. Angel, now of the Smithsonian Institution, for the information regarding the trepanation. Another and cruder example is now reported from Lerna.

[62] Mylonas, *Ancient Mycenae*, figs. 56, 58, 59. Our Figs. 99, 136.

[63] Schliemann, *Mycenae*, p. 201 and nos. 309, 310.

in with moisture through the roof, the bones were well-preserved.

In the northwest corner of Grave Epsilon, a grave of women, a bronze crater some 75 cm. high, excellently preserved, was found lying on its side and within it a bronze jug, some 44 cm. tall, equally well-preserved. Both are similar to those found in Grave IV, and what is more interesting, they were found in exactly the same relative arrangement—the jug in the crater.[64] In Grave IV two women were buried along with men; in Grave Epsilon the last person buried was a woman. And one wonders whether bronze vases of the type found were placed in graves of women; yet no bronze vases came from Graves Mu, Omikron, and Upsilon, which proved to contain the remains of women.

A child burial was disclosed in Grave Xi.[65] The remains of the person who was buried first in the well-like shaft grave were pushed aside even before they were fully decomposed. On the cleared floor the body of a little girl, some five or six years of age, was laid out in an extended position. Around it were placed some ten vases, stemmed goblets, jugs, and a large matt-painted amphora, which was placed immediately above the head. Around the skull there was placed a diadem made of a gold band on which were secured at short intervals three cruciform rosettes of thin gold foil decorated in repoussé. All were kept in place by means of bronze pins. Along the temples were suspended loops of beads of rock crystal, carnelian, and amethyst, while thin gold bands coiled in small rings originally kept her curls in place. Around her neck was found a necklace made of rock crystal beads with a rectangular pendant of bluish faïence decorated with lozenge-shaped elements, reminiscent of the Masonic emblem, and parallel small bars along its short edges. A pair of simple earrings and a ring of coiled gold wire around the little finger of the left hand completed her attire.

One more object should be noted: a small gold, nut-shaped article, which was hollow. Perhaps tiny pebbles that would rattle when shaken were placed in it. Could it be a Mycenaean rattle, a cherished toy which a loving mother, perhaps, placed in the grave of a beloved girl? The exploration of Grave Xi gave us a few sentimental hours, and the small, pathetic-looking bones of the tiny girl—of our little princess, as we called her—brought home the sense of helplessness which lies upon human beings, great or small, famous or lowly, when the hour of death arrives. Today the visitor will find but a deep hole in the ground when he visits Grave Xi, but when on its floor were still lying the remains of our little princess, decked in her ornaments and surrounded with vases, it presented a striking picture of the life and customs of a remote and forgotten past.

DESPOILING OF GRAVES

We have noted repeatedly how objects belonging to older burials were removed from the grave and some even carried away by relatives. Apparently despoiling a grave was not considered a religious offense. Grave Lambda has given us the best and most complete example of such a spoliation carried out in Early Mycenaean times. Lambda is one of the large sepulchers of Circle B, measuring 3.65 by 2.68 m. Its roof, made of flagstones covered with a layer of *plesia* averaging 15 cm. in thickness, had caved in before the area over the floor was filled in with earth. The skeleton of the last burial was found, crushed by the flagstones, lying on a layer of pebbles in the center of the grave. To our great surprise we found absolutely nothing on the body or around it. By the east side of the grave we found bones of a skeleton which had been brushed aside at the time of the last burial, although there was room enough on the floor for two persons. Among and under the piled bones were disclosed a bronze knife and three complete bands of gold decorated in repoussé with holes for attachment. These finds proved that the family using the grave had no objection to the custom of placing furnishings in it. It became evident therefore that the furnishings of the last burial had been removed. Above the north end of the west side of the grave immediately under the roof construction was detected a hole (75 x 55 cm.) which apparently was made by the makers of Grave Lambda I (Fig. 88). Under the hole on the floor of Lambda along its west side, we found a small pile of earth and stones. When we removed this pile, we found a number of weapons which had luckily survived. The most important of these was a bronze sword over the upper part of which were piled the following articles: a broad knife with a handle of ivory apparently in a wooden scabbard, a triangular dagger whose handle seems to have been decorated in silver, and a bronze spearhead with remnants of its wooden shaft and gold decoration. Under the shoulder of the sword was a moon-shaped ornament of gold foil; a little farther down was another elongated oval ornament of gold decorated with

---

[64] *Ibid.*, pp. 274-275 nos. 436, 437.

[65] Mylonas, *Ancient Mycenae*, figs. 62-63.

twisted gold bands at its end, and outlined at the tip with gold cord. These gold ornaments decorated the leather scabbard of the sword. The handle was gone; apparently it was made of perishable material that decayed completely; but the gold ring, in two sheets, which formed the connection between the handle and the ivory pommel, as well as the pommel itself, were found. A band of gold, in two sheets, was also found near the handle, perhaps forming the decoration of the *telamon* or baldric, from which the sword was suspended. Near the pommel were disclosed twenty-four stone arrowheads, twenty of which are of obsidian, grouped together as if they were originally held in a bag. These furnishings definitely indicate that the person buried last was originally provided with rich furnishings.

These objects, the pile of earth and stones covering them, the hole under the roof, and the complete absence of furnishings around the person buried last, prove definitely that Grave Lambda was despoiled before its roof had caved in. The hole indicates the means through which access was obtained by the people who entered and despoiled the grave. The pile of earth and stones over the objects, which covered them up and protected them against detection, was made when the hole was accidentally cut and perhaps intentionally enlarged and when the despoilers entered the grave. There can be little doubt that the despoilers were the makers of Grave Lambda I, whose vases will indicate that the robbery occurred in the early years of the Late Helladic I period, a few years, in other words, after the last burial was consummated.

The second case is a striking example of rebuilding and spoliation at a later period. It is connected with Grave Rho. Originally this was a shaft grave. Many years later its shaft was increased considerably and within it a new grave was built of poros stones. The remnants of the person or persons buried in the shaft grave, a few bones, were found piled up against the side of the grave and on top of its roof shelf. Of the furnishings the shaft grave might have contained, only a broken goblet and a cup were stacked with the bones. The built sepulcher within the enlarged shaft grave is composed of a passage leading to a burial chamber (Fig. 103). The roof of the chamber is completely preserved, but that of the passage was removed in the past. The side walls both of the corridor and of the burial chamber are vertical up to a certain height and then incline inwards, reducing the area to be spanned to only 30 cm. That span was covered by horizontal slabs; thus resulted the type we called saddle-roof. The joints of the poros blocks of the passage were filled with *plesia* to make them water tight, while those of the blocks of the burial chamber in addition were

covered with strips of stucco on which were painted broad bands alternately red and black in color. The floor of the burial chamber, though cut in the rock, was paved with poros blocks. Its doorway to a height of about a meter above the floor is vertical; above that height its courses incline inward to form a pointed arch over the apex of which projects the edge of the first slab of the roof, like a terminating cornice of a façade. One feels that the arched upper part of the door-opening corresponds to the relieving triangle of the façades of Late Mycenaean structures. The face of the door opening was covered with solid red color. It should be noted that the opening was not found blocked by a wall. This elaborate and unique sepulcher built within a shaft grave, gave rise to high expectations but it was found to be completely empty. Even the bones of the person or persons buried in it had been removed. That it was used for burial was indicated here and there, especially by a fragment of a skull bone found in the chamber. In the northeast corner of the burial chamber and in a worn-out spot of its poros floor we found a carved gem, a bead of chalcedony on which in intaglio was represented a horned animal running with head turned backward. Gold foil found in the fill at its north end and by its west side, and fragments of pottery found in that loose and peculiar fill also indicated that the grave had been used, that it was emptied of its contents some time later.

The story of Grave Rho emerged clearly from its remains and its fill. Long after the shaft grave was sealed, it was accidentally found by someone who wished to have his grave built in that area. The shaft was then more than doubled in extent. The bones of its early occupant or occupants were removed from the floor and some of them were packed against the side of the grave and on top of its shelf. Of the furnishings found with the bones only one broken goblet and a cup were stacked with the bones; the rest apparently were taken away or were thrown out of the grave. Within the enlarged shaft was built in poros the grave with the passage and the chamber. Within that burial chamber the body of a person of means was deposited and around it were arranged perhaps rich funeral furnishings. The roof slabs of the passage were secured and the shaft was filled with earth. Years later, exactly when we cannot know, intruders dug up the northern half of the grave—the half over the passage where the loose fill was found—removed its roof slabs, descended into the grave, and emptied its chamber. The gold foil and the broken pieces of pottery found at the northwest area of the fill indicate that through that section of the grave its contents were removed. Then the opened part of the shaft was filled again and remained untouched until our times.

A number of questions arise in connection with this grave. The most pressing has to do with the reason for its clearing. To my mind there can be no doubt that the grave was robbed and its contents were appropriated by living Mycenaeans. But if the grave was robbed, why was it emptied of its bones as well? It seems reasonable to assume that the despoilers wanted to make sure that nothing was left of the gold foil ornaments which may have covered the body, that consequently they took the bones out to the light before they removed the last particle of gold. It has been suggested also that perhaps the descendants of the person buried in the built grave at a later date removed the skeletal remains of their ancestor and his furnishings to deposit them again in a more sumptuous family grave, in a tholos tomb for example. This assumption, however, will leave without an answer a number of questions. In 1951, 1952, and again in 1953, in the area beyond the northwest side of the grave toward the center of the circle more foil was found, fragments of vases, a number belonging to three large palace-style amphoras, pieces of ivory, among which an almost complete ivory rosette, fragments of vessels made of alabaster, a small piece of lapis lazuli later proved to be an Egyptian carved scarab, and the like. There can be no doubt that these objects were part of the furnishing of the built grave since the fragments of pottery among them matched those found over the northwest section of the grave and were put together to result in the completion of two amphoras now in the Nauplia Museum.[66] If the furnishings were removed to be deposited in a new grave they would not have been dispersed and broken. Between Graves Alpha and Delta, that is, in the area immediately beyond the

northwest corner of Rho, was found in 1952 a pile of bones without any furnishings laid in the earth; we called them a bundle burial. No other example of such a burial was found and we could maintain with reason that the bones found are the remnants of the person who was buried in the built grave, whose skeletal remains were removed when the chamber was emptied of its contents. This, too, will indicate that the grave was despoiled.

In spite of the fact that its contents were not preserved, Grave Rho remains a most important example of Mycenaean grave architecture. It has no parallel in the mainland of Greece. Striking parallels are to be found in the built graves of Trachona in Cyprus,[67] of Ras Shamra, and of Minet-el-Beida. Of course, absolute equation is not possible, since the last two possess steps in the dromos, niches and windows in the chamber, and exhibit differences in the details of the construction. One of the striking similarities, beyond structural details, is that the doorways of the Ras Shamra examples are never blocked by a stone wall, a feature so typical of Mycenaean graves; however, Grave Rho also lacks a blocking wall. Since the Ras Shamra built graves have long antecedents and Grave Rho is the only example found in Greece, one may assume that it was the result of Syrian influences. There can be little doubt that by LH II close contact existed between Greece on the one hand and Syria and Egypt on the other. To these contacts may be attributed the construction of Grave Rho, which is unique for Greece.

The date of the grave, sometime in the fifteenth century B.C., is well established. The date of its spoliation will remain unknown, as well as its despoilers. But its spoliation will give us another example of the practice in Mycenaean times.

STELAI FROM GRAVE CIRCLE B

The stelai found in Grave Circle B are comparatively few, for apparently a grave was usually marked by a pile of stones. Stelai were found, as we have seen, over Graves Alpha, Gamma, Nu, and Omikron. Of these only two, over Graves Alpha and Gamma, were sculptured. The poros stele of Grave Alpha bears on its upper section an incised representation of a charging bull attacking hunters (Fig. 87). The work is

rather crude, but compares well with that on fragments x and xi of Grave Circle A.[68] One of its fragments was found still standing on the base, consisting of a thick slab bearing along its longitudinal axis and in the middle of its width a rectangular cutting in which the stele was inserted and made secure.

Of somewhat higher artistic merit is the sculptured stele found over Grave Gamma (Fig. 104). The stele

[66] *Ibid.*, fig. 86. For additional pictures of Grave Rho see figs. 83-85.

[67] C. F. A. Schaeffer, *Mission de Ras Shamra*, II, pp. 30-92, figs. 75-85, and pls. xv-xvii; "Reprise des recherches archéologiques à Ras-Shamra-Ugarit," *Syria*, 28 (1951), pp. 1-21 and especially fig. 1. H. Th. Bossert, *The Art of Ancient Crete*, figs. 493-494. E. Gjerstad *et al.*, *Swedish Cyprus Expedition*, I,

pp. 461-466. Papadimitriou, *Praktika*, 1954, pp. 244-259. For the Grave of Isopata near Knossos, to which Grave Rho could be compared, see Evans, *The Prehistoric Tombs of Knossos*, and *Palace of Minos* IV, part 2, pp. 771 ff.

[68] Heurtley, *BSA*, 25 (1921-1923), pp. 126-146 and especially pp. 136 ff.

evidently was used later as a base block, since a rectangular cutting was made on its face, characteristic of stelai bases. It is made of poros and its face is covered with carved decoration in technique similar to that in the stelai of Class II from Circle A; in other words, the design is produced by cutting away the immediate background around the figures and patterns. Consequently, the figures are flat, but they have strong contour lines and some decorative quality. The area to be decorated, almost the entire face of the stele, is framed by two fillets and is divided by a raised band into an upper, larger register decorated with connected spirals and a narrower lower register filled with a figured composition. A good deal of the decoration was cut away when the stele was transformed into a base, but the compositions are clear. The spiral motif is well known from Stele 1428 from Grave V; the figure decoration has no parallel. In the lower part of the composition two lions stand on their hind legs on either side of a central unit now mostly missing. Beside the rear legs of the lion to the left we find the rear legs and the end of the tail of another animal. Above the lions on either side are two human figures. The one to the right stands brandishing an object with both hands, perhaps a long knife similar to those found in Grave IV or to the one held by the standing figure on Stele 1428. Since it is held by both hands, it may be better perhaps to see in it a short, stout club. The other man is represented as wounded or dying, but certainly hurled on his back, with legs still in the air and arms outflung. Over the fallen man, to fill the space, the sculptor added another of those geometric forms which is usually interpreted as an altar, while at the lower left corner of the composition, behind the legs of the lion, he inserted what looks like the Egyptian sign WAZ.[69]

The tail and rear legs in front of the lion to the left must belong to a large animal, possibly a bull or a cow or even a horse, rearing up on its hind legs and thus filling the space between the two lions and the two men—a large animal which is being attacked by lions. The subject of an animal being attacked by two others is a common Minoan theme, here treated in a typical Mycenaean fashion and perhaps given a narrative content. We may now note that while the lion to the left is standing vigorously on its hind legs and is bending its neck in a characteristic attitude of attack, the lion to the right seems to be lying on its haunches with its tail on the ground line and head fallen back. While the one lion is attacking briskly, the other is perhaps lying stunned or wounded. If we bring the human forms into the composition and relate them to the

animal scene—and there is no reason why we should not—then we may conclude that one of the men, having successfully attacked one lion, is continuing his assault, while the other is disabled by the wild animals. The story told by the relief is clear: two lions attacking a herd, are set upon by two men and in the skirmish that follows one of the men is killed or seriously wounded. Thus the stele may perhaps represent the activities or death of one of the first men buried in the grave.

Along with the sculptured stele, over Grave Gamma, were found a large segment of an unsculptured stele of shelly sandstone and a half of another base. These do not offer us additional information regarding the setting up of stelai since they were not found *in situ*. The fragments of the unsculptured stele found over Grave Omikron are not very helpful either since they were removed by the peasants from their original place in 1946. We get some information from the stele of Grave Nu although it is preserved in fragmentary condition. As a matter of fact, only four small pieces of its lowest part are preserved, but these were found still standing on the base. Of that base only one segment survives; the fragments of both stele and base, however, are in their original position and illustrate the way the stelai were set up (Fig. 105). The stele is of shelly limestone, and the fragments found do not show any signs of relief work. However, these are so small that definite conclusions as to whether the stele was sculptured or not are impossible. It was definitely established that the stele was oriented east and west. On the basis of the information provided by these fragments Papadimitriou was able to recognize a number of blocks found in Circle A, now lying around its area, as belonging to the bases of stelai which stood over the shaft graves in that circle.

A glance at the plan of Circle B (Fig. 88) will indicate that the graves were arranged around its perimeter, that an area in the center was left unused. At first we thought that perhaps that area was reserved for a shrine or altar where the funeral rites were held. However, the complete excavation of the area proved that such a shrine or altar was never constructed. Perhaps the circle was abandoned before it was entirely filled with graves. The position of the entrance to the circle is equally uncertain. It is evident that it could not have been located on the north, east, or south side, because in those sides its area is occupied by graves which left no room for a passage. The west side, lying below the modern road remains unexplored. We rather favor the southwest section. In that section we find a free passage between Graves Epsilon

---

[69] For the use of that Egyptian symbol in Mycenaean Greece see Marinatos, *BSA*, 46 (1951), pp. 106-108. For the interpretation of the composition of the stele, *Geras*, p. 74.

and Gamma on the one hand and Mu on the other. Furthermore, below Grave Mu we have an area known as Kappa[2] where a peculiar horseshoe-shaped enclosure made of mud brick was found. The function of this structure and area remains unknown. Perhaps it

was used in connection with the burial ritual, in which case it must be located near the entrance of the circle. Here we may add that nowhere in the area of the circle was evidence uncovered to indicate, let alone prove, the existence of a cult of the dead.

CHARACTERISTICS OF MYCENAEAN BURIAL

The summary description of the graves found in Circle B will permit only a few generalizations; final conclusions will be possible only after the complete and definitive study of the objects found and the publication of the architectural plans. We have already made whatever generalizations are possible, but these should be considered as preliminary and subject to revision and correction. The burial customs, however, of the period emerge clearly even from the preliminary report. It is established that the only mode of burial was inhumation; no traces whatever of cremation were found. The graves were occasionally used for the burial of one person, but usually more members, presumably of the same family, were laid in the same grave. Very often the bones of the previous burial were swept aside and left in a pile by the side of the grave or in one of its corners to make room for the later burials. At this time some of its furnishings were destroyed, smashed, put out of the grave, or even carried away by relatives. The last conclusion is justified when a comparison of furnishings found with the piled bones and those around the skeleton of the person buried last is made. The latter were carefully arranged around the body, which was usually deposited in an extended position on pebbles with which the floor was covered. Sometimes the body was lowered on an animal pelt which was left in the grave. It seems that spoliation of graves and bodies, even by relatives, was not considered an impious act. Some of the furnishings may have been articles used in actual life, such as the swords and knives; others, such as the gold bands and trimmings decorated in repoussé, may have been made especially for the grave. After burial a funeral meal was always held, a low mound was piled over the grave, and then a marker was erected, either a stele or a pile of stones.

The date of the various graves has to be determined in the final publication. Here it may be suggested that the earliest burials in Circle B must be placed in the latter half of the Middle Helladic period, in the closing years of the seventeenth century B.C. The latest burials belong to the LH I period in the sixteenth century. It is evident that some of the graves of Circle

B are contemporary with those in Circle A, which are usually dated from 1600 to 1510 B.C. Consequently for some time at least the two circles were used concurrently. Marinatos has made the suggestion that such a use may indicate the existence of two branches in the royal family of Mycenae—each circle belonging to one of the branches, reflecting the practice of the succession of kingship from brother to brother and then to the son of the first.[70] An example of this practice in Mycenae itself is recalled in the tradition preserved in the *Iliad*: Atreus was not succeeded by his son Agamemnon, but by his brother Thyestes, after whose death Agamemnon became the king. At any rate, both sets are graves of the ruling family of Mycenae of the end of the seventeenth and the sixteenth centuries B.C.

As was the case in Circle A, most of the graves of Circle B belong to mighty warriors. According to Dr. Lawrence Angel, of the Smithsonian Institution, who studied the skeletal remains, these chieftains "had massive as well as tall bodies, since both the vertebrae and the thickness of all long bone shafts are extra large." They average 1.706 m. (5′ 7⅛″) in height, "over 0.06 m. taller than Middle Bronze Age commoners," and at least three of them, in Graves Gamma, Zeta, and Nu, were over 1.80 m. (about six feet) tall.[71] Perhaps we have the appearance of one of them in the amethyst bead from Grave Gamma, and maybe a general indication of features in the electrum mask from the same grave. All the available evidence proves that they do not belong to the Minoan type; they certainly belong to the group of people who laid the foundations of the greatness of the Mycenaean state. It is evident that they will remain nameless. We noted the example of trepanation, one of the earliest skull operations on record in the history of European medical practice. Funeral furnishings were not found with the skeleton of Grave Sigma. Perhaps they were removed when Grave Lambda was constructed. But between the lower right ribs and the iliac crest two green-brown, faceted, and polished "stones" came to light. In the words of Dr. Angel: "They are gallstones, suggesting a rich and perhaps truly 'Homeric hero' diet." The man suffered also from arthritis.

[70] Marinatos, *Geras*, pp. 83-86.
[71] To Dr. Angel I am indebted for the information regarding the skeletal remains.

The shaft graves seem to be characteristic of Mycenae. The only other examples known are reported from Lerna, Berbati, and Pylos; but those graves were found empty.[72] Their form seems to have developed from the Middle Helladic cist grave and the development was influenced by the existing local conditions. Elsewhere, different conditions imposed a different development of the Middle Helladic cist grave. This is excellently illustrated by the sepulchers of the west cemetery of Eleusis. The rock of that locality is extremely hard, perhaps almost impossible to cut as required in the making of the shaft graves. The sepulchers had to be constructed in the soft earth. Consequently they developed along the lines we discussed above and resulted in long rectangular graves covered by huge slabs with a side entrance, differing from the shaft graves.

The grave circles of Mycenae are the only ones of their kind known from the mainland of Greece, and their antecedents remain uncertain. One may wonder why the area of the royal graves was given a circular form; was the shape imposed by superstitious beliefs or religious traditions? A rectangular area could have served as well and a fence around it would have been simpler to construct. The Minoan cemetery at Mallia has a rectangular form and contains a multitude of graves.[73] The circles at Mycenae were not derived from the circular ossuaries of Messara, which precede them in date, since their shaft graves indicate that they have no relation to the Cretan structures.[74] Perhaps in the round graves of Nidri, in the island of Lefkas, disclosed by Dörpfeld[75] we may have an early prototype; the cists within the stone circular enclosures could have been developed into shaft graves and their numbers increased. We may even believe that in the tumuli, such as the one at Drachmani cleared by Soteriades or the tumulus of Aghios Ioannes in Messenia discovered by Marinatos,[76] we may have the structures which influenced the making of grave circles. For the time being the solution to the problem is not forthcoming and the circles at Mycenae remain the unique royal burial grounds of the Early Mycenaean period.

---

[72] J. Caskey, *Hesperia*, 24 (1955), pp. 32-34, considered to be as old as Grave VI. For an example from Berbati see Caskey, *op.cit.*, p. 34 n. 16. See also N. Platon, Κρητικὰ Χρονικά, 3 (1949), pp. 534-573. For the Pylos' example, Blegen, *AJA*, 67 (1963), p. 159 and pl. 31, fig. 13. There it is dated LH I-II or even Middle Helladic. For possible prototypes for the shaft graves from Anatolia cf. Mellink, *Aegean and the Near East*, p. 39. In the closing days of the summer of 1965 Marinatos discovered a shaft grave at Peristeria in Triphylia with some of its original furnishings.

I am indebted to Professor Marinatos for this information.

[73] P. Demargne, *Mallia. Exploration des nécropoles*, pl. 38, plan 1.

[74] S. Xanthoudides, *The Vaulted Tombs of Messara*, 1924.

[75] W. Dörpfeld, *Alt Ithaka*, 1927, Beil. 37-41.

[76] G. Soteriades, *Ephemeris*, 1908, pp. 93-94. S. Marinatos, in *Ergon*, 1954, pp. 42-43, fig. 55 and *Praktika*, 1954, pp. 311-315, fig. 12.

THOLOS AND CHAMBER TOMBS

Menippos: . . . Show me Helen; I shall never be able to make her myself.

Hermes: This skull is Helen.

Menippos: And for this a thousand ships carried warriors from every part of Greece; Greeks and barbarians slain, and cities made desolate?

Hermes: Ah, Menippos, you never saw the living Helen; or you have said with Homer,
> *"Well nigh they suffer grievous years of toil*
> *Who strove for such a prize."*

We look at withered flowers, whose dye is gone from them, and what can we call them but unlovely things? Yet, in the hour of their bloom these unlovely things were things of beauty. (Lucian: *Dialogues of the Dead*, XIX; tr. F. G. Fowler.)

While the shaft graves were still in use, two new types of graves make their appearance in the Mycenaean world and are used concurrently for the better part of a century. These came to be known as chamber tombs and tholos tombs. The former were used by the people in general; the latter were used for the burial of the king and the immediate members of his family. Unlike the shaft graves, which seem to be characteristic of Mycenae and whose life span covered a century, chamber and tholos tombs were made in the entire Mycenaean area to the end of the Mycenaean era. Only where geologic conditions were prohibitive, chamber tombs were not constructed. Again, Eleusis' west cemetery can be used to illustrate the point. Since the hardness of the rock prevented the Eleusinians from building chamber tombs, we do not have such rock-hewn graves there, but elsewhere in Attika—at Spata, for example, at Perati, Varkiza, Voula, the Agora of Athens—chamber tombs cut in the rock of the hillside are common. However, the type was so popular that even at Eleusis, towards the end of the period, a few chamber tombs were made, but they were dug in the earth and not hewn in the hillside.[1]

Both types of graves are well known and have often been described. At the very beginning we must stress the fact that they did not follow the shaft graves, as it was maintained until recently, but for a time were used concurrently with them. That is, the notion that the first tholos and chamber tombs were made when the last shaft graves were no longer in use, does not correspond to the facts.[2] Again, it has been maintained that the new graves mark a change in the burial customs of the people.[3] The shaft graves come down to the end of the LH I period, while some of the chamber tombs and at least a few of the known tholos tombs go back to the very beginning of LH I.[4] The different types of graves were used concurrently during the LH I period. We shall see that the burial customs illustrated by the contents of the chamber tombs do not differ from those presented by the remains of the shaft graves. Only the types of graves differ, and to that we shall return after our description, but we may now state that the chamber and tholos tombs, as far as the type is concerned, could not have developed from the cist graves of the Middle Helladic period or from the shaft grave type and that they appear suddenly and with parts and functions fully developed.

CHAMBER TOMBS

The chamber tombs are underground, cave-like graves cut horizontally into the slope of a hillside (text fig. 23). They are composed of two parts: a chamber and a *dromos*, which is the horizontal approach or passage to the chamber. The *dromos* was left open to the sky and usually almost at right angles

---

[1] Mylonas, *Praktika*, 1954, pp. 50-53.

[2] Wace, *BSA*, 25 (1921-1923), p. 391.

[3] Tsountas, Μυκῆναι καὶ μυκηναῖος πολιτισμός, pp. 146-147, 242 ff. Adler in Schliemann's *Tiryns*, p. xxxi. Wace, *BSA*, 25 (1921-1923), pp. 119-120 and *Mycenae*, p. 22.

[4] Cf. Blegen, "An Early Tholos Tomb in Western Messenia,"

Hesperia, 23 (1954), pp. 158-162. For chamber tombs cf. Blegen, *Prosymna*, p. 388, where it is specifically stated that the oldest group in Chamber Tombs XXV and XXVI is "contemporary with the early shaft-graves at Mycenae." And Wace, *Chamber Tombs*, pls. I-IV. In Chamber Tomb 1 at Volimidia-Pylos, I found LH I sherds with packed bones and Marinatos reports that a vase

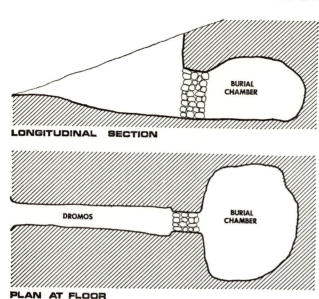

LONGITUDINAL SECTION

PLAN AT FLOOR

23. Mycenae. Plan of chamber tomb (after Wace)

to the chamber and the slope.[5] Its floor inclines either gradually or sharply, depending on its length, so as to allow enough depth to make possible the carving of the chamber completely in the rock. Sometimes the required depth is attained by means of steps. In LH III times the *dromos* is usually long (Tomb 505 at Mycenae has a *dromos* 35 m. in length) and its sides, at least in the territory of Mycenae, incline inwards so that the opening of the *dromos* is very much narrower at the top than at the bottom. Sometimes niches are cut in the walls of the *dromos*, as a rule near the floor line or a little above it. The *dromos* leads to a rectangular doorway, with a horizontal lintel and sides inclining slightly inward, thus making the opening at the top somewhat narrower than at the bottom. No thresholds or arrangements for a door are known, but occasionally the façade of the doorway was covered with plaster and decorated in color with rosettes or other geometric patterns. The doorway is often deep, looking like a small passage, and this is known as the *stomion* of the grave. It recalls the deep entranceway of Grave Circle A. The chamber, hewn entirely in the living rock, presents a variety of shapes ranging from oval to round to rectangular, and of varied dimensions. The largest chamber tomb at Mycenae measures 5.50 by 6.50 m. and has a height of

6.50 by 7 m. The roofs of the chambers are also varied and their shape depends in the main on the quality and hardness of the rock in which they were hewn. Most of the Mycenaean roofs are "slightly hipped." Some of the chamber tombs of Messenia and of Triphylia, explored by Marinatos, have an almost round chamber and a domed roof. In some examples side chambers are to be found; in others, niches are cut in the walls. Again, on the floor of some, both in the *dromos* and in the chamber, pits or cists were dug; in others a bench is to be found in the chamber, built or carved out of the rock.

Burial Customs

The chamber tombs were family graves and were used over and over again in the course of the centuries. It is a well-established fact that in Mycenaean times inhumation was the general mode of burial. Thus far a unique cremation was found at Traghana in Triphylia, dating from LH II times.[6] A pot containing the ashes from a cremation was found in the door packing of Grave 41 of Prosymna, apparently dating from the closing years of the Mycenaean Age,[7] and at Perati eleven examples of cremation were found belonging to the LH III C period.[8] These are but very few examples compared to the hundreds of burials thus far explored, and they tend to prove that although cremation may have been known, especially in LH III C times, inhumation was the well-nigh universal mode of burial. The dead were placed in a more or less extended position on the floor of the chamber without regard to a fixed orientation; sometimes the lower limbs were pulled up, at other times the legs were bent at the knee and feet placed side by side. Sometimes the head was raised on a support. We have no evidence from Mycenae or Prosymna that coffins were employed for the burial, but sometimes the bodies were left on the wooden litters on which they were taken to the grave.[9] Possessions, gifts, and vessels containing supplies, the grave furnishings, were carefully arranged around the body. Vases were the most common objects deposited in the grave; ornaments and personal possessions were also common; sometimes even tools were placed by the body. Apparently after the burial a toast was drunk in honor of the interred, and the goblet used for the purpose was

from Grave 3 of the same cemetery is identical with one from Shaft Grave III; *Praktika*, 1952, p. 479.

[5] For descriptions and discussions of these tombs see especially: Tsountas, *Ephemeris*, 1888, pp. 119-180. Wace, *Chamber Tombs at Mycenae*, especially pp. 121-146, and *Mycenae*, pp. 13-19, 26-46, 119-131. Blegen, *Prosymna*, pp. 228-263. Persson, *The Royal Tombs at Dendra Near Midea*; *New Tombs at Dendra*; *Asine*, pp. 356-359.

[6] Marinatos, *Praktika*, 1955, pp. 251-254.

[7] *Blegen, Prosymna*, p. 242.

[8] I am indebted to Dr. S. Iacovides, their discoverer, for the information. See also *Praktika*, 1953, p. 68; 1955, pp. 102, 104; 1956, p. 68 and *Ergon*, 1963, p. 21.

[9] Persson, *The New Tombs at Dendra*, p. 162 where the grooves occurring in the *stomion* of tombs are declared to have been used for skid poles.

smashed against the doorway of the chamber.[10] Fragments of these shattered cups found in a number of graves attest to the custom. Then the *stomion* and door were completely blocked by a stone wall; sometimes, however, the wall was not carried to the lintel but a small opening was left at its very top.[11] Next the *dromos* was filled with earth, recalling the χεύειν χυτὴν γαῖαν, the piling of earth, typical of Homeric burials. A funeral meal seems to have concluded the burial rites, and a marker was placed over the grave for identification. This was either a stele or a mere boulder.

When a second death in the family occurred and the grave was to be used again, the earth from the *dromos* and the wall blocking the doorway were removed and the body with its funeral furnishings was laid on the floor at the side of the earlier burial. The door and *stomion* were blocked, a toast was offered, and the *dromos* was filled again, the funeral meal eaten and the marker erected. This procedure was repeated over the years as the need arose and as long as the grave remained in use. When the floor was filled with bodies, the remains of those buried previously and their furnishings were swept aside against the walls of the chamber, or were placed in side chambers and niches, or swept into holes and cists cut in the floor of the chamber or of the *dromos*. In a few cases the bones of ancestors were carefully packed, and in even fewer instances individuals were buried in cists so that their skeletons remained undisturbed. As a rule, however, the bodies were laid on the floor of the chamber and the skeletons were later brushed unceremoniously aside. In a few cases, bones and shattered furnishings were thrown out into the *dromos*, in order to make room for later burials. In general, the operation of clearing the floor of the chamber was characterized by complete indifference and disrespect for the bones of ancestors. Wace, who cleared a good many chamber tombs and had a chance to formulate the burial customs of the people, states: "Sometimes in clearing the chamber for new occupants the remains of previous interments were quite obviously thrown out pell-mell into the *dromos* . . . by the later members of the family without much regard for the remains of their ancestors."[12] Blegen, who cleared some fifty chamber tombs at Prosymna and noted their peculiarities and characteristics, remarks that bones and furnishings were swept into a heap to make room for later burials, "the bones and other objects in the heaps were always found to lie in utter confusion and disorder; and it was clear that the actual

physical remains of the dead were held in little respect, when the time came for a subsequent burial."[13] It should be especially noted that on the occasion of the clearing up of the floor, the older furnishings were shattered, and apparently objects of value, such as weapons of metal, jewelry and the like, or of use, seem to have been carried away by the very relatives of the deceased.

This behavior, in contrast to the reverence and care exhibited for the bodies and their furnishings at the time of burial, perhaps sheds some light on the beliefs of the Mycenaeans regarding an existence after death. It can be explained only if we assume that the Mycenaeans believed that the spirit of man, what Homer called the "psyche," was sentient and remained in the grave as long as the flesh was in existence. During this time, apparently, the corpse had to be treated with respect; it had to be provided with supplies; it had to be given favorite objects which belonged to it in life. The moment the flesh was dissolved and the body was transformed into a pile of bones, it was apparently believed that the spirit was released from this world, that it had descended into its final abode in the realm of the spirits never to return to the world of the living. It was believed perhaps that it was no longer interested in the affairs of living men, nor could it influence their future. So the bones could with impunity be swept aside or even thrown out of the grave. The fact that the furnishings were stolen and broken when the flesh had disintegrated indicates that it was believed that the deceased needed them no longer; that they were not meant for use in the lower world but only for the trip to that world. The end of the journey was indicated by the complete decay of the flesh. The fact that ornaments of precious metal and even weapons of bronze were taken by the descendants seems to indicate that personal objects were laid in the grave with the body, not to serve it in the lower world, but because of fear of exciting the anger and revenge of the dead by withholding objects in which he had pleasure in life—anger which could be a potential carrier of disaster during the period when the dead were still sentient and abode in the grave, during the time, in other words, when the flesh was still intact. We must also note that the grave furnishings were not renewed from time to time, nor were additional offerings placed in the graves in the years which followed burial.

Signs of fire, remnants of charcoal and ashes found in chamber tombs, are now regarded as the results in the main of fumigation and purification of the cham-

---

[10] Blegen, *Prosymna*, p. 238. Wace, *Chamber Tombs*, p. 131.
[11] Tsountas, *Ephemeris*, 1888, p. 129. One of the chamber tombs excavated in 1964 at Mycenae presented such an opening.

It was used for a single burial.
[12] Wace, *Chamber Tombs*, p. 130.
[13] Blegen, *Prosymna*, p. 247.

ber necessitated by its long use and the repeated burials over many years. Some may be attributable to the rites of burial performed in the graves. Often enough the fires were lighted on the floor of the grave without regard to the skeletal remains and furnishings existing there and so bones and sherds were blackened and disfigured.[14] This again indicates a disregard for the bones of those who had been buried previously. No evidence of embalming was found in the chamber tombs excavated thus far, and it seems certain that this art was not practiced by the Mycenaeans. The number of buttons of terra cotta or of steatite found in the graves proves that the bodies were laid fully clothed on the floor. Among the furnishings vases are the most usual and conspicuous. Usually of excellent quality, they are often decorated with brilliant painted designs. The spiral was a favorite motive throughout the age, but plant and marine motives were common, especially in Late Helladic II times. They were at first rendered in a realistic manner, but with the passing of years they were more and more stylized until they became mere decorative patterns.[15]

Figurines Found

Small terra-cotta figurines are characteristic grave furnishings of the Late Helladic III period[16] (Fig. 106). The meaning of these figurines has not been established as yet to the satisfaction of all, and at times various interpretations have been advanced. They seem to appear abruptly perhaps in LH III A times and are characteristic of the closing centuries of the Mycenaean era. There are long-horned animals, a few chariots, three-legged chairs, a man making bread, but the majority represent female figures. These have been divided into various types, the most important of which are types Φ and Ψ and the *kourotrophos* type. All three types possess a cylindrical lower part, in earlier examples solid, in later hollow, but type Φ has an oval, flat torso which lacks arms, a pinched-in face, and a flat, triangular head. Occasionally figurines of this type are modeled with a *stephane*, or wreath, on the head. Their sex is clearly indicated by well-modeled breasts placed high on the flat torso. Figurines of type Ψ possess an equally flat torso with

less prominent but still well-defined breasts, but their shoulders are drawn out sharply to form wing-like projections, giving the torso a crescent or sickle shape. They also have pinched-in faces with prominent noses and triangular, flat heads which as a rule are covered with a stephane or polos. From the rear edge of the headgear originates a narrow and flat plastic band, dotted horizontally with color, reaching from neck to the waist. The *kourotrophos* type (Fig. 107), as the name implies, are female figurines identified by the form of a baby thrust against the breast and held there by atrophied hands, or precariously stuck against the stripes below the breasts. A variation of the *kourotrophos* type are "multiple figurines" (Fig. 108), two examples of which are thus far known, both coming from graves. Two figurines of type Φ are attached to each other at the side, like Siamese twins, and bear a child on their common shoulder.[17]

Of the odd examples found in graves we may mention a figurine representing a man or woman kneading dough, a figurine that originally was perhaps seated on a three-legged throne, and a female figurine of the crescent type seated on a weird animal in the collection of Mme. Stathatou of Athens.[18]

Figurines of the various types were also found in settlements and in what seem to have been shrines, but the majority in our collections were discovered in graves. Unfortunately there is no record of the conditions under which most of the figurines known to be from graves were found. Some were discovered in the piles of bones swept aside and against the walls of tombs, and therefore their original position will remain unknown. Others were found in disturbed context; of still others we have no information whatsoever. Only a few were actually found in primary burials and of these only rare photographs exist (Fig. 110). And yet the conditions under which figurines in graves were discovered will, I believe, help us considerably in determining their meaning and function. Long ago Kandanes remarked that a good many of the figurines found in the Nauplia district came from graves of children.[19] Recently Blegen observed that the majority of the figurines he found in Prosymna came from child burials.[20] All the figurines we found

14 Cf. for example Wace, *Chamber Tombs*, pp. 140-141. Nilsson, *Minoan-Mycenaean Religion*, 2nd ed. pp. 595 ff. *Prosymna*, p. 251. In some graves were found incense burners in which perhaps aromatic gum was burned; clay and bronze scoops, which may have served as lamps; braziers and typical lamps. All these apparently were used in the burial rites. Sometimes the partly decomposed remains were covered up with earth for further protection of the living. Wace, *op.cit.*, p. 137. Blegen, *op.cit.*, pp. 251-252.

15 *Infra*, pp. 198-201.

16 Tsountas, *Ephemeris*, 1888, pp. 168-169. Blegen, *Zygouries*, pp. 203-206 and *Prosymna*, pp. 355-360. Wace, *Chamber Tombs*,

pp. 215-217. Furumark, *The Chronology*, pp. 86-89. A figurine from the Pylos tholos tomb is reported to belong to the LH II/III times; Lord William Taylour, *The Mycenaeans*, pp. 80-82.

17 Mylonas, "Seated and Multiple Mycenaean Figurines," in *The Aegean and the Near East*, p. 120, pl. xv, 9 and n. 43.

18 Blegen, *Annuario*, 1946-1948 (= 1950), pp. 13-16. From the tablets we learn that the bakers were men. For the figurine in the Stathatos collection see Doro Levi, *Studies Presented to David M. Robinson*, I, pp. 108-125, pl. 4, a,b. Mylonas in *The Aegean and the Near East*, pp. 112-113. *Infra*, p. 115.

19 Kandanes, Ἀθήναιον, H (1880), p. 520.

20 *Prosymna*, p. 256.

in situ in the Mycenaean graves of Eleusis were among furnishing provided for children[21] (Fig. 110). Papadimitriou found figurines in children's graves in the chamber tombs of Varkiza and Voula, and Iacovides reports figurines only in children's graves in the cemetery of Perati.[22] In spite of all the cases noted in the last twelve years, we cannot prove that such figurines were never placed in the graves of adults although I could find no verified undisturbed male burial containing figurines. We can, however, definitely assert that they are characteristic finds of children's burials.

Based on the evidence obtained at Prosymna, Blegen suggested that some at least of the terra-cotta figurines found in graves are toys for children, while others could be representations of nurses. This suggestion was rejected by Persson, who compared the Mycenaean figurines to the *ushebtis* of Egypt and attributed to them a similar function.[23] Nilsson, accepting Persson's interpretation, suggested that figurines of the Φ and Ψ types when found in shrines should be interpreted as votaries and representations of divinities, respectively, but when found in graves as filling a function comparable to the *ushebtis*. Noting especially Tsountas' observation that figurines were found only in a few graves and that most of these were proved to be the poorer sepulchers, he maintains that "anyone who was unable to procure jewelry and costly things, thought to make up for the want by these cheap figures which, however, it was imagined would procure a luxurious afterlife for the man who had not known much but work and necessity in this life."[24] This interpretation seems to us unacceptable. If these inexpensive figurines were capable of securing comfort and ease in the lower world, then we would expect to find them in every grave. Human beings, rich or poor, have always been anxious to secure a future of comfort and ease and to pile up assurances for the days to come. That no religious or other scruples prevented the rich from using figurines is indicated by the fact that such figurines were found in some rich graves. The fact that they are found in some but not in all the graves, I believe, nullifies Nilsson's interpretation. The fact that they are found in graves of children will account for their discovery in poorer graves. It is evident that children's graves would be less well-equipped with belongings and gifts than those of the adults.

Their equation with the *ushebtis* is also untenable. If they performed a similar function, then we would expect to find that the ideas of the Mycenaeans of what happens after death would parallel in some way those of the Egyptians. That certainly does not seem to be the case. The fact that such figurines, along with the other funeral furnishings, were swept away after the decomposition of the flesh, indicates that they were not meant for the lower world but only for the trip to the lower world. The fact that they were found in children's graves excludes the supposition that they stood for concubines and slaves meant to serve their masters in that capacity in the lower world. They could not be symbolic representations of mothers who were still living. Furthermore, it remains unexplained why the same types were used to represent votaries and a divinity on the one hand (figurines found in shrines) and on the other slaves, servants, and even concubines (figurines found in graves). And again why are all the figurines female? Did not the women need comforts in the lower world comparable to those for men?

The only interpretation possible must take into consideration that in all occasions the figurines filled a similar or comparable function. Figurines of type Ψ were representations of divinities whether found in settlements, shrines or graves. The type, as has been pointed out long ago, evolved from the Minoan Goddess with raised hands and represents a divinity perhaps in the attitude of blessing.[25] Figurines of type Φ found in graves are representations of nurses. The "multiple figurines" and the *kourotrophoi* will certainly confirm this identification. We may assume that the *kourotrophoi* were placed in the graves of infants.

The evidence from Crete, we believe, will further strengthen our interpretation. Of the many figurines found in the houses and shrines of that island, the idols known as "bell-shaped" have been considered by Nilsson as "cult objects" and representations of divinities.[26] And yet bell-shaped figurines were found in the Late Minoan III graves of the Mavro Spelio cemetery (Nos. III and VII). One of these could be considered as a *kourotrophos*, since the female form represented holds an infant in her arms. Nilsson explains their presence as "a sign of the Mycenaean influence," and states further that "the common Mycenaean idols being very rare in Crete, the Cretan type was used instead." But the Cretan type represented a divinity; how then could the Cretans use it instead of the Mycenaean if the latter stood for mortal slaves, concubines, and the like? The substitution, we believe, indicates

21 Mylonas, *Ephemeris*, 1953-1954, A., *Volume in Memoriam G. P. Oikonomos*, pp. 35-44.

22 To Dr. Iacovides I am indebted for the information.

23 *Royal Tombs at Dendra*, p. 89; *New Tombs at Dendra*, p. 33.

24 Nilsson, *Minoan-Mycenaean Religion*, 2nd ed., pp. 307-308.

25 Σ. Ἀλεξίου, Ἡ μινωϊκὴ θεὰ μεθ' ὑψωμένων χειρῶν, 1958. Marinatos, *Ephemeris*, 1927-1928, p. 20. R. Dussaud, *RHR* 51 (1905), pp. 43 ff. For figurines in general see Mylonas, *Yearbook University of Athens* School of Philosophy, 1954-55, pp. 139-152.

26 Nilsson, *op.cit.*, p. 309.

the divine or semidivine character of the Mycenaean figurines of the Ψ type especially, for otherwise it would never have taken place.

The belief that motivated the placing of these figurines in children's graves is easily determined. Death has always been considered a mystery by human beings, and the efforts of man's intellect from the beginning of time have been concentrated on developing ideas that would provide a measure of assurance against the inevitable. The Mycenaeans, too, developed such beliefs, which we have outlined briefly, and seem to have felt confident that the adult who was well equipped with supplies, weapons, and the possessions he liked in actual life could negotiate comfortably the trip to the lower world. The fate of small children must have seemed hopeless indeed. In their few years they had depended for guidance and for life itself on their parents, and suddenly they were left alone to face a long, uncertain, and terrifying trip to the unknown. Placing these children under the protection of the Goddess of Blessing and under the care of divine nurses would appear natural and even essential, an act which would ease the worry of parents who felt helpless to be of service to their little ones. In this idea, perhaps, originates the tradition current in historic times according to which a number of gods and heroes were brought up by semi-divine nurses.

Figurines representing chariots could well have been toys, while female animals could have been considered as means to supply milk needed for the trip. In this function animal figurines would correspond to that attributed to the Egyptian *ushebtis*, but their use was limited to the time required for the trip to the lower world. Thus, I believe, we can suggest a consistent meaning and function for these figurines, confirmed by the facts known to date. Another question regarding these figurines, however, will have to remain unanswered—that of their origin. We have noted above that they appear suddenly during the LH III A period, and, although some types are proved to be later than others, the earlier ones appear fully developed and in common use. What were their antecedents? They could not have developed from Minoan prototypes, since such figurines are not to be found in

Crete. The Cycladic figurines, made and used in the Cyclades in the Early Bronze Age, apparently with a similar function, could have served as prototypes, but, as far as we know at present, a chronological gap of many centuries separates the two groups.[27] We can only hope that further research and excavation will provide an answer to this question.

Animal Sacrifice

In a limited number of graves remains of animals were found among the funeral furnishings and the skeletal remains. Bones of dogs were found by Persson in Tomb I of Asine and the royal tomb of Dendra, by Keramopoullos in the *dromos* of Tomb 6 at Thebes, by Wace in Tombs 505 and 533 in the Kalkani cemetery of Mycenae; dog's teeth were among the finds from the Vapheio tomb. The skeleton of a horse was found in one of the tombs of Nauplia. Papadimitriou discovered the skeletons of two horses laid facing each other in the *dromos* of the tholos tomb of Marathon (Fig. 111). Another skeleton possibly of a horse was found in 1956 at Argos.[28] Perhaps these few instances indicate that occasionally a favorite dog or horse was killed so as to accompany his master on the trip to the lower world. In a number of the tombs of Triphylia Marinatos found skeletons of horses which were sacrificed later in honor of the dead; as he kindly informs me, all those examples belong to the Historic era and mostly to the Hellenistic period.[29]

Evidence for the immolation of human beings is more flimsy and indefinite. Six skeletons found by Tsountas in the fill above the door of Chamber Tomb 15 in the Lower City of Mycenae, a skeleton found by Blegen above the door of Tomb VII at Prosymna, and a skeleton found by Wace in Tomb 505 of the Kalkani cemetery, may be considered as examples of such immolations.[30] But even in these cases we cannot be sure. When Tsountas wrote his *Mycenaean Age*, he was convinced that human sacrifices formed part of the burial customs of the Mycenaeans.[31] In 1928 when we were discussing the problem in one of those friendly sessions which his students and friends so greatly cherished, he was no longer sure. For meanwhile, it was indicated that the human bones found in such

[27] Cf. Tsountas, Κυκλαδικά, *Ephemeris*, 1898-1899; D. G. Hogarth, "Aegean Sepulchral Figurines," *Essays in Aegean Archaeology Presented to Sir Arthur Evans*, pp. 55 ff. S. S. Weinberg, "Neolithic Figurines and Aegean Interrelations," *AJA*, 55 (1951), pp. 121-133. Picard, "Oushabti Égéens," *REA*, 32 (1930), pp. 97 ff. Nilsson, *op.cit.*, pp. 293-294. Mylonas, *Aghios Kosmas*, pp. 138-142.

[28] *The Mycenaean Age*, p. 152. Froedin-Persson, *Asine*, p. 358 and *Royal Tombs at Dendra*, p. 18. Wace, *Chamber Tombs*, p. 116. Keramopoullos, *Deltion*, 3 (1917), p. 137. *BCH*, 80 (1956), p. 365, fig. 7 and *BCH*, 83 (1959), p. 585 fig. 7. *Ergon*, 1958, p. 23. At my suggestion parts of the skeleton were filled

in with clay. Unfortunately the remains left in the *dromos* under lock and key have been lifted by visitors.

[29] To Professor Marinatos I am indebted for the information covering his discoveries to date, and the permission to mention them. In the tholos tomb of Akona in 1963 he found the remnants of a stag sacrificed around 700 B.C. Cf. *Ergon*, 1963, p. 82, fig. 83.

[30] *Ephemeris*, 1888, p. 130. Blegen, *Prosymna*, p. 235. Wace, *Chamber Tombs*, p. 145. Persson, *Royal Tombs at Dendra*, pp. 68 ff. Volgraff noticed some evidence favoring human sacrifice in the graves of Argos, *BCH*, 28 (1904), p. 370.

[31] *The Mycenaean Age*, pp. 97 and 151.

abundance in Grave Circle A actually belonged to burials disturbed during the rearrangement of the circle in LH III B times. At best we can only suppose that in very rare cases and for particular reasons a favorite slave or a captured enemy, a dog or a horse, was killed over the grave of the master. But the regular practice of human sacrifice seems to be foreign to the Mycenaean World.

The Cenotaph at Dendra

We may conclude our account of the chamber tombs and their contents with a brief description of a unique case revealed at Dendra, in Chamber Tomb 2.[32] On the floor of that grave Persson found a stone slaughtering block, a sacrificial table, a hearth, two *menhirs* of stone, and two pits cut in the hardpan. One of the last, located in front of the hearth, contained animal bones, while the other was found empty; a third pit in the *stomion* was found packed with large and small bronze vessels. Not a human bone was discovered in it, and with good reason Persson has maintained that the sepulcher was a cenotaph erected for the benefit of two persons (equated with the two stone *menhirs*) who had perished away from their native land. He further suggested that the "tomb was fitted as comfortably as possible, with a strongly built hearth to warm oneself at, with the dead person's household goods," so as to make a good resting-place for those who perished abroad. However, a grave fitted as a home, with a well-built hearth, was foreign to the Mycenaean beliefs; otherwise we should be finding more graves with hearths. The fact is that only the Dendra tomb exhibits this unique feature. And yet, as Persson states, in all respects and outside of its funeral gear, the tomb was treated like any other grave. Its door was carefully blocked and its *dromos* was filled after the rites held in it. This certainly would indicate that the hearth and the rest of the funeral gear, so different from that found in all the other graves, was needed for a special rite, apparently the rite of inducing the wandering "spirits" of the two persons who perished abroad, and possibly remained unburied, to go to the grave prepared for them. It seems to me that the funeral gear found in the tomb and the rites it suggests have many points in common with the acts and rites performed by Odysseus at the edge of Hades to induce the "spirit" of Teiresias to leave the lower world temporarily and go to the place where the rites were held. On that occasion Odysseus dug a pit of a cubit's length "this way and that and

around it poured a libation to the dead; first with milk and honey, thereafter with sweet wine." Then he cut the throat of animals whose blood, poured in the pit, was to attract the "spirit" of Teiresias among others. The order to his companions to flay and burn the animals followed. Finally Odysseus with a drawn sword sat there and "would not suffer the powerless heads of the dead to draw near to the blood" until he had inquired of Teiresias about his homeward journey.[33] The great seer was induced by these means to abandon temporarily his present abode and to approach Odysseus.

The slaughtering block and the sacrificial table found in the Dendra tomb were the necessary equipment for the killing and sacrificing of animals. Over the hearth, filled with burning charcoal, the animals flayed and made ready, could be burned on the spot. The pit in front of the hearth was there to receive the blood, the bones and the ashes of the sacrificial animals. In the same pit and with the animal bones were found a sacrificial knife and a silver cup with a gold rim, that apparently were used for libations and for the sacrifice. It seems to me that in the Odyssey we have the memory of the special Mycenaean ritual used to invoke the "spirits" of those perished abroad to return to a cenotaph. Of course, there is a difference in purpose in the act of Odysseus and in that of the builders of Chamber Tomb No. 2 at Dendra. The former was trying to induce the appearance of the "psychai" which were already in Hades. The latter, if Persson's conclusions are correct, were trying to induce their dead countrymen, who perhaps had remained unburied in a foreign land, to return home and repose in the grave prepared for them. Yet, the similarity in objective—the inducement of the dead to come to a specific spot—justifies the comparison. The special rite of the killing and burning of the animals, the pouring of their blood in the pit, and the use of libations accompanied, of course, with appropriate ἐπικλήσεις, perhaps were believed to be adequate to bring the persons who had perished abroad to the grave built for them and perhaps some other rite performed in the grave, not included in the acts of Odysseus, was believed to induce them to stay in it for whatever period was considered necessary. The hoard of bronze vessels placed in the pit of the *stomion* would have acted as added inducement. In a final act, the door of the grave was blocked by a wall, as was customary at the end of a regular burial, the dromos was filled up and perhaps a marker was erected in the

---

[32] Persson, *Royal Tombs at Dendra*, pp. 73 ff. and 108 ff. On the wall of the grave high above the hearth Persson found seven holes which "could have served for fastening metal stars or perhaps an object representing a constellation." This recalled

to him the "Great Bear" representations in Egyptian tombs. *Ibid.*, p. 115.

[33] *Odyssey*, 11, 25 ff.

normal way. This tomb is generally accepted as a cenotaph.

Some years ago, I suggested that Tomb 528 of the Kalkani cemetery at Mycenae, in which no bones were found, may have served as a cenotaph. Now I want to draw attention to the fact that Wace noted in three other tombs (Nos. 514, 519, 530) that "although all the earlier interments had apparently been removed or brushed aside to make ready for newcomers and the walling of the door was intact, no skeleton was found lying *in situ* on the floor," and in the space prepared. Blegen reported a similar experience from Prosymna. In Tomb XXVII, besides, he found a "capacious cist" which he calls a "peculiar feature."[34] That cist was "filled with soft black earth and contained nothing except a few fragmentary bones." One wonders whether it is possible to suggest that these tombs, which present a puzzling problem, were finally used as cenotaphs and consequently never again employed for burials. In that case, the cist in Tomb XXVII might have served for the special rites that were needed. Of course, in the tombs mentioned we do not find the elaborate equipment of Dendra, but we could perhaps assume that the Dendra tomb was a special case requiring special, individual treatment. At any rate we point out these tombs of Mycenae and Prosymna since they present a peculiar problem worthy of study by those who will be privileged to excavate Mycenaean tombs in the years to come, with the hope that they will be able to provide a definite solution to the problem presented by them.

THOLOS TOMBS

The chamber tombs were family graves, used over a period of many years by the people of the Mycenaean sites. The kings, and the immediate members of their families were buried in the tholos tombs.[35] In essence these royal sepulchers are similar to the chamber tombs and have the same number of parts. They are underground structures, generally, but not always, hewn in the living rock of a hillside, and are composed of a *dromos*, a passage cut at right angles to the slope, a *stomion* or deep doorway, and a round chamber (text fig. 24). This round chamber, the *tholos*, was hewn vertically from the top, like a huge well, and it was roofed by means of a stone corbel vault, i.e., by tiers of ashlar masonry laid in rings and in such a way that each tier projected slightly beyond the edge of the course below it. Thus the distance to be covered was gradually reduced until a small opening was left at the apex, which was closed by a single slab, the underside of which was usually hollowed to give the impression that the vault came to a point. Behind the rings of stone, loose earth and rubble were piled to weigh them down, and then the area between the walls of the shaft and the loose earth and stones was filled with thick layers of water-resisting clay. This was the method employed especially at Mycenae. The projections of the masonry in the interior of the round chamber were cut away and the surface smoothed. The resulting vault is conical in shape and in section looks like the old-fashioned beehive; hence these graves are often called beehive tombs. Holland has proved that, in the examples found at Mycenae, the lintel of the doorway lies at about the level of the hillside and that consequently the stone vault projected above that surface. That projection was covered over with earth forming a mound, making the round chamber a completely underground structure. Sometimes a circular wall, a *Krepis*, surrounded the base of the mound, thus giving it strength and permanency.[36] A stele must have been placed over it. In a number of tholoi of a more advanced type structurally, cists cut in the rocky floor of the chamber were made, and in them the dead were deposited along with some of their furnishings. After each burial, as was the case with the chamber tombs, the *stomion* of the grave and its doorway were blocked by a wall and the *dromos* was filled with earth. Such a formidable blocking wall was found intact in the *stomion* and in front of the entrance of the tholos tomb at Dendra (text fig. 24). The fact that remnants of a blocking wall survived to the days of Schliemann in the doorway of the so-called Tomb of Klytemnestra would indicate that even in the more elaborate and ornate tombs the practice was followed. A wall is preserved across the end of the *dromos* of a number of tombs (for example, the Tomb of Kly-

---

[34] Wace, *Chamber Tombs*, pp. 50, 88, 108. Blegen, *Prosymna*, pp. 99-100.

[35] For a discussion of the Tholos Tombs and their subdivision in groups see especially Wace, *BSA*, 25 (1921-1923), pp. 283-402, and *Mycenae*, pp. 13-19, 26-46, and 119-131. Mylonas, *Ancient Mycenae*, pp. 96-97. My suggested dates differ from those given by Wace. The whole problem of chronology of the tholos tomb groups should be re-examined. See *contra* Sir Arthur Evans, *The Shaft Graves and Bee-Hive Tombs*, 1929. For Holland's views, *BSA*, 25 (1921-1923), pp. 397 ff. See also *Ephemeris*, 1889, pp. 136-137. *Royal Tombs at Dendra*, p. 20. N. Valmin, "Tholos Tombs and Tumuli," *Corolla Archaeologica*, 1932, pp. 216 ff.

[36] Wace, *JHS*, 74 (1954), p. 170; *BSA*, 48 (1953), pp. 5-7; 51 (1956), pp. 117-118; *Mycenae*, pp. 13-19, for the division of the tholos tombs of Mycenae in three groups. For the location of some of these tombs cf. Fig. 68.

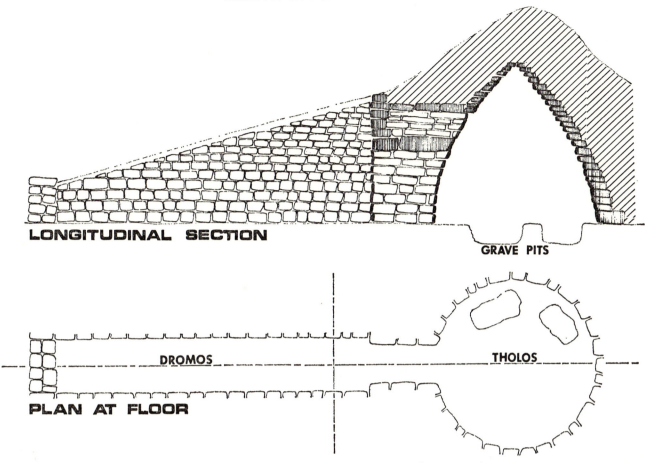

LONGITUDINAL SECTION

GRAVE PITS

DROMOS

THOLOS

PLAN AT FLOOR

24. Dendra. Plan and section of tholos tomb (after Persson)

temnestra, the Tomb of Menidi, etc.), indicating that the *dromoi* were filled after burials.

The brief description of the general type will make evident the fact that the tholos differs from the chamber tombs in having a round chamber roofed over artificially. Sometimes the walls of their *dromoi* were lined in ashlar masonry and in only two instances— the Treasury of Atreus at Mycenae and the Treasury of Minyas at Orchomenos—a smaller side chamber, cut in the rock, was added to the tholos. The parts of the tholos tomb described existed even in the earliest examples found thus far. However, the construction exhibits a gradual but constant improvement. Wace succeeded in defining this progressive development and in classifying the examples found at Mycenae into three groups or categories. To the first group belong the older known tombs of that site, the Cyclopean, the Epano Phournos, and the Tomb of Aigisthos. They lack a relieving triangle, their tholoi are built of rubble masonry and the walls of their *dromoi* are unlined. To the second group belong the Panaghia Tomb, the Kato Phournos, and the Lion Tomb. The appearance of the relieving triangle, the practice of

dressing the stones employed in the construction of the vault, the lengthening of the *dromos*, the lining of its sides with rubble masonry, and the facing of the façade with poros blocks (in two out of three examples) form the characteristic features of this group. Cists cut in the floor of the chamber now seem to be usual (two out of three examples, Kato Phournos and the Lion Tomb). To the third group belong the Tomb of the Genii, known to the villagers as the Tomb of Orestes; the Treasury of Atreus, known to the villagers as the Tomb of Agamemnon; and the so-called Tomb of Klytemnestra, built of conglomerate and marking the culmination of tholos tomb construction. Wace dates the three groups from ca. 1510 to ca. 1300 B.C. I think that the chronological limits within which each of these groups has been placed has to be revised, and the lower limit brought down to 1220 B.C.

Not a single one of the nine known tholos tombs of Mycenae were found wholly or even partially intact; their dates, therefore, have been based on scanty evidence. The upper chronological limit, ca. 1510 B.C., was based on the assumption that the earliest tholos tomb followed the last of the shaft graves.[37] This is

[37] *The Mycenaean Age*, p. 146. Wace, *BSA*, 25 (1921-1923), p. 391.

no longer tenable. Beyond Mycenae, the tholos tomb of Koryphasion (in the territory of Pylos), explored by Kourouniotes and published by Blegen, proves that tholos tombs were being constructed at the beginning, at least, of LH I, early in the sixteenth century if not earlier. It would be strange indeed if this more impressive type of grave had not been adopted at once by the rulers of the most prosperous sites of the Mycenaean world. Besides, the construction of the shaft graves seems to have continued in the LH II period as the treasure found by Drosinos and the shaft under the granary discovered by Wace would indicate.[38] Similarly, the lower limit, the date of the last group was based on the belief that the Treasury of Atreus dated from around 1330 B.C. We shall find later that the date of this sepulcher has to be lowered to the middle of the thirteenth century, B.C. Since this group contains the last tholos tombs built at Mycenae, it must cover the closing years of the Mycenaean power and prosperity; and its latest grave must have served the latest kings of Mycenae who ruled over the city before its destruction.[39] The dates have to be revised, but the progressive development of construction has been well established by Wace.

The building of tholos tombs, like that of the chamber tombs, was universal in the Mycenaean area. Some sixty-five examples found and explored thus far are distributed widely over that area. Nine are known from Mycenae; a good many are reported from Triphylia, others from Achaia and Lakonia, while examples are known from Boiotia and Thessaly. In Attika we have five excavated examples. The small number of examples of tholos tombs as compared to the hundreds of excavated chamber tombs, natural though it may be since the former are sepulchers of kings, is not the only difference existing between the two types. Of greater importance is the difference in the number of graves of the two types which have been found with their original contents intact. More than two hundred chamber tombs were not detected

or cleared of their contents before the age of scientific excavation; in contrast thus far only four tholos tombs have been found whose contents were fully or partially preserved to the present time—the tombs at Vapheio, Dendra, Myrsinochorion-Routsi, Pylos. These four examples certainly are inadequate to furnish us with a complete picture of the ritual followed in the burial of kings. It seems to me, however, that any difference between the ritual and customs followed in the burial of the kings and the immediate members of his family on the one hand and those followed for people in general on the other, was one of degree and not of quality or essence; the burial of the king, that is, was more magnificent; his grave was larger, structurally more elaborate and more impressive; his grave furnishings were more numerous and more valuable, but the underlying ideas and beliefs were the same, the essence was the same. The remains of the chamber tombs, therefore, provide the basic material which helps to formulate the burial customs in general of the Mycenaean period, throughout its extent. The validity of using this material is also indicated by the fact that no discrepancies seem to exist in the details revealed in the few instances of undisturbed deposits in tholos tombs and in many of the chamber tombs. As a matter of fact the tholos tombs found in Messenia seem to parallel very closely the customs exhibited in the rock-cut chamber tombs. Before we discuss these details, it may prove profitable to describe a few of the best known examples of the tholos tombs.

The Treasury of Atreus

The so-called Treasury of Atreus is certainly the most outstanding example of a tholos tomb and perhaps the most ornate.[40] It is excellently preserved, and has been noted since the days of the early travelers (Fig. 112). Its *dromos*, cleared by Stamatakes in 1878 and most recently investigated by Wace, exhibits walls lined with conglomerate blocks of ashlar masonry

[38] Blegen, *Hesperia*, 23 (1954), pp. 158-162. For the treasure of Drosinos cf. Thomas in *BSA*, 39 (1938-1939), pp. 65 ff. and Wace, *BSA*, 25 (1921-1925), p. 59. Late MH ware is reported to have been found at the tholos tomb of Karditsa: *AJA*, 62 (1958), p. 324 and *Deltion*, 1960, p. 171, and at Pylos—the tholos tomb in the *aloni* of E. Vayeanas—*AJA*, 62 (1958), pp. 178-179, figs. 12 and 13. Cf. also Taylour, *The Mycenaeans*, pp. 80-81.

[39] Persson has stated categorically that the tholos tomb of Midea-Dendra, which he excavated, morphologically belongs to the second group of Wace, but that "the things found in the tomb undoubtedly bring the date down to Late Helladic III and so they assign it to the period after 1400 B.C." This, of course, seems to indicate that Wace's date for the second group should be lowered. However, Persson's dating of his tholos tomb seems to need revision and consequently its evidence is not binding. Cf. *infra*, p. 129. Mrs. Vermeule seems to accept my date of the Treasury of Atreus since she states that "it was

built sometime after 1300 B.C." (*Greece in the Bronze Age*, p. 123). In that case her statement (on p. 123) that "the first great architectural complexes do not rise in Greece until tholos tombs have almost stopped being built," is misleading since the most monumental tholos tombs—the "Treasury of Atreus," the "Tomb of Klytemnestra," the "Treasury of Minyas" at Orchomenos, even the tombs of Marathon and Menidi—were constructed long after the early palaces were built and brilliantly decorated with frescoes.

[40] Wace, *BSA*, 25 (1921-1923), pp. 338-357, and *Mycenae*, pp. 28-33 and 119-131. Mylonas, *Ancient Mycenae*, pp. 85-91. For an illustration of the entrance to the tomb before the clearing of its *dromos* by Stamatakes cf. Schliemann, *Mycenae*, pl. IV. The *dromos* measures 36 m. in length and 6 m. in width. The doorway is 5.40 m. high, 2.70 m. wide at the ground and 2.45 m. at the top. The tholos has a diameter of 14.60 m. and its vault a height of 13.30 m.

fitted carefully in horizontal courses. Some of the blocks employed in the lining are of great size and a few were taken from an older building. Its east end, the opening of the *dromos*, was blocked by a wall of well-cut poros blocks of the sandstone variety, some of which were reused stones, while its west end is blocked by the façade of the grave. At that end its lined sides tower some 10 m. above its floor, which originally was paved with hard whitish earth, packed over the rock.

The façade is well preserved, although its decoration has been removed. It exhibits a doorway of monumental proportions. Above the lintel is the characteristic relieving triangle, and above this, completing the façade and crowning its upper section, a projecting double row of conglomerate blocks. On either side of the doorway two rectangular bases remain *in situ*. They are made up of three superposed and graduated plinths, which originally supported engaged half-columns secured to the façade by means of dowels, for which the dowel holes, seen beyond the door opening, were cut in the masonry. Fragments of these carved half-columns are now in the National Museum of Athens and in the British Museum.

The depth of the *stomion* is imposing and measures 5.40 m. in height and 5.20 m. in length. The double door closing the opening was placed in the middle of the *stomion*, as can be proved by the threshold (some 1.20 m. in width made up of two conglomerate blocks hemmed in place by a small rectangular piece of poros and a smaller poros wedge) and the corresponding parallel rows of bronze nails on the wall and on each side which held the wooden door frame in position. The threshold was covered either with wood or bronze. The façade lintel covers only a section of the depth of the *stomion*; the balance is covered by an immense block, weighing an estimated 120 tons. In spite of its gigantic size and weight, it is beautifully fitted into position, and its inner face is worked to carry the curve of the wall at either end.

The tholos is enclosed by thirty-three superposed courses of perfectly joined conglomerate blocks (Fig. 113). On the face of its wall from the third course to the fifth and at regular distances horizontally, ranging from 1.05 to 1.22 m., we find small holes with remnants of bronze nails in them. More holes are to be found at irregular distances in higher courses. Dörpfeld suggested that the nails held bronze rosettes and

other decorative elements in bronze to enliven the interior of the tholos. Its floor, which is of solid rock, once was covered with hard-packed whitish earth. A doorway, surmounted by a large lintel and relieving triangle, cut on the north side of the tholos (Fig. 113), led through a passageway to a side chamber, hewn out of the living rock and in all respects is reminiscent of the rock-cut chamber tombs. Its crumbled sides and roof today are bare of any decoration which once might have covered them, but in the center of its floor was found a rather irregular cutting, and two worked blocks which seem to indicate that a wooden pillar originally may have stood there to support a lining of the roof. Since the sides of the chamber most probably were lined with a rubble wall, traces of which are mentioned by Tsountas, we may naturally conclude that this side chamber was lined with slabs perhaps decorated in sculpture. We may suggest that the carved slabs with bulls in the British Museum formed part of the decoration of the side chamber. Evans originally suggested that these formed part of the decoration of the *dromos*. Marinatos placed them on the façade above the lintel. Both suggestions seem untenable. The dowel holes on the façade make impossible the placing there of the fragments of the Elgin slabs.[41] Furthermore Papadimitriou discovered additional fragments in 1952-1953, apparently belonging to the same composition as the Elgin slabs. We therefore have now too many pieces for the available area on the façade. On the other hand, since these slabs were worked near the Treasury,[42] they must belong to it, and the only available place for them is on the walls and ceiling of the side chamber. That the chamber could have been decorated in spite of the darkness that prevails is suggested by the carved stone slab which formed the ceiling of a side chamber in the Treasury of Minyas at Orchomenos.

Only fragments of the decoration of the façade of the Treasury of Atreus have survived, and these are scattered in a number of museums: Athens, London, Munich, Karlsruhe, and Berlin. These fragments indicate that the façade was covered with slabs of stone of various colors bearing elaborate carved designs.[43] The fragments in the British Museum are the most important; they were part of Lord Elgin's collection and form the basic elements upon which a restoration has to be based. Until recently the restoration of Perrot

---

[41] Evans, *Palace of Minos*, III, pp. 192 ff. *Catalogue of Sculpture in the British Museum*, I, part 1, pp. 14-31. Wace, *Geras*, pl. 20, p. 312. For his initial arrangement *Mycenae*, fig. 51. Marinatos, *Volume in Memoriam of G. P. Oikonomos, Ephemeris*, 1953-1954 A, pl. 1 opposite p. 16.

[42] Marinatos' latest investigations around the Treasury have proved that gypsum slabs had been worked in the neighborhood of that monument and that therefore the Elgin slabs could belong to it. Rejecting with reason Sir Arthur's suggestion

that they decorated the *dromos*, he placed on the façade the fragment in the British Museum. Wace, who originally thought that the slabs might have belonged to the Tomb of Klytemnestra, later suggested (*Geras*, p. 314) that perhaps they were part of the decoration of the side chamber of the Treasury of Atreus. I agree with his later conclusion.

[43] The fragments in Athens have been rearranged in the Mycenaean Room of the National Museum by Dr. C. Karouzos.

and Chipiez was more or less accepted, although it was considered overloaded with ornament.[44] The restoration proposed by Wace, with slight additions, seems to us to be the one indicated by the existing evidence. The restoration offered in Fig. 114 is a repetition of Wace's restoration with the necessary slight additions.

Over the tholos a mound of earth was erected surrounded at its base with a low retaining wall, fragments of which were found by Wace.[45] He suggested that this mound must have been of the same size approximately as the one which covered the so-called Tomb of Klytemnestra, which is calculated to have had a diameter of 50 m.

A mere glance at the Treasury of Atreus will be sufficient to prove that it is one of the most impressive monuments of the Mycenaean world. The planning and skill in construction, its proportions and lofty vault, the care with which its rings of stone were fitted and smoothed, the precaution taken to free it from the seepage of rain water, the apparent facility and thoroughness with which huge blocks were carved to fit a round structure, the way in which they must have been eased into their positions—all indicate the high degree of excellence which the architects of Mycenae had reached in the thirteenth century B.C. We wish it were possible for us to visualize the burial ritual held in this magnificent sepulcher, to recover its interior as it was left when the body of the last king was deposited on its floor or in the side chamber, and a solid wall of stones was built across the *stomion*. But the contents of the grave were gone long before the days of Pausanias, and all we have left is the varied pictures our imagination can conjure up as it is stimulated by the impressive and massive architectural remains.

The date of the Treasury of Atreus has given rise to a great many arguments and theories. The detailed investigations and studies of Wace, however, have definitely proved that the early date for its construction,

the seventeenth century B.C., advanced by Evans and Myres is untenable.[46] There can be no doubt that the Treasury of Atreus marks the latest development in the construction of tholos tombs and should be placed much later. Wace suggested the latter half of the fourteenth century, the years around 1330 B.C., as the date of its construction. He based his conclusion on the date he suggested for the construction of the Lion Gate. It seems to us that all the available evidence will place the Treasury around the middle of the thirteenth century, ca. 1250 B.C.[47] Perhaps the same ruler was responsible for the construction of this tholos tomb and the Lion Gate, with which the treasury is considered as contemporary by Wace. The construction of that gate, as we have seen, must be placed around the middle of the LH III B period.

The Tomb of Klytemnestra

Slightly later in date, perhaps ca. 1220 B.C., seems to be the so-called Tomb of Klytemnestra, a monument which, along with the Treasury of Atreus, marks the highest development in tholos tomb construction (Fig. 115). It lies only some 120 m. to the west of the Lion Gate and near an older tholos tomb that is known under the name of Aigisthos. Unlike the Treasury of Atreus, the Tomb of Klytemnestra is not preserved in its original state although it was buried and well hidden, and it apparently remained unknown to the people of Mycenae of the Historic Age. Across its *dromos* a theater was constructed in Hellenistic times, a few seats of which are still to be seen *in situ*. The locality of the tomb was apparently detected during the closing years of the Turkish occupation of Greece and between 1807 and 1812 Veli, the pasha of Nauplia, destroyed the top of its vault and through it cleared the tholos of its contents; but he left the *dromos* intact. The *dromos* was investigated by Mme. Schliemann in 1876 and was cleared completely in 1897 by

[44] Perrot and Chipiez, *History of Art in Primitive Greece, Mycenaean Art*, 1894, II, pls. opposite pp. 63 and 73. For a full discussion of the fragments in the British Museum, see catalogue *loc.cit.*

[45] *BSA*, 51 (1956), pp. 117-118.

[46] Wace, *Mycenae*, pp. 28-33 and especially 119-131. Evans, *Palace of Minos*, III, p. 201; IV, p. 244 and *Shaft Graves and Bee-Hive Tombs of Mycenae*. Myres, *Who Were the Greeks*, pp. 282-284, 381-382, 574. Cf. also *Catalogue of Greek and Roman Sculpture in the British Museum*, I, part 1, p. 14.

[47] We have detailed the evidence in our recent study on the Akropolis of Mycenae published in *Ephemeris*, 1958 (1961), pp. 194-200. Mrs. David French has recently, *BSA*, 58 (1963), p. 46, stated that the sherd found under the threshold "is late L.H. III B in style." A similar sherd is reported to have been found by Stamatakes in the doorway of the Treasury. Some of the figurines found under the blocks of the *dromos* she assigns to LH III A types. However, it is a recognized fact that figurines whose type may have been started in early years continued to be produced and to be used in later times. Before they are ac-

cepted as indicating an early date, it has to be proved that figurines of their type were not being produced in LH III B times. As far as I know this has not been done, and consequently the sherds remain our main evidence. The suggestion that the threshold may have been disturbed "when the doors were refurbished on the occasion of a later interment," is highly improbable. Before we can admit the argument we have to be assured that such a refurbishing was necessary, that it did take place, and in addition that in the course of it the threshold was disturbed. We must recall that the threshold and door are at some distance from the façade and the wall which blocked the entrance and that the threshold, as Wace pointed out, was covered "either with wood or with bronze"; consequently it could not be disturbed so easily. Blegen, who was present at the time of the investigation of the threshold, assures me that no disturbance was apparent nor indication of refurbishing was suggested by the remains as then revealed. For Holland's view on the date, late thirteenth century B.C., cf. *BSA*, 25 (1921-1923), p. 272 n. 2.

Tsountas.[48] Later, the monument fell into disrepair and rain water almost completely ruined it. Its restoration became imperative, and at the suggestion of Papadimitriou it was undertaken by the Greek Service for the Restoration and Preservation of Ancient Monuments, under Orlandos and Stikas, in the spring of 1951; and completed in the fall of 1951.[49] With its vault restored and the sides of its *dromos* relined, the monument rivals in impressiveness the Treasury of Atreus.

The tomb is oriented north and south, and its *dromos* is some 37 m. by nearly 6 m. The sides of the *dromos* are lined with conglomerate blocks laid in horizontal courses. The south end of the *dromos*, its opening, is blocked by a low wall built of poros stone. Its north end is well-bonded with the façade of the tomb. This façade again shows a double division, the lower section pierced by the doorway and the upper section, or *tympanon*, pierced by a relieving triangle.

The doorway narrows slightly upwards. On either side of the doorway half-columns of gypsum were originally attached to the wall. Their semicircular bases of polished conglomerate are still *in situ*. The bases, as well as the half-columns, are fluted; thirteen flutings are clearly to be seen on both. Part of one of the columns is still preserved; it tapers slightly downwards, like the half-columns of the Treasury of Atreus. Apparently the section above the lintel, the *tympanon*, was lined with slabs of stone or colored marble bearing carved designs. Still to be seen across the base of the *tympanon* is a band of bluish limestone decorated with the well-known beam ends or raised discs motive. The *tympanon*, in this case also, is crowned by projecting blocks which form a terminating cornice.

The *stomion* is some 5.40 m. deep and is spanned by three blocks of stone, the outer two being the lintels of the façade and of the tholos, respectively. In the central block, and at a distance of 3.50 m. from the façade, pivot holes can still be seen, proving that once a door existed there and indicating the threshold made up of two large conglomerate blocks, which possibly were covered with a bronze or wooden casing. For the round chamber and its vault, I am indebted to Stikas who was kind enough to furnish the following information. At the time of the restoration the vault was standing to a height of 8.55 m. Around the sepulcher was found a little over one fifth of the total amount of stone used for the reconstruction of the part that had fallen, actually 37 running m. out of 170. These stones, however, because of the character-

istic curvatures exhibited on their face, were instrumental in determining the shape of the upper part of the vault. When they were placed in their original position, they proved that the curvature of the vault from the floor to top was not a continuous one, as it is usually drawn, but that toward the top it exhibits a change in curve, as indicated in Fig. 116. Stikas states that he noticed a similar change in the curvature of the vault of the Treasury of Atreus. The vault as restored is 12.96 m. in height and it covers a circular room 13.52 m. in diameter. The blocks employed for the construction of the vault are comparatively small (greater in depth than in frontage), but the height of the lintel (65 cm.) is continued around the vault by thirteen blocks, thus forming a wider band in the masonry, relieving the uniformity of the courses and providing a firm base for the vault. In the floor of the north sector of the tholos an oval pit was dug at the time of its construction, apparently to take care of water rising through the rock. An underground drain, cut in the rock and passing under the threshold and the *dromos* carried the water beyond the poros wall blocking the entrance to the *dromos*. To the time of the investigation of the grave by Tsountas a wall of poros stones,[50] standing to a height of nearly 1.50 m., was still blocking the doorway, proving that the custom of blocking the doorway after burial was prevalent in the tholos tombs as well.

In the *dromos*, at a point some 5.50 m. from the façade, Tsountas, in 1892, discovered and explored an intact pit grave, apparently belonging to a woman. Two richly carved ivory handles of bronze mirrors, ornaments of gold leaf, and beads of various materials were found in the grave.[51]

In the summer of 1954, Papadimitriou and I while investigating Grave Circle B, removed the fill to the south of that circle; it proved to have been the dump of previous excavations. Its position seems to indicate that in all probability it was made up of the earth removed either by Mme. Schliemann or by Tsountas from the *dromos* of the Tomb of Klytemnestra. This, of course, is by no means certain nor can it be proved; it could be assumed with equal probability that some of the earth was removed from the Tomb of Aigisthos. Among other objects found in this earth were two carved gems, one of which bears the figure of an animal, and the other a design not only interesting because of the excellence of its workmanship but also important because of the subject represented (Fig. 117).

[48] *The Mycenaean Age*, pp. 122-124. Wace, *BSA*, 25 (1921-1923), pp. 357-376, pl. 56 and *Mycenae*, pp. 35-38.

[49] The final publication of the monuments as restored has not appeared as yet. I am indebted to Professor A. Orlandos and Dr. E. Stikas for their permission to mention their work and

for the drawing of fig. 116. The story of the early work in the *dromos* of this tholos tomb is told by Papadimitriou in *Ephemeris*, 1948-1949, *Chronika*, pp. 43-45.

[50] *The Mycenaean Age*, p. 124.

[51] Tsountas, *Praktika*, 1892, pp. 56 ff.

This second gem, a clear chalcedony, is lentoid in shape. The work, as usual, is done in intaglio in a crisp and precise manner typical of Minoan-Mycenaean gem carving. On an exergue, formed by repeated half-moon shapes, a female figure, with arms bent at the elbow and raised in the familiar Minoan attitude of blessing, rides sidewise on a mythical animal with the muscular body of a lion and the hairy neck and head of an animal which looks like a wild horse. The female figure with elaborately arranged hair is dressed in the Minoan fashion, with a tight girdle around her tiny waist, a tight bodice with prominent breasts exposed, and a voluminous, apparently flounced skirt. There can be no doubt that a divinity is represented riding on a mythical, hybrid animal. The composition brings to mind the terracotta figurine in the collection of Mme. Stathatou of Athens, published by Professor Doro Levi, and even more so the compositions on a sealing from Aghia Triada and on the well-known glass plaques from Dendra found by Persson.[52]

The latest discovery around the Tomb of Klytemnestra was made by Wace. In the course of his excavations in 1952-1954 he discovered an ashlar poros foundation that formed "the supporting wall which held up the base of the mound of earth piled over the dome of the tomb."[53] He estimated that the original mound, supported on the east by the poros wall, must have had a radius of 25 m. Wace further suggested that there is good reason to suppose that this mound, not far from the Lion Gate, was pointed out to Pausanias as the Tomb of Agamemnon.

The Treasury of Atreus and the Tomb of Klytemnestra are the only tholos tombs thus far discovered that have their façades decorated with scuptured slabs and columns. Perhaps the Treasury of Minyas at Orchomenos may have been so decorated,[54] but the upper section of its façade is not preserved. These decorated façades induced the supposition that they were intended to be visible at all times; that consequently the *dromoi* of these graves were not filled in after every burial, as was customary with the chamber tombs. Persson, who opposed the view that the *dromos* of a tholos tomb stood open, even after the burial of the prince, seems to believe that the *dromos* was filled up only after the king himself was buried.[55] What happened, however, if the king died first and later the immediate members of the family were to be buried in the same grave? In three out of the four examples of partially or wholly preserved tholos tombs the skeletal remains of more than one person were found. Must we believe that in all the known cases the king died last? If he did not, then, according to Persson's conception the *dromos* had to be filled up after his burial and had to be dug up again when the other members were to be deposited in the same grave. This will amount to the same practice as that presented by the chamber tombs. It is, of course, possible to suppose that a sepulcher, constructed early in the reign of a king, stood open and visible until the first interment in it was made, whether the king himself or someone else of his immediate family was buried; that only after the first interment its *dromos* was filled and the façade of the tomb was no longer visible.

We have already noted that a blocking wall closed the entrance of the so-called Tomb of Klytemnestra. This would have destroyed the decorative effect of the façade and its grandeur if the grave was left open to view even if the *dromos* was not filled up. Custom required that after each burial the door opening had to be closed; this is indicated by the blocking walls of the three out of the four examples found more or less intact. Consequently after each burial the opening would have been blocked and not only after the last. Certainly that blocking wall, a blank face some 5.50 m. by some 2.50 m., would have added an ugly element. We would expect that some solution to eliminate that shortcoming would have been devised by the builders of the tholos tombs, who had proved their ability to improve on their structures and had demonstrated their delicate aesthetic sense. It would have been easy and natural to move the door to the line of the façade and to build the blocking wall behind it. Then the opening would have been solidly closed, as the custom required, and at the same time the artistic effect would have been helped by an elaborate door masking the ungainly sight of a blank wall. This was not done because the façade of the grave after the blocking of its entrance was not exposed to view; and it was not exposed to view because the *dromos* was filled up after every burial.

More corroborative evidence is available from the proved practice in chamber tombs. A few of these tombs had a façade covered with plaster and decorated with color.[56] These correspond to the two tholos tombs whose façade was decorated in a grander scale, befitting the exalted position of the king. If the decorated royal tombs were left exposed to view because of their decoration, one would expect that the decorated chamber tombs would have been left exposed to view

---

[52] *Infra*, p. 154.
[53] Wace, *JHS*, 74 (1954), p. 170; *BSA*, 48 (1953), pp. 5-7 and Taylour, *BSA*, 50 (1955), pp. 209-223 fig. 3 and pl. 36.
[54] *Infra*, p. 125.

[55] *Royal Tombs at Dendra*, p. 26.
[56] *The Mycenaean Age*, p. 61 fig. 16, p. 133 fig. 49. *Ephemeris*, 1888, p. 122 fig. 3; 1891, pl. 1. Blegen, *Prosymna*, plan 39. *BCH*, 79 (1955), p. 310.

in a similar manner. Yet Tsountas proved definitely that the *dromoi* of these chamber tombs were filled up almost as soon as the artist had finished decorating their façades, for on the face of the plaster of the façade imprints were left by the pebbles and stones contained in the earth used to fill up the *dromos*.[57] These imprints could have been left only if the *dromos* was filled up immediately or shortly after the completion of the decorated façade. Since the *dromos* thus is proved to have been filled, the façade was no longer visible; it was not decorated because it was to be left exposed and was to be viewed by the survivors. I believe that all available evidence tends to vindicate the view that the *dromoi* of the tholos tombs were also filled up after each burial.

The Treasury of Minyas

Beyond the area of Mycenae, as we have seen, a number of tholos tombs have been found, some of which are of monumental proportions and workmanship. The best known is the tholos tomb at Orchomenos in Boiotia cleared by Schliemann in 1881-1886.[58] Even in the days of Pausanias this sepulcher was known as the Treasury of Minyas, one of the wealthiest men of the Heroic Age, who is reputed to have been the first to build a treasure-house to store his riches. Apparently the monument was in those days intact since the traveler in describing it states that "its shape is round, rising to a rather blunt apex; they say that the topmost stone is the keystone of the entire building." Comparing it to the Pyramids, he wrote "the Greeks are apt to regard with greater admiration foreign sights than sights in their homeland; for whereas their eminent writers have seen fit to describe minutely the Pyramids of Egypt, they have not made even the briefest mention of the Treasury of Minyas and the walls at Tiryns, though these are no less marvelous." (IX, 36, 5 and 38, 2)

The *dromos* of this tholos tomb is completely destroyed, but its doorway survives. The round chamber is built of well-wrought marble blocks; its corbel vault is now preserved to the height of the lintel. Bronze nails at regular intervals can be seen on its blocks from the fifth course upwards, and these apparently held bronze elements, possibly rosettes, with which the interior was decorated. A side chamber, placed within a shaft cut from the top, is attached to the tholos. Its walls were lined with rubble masonry that supported, at a height of 2.40 m. from the floor, a ceiling of green schist slabs, the lower face of which was carved with a superb composition of rosettes, spirals, and plant forms. The rubble walls of the sides were perhaps lined with slabs decorated in relief, but these have not survived. Above the ceiling the side walls were carried to a certain height and the cavity thus formed was covered with superposed slabs. Then the shaft was filled with earth. The upper cavity was designed to relieve the supporting structure from weight. It performed its task excellently since, according to Schliemann, the ceiling did not cave in until 1870.

The Tomb of Peristeria

The latest monumental tholos tomb to be discovered is in Triphylia at the site known as Peristeria.[59] It was found by Marinatos in 1960 and its exploration was continued in the summer of 1962. It is one of the largest tombs of the district, and its sides, to a distance of a meter from the doorway, are lined with a rubble wall. The façade built of cut poros stone, brought to the site from elsewhere, excellently worked and fitted, gives the sepulcher a monumental and impressive appearance. On the left-hand doorpost two mason's signs, a double axe and a branch, are deeply cut in the poros. The *stomion* was covered with three lintel blocks—one of poros, two of conglomerate, worked on all four sides. The vault of the round chamber seems to have collapsed sometime in the third century B.C.

The contents of the grave were removed (plundered) in antiquity, perhaps in late Mycenaean times. In the fill were found matt-painted sherds and others belonging to the LH I and II periods. On the floor, however, were found stems of kylikes typical of LH III times. Because of the matt-painted sherds, its discoverer placed the construction of the grave in the sixteenth century B.C., although typologically it belongs to the second group of Wace's classification. In Hellenistic times the grave became the center of a cult and within its vault were held numerous animal sacrifices.

The Tomb of Vapheio

It may be profitable to review briefly the remains of the tholos tombs that were found wholly or partially intact before we attempt to summarize the burial customs exhibited by these sepulchers. One of the earliest to be discovered and perhaps the best known because of its contents, is the tholos tomb explored by Tsountas in 1888 near the village of Vapheio in Lakonia.[60] Not cut in the hillside but built on top of

---

[57] *The Mycenaean Age*, p. 142.

[58] Schliemann, *Orchomenos*, 1881. *The Mycenaean Age*, pp. 126-129. Schuchhardt, *Schliemann's Excavations*, pp. 299-303.

[59] See brief summaries in *Ergon*, 1960, p. 153; 1961, pp. 164-

167; 1962, pp. 110-114. To Professor Marinatos I am indebted for the additional information of his discovery.

[60] *Ephemeris*, 1889, pp. 130-172.

the hill and originally covered by a mound of earth, the tomb seems to have been noted for the first time in 1805 by Gropius, but it was known to the villagers all along, and of course it had been robbed. The walls of its *dromos* are lined with stone masonry. In its fill were found many potsherds, all of them Mycenaean in date, two small leaves of gold, and a fragment of electrum. Its *stomion* contained a pit, which had been cleared before by illicit diggers, but at its bottom a layer of ashes 10 cm. deep was found. The tholos proper is circular with a maximum diameter of 10.35 m. Its floor was not level, but exhibited irregular depressions indicating that the removal or sweeping aside of burials produced the irregularities. A few bones were scattered on the floor and some furnishings were found grouped together in three areas. Among them were 9 carved gems, 2 silver pins, 2 gold rings on the bezel of one of which we find a representation, perhaps of a religious rite, a quantity of gold foil, and other smaller articles. Among the objects found scattered on the floor were some 30 beads of amethyst that originally formed a necklace, 3 gold beads, 19 gold rosette beads, some fragments of daggers with inlaid decoration, and some fragments of ivory. These articles had been overlooked by the despoilers of the grave. Fortunately the robbers also failed to detect a cist cut in the floor of the chamber.

The sides of the cist were covered with small stone slabs placed horizontally. The slabs of its roof were discovered some 30 cm. below the level of the floor. Very little earth had gained access to the cavity of the grave, but strangely enough neither bones nor ashes were found in it; evidently the body was not cremated but the skeleton has dissolved completely. The placement of the furnishings, however, indicated to Tsountas its position. At the west end of the grave, apparently beyond the head, lay two bronze vessels, a bronze sword, whose handle was secured by three gold rivets that survived, six bronze knives, a bronze pipe which may have covered a wooden scepter, a bronze ladle, a knife or tool, two bronze spear points, a thin disc of bronze, perhaps a mirror, 15 small discs of bronze and lead, 2 stone vases, 2 vases of alabaster one of which contained a small silver dipper, 2 fragments of a small silver vessel, 4 clay pots, 3 lamp-like clay vessels.

In the area of the neck and chest of the assumed body were found 80 spherical beads of amethyst forming two rows of a necklace and 2 carved gems. By the right side of the assumed body, a dagger with inlaid decoration was found and a fragment of a blade with an inlaid gold band. In the fill surrounding the dagger were found a great number of very small, just visible, gold nails which perhaps covered the face of a wooden

scabbard. By the dagger, but rather towards the middle of the pit, was found a silver phiale with rim inlaid with gold. Where the hands of the assumed body would have been the grave furnishings were found as if arranged in two symmetrical groups. In the position of the right hand was found one of the magnificent gold Vapheio cups decorated with the hunt of wild bulls, another silver cup similar in size and shape to the gold cup but without decoration, and a heap of carved gems. An identical group of objects was found in the area where the left hand would have been; i.e., the second gold cup with the scene of tame bulls (Fig. 120) worked in the repoussé technique, a silver cup, and a heap of carved gems. A silver vessel, in the shape of a deep phiale without handles, was found near the second silver cup, and two or three additional carved gems were found in the fill between the two heaps. Finally, a ring of gold, one of bronze, and one of iron were found in the same area. Thus was the dead laid to rest with this magnificent group of furnishings. At the west end of the grave were found two bronze axes, one bronze knife, and four discs of lead. The Vapheio tomb was the first to illustrate the wealth of objects placed in tholos tombs; but except for the famous gold cups, its furnishings remained unknown and their importance overlooked. Neither the time when the vault of the grave collapsed nor when the grave was robbed could be determined from its remains.

The presence of the mirror and the necklace as well as that of swords and knives made Tsountas wonder whether a prince of effeminate tastes or even a mighty warrior under the influence of oriental customs had decreed to be buried with finery such as is usually attributed to women. We would like to suggest in explanation that at least two persons, a man and a woman, were buried in the cist at different times. Since all traces of bones have disappeared, we cannot in reality know how many bodies were buried in the cist. The place of discovery of some of the furnishings would suggest the position of the person buried last. It is to be noted that all six knives, the two spearheads, the only sword, the fragment of what was taken to be the sheathing of a scepter, were found at the west end of the grave. Furthermore two battle axes and a knife were found at the east end of the cist. In other words the objects which could be considered as weapons of a warrior were found piled at the two ends of the grave. It is to be noted that the only sword in the cist was not found along the right arm, the usual position of such a weapon. Instead, there was found a dagger with an inlaid blade. Tsountas was the first to point out that inlaid daggers seem to have been used by women.[61] It is, furthermore, interesting to note that three rings were found near the hands of the assumed body. Karo has pointed out that most of the rings we have from LH I and earlier times were found in the graves of women.[62] The rings from Grave Circle B come from sepulchers of women. In view of all these indications we may be allowed to suggest that a man was buried first in the cist. After some time, which cannot be determined from the evidence, the cist was used again for the burial of a woman. It was then that the bones and some of the furnishings of the previous burial, including sword, knives, spearheads and battle axes were pushed to the two ends of the grave to make room for the newcomer. Perhaps then articles were burned in the cist in propitiation of the disturbed possessor of the cist. The furnishings found in the middle of the grave, including the gold cups, would belong to the woman.

The Tomb of Dendra

Fifty years after Schliemann's epoch-making exploration of the shaft graves of Mycenae, the tholos tomb of Midea-Dendra was accidentally discovered in 1926 by Mrs. Dorothy Burr Thompson and was excavated by a Swedish expedition headed by the late Professor Axel Persson.[63] The tomb is typical of its type and exhibits characteristics belonging to Wace's second group (text fig. 24). It was built in the side of a hill composed of soft clay-slate. Its *dromos* is lined by walls that narrow upwards. Its doorway is also built of small stones, with the exception of its door jambs which are monoliths of poros stone. Its *stomion* has a depth of 3.50 m. Three slabs formed its lintel, with one still in position. Above them once stood a relieving triangle. The tholos itself, built in the main of relatively small flat pieces of schist, has an irregular circular form measuring 7.30 m. in maximum diameter. Since the top of its vault has caved in, its original height is not known, but its highest preserved section stands 5.10 m. in height. It is interesting to note that the dimensions of its *dromos* and tholos are about half as much as those of the Treasury of Atreus.

Its floor was paved with a very thin coating of plaster and was broken by four pits which had been dug in it, all presenting an irregular form. On the floor were found a number of human bones, scattered about in disorder; they are stated to have belonged to at least three burials. Besides were found some "late Mycenaean vase fragments, a number of small gold objects, some long pierced agate beads, a hundred or

so faïence beads shaped like grains of wheat, an almond-shaped stone engraved with a deer, etc." From the disorder exhibited by bones and objects the excavators concluded that the grave was robbed, at least that part of its contents deposited on the floor. Finds dating from the Proto-Geometric period, including a burial place in a niche by the inner upper edge of the *stomion*, indicate that the vault of the tholos collpsed sometime around 1050 B.C.

Of the four pits in the floor, two contained burials and these had escaped spoliation. The largest, the west pit, contained the remains of a man and a woman, the "King" and the "Queen." The skeleton of the Queen occupied the south end of the grave, lying supine on a layer of plaster. A great carnelian gem, decorated in intaglio with two wild boars, was found by her left wrist and between her breast and her right arm was revealed a silver cup, lined with gold. Its silver face was decorated with inlaid bulls' heads in gold and niello.

The extended skeleton of the King occupied the north end of the west pit. A great number of small objects of greenish paste, evidently the decoration of a helmet, were found round his head. A large gold cup, magnificently decorated in repoussé work with octopi, dolphins, and argonauts in a marine landscape was found on his breast (Fig. 121). Inside the cup were found rings, three of which had bezels made up of thin plates of silver, lead, copper, and iron. The cup also contained six gems with designs in intaglio. Lower on his breast lay a silver goblet, adorned with animated hunting scenes, a shallow silver cup, and a cup of the Vapheio type lined with gold and having representations of bulls on the outer silver covering. Over the lower part of the body lay a shallow bronze vessel. A short bronze sword with a gold-mounted hilt was at the king's right, while at his left were found three bronze swords, all with gold-mounted hilts; one had a pommel of agate, the other two pommels of gold-mounted ivory. A disorderly heap of objects—a gold-mounted sword, four spearheads, two bronze knives, and two lead horns—was revealed beyond the king's feet. Above the head of the King was found "a wooden vessel mounted with broad bronze hoops." In the middle of the grave, between the skeletons of the King and the Queen, was revealed (at a depth of only 75 cm. from the floor, while the floor of the grave was found at a depth of 1.50 m.) a broken shell of an ostrich egg in a silver neck mounting adorned with bronze bands with gold borders and applied multicolored glass ornaments. Also near the middle of the

---

61 *The Mycenaean Age*, p. 232.

62 *Schachtgräber*, pp. 180, 193, 332 and *Religion des aegäischen Kreises*, p. x. H. Thomas, *BSA*, 39 (1938-39), pp. 81 ff. Persson,

The Royal Tombs of Dendra, pp. 13, 39, with a ring coming from the grave of the princess.

63 Persson, *The Royal Tombs of Dendra*, pp. 8 ff.

pit were found a lamp of steatite and a necklace of 61 small beads. "Low down at the bottom of the pit" was found a fragment of a clay stirrup jar.

In the east burial pit were found the remains of "a young princess" on a layer of clay. A necklace made up of 18 large and 18 smaller gold rosette beads was found around her neck and on her breast; the gold binding of a girdle and 35 spiral pendants of thin gold which adorned it were found below the chest. Eight gold beads were revealed on the layer of clay at the bottom of the pit. In the earth above the covering slabs of the pit, some 30 cm. below the floor level, a massive gold ring with a carved bezel was found.

The remaining pits were taken to be sacrificial and are so called by Persson. The larger of the two, the south pit, dug in front of the inner opening of the *stomion*, measures about 2 m. square and 1 m. deep. It was found filled with "a mixture of charcoal and earth" and contained "pieces of gold mountings, bronze fragments, bits of burnt ivory, beads of faïence and of semi-precious stones, etc., etc."

The fourth pit on the north section of the floor, measuring 1.50 by 50 cm. and 70 cm. deep, contained "only unburnt bones of human beings and animals, including the well-preserved skull of a dog." In it were also found some faïence beads, fragments of gold foil, decayed blue glass paste, fragments of bronze including nails, portion of a big stirrup vase, the other fragments of which were found on the floor of the tholos, in the third pit in the *dromos*, and "low down" in the west pit in which the King and the Queen were buried.

The tholos tomb of Dendra has provided us with another clear picture of the burial of a king and members of his immediate family in a cist and the articles which were laid with their bodies. It has preserved, however, much more interesting evidence if we can read it. A number of people were buried in it, and it is essential that we determine the order of their interment. Persson maintained that "the King and the Queen" had been buried at the same time and "later than the Princess."[64] He has failed to point out clear evidence on which his conclusions were based, although he built on them further deductions that led him to suggest that we are dealing here "with a case of suttee"—the widow following her dead husband to the grave. There is clear evidence, I think, that the Queen was buried after the burial of the King.

Beyond the feet of the King were found a number of weapons in a confused heap. Persson invokes a grandiose picture to account for it; "those who follow him (the King) on his last journey," he writes, "throw other treasures at his feet as a last token of respect,

swords, spears, knives, helmets, etc., exactly as in our days flowers accompany the dead into the grave." This throwing of swords and knives is hard to conceive and certainly too imaginative. The simpler and most probably the real explanation is that these weapons were pushed from their original position, as they were originally laid beyond the feet of the King, and thus formed the heap. And they were pushed towards the center of the pit to make more room for a later burial, the burial of the Queen. Thus, I believe, that the burial of the King preceded that of the Queen; this is also indicated, as I explain below, by the cups of precious metal found with the bodies.

Large and small terra-cotta vases, which are among the most usual funeral furnishings, were not found in this grave. Perhaps this should be attributed to the fact that only the contents of the burial pits were found intact, and in these there was room for only the most valuable of the furnishings. Vases perhaps originally filled the south half of the west pit, and these were placed outside the cist on the floor of the grave when the Queen was buried. Other vases perhaps were placed on the floor of the chamber at that time and were carried away by the robbers to make sure that they did not contain treasures. The scattered bones found on the floor of the chamber were assumed to have belonged to slaves or dependents, sacrificed over the grave of the King. No evidence has been shown to indicate this interpretation. They most probably belong to other burials. That articles of substantial value and artistic merit were included among their furnishings is indicated by the objects found scattered on the floor which had escaped the despoilers of the tomb: fragments of gold—discs, beads, mountings—of glass paste, of faïence, of ivory, beads of semiprecious stones, a gem of lapis lazuli. To these must be added the massive ring found in the east pit and in earth only 30 cm. below the floor line. The scattered bones of three individuals found indicate that more people than those discovered in the cists were buried in the tholos and that they were laid on the floor of its chamber like the dead of the chamber tombs.

The north pit is assumed by Persson to be a sacrificial pit, and the unburnt bones, human and animal, found in it are taken to be the remains of a servant and a dog, who were sacrificed to "accompany their master in death." What evidence imposes this conclusion? Such evidence does not exist. If indeed the shaft was a sacrificial pit and if the skeletal remains in it belonged to persons and dogs sacrificed at the burial of the King, then at least the most easily identifiable bones of "the servant" would have been found in the pit and mentioned, as the head of the dog was mentioned. We can scarcely even imagine that the sacrificed man and animals were dismembered and their fragments scattered with only a few deposited in the sacrificial pit. And then how would we explain the portion of the stirrup vase, and the beads, etc., found in the pit? I believe that it is nearer the truth to maintain that into the pit were swept the remnants of previous burials; the bones in it recall the *disiecta membra* found in the pits of the chamber tombs. It will follow that the portion of the stirrup vase formed part of the furnishings and was shattered at the time of the sweeping. Other fragments of that vase were found on the floor of the chamber, outside the tholos in the *dromos*, and "low down" in the pit in which the King and the Queen were buried. The last-mentioned fragment suggests that the bones were swept away from their original position and some of them perhaps into the north pit. It seems reasonable to assume that the skeleton to which these vases belonged along with other furnishings was lying over the area of the floor in which the pit for the King was to be dug. It had to be swept aside and its furnishings removed. Then the pit for the King was dug; accidentally a fragment of the shattered stirrup, which belonged to the skeleton that had been swept away, dropped into the completed pit which must have been empty at the time, since the fragment was found "low down at the bottom of the pit." Other fragments of the same vase were thrown out of the grave into the *dromos*, and in the process another piece dropped in the large "sacrificial pit" in front of the *stomion*. The reading of the evidence preserved and observed by the excavators leads us only to the interpretation outlined, and this interpretation finds additional support in the furnishings of the grave.[65]

Persson maintained that the gold cup with the octopus decoration, as well as the silver cup with the bull composition and the silver goblet with the hunting scene found over the body of the King, must date from ca. 1500 B.C., and that they were made by Cretan artists for actual use. Yet, he places the burial of the King after 1400 B.C. It will be difficult to maintain that these cups and goblets were in use for a century before they were placed in the grave, that they were passed from one king to the next as heirlooms for some three generations; it will be more in agreement with the customs of the age for the king who had ordered and used them in his lifetime to have them placed with the other furnishings in his grave. The suggested date of these objects will stand modification. The closest parallel to the octopus decoration is to be seen on a wooden lid now in Berlin, found in a grave at Sakkara and placed by Fimmen in the fourteenth

century B.C. Persson, on stylistic grounds places the lid at an earlier time, a date before 1400 B.C.

The Queen's cup with the inlaid bulls' heads he places, on stylistic grounds, ca. 1400 B.C.; it seems to us that it belongs to much later times. The difference in date of the gold and silver cups from the grave, suggested by Persson, would indicate that the burial of the Queen took place at a later date than that of the King. We have, however, additional evidence in the stirrup vase pieced together "out of fragments found on the floor of the chamber, in the pits, in the *dromos*." The excavator states that this vase is "contemporary with L M Ia" ware in Evan's classification; in other words, it belongs to a period older than that indicated by the objects found in the royal cist. Since this stirrup vase is complete it must have found its way to the grave as a grave furnishing and consequently it dates the burial for which it was used. Thus it seems that the objects found in the tholos tomb at Midea-Dendra indicate at least three successive periods of use for burials. To the first and oldest belongs the burial of the stirrup vase; to the second the burial of the King with the gold and silver cups antedating the third burial, that of the Queen, to which belongs the silver cup with the inlaid bulls' heads to be dated after 1400 B.C.

The survey of the evidence preserved in the tholos tomb of Midea-Dendra proves that in the sepulcher we find practices customarily followed in the chamber tombs used for the burial of the common man. We find, that is, less important burials on the floor of the grave and special ones in cists; the sweeping up of skeletal remains to make room for later burials (in this instance to make room for the pit in which the King and the Queen were buried); the careful arrangement of furnishings at burial; the indifference toward the bones of those previously buried and the smashing of the furnishings no longer considered necessary. The apparently unrelated bones found in the north pit, which do not seem to have formed one or more complete skeletons, parallel the *disiecta membra* found in the pits of the chamber tombs, and indicate that some of the remains were left outside the pit, proving indifference towards the bones of previous burials.

The pit in the direct line of the *stomion*, No. IV of Persson's plan, presents a special problem and great interest. It was found filled with charcoal and earth containing burned remnants of objects. Persson suggests that over it "great logs of wood were piled up to form a pyre." After the burial "goodly gifts" were burned on the pyre, which finally subsided and its "half charred bits of wood, burnt gold and bronze mountings, burnt ivory, bits of glass and broken ves-

---

[65] The discussion of the furnishings is based on the statements of Persson, *op.cit.*, pp. 45-52 and 66.

sels filled the greater part of the pit." Attractive though this picture is, it does not seem to correspond to the facts as revealed by the evidence. That some objects were burned over a fire and their remains were swept into the pit is evident. But that a pyre of "great logs of wood" was made is not indicated by the mountings of "thin gold leaf" some "0.018 m." in thickness. One would expect that these objects made of "thin gold leaf" would have melted in a fire of great logs made strong by a "good draught." The explanation for the existence of the fragments of the stirrup vase found in the pit, indicates again the impossibility of the arrangements suggested. "One of the dead man's kinsmen" it is stated, "takes a large vessel of wine, a stirrup vase, and shatters it against the logs of the pyre, so that the contents are poured out. The upper part of the shattered vessel falls into the fire; he stands there with the bottom in his hands, he throws it down to the dead man in the grave—so we found the fragments." The picture is impressive, but it cannot be true. As he imagines it, all this happened after the burial of the King and of the Queen. Over them a good many gifts were placed; even a good many weapons were thrown in the grave beyond the feet of the King. And then the pyre was lit and the fragment of the stirrup vase was thrown in the grave. The difficulty is that this fragment would naturally have landed on top of the bodies and their furnishings. But actually it was found "low down in the bottom of the pit." How did it get there? The grave was not disturbed and bodies and furnishings remained as they were left at the time of burial. And then must we assume that after throwing the fragment in the pit of the King, the "kinsman" threw another across the chamber to the north pit, and then turning around threw a third piece into the *dromos* since sherds from the same pot were found in all those places? Fragments of the same vase found in the bottom of the burial pit and elsewhere would indicate that Persson's conception does not correspond to actuality.

There can be no doubt that objects were burned beside the *stomion* in a pit called the sacrificial pit, but which I would call a ritualistic pit. This burning of objects seems to have formed part of the burial ritual. As early as 1888, Tsountas reported the discovery in some chamber tombs of various burned "offerings—trinkets and toilet accessories," with the further remark that "the fact that these objects are not consumed shows that the pyres were usually slight

and intended only to consume the cloth."[66] It is evident that here again we have a practice present both in the tholos and the chamber tombs.

We may now draw a comparison between the tholos tombs of Vapheio and of Dendra. The contents of both were only partially preserved. Both belong to Wace's second group of the tholos types. The date of the former, as indicated by its pottery, falls within the early part of the LH II period, whose lower chronological limit is usually placed around 1400 B.C. But the date of the latter is stated to be after 1400. Perhaps the date of the construction of the tholos tomb at Dendra should be placed in the late fifteenth century B.C. Both tombs have ritualistic pits; that at Vapheio is in the *stomion*, at Dendra on the floor of the chamber immediately in front of the inner end of the *stomion*. In both tombs there were a number of burials on the floor and the most important ones in cists. The roofs of the cists of both tombs present an interesting feature; their slabs were placed considerably below the floor level (some 30 cm. at least) and the empty space above them to the floor was filled with well-packed earth as if to defy detection. In both tombs very few vases were found, but rich grave furnishings were laid with the bodies in the cists. These furnishings consisted of cups made of precious metals, weapons, and articles of personal adornment.

The Tomb of Myrsinochorion

The third tholos tomb that escaped spoliation was discovered by Marinatos in 1956 near the village of Myrsinochorion at the site of Routsi in Triphylia.[67] A complete account of the contents of the tomb will have to await final publication but from the preliminary report we can draw information sufficient to our purpose. The grave contained six or seven burials made between ca. 1500 B.C., when the tholos tomb was constructed, to ca. 1400 B.C., when it was abandoned. It contained two cists. Apparently a princess was buried in Cist 1. Among her remains was found a long necklace made of spherical, multi-colored beads of glass. Cist 2 was found securely closed by three slabs. It contained a pile of bones and on the top the skeleton of a woman placed in it last. Over the neck and chest bones was revealed a necklace of some 54 amber beads. By the left hand was found a bronze dagger with inlaid decoration of alternating gold and silver nautili set in a deep blue niello. Another dagger was found within the right armpit, with a handle made of

---

[66] Tsountas, *Ephemeris*, 1888, p. 134, and *The Mycenaean Age*, pp. 147-148, where he recalls the story of Periander, the Corinthian tyrant, his pledge to his wife Melissa and the burning of the clothes of the Corinthian women for the benefit of Melissa (Herodotos, v, 92).

[67] *Ergon*, 1956, pp. 93 ff. *Praktika*, 1956, pp. 203-206 and pls.

97-102. Marinatos-Hirmer, *op.cit.*, pl. XXXVIII, a, b, fig. 171 and p. 167. The fourth tholos tomb in the vicinity of Nestor's palace presents some peculiarities and difficuties which perhaps will be explained in the final publication. Consequently its description is not included here. Meanwhile, see Taylour, *op.cit.*, pp. 80-82.

gold decorated with embossed circles and a bronze blade decorated with inlaid gold leopards in a rocky and wooded landscape. Thirteen gold beads in the form of snails were found near the dagger, while at the left side was revealed a small mirror and over it a third dagger with gold rivets and a gold ring at the end.

Among the bones below the skeleton were found mirrors, the ivory pommel of a sword, a gold ring, beads of gold, a silver cup, a gold and silver pin with a head of amethyst, and a number of beautifully engraved gems, etc.

On the floor of the grave was revealed the skeleton of the last burial, surrounded by grave furnishings. Among these were a heavy necklace of amber, 15 engraved gems piled near the hands, 10 swords and knives at the right side of the skeleton, and some 12

vases deposited by the head and by the feet. Beyond this burial and its furnishings the floor of the grave was covered with the shattered belongings of previous interments, whose bones had been pushed aside. Of the 40 vases which were found on the floor only a small askos was intact. It is interesting to note that the excavator pointed out that at least half a dozen vases are direct imports from Crete.

The discussion of the contents of three of the four tholos tombs found thus far with contents partially or totally preserved, I believe justifies the statement made above that the burial customs exhibited by the remains of the chamber and tholos tombs are identical, that there is no conflict in the ideas which motivated them. Versed in these customs we may now proceed to the consideration of a number of problems which have vexed scholars for more than a generation.

The Origin

PROVENIENCE OF THE TOMBS

It has been maintained that the chamber and tholos tombs exhibit burial customs that are different from those of the shaft graves. There can be no doubt that the types of graves are different, that the chamber and tholos tombs could not have evolved from the cists and shaft graves. Wace has suggested that the chamber tombs were developed from Early Helladic rock shelters similar to those excavated at Zygouries, as the chamber tombs of Crete seem to have developed from comparable rock shelters.[68] Thus a mainland prototype was suggested. However, the Zygouries examples have few parallels thus far in the funeral architecture of the Early Helladic period, and then the entire Middle Helladic period, of which the cist grave is the characteristic type, intervenes between them and the chamber tombs of the Mycenaean Era. Evans has naturally postulated a Minoan prototype, pointing out that in the cemetery of Mavro Spelio the custom of deepening natural caves for burial use was current as early as the Middle Minoan II period.[69] These, as Pendlebury puts it, "foreshadow" the construction of the later chamber tombs. The earliest examples of the regular chamber tombs of Mavro Spelio, however, belong to the Late Minoan period,[70] and, according

to Evans, find their real prototypes in graves of the Middle Kingdom in Egypt. To Egyptian influence Persson attributes the beginning of the chamber tomb construction in the mainland of Greece, and in Egyptian rock-cut graves he finds their closest parallels.[71] There can be no doubt that toward the end of the Middle Helladic period connections between Mycenae and Egypt were very close, and that Egyptian practices influenced the burial customs of the Mycenaeans. Wace and Blegen have shown that "more than eight times as many Mainland (Helladic) as Cretan (Minoan) vases are known from Egypt" dating from the Late Bronze I and II periods, from the sixteenth and the fifteenth centuries B.C.[72] The increased number of funeral offerings placed in graves, the one example of embalming found in Grave v, the death masks, the ostrich eggs, the box of Egyptian sycamore with the applied figures of dogs in ivory, the Nilotic scene on the Mycenaean inlaid dagger, the sign of Waz on the stele from Grave Gamma, even perhaps the idea of sculptured compositions on stelai indicate strong Egyptian influence. The suggestion is now made, and on good ground, that the gold found in the shaft graves of Mycenae was brought from Egypt.[73] In view

---

68 *Chamber Tombs*, p. 125.

69 Evans, *Palace of Minos*, II, pp. 555-557. Pendlebury, *The Archaeology of Crete*, p. 133.

70 Cf. Forsdyke's comments in *BSA*, 28 (1926-1927), pp. 243 ff.

71 Persson, *New Tombs at Dendra*, pp. 164-175. Mylonas, *Ancient Mycenae*, pp. 98-99.

72 *Klio*, 1939, p. 147. Stubbings, in his study in the revised edition of the second volume of the *Cambridge Ancient History*, has connected the shaft graves with the arrival of the Danaans in the Argolid—with the arrival of a new dynasty with some of the displaced Hyksos leaders who were expelled from Egypt. I believe that it would be difficult to explain

how these assumed foreigners adopted *in toto* the MH burial customs of the people they conquered, and this has to be done before any validity can be granted to the suggestion. If the expelled Hyksos had reached the Argolid they would have imposed their rule only by force and this would have required overseas transportation, which they did not possess. Also, one would expect that they would have introduced writing if nothing else and inscriptions on their tombstones.

73 Persson, *New Tombs at Dendra*, pp. 146 and 195. Marinatos-Hirmer, *op.cit.*, p. 55. Cf. Herodotos, III, 23. Mylonas, *Ephemeris*, 1958. (1961) p. 162.

of the evidence available to date, we may feel safe in accepting Persson's suggestion that the chamber tombs of Mycenae are derived from the Egyptian rock-hewn graves of the Middle Kingdom.

The problem involving the provenience of the tholos tomb is not so easily solved. The Minoan derivation of this type, which enjoyed a brief popularity, is rapidly losing ground. Some scholars tried to see a similarity between the tholos tombs of Mycenae and the round ossuaries of the Messara of Crete. But it has been pointed out that the ossuaries were not roofed over by a stone vault, that consequently they could not have served as prototypes for the Mycenaean tholos tombs. At best they could be conceived as having influenced the construction of the Mycenaean grave circles. Recently the view favoring a Cretan origin was revived by the discoveries and preliminary reports of Hood and Levi.[74] Their final publication perhaps will elucidate the problem. However, we must bear in mind that the contents of the tomb of Koryphasion, excavated by Kourouniotes and published by

Blegen, seem to place the early tholos tomb well above 1510 b.c., which is usually considered as their starting date in the discussions of the provenience of the tholos tomb. The suggestion that the vaulted chamber tombs of Messenia may have served as prototypes for the tholos tombs has been disproved by Iacovides, who ably demonstrated that the former were constructed in imitation of the latter.[75] Perhaps the tumuli of the Middle Helladic period suggested the form of the tholos tombs. Nordic and Iberian provenience seem to me rather far-fetched,[76] and I still believe that the complete evidence will confirm the suggestion that the tholos tomb is a mainland creation developed to provide a sepulcher for the rulers when the chamber tombs began to be made and used for the burial of the common people. After all, the tholos tomb is a rock-hewn structure approached by a *dromos* as is the chamber tomb. In a similar manner the shaft grave was developed to provide a fitting sepulcher for the kings, while the cist, basically similar in type, was used for the commoners.

CUSTOMS COMMON TO ALL TYPES OF TOMBS

We have admitted freely that the types of graves are different and the provenience of the tholos tomb at present cannot be established to the satisfaction of all scholars. Are the customs exhibited by the shaft graves on the one hand and by the chamber and tholos tombs on the other different as it has been assumed until recently? The notion seems to have been based upon certain points, raised by Tsountas long ago; these were never challenged nor dismissed, but taken for granted. "The beehive dead are never embalmed, nor do they wear masks, nor are laid on pebble beds"; not a sword was found in some sixty-odd chamber tombs he explored,[77] and the wealth of objects found in the shaft graves has no parallel in the explored tholos and chamber tombs. In considering the points raised we have to recall that at the time Tsountas was raising his objections only one royal burial with partially preserved furnishings was known to him, the burial in the cist of the Vapheio tomb he had excavated; we also have to bear in mind that in his evaluation he actually compared the contents of the shaft graves, sepulchers of kings, with those of the chamber tombs, sepulchers of the people. But even so, the objections do not seem justified.

Let us consider in order the points raised. In the shaft graves of Circle A the remains of 19 persons were

found; at least 24 skeletons were cleared in the shaft graves of Circle B, making a total of 43 burials. Of these, only the skeleton found in Grave v yielded evidence of embalming. Certainly one instance in 43 cases does not indicate a custom; on the contrary, it proves that embalming was an intrusive element, imported presumably from Egypt, tried but once and then abandoned. It may even be suggested that the person whose body was embalmed was an Egyptian princess, who marrying and dying abroad, asked to be prepared for burial in accordance with the customs of her native land.

We shall be led to the same conclusion by the consideration of the masks. Such masks were unknown in Middle Helladic burial practices but appeared suddenly, fully developed, in the shaft graves. Five masks were found in Graves iv and v and one in Grave Gamma, a total of 6 against a total of 27 skeletons of men revealed in the shaft graves. This proportion again seems to indicate that placing masks in the graves of men was not a prevalent custom, if it was a custom at all. It certainly has no antecedents in Greece, nor did it have a place in the traditions of the people; it was an intrusive element, an innovation whose abandonment after its novelty wore off was rather natural. The novelty perhaps was introduced

---

[74] S. Hood, "Tholos Tombs of the Aegean," *Antiquity*, 34 (1960), pp. 166-176. Mr. Hood in his discussion has overlooked the graves of Nidri in Lefkas.

[75] S. Iacovides, in *Charisterion* (Festschrift for A. K. Orlan-

dos), vol. B, pp. 98-111.

[76] Persson, *The Royal Tombs at Dendra*, p. 26; cf. *Alteuropa³*, pp. 68, 260.

[77] *The Mycenaean Age*, pp. 146-147, 344-345.

from Egypt; we must recall that two of the masks were found in Grave v in which were also found the embalmed body, the inlaid dagger on which is represented a Nile scene, and the ostrich egg. Grave v contained the remains of three individuals. If, as we suggested, the embalmed body is that of a woman, then the other two were men to whom the masks belonged. Of course Schliemann stated that the mask was over the face of the embalmed body, but certainty on that score cannot be established.

The floors of the shaft graves were covered with pebbles, following a long-established Middle Helladic custom. The purpose of these pebbles was to provide drainage. How anxious people were to prevent seepage is indicated by the thick layer of water-tight *plesia* with which they sealed the roofs of their shaft graves. In a tholos or a chamber tomb the need for providing such drainage is practically nonexistent since they are well-roofed sepulchers; but even in the case of the tholos tomb we find again water-tight clay sealing the vault. The discontinuation of pebbly floors was natural. In the tholos Tomb of Klytemnestra, where water collected on the floor, special drainage was provided by means of a catch-pit and drain.

The argument based on the scarcity of weapons in the chamber tombs and tholos tombs is no longer valid. Tsountas, Wace, Blegen, and Marinatos, among others, noted the practice of descendants to remove objects of value or of use from the grave when it was visited for subsequent burials.[78] This practice would account for the lack of weapons in the chamber tombs. When Tsountas was making his assertions, he had only the furnishings of the Vapheio cist in mind; in that cist he found only one sword, six knives, and two spearheads. However, since then, other burials in tholoi have been found. Persson discovered in the king's pit 5 swords, 4 spearheads, and 2 knives, and these belonged to one person. Marinatos found by the body of the person buried last in the tomb of Myrsinochorion-Routsi 10 swords and knives.[79] In contrast to these weapons found in tholos tombs, we have in the shaft graves of Circle B at Mycenae but one dagger from Grave Beta, 2 swords from Grave Delta, one sword and one knife from Grave Iota. It is evident that the point is not valid. Similarly the wealth of objects found in the single burial in the Vapheio cist and in the double burial of the Dendra cist, not to mention the furnishings of the Myrsinochorion-Routsi cist, compare well with the objects found for single burials in the shaft graves of Mycenae. Furthermore, it is

natural to maintain that after some time moderation had set in to curb the exuberance experienced possibly under Egyptian influence and sudden wealth. But characteristic furnishings continue to be laid with the dead and even weapons appear constantly from the time the custom of placing offerings in graves commenced until the end of the Mycenaean Age. As a matter of fact, no cups surpass in value or beauty the Vapheio cup or the gold cup found at Dendra, and the inlaid daggers from Myrsinochorion-Routsi compare well with those of Mycenae; and these were found in tholos tombs which belong to LH II and III times.

This reexamination of the points raised proves that the differences assumed to have existed between the burial customs exhibited by the shaft graves and the cist graves on the one hand and by the tholos and chamber tombs on the other in reality do not exist. Both groups are family graves. More bodies were laid in the chamber tombs, but this was natural; they were large structures requiring a great deal more effort in their construction than the cists and they could accommodate many more burials. We find the same custom of interment: the sweeping aside of the bones of previous burials to make room for later occupants; the placing of furnishings carefully around the body at the time of burial, but sweeping them away, shattering them, and even throwing them out of the grave after the body was transformed into a pile of bones; the same indifference for the bones of ancestors; the same practice of removing objects from the grave; the same practice of the funeral meal, of pouring earth over the grave, of erecting a σῆμα over it. The similarity of the burial customs and practices in their entirety as far as we can determine them now is so complete that to maintain that a difference exists in the burial customs of the two groups is, I believe, unwarranted.

Let us consider now another notion. It is often assumed that the tholos tombs especially were erected to serve as the eternal abode of the deceased. The truly monumental character of the Treasury of Atreus and of the Tomb of Klytemnestra with their decorated façades helped create the impression that they were so constructed to serve as the permanent abode of the king, as the place where the dead *wanax* would continue to receive the homage and worship of his subjects.[80] The chamber tombs, however, as sepulchers of the common people, are equally monumental. When we stand outside the *dromos* of Chamber Tomb 505 at Mycenae, we at once grasp its monumental character, for its *dromos*, 35 m. in length, is excellently cut

---

[78] Tsountas, Μυκῆναι, p. 147. Wace, *Chamber Tombs*, pp. 138, 145. Blegen, *Prosymna*, p. 247. Marinatos, *Praktika*, 1956, p. 204.

[79] For the tomb of Myrsinochorion-Routsi, *supra* n. 67. For

the tomb at Dendra, cf. *supra* n. 63. Cf. also *Ergon*, 1956, p. 94.

[80] This notion was originated at the very beginning of the Mycenaean studies, cf. *The Mycenaean Age*, p. 142.

in the rock of the hillside.[81] A simple comparison of the pictures published by Persson of the tholos tomb of Dendra and of Chamber Tomb 2 of the same site will demonstrate at once their close relation and their equally impressive monumental character.[82] The sculptured decoration of the façade of the Treasury of Atreus and of the Tomb of Klytemnestra find their parallels in the painted façades of some of the chamber tombs.[83] It is true that only a few chamber tombs are so decorated, but of the sixty-five examples of tholos tombs known, only two and possibly a third (the Treasury of Minyas at Orchomenos) present sculptured façades. Certainly, if the tholos tombs were meant to serve as the permanent abode of a dead king, then the chamber tombs would have been built to serve as permanent abodes for the citizens. But how is it possible to accept this notion when we can see in the excavated chamber tombs the bones of those who were buried first swept unceremoniously to the corners, or brushed into pits, crushed by visitors, burned by the fires lit for fumigation, and sometimes thrown out of the graves not by invaders or robbers, but by the members of their families? The Mycenaeans visited their graves at intervals to deposit in them those who followed one another in death. They were familiar with what happens to the body after it lies dead for some time. They could see that the body was no longer there, that it was transformed into a chain of bones, and these were swept away. How then could they believe that the dead were still abiding in the grave? If the chamber tombs were not considered as the permanent abode of the dead whose bones could be swept aside unceremoniously and sometimes thrown out of the grave with impunity, then in the same way the tholos tombs could not have been considered as the permanent abodes of the kings.

Another observation on the notion is possible. The furnishings for the dead included large vases which must have contained supplies. In the Prosymna graves jars were found still covered with tightly fitting lids, and, as Blegen remarks, "It is not probable that such care would be taken to close an empty pot."[84] In Tomb 530 of Mycenae Wace found two "alabastra" filled with a "peculiar greyish-yellow earth with a curious greasy feel."[85] The fact that the biscuit of pots found in graves was impregnated with oil proves that olive oil was stored in them. The inclusion of pots with supplies among the furnishings of the dead indicates that the Mycenaeans believed that the dead needed

them when they were deposited in the graves. If they also believed that the dead continued to remain in the grave forever, they had to believe that the occupants of the grave would continue to need supplies as long as they remained there; we would, therefore, expect them to have these supplies replenished from time to time. This was the case with the Egyptians, who believed that the grave was to serve the dead, or its *ka*, until the day when all parts would come together in a new life. And so we find rulers making provision in their "wills" for supplies to be furnished to their graves for generations. As far as I know, nowhere in the Mycenaean world was evidence found even to suggest, let alone prove, that such supplies were periodically brought to the graves of the rulers. But how could we assume that such supplies and gifts were provided when we find that the supplies and gifts so carefully placed around the bodies at the time of burial were later, after the flesh had decomposed, swept away, shattered, and not infrequently thrown out of the grave, that some of the most valuable and useful were carried away?[86] I believe that all the evidence that is obtainable to date from the remains of graves definitely points to the fact that the graves, in spite of their monumental character, were not considered as the permanent abodes of the dead ancestors, but temporary stations on the way to the lower world.

The survey of the burial customs and of the graves of the Mycenaean period indicate their variety, I believe, and explain their details. These burial customs and the two types of graves remained in use to the end of the age. One feature must be commented upon once more. The contrast existing between the scrupulous care which apparently was exercised in the deposition of the body and in the arrangement of its belongings and furnishings at the time of burial and the summary treatment of the skeletal remains of the same dead and their furnishings after the flesh had decomposed. This sharp contrast of attitude seems to indicate that the dead needed his supplies or had to have the objects which he used in his lifetime when he was placed in the grave, but had no need of them after the flesh had dissolved; that the dead was to be feared until that decomposition, that until that stage was reached he could interfere in the life of the living. But when the body was transformed into a pile of bones, his gifts and furnishings could be shattered, his bones could be swept away and even thrown out of the

---

[81] Wace, *Chamber Tombs*, p. 12 and fig. 7.

[82] Persson, *Royal Tombs at Dendra*, figs. 17-19. The *dromos* of the tholos tomb has a length of 17.90 m., while that of the chamber tomb has a length of 20 m.

[83] *Supra*, n. 56.

[84] *Prosymna*, p. 259.

[85] *Chamber Tombs*, p. 143 n. 1.

[86] Even in the tholos tomb of Dendra we found evidence indicating the shattering of the possessions of those buried previously, *supra*, p. 129. Now see the important conclusion of Professor Marinatos on the matter, *Praktika*, 1956, p. 204.

chamber, his valuable ornaments and weapons could be stolen by the descendants with impunity. This attitude seems to imply the belief that after the decay of the flesh the dead had reached the world where all "spirits" go, that he could no longer influence the life of the living, that he had no need of their attention or of supplies. This belief seems to be echoed by the Homeric conception of the hereafter, of a Hades occupied by "psychai" no longer interested in their living descendants, powerless to influence the lives of those still in the upper world. As a matter of fact, many a Mycenaean custom finds a parallel in the burial customs delineated in the *Iliad* and the *Odyssey*.[87] The type of supplies given to the dead, the occasional deposition of the tools of the trade with the body of a deceased artisan, for instance, parallels the placing of his oar over the grave of Elpenor; the raising of a τύμβος over the pyre which consumed the bodies of the Homeric heroes, repeats the practice of pouring a mound of earth over the tholos tombs. A stele is the γέρας θανόντων in Homer; it was also the means used by the Mycenaeans to identify their graves. Funeral meals were held in both ages. Occasionally human beings and animals were sacrificed over the grave of a chieftain. In both we find cenotaphs built to honor those who perished away from home, indicating the common idea that the "spirits" of the dead could not descend to Hades unless their corpses were properly buried. In both we find libations poured in honor of the dead. In both we find the lack of rites held in honor of the dead ancestors at specified intervals, i.e. a cult. If our interpretation of the unique funeral gear of Chamber 2 of Dendra is correct, then we have another parallel to a unique Homeric act reflected in Odysseus' performance at the gate of Hades and his effort to lure the "psyche" of Teiresias.

The only and very important difference existing between the Mycenaean and the Homeric burial customs is that in the disposition of the dead; the former used interment generally while the latter used cremation. This difference resulted, I believe, from the adoption by Agamemnon's Achaeans of the Trojan custom of cremation, and this is proved by Blegen's excavations of Troy.[88] Those warriors fighting away from home would have no difficulty in adopting the custom, since it did not conflict with their ancestral beliefs and practices. The fire consumed the flesh faster and so enabled the body to descend into Hades more quickly, and that descent was the ultimate purpose of the interment of the dead body in the grave. It is impossible, I believe, not to be impressed by the parallels apparent between the customs described in epic poetry and those revealed by the excavations of the graves of the Mycenaeans. The evident conclusion to be drawn from these parallels is that the Mycenaean tradition was the source from which were drawn the details of the epic descriptions.[89]

The work of Tsountas, of Wace, of Blegen, and of Marinatos has revealed the important features of the burial customs of the later periods of the Mycenaean Age. Unfortunately, the data found in the royal sepulchers are not sufficient to picture in its details the ritual followed in the burial of kings and princes. This is left to our imagination. The vaulted tombs, the few but precious furnishings that escaped spoliation, the military valor and political preeminence of the *wanaktes* indicate that the ritual must have been of a splendor commensurate with their imagination and ambition. The grandiose scenes, however, conjured up by Persson and others are tinged with a great deal of fantasy and may only serve to spur our imagination to more colorful stagings.

87 For a more detailed account of the existing parallels see Mylonas, "Homeric and Mycenaean Burial Customs," *AJA*, 52 (1948), pp. 56-81 and "Mycenaean Burial Customs," *Yearbook of the University of Athens*, The School of Philosophy, 1962, pp. 291-355.

88 Nilsson, *Minoan-Mycenaean Religion*, 2nd ed., p. 617, in explaining the divergencies of his views and mine "as regards the similarities and dissimilarities of Mycenaean and Homeric burial customs," which in the main are in agreement, remarked that I attribute "great weight to Blegen's discovery of a cemetery with cremation-burials belonging to the sixth city of Troy; but epic poetry originated in the mainland and when, much later, it came to Asia Minor, these graves were concealed and forgotten, while the landscape was there and the walls of Troy were standing." Without entering into the argument of where and how Homeric poetry originated and developed, I may state in answer that the early poems composed on the subject of the Trojan war were based apparently on the legends, memory, descriptions, and factual accounts carried back to the homeland from the wars. Among these must have been stories of burials of important leaders, and these stories or their echoes, along with the other stories of the warfare, found their way into the epics. Those stories were based on facts; those facts contained the knowledge of

the practice of cremation in the Trojan area that is proved by the archaeological discoveries to have existed in the Sixth City. In consequence the concealment of these graves when epic poetry "came to Asia Minor," while the landscape and remnants of walls were there, has no bearing on our problem unless we wish to maintain that all the details enumerated in the poems and in fact their substance was inspired by the landscape and the ruins which were visible at the site in later years. Such a view seems to me to be untenable since it will leave unexplained so many details of material culture indicated in the poems, but invisible in the ruins of Troy even today after its excavation. Incidentally, Lorimer, *Homer and the Monuments*, p. 107, also accepted the view that the Achaeans learned cremation from the Trojans. That no cremations contemporary with Troy VIIa were found could be countered by the fact that no other graves of that city were found and yet its people must have died and were buried. Lorimer is correct in maintaining that even if the cremation habit was abandoned, it could have been revived under the stress of war and a long siege.

89 Professor M. Andronikos finds in the burial practices of the Geometric period the background of the Homeric practices, *Hellenika*, 17 (1962), pp. 40 ff., but see Mylonas, *Yearbook*, University of Athens, 1962, pp. 291-355.

SHRINES AND DIVINITIES

OFFERINGS	For Poseidon:	one gold cup, two women
	For Zeus :	one gold bowl, one man
	For Hera :	one gold bowl, one woman
	For Hermes :	one gold cup, one man

(Pylos Table Tn 316)

We know very little that is definite about the religion of the Mycenaeans although we know a great deal about certain aspects of their burial customs that pertain to religious rites and practices. Sanctuaries or shrines are few and poorly documented, and no cult statues exist about which we may be absolutely sure. We do have a good number of small objects bearing religious representations and these may be likened to the illustrations of a picture book for which the scholar must provide the text. This text, however, can be widely divergent in its interpretations and highly subjective. Furthermore, since these small articles are either Minoan products or work done under influence from Crete, we are faced constantly with the question of what is Mycenaean and what is Minoan and how much of the evidence found in Crete can be used in the writing of our text of the religious rites and beliefs of the Mycenaeans.

THE RELATIONSHIP BETWEEN THE MYCENAEAN AND MINOAN RELIGIONS

The problem, a serious one, was pointed out some years ago by one of the pioneers and founders of the study of the Minoan-Mycenaean religion, Martin P. Nilsson. In the second edition of his monumental work on that religion he again posed the question: "What was the relation of the Mycenaean to the Minoan religion? . . . Is Mycenaean different from Minoan?" And his answer, succinctly stated, indicated the general attitude towards that problem. "Scholars," he continued, "who have paid attention to this problem state almost unanimously that no difference exists, the monuments with religious representations from the mainland being absolutely undistinguishable from those found in Crete." And again he stated: "We have reason to suppose that the Minoan and the Mycenaean religions were identical in their outward forms. Practically, in the details of research, we must treat both as one; for no separation can be made between the small monuments, gems, etc., whether found in the mainland or in Crete."[1] On page 30 of the same edition, however, Professor Nilsson admits that the situation is not as simple as that and adds: "In the first edition of this book" (but also in the second), "I regarded Minoan and Mycenaean religion, on the strength of the monumental evidence, as almost identical, though not without pointing to certain differences. This was rash, for images may cover different ideas and conceal them." He furthermore points out most aptly that "the art of a cultured people develops a number of fixed art types which are used constantly. When an unlettered but gifted people having only the rudiments of art comes in contact with such a store of fixed types it takes them over, but the underlying religious ideas may be of quite a different order." The "unlettered but gifted people" in our situation are the Mycenaeans, and the cultured people from whom they may have borrowed the "fixed types" are the Minoans. We may also emphasize the possibility that a definite religious significance conveyed to a Minoan by a composition may not have had the same meaning for a Mycenaean or may have had no religious significance at all for him. This being the case, it becomes fundamental to base our conception of Mycenaean religion on objects found in the Mycenaean territory alone, determining cautiously whether or not they may have a religious significance. As a rule, scholars from Evans and Nilsson to the present have been indiscriminate in their use of materials on which to

[1] M. P. Nilsson, *Minoan-Mycenaean Religion*, 2nd ed., pp. 5-7. The pioneer study of Sir Arthur Evans, "Mycenaean Tree and Pillar Cult," *JHS*, 21 (1901), pp. 99-204, is still of fundamental importance to the study of religion. Cf. also *JHS*, 32 (1912), pp. 282 ff. The gold rings known up to 1939 were collected, studied, and published again by Axel W. Persson in the Series of Sather Lectures under the title, *The Religion of Greece in Prehistoric Times*, 1942 (hereafter referred to as *Religion*).

base their conception of the Mycenaean religion, disregarding whether it was found in the mainland or in Crete. I believe that the time has come when, with our increased knowledge of the Mycenaean achievement, an attempt should be made to try to write a text to the illustrations presented by objects found in the Mycenaean territory, excluding such discovered in Crete.

It is now generally conceded that the Mycenaean citadels were not outposts of the Minoan state ruled by Minoan princes, as it was believed some time ago; that they were strongholds of states ruled by the Achaean Greeks. These rulers and their people had a language different from that of the Minoans and belonged to tribes ethnically different from those of the Cretans; they must have had also their own ancestral religious beliefs which differed from those of the Minoans. The view, furthermore, is generally accepted that the descendants of the early Greek-speaking Indo-Europeans who settled on the mainland of Greece received and adopted in the course of time many Minoan elements under the influence of which they developed their more or less primitive indigenous culture into the brilliant Mycenaean civilization. We may even assume that they employed Minoan artists to work for them, and naturally they must have imported a good many objects from the island of Crete, which was much more advanced in artistic and cultural matters. They seem, however, to have kept many of the ancestral traits (the megaron is a striking illus-

tration of this), and as time passed they diverged more and more from the Minoan norm.

Why can we not assume that the same process was followed in the realm of religion? It is generally believed that the Greek-speaking Mycenaeans were the descendants of the people who settled in the mainland of Greece in Middle Helladic times. Of the religion of the Middle Helladic people, of the ancestors of the Mycenaeans, we know practically nothing. We are familiar with their burial customs, but beyond these we cannot proceed. Nilsson emphasized our almost total ignorance of their religion when he wrote, "Our knowledge of the religion of the invading Greeks amounts almost to one word only . . . the name of Zeus." But this people gradually came in contact with the Minoans, who already possessed an elaborate ritual and different religious beliefs. It is natural to assume that the mainlanders, the immediate ancestors of the Mycenaeans, were exposed to, were influenced by, and perhaps even adopted some part of that ritual and those beliefs, primarily those which did not conflict with their own. The question, however, remains: Did these influences and even adoptions change their religious beliefs and practices so much as to make them indistinguishable from those of the Minoans? The newly obtained evidence from the Pylos tablets, where we find that Zeus and Poseidon and others of the Olympians were honored with offerings, seems to indicate that the ancestral Great Gods of the Mycenaeans were neither forgotten nor supplanted by the Minoan Great Goddess.

MAINLAND EVIDENCE

At any rate, it will be interesting to find out what conclusions and assumptions will be made possible by the study of the objects and remains found in the mainland of Greece only. The material from which we have to draw our information consists in the main of small works of art which have survived. These may form but a small proportion of what was originally created and may possibly give us at best but a vague outline of the facts. Two groups of objects bearing engraved and carved designs are especially important to our quest: rings and semiprecious stones and gems. Some of the rings and gems were actually found by excavators in well-known Mycenaean sites and their testimony is beyond dispute. Others are reputed to have been accidentally found by peasants in such sites: the pedigree of these has to be carefully scrutinized and their testimony has to be used with great caution since it is always under serious suspicion.

The rings, as a rule, have a rather small hoop and a large bezel set at right angles to it. Evidently most of them were not meant to be worn on the fingers but probably were secured as pendants to chains. The massive gold ring from the Argive Heraeum was found below the wrist bones, indicating that it was worn on a cord tied around the wrist. Some scholars believe that they were mere ornaments, others that they were actually used as signet rings serving a practical need. Persson has pointed out that rings which bear cult scenes are often badly worn and Evans before him noted that we have a number of seal impressions from the same ring, which must have been worn and used by some religious functionary.[2] There can be little doubt that the rings were actually used and were not mere ornaments. Evans, furthermore, stressed the fact that if these rings were personal and their compositions identified their owners, the meaning of these

2 Blegen, *Prosymna*, p. 209, fig. 576 from Tomb XLIV. Evans, *Palace of Minos*, IV, part 2, p. 596 and fig. 597 A, e.

compositions must have been well understood by the person for whom the ring was made. The compositions both on the rings and on the gems are always in intaglio. In some cases the impression has been published, in others the original carved surface. Consequently a reversal of positions is often apparent in the various publications. I agree with Persson that "we must regard the impression to be taken from the ring as the desired end result of the artistic engraving," and I shall have the impressions in mind when I describe their representations.[3]

The engraved gems, known as island stones, for which a variety of material was used—agate, amethyst, carnelian, rock crystal, steatite—are more numerous than rings and as a rule are perforated. The perforation of the great majority is set at a right angle to the design but in some the perforation is parallel. Persson suggested that the former was for the wrist, the latter for necklaces. His suggestion found wide acceptance.[4] In the Vapheio cist Tsountas found a number of gems piled together in two groups, each group in the position presumably occupied by the wrist and hand of the body. Marinatos discovered some 15 engraved gems near the hand of the person buried last in the tholos of Myrsinochorion-Routsi. Persson found a lentoid gem by the "Queen's" left wrist in the royal tomb of Dendra, and Blegen discovered a gold ring in Tomb XLIV of Prosymna apparently worn at the wrist.[5] Some time ago Evans suggested that the ornament worn at the left wrist by the Cup Bearer of Knossos is an agate gem mounted with silver bands. Similarly, the male votary holding a dove from the "Shrine of the Double Axes" is wearing a gem at the wrist. That women also wore such gems at their wrists is proved by the "Dove Goddess" from the same shrine.[6] We now have an example from Mycenae itself illustrating the use of these gems. A female terra-cotta figurine found in the citadel in the summer of 1962 is represented with gems worn not only around the wrists but also around the arms (Fig. 128). It is evident then that these carved gems were used for adornment, and the question arises whether or not they were also used as seals and served to identify possessions of their owners. Tsountas maintained that they should be considered merely elements used for adornment since no attachments were found or projections were left to transform them into seals and since a number of them were sometimes found associated with the body. The case of the Vapheio and the Routsi finds seems to corroborate this view. The

representation of the way in which gems were worn, illustrated by the figurine from Mycenae, will again suggest that they were not used as seals since four of them would be too many to identify the owner and the way they are worn would prove a handicap to the act of sealing. Whatever the use of the gems worn around the wrist may have been, it seems safe to maintain that those worn in necklaces were mere ornaments; at the most amulets. This distinction is of importance because the owner of a seal necessarily had to know precisely the meaning of the carvings by which he was identified; ornaments forming a pendant in a necklace often enough are used though the exact meaning of their carvings may be unknown or vaguely remembered by the wearer. It is not infrequent that even in our day people wear ornaments because they are striking, bizarre, even barbaric; exotic ornaments imported from lands where their meaning is understood but whose meaning is partially understood or even totally misunderstood by the wearer in another land. A good many of the carved gems bear designs of a secular nature, animals in combat, or tending their little ones, or standing by a tree, etc.; a few bear scenes of a religious nature and these are of great importance to our quest.

Objects from the Grave Circles

The oldest rings and gems we have from the Mycenaean world were found in the shaft graves of Circles A and B at Mycenae. These, however, bear compositions that do not seem to reflect religious activities or beliefs. We have, however, other objects from Grave Circle A which certainly bear religious representations. Most important are representations in gold foil from Graves III and IV of what is generally accepted as the façade of a tripartite shrine. The sacred character of the structures is indicated by the horns of consecration placed on top of the roof and in front of the base of the columns (Fig. 122, e). Upon a platform of ashlar masonry stand the three sections, or *cellae*, of the shrine, each provided with a column. Over the higher roof of the central room we have two sets of horns of consecration (possibly one set for each of its two façades), while birds with outspread wings perch on the horns placed over the roof of the side *cellae*.[7] On a fragmentary representation in gold leaf from the tholos tomb of Volos in Thessaly we seem to have a tripartite shrine, constructed in ashlar masonry.[8] A high door is represented at the center, on either side of which we have a section whose shorter height is

---

[3] Persson, *Religion*, p. 30.

[4] *The Royal Tombs at Dendra near Midea*, p. 58.

[5] *Prosymna*, p. 273. *Ephemeris*, 1889, pp. 146-148. *Praktika*, 1956, p. 204. *The Royal Tombs at Dendra*, p. 58.

[6] Evans, *Palace of Minos*, II, part 2, pl. XII, p. 705, fig. 441

and part 1, pp. 337 and 340, figs. 192b and 193a,1.

[7] Karo, *Schachtgräber*, pl. XVIII nos. 242-244 (Grave IV), pl. XXVII no. 26 (Grave III).

[8] *Ephemeris*, 1906, pl. 14.

indicated by an intermediate course of roundels. The construction seems to be crowned by horns of consecration.

In gold leaf also are nude female figures from Shaft Grave III of Mycenae (Fig. 122, a, b). One (b), is a single gold plate decorated in repoussé and hollow at the back. The other (a), is made up of two plates, front and rear, finished on both sides. On each figure a single dove is perched on the head. Two more doves, one at each elbow of the second figure, seem to take off in flight. Schuchhardt suggested that the second lady, finished on both sides, may have formed part of a hairpin, somewhat similar to a hairpin with a lady and flowers found in the same grave. It is not definitely established that these ladies are representations of divinities, although for quite a while they were called Aphrodite with her dove. Nilsson has pointed out that the gold leaf, in one case, shows the heads of two nails, while in the other six holes are evident. These figures were attached to some other objects; they are therefore mere decorative designs and consequently "their cult significance is somewhat doubtful." He further pointed out that their nudity would exclude their cult significance, since all Minoan divinities are represented clothed. He attributes them to "foreign, viz. Oriental influence."[9] It is interesting to note in this connection that on an ivory accessory of a bronze mirror, found by Tsountas in the cist grave from the *dromos* of the so-called Tomb of Klytemnestra, we find two women, shoulder to shoulder, dressed this time, each holding a dove. Tsountas noted that the women have short curly hair, thick lips, and flat noses, and concluded that they are representatives of the Semitic type.[10] Consequently the doves and figures of the ivory plaque do not have any religious significance for the Mycenaeans. In spite of the difference in age between the gold leaf (LH I) representations and those on the ivory plaque (LH III), the same explanation may be true for both. Notable also is the fact that the nude figures with the doves were found in Grave III in which only women and children were buried. Like the gold discs, some 700 pieces of which were found in that grave, they may have been ornaments attached to the garments of the women, and may have had no religious significance.

In the same grave were found gold discs decorated with butterflies, which were used as scales in a model of a balance, and some pendants, identified by Evans as chrysalises. I believe that Nilsson is right in his conclusion that the former are most probably "models of implements from daily life deposited in the grave," and that the latter cannot "symbolize the resurrection of man," since this conception "is of late date and associated with the syncretistic religions in which the hope of a happy after-life was very prominent."[11]

Among the furnishings of Shaft Grave IV of Mycenae were three pairs of what have come to be known as sacral knots in faïence. They were found with fragments belonging to a gaming board, and it was suggested that they, like the pieces of rock crystal, were inlaid in the board. Evans attributes a religious significance to the knots and calls them sacral; Persson accepted that view and explained that they were symbols indicating "that the object to which it is appended is connected with the divinity." But Nilsson denies that the knots had a sacral significance and suggests that they were merely ornaments that could be placed as decoration on a gaming board or on the apparel of a woman.[12] In any case, these are the only examples of the knots found thus far in the mainland.

Gold Rings

We find representations of shrines in 19 gold rings, all but five of which we illustrate. Some were actually found at Mycenae, others are reputed to have been found there. In 1892 Tsountas discovered in a chamber tomb at Mycenae a ring (Fig. 125, No. 1) on which a shrine is certainly represented. Three figures—female according to Tsountas, male according to Persson—are represented approaching a structure.[13] Its sacred character is made clear by the horns of consecration placed over its central section. In that section we find a column with a double capital standing on a double or two-partite pyramidal base. On either side of the central section we see a smaller section; a gate perhaps at the right, a small chamber at the left. The figures, wearing voluminous flounced skirts, are represented in identical attitudes: left arms raised, right lowered at the side and holding branches with the exception of the third, who holds a knife. Behind the figures is represented a strange element interpreted by Persson as a bee or other insect in flight, but which, we shall find later, may stand for a tree with three branches on its top (p. 172 n. 81). In the same grave was found an ivory handle with two female figures of the Semitic type that possibly should be dated in LH III times.[14]

Another gold-plated silver ring from a chamber

---

9 Schuchhardt, *op.cit.*, p. 200. Nilsson, *op.cit.*, pp. 397-398.
10 *Mycenaean Age*, p. 189.
11 Nilsson, *op.cit.*, p. 47.
12 Karo, *op.cit.*, pl. CLII nos. 553 and 554. Persson, *Religion*, p. 92. Evans, *Palace of Minos*, I, pp. 430 ff. Nilsson, *op.cit.*, pp. 162-164.

13 Μυκῆναι, pl. V, 3. *RA*, 37 (1900), pl. VIII, 2. Persson, *Religion*, pp. 56-59 and 175 no. 13.
14 Tsountas and Manatt, *Mycenaean Age*, p. 188 fig. 84; compare with fig. 82 from the grave in the *dromos* of the Tomb of Klytemnestra.

tomb at Mycenae (Fig. 123, No. 2) gives us the representation of a building whose sacred character is again indicated by horns of consecration placed on its roof. Evans considered it a sacred gateway. Nilsson accepts it as a shrine; Persson interprets it as a tripartite shrine, the double architrave indicating the roof structure of the lower and the elevated sections respectively of the shrine.[15] Three women are approaching the shrine holding their arms and hands in different positions. Interestingly enough, the skirts they are wearing are not flounced as usual, but exhibit small vertical pleats. Around their necks are to be seen two lines which are taken to be a double necklace. One wonders whether only one of those lines, that also seems to be dotted, is a necklace; the other, strongly embossed, may be the hem of a bodice.

A religious scene is represented on the bezel of a gold ring found by Persson in the Queen's tomb at Dendra in the summer of 1939 (Fig. 124, No. 3).[16] At the extreme left of the composition is represented a low building in ashlar masonry apparently in two sections, which Persson interprets as a tripartite shrine. Behind this structure a complete column supports a double entablature on which a set of horns of consecration is to be seen. This indicates the sacredness of the structure and of the colonnade, indicated by a single column. In front of the structure we find indistinct traces of a worshiper; in spite of Persson's ingenious surmises, the representation is too worn out for a reliable identification and interpretation. He believes that in this section we have a worshiper wearing a baggy skirt made of an animal pelt. On the extreme right of the representation we find an enclosure within which there seems to be a "baetyl" and beyond it a tree. Between the shrine to the left and the enclosure to the right two women, similarly dressed and in a similar pose, evidently engage in a ceremonial dance. The left arm of one is extended over the enclosure to the right and her hand seems to be touching the tree in the enclosure.

The three examples of gold rings bearing representations of shrines indicated by the horns of consecration were found in excavations and their pedigree is known. We have, however, additional rings whose history remains vague. A ring (Fig. 127, No. 4) now in the Berlin Museum, was first published by Furtwängler and Loeschcke. It is reputed to have been found at Mycenae. At the extreme right a structure, apparently built on a raised platform, is surmounted by two sets of horns of consecration. Within the building, which seems to have two lateral walls and two entablatures, is a column with a tripartite capital and a set of horns of consecration in front of its base. Before the shrine is seated a woman, wearing a flounced skirt and holding up a round mirror. A woman stands before her, with right hand raised in a gesture of adoration or greeting. Nilsson calls the seated woman "a most enigmatical goddess," while Persson finds her in Syro-Hittite reliefs seated at the side of the weather god Teschub, and also on seals, where she is seated on a tabouret, holding up a mirror and receiving the adoration and gifts from worshipers. The mirror, according to Persson, would indicate that her province is sun magic: by creating heat with the mirror she influences the sun, the great source of light and heat in nature. Neither the date nor the exact provenience of the ring is ascertainable.[17]

A gold ring found in a tomb near Thebes, No. 5 in our series, shows a woman seated in a similar fashion in front of a structure with a set of horns of consecration on the roof.[18] Before her stands a man with right arm bent at the elbow and forearm raised in an attitude of adoration. From the middle of the horns of consecration five dots rise vertically; they may stand for a bough either decorating the horns or growing beyond the shrine. A dotted line above the human figure perhaps symbolizes the sky and above it we find the rayed orb of the sun. There can be little doubt that in this composition we have a shrine in front of which a goddess is seated and worshiped; or, as Nilsson so expressively stated it, "this is a very fine representation of the epiphany of a goddess before her shrine."

A second ring from the same grave (Fig. 127, No. 6) bears an equally interesting composition although the structure represented on it does not exhibit the horns of consecration.[19] On the left side of the composition a structure consisting of two sideposts and a thick central member supports two superposed slabs, the upper being a little longer than the lower. It is constructed on a rocky ground clearly indicated by boulders arranged in a mounting line. Before it a huge bull is crouching on the ground under a tree. The branches of the tree, following the edge of the bezel, are bent horizontally over the back of the bull. Nilsson identifies the structure on the left as an altar. If it is, then the bull may represent a sacrificial ani-

---

[15] Tsountas, *RA*, 37 (1900), pl. VIII, 3. Evans, *JHS*, 21 (1901), p. 184 fig. 58. Persson, *Religion*, pp. 59-60 and 175 no. 14.

[16] Persson, *op.cit.*, pp. 40-43 and 172 no. 5.

[17] Nilsson and Evans state that it came from Mycenae; Persson could not find "verification of this statement"; *Religion*, pp. 43-46 and 172 fig. 6. Nilsson, *op.cit.*, p. 354. Perhaps the two women are priestesses conversing outside the shrine; the duties of the one may have included sun magic, indicated by the mirror.

[18] Nilsson, *op.cit.*, p. 179 fig. 83; *AA*, 1939, p. 231 fig. 3. It is now in the Benaki Museum.

[19] Nilsson, *op.cit.*, p. 178 fig. 82.

mal. The terrain and the tree would indicate that the setting is rural and mountainous.

Marinatos suggests that an altar is represented on a gem found in the vicinity of Pylos;[20] I would see instead a shrine. A set of horns of consecration appear on top of the structure decorated with two leafy branches. A woman approaches the altar-shrine bearing lilies. A full description of this example, No. 7 in our series, will be given in the final publication to appear shortly.

A gold signet ring in Evans' collection (Fig. 125, No. 8), first published by him in 1901, is also reputed to have been found in Mycenae.[21] At the extreme left on rocky ground stands a shrine, identified as such by the set of horns of consecration on top of its roof. The pair of slender pillars and the double entablature led Persson to recognize in this structure a "tripartite cult building, the *aedicula,* seen in side view." Between the horns of consecration and on either side of the base of the construction rise branches. In the middle of the representation stands a woman in a flounced skirt; the lower part of the body is turned to the right, the upper is in full front, and the head is turned to the left, to the shrine. She is extending her right hand to that shrine in a gesture of adoration. A tree is represented to the right of the woman and at some distance from her, while details of the soil are indicated by segmented lines. (One wonders about the pedigree of this ring.)

We may add here the fragment of a fresco from Pylos on which a single open hall with a central column, surmounted by two sphinxes. Similarly on a crater from the Agora of Athens, attributed to the LH III A period, we find the façade of a shrine with a pillar in the middle and horns of consecration on top. A slender stand between the horns evidently terminated in three leaves, like the stems represented on either side of the shrine. In the two apertures of the shrine we find baetyls standing by themselves.[22]

Sacred Enclosures

The identification of the structures on the rings and fresco fragments as shrines or cult buildings is put beyond doubt by the horns of consecration which surmount them. Some representations, however, seem to indicate the existence of enclosures of a religious nature, although no emblems characterize them as such. One of these (Fig. 124, No. 9), reputed to have come from Mycenae, was first illustrated by Evans.[23] At the extreme left we find what apparently is a built

enclosure or "a portal shrine," as stated by Evans, within which Persson identifies a baetyl, and a tree with rich foliage. Facing the enclosure and the tree stands a man wearing trunks and leggings. Both arms are bent at the elbow; the right forearm and hand, however, are raised in an attitude of adoration, while the left is extended across the chest. A large animal, identified as an *agrimi* (wild goat), with long horns, stands behind the worshiper, and beyond, in the background, a tree with rich foliage is depicted. While the man and the *agrimi* stand on a straight line, the structure to the left is raised on a rocky ground.

Of greater interest and importance is a ring (Fig. 123, No. 10) first published by Furtwängler in his monumental book *Antike Gemmen.* It is reputed to have been found at Mycenae and has caused a good deal of discussion. On the extreme right of its oval bezel we find what has been accepted as an enclosure or a portal upon a high base, within which there is a baetyl and beyond which a tree rich in foliage. As a pendant to this on the extreme left we find another rectangular structure of three upright members supporting two superposed slabs. The structure continues beyond the third upright member. An upright stone appears between the first two supports and a small unidentifiable object between the second and third support. Over the upright stone, as a rule interpreted as a baetyl, hangs a garland. The small object was taken by Evans to be a Mycenaean shield.[24] Between the two structures two women and a man engage in a violent, orgiastic dance. The entire composition is placed on a straight line below which the area that may be called an exergue is filled with elongated dots. A comparison of this exergue to the way rocky, uneven ground is represented on rings will make it evident that the structures do not stand on a mountainous terrain, but on even ground. Two lines above the standing woman and the man would indicate the firmament, while branches strewn above the bending woman may stand for a grove.

The various units of the composition are widely interpreted by scholars. The construction to the left, for instance, Persson, who follows Evans in this, takes to be a tomb since "the tall, narrow, phallos-like stone occurs as a gravestone in Phrygia, on Attis' grave, and elsewhere."[25] However, upright stones similar to this, interpreted as baetyls, are to be seen in the enclosure at the right edge of this ring, in the enclosure at the right edge of the ring from the Queen's Tomb at Dendra, and in the enclosure on the ring now in the

---

[20] Marinatos-Hirmer, *op.cit.,* fig. 208, second line right.

[21] *JHS,* 21 (1901), p. 182 fig. 56. Persson, *op.cit.,* pp. 54-56 and 175 no. 12.

[22] *Archaeology,* 13 (1960), p. 8 fig. 7 and p. 37 fig. 5. *AJA,* 65 (1961), p. 157 pl. 60 fig. 16; *AJA,* 66 (1962) pl. 40 no. 12.

[23] *JHS,* 21 (1901), p. 182 fig. 55. Persson, *op.cit.,* pp. 52-53 and 174 no. 10.

[24] Persson, *Religion,* pp. 38-39 no. 4. Evans, *Palace of Minos,* I, p. 161.

[25] Persson, *op.cit.,* p. 39. Evans, *Palace of Minos,* II, pp. 838 f.

museum in Candia in which we have three dancers between two enclosures. It is true that the genuineness of the last ring has been successfully challenged,[26] but the other examples of baetyls in enclosures definitely prove that we do not have to invoke the evidence of the phallus-like stones of Phrygia for analogies. It seems to me self-evident that the structures represented on these rings must correspond to real buildings well-known to the owners of the rings. I fail to find any similarity between the structure taken to be a grave and the contemporary Mycenaean sepulchers familiar to us from hundreds of examples excavated thus far, and even more familiar to the Mycenaeans. Furthermore, the three upright posts of the so-called grave are certainly trunks of cut trees; they are identical in appearance to the doorposts and entablature blocks of the structure to the right which certainly are made of wood and resemble the representation of a palm tree on the round sard No. 8 from the tenth chamber tomb of Mycenae (*Ephemeris*, 1888, pl. 10). A grave of Mycenaean times made of wood is an impossibility, I believe. The structure is not a grave; it must be something else. Its scale in relation to the human forms, which may be questioned, follows the Minoan-Mycenaean convention of magnifying the size of the latter and reducing the dimensions of the former to be seen in practically all the compositions on rings in which figures and structures are represented; consequently the scale is not a decisive element.

The female figure bending over the structure gave rise to the suggestion that it is a tomb. Evans recognized in the bending figure the "Great Mother or her attendant mourning over her mortal consort."[27] Nilsson seems to be unwilling to accept the structure as a tomb, but thinks that "the interpretation of Sir Arthur Evans is substantially correct. The woman to the left," he writes, "is certainly represented as mourning or lamenting and the one in the middle as dancing, while the man is shaking the tree. . . . Consequently" he concludes, "we have a tree cult with on the one hand joy and dancing, on the other mourning." This explanation is preferable to Persson's. One, however, could ask how we can be sure that the bending woman is mourning or lamenting. Do we have any other examples from the Minoan-Mycenaean world that would strengthen this assumption? On some rare Larnakes of LH III C times we find women mourning and from the same period we have figurines of mourning women.[28] They express their lamentation by plac-

ing their hands over the top of their heads, a position reminiscent of the gesture of the women on the Warrior Vase. There can be little doubt that the woman on the ring is bending over, but is it altogether impossible to see in that position a violent movement in her orgiastic dance, corresponding to the violent movement of the man at the right end of the composition? The movement at the one end goes to the right, at the other to the left. People engaged in such ecstatic dances take all kinds of exaggerated positions which when crystallized may be completely beyond our conception of the norm. Compare, for example, a camera shot of a modern youngster going through the gyrations of the so-called modern dances. I would like to suggest that the woman is represented bending with elbows apart in her wild dancing.

The man to the right is in an equally violent posture; he has thrown his hands upwards, his head backwards, his feet in an almost kneeling position. He is believed to have grasped and bent down the stem of the tree which should be accepted as growing beyond the enclosure. Evans proposed the explanation that the "man is pulling down the branches of the tree to pluck a fruit and to offer it to the hungry goddess." Persson maintains that the man is dancing but "seems to grasp the trunk of the tree," a gesture that would "attract the attention of the great Tree Goddess."[29] Professor Nilsson states that "the man is shaking the tree." Actually his hand does not grasp the trunk of the tree, which must be conceived as growing beyond the enclosure. Certainly the tree is bent in the direction of the man as if it is being pulled; but the tree has to follow the oval shape of the bezel. That the bending of the tree could have nothing to do with the dancing man is indicated by other representations where trees are so bent although no man is there to pull them down. A striking illustration of this we find on the gold ring in the State Museum in Berlin.[30] A tree grows beyond a portal or enclosure in front of which a man, with his back to tree and enclosure, stands worshiping a goddess. The branches of the tree bend even more violently than those on our ring. On one of the gold rings from Thebes (Fig. 127, No. 6), behind the couchant bull a tree bends over the back of the bull; no man is there to pull it that way or to shake it. On the famous ring of Knossos, on which the epiphany of the young male god is invoked by a woman worshiper, we find trees beyond a built portal;[31] they bend in two differ-

[26] Nilsson, *Minoan-Mycenaean Religion*, p. 277 n. 55. Schweitzer, *Gnomon*, 4 (1928), p. 171.

[27] Evans, *Palace of Minos*, I, p. 161. *JHS*, 45 (1925), p. 13.

[28] Nilsson, *op.cit.*, p. 277. For the figurines of women mourning see the forthcoming article in *AJA* of S. Iacovides. For the larnakes see E. Vermeule, *Greece in the Bronze Age*, pp. 210-

214. See our Fig. 152.

[29] Persson, *op.cit.*, p. 39. Nilsson, *op.cit.*, p. 277.

[30] Nilsson, *op.cit.*, p. 266 and n. 16, fig. 130. Persson, *op.cit.*, no. 20.

[31] Evans, *Palace of Minos*, I, p. 160 fig. 115. Persson, *op.cit.*, p. 176 no. 15.

ent directions to fit into the ground reserved for them. It is evident that the bending of the tree is imposed by the nature of the section of the oval bezel on which it is represented.

In connection with the position of the hand by the tree, it may be instructive to note how the hand of one of the women dancers on the ring from Dendra (Fig. 124, No. 3) seems to touch the tree growing beyond the enclosure, the way the man's hand on our ring seems to extend to the tree. From that position we may surmise that the woman is shaking the tree. That the surmise is wrong is indicated by the position of the right hand of the other woman which is extended in the same way but at a distance from the tree. Both hands are where they are because of the measure and figure of the dance. The same can be maintained for the man on the ring from Mycenae.

Summarizing our discussion, we may conclude that on that ring we have an orgiastic dance performed by two women and a man. As for the structures represented at the two ends of the composition, I would like to maintain that they belong to the same sacred enclosure. Nilsson has suggested that the scene of the dancing was actually held within the enclosure where the tree stood and in front of which the ritual was performed.[32] If the artist represented the rite as it actually occurred, then part of the scene at least would have been concealed by the surrounding construction; consequently the worshiper would have been partially concealed, at best "his head and the upper part of his body" would be visible. But that would have been against the desire of the artist to give an "explicit representation," to represent "all the features that are significant: the dancing figures had to be represented in full and this necessitated their placement outside the enclosure, while their action should be conceived as taking place within." Following this suggestion we may maintain that the representation of the wall of the enclosure was interrupted in order that the figures of the worshipers and their action be made more explicit. On the right the artist placed the portal of the enclosure, on the left we have the wall which surrounded the area within which stood the sacred tree or grove. Both structures have an entablature of two superposed slabs and should be considered as attached to each other in reality, the enclosure continues beyond the third upright post on the left as indicated by the entablature. Only one sacred enclosure therefore is represented, within which a rite of the tree cult is being performed. If this interpretation

is correct, then the structure to the left is shown once more not to be a grave; the bent woman should be understood to be within the enclosure, and her attitude is not one of lamentation over a grave but that of a figure engaged in vigorous dancing. Within the enclosure the baetyl and the "shield" are represented in the apertures of the structure to the left.

A similar representation, that is, two women and a man dancing between two sacred enclosures with trees, is to be seen on a gold ring, No. 11, now in the National Museum of Athens. Certainly, on it we have no scene of mourning and lamentation. Unfortunately, however, the pedigree of this ring is uncertain. It, along with another now in the Museum of Herakleion, was bought from dealers and was presented to the Museum. Schweitzer rightly, I believe, casts doubts upon their authenticity and Chapouthier joins him in believing that the ring in the National Museum is not authentic.[33]

A dancing ritual is represented on the well-known gold ring found by Tsountas in the cist of the Vapheio tholos tomb (Fig. 123, No. 12).[34] On the extreme left of the representation the bent branches of a tree follow the oval edge of the bezel. The tree grows from rocky ground beyond a conical element that has been interpreted as an "elongated vessel" by Tsountas, as "a baetylic pillar" by Evans, as "an upturned pithos" by Persson, as an "undefinable construction" by Nilsson. It seems to stand on a platform before which the ground is rocky and ascending. On this rocky ground we find a man, wearing loin cloth and leggings, in an almost half-kneeling position with arms extended beyond the body and bent at the elbow, and forearms raised. Like the dancing man on the ring from Mycenae (Fig. 123, No. 10), he turns his head towards the center of the composition and away from the tree. In the middle of the representation is a woman wearing an elaborate skirt with flounces and vertical pleats (cf. Fig. 123, No. 2, the gold-plated silver ring from Mycenae). The position of her arms, her flying hair, indicated by dots, the turn of her body, prove that she is also dancing. Above her left shoulder a small object is identified by Evans as a chrysalis, but which in reality remains unexplained. To me it resembles the object on the left enclosure of the ring from Mycenae, and suggests a shield. Apparently Nilsson does not think that it is a chrysalis. To the right is a leafy branch and an *ankh*-shaped variant of the double axe. On the extreme right lies a figure-eight shield and by it an object interpreted by Evans

---

[32] *Minoan-Mycenaean Religion*[2], p. 271.
[33] *Ibid.*, figs. 131 and 132. Persson, *op.cit.*, pp. 64-65 and 176 no. 17. Schweitzer, *Gnomon*, 4 (1928), p. 171. Chapouthier, *Les Dioscures au service d'une déesse*, p. 187 n. 4.

[34] *Ephemeris*, 1889, pl. 10 no. 39. Persson, *op.cit.*, pp. 36-38, 171 no. 3. Nilsson, *op.cit.*, pp. 211 and 275. Evans, *Palace of Minos*, III, p. 140.

as a "prostrate mourning woman," by Persson as a "pair of the so-called sacral knots," by Nilsson as a "cuirass or a sacral knot." We shall have a chance to discuss it later.

Again, as we have seen, a number of elements in this composition have provoked argument. Is the element to the left an upturned pithos? In this case it would stand for a grave, for a pithos burial, as Persson maintained. The object reminded him of the "burial jars" from the site of Sphoungaras in Crete which were placed in the earth upside down. But we have to remember that on these rings structures would be represented of a type familiar to the people who owned them; and then the element is represented as standing on the ground and not in it. Do we find such burials as the Sphoungaras pithoi or pithos burials above ground in Lakonia in the LH IIa period to which the tholos tomb of Vapheio belongs? Even if we admit that a Minoan artist carved the ring, we shall still have to accept the view that he would have used elements current in the life and knowledge of the future owner. Although we find intramural burials in LH II settlements, there is not a single example of an inverted pithos burial for an adult in a cemetery or a glen. Nor could it be emblematic of death and dying vegetation, since the tree beyond this and the representation on Ring 10 (Fig. 123) is as full of leaves as any other tree represented on any ring, and consequently it could not indicate winter when vegetation dies, as Persson wishes. Perhaps it would be wise to follow Nilsson and accept the "elongated vessel" as an "undefinable construction." But I would like to see in it a rustic mound or a cairn made of earth near a sacred grove symbolized by the tree. The existence of such cairns of stones is indicated by the well-known pressed glass-paste plaque from the Tholos Tomb of the Genii at Mycenae. Perhaps the famous altar of Lykosoura of historic times is an example of such a mound serving a religious function, not a ritual of obsequies.[35]

It is assumed that the man is shaking a branch of the tree. It seems to me that the man's hand does not even reach the branch, which should be considered beyond it. The position of his arms, the turning of the head and body, the semi-kneeling position, indicate clearly that the man is in the midst of a vigorous dance. His stance corresponds to that of the dancing man on the ring from Mycenae (Fig. 123, No. 10) and neither is pulling down a tree; the bent branches of the trees were so drawn because of the limitations

presented by the oval bezel. In both rings we have a tree cult ritual in which dancing played an important role. The rocky ground will indicate that it takes place on a mountainous terrain to which the two worshipers journeyed. The man left his shield and garment to one side before engaging in the vigorous ritual.

A gold ring discovered by Tsountas in a chamber tomb in 1895 (Fig. 127, No. 13), has on its bezel an interesting and unique composition.[36] Both Evans and Persson see on it a sacred spring and a cult building with a grove of cypress trees. Two women, each wearing the typical flounced skirt and a bodice leaving the breasts naked, stand on either side of the spring in an attitude of worship. A rocky area is indicated behind the woman to the left, while behind the woman to the right is what is assumed to be a baetyl. The composition, representing perhaps a cult scene taking place in front of a sacred spring, is in an open, rocky landscape.

We may end our discussion of the gold rings from the Mycenaean world by noting the ring left to the Ashmolean Museum, by E. P. Warren (No. 14 in our series).[37] The only detail in its history is the statement of Hogarth, sometime Keeper of the Museum, that Warren knew of its existence "almost as long as the contents of the Vapheio tomb have been known." The inference drawn by some scholars is that probably "the ring once belonged to the contents of the tomb." Thus the pedigree of the example is rather vague. Its comparison to the gold ring actually found by Tsountas in that tomb will bring out striking differences. The hair of the women, indicated by long, rather snaky lines instead of dots, the thick waists, the massive form of the kneeling woman, the fuzzy rendering of the pleats of the skirt below the waist of the standing woman, the unique representation of an ear in the background, reminiscent of Egyptian prototypes, all these details seem to us to cast definite doubts on the authenticity of the ring. It is interesting to compare the small male figure hovering in the air with the small male figure invoked by the woman worshiper on the signet ring from Knossos.[38] The stance of the little figure, his bow instead of a spear, the raised left arm, the dots below his right arm that should have been behind his head, as it is in the ring from Knossos and as it would naturally be for a figure descending, inspire further doubts as to its genuineness. The vertical lines on the platform of the composition are paralleled by a similar arrangement on the ring from Knossos, which may have been the prototype from which the

---

[35] Cf. Pausanias, VIII, 38, 7. Kourouniotes, *Ephemeris*, 1904, pp. 153 ff.
[36] Evans, *Palace of Minos*, III, p. 137, fig. 89. Persson, *op.cit.*, pp. 62-64, 176 no. 16.

[37] Nilsson, *op.cit.*, pp. 342 ff., fig. 155. Persson, *op.cit.*, pp. 32-34 and 171 no. 1. Evans, *Palace of Minos*, II, p. 842.
[38] *Palace of Minos*, I, p. 160 fig. 115.

little hovering figure was drawn. But even if the ring is genuine, it first has to be proved that it represents a mourning scene instead of a dancing ritual, and the appearance of the descending male figure in a scene of this kind has to be justified. The identification of one of the boulders as a pithos is also doubtful. On the ring from Vapheio Persson identified an upturned pithos; here, however, he identifies a pithos standing on its base. Why the difference? Again, the suggestion that in the standing woman we have the Great Mother herself who comes to the scene through the invocation of the prostrate woman will raise the question, why the divine epiphany? If Persson's assumption is correct that the "pithos" contains a burial, then what would the presence of the goddess mean? Usually it is believed that the divinity approaches the worshipers to hear their prayers and demands. Why should the goddess appear in burial rites or obsequies? The assumption of Persson that this indicates the belief that "the dead shall arise" is too imaginative and not justified by the facts. One wonders whether in the hundreds of graves excavated any evidence was found suggesting, let alone proving, such a belief. The very fact that Persson does not mention evidence that would have strengthened his interpretation is proof that such does not exist; and we must remember that he excavated and published a good number of Mycenaean graves.

Perhaps we should also repeat that no evidence for a cult of the dead has been revealed thus far in any Mycenaean site or grave; the effort, therefore, to interpret scenes on the gold rings as ritual obsequies over the graves of a hero or an ancestor and to see in them the promise for resurrection is actually not only in variance but in conflict with the evidence preserved by the actual graves and brought to light by excavators. Again we may point out the fact that Persson's division of the ring representations into winter, spring, and summer scenes is quite arbitrary. Except for the ring in the Ashmolean Museum, all his examples of winter scenes have trees as loaded with leaves as those in his examples of spring and summer. And one wonders why the scene on the Vapheio ring, or the Mycenae example is set in winter? The study of these rings, I believe, leads to the only possible conclusion, expressed by Nilsson so succinctly: on the rings we have representations of forms of the cult devoted to the sacred tree that belongs pre-eminently to the countryside.[39]

From the gold foil specimens of the shaft graves and from the rings that seem to range in date from all the three subdivisions of the Mycenaean age, we learn that sacred buildings did exist in that age. Some of them

could have been tripartite; their religious nature is always indicated by the horns of consecration on the entablatures. Only in one example, on the ring in the collection of Evans (Fig. 125, No. 8), we find the "tripartite shrine" decorated with branches and beyond it a tree standing by itself. In the other five examples no trees or plants are associated with the "tripartite shrine." In contrast, in the three examples where enclosures or portals are represented we always find associated with them a tree, which may stand for a grove, but no horns of consecration. Trees are also connected with what has been called a sacred spring house with its doubtful roof ornament. In two out of the three representations of these enclosures and groves we find worshipers, two women and one man, engaged in a vigorous orgiastic dance. A similar orgiastic dance is performed by one man and one woman on the Vapheio ring before a tree and "a mound"; it is perhaps legitimate to assume that the mound takes the place of the enclosure and that both indicate sacred groves. The sacredness of the enclosures perhaps is also indicated by baetyls which are seen standing in at least one of the examples. It is also possible to assume that by means of the orgiastic dancing the divine presence is invoked. In contrast to the dances performed by men and women, in front of these enclosures and groves, the worshipers approaching the structures embellished with horns of consecration are represented in a stately, almost hieratic attitude, expressing their reverence by means of measured gestures. Only in one instance (Fig. 124, No. 9) does a worshiper stand in front of an enclosure and a sacred tree in a measured, respectful attitude, raising his forearm in adoration. In all three examples of enclosures and dancing scenes the men represented wear leggings, and in two out of three the enclosures are built over rocky ground. The standing man of Ring 9 is also wearing leggings. Could this detail, along with the rocky ground on which the enclosures stand, indicate that these are on hilly sites far from regular settlements? Another even more remarkable detail is that neither in the shrines with the horns of consecration nor on the enclosures do we have a double axe represented. And with the exception of the tripartite shrine in gold foil from Graves III and IV, we have no birds standing for a divine epiphany. Finally, we may note that the shrines represented seem to be very small.

Shrines Revealed by Excavations

If from the representations on works of art we turn to the architectural remains of the Mycenaean world, we shall find that no foundations of a tripartite shrine have thus far been discovered, not even in the Minoan

[39] Nilsson, *op.cit.*, pp. 272 and 274.

area. Marinatos suggests that in the villa of Vathy-petro we may have the foundations of a tripartite shrine, but his evidence is not definite.[40] Remains of shrines have rarely been found in the mainland of Greece, in the Mycenaean area. In the ruins of the palaces archaeologists have suggested possible sites of shrines, but again evidence is lacking. Thus, Wace identified as a shrine a room in the upper terrace of the palace at Mycenae. But we have seen that most probably that room was a gallery. With greater reason Blegen, as we have already noted, identified as a shrine Room 93 in the northeast wing of the palace at Pylos. It stands higher than the court it faces, and its front is completely open. No relics whatever were found in it to indicate its identity, but in the court and on its axis a rectangular block was found and identified as an altar. What may be a fragment of a set of horns of consecration found in the palace may come from the shrine.[41] At Asine Persson discovered a house shrine in one of the late Mycenaean houses in what may be called the *domos* of that house. Against one of its corners a shelf was revealed on which were standing cult objects and figurines at the time of the excavation.[42] The pottery found is of the granary style, indicating that this house shrine was in use to the very end of the Mycenaean era.

Another house shrine was found by Persson at the site of Berbati. Its final publication is forthcoming, but in a brief report given by Nilsson we find that again in one of the corners of the house stood a small bench of unworked stones on which fragments of two small female figurines and bases were found. When the house was later remodeled, the small bench was replaced by a construction consisting of two large stones and other stones formed a kind of channel. The foot of a pedestaled goblet was fixed in this construction, which could be accepted as an altar.[43]

We may perhaps have a house shrine in the citadel of Mycenae. Above the House of Tsountas, Wace cleared a large room with stuccoed floor, with benches along two of its walls, and a large hearth at its south end. At the southwest angle of this hearth was disclosed a depression in which the pointed end of a libation vessel could have been accommodated. A shallow channel in the floor connected this with a two-handled jar sunk in the floor. The arrangement parallels the channel and hollows found by Blegen at the side of the throne in the megaron of Pylos. Wace noted that near this stuccoed room Tsountas found the

painted tablet of the war goddess, to be described below, and at a small distance the fragment of fresco on which three daemons or genii are represented. These finds may suggest that the room served as a house shrine although no idols or other cult objects were found in it.

John Caskey now reports (text fig. 25) a temple of the Late Helladic I period at the site of Aghia Eirene on the Island of Keos.[44] With the exception of its

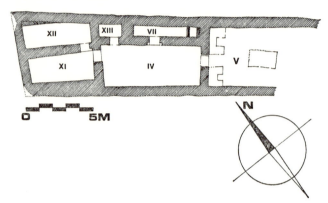

25. Keos. Plan of temple (after Caskey)

southeast end, lost by the encroachment of the sea, the temple is well preserved and some of its walls, made of schist stones, still stand to a height of two m. Its greatest preserved length amounts to about 23 m., while its width is 6 m. Two long connected rooms are its most conspicuous apartments. In the middle of the outer room (v) is preserved a stone rectangular platform around which were found fragments of terra-cotta figures. Against its northwest wall are to be seen benches flanking a doorway which gave access to the inner Room IV. The north side of that room is occupied by a corridor (VII) and a cupboard (XIII), while beyond its west side are to be found two small rooms or cells (XI and XII), differently oriented perhaps because they were laid out and used before the main axis of the building was established. Their contents and the relics preserved below their floors indicate that these cells are the oldest part of the structure. Cell XI seems to have served as the *adyton* or the inner sanctum of the temple at the time of its construction; its approach from Room IV is provided with a marble step, while stone thresholds are found in the door openings of the other rooms. On the floor of Room XI were found among potsherds many battered fragments of terra-cotta figures, lying about in confusion, a small clay jug with a double rim, and another with a

[40] Marinatos, *Praktika*, 1952, pp. 608-609. Of course we seem to have a parallel in the Cretan examples in the Late Minoan frescoes from the Palace of Knossos.

[41] Blegen, *AJA*, 65 (1961), pl. 55 fig. 15.

[42] Frödin-Persson, *Asine*, pp. 298 and 308. Room XXXII of House G; plan on page 75. Nilsson, *op.cit.*, pp. 112-114 fig. 32.

[43] Nilsson, *op.cit.*, p. 116. For the possible house shrine of Mycenae cf. *JHS*, 71 (1951), pp. 254-55.

[44] Caskey, *Hesperia*, 31 (1962), pp. 278-283; 33 (1964), pp. 326-328, fig. 2; *Archaeology*, 15 (1962), pp. 223 ff. and 17 (1964), p. 277.

long neck and handle, probably for ceremonial use. In corridor VII part of a bronze boat was found and on a higher level the upper part of a solid bronze figurine of a youth raising his hand to his forehead in Minoan fashion.

The temple seems to have been constructed not later than the fifteenth century, since below the floor of its *adyton* the fill is characterized by Middle Helladic sherds. It was destroyed, perhaps by earthquakes, was built again in the thirteenth century and remained in use to the end of the Mycenaean period. Even in the Historic era the *adyton* (Room XI) seems to have been regarded as a sacred place. In it, as we have noted, and in the connected rooms were found many battered fragments of female terra-cotta figures; "not less than 15" reports Professor Caskey, "and the total may approach 20." This multitude of figures makes it impossible, at least for the time being, to determine whether there is among them a cult figure of the divinity that was worshiped in the temple and to attempt to identify that divinity. It should be noted specially that a severed head of one of the broken terra-cotta figures, perhaps handed down from generation to generation as a sacred object, was set in a clay ring acting as a base on a level about one meter above the floor of the original *adyton*. Finally, Dionysos was worshiped in the shrine from the sixth into the fourth century B.C. In the temple of Keos we have a most striking example of the erection and maintenance of a shrine over an area traditionally held sacred.

One of the most ambitious sacred buildings of the Mycenaean age in the mainland is to be found at Eleusis, but its identification rests on its peculiarities as a structure and on circumstantial evidence. No relics were found within it to prove its identity, yet the structure seems to have served as a temple.[45] It was found on the east slope of the hill of Eleusis and below the floor of the later *Telesteria*, that is, in an area over which substantial buildings were constructed, because it had been sanctified by a special divine act. In plan it is a megaron and in front of its *aithousa* stretched a platform some 2 m. in length (text fig. 26). Its yard was surrounded by a *peribolos* wall. It seems to us that this small building, with its platform, its yard surrounded by wall, in the area that tradition maintains was used for the construction of the first temple to Demeter, over which in successive buildings and generations the *anaktoron* or holy of holies of the sanctuary of Demeter was constructed, could have served no other but a religious purpose. Still its iden-

tification as a temple rests, as we said, on circumstantial evidence. It was built to serve a special cult, and characteristically it is not tripartite.

At Malthi Dorion a "Shrine of the Double Axe" was recognized in the ruins of a house belonging to the late Mycenaean period.[46] Its identification rests on the discovery of a bronze double axe and packed vases on its floor. In size it is no different from the

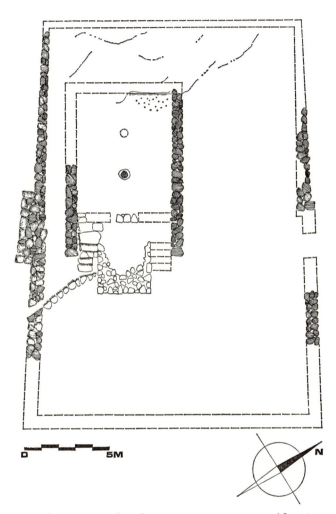

26. Eleusis. Temple of Demeter in megaron (drawing Travlos)

known Mycenaean bronze double axes which were used as tools. A similar axe with blunted edges was found by Tsountas in one of the rooms of the palace of Mycenae, which certainly was not a shrine, and the packed vases recall the potter's shop of Zygouries and the cellar of the house at Mycenae excavated by Papadimitriou and Petsas. We shall see shortly that votive axes are known from Crete and their nature is

[45] Mylonas, *Eleusis and the Eleusinian Mysteries*, pp. 34 ff., fig. 11. On the evidence of Ring 4 and of the fresco fragment from Pylos, we should restore one instead of two columns in the façade of the *aithousa*.

[46] M. N. Valmin, *The Swedish Messenia Expedition*, 1938, pp. 178-180. For a sample of a Mycenaean bronze double axe used as a tool, see Mylonas, *AJA*, 66 (1962), pl. 121 fig. 5.

indicated by the thin plate of metal used in their making or by their small size; they could not serve a practical purpose. This has also been noted by Dr. N. Valmin. The axe from Malthi-Dorion is a typical Mycenaean tool, not a votive offering or a religious symbol. The evidence for identifying the room as a shrine does not justify the assumption and certainly is most inadequate to prove it.

In the Island of Delos Professor Hubert Gallet de Santerre identifies as "Mycenaean" temples three structures indicated on his drawing by the letters Ac, Γ, and H. The first is to be found below the floor of the later *Artemision* and is preserved in a fragmentary form. It is assumed to be composed of a long *cella* measuring about 15.30 by 2.65 m. Nothing was found in it to indicate its function.[47] But it is reasoned that the objects in gold and ivory found in 1928 and 1946, among which is to be seen a double axe of thin plate of bronze evidently made for cult purposes, must have belonged to a shrine and that the foundations Ac are what survives of that shrine. One may wonder, however, how we can be sure of the plan of the building since only one of its long sides is preserved, and what can prove that the precious articles found were not a treasure buried by a wealthy citizen, even a wealthy priest.

The foundations of "Shrine Γ" are well preserved and reveal a rectangular shape. Nothing was found in it to prove its sacred character. It is assumed that it was surrounded by a peribolos wall, but only a few stones in two widely separated points are taken to indicate the existence of that wall. Very few pieces of pottery were found in and around the structure to indicate its date—one sherd found by Vallois, others found in 1948. However, its plan is comparable to that of the shrine of Keos, in its long and narrow form. The case for "Shrine H" is even weaker, with no evidence whatever to prove its claim. Consequently, for the identification of the buildings on Delos, also, we shall have to depend on reasoning and circumstantial evidence.

In the other famous site of Apollo, at Delphi, a sanctuary must have been located at Marmaria. No traces of a structure were revealed, but on a big stone some thirty terra-cotta figurines of the known Mycenaean types were found. These and other objects possibly indicate that in LH III B times a shrine or a sacred enclosure must have existed there. Deeper in the fill, along with a core of obsidian and a perforated sea shell, was found a votive double axe. Unfortu-

nately, the exact context in which this was found is not determined, and apparently the fill of the stratum was not undisturbed.[48]

We meet a similar situation at the site of Amyklai, in Lakonia, where no sacred structure was found, but a good number of female and animal figurines, indicating perhaps the existence of a Mycenaean sacred enclosure still in use in LH III C times. On that site was later built a temple of Apollo.[49]

The survey of the remains in the Mycenaean area suggested as belonging to shrines proves that they are neither numerous nor very definite. Verified religious structures are house shrines, the temple of Keos, and perhaps that of Eleusis. The identity of other remains assumed to belong to temples standing by themselves is subject to argument and is based, in the main, on reasoning and circumstantial evidence. We may, however, on the evidence of Keos and Eleusis, maintain that separate buildings serving as temples, such as are shown in the representations on the rings we have discussed, did exist in Mycenaean times.

Sacred Columns and Boughs

Within the shrines observed on gems and rings we often find a single column with capital and entablature; in the case of the tripartite shrines in gold foil we find a column in each of the three divisions. The sacred character of these columns seems to be indicated by the horns of consecration which we find in front of their bases in the examples from the shaft graves and on the ring of the "Priestess or Goddess with the mirror." In the sacred enclosures or portals we find baetyls whose nature as cult objects is well established. Evans long ago suggested that the columns and pillars stand as the aniconic image of a deity; they are its embodiment. However, in all the cases we have seen thus far the columns certainly have a structural function, and this is incompatible with their being embodiments of a divinity. There are a few instances in which free-standing columns are represented. On a seal cylinder from Mycenae are carved in intaglio six columns among which stands a man in an attitude of adoration (Fig. 124, No. 20).[50] Although the columns have capitals and bases, they do not carry entablatures.

We are carried a step further by the interesting scene represented on one of the impressed glass plaques found by Tsountas in the so-called Tomb of the Genii at Mycenae (Fig. 126, No. 22).[51] Two pairs of strange-looking genii, which we shall discuss later,

[47] H. Gallet de Santerre, *Délos primitive et archaïque*, 1958, pp. 91, 92-93 drawing B and p. 93 n. 1.

[48] Demangel, *Fouilles de Delphes*, II, "Le sanctuaire d'Athéna Pronaia," fasc. 3, pp. 5 ff. For the double axe see fig. 13, 3.

[49] *Ephemeris*, 1892, pl. 3 nos. 1, 3, 4 and *Ath. Mitt.*, 52 (1927), Beilage, VI.

[50] Nilsson, *op.cit.*, p. 245. *JHS*, 21 (1901), p. 141 fig. 24.

[51] Evans, *JHS*, 21 (1901), pp. 117-118.

stand on their hind legs, holding beaked jugs evidently used in Mycenaean times for libations. Between the first two genii stands a low unit, and another like it between the two pairs of genii. Evans, who first published the plaque, suggested that the element we call a low unit is a bowl resting on a "tripod with a central stem," that the bowl "might be regarded as a capital of the column, but this would not explain the side supports." But the "side supports" are two in number, and this would eliminate the tripod notion. On the other hand an accentuation of the shaft of a column, as represented in gems and rings, is sometimes rendered by means of lines drawn vertically along the edge of the columns. The clearest example of this practice is illustrated on the so-called fleur-de-lys column on a gold ring from Mycenae (Fig. 124, No. 43). There the lines are taken to indicate a "fluted pillar." Similarly, the vertical edges of a foliated "pillar tree" on a crystal signet ring in Evans' collection, reputed to have been found at Mycenae, are emphasized by straight lines.[52] The column with the griffins attached to it on a lentoid gem from Mycenae published by Tsountas seems to have its vertical edge strengthened by a line. Again the so-called central stem definitely tapers downwards, a characteristic feature of a column; it is doubtful that a central support would have been made that way. Finally, one may wonder why a comparatively tremendous central support would be needed for a comparatively small bowl, already supported by the assumed tripod. A comparison of the so-called bowl to the bulging capital of a well-defined column represented on the sealing from the Rhyton Well of Mycenae (Fig. 127, No. 38), found by Wace and discussed below, will prove that it too is the capital of a column. The facts pointed out are illustrated more definitely on a fragment of a glass paste plaque we found at Mycenae in the summer of 1963. It is obvious, we believe, that the central unit on the plaque is a column standing by itself. The fact that the "genii" are ready to pour a libation over it would indicate its sacred character.

A remarkable composition is to be seen on a sealing found by Wace in what came to be known as the "Rhyton Well" some 50 m. southeast of the great ramp in the citadel of Mycenae (Fig. 127, No. 38).[53] On that small piece of clay, only 3 cm. long and 24 mm. wide, we find impressed an unfluted Mycenaean

column with a kneeling quadruped on either side of it. The species of animal cannot be definitely determined, but to Wace they seem "more like goats than horses." I think that they are sheep. The bulbous capital of the column is surmounted by a number of crescent-shaped elements the most obvious of which are two sets of horns of consecration, one inside the other. On top of the uppermost pair a bird is pecking, while two more birds are represented in flight, one over each of the kneeling quadrupeds. Between the upper and the lower set of horns of consecration is a row of round dots "intended to indicate a row of beam ends," explains the discoverer of the sealing, but rather serving to separate the two sets of horns. Here perhaps we have another example of a sacred column.

"Genii" are again represented on a gem from the cist of the Vapheio tholos tomb, holding libation jugs over boughs whose sacred character is indicated by horns of consecration placed in front of them on a stand (Fig. 126, No. 27).[54] Branches are again represented between three men who raise their hands in a gesture of adoration on a gem found on the citadel of Mycenae and now in the National Museum of Athens.[55] There can be no doubt that, like the trees of the enclosures pictured on the rings, the boughs here are cult objects. So we find that trees, boughs, baetyls, sacred stones, and columns were objects of cult in Mycenaean times. The question naturally arises whether or not we have representations of the deities who were worshiped in these shrines and enclosures, who were invoked by worshipers either by prayers and gestures of adoration or by dancing. We have a few objects on which beyond doubt a divinity is represented.

The Tree Goddess

Most interesting and important is the great gold ring, the second largest found thus far in the mainland, found by Drosinos to the south of Grave Circle A (Fig. 123, No. 15). It is generally assumed that it formed part of the furnishings of a shaft grave and has been repeatedly described from the day of its discovery to the present.[56] The design on its bezel, cut in intaglio, is remarkable both for its technical perfection and its subject. Under a tree laden with foliage a woman is seated, holding in her right hand three poppy heads on long stalks. Two women approach

[52] *JHS*, 21 (1901), p. 155 fig. 33 and p. 156 fig. 34. See also the trunk of the tree on the gold ring from the akropolis of Mycenae, Marinatos-Hirmer, *op.cit.*, fig. 207, and our Fig. 123, no. 15.

[53] *BSA*, 24 (1919-1921), p. 205. *Mycenae*, fig. 110e. Nilsson, *op.cit.*, p. 174 fig. 78. The horns of consecration on the sealing can be compared with profit to those on the roof of the tripartite shrines of Fig. 122e.

[54] *Ephemeris*, 1889, pl. 10 no. 35. Nilsson, *op.cit.*, p. 146

fig. 53.

[55] National Museum, Athens no. 5409. Wace, *Chamber Tombs*, p. 204 pl. xxa.

[56] It was first published by Schliemann, *Mycenae*, p. 354 fig. 530; then by Tsountas, *RA*, 37 (1900), pl. VIII, 1. Persson, *Religion*, pp. 70-76 and 178 no. 22, who states wrongly that the ring was found by Schliemann. Nilsson, *op.cit.*, p. 347 fig. 158. Helen Thomas, *BSA*, 39 (1938-1939), pp. 79 ff.

her; one holds flowers, probably lilies, while the other has apparently handed her poppy heads to the seated woman. A little girl holding lilies stands in front of her, while behind the tree a second little girl raises her arms either in adoration or to touch the tree. A cairn of stones is to be seen between the seated woman and the first votary approaching her. A ceremonial double axe and a figure behind a figure-eight shield holding a spear are to be seen above the women. Six animal heads without horns, one above the other, occupy the left edge of the bezel, while above shine the sun and the crescent, separated from the rest by a triple wavy line, which has been interpreted as a rainbow or the Milky Way but which perhaps stands for the firmament.

It is generally accepted that the seated woman is a deity approached by votaries, but her identity is not established. She has been variously identified as Earth, Rhea Cybele and her nymphs, Aphrodite Ourania, a mortal princess with her attendants in the garden, the Great Minoan Goddess, the Tree Goddess, a Goddess of Healing, Demeter, and the Goddess of Nature in general. Since she is seated below the tree and since the tree is the important element in a well-documented cult, we believe that Persson's suggestion that she is the Tree Goddess seems nearest the mark.

The scene on the ring may be conceived of as set in a sacred enclosure. However, Persson's suggestion that it is the interior of the great shrine on the summit of the akropolis of Mycenae and that the sacred tree of the site is represented, like the tree of Athena on the Akropolis of Athens, seems rather far-fetched. Nilsson has suggested that the Goddess is represented in her "holy grove."[57] We have already seen that the shrines on works of art are always represented with horns of consecration; these are absent from our composition. Horns of consecration are also absent from the representations of sacred enclosures within which a tree is always represented. Here also, as the sun, the crescent, and the firmament indicate, the tree stands in a roofless area. If the animal heads are supposed to be nailed on a wall, then that wall would be the one enclosing the area of the sacred tree. Within the enclosures we noted that baetyls are standing the way the double axe is standing in our composition; and on the ring from Mycenae (Fig. 123, No. 10) in the second compartment, Evans saw a shield in the object represented there. That would give us the counterpart of the figure behind the figure-eight shield in our

composition. The cairn also will bring to mind the mound of earth on the Vapheio ring (Fig. 123, No. 12), behind which a tree is growing. I believe that all these common elements indicate that on the ring from the akropolis of Mycenae the interior of a sacred enclosure with its sacred tree and other elements is represented. The deity within it therefore should be the Tree Goddess, who is accepting the offerings of her votaries. The examples cited above represent orgiastic dancing held in her honor or in the course of invoking her epiphany.

On the analogy of a gold ring from Knossos, the figure behind the figure-eight shield is often identified as a male god, the consort of the Great Goddess, hovering in the air or descending to reach her. Persson sees in it a figure-eight shield appended to a standard, and we shall see shortly that if it is actually a divinity hovering in the air, it cannot be a male god. There is one detail, however, that may indicate that the figure is static. On a gold ring from Knossos we have an air-borne figure. There we see that the artist was aware of and able to suggest the air currents created by the downward motion of such a figure; the hair of the descending male god is represented by a number of dots flying in all directions. If the figure with the shield on the ring from Mycenae is air-borne, we would expect to find a similar arrangement in a representation of which every detail suggests exceptional technical ability. Such an arrangement does not exist. The two lines by the shield, like the similar two lines by the shaft of the double axe, are, as Persson suggested, symbolic of the ground on which these figures stand.

It is difficult to prove whether or not all the elements seen in the composition justify the suggestion that on the ring we have the Mycenaean pantheon. But we can maintain with a degree of confidence that the ring from the citadel of Mycenae represents a sacred enclosure within which are to be found the sacred tree and other sacred emblems—a cairn, the double axe, and perhaps the figure-eight shield standard. The Tree Goddess, seated under her sacred tree, receives the adoration of her votaries. The whole scene is depicted under the brilliant light of a morning sun.[58]

Another gold ring with a striking representation of a goddess comes from the neighborhood of Tiryns (Fig. 123, No. 16). It formed part of a treasure accidentally found by villagers in a large geometric cauldron.[59] It is the largest ring known thus far, the

---

[57] Nilsson, *op.cit.*, pp. 235 and 347 n. 22.

[58] Perhaps we should note that Herkenrath, *AJA*, 41 (1937), pp. 411 ff., suggested that the two small figures are idols; the suggestion seems impossible. Persson held that they were women represented on a smaller scale (*op.cit.*, p. 71). This is also im-

possible to maintain since the other women votaries are in full scale. Evans thought that they were attendants of the Great Goddess (*Palace of Minos*, II, pp. 339 ff.).

[59] Published by Karo, *Ath. Mitt.*, 55 (1930), pp. 121 ff. Nilsson, *op.cit.*, p. 147 fig. 55. Persson, *Religion*, pp. 76-79, 99, and 179

bezel measuring 32 cm. in extreme length. Seated on a camp-stool with a high back a Goddess, dressed in an elaborate, close-fitting, long garment, holds in her raised hand a tall, pointed goblet of the variety called by Evans sacramental pedestal goblet.[60] She wears on her head a plate-shaped cap and rests her feet on a footstool. In front of her stands a small column with a *thymiaterion* (incense burner) on top, while behind her stool, and over a small structure, is represented a bird perched on an unidentified object; Persson suggests that it is a sacral-knot. Towards the Goddess are moving four lion-shaped genii or daemons, walking on their hind legs, each holding aloft a beaked jug. Each seems to wear a hide on his back, covered by a net that is held in place by a belt. Behind each of the genii are placed leafy branches secured in their upright position by double or triple rings, apparently based in two or three superposed tiers. Above the skyline the sun and a crescent moon with horns pointed downwards are shown in a dotted field where four branches or trees are also represented. Persson accepted the dots as stars, but a comparison of the dotted area with the exergue of a ring from Mycenae (Fig. 123, No. 10) will show that an actual field is represented with plants growing in it over which the sun shines brightly. The composition is placed over an exergue decorated with the typical Mycenaean half-rosettes.

It is impossible, of course, to establish definitely the meaning of this intriguing composition. The daemons bring to mind the impressed paste plaques found by Tsountas in one of the tholos tombs of Mycenae, with similar genii holding identical beaked jugs, ready to pour libations over a cairn, over sacred columns, over square altars. Here the libations are being brought to the goddess, and apparently they will be poured into the sacramental goblet she is holding. Persson suggested that on this ring "we have a scene representing a libation of the first wine of the season" to the Great Goddess "and that the daemons are wine genii"; that "possibly we have a sacramental act, and it can scarcely be merely rain magic, as has most often been proposed." It will, of course, be impossible to prove that here we have the offering of the first wine,

but there can be little doubt that an offering in the form of a libation is being presented to the goddess whose personal epiphany is not to be doubted. The genii, the branches, would indicate that the goddess is a nature deity, perhaps the same one to be seen seated under her sacred tree on the ring from Mycenae.

The Mistress of Animals

Closely associated with the Tree Goddess is what has been called the Mistress of Animals (Πότνια Θηρῶν). Both are nature goddesses. In contrast to the former, the latter is not represented on the known Mycenaean rings, and as a matter of fact she is rarely represented on gems found in the Mycenaean territory. On a carnelian found in the tholos tomb of Vapheio we find a woman holding up a large ram whose head rests on her right shoulder. On a chalcedony gem from the same grave we find two women, one of whom grasps an animal standing erect before her.[61] Of course, we cannot be absolutely sure that these women are representations of the Mistress of Animals; they may be mortals playing with their pets; but we cannot deny the possibility. We have to bear in mind that the grasping of the animals indicates the power exercised over them by a deity and is the characteristic feature of the being who, in later times, became known as the Mistress of Animals.[62] The presence of animals, even wild and powerful like the lion or imaginary like the griffin, may indicate merely that they are guardians of a deity, not necessarily of the Mistress of Animals, or even guardians of an important mortal who wishes to stress his exalted position. We find them, for example, painted on the wall on either side of the throne of the king at Pylos.

Representations of a female deity grasping animals on either side of her are not extant in the Mycenaean world. The closest representation of the kind is on a red jasper ring found in 1892 at Mycenae and published by Tsountas. On this almost unique ring not a female divinity, but a long-haired, bearded man holds at arm's length two lions, one by the throat, the other by the hind leg (Fig. 125, No. 40).[63] He seems to be the counterpart of Gilgamesh rather than a god. We find a similar representation on a lentoid

no. 24. Persson's interpretation, of course, is inspired by his vegetation cycle theory. For a summary and evaluation of this untenable theory, see Nilsson, *op.cit.*, pp. 287-288.

[60] Evans, *Palace of Minos*, IV, p. 390. A similar goblet of alabaster was found in Shaft Grave V (Karo, *Schachtgräber*, pl. CXXXVIII) and one of silver in the royal tomb at Dendra (Persson, *The Royal Tombs at Dendra*, p. 51 fig. 30).

[61] Tsountas, *Ephemeris*, 1889, pl. 10 nos. 33, 34. Perhaps a similar secular scene should be recognized on the ivory plaque found by Tsountas at Mycenae on which we find represented an animal jumping up to reach a plant held in the raised hand of a woman, *Ephemeris*, 1888, pl. 8 no. 1, and Kantor in *Archae-*

ology, 13 (1960), pp. 23-24 fig. 23. We may note the clay sealing Wt 501 from Mycenae on which we find represented a man between two jumping goats, *Archaeology*, 13 (1960), p. 32 no. 15. In this last example we certainly have a secular scene.

[62] Nilsson, *op.cit.*, p. 360.

[63] *Mycenaean Age*, p. 160 fig. 54. Evans stresses the fact that he wears a Syrian loin cloth. His beard and hair, however, would identify him as a Mycenaean perhaps masquerading as Gilgamesh. Miss Chittenden maintains that he is the Master of Animals and a god to be found also on the Castellani gem—*Hesperia*, 16 (1947), pp. 109 and 110. One wonders, however, about the pedigree of that gem (see *infra*, pp. 166-167).

gem of agate discovered by Blegen in Tomb xxxiii of Prosymna. The human figure in the center now is a beardless youth who wears a typical Minoan loin cloth. On either side of him the youth holds a lion, one by the mane and the other by a hind leg.[64] The gem belongs to the LH III period. In this again we may have a reflection of the Gilgamesh prototype. On a gem from Kydonia in Crete, we have a beardless youth holding at arm's length two lions which seem to be "sitting upright," and Nilsson mentions a number of seal impressions bearing similar if not identical representations. But all these examples come from Crete, not from the mainland.[65] From the mainland we have an amethyst bead from the Vapheio tomb on which we find a woman holding in each hand a bird by the neck.[66]

On a lentoid ring-stone of pale yellow carnelian "which formed the bezel of a gold ring," a woman is seated on a lion's head, with a lion on either side of her (Fig. 126, No. 26). Nilsson gives Mycenae as its site, but Evans, who first published the gem, specifically states that "its provenience is unknown."[67] Evans also specifically states that the amygdaloid agate gem with a "female divinity" between a lion and a lioness, was found at Mycenae (Fig. 124, No. 21).[68] It formed part of his collection. It is unfortunate that the gem was not discovered in an excavation, since it exhibits certain features that are disturbing. The female figure between the lions apparently is represented kneeling and holds "her two hands in an evenly balanced attitude." The animals seem to be kissing or licking those hands in a very unique fashion. Equally unusual is the kneeling position of the woman and even more so the indication of the sex of the animals. A good many representations of lions on a variety of objects and in various techniques have survived; in no other example do we find this differentiation by means of the teats for the female and the genital organs for the male animal. In contrast, female griffins and bitches (in Minoan art) are clearly indicated. One wonders whether this interesting agate is an original.

The So-called Snake Goddess

Perhaps the most remarkable representation of lions on either side of a female figure comes from Chamber Tomb 515 of the Kalkani Cemetery at Mycenae (Fig. 125, No. 32). On two carnelian lentoid gems found

there by Wace we have a practically identical representation succinctly described by their discoverer. "The intaglio design," he wrote, "shows a standing woman; her hands are raised and support above her head an object shaped like two pairs of horns, but ending in snakes' heads; from its center rises a double axe. . . . On either side stands a rampant lion." Again, he states that "the object which the goddess holds above her head is clearly intended to represent snakes, but perhaps not actual snakes so much as a ritual object imitating snake forms." This "ritual object" consists of two bow-shaped superposed tubular members whose middle parts and ends curve upwards; the ends rise almost vertically to terminate in what resemble snake heads, but they have a ring beneath them. A similar ritual object is carried by a woman on four other gems; one in Cassel reputed to have been found in the tomb of Menidi, the other from the Diktaean cave, a third from the neighborhood of Knossos, and a fourth from Tomb xx of Ialysos. It is also carried by a woman on three sealings recently discovered by Blegen at Pylos. Wace remarked that all these gems are perforated along their horizontal axis and they seem to have belonged to necklaces.[69]

The same "ritual object" is certainly depicted on the bezel of the gold ring found above the roof slabs of the Princess' cist in the royal tholos tomb of Midea-Dendra.[70] Above an exergue where two quadrupeds are arranged symmetrically, we find two rather peculiar animals, represented in full front, standing over the middle of an object similar to that on the gems from Mycenae (Fig. 125, No. 31). Persson, who published the ring, carefully describes the "ritual object" as composed of "three stalks with a bud or a seed-vessel at the point; below the animals, they are bound together in an elaborate way." He therefore concludes that the ritual objects on the ring from Midea-Dendra are made up "of plants" and compares them with the three stalks on each side of a woman in the well-known hairpin from Shaft Grave IV.[71] In the latter case he notes that the stalks are "hanging downwards round the central figure." He could have compared his objects to the gold pendant from Aegina, of a later period, where we find the two parallel, tubular members issuing from behind the thighs of a male figure who holds a water bird by the neck with each hand. The birds are pecking the ends of the tubular mem-

---

[64] *Prosymna*, p. 274 fig. 581.

[65] Cf. Nilsson, *op.cit.*, p. 357 fig. 168.

[66] Tsountas, *Ephemeris*, 1889, pl. 10 no. 5.

[67] *JHS*, 21 (1901), p. 165 fig. 45, n. 2. Nilsson, *op.cit.*, p. 359. The gem is now in the British Museum. Originally in the hands of a Swiss collector, it found its way into the collection of Sir Wollaston Franks. Its pedigree is uncertain and Evans favors an east Cretan origin.

[68] *JHS*, 21 (1901), p. 165 fig. 44. Similar uncertainty as to

genuineness applies to the carnelian gem, acquired by Evans in Athens in 1931 and said to have been found at Mycenae, on which a woman is represented between lions, *Palace of Minos*, IV, part 2, p. 402 fig. 334.

[69] *Chamber Tombs*, p. 59, and p. 200 pl. XXVIII, 31 and 32. Nilsson, *op.cit.*, pp. 360 ff. Blegen, *AJA*, 65 (1961), pl. 60 c,d.

[70] Persson, *The Royal Tombs at Dendra*, p. 56. Evans, *The Palace of Minos*, IV, part 1, fig. 134 and pp. 170-171.

[71] Karo, *Schachtgräber*, pl. XXX no. 75.

bers. In the catalogue the tubular members are described as "branches."[72] On the sealings from Pylos we seem to have a woman supporting or holding aloft over her head the same ritual object, now made up of three tubular units, surmounted by a pair of horns of consecration. Over the horns there is a blob which cannot be identified. Instead of lions, horned animals stand on either side of the woman.

The nature of the "ritual object" held by the woman has created a problem that even now cannot be considered as solved. Wace suggested that the object was made up of snake forms. Others maintained that it was made up of snakes, even suggesting that these snakes had heads at both ends. Nilsson, however, pointed out that the "ritual object" seen on the gems from Mycenae, at least, could not have been made up of snakes since "the two parallel objects (the assumed snakes) . . . are connected with each other by three cross bars in each of the two lower curves. This is evidently impossible, if snakes are intended." Furthermore, the way the three tubular members are plaited into a single band in the ring from Dendra will definitely exclude their identification as snakes. The same cross bars and the thickened ends will rule out the suggestion that they represent bows. The final conclusion reached by Evans, after a thorough discussion of the problem, is that in fact they are "snake frames" influenced in form both by the bow of the goddess and by the horns of consecration; that the object is formed of the stuffed skins of two or three sacred snakes. Nilsson finds this explanation "too beset with difficulties," but, as he admits, he cannot "find another more probable." He, however, remarked that the "ritual object" is "reminiscent of the horns of consecration, and this resemblance is strengthened by the position of the double axe between the ends, just as it is placed between the horns of consecration" and suggests as an alternative "that the characteristically vivid imagination of the Minoans effected a formal modification of the object under the influence of the horns of consecration."[73] I believe that we shall be nearer the meaning of the "ritual object" if we combined Persson's and Nilsson's interpretations and suggestions: that the "ritual object" is made up of two or three pairs of horns of consecration made of stalks with a seed vessel at the ends bound together and plaited at the center. Thus, in this "ritual object" we have a combination of two emblems sacred to the Minoan-Mycenaeans, the horns of consecration and the sacred boughs. One thing, however, seems clear:

the "ritual object" is not made up of snakes. Consequently the woman who supports it cannot be conceived as the Snake Goddess, but possibly a priestess.

Perhaps it may prove profitable to compare the objects made of tubular units to the representation of the horns of consecration over the column represented on the sealing from the rhyton well of Mycenae (Fig. 127, No. 38). There too we seem to be having tubular members and interestingly enough the ends of the horns are emphasized by dots which would correspond to what are taken to be "snake heads" or "seed vessels" of the ritual object. Above the lower set of the horns on the sealing from Mycenae we find two straight vertical lines reaching a horizontal line. This linear pattern seems to be reflected in the pattern over the tubular object on the lentoid bead-seal from Ialysos; in that example, however, we have three vertical lines rising above the tubular upper horizontal member to a horizontal line. Could these linear patterns represent another ritual article placed on top of horns of consecration? It is interesting to note that on some small glass paste plaques exhibited in the National Museum at Athens,[74] we find represented a woman with the well-known flounced skirt holding in her right hand a three-pronged object identical to the linear pattern on the sealing and on the Ialysos gem. In the plaque the three-pronged object must certainly have a ritualistic meaning. When we find it elsewhere, it may indicate similarity of the objects on which it is placed. It seems to us that these observations strengthen the conclusion that the tubular ritualistic object is formed of horns of consecration made of boughs tied together at the center. Of course, the middle part of the horns of consecration on the Mycenae sealing does not curve upwards; but this in the examples on gems was due to the necessity of placing the objects over the head of the woman in a small lentoid space. In the sealings from Pylos the middle part of the "ritual object" is almost straight and this may indicate that the upward curving of the central section was due to technical reasons rather than to an attempt on the part of the artist to represent the object exactly as it was in reality. As a matter of fact variations do exist among the representations as to this section of the object.

Later in our study we shall return to the double axe over the "ritual object" on the gems from Mycenae. We may now note that the exergue is filled with dots which could only indicate the surface of the earth. In a similar manner the earth was indicated on the

[72] Nilsson, *op.cit.*, p. 367. Higgins, *Greek and Roman Jewellery*, places the pendant in the seventeenth century B.C., p. 65 and color plate B1.

[73] Nilsson, *op.cit.*, pp. 364-366. We consider the full description

of the views held by scholars regarding this representation necessary since the conclusions based on it are of extreme importance.

[74] Accession no. 2450.

ring from Mycenae and on the ring from Tiryns (Fig. 123, Nos. 15 and 16). The position of the rampant lions on either side of the woman may suggest that she is a goddess. One wonders, however, whether she may not be a priestess holding aloft sacred objects towards which is directed the adoration of the animals. I prefer this interpretation.

The Goddess of Blessing

A goddess is certainly represented riding a mythical animal, moving above the earth, on a clear chalcedony gem almost circular in shape, found by Papadimitriou and myself in an old excavation dump piled beyond the south side of Grave Circle B (Fig. 117).[75] The goddess wears a flounced skirt and the upper part of her body is nude. The animal seems to have the body and tail of a lion, and the head resembles that of a horse or even of a camel. The goddess raises her hands in the well-known gesture of blessing or benediction.

We find the goddess seated on an animal in the same attitude on some of the eight glass plaques found in the King's cist of the tholos tomb of Midea-Dendra.[76] Persson identified the animal as a bull and interpreted the scene as the prototype of Europa and the Bull. Unfortunately, the head of the animal is missing or is not well preserved in the plaques of Midea; consequently its identification is impossible. However, the female figure can be made out clearly, and she holds her arms and hands in exactly the same position as the goddess on the gem from Mycenae; she certainly does not hold the animal by the horns, which in fact do not seem to exist. The plaques date from the LH III A period, ca. 1400-1300 B.C., and they indicate that the type was current in the fourteenth century. If the gem from Mycenae came from the tomb of Klytemnestra, then we may feel justified in assuming that the type continued into the thirteenth century.

More striking than the glass plaques of Midea-Dendra is a terra-cotta figurine in the collection of Mme. Stathatou (Fig. 118). It is reported to have been found in a grave at Charvati in Attika.[77] A goddess is represented riding on her mythical animal. The attitude of the figure is the same as that on the gem from Mycenae, but now the head is stylized completely and the raised arms and hands have been transformed into wing-like projections. Furthermore, the figure is represented *en face* and apparently fully clothed. The animal on which she is riding looks like a horse, although

its pointed muzzle would indicate that this too is a mythical animal. Doro Levi, who published the figurine, maintained that the figure was seated on a saddle. A study of the example, however, especially its rear side, would indicate that she is placed on a set of horns of consecration. This would identify her as the Goddess of Blessing.

Mme. Stathatou's figurine carries us to the next step in the evolution of the type, to the representation of a seated female figurine found by Tsountas in a chamber tomb at Mycenae.[78] Unfortunately, the object on which she was seated was not found. I doubt that the figure was seated on an animal; in that case we would have had a solid attachment that would have left traces on the figurine. Most probably she was seated on a three-legged throne similar to examples known from a number of sites. The similarity of the figurine to that of Mme. Stathatou's is evident, and there can be no doubt that in this sequence we have the same goddess now riding on her mythical animal through the ether, now seated on her throne, now standing. The figurines of the standing or Ψ type, which we have studied in connection with the burial customs of the Mycenaeans, form the final stage in the development of the type. Such figurines, along with others of the Φ and T types, as well as bovine representations, have been found not only in graves but in settlements and in areas which have rightly been considered as precincts of sanctuaries.[79] Delphi and its sacred area has yielded many examples of such figurines, some of which, type Ψ, should represent a divinity, some votaries. It is perhaps interesting to remark that type Ψ, the Goddess of Blessing, continued in use during the LH III C period but is as well as all the other types disappears abruptly after the end of the Mycenaean Age.

Perhaps one of the most striking examples of a figurine representing a votary was found in the summer of 1962 at Mycenae in one of the rooms by Corridor C of the gallery and storeroom system which we have proved existed along the north Cyclopean wall (Fig. 128). It stands 18 cm. in height, and, unfortunately, the top of its head is missing. It represents a woman elaborately decked, with both hands held in front of her chest, dressed in a bell-shaped or rounded skirt that covers the lower part of her body completely. It is decorated with broad circular bands.

The Minoan antecedents of the Goddess of Blessing as represented by the figurines of the Ψ type are well known.[80] That she was worshiped to the end of the

[75] Mylonas, *Ancient Mycenae*, fig. 35.
[76] Persson, *Religion*, p. 133 fig. 24. Nilsson, *op.cit.*, pp. 36-37.
[77] Doro Levi, "La dea Mycenea a cavallo," *Studies Presented to D. M. Robinson*, I, pp. 108 ff. pl. 4, a-b.
[78] Mylonas, "Seated and Multiple Mycenaean Figurines,"

The Aegean and the Near East, pp. 110 ff. Our Fig. 109.
[79] *Supra*, p. 148. For the Minoan origin of the Goddess with raised hands see S. Alexiou, Ἡ μινωϊκὴ θεὰ μεθ' ὑψωμένων χειρῶν, 1958. Also S. Marinatos, *Ephemeris*, 1927-1928, pp. 7 ff.
[80] Nilsson, *op.cit.*, fig. 32, and note 79.

Mycenaean period is indicated by the sacred objects found by Persson in the house-shrine of Asine. Among them are two figurines of the goddess with raised arms, now in a standing attitude. Two more figurines are among the objects found in the sanctuary of Berbati; others are known from Amyklae; these also belong to a late Mycenaean period.

In the shrine of Asine was also found a large terra-cotta head which may belong to a male figure. Persson at first called it the "Lord of Asine," but under Evans' influence he later identified it as belonging to a female idol. Its similarity to the terra-cotta heads from Keos may indicate that Evans' identification is the correct one. Nilsson accepts it as a male head. From Mycenae comes a painted plaster head of a male figure. Wace discovered it along with the beautiful ivory group of two women and a boy in the fill of Room 5 below the north terrace wall of the Hellenistic temple.[81] A fragment now in the Museum of Classical Art and Archaeology at the University of Illinois, reported to have been found at Mycenae, is the head of a male figurine.[82] It is not a very exciting work of art, but there can be no doubt that it belongs to a male figure; the beard is indicated not only by the projection of the chin, but is also emphasized by a band of color. The mustache also is indicated by a band of color. Whether or not the plaster and terra-cotta heads belonged to a representation of a male divinity cannot be now determined; they may have belonged to male votaries. Incidentally, a terra-cotta male figurine was discovered in 1964 in a drain serving the northwest section of the hill of Mycenae. The man seems to hold his hands below his forehead in an attitude of prayer.

The figurines enumerated are small in scale. That the Mycenaeans occasionally modeled figures larger than these is indicated by the head made of plaster and gaily painted, found by Tsountas at Mycenae (Fig. 132).[83] It is almost life size and belongs to a female figure. The modeling is broad and vigorous, and its effect is enhanced by color. The face is covered with white, indicating that we are dealing with a woman; the eyes, the hair, the flat cap over the hair, and the lips are painted. Furthermore, a dotted rosette is painted on each cheek. It is usually assumed that the head belongs to a sphinx, whose popularity as an art motif is well known in late Mycenaean times. However, Evans has reported a "clay head of a Goddess" found above the Villa Ariadne at Knossos, now in the Ashmolean Museum. It has a flat-topped head

gear and tattoo marks on cheeks and nose; these recall the details of the plaster head from Mycenae. He believed it to have belonged to a very late shrine, perhaps from the period when Knossos was under the domination of Mycenaean rulers.[84]

In his excavations at Keos, Caskey found numerous fragments of terra-cotta figures of almost life size, as we have seen. All are female. They are made of local coarse clay and the surface is covered with a coat of finer clay; traces of white color found in some fragments seem to indicate that the nude parts of the figures were painted white. The figures were made in sections and contained wooden armatures to support the parts until the firing was completed. They are frontal and wear typical flaring Minoan skirts that reach to the ground thus giving a solid base to the figures. Around slim waists the skirts are secured by heavy bands. The upper part of the body in some examples is bare, in others covered by the typical Minoan bodice open in front to expose the breasts. Some figures wear what seems to be a collar, others a garland. The hands rest on the hips; thus the figures have a posture characteristic of dancers. They hold their heads erect and their long and oval faces exhibit high cheek bones, sharp noses, small eyes, and arched brows. Some seem to smile, others are serious. Thick braids of hair are hanging down their backs.

Whether or not all these figures were made at one time and when, remains undetermined, although they seem to belong to the shrine of the fifteenth century B.C. They seem to represent votaries, perhaps dancers, and no fragments have been identified as belonging to a cult statue. How these figures were arranged in the shrine cannot be determined, but they must have presented an awe-inspiring sight. They have no parallels in the Mycenaean world and they seem to point to Crete for antecedents and inspiration. But even in Crete the nearest figures, those found by Marinatos at Gazi, belong to the closing years of the Minoan era.[85]

Ivory Figurines

We mention finally the ivory group of two women and a boy discovered by Wace in 1939 in the same fill in which the male head of clay was found (Fig. 129).[86] It is a lovely and very interesting piece of work, but there is no evidence proving that it belonged to a shrine or that it represents goddesses. The shawl of the one woman rests on the hip of the other. Whether

[81] Persson, *Religion*, p. 100 n. 1; *Asine*, p. 308 fig. 211. Evans, *Palace of Minos*, IV, p. 756. Wace, *Mycenae*, fig. 104, b.
[82] Mylonas, *AJA*, 41 (1937), pp. 237-247.
[83] Tsountas, *Ephemeris*, 1902, pls. 1, 2. Marinatos-Hirmer, *op.cit.*, pls. XLI-XLII in color.
[84] Evans, *Palace of Minos*, IV, part 2, pp. 756-757 fig. 738.

[85] Caskey, *Hesperia*, 33 (1964), pp. 328-331, pls. 57-61. *Archaeology*, 15 (1962), pp. 223-226. Marinatos-Hirmer, *op.cit.*, figs. 128-131 and 135-137.
[86] Wace, *JHS*, 59 (1939), p. 210; *Mycenae*, pp. 83-84 and 115 figs. 101-103.

this is an attribute of divinity cannot be proved by the existing evidence from the Mycenaean world; in this group we have its only appearance. But this connection of the two figures by a shawl is reflected by the so-called Siamese figurines in terra-cotta, two examples of which have been found thus far in graves, one at Mycenae itself (Fig. 108). In both, the two females are tending a child, perhaps a boy;[87] in both they are attached to each other at the shoulder, hence the appellation "Siamese twins," as the figures in the ivory group are connected by the shawl. Wace identified the two women as Demeter and Persephone and the boy as "both Iakchos and the young male god of the Minoan-Mycenaean religion." Nilsson has already objected to the identification of Iakchos, since that divine being "came into existence only after the annexation of Eleusis by Athens" and has pointed out that "there is no definite evidence that this group represents two goddesses and the divine child."[88] Palmer's identification of the boy as Triptolemos is even less fortunate, since that hero was introduced rather late (after the end of the sixth century?) into the Eleusinian pantheon.[89] As we noted above, there is neither evidence nor indication that the women are divinities; on the contrary their comparison, even by Wace, to the so-called "Siamese twins" tends to strengthen the view that they are secular in character. The group was not found in a shrine nor is it associated with other cult objects. Consequently the lovely ivory group of Mycenae cannot be used in the development of our conceptions regarding the goddesses of the Mycenaean Pantheon.[90]

On the under side of the group appears a hole by means of which the figures were attached to a stand or another object (Fig. 130). It has been suggested that it was placed atop a scepter. Perhaps the ivory group was mounted on or near the cradle of a child scion of the ruling family and was meant to represent that infant in the care of divine nurses. From the tablets of Pylos we learn how elaborately chairs and thrones were decorated with applied figures in gold and ivory, including figures of men and of horses; other furniture would have been similarly decorated with appropriate figures. Of course, no evidence was found proving the use of the group and we can only be sure that it was attached on another object, that it was not made to stand on a ritualistic bench or hearth.

War Goddess

Our next representation is painted on a plaster tablet, some 19 cm. in extreme length, that was found by Tsountas in the house named after him in the southwest section of the lower citadel at Mycenae (Fig. 131).[91] The painted surface is damaged extensively, yet the representation in its main lines seems to be clear. Its painter followed the conventions current in fresco work in the Minoan-Mycenaean period, and these help considerably in the identification of its units.

In a rectangular field limited by a double border of three parallel horizontal lines and with numerous

---

[87] Mylonas, in *The Aegean and the Near East*, pp. 120-121.

[88] Nilsson, *op.cit.*, pp. xxiv and 314 n. 20. Wace's interpretation was accepted by Picard (*Relig. prehelleniques*, p. 83). The statement: "The Palace of Mycenae seems to have kept its ivory divine triad on display until the latest period of its power, stored in a strong room with other valuables," (E. Vermeule, *Greece in the Bronze Age*, p. 220) is based on fantasy and not on archaeological evidence.

[89] L. Palmer, *Mycenaeans and Minoans*, p. 124. Mylonas, *Eleusis*, pp. 238, 308, etc., and entry, Triptolemos, in index. In the Homeric Hymn to Demeter he is one of "the Kings who deal justice," but by 423/2 B.C. he was included in the list of the divinities who received sacrifices. We cannot assume that they are goddesses because of their garments since the votaries of the Tree Goddess also are garbed in the same fashion.

[90] We may now note that ivory carvings in which one or more women are represented in relief are not unusual. From Mycenae itself we have two women represented on the handle of a mirror; two seated women represented in low relief on a plaque which was attached to the handle of a mirror; a woman, perhaps standing, holding a branch is the subject of another relief, while another dressed in the flounced skirt is seated on a rocky bench. (*Ephemeris*, 1888, pp. 162-163, pl. 8 nos. 1, 2, 3, 4, 5 from Tombs 27, 29, 42, and 49.) All these fragments were found in graves and are in relief. Half of the back view of a female figure in the round was found in Tomb 27 and recently another ivory figurine was pieced together from fragments by Mrs. Sakellariou (*infra*, n. 93). An almost complete female ivory figurine in the round, belonging to LH III times, comes from Tomb LI of Prosymna (Blegen,

Prosymna, pp. 461-462, figs. 729-731). It is 11.8 cm. in height and is badly preserved. The woman is standing stiffly, wears the regular Minoan bodice and a flounced skirt. She holds the left arm hanging down at the side with elbow bent and the forearm and hand across the abdomen. Her right hand rests above the right breast. No attributes are evident. Among the debris of the structures on the north slope of the citadel of Mycenae we found in the summer of 1963 a small female ivory figurine in the round. It measures but 3.5 cm. and represents a woman votary perhaps, wearing the typical flounced Mycenaean skirt, resting her hands in front of her bare bosom. This and other figures prove that in Mycenaean times women, some of them votaries perhaps, were made in ivory without reference to divinities and these cast doubt on identifications that are not based on clear and definite evidence. Thus far such evidence does not exist, and neither the valuable material used for the carving of these figures nor their elaborate dresses proves their divinity. We may note that similar representations of women in glass paste are common and have been found in Mycenae, Dendra, even at Knossos. Certainly these figures are not divine (Tsountas, *Ephemeris*, 1888, p. 165 pl. 8 no. 9. Persson, *New Tombs at Dendra*, pp. 57-58 fig. 65. Evans, *Palace of Minos*, II, p. 702 fig. 440).

[91] *Ephemeris*, 1887, pl. 10 no. 2. Rodenwaldt, *Ath. Mitt.*, 37 (1912) pp. 129 ff. and pl. VIII. Herkenrath, *AJA*, 41 (1937), p. 413. Nilsson, *op.cit.*, fig. 156 and pp. 344-345. He calls it a "limestone" tablet wrongly. Similarly Mrs. Vermeule calls it "limestone plaque" (*op.cit.*, p. 284); actually it is of plaster. Persson, *Religion*, p. 74. Evans, *Palace of Minos*, III, p. 135 fig. 88.

vertical strokes filling the bands thus formed, we find a figure composition of two women facing and extending their hands forward towards a central figure. A typical Mycenaean altar with incurved sides is to be seen in front of the woman on the right side. The central figure is covered almost completely by a huge figure-eight shield—so completely, indeed, that Tsountas in the first publication of the tablet stated that the central figure could not be identified, that it was either a human form or an idol with its head and feet missing. Rodenwaldt, some twenty-five years later, noticing some white color above the shield at one side, maintained that a female divinity was represented behind the shield. His observations and identification are generally accepted. Nilsson states definitely that, though the feet have vanished, "above the shield appear the neck and the head, which is turned to the left, but great parts of both are wanting; further, the horizontally outstretched right arm and the left arm, visible from the elbow appear from beneath the shield." I reexamined carefully both the tablet and the color reproduction made by Gillieron *père* as published by Tsountas and failed to find the members indicated. But if they were there when the tablet was found, then the divinity represented would be female, a goddess, since the color of the face and arms is white. The shield would identify her as a War Goddess and would bring to mind the figure-eight shield on the gold ring (Fig. 123, No. 15), from the akropolis of Mycenae. The few traces of color along the side of the shield may indicate an outstretched hand holding a spear in a manner similar to that on the ring. The similarities between the two are so striking that in the ring, too, we must see a female goddess and not the male consort of the Great Goddess of the Minoan world. But we have seen that Persson maintained that on the ring we have a "figure-eight shield appended to a standard firmly fixed in the ground," and in the same manner he explains the figure on the tablet as a shield which stands secure on a standard and does not cover a Goddess of War.[92] In view of what seem to have been the aniconic tendencies of the Middle Helladic people and the lack of a prototype in the Minoan world, Persson's suggestion is valid and to be preferred. Perhaps the standard was painted in white color and this gave rise to the idea of a goddess.

It is interesting to note that here the women wear the usual many-flounced skirts, but they have the upper part of their bodies covered completely by a garment. This is clearly indicated by the color of that garment and by the line below the neck of the woman on the left side, the termination line of a blouse or other garment.[93]

Figure-eight Shields

The shield represented on the tablet will serve to place before us a difficult question that has been answered differently by our authorities. The figure-eight shield was used as a piece of protective armor especially in the earlier years of the Late Helladic period; it was also used as a decorative motif. Was it also used as a religious symbol? The question was raised and an affirmative answer was given in 1893 when E. Gardner put forward the view that the small armed figure on the gold ring from the citadel of Mycenae (Fig. 123, No. 15), was a palladium and that the shield was a symbol or an abbreviated form of the armed deity. Other scholars, including Reinach, Blinkenberg, Evans, Picard, Persson, followed and developed the thesis that hoplolatry, the veneration of arms and armor, was current in Mycenaean times. Nilsson summarized the evidence succinctly and concluded that the shield was a favorite decorative motive and had no religious significance.[94] One wonders, however, why such a representation was placed on weapons and why the type persisted long after the figure-eight had been replaced by a smaller shield. We find it represented in relief, for example, on a bronze axe from Vapheio[95] and its presence there was taken to imply a strengthening of the metal tool. On a sword blade from Shaft Grave IV it is represented a number of times.[96] We seem to have it standing in sacred enclosures, as perhaps on Ring 10 (Fig. 123), the way baetyls are erected. Whether or not we accept Persson's assertions that on Tsountas' tablet and on Ring 15 from Mycenae we have shields on standards, or prefer the explanation that a War Goddess is represented on those articles, the fact remains that the figure-eight shield is the most conspicuous and striking element of the composition, the all-important piece of armor of the War Goddess. On a fragment of ivory discovered in 1964 in the northeast extension of the citadel of Mycenae, the figure-eight shield is the dominant carved

---

[92] Persson, *Religion*, p. 73.

[93] Cf. our Fig. 131. Recently an ivory female figurine was pieced together by Mrs. Agnes Sakellariou from fragments apparently found by Schliemann at Mycenae and now kept in the National Museum at Athens. It is not completely preserved and stands to a height of 8.5 cm. The woman is wearing the typical, elaborate, flounced skirt but, unlike other figurines, has the torso covered by a heavy, unadorned blouse, similar, it seems, to those worn by the two votaries on Tsountas' painted plaque. The features of her oval face are well modeled and are very expressive, while over her broad forehead a lock of hair is carved, reminiscent of the coiffure of the ladies on the fresco from Tiryns. The arms of the figurine are missing but it is evident that the woman did not hold her hands in front of her chest (*Ephemeris*, 1957, Chronika, pl. B, a).

[94] *JHS* 13 (1893), pp. 21 ff. Nilsson, *op.cit.*, pp. 406-412; his conclusion is negative.

[95] *Ephemeris*, 1889, pl. 8 no. 2.

[96] Karo, *Schachtgräber*, pl. LXXXV no. 404.

motive. On a sealing from Crete we find shields framing the representation of three examples of what can be identified as sacerdotal stoles.[97] On a sealstone of glassy substance from Midea-Dendra we find a horned animal (a sheep or a goat) with a figure-eight shield between its legs and below its head.[98] We find it represented on the rock crystal gem from Mycenae on which the severed head of an animal seems to indicate that the representation deals with sacrificial animals.[99] It is true that definite proof of the shield as a cult object does not exist, but the indications are that it seems to have been considered as such, although it was also used as a decorative motif.

The Heavenly Bodies

On rings from Mycenae and Tiryns (Fig. 123, Nos. 15, 16) and on Ring 5 from Thebes, the sun is represented, and on the first two examples also the crescent. Does that imply the existence of a cult of the heavenly bodies in Mycenaean times? Nilsson in discussing the problem reached the conclusion that in the "Minoan world there are no certain traces of a cult of the Heavenly Bodies" but that the representations indicate the existence of "some cosmogonic myths or at least beliefs relating to the Heavenly Bodies" inspired possibly by Babylonian conceptions.[100] Even this very cautious conclusion, I believe, goes beyond the existing evidence. The sun and the crescents represented on the few Mycenaean monuments may actually indicate the natural conditions existing during the time the scene takes place: i.e., in the morning when the sun is in full glory but the moon may still be visible. The wavy lines that have been interpreted as the Milky Way or the rainbow may be a purely artistic device to indicate the sky over which the sun courses. We find this attempt to represent the "ether" in the gem from Mycenae where the goddess is riding on her mythical animal (Fig. 117, No. 19). The dots filling the segment in which the sun and moon are depicted have been interpreted as stars. We have seen how dots were used in filling the exergue of the ring from Mycenae (Fig. 123, No. 10). There they indicate the level ground. A similar explanation should hold valid for the ring from Tiryns; the sun and the moon shining over the fields, further indicated by the branches rising over the dotted ground. How could

the branches be interpreted if the dots represent stars? Branches in the starry sky? The Mycenaeans, of course, may have had cosmogonic myths, but I do not think that these are represented on their rings or gems. I fully agree with Nilsson that the cruciform patterns on pottery and gold work, even the actual representation of crosses are merely decorative and have no sacred or religious significance. As for the bull sports and their possible religious significance, we have so few representations on late Mycenaean works of art that the conclusion is inescapable: whatever their meaning in the Minoan world, in the Mycenaean area bull sports were devoid of religious significance; they were mere sports, like hunting. The bull, however, seems to have been the favorite sacrificial victim.

We may finally add to our list of representations the electrum signet ring found by Tsountas in 1893 in one of the Chamber Tombs of Mycenae (Fig. 123, No. 18).[101] A large woman, seated on a "simple seat or a small shrine," has turned her back to what has been interpreted as a bush or as a rocky landscape, but which perhaps could be a cairn. Before her stands a male figure, wearing only a belt (perhaps a loin cloth?) and anklets, holding a spear. He is rendered in a smaller scale, but this perhaps was imposed by the area in which he had to be drawn. He extends his right arm towards that of the woman, held in the same attitude. Both man and woman perform the same gesture in which a forefinger and thumb are pressed together. The impression conveyed is that the two figures are engaged in an animated conversation. The scene has been identified by Evans first and then by Persson as a *sacra conversazione* between the Great Goddess and a male god, her consort. Persson further claimed that "the Goddess had accepted a promise from the lesser god." However, Nilsson is inclined to accept the scene "as entirely secular in character," and as such it has little value to our quest.

Contributions of the Tablets

Additional information regarding the divinities worshiped by the Mycenaeans is provided by tablets in Linear B found at Pylos and at Knossos.[102] The latter, of course, were inscribed at the time when the capital of Minos was under the control of mainlanders, and consequently they do not refer to Minoan

[97] *Palace of Minos*, IV, part 2, p. 608 fig. 597 A. K.
[98] Persson, *New Tombs at Dendra*, p. 29 fig. 31.
[99] *Ephemeris*, 1888, pl. 10 no. 28, from Chamber Tomb 42.
[100] Nilsson, *op.cit.*, p. 420.
[101] *JHS*, 21 (1901), p. 175 fig. 51. Nilsson, *op.cit.*, pp. 351-352. Persson, *Religion*, pp. 69-70 and 178. Evans, *Palace of Minos*, III, p. 464 fig. 324.
[102] The chief publications covering the subjects are: M. Ventris and J. Chadwick, *Documents in Mycenaean Greek*, 1956. E. Bennett, *The Pylos Tablets*, 1955: *The Olive Oil Tab-*

lets of Pylos, 1958 (Minos Supplement 2). E. Bennett, *The Mycenae Tablets*, II, 1958 (*TAPS*, vol. 48). J. Chadwick, *The Mycenae Tablets*, III, 1963 (*TAPS*, vol. 52). M. Lang, "Palace of Nestor Excavations" in *AJA*, 62 (1958), to 67 (1963). L. R. Palmer, *The Interpretation of Mycenaean Greek Texts*, 1963. For a brilliant popular account of the decipherment and its implications see J. Chadwick, *The Decipherment of Linear B*. 1958. For a good summary of the publications and progress to 1954 cf. S. Dow, *AJA*, 58 (1954), pp. 77 ff. Periodicals devoted to the study: *Minos, Nestor, Kadmos*.

but to Mycenaean religious practices. In these tablets we do not find fragments of invocations, or hymns, or religious precepts but records of proportional tribute and ritual offerings to the gods or disbursements of perfumed oil to shrines, gods, and even priests and attendants. Some of the tablets from Pylos contain also brief introductory statements or specifications for the use of the scented oil. Unfortunately, these statements are neither clear nor explicit and afford room for wide divergences in interpretation that cancel, at least for the time being, their usefulness.[103]

The tablets, however, provide us with a list of the gods who are the recipients of offerings. Among them we find the names of Olympian gods and goddesses worshiped in the historic period of Greece; Zeus and Hera, Poseidon, Hermes, Artemis, and possibly Dionysos (?). Some gods are indicated only by an epithet known to us from epic poetry: *Paiawon* for Apollo, *Enesidavon* for Poseidon, *Enuwarijo = Enyalios* for Ares in tablets from Knossos. On the tablets from both areas we find female counterparts of Zeus and Poseidon: *Diwia* and *Posideia*. In both areas we have a goddess referred to not by name but by the form of respectful address: *Po-ti-ni-ja*, Potnia, Lady or Mistress. Sometimes the name of the locality where her shrine perhaps was located, precedes the form and so we have *Upojo Potinija*, *Newopeo Potinija*, *Asiwija Potinija*, and even *Dapu₂ritojo Potinija* or the Lady of the Labyrinth in a tablet from Knossos. On one tablet (V₅₂) we read *Atanapotinija*, with no word divider, The Lady of Athana; apparently Athena. On tablet Oi 701 from Mycenae we find *sitopotinija* which may indicate an agricultural divinity. On a number of tablets from Pylos we find *Po-ti-ni-ja* without any qualifying words; she seems to be a major divinity who had an important shrine at *Pakijanes*, a site apparently near Pylos. Her name was so well known to the scribe and the reader that it was not considered necessary to add it to the record. Chadwick suggests that *Potinija* was the Mother Goddess of the Mycenaeans. In a similar manner *theos* or *theoi* are re-

corded without any specific name and at Knossos we find a record of offerings to *pasiteoi*, to all the gods (Tablet Fp. 1).[104]

Again we seem to be dealing with a form of respectful address in the titles *wanassoi, wanakate* (to the Two Queens to the King), which figure especially in the Oil Tablets. Who the two queens were cannot be ascertained from the evidence at hand. Palmer has suggested that *wanassa* was the cult title of the Great Mycenaean Goddess.[105] The title, however, in the majority of cases is in the plural and is applicable to at least two goddesses. Furthermore, he maintains that *wanax* is the title of a "young god, the son and consort" of the Great Mycenaean Goddess. But there is nothing in the text to indicate the age of the god mentioned. His association with the two goddesses, the two queens, does not indicate a family relationship with the one only, since we find Poseidon associated with the queens in a similar manner; and evidently he cannot be considered as a young god, the son and consort of the one or of both the queens. For the time being the identity of the divinities addressed as *wanassoi* and *wanax* will have to remain undetermined. The offering recorded on Tablet Un2 surpasses in magnitude that given to any other god[106] and evidently would not have been offered to an infant or a youth but to a major divinity of the district. I believe that the title *wanax* is best suited to Poseidon, the special divinity of Pylos, and the offering of Un2 is in line with others dedicated to that god.

Perfumed oil is sent to *Matere-Teija*, to the "Divine Mother" (Fragment 1202). Who that goddess was is not specified further. We also have a *Potinija Iqeja*, identified as *Potnia Hippeia*, a "Horse-Goddess";[107] her status as well remains uncertain.

The records give us the names of other divinities, perhaps of lesser rank, who cannot be identified or equated with gods and goddesses of the classical era: *Manasa, Iphimedeia, Peleia, Dipsioi, Drimios, Pipituna*, in Knossos, *Triseroe, Dopota*, etc., and also what

---

103 Cf. Ventris and Chadwick, *op.cit.*, pp. 284-287, for the interpretation of the introductory statements on the reverse of Tablet Tn 316 translated by them as: PYLOS: *"Perform a certain action* at the (shrine) of Poseidon and . . . the town, and bring the gifts and bring those to carry them." The same statement is interpreted by Furumark: "Let them be sent to the shrine of Poseidon, and bring the gifts and cupbearers to the city" (*Eranos*, 51 [1954], pp. 51-53); by Meriggi: "They were sent to the shrine of Poseidon, and the city sent gifts and acolytes" (*Glotta*, 34 [1954], pp. 19-22); by Palmer: "A ceremony of consecration was held (or "sacrifice was made") in the shrine of Poseidon and the town was purified, and gifts were brought and the *po-re-na* were purified." (*Interpretation*, p. 262). This illustrates the difficulties and uncertainties involved in the interpretation. Again the briefer statement on the obverse of the same tablet Tn 316 and the word *po-ro-wi-to-*

jo, is interpreted by Professor Palmer (*op.cit.*, p. 262) as "Navigation Month," but by Professor Jameson in his article on "Mycenaean Religion" (*Archaeology*, 13 [1960], p. 35) as "[The benefactions] of Proitos."

104 Palmer, *op.cit.*, p. 239, Chadwick, *The Mycenae Tablets*, III, p. 58; *Minos* 5 (1957), pp. 117-129.

105 Palmer, *Minoans and Mycenaeans*, p. 232; *Interpretation*, p. 249. He seems to equate the Queen with the Mother Goddess of the ancient Near East and on that he bases his interpretation of *wanax* as a young God. But on the tablets from Pylos not one but two queens are associated with the *wanax* and furthermore a "Divine Mother" (Fr. 1202) different from the Queens.

106 Cf. Palmer, *Interpretation*, p. 258. Ventris-Chadwick, *op. cit.*, p. 221.

107 Palmer, *op.cit.*, Glossary, p. 422.

seem to be religious festivals held in various months. These, too, are not fully understood.[108]

That the gods and goddesses had places where they were worshiped becomes clear from the available texts. We find, for instance, that Potnia had a place at *Pakijanes* and Poseidon at Pylos. Whether these places were shrines or sacred enclosures is nowhere specified and the word temple or shrine is not to be found on the tablets. We read, however, that the gods had slaves and sacred land that was rented out to tenants, herds of animals, and apparently other properties such as produce, cheeses, and pelts of animals. Their shrines or enclosures must have been very rich and apparently the properties of the gods and goddesses were managed by priests and priestesses.

We may now try to equate the divinities represented on works of art with those named in the tablets although this requires a good deal of imagination. Nilsson has proved very convincingly that the Mistress of Animals of the Minoan-Mycenaean world can be equated with Artemis, who is also among the recipients of offerings in the Pylos tablets. But, as he adds, "this Artemis is not the goddess of classical mythology, the sister of Apollo, but a ruder and more primitive type of deity, which was wide-spread especially in the Peloponnesos. . . . Artemis, the goddess of wild nature, which has not been touched or altered by the hands of man and who was worshiped with orgiastic dances."[109]

Athena or her palladium could be recognized in the armed goddess of Tsountas' tablet, and Nilsson's ingenious reasoning that she was originally "the house-goddess of the king" who gradually became a warlike goddess" is very convincing.[110] However, we still have to prove the nature of the house-goddess of the king in the Mycenaean world; her role in the Minoan hierarchy is well defined. The fact that Demeter is not named among the gods who are the recipients of offerings may indicate that she cannot be equated with the Tree Goddess whose cult is so often depicted on Minoan works of art. And Hera's claims seem to be based on the fact that her temple at Tiryns was built over the ruins of the Mycenaean Palace. We may here note that what might be considered as a house cult of the οἰκουρὸς ὄφις is suggested only by two pieces of

pottery: one reported from Mycenae, a ring vase to which we find a serpent attached and the other vase from Naxos on which two snakes attached to the shoulder are moving towards a small saucer.[111] We have house-shrines, such as that of Asine, even with objects of cult, but we cannot be sure what divinity was worshiped there, a female divinity of blessing or some other. But we certainly have no evidence of a domestic cult of the Snake Goddess.

Beyond the two equations we cannot go. It is evident from the tablets that the Mycenaeans of the thirteenth century B.C. worshiped a number of male gods. But, as we have seen, no representations of a male god are to be found on the works of art that have survived. There can be little doubt that Zeus and Poseidon and a number of others perhaps came to Greece with the early Greek-speaking Indo-Europeans; they were not represented in human form then, and it seems that they were not so represented to the end of the Mycenaean era. Their descendants found no prototype to follow in the rendering of their major male gods in the religious repertory of the Minoans. The male attendant or consort of the Minoan Great Goddess did not appeal to them and such a subordinate figure could not be used as a prototype for the representation of their great male god. One wonders whether the introduction of this subordinate figure in the Minoan pantheon was not the result of mainland influence and accommodation during the period when at least part of Crete was dominated by the mainlanders. The Mycenaeans borrowed, from what was available, what would not conflict with their basic religious conceptions; they adopted the Tree Goddess and perhaps the Mistress of Animals, nature goddesses of universal appeal to agriculturalists and pastoral peoples; they adopted the "Goddess of Blessing," the benevolent divinity whose beneficial role is easily welcomed by all peoples; but they do not seem to have gone further.

Their only creation seems to have been the War Goddess; they found no prototype in Crete for that divinity which they could follow. It is reasonable to assume that due to their aniconic tendencies they could not visualize that divinity in human form but built her up from the armor they employed, the shield,

---

[108] *Ibid.*, pp. 248-255. Following Guthrie, Palmer identifies the "Dipsioi" as the "thirsty ones," (the dead) and formulates a festival of the dead comparable to the classical festival for the dead which began on the evening of the *choes* in the Athenian Anthesteria. One wonders whether, before this interpretation is accepted, it should first be proved that in Mycenaean times there existed a cult of the dead similar to that current in historic Greek times; whether first it is not necessary to point out where in the many hundreds of Mycenaean tombs excavated thus far we have concrete evidence proving the existence of such a cult. I know of no concrete

evidence even suggesting that cult.

[109] Nilsson, *op.cit.*, p. 503. It is doubtful that Artemis was the *Potinija* of the tablets since we find her mentioned by name in the documents.

[110] Nilsson, *op.cit.*, p. 499.

[111] *Ibid.*, p. 141 fig. 50. National Museum at Athens inventory number 5427, reported to have been found at Mycenae. For the example from Naxos see Kontoleon, in *Ergon*, 1959, p. 127 fig. 136 and Desborough, *The Last Mycenaeans and Their Successors*, 1964, pl. 7, b.

the spear, perhaps the helmet, mounted on a standard. This creation must have been completed at an early date when the figure-eight shield was still in use, perhaps in LH I times; we find it completed on the gold ring of early LH II times from the Drosinos treasure of Mycenae (Fig. 123, No. 15). But their important and ancestral male deities remained without representation. Perhaps in the baetyls and free-standing columns they may have found their aniconic representations. Perhaps in the cairns the Mycenaeans may have seen, as Miss Chittenden maintains, the God of the Heap, Hermes, and in mounds Father Zeus.[112] The fact, however, remains that they neither borrowed from Minoan Crete nor developed images in the form of man to represent their ancestral male gods. The worship of male gods with an ancestral origin and tradition proves that the Mycenaean religion differed from that of the Minoan Cretans.

[112] "The Master of Animals," *Hesperia*, 16 (1947), pp. 89 ff. Unfortunately, the two gems, the Castellani and the Phygalia, on which she relies have first to be proved genuine works of art of the Mycenaean period and area. The cairn on the glass plaque from the Tomb of Genii at Mycenae will not prove sufficient to establish Hermes' mastery over wild life nor that the "Genii" are his servants exclusively. We find them ministering to a goddess on the ring from Tiryns and watering boughs which may stand for the Tree Goddess. Cf. also Nilsson, *op.cit.*, p. 515. The altar of Zeus Lykaios may associate Zeus with the mound.

CHAPTER VII

CEREMONIAL EQUIPMENT AND THE CULT OF THE DEAD

"And to Thee . . . will I sacrifice a sleek heifer broad of brow, unbroken. . . .
Her will I sacrifice to Thee and will overlay her horns with gold."

(*Iliad*, x, 291 ff.)

CEREMONIAL EQUIPMENT

Horns of Consecration

The Mycenaeans seem to have adopted very few of the Minoan divinities, but they borrowed a good many articles used in their religious rites. The most conspicuous of these are the horns of consecration, which are found in all the representations of shrines. Whether or not horns of consecration were placed over the palaces of the Mycenaean rulers, the way Evans pictures them on top of the palace of Knossos, cannot definitely be decided. But the fact that no real examples were found in the palaces excavated thus far in the Peloponnesos may perhaps indicate that they did not form part of the decoration of a palace; certainly they were not used in the decoration of the façades of graves. The fragment from the palace of Pylos may belong to the shrine identified by Blegen. In the citadel of Gla an undisputed fragment of horns of consecration was found by Threpsiades.[1]

Altars

Closely associated with shrines are altars, attested by a number of monuments. We have already noted that in the court in front of Room 93 in the northeastern wing of the Palace of Nestor at Pylos Blegen discovered a rectangular stone block covered with painted stucco on all four sides and on top.[2] It was tentatively identified as an altar, an identification which I consider correct. Such a rectangular altar is represented on one of the impressed glass plaques found by Tsountas in the tholos Tomb of the Genii at Mycenae (Fig. 126, No. 23). On either side of rectangular altars, called by Evans sacred pillars, are represented the same daemons, which we have seen on the ring from Tiryns (Fig. 123, No. 16), standing on their hind legs and holding aloft the familiar beaked jugs used in pouring libations.[3]

In the *aithousa* of the megaron at Mycenae, and by the south base of its column, Papadimitriou uncov-

ered the remnants of a built altar apparently of a rectangular form.[4]

A small round altar with strongly incurving sides seems to have been usual in Mycenaean times. Actual examples of this type were not found in the mainland, but we find them represented on a number of decorated articles. The most important representation of it is to be seen on the plaster tablet from Mycenae, already discussed, of which the religious meaning is universally accepted (Fig. 131). It stands between the figure-eight shield and one of the female votaries. Nilsson recognizes an example of the round altar on the gem from Vapheio on which we find genii with jugs standing on either side of a construction supporting horns of consecration, above which rise three boughs (Fig. 126, No. 27).[5] The base of that altar, he remarks, "is reduced to a button-like shape." It could be maintained that the boughs are rising from a large flower pot on the front of which the horns of consecration were set. We find, however, this type of altar in a number of compositions of antithetic groups, including that over the Lion Gate, to which we shall return shortly. There can be little doubt that this type of altar was derived from Crete, and in the stone altar from Mallia with incurved sides and with the star and cross incised on it we have a good prototype.[6] There is another example from the "High Priest's House" at Knossos itself.[7] Perhaps even more instructive is the representation in relief on a fragment of a pithos from the cave of Psychro. There can be little doubt that we have here an altar with incurving sides, the nature of which is proved by the sacrificial offering, perhaps fruits, placed on top of it. There is also a clear representation of the altar on the stone rhyton from the palace of Kato Zakro discovered by Platon.[8]

The most striking altar usually attributed to the Mycenaean period is the circular pit or *bothros* found in the court of the megaron of Tiryns by the north

[1] *Ergon*, 1960, p. 48 fig. 58. *AJA*, 65 (1961), pl. 55 fig. 15.
[2] *Supra*, p. 57.
[3] *JHS*, 21 (1901), p. 117 fig. 13. Nilsson, *op.cit.*, p. 121.
[4] Papadimitriou, *Praktika*, 1955, pp. 230-231.
[5] Tsountas, *Ephemeris*, 1889, pl. 10 no. 35. Nilsson, *op.cit.*, p. 122.

[6] *BCH*, 53 (1929), p. 523.
[7] *Palace of Minos*, IV, part 1, pp. 202 and 209 figs. 157 and 160a.
[8] *BSA*, 6 (1899-1900), p. 104 fig. 34. Nilsson, *op.cit.*, p. 169 fig. 69. For the example from the palace of Kato Zakro cf. *Ergon*, 1963, fig. 187.

inner anta of the propylon. It is known to have consisted originally of a round pit, built of sandstone, 1.16-1.21 m. in diameter and some 90 cm. in depth. At a later time a rectangular stone podium was constructed around its opening. The round pit itself was found and explored by Dörpfeld, who gives a brief but useful description of his investigation.[9] The round pit is usually called Mycenaean, but on what evidence is not mentioned. Dörpfeld does not mention any finds from it or pottery which might indicate its date. He stressed the fact that the rectangular construction in limestone was later than the Mycenaean period, since it sits on the plastered surface of the court. But the pit was dug through that surface, and some of the stones of its round section above the floor do rest on the broken edges of the Mycenaean floor. Judging from the way the plaster of the floors was carried around the column footings in the palace of Pylos, we would expect to find the course of stones near the level of the surface covered with the plaster of the court if pit and court were contemporary; this is not mentioned by Dörpfeld and does not exist today. On the contrary some of the stones rest on top of the plastered pavement. The date of the pit was deduced from its similarity to the so-called altar over Grave IV of Grave Circle A at Mycenae. But that monument was deeply buried in the earth at the time when the palace at Tiryns, to which the pit-altar is presumed to have belonged, was being built. And then, we still have to prove that the structure over Grave IV was actually an altar. Before we base any inferences or conclusions on the pit-altar of Tiryns we must definitely prove its date. That date seems to be after the Mycenaean era. We must note that besides the palace at Tiryns two other palaces similar to it and one of a different plan have been fully excavated: the palaces of Mycenae and Pylos on the one hand and that of Gla on the other. The courts of these palaces have been cleared fully. In none has a round pit or bothros been disclosed. If this type of altar, as it is called, was a Mycenaean creation, we would expect to find other examples in the palaces that have been excavated. Instead of pits or bothroi we seem to have shallow depressions in the *aithousa* of the megaron of Mycenae and near the throne in the palace of Pylos where libations might have been poured.

Tables of Offerings

From the small altar, which could have been portable, may have developed the small, three-legged, round tables of offerings found in Mycenaean sites. Wace put together such a table from fragments he found in Room 16 of the palace of Mycenae[10] (Fig. 133), and other fragments were found by Tsountas, Papadimitriou, and myself. Some are known from Tiryns. A three-legged round table of offerings was found by the west column base in the *domos*, or room of the hearth, of the megaron of the palace at Pylos. It is made of clay and was coated with stucco.[11] It is interesting to note that not only these tables of offerings but also miniature clay thrones, apparently used in combination with seated female figurines, have three legs and perhaps this may have some ritualistic significance. On a rectangular flat cylinder from the Island of Naxos found by Professor N. Kontoleon we have a low table of offerings on which are stacked a rhyton, a libation jug, a deep open-mouthed jar without handles, and a sword in its scabbard set on its broad, perhaps pommeled hilt. In front of the table stands a military man, a "prince," wearing a Minoan loincloth, leggings, perhaps a corselet, and a hat with a plume. He holds his right arm at his side and in his left hand he holds a spear at arm's length. Beyond this weapon rises a palm tree.[12] There can be little doubt that on this flat cylinder we have the representation of a ritual act in an out-of-doors sanctuary before a table of offerings. The table and the tree bring to mind, as Kontoleon noted, the altar of Apollo and the sacred palm tree of Delos known even to Homer (*Odyssey*, VI, 162). The warrior or prince, with his rigid stance and extended left arm, reflects the attitude of the chieftain on the steatite vase from Aghia Triada, while the plumed hat finds a parallel in the headgear of the "Lily Prince" of Knossos. It seems to me that this engraved flat cylinder, placed by its discoverer in the fifteenth century B.C., illustrates a Minoan ritual.

The three-legged tables of offerings are small, portable, and were found in palaces; on them were placed probably fruit, cereals, perhaps liquids, and even small parts of a sacrificial animal. On a fresco fragment from Pylos we seem to have a procession of women bearing fruits to be offered. The existence and use of sacrificial tables in Mycenaean times is indicated by two representations on gems, one of which was found in an excavation. The first, on a carnelian lentoid gem now in the Berlin Museum (from the de Montigny Collection), is reported to have been found at Mycenae; a slaughtered bull with a dagger stuck into the back of its neck is lying on a sacrificial

---

9 Schliemann, *Tiryns*, pp. 337-340.

10 *BSA*, 25 (1921-1923), p. 225. *Tiryns*, II, p. 63.

11 Blegen, *AJA*, 57 (1953), p. 61 and pl. 35 and *Guide*, p. 10 fig. 7.

12 Mylonas, *"The Aegean and the Near East,"* pp. 118-119.

Cf. the crater in the Louvre where votaries are represented approaching a Goddess seated on a three-legged throne: Karageorghis, *AJA*, 62 (1958), pl. 99. For the flat cylinder from Naxos cf. Kontoleon in *Ergon*, 1959, p. 127 fig. 135.

table with sturdy legs (Fig. 125, No. 34). Over its body is carved a bent palm tree with foliage so conventionalized that Evans assigned the gem to advanced Late Minoan times.[13] The second example, an agate lentoid gem, is better documented since it was found by Tsountas in Chamber Tomb 47 of the Cemetery of Mycenae.[14] On a table is represented a boar on its back, already slaughtered. A long-robed figure with knife in hand is about to make an incision in the abdomen of the animal (Fig. 125, No. 35). Tsountas, influenced by the attire, identified the individual as a woman, but there can be little doubt that it is a man wearing a long and heavy ceremonial robe, evidently required by the occasion. Evans suggested that the man, "belonging to the priestly caste," was getting ready to examine the intestines of the animal to predict the future, that he was what later came to be known as a *haruspex*. Perhaps we should note that the table seems to have three legs, the same number we find on the sacrificial table in the lentoid gem from Arkhanes,[15] but this may be due to the angle from which the table was depicted.

Sacrificial Animals

That the sacrifice of animals was part of the religious practices of the Mycenaeans is also indicated by a gold ring from the treasure found by Drosinos in the citadel of Mycenae.[16] It is rather worn, but the representation can be made out clearly. It is composed of six animal heads arranged in two fields over and below a horizontal row of eleven large dots. At the extreme left is a huge rock, beyond which stand three leafy branches. Three of the heads evidently belonged to bulls, the other three exhibit no horns and recall the heads at the left edge of the ring with the Tree Goddess and her votaries (Fig. 123, No. 15), from the same treasure of the Mycenaean citadel. We may surmise that the heads are attached to the wall of a precinct, as are the large dots, but there can be no doubt that they indicate animals that have been sacrificed. The large dots recall those between the two pairs of sacred horns on the sealing from the Rhyton Well at Mycenae.

On a gem from the Vapheio tomb, we find as the sole decoration four rams' heads.[17] In Grave 42 of Mycenae Tsountas found a rock crystal lentoid gem

on which is engraved an "antelope" with head turned to the right. Before its chest there is a head of an animal, while below its belly and above its back are to be seen representations of figure-eight shields.[18] From Grave 26 of the same cemetery comes an agate lentoid gem on which we find a bull standing with its neck and head severed. Over its back are represented two heads of wild goats, while under its belly perhaps a severed limb of an animal.[19] A bull's head with a double axe in a reversed position between its horns, in gold foil, from Shaft Grave IV would indicate the sacrificed animal and the tool used in the sacrifice.[20] We find a similar composition on an onyx lentoid gem from the Argive Heraeum (Fig. 125, No. 41);[21] a double axe, in a reversed position, is to be seen between the horns of a bull. Again the axe stands for the tool used in the sacrifice. On either side we find the object which has been interpreted either as a corselet or sacral knots. As we have seen, some scholars believe that the sacral knots have a symbolic meaning. Persson writes that "the object to which it [the sacral knot] is appended is connected with the divinity,"[22] and he points out that to date, as well as in ancient Greece, the magical virtue of the knot is widely accepted. Evans, of course, proclaims the knots as sacral. Nilsson seems to deny the sacral significance of the knot and accepts the objects as corselets or cuirasses, but candidly remarks that the "cuirass" is an enigmatical piece of apparel.[23]

Sacerdotal Stole

It seems to me that these objects must have a direct bearing on the sacrificial act symbolized by the double axe and the bull's head. A corselet certainly would have no place in such an act. Unfortunately we have no representation of an actual sacrifice. The nearest to it is the scene on the agate lentoid gem from Chamber Tomb 47 of Mycenae (Fig. 125, No. 35). There the slaughtered animal is being opened up by a presumably priestly personage, who wears a long and heavy robe as he performs this sacred duty.[24] On a haematite bead seal from the Vapheio tholos tomb we find a priest heavily attired holding over his shoulder a single-bladed Syrian axe (Fig. 127, No. 36), while on a jasper lentoid gem (Fig. 127, No. 37) a priest is represented leading a tame griffin.[25] The garments

---

[13] Evans, *Palace of Minos*, IV, part 1, p. 41 fig. 24.
[14] *Ephemeris*, 1888, p. 179, pl. 10 no. 36, printed upside down as mentioned by Tsountas. Evans, *Palace of Minos*, IV, part 2, p. 572 fig. 550.
[15] Evans, *Palace of Minos*, IV, part 1, p. 41 fig. 25.
[16] H. Thomas, *BSA*, 39 (1939), pp. 82 ff. Schliemann, *Mycenae*, p. 360 no. 531. Nilsson, *op.cit.*, p. 233 fig. 114.
[17] *Ephemeris*, 1889, pl. 10 no. 25.
[18] *Ibid.*, 1888, pl. 10 no. 28.
[19] *Ibid.*, 1888, pl. 10 no. 18.

[20] Karo, *Schachtgräber*, pl. XLIV no. 353.
[21] Furtwängler, *Antike Gemmen*, pl. II, no. 42. *Palace of Minos*, I, fig. 312 c.
[22] Persson, *Religion*, p. 92.
[23] *Palace of Minos*, I, pp. 430 ff. Nilsson, *op.cit.*, pp. 162-164.
[24] *Ephemeris*, 1888, p. 179 and pl. 10, no. 36.
[25] *Ephemeris*, 1889, pl. 10, no. 26. *Palace of Minos*, IV, part II, p. 412 fig. 341 c. We find almost similarly attired priestly personages on the gem from Mallia—*BCH*, 70 (1946), pp. 148-153, fig. 1—and on two gems from Knossos—*Palace of Minos*, IV,

which these priestly personages are wearing are long and heavy, decorated with broad bands, and in many ways resemble garments worn by women. We may assume that in the course of the sacrifice the men entrusted with the task of stunning and killing the animal were dressed in a special stole, since even the priestly personage who seems to be making an incision in the abdomen of the wild boar is wearing one. The garment, therefore, seems to have been an essential article in the sacrificial act, and along with the head of a bull and the double axe had a place in a composition in which objects with direct bearing on the sacrifice were to be represented. Like the head of a bull, the sacerdotal dress could be represented by itself to imply the sacrifice, as it is in the gem from Argos published by Vollgraff,[26] or could be held by priestesses and priests in preparation for the act of sacrifice.[27] In the case of the representation on the ring from Vapheio (Fig. 123, No. 12), we may surmise that a priest took off his robes and placed them by the figure-eight shield before engaging in the ritualistic and orgiastic dance; indeed it would have been impossible for him to execute that dance if he wore a long and heavy garment (compare the long-robed priestly figures on the Vapheio gems, Fig. 127, Nos. 36, 37).

Libation Basins and Jugs

In the palace of Pylos by the area of the throne Blegen found what he calls a "curious installation"— a shallow basin-like depression in the floor connected by a narrow channel with a second depression some two m. distant. Two similar depressions were found by Papadimitriou in the south section of the flooring of the *aithousa* of the megaron at Mycenae and by Wace in a room above the "House of Tsountas."[28] Perhaps these were used for the pouring of libations. That such libations were customary is indicated by the large "jug" whose bottom was missing, "and had certainly been deliberately broken off," found upside down on the ledge of the house-shrine at Asine, which "had evidently served for libations."[29]

The beaked jug, illustrated in the impressed glass plaques from Mycenae, on the gem from Vapheio, and on the ring from Tiryns (Figs. 123, No. 16; 126, Nos. 22, 23, 24, 27) were perhaps used to pour libations. Nilsson discussed this ritualistic jug fully and found its prototypes in clay vessels used in Crete in Middle Minoan times, developed from an Early Minoan form.[30] Actual examples in silver were found in Grave IV of Circle A and in Grave Alpha of Circle B.[31] The comparatively few rhyta found in the Mycenaean world are seldom pictured in scenes of a religious nature on works of art.[32] From Grave IV, we have a silver rhyton in the form of a bull's head, with a hole on top of the forehead and between the horns to admit the liquid, and another in gold, in the form of a lion head;[33] both are masterfully made, the former in solid silver, the latter in hammered sheets of gold. In the fill of the Rhyton Well of Mycenae, Wace found three fragments of bull-rhyta of stone; another fragment was found by Tsountas and a fourth by Wace below the floor of the closet in the corridor beyond the northwest corner of the court of the palace.[34] A fragment of a marble rhyton in the form of a lion's head was found at Delphi, similar in all respects to an example from Knossos.[35] These rhyta may have been used for religious rites, but as Nilsson cautions, some of these animal-headed rhyta "may have been fanciful vessels of luxury which were sometimes also dedicated to the gods or used in the cult."[36] In an interesting study Seltman maintained that bull-rhyta of stone, such as we find represented in Egyptian tomb paintings, were only most ingenious vessels for pouring liquids, wine for example, at banquets.[37] Whether or not ring-shaped vessels played any role in the ritual cannot be determined. From the Mycenaean world we have only a fragment, now in the National Museum. It seems to belong to the closing years of the Mycenaean Age. Vases with mourning women on their rim (Fig. 152) belong to the burial ritual, while those from Naxos and Ialysos with serpents feeding from small cups attached to a jug may indicate the survival of Minoan traditions.[38] Again, it is interest-

---

part II, p. 414 fig. 343a and b. On another gem from Knossos a young man similarly attired holds a bird; *ibid.*, p. 405 fig. 336.

[26] *BCH*, 28 (1904), p. 389 fig. 32, stated to be a "palm" but placed upside down.

[27] *Palace of Minos*, I, fig. 312a, b. *Annuario*, VIII-IX (1925-1926) pl. XII no. 123 and p. 130 fig. 139, all from Crete.

[28] Papadimitriou, *Praktika*, 1955, pp. 230-231. Blegen, *AJA*, 57 (1953), p. 61.

[29] Nilsson, *op.cit.*, p. 113 fig. 32.

[30] Nilsson, *op.cit.*, p. 153.

[31] Karo, *Schachtgräber*, pl. CIII no. 74 (Grave III). Schliemann, *Mycenae*, p. 280 fig. 353. Cf. *Ergon*, 1959, fig. 135, for a similar jug on the flat cylinder from Naxos.

[32] Karo, "Minoische Rhyta," *Jahrbuch*, 26 (1911), pp. 249 ff. Nilsson, *op.cit.*, p. 144.

[33] Karo, *Schachtgräber*, pls. CXIX-CXXI, CXVII-CXVIII.

[34] Wace, *BSA*, 24 (1919-1921), p. 205.

[35] P. Perdrizet, *Fouilles de Delphes*, V, p. 3 fig. 13. *Palace of Minos*, II, part 2, pp. 827-833 and figs. 542 and 549. Cf. also Karo, "Minoische Rhyta," *Jahrbuch*, 26 (1911), pp. 254-255 fig. 7.

[36] Nilsson, *op.cit.*, p. 146.

[37] In *Studies Presented to David M. Robinson*, I, pp. 6-14 and especially 12-13.

[38] Nilsson, *op.cit.*, p. 141 fig. 50. Inventory no. 5427. It is reported to have been found at Mycenae. The example from Perati of a vessel with mourning women on its rim is illustrated in V. R. d'A. Desborough, *The Last Mycenaeans and Their Successors*, 1964, pl. 7, b. These vessels with figurines attached to their rims, sometimes called Kalathoi, are proved to be grave furnishings used in LH III C times. See Iacovides, "A Mycenaean

ing to note that multiple vases known as *kernoi*, which are rather common in the Minoan territory, are rarely found in the Mycenaean. "A composite vessel . . . consisting of three cups" is among the objects found in the house-shrine of Asine.

Surviving monuments indicate that liquids to be used in libations, fruits and other produce, sacrificial animals, and even human beings were offered to the gods. This is corroborated by the evidence to be found in tablets of Linear B from Pylos and Knossos. For example, from the Pylos tablet Tn 316 we learn that gold cups and bowls, women, and men were offered to the gods. The offerings recorded in tablet Un 2 include barley, cyperus, flour, olives, honey, figs, wine, one ox, 26 rams, 6 ewes, 2 he-goats, 2 she-goats, one fat hog, and 6 sows. The gifts to Poseidon recorded in Un 718 include wheat, wine, flour, cheeses, honey, one ox, two rams, two sheepskins, and a quantity of unguents.[39] It is not clear, however, whether this record is one of ritual offerings or a tribute paid to the god for the use of his sacred land. As a result of these munificent offerings the gods and goddesses had slaves that worked in the fields or in various crafts, herds of animals, some of which served for the sacrifices, and a good supply of produce which could be sold or used in connection with the ritual. The sheepskins could have been used in the making of various industrial articles or for the making of priestly vestments such as those worn by the attendants in the sarcophagus of Aghia Triada and those which are said to appear in fragments of frescoes from the palace at Pylos.[40] Unguents were used to scent the oil that was sent to the shrines to be used for ritual in many ways and which was perhaps exported as a commercial commodity.

Cairns

On one of the impressed glass plaques from the "Tomb of the Genii," two daemons are holding aloft their beaked jugs ready to pour a libation over a cairn (Fig. 126, No. 24). It seems, therefore, that cairns also, as well as altars and shrines, were tended with libations. If my interpretation of the signet ring of Vapheio (Fig. 123, No. 12) is correct, cairns were also to be found, instead of altars, connected with

sacred groves. I believe that in the Sanctuary of Lykosoura in Arkadia, mentioned by Pausanias (VIII, 38, 7) and excavated by Kourouniotes, this association of cairn and sacred grove survived.[41]

Daemons

Daemons are intimately associated with Mycenaean (and Minoan, of course) cult practices. We have seen them raising their beaked jugs ready to pour libations over rectangular altars, sacred columns, sacred boughs, and cairns (Fig. 126). They are pictured with libation jugs approaching a seated goddess on the gold ring from Tiryns (Fig. 123, No. 16). On a gem from the Vapheio tomb we find a single daemon holding his jug.[42] On a lentoid gem found by Tsountas in a chamber tomb we find the creature, again wearing a coat made of hide attached by a belt at the waist, standing on its hind legs. On either side lions are seated symmetrically turning their heads backward (Fig. 126, No. 25). The daemon extends its hand over the head of the lion in front of him.[43]

Instead of lions we find two men standing on either side of a daemon on a bead seal reputed to have been found in the Island of Hydra and now in the British Museum (Fig. 126, No. 29).[44] The men as well as the daemon hold their arms and hands in a similar attitude of adoration or greeting. A man between two daemons is depicted on two other gems; one of these has disappeared since its publication and the other is in the Museum in Berlin. The pedigree of both is doubtful. The former was in the Castellani collection and was published originally in 1885.[45] It was then stated that it was found in the excavations at Orvieto, but its owner in March 1884 affirmed that it was found at Corneto. Both sources indicate that Etruria was the place of its provenience. Since it was considered to be of Greek workmanship, it was usually taken to be a Minoan-Mycenaean product in spite of its reputed discovery in Etruria. The design carved on it presents difficulties. At the present time, it is believed that on it a man stands between two daemons holding libation jugs and that "the man grasps the daemons by their heads." But in the early publications, at a time when the gem could perhaps be seen in the collection, it was stated that two bulls were

Mourning Custom," *AJA*, 70 (1966), pp. 43 ff. and our fig. 152. For the jugs with serpents cf. Desborough, *op.cit.*, pl. 7, c, d.

[39] Cf. Ventris-Chadwick, *op.cit.*, pp. 221, 282-284, 286-287, and Palmer, *op.cit.*, pp. 258, 262-263.

[40] I am indebted to Professor Mabel Lang for the information.

[41] *Ephemeris*, 1904, pp. 153 ff. In a very stimulating study Miss Chittenden discusses the prehistoric cairn and concludes that it is the aniconic form of Hermes—"he of the heap." *Hesperia*, 16 (1947), p. 113.

[42] *Ephemeris*, 1889, pl. 10 no. 36.

[43] *JHS*, 21 (1901), p. 168 fig. 46.

[44] Furtwängler, *Antike Gemmen*, pl. VI no. 16. Evans, *Palace of Minos*, IV, part 2, pl. 466 fig. 390. Nilsson, *op.cit.*, p. 378 fig. 186. *JHS*, 17 (1897), pl. III, 5.

[45] *Annali dell'Istituto*, 57 (1885), pl. GH, 8, p. 195. Furtwängler, *op.cit.*, III, pp. 37-38 and n. 1. Cook, *JHS*, 14 (1894), p. 120 fig. 14. J. Chittenden, *Hesperia*, 16 (1947), p. 109 pl. XVI, d. Nilsson, *op.cit.*, p. 379. The full discussion of this gem is necessary, since on it and on the one in the Berlin Museum is based the notion of the existence of a "Master of Animals."

represented and that the man grasped each bull by the horns. This interpretation is pictured on the drawing of the gem which is now available (Fig. 126, No. 28). But scholars maintain that the artist who made the drawing did not copy the original faithfully and that the horns are his contribution to the design. However, a close scrutiny of the design will bring forth other facts which are disturbing. All agree that behind each daemon is depicted "a slender bough." These boughs have branches or leaves only on one side of the trunk, the side towards the edge of the gem and away from the back of the creatures. It is evident, I believe, that these "boughs" were formed when the prickly edge of the skin usually covering the back of the daemons was separated from them, and this separation resulted from misunderstanding of the nature of the artistic type. The paws on which the creatures stand were rendered as hoofs and perhaps on this detail was based the idea that bulls were represented; this too is at variance with the way the paws of these creatures are rendered in genuine Mycenaean examples. On the well-known gem from Vapheio on which two daemons are holding libation jugs over boughs attached to a set of horns of consecration, the hides that cover their backs project above their heads in a way suggestive of horns (Fig. 126, No. 27). A similar representation whose meaning was misunderstood may account for the horns on the Castellani daemons, if such horns really did exist on that composition. Finally the jugs held by the Castellani daemons are certainly far removed from the type illustrated on all the existing genuine gems and rings; they are nearer Panathenaic amphoras, as a matter of fact, than libation jugs of the Mycenaean period (cf. Fig. 126, Nos. 27 and 28). Because of all these divergences and because of the reported discovery of the gem in Etruria, I maintain that it is a late attempt by some artist to imitate a Mycenaean original which he did not fully understand; that the gem is neither Mycenaean nor prehistoric, but an object made in the course of the Etruscan period, if it is not an outright forgery.

The gem in the Museum of Berlin is of rock crystal and is reputed to have been found at Phigaleia.[46] A daemon stands on either side of a bird-headed man who holds them by the lower jaw (Fig. 126, No. 30). A comparison of this gem with that in the Castellani collection will prove very interesting. The bird-headed man of the gem reflects that of the Castellani example; one of its daemons seems to have hoofs, while the feet of the other end in what could be taken for bird's claws. Cook long ago noted that "oddly enough the

daemons seem to have the legs of birds"; their heads are definitely those of horses. The upper part of the torso of the man is not rendered in full front as is customary, but more nearly in side view, as would be natural, and the pinched waist usual in Mycenaean-Minoan art is lacking. Again one wonders whether the similarity of the heads of horses' heads did not suggest Phigaleia as the place of provenience to the early writers of the catalogues of the Museum, who were versed in the historic period of Greek art and culture. All these details are disturbing, and before we could accept and use as evidence the composition carved on the Berlin gem we would first have to prove its pedigree and authenticity.

We may now note the fragment of a wall painting unearthed by Tsountas in the house named after him at Mycenae, where we find parts of three animal-shaped creatures marching in file carrying a long pole (Fig. 124, No. 50).[47] Commonly they are described as having heads of asses, but as Nilsson pointed out, the "same loose skin covers their backs" and this is differentiated by color (blue and red) from their bodies rendered in yellow. We may add that the top edge of the skin projects over the forehead of the creatures in a manner paralleled by representations of the Mycenaean daemons. We cannot be sure of the subject of the composition, but we can imagine that from the pole were suspended the carcasses of animals killed in hunting. On a Cretan seal stone we find two animals, possibly lions, suspended from the ends of a pole carried by a daemon, and representations of similar daemons carrying an apparently dead animal over their heads are not unknown.[48]

Scholars agree in general as to the meaning of these fantastic creatures. Tsountas long ago suggested that they were "daemons of forest, mountain and stream" and compared them to the satyrs of the historic era.[49] Nilsson, summarizing the evidence discussed by Evans, Isaac, Picard, and others, concluded that these daemons are the ministrants of the cult, the servants of the deity. But since they sometimes appear as the central figure exerting their power over other animals, and in one rare case even over a man, they may be conceived of as "at least semi-divine in nature. . . . They are not gods themselves, but the stuff of which gods are made, daemons or beings of popular belief, roaming the land and haunting the sacred places and groves, superior to animals and to man . . . but subject to the gods."[50] It is interesting to note that although they seem to be connected with the tree cult and to be the servants of the Nature Goddess, whether

[46] Furtwängler, *op.cit.*, pl. II no. 34. Cook, *JHS*, 14 (1894), p. 138 fig. 18. Nilsson, *op.cit.*, p. 379 fig. 187.
[47] *Ephemeris*, 1887, pl. 10 no. 1. Nilsson, *op.cit.*, p. 377.
[48] *Palace of Minos*, IV, p. 442 fig. 367, p. 441 fig. 364, p. 431

fig. 354. Nilsson, *op.cit.*, p. 378 fig. 185.
[49] *Mycenaean Age*, p. 301.
[50] Nilsson, *op.cit.*, pp. 381, 376 n. 22.

a Tree Goddess or the Mistress of Animals, we do not find them in the ritual scenes honoring the same goddesses in which human beings participate.

The origin of the type has given rise to extensive discussion. Wolters was first to suggest that the daemon was a Minoan adaptation of the Egyptian Hippopotamus Goddess Ta-urt, who was known in Middle Minoan I times, as a steatite scarab from Platanos proves. Evans developed this Egyptian origin further, while Doro Levi projected a Babylonian ancestry. Nilsson, in summarizing the discussion, concluded that "the daemons were created by Minoan fancy and the only influence that we can allow from abroad is purely secondary and concerns the manner of representation alone; the functions of these daemons are not derived from abroad, but are Minoan in origin and manifestly belong to Minoan belief."[51] Whatever the origin of the Minoan daemons may be, the fact is that the Mycenaean version did not originate in the mainland but was imported from Crete.

Priests and Priestesses

The daemons seem to have been creatures of the imagination and in the world of fantasy they served the Mycenaean divinities. In reality the ritual and the affairs of the gods were administered by priests and priestesses. The meager information preserved in works of art[52] is now enhanced and clarified by the evidence contained in the tablets found by Blegen at Pylos. On those tablets priests and priestesses are often mentioned. We even know the names of three priests: Wetereu, Risowa, and Newokito, who seem to have been persons of influence and wealth. The priestesses in general are not named but we know at least one by name—Erita—a remarkable woman who not only was wealthy (she had two men slaves and one girl) but also dared to argue with the *damos*, the community, over the status of land, claiming that it should be tax-exempt since it was held on behalf of the god; a claim which the *damos* denied.[53]

Lesser officials did exist and among them we find the *klawiphoroi* or keybearers who seem to be women, the *hieroworgoi* who seem to be male officials, and the *dakoroi* temple attendants, the *aketirijai, dipteraporoi, akawone*, etc. The exact functions of these are not

known, but apparently the divinities had different lesser officials assigned to them. Palmer believes that the *eqetai* too had cult connections.[54]

The scenes of dancing represented on rings and gems would indicate the use of music in religious rites. No references to musicians are to be found on the tablets discovered thus far, but perhaps the "lyre player" fresco from the palace at Pylos and the ivory lyre found in the tholos tomb of Acharnae-Menidi may indicate the instrument most commonly employed.[55] We find both lyre and flute players on the sarcophagus of Aghia Triada,[56] and it could be maintained that along with so many other Minoan articles employed in the ritual the use of music for religious functions was also introduced from Crete to the mainland in Mycenaean times.

Scholars seem to follow Evans in the belief that in Minoan-Mycenaean times the king was also the high priest of the state.[57] Nilsson affirms that the "Mycenaean king carried on the cults of the gods in his palace sanctuary," that "certain sacral functions were so firmly bound up with him and his title that the latter was not abolished when the kingship was, since "religious scruples forbade its discontinuance," but was bestowed upon the functionary entrusted with the performance of religious rites and services. Thus the second archon of Athens, charged with the care of sacrifices inherited from old times, of the Linaea, and even of the Greater Eleusinian Mysteries, was known as *basileus*. Furthermore, Aristotle states that the *basileus* was a functionary with sacred office. This reasoning seems to have established as a fact that the Mycenaean chief of state was also its highest religious functionary.

It seems to us that this concept does not agree fully with the picture of the Mycenaean state furnished by the Pylos and Knossos tablets. There we find that the official title of the supreme ruler of a Mycenaean state, the title of the official who resided in and was the master of the palace, was *wanax*. If the cult of the supreme ruler, held in his palace, gradually became public as is maintained, then the *wanax* would have been its functionary. If the title of that functionary was continued because of religious scruples, then the official of later times charged with the continuation of

---

[51] Wolters, *AA*, 1890, pp. 108 ff. Evans, *Palace of Minos*, IV, part II, p. 439 n. 2 and *JHS*, 21 (1901), p. 169. Nilsson, *op.cit.*, p. 381. Doro Levi, "Le cretule di Zakro," *Annuario*, VIII-IX, (1925-1926), pp. 190 ff.

[52] On the gems of Vapheio, *supra*, n. 25. In Grave XLIV of the cemetery at Prosymna Blegen found interred with a "priest" or "priestess," equipment comprising a "table of offering" and libation vessels, *Prosymna*, pp. 213-214.

[53] Palmer, *op.cit.*, on Ep. 704 and 297, pp. 210-212.

[54] Ventris-Chadwick, *op.cit.*, p. 128. Tablets A2, 29, En 03, cf. especially tablet Un 219. Palmer, *op.cit.*, pp. 259-260. On the

di-ri-mi-jo, di-wo i-je-we of Tn 316 see now Palmer, *op.cit.*, pp. 262-263 where it is interpreted as "*Di-ri-mi-jo* son of Zeus."

[55] Of course in the "lyre player" we have a secular scene and not a religious rite. For it see Blegen, *AJA*, 60 (1956), pl. 41 fig. 3. *Reconstruction of Piet de Jong*. For the Menidi lyre, see Lolling, H. G., *Das Kuppelgrab bei Menidi*, 1880, pl. VIII.

[56] *Infra*, pp. 176 ff.

[57] Nilsson, *op.cit.*, p. 484. Palmer, *TAPA*, 1954, pp. 37-50. See recently Taylour, *The Mycenaeans*, p. 69, in spite of Bennett's remarks "On the Use and Misuse of the Term 'Priest King,'" Κρητικὰ Χρονικά, 15-16 (1961-1962), A., pp. 327-335.

the cult practices would have been called *archon wanax*; instead he is known as *archon basileus*. On the other hand we find on the tablets an official called *pa₂-si-re-u*, who, according to Ventris, Chadwick, and Furumark is clearly to be connected with the Homeric *basileus*; as a matter of fact a number of persons in the state of Pylos bear that title. But the title seems to be that of a lesser provincial official, perhaps the title of the governor of a small district, of a feudal lord. We may surmise that the *pa₂-si-re-u* was in charge of religious matters in his district,[58] although these seem to have been in the hands of priests and priestesses. We may even assume that at the end of the Mycenaean Age, when the political system disintegrated and the office of the *wanax* was abolished, the feudal lords who survived took for themselves the prerogatives and duties of the king, including the exercise of religious supervision; that this was remembered at Athens in the historic period.

The difficulty in accepting this argument lies in the fact that the Mycenaean state of Athens was not destroyed, that consequently its *wanax*, staying on the Akropolis of Athens was not superseded by a minor dignitary, by a *pa₂-si-re-u*, and if he had been a high priest in late Helladic times he would have continued in that office until central authority—both that of the *wanax* and that of the *pa₂-si-re-u*—was abolished. The office, therefore, would have been remembered as that of the *archon wanax* at Athens. Furthermore, Palmer now maintains that *pa₂-si-re-u* was an "official responsible for royal bronze-smiths."[59]

Temples to the Olympian gods were built over the ruined palaces of Mycenae, Tiryns, and Athens. One wonders, however, whether, as is maintained, "the reason why the temples are built upon the ruins of the Mycenaean palaces is the sacred character of the king's palace, which remained always attached to the place through the tenacity of religious tradition."[60] I believe that this reason, far from being convincing, is very doubtful and does not agree with the evidence. We have to remember that over the ruins of the palace both at Mycenae and Tiryns small houses were also built in Geometric times, used by the descendants of those who survived the catastrophe. It was natural for those people to build the temple of their god in the area in which they had their homes, and that was within the limits of the palace. Again the top of the Mycenaean citadels was the most appropriate place for the location of the protecting divinity of a settlement centered around that hill. Before we can accept

the continuity of cults at Mycenae, Tiryns, and Athens, we have to prove the transition from Mycenaean times and the existence of the cult in the locality in sub-Mycenaean and Proto-Geometric times. There is no evidence to indicate that existence. And there is no evidence even to suggest that the reason for the construction of the temple over the ruins of the palace was the sacred character of the king's domicile. The argument, therefore, in favor of the king's sacred status based upon the existence of temples on Mycenaean citadels does not seem to be valid, for its base has first to be proved. The available evidence to date will not permit the assumption that the chief of the Mycenaean state, its *wanax*, was also the high priest or the chief religious functionary.

The Double Axe

The description of the religious apparatus used by the Mycenaeans will not be adequate without the discussion of the double axe as a religious symbol in the mainland of Greece. Generally it is stated that the double axe is an emblem of Minoan-Mycenaean religion. There can be no doubt that it served that purpose in the Minoan religion of Crete. Years ago Nilsson emphasized the fact when he wrote that the double axe is "the real sign of Minoan religion and as omnipresent as the cross in Christianity and the crescent in Islam."[61] But was it such a "real sign" of the Mycenaean religion also? Nilsson pointed out the difference in form and material of the double axes used as tools and those which, because they are unfit for use or because of their religious associations or both, served as religious symbols and emblems; then he gave a long list of examples found in Minoan sites which justifies the opening statement of his discussion quoted above. If we turn from Crete to the Mycenaean world in the mainland we shall find comparatively few examples. These it may perhaps be well to list chronologically as far as it is possible.

To the Late Helladic I period belong examples which were found in the shaft graves.[62] Miniature double axes of gold foil were among the furnishings of Grave IV. With them was found a double axe between the horns of a bull, representing a sacrificial victim and the tool with which the animal was stunned. The double axe is used as a motive on LH I vases. A number of examples exist, the best known being the double axes on amphoras found in Shaft Grave I. However, these representations are characterized by Evans as "degenerations of the Double Axe motive" and by

---

[58] Ventris-Chadwick, *op.cit.*, pp. 121-122. Carratelli, *La Parola del Passato*, 1954, p. 217, accepts the *pa₂-si-re-u* as a religious functionary corresponding to φυλοβασιλεῖς.

[59] Palmer, *op.cit.*, glossary, p. 442, where references to the text.

[60] Nilsson, *op.cit.*, p. 487.

[61] *Ibid.*, p. 194.

[62] Karo, *Schachtgräber*, pl. XLIV nos. 353-354.

Nilsson as paintings in which "all feeling for the real significance of the emblem is totally lost."[63] In other examples from the Mycenaean world we find a more accurate representation of the double axe.

In the Late Helladic II period the motive of the double axe continues to be used on vases, in the early part of the period especially. But in addition it appears on other articles. Most conspicuous is the double axe carved on the gold ring from the treasure found by Drosinos in the citadel of Mycenae (Fig. 123, No. 15). The date of the ring cannot be definitely proved, but we can accept Miss Thomas' conclusion that it belongs "to the early part of LH II, soon after the transition from LH I."[64] At least we cannot place it below the early years of that period. Another representation of the double axe has been recognized on the gold ring from the Vapheio tholos tomb (Fig. 123, No. 12). That ring, too, and the contents of that tomb are generally placed in the early years of LH II. A representation of a ceremonial double axe is to be seen on the gems found by Wace in Chamber Tomb 515 of the Kalkani cemetery (Fig. 125, No. 32). It rises above an enigmatical ritual object supported by a priestess or a goddess.[65] Those gems were also placed in the early years of the LH II period. These engraved gems were horizontally perforated and therefore they most probably formed part of a necklace; they are almost identical and could have been objects imported from Crete and worn by their owners as rare articles with unusual and curious motives whose original meaning was no longer remembered or was even unknown to the wearer from the very beginning. Until recently peasants in Crete attributed to Minoan gems miraculous powers never dreamed of by the artists who created them. Whatever the truth of the matter may be, the fact remains that in these two rings and in the two gems we find representations of the double axe as a religious symbol. On the imposing façade of the tholos tomb of Peristeria in Triphylia, cleared by Marinatos, we find incised the double axe and above it a branch. Certainly these were masons' signs. Even before the LH II period ends the double axe seems to disappear from the repertory of the vase painter. An example from Thorikos may belong to the later part of the period.[66] But we find no traces of the double axe in the monumental amphoras of the Palace Style which became so characteristic of the period and which provided ample space for its representation.

Examples of the double axe from the Late Helladic III period, which is accepted as comprising three centuries, are almost nonexistent. A double axe was found incised on a stone block of the wall of Room 7 of the archives suite in the Palace of Pylos. It could certainly be accepted as a mason's mark.

In contrast to the few instances of masons' signs from the mainland we have a long list of examples from Crete brought together by Nilsson.[67] Characteristically, double axes were found in Crete in rooms that are proved to have been shrines. In the Shrine of the Double Axes a small example of steatite was found against one of the two sets of horns of consecration, and miniature bronze axes, originally gold plated, were found in the Treasure Chamber near that shrine.[68]

In Mycenaean territory there is a house shrine at Asine whose cult objects have survived.[69] Among them we do not find a double axe, although we do find a stone celt, and there is no mention of an axe from the shrine of Berbati.[70] From the mainland we have one example of a votive double axe of bronze from Delphi, which seems to belong early in the Mycenaean period; and from the Cyclades a bronze example from Delos, found, along with a good many small objects of ivory and gold, below the floor of the Artemision.[71] We have to remember, however, that the former site seems to have been under Minoan influence, as indicated by the fragment of the marble rhyton in the form of a lioness' head found there and by the tradition preserved in the Homeric Hymn to Apollo, while the position of the Cyclades vis-à-vis Mycenae and Crete is not fully and definitely established. The remains of the shrine of Keos and those recently found at Kythera seem to indicate that the islands retained their Minoan tradition to the beginning at least of the LH III period. No remnants of votive double axes have been found thus far in the better known major sites of the Mycenaean world—at Mycenae, Tiryns, Pylos, Athens. One could, of course, maintain that votive double axes, being made of valuable metal, were carried away by the enemies who plundered the Mycenaean palaces and citadels; we would, however, expect a fragment of an example to have escaped the general catastrophe. A talent of copper was found on the citadel of Mycenae itself, and hoards of metal were found there and on the Akropolis of Athens including double axes used as tools, but no fragments of votive

63 *Ibid.*, pl. CLXVII nos. 190-192, 195. Evans, *Palace of Minos*, IV, part 1, pp. 292-293. Nilsson, *op.cit.*, p. 209.

64 *BSA*, 39 (1938-1939), p. 86.

65 *Supra*, p. 152 and Wace, *Chamber Tombs*, pl. XXVIII nos. 31 and 32; pp. 59 and 200, for the date.

66 *Ergon*, 1960, p. 154, figs. 168-169. *Ephemeris*, 1895, pl. 11 no. 2.

67 Nilsson, *op.cit.*, p. 215.

68 Evans, *Palace of Minos*, II, p. 337 fig. 189.

69 Frödin-Persson, *Asine*, fig. 206.

70 Nilsson, *op.cit.*, p. 116.

71 P. Perdrizet, *Fouilles de Delphes*, II, 5, pp. 4, 8, 119-121. For the example from Delos: H. Gallet de Santerre and J. Tréheux, *BCH*, 71-72 (1947-1948), p. 232 pl. XL, 1.

axes. On a fragment of a wall fresco from Mycenae found by Schliemann outside Circle A possibly in the area of the Ramp House we have represented what seems to be a loggia in which ladies are sitting. Garlands suspended over their heads are attached at the ends to some objects, painted white, stuck into the upper corners of the boxes. These objects were identified as double axes by Rodenwaldt and Evans on the basis of some white objects stuck into columns represented on a fresco from the northwest hall of Knossos and considered to be double axes. The identification is doubtful and arbitrary, and as Nilsson pointed out "it is very doubtful whether the building on the fragment of Mycenae is a shrine at all."[72] The example in the central position is closer to the representation of a figure-eight shield as we find it on gems than to a double axe, and the other two examples are not sufficiently well preserved for identification.

Stone Pyramidal Base from Mycenae

From this period the only remnant that has caused general excitement is a stepped pyramidal stone base found by Boëthius at Mycenae near the top of the great ramp in a pile of stones apparently collected there in the course of the early excavations in the citadel. It comprises three steps and measures 30 cm. in height and 20 cm. by 19 cm. at the base. It has a socket on top in which the stand of some object was secured. Its similarity to stepped bases found in Crete led scholars to maintain that it supported a double axe and to conclude that the double axe of the Great Goddess was to be seen in the palace of Mycenae itself.[73] The question is how do we know what object the base supported. First of all, since even on Minoan representations the double axe is not always based on a pyramidal stand, it cannot be claimed that the stand is peculiar to it. On a sealing from Zakro a ceremonial double axe rises from the ground without the intervention of a base.[74] In the larnax of Palaikastro the stepped base supporting the double axe is composed of two superposed rectangular blocks.[75] In a similar manner the stand of the double axe on one side of the sarcophagus of Aghia Triada rests on a two-sectioned pyramidal base, but on the other it stands upon a platform without the aid of a base.[76] The double axe is represented as secured to the ground without the intervention of a base on the monumental painted pithos from the fill above the tenth magazine of

Knossos, on the larnax from Mochlos, on the basket-shaped pot from Pseira, in sherds from Phaestos and on the false-necked amphora of Myrsinochorion-Routsi,[77] stated to have Cretan affiliations. On the sides of a small limestone altar found some 33 m. northwest of the palace at Knossos, we find carved double axes rising from a single base-block.[78] Certainly this and the examples quoted above seem to indicate that the double axe was not always erected on a stepped pyramidal base, which thus had become its characterizing element.

If we turn our attention from Crete to the mainland, we shall find in the few representations of the double axe that it is not equipped with a pyramidal base. On the gold ring from the citadel of Mycenae, where we have our most convincing representation of a ceremonial double axe, the symbol is embedded in the earth without a base (Fig. 123, No. 15). Because of this it is usually assumed to be hovering in the air, an explanation that was successfully refuted by Persson. On the other hand, our survey of finds indicates that other objects were commonly erected by the Mycenaeans in their sacred enclosures and shrines. What Nilsson calls the "sacred boughs" are usual; certainly they are depicted on works of art much more frequently than the double axe. These boughs had to be secured in a base to hold them upright. As a matter of fact, the boughs on the signet ring from Tiryns (Fig. 123, No. 16), are secured by means of bases which exhibit two or three superposed members. And if Persson's suggestion is correct that the palladium-like figure with the figure-eight shield on Tsountas' tablet (Fig. 131) and on the ring from the citadel of Mycenae are ceremonial shields supported on a standard, we would have another sacred object which had to be provided with a base. We must always bear in mind the stepped bases on which stand the attached columns of the Treasury of Atreus, indicating that such bases were not uncommon in Mycenaean practice. To conclude, therefore, on the evidence of the stone stepped base that the double axe stood on the citadel of Mycenae is not warranted by the facts. I could maintain with better reason that a sacred bough stood on that base.

The enumeration of the examples of ritual double axes from the mainland indicates that the available evidence does not permit even the assumption, let alone the conclusion, that the double axe was a re-

[72] Nilsson, *op.cit.*, p. 249. Evans, *Palace of Minos*, I, p. 443 fig. 319 and p. 446 fig. 321. *Ath. Mitt.*, 36 (1911), pp. 228 ff., and pl. IX, 2.

[73] Wace, *Chamber Tombs*, p. 201 and pl. LVII d. Nilsson, *op.cit.*, p. 218, fig. 111. Webster, *From Mycenae to Homer*, p. 41.

[74] Nilsson, *op.cit.*, p. 157, fig. 64.

[75] *Ibid.*, p. 170 fig. 71. BSA, 8 (1901-1902), pl. XVIII.

[76] Marinatos-Hirmer, *op.cit.*, pls. XXVII-XXIX A and Nilsson, *op.cit.*, p. 247 and fig. 196. *Infra*, pp. 176 ff.

[77] Evans, *Palace of Minos*, IV, part 1, p. 290 fig. 226 (Pseira); p. 343 fig. 285. BCH, 52 (1928), p. 150 and pl. IX. Nilsson, *op.cit.*, p. 203 fig. 96. Marinatos-Hirmer, *op.cit.*, fig. 230.

[78] Evans, *Palace of Minos*, IV, part 1, p. 201 fig. 154.

ligious symbol of the Mycenaeans. Its complete absence in works of art and buildings of the Late Helladic III period would indicate that its sporadic appearance in the earlier eras was an intrusion and the result of Minoan influence, which was then very strong. Furumark has aptly pointed out that in the first half of the LH II period Minoan influence reached its apogee, that in the second half of the period the mainland elements reassert themselves; then contact between Crete and the mainland almost ceased.[79] To that resurgence of the native Mycenaean elements, therefore, can be attributed the eclipse of the double axe, which thus seems not to have been the emblem of the Mycenaean religion.

Antithetic Groups

In our discussion of the daemons we often met with compositions of two elements arranged on either side of a central unit. These antithetic groups, as they could well be called, are of importance to us since a religious significance has been attached to them. Evans was the first to collect the known examples in his pioneer and monumental work on the "Mycenaean Tree and Pillar Cult."[80] In general, in these groups we have a real or mythical animal standing on either side of a tree or a column. Some of the representations may be secular in character with counterparts to be seen even today in the Greek countryside.[81] Others are not drawn from life experiences.

On a gold ring from Mycenae, formerly in the Tyszkiewicz collection (Fig. 124, No. 42), the central unit is a column, rising from a flat slab. It has a double bulbous capital over which rests a broad entablature composed of two superposed members, recalling the superposed slabs of the sacred enclosures of the signet rings. From either end of the entablature is suspended an unidentifiable object. On either side of the column lions are represented antithetically, facing outwards but with their heads turned towards the column, to which they seem to be attached by long ropes.[82]

Elsewhere two sphinxes confront each other, seated on either side of what has been called by Evans a fleur-de-lys column (Fig. 124, No. 43).[83] Sphinxes are confronted above and on either side of the capital of a fluted column on the magnificent ivory carving found by Wace in the House of Sphinxes.[84] They are seated on a structure the sacred character of which is indicated by the horns of consecration that decorate its façade. Four sphinxes symmetrically arranged in groups of two are represented standing on either side of a column in an ivory plaque from the tholos tomb of Menidi.[85] Not only sphinxes and lions but also griffins were employed in antithetic arrangements. In Tomb XLIV of Prosymna Blegen found a fine gold ring on the bezel of which are represented two crouching crested griffins heraldically opposed, on either side of a spirally fluted column with an elaborately engraved capital. The ring, dating from an early phase of the LH III period, was secured by a cord around the wrist of a priest perhaps.[86]

Also of great decorative quality and excellent workmanship is the design on a lentoid gem found in a chamber tomb at Mycenae (Fig. 124, No. 44). This design carries us a step further towards the representation on the Lion Gate. On either side of a central column with spiral flutings stands a griffin resting its forefeet on an altar with incurved sides. The column rises from that altar to a bulbous capital that supports a broad entablature composed of a strip of roundels, evidently beam ends, and a broad member perhaps standing for the coping of the façade. The griffins turn their heads backward and seem to be tied to the column by ropes.[87] One may easily admit that the column could be conceived as standing in the background, but the griffins certainly have to be accepted as having their forefeet on the altar. We find the same position of the forefeet of animals on two gem carvings from Mycenae. On these the central column has been omitted, but the altar with the incurving sides is there and two animals with a common head rest

---

[79] A. Furumark, *Opuscula*, 6 (1950), pp. 249 ff. Of course, votive double axes are known from a number of sites of the historic Greek period, cf. Amandry, *BCH* 62 (1938), p. 314, n. 6, p. 315.

[80] *JHS*, 21 (1901), pp. 99-204.

[81] For example, the *agrimia* locking horns on either side of a tree on a banded agate from Mycenae (*JHS*, 21 (1901), p. 153 fig. 30); the couchant bulls on either side of a tree in Evan's collection (*ibid.*, p. 156 fig. 34); the wild horses (?) on either side of a tall tree with a trifoliate top on a gem from Mycenae (*Ephemeris*, 1888, pl. 10 no. 43). Interestingly enough, the three branches (?) or divisions of the top are edged with small parallel lines; they present a striking similarity to the object behind the three male votaries on the ring from Mycenae (Fig. 125 no. 1). Perhaps in that ring the artist wanted to indicate a tree in the background, but for lack of space inserted

sidewise only its trifoliate top. That this "trifoliate" design was inserted in compositions on gems is indicated by its existence below the belly of a bull on chalcedony lentoid gem from Grave 25 of the cemetery of Mycenae (*Ephemeris*, 1888, pl. 10 no. 15). We have wild goats standing on either side of a tree on a gold signet ring found by Wace at Mycenae (*Chamber Tombs*, p. 27 fig. 13).

[82] *JHS*, 21 (1901), pp. 159-160 fig. 39.

[83] *Ibid.*, p. 155, fig. 33.

[84] *BSA*, 49 (1954), pl. 38 c.

[85] H. G. Lolling *et al.*, *Das Kuppelgrab bei Menidi*, p. 20 pl. VIII, 10. Nilsson, *op.cit.*, p. 251 fig. 121.

[86] Blegen, *Prosymna*, p. 266 fig. 576.

[87] *Mycenaean Age*, p. 254 fig. 131. *JHS*, 21 (1901), p. 158 fig. 36.

their forefeet on it: in the one example, two lions; in the other, two griffins.[88]

The Lion Gate Relief

The gem from Mycenae with the tied griffins on either side of the column brings us to the impressive relief over the Lion Gate of Mycenae (Fig. 16). The relief, considered one of the earliest pieces of monumental sculpture of the Greek prehistoric world, has often been described and discussed. Its subject therefore is well known.[89] A lion stands on either side of a column, tapering downwards, bearing a symbolic entablature and based firmly on top of two altars with incurved sides, placed side by side and covered by plinths. The lions rest their forefeet on these plinths and turn their heads towards the visitor approaching the gate; the heads were apparently made of different material and are now missing. It was customary to believe that they were made of bronze and were compared to "the golden and silver dogs, which Hephaistos had fashioned with cunning skill to guard the palace of greathearted Alkinoos." However, the dowel holes used to secure the heads are so large and deep that they indicate not bronze, but a heavier material, probably steatite. It would have been rather difficult to model the heads with their elaborate details of mane, etc., on the hard limestone of the slab. Sometimes the animals are taken to be lionesses, apparently because of the omission of genital organs. However, equally missing are the teats of the female animal which would have identified its sex. We must remember that the Mycenaean artist did not indicate the sex of lions by the genital organs, which he generally omits. We can find but one case, on the amygdaloid gem in Evans' collection of a lion and lioness on either side of a kneeling "Goddess", where the sex is indicated by the genital organs of the male and the teats of the female. The provenience of that gem is uncertain, since it was not found in an excavation, and its authenticity is suspect. Furthermore, on the Lion Gate relief, cuttings on the side of the neck of the lion to the left of the spectator indicate that the animal represented is male. For the cuttings were of a certainty the ends of the mane of the animal cut in the slab to provide additional support to the block, perhaps of steatite, on which the head and face of the animal was carved. Unfortunately the same section of the neck of the lion to the right has weathered badly. However, there too we have at least the remnants of one cutting which would indicate that a similar pro-

vision was made for the head of that lion. Consequently, both animals can be considered as lions and not lionesses.

Scholars agree that the Lion Gate relief follows a traditional design, but they disagree as to its significance, if indeed it possesses any. Tsountas long ago pointed out that the composition could be either symbolic or purely decorative, and inclined towards the latter.[90] Evans believed in its religious and symbolic significance, and saw in the column the aniconic form of a deity and in the presence of the relief over the gate a symbol which placed the citadel under the protection of the Great Mother Goddess, who thus became the founder of Mycenae. Wace, following Evans, accepted the column as a sacred pillar, an aniconic form of a deity, a symbol of protection.[91] According to his interpretation, the position of the relief showed that the gate and the walls of Mycenae were placed "under the protection of the divinity indicated by the pillar, perhaps the Great Mother Goddess, who is often associated with lions." However, he did not exclude the possibility of a heraldic interpretation, and added: "The lion was probably the badge of Mycenae and thus this relief may have a kind of heraldic as well as religious significance."[92]

I believe that the composition can have only a heraldic significance. The column in the center cannot be conceived of as an aniconic representation because of its entablature, which will prove that it had a structural function. We have noted that sacred columns did exist in the Mycenaean world, but they are free-standing and bear no entablature. On the other hand, columns with entablature standing in lieu of a building are rather common. In rejecting Evans' interpretation, Nilsson has pointed out that signs to which religious significance could be imparted, such as the double axe, perhaps were used "to put the construction under divine protection and impart to it divine strength in addition to its material strength."[93] Such symbols, however, are not to be seen in our composition or on the wall, and perhaps the Mycenaeans felt that the massiveness of their construction did not need divine aid to withstand enemy assaults.

Nilsson suggested that the column with its entablature represented a shrine and that the lions, therefore, may be guarding the shrine. However, if a shrine was represented we should find it indicated in the usual way in which a shrine is depicted in Mycenaean works of art. We have seen above that the horns of consecration are always present in shrine representations.

---

88 Furtwängler, *Antike Gemmen*, pl. III nos. 23 and 24. *JHS* 21 (1901), p. 159 figs. 37 and 38. Nilsson, *op.cit.*, p. 253 fig. 122.

89 For a recent discussion see Mylonas, *Ancient Mycenae*, pp. 26 ff. and P. Åstrom, *Opusc. Athen.*, 5 (1964), pp. 159-191.

90 *Mycenaean Age*, p. 31.

91 *JHS*, 21 (1901), pp. 157-158. Wace, *BSA*, 25 (1921-1923), p. 16.

92 *Mycenae*, p. 53.

93 Nilsson, *op.cit.*, pp. 245, 247, 255.

We may recall that in the tripartite shrines in gold foil from the shaft graves not only on the roof but in front of the bases of their columns horns of consecration were placed. The shrine in front of which the goddess or priestess with the mirror is seated (Fig. 127, No. 4) exhibits horns of consecration not only on its roof but also in front of the base of its column. Similar horns of consecration could have been placed by the sculptor on top of the altars and in front of the footing of the column in the Lion Gate relief. In the elegant ivory plaque of confronted sphinxes found by Wace in the house named after them, horns of consecration are carved on the base on either side of the central column; in a similar manner horns of consecration could have been carved on the altars over which rises the column of the Lion Gate relief. On the sealing from the Rhyton Well of Mycenae a set of horns of consecration was placed directly on top of the capital of the column; a similar arrangement would have been possible if the Lion Relief represented a shrine. Furthermore other emblems, such as birds and even sacred boughs could have been added.

It could be argued that the carved slab does not close the relieving triangle entirely, that above it in the empty space there originally was another slab on which may have been carved additional elements, perhaps horns of consecration, a bird or even sacred boughs. This argument is valid. According to measurements taken at the site the empty space of the relieving triangle left above the existing slab is about 1.085 m. at the base and has a maximum height of 85 cm. A slab of these dimensions provided sufficient space for sculptured elements. However, we have first to prove that the space was filled with a slab. Perched on top of the existing large slab it would have had a precarious existence. Deep dowel holes would have been necessary to anchor it, and if such dowel holes were made for the heads of the animals we would expect even bigger ones on top of the existing slab on which the second slab would have been based. Such dowel holes do not exist. There is one small, irregularly shaped and shallow hole to be seen on top of the existing slab, but it is debatable whether it is artificially made. It rather seems to be a natural flaw in the stone. But even if we accept it as artificial, it is too small and shallow to provide sufficient room for a strong clamp.[94] On top of the Elgin slabs with the

bull reliefs in the British Museum we find cuttings evidently serving the attachment of superposed slabs. We would expect similar cuttings on top of the existing slab, but they do not exist. The way in which the relieving triangle of the Treasury of Atreus is completed would exclude the supposition that a capping block with a triangular projection was based on the stones on either side, like a keystone, with its projection filling the space over the existing slab; that in the projection a relief was cut. Perhaps the empty space was not filled by a single slab but by three blocks with a central smaller block acting as a wedge holding the side stones; or, if this was considered not aesthetic enough, by regular large rectangular blocks diminishing in size as they went upwards. In that case one wonders whether the arrangement would permit relief decoration on different blocks.

These considerations rest on hypothetical grounds. There is a solid and to us a convincing argument against the supposition of the existence of additional sculptured elements over the preserved relief. The composition over the Lion Gate is neither unique nor original; it actually is a monumental rendering of a theme common to miniature carving that was used long before the gate was erected. We find the theme carved on rings and gems, and in all instances the design ends with the entablature. On the lentoid gem from Mycenae with the griffins attached to the column (Fig. 124, No. 44), which is the composition closest to that of the Lion Gate, the entablature is the topmost element of the design. Incidentally, in the compositions on the small articles the horns of consecration are not depicted; one more reason why we believe that a shrine is not represented on the relief of the Lion Gate. The column with its entablature gives the impression of symbolizing a substantial and even majestic building, an individual structure. But we have seen that Mycenaean shrines seem to have been of small dimensions, that sometimes they were attached to palaces and formed part of them, rather than being individual buildings. The impressive column could stand only for the most majestic building erected by the Mycenaeans and that is the palace of their rulers.

Marinatos has recently suggested an ingenious interpretation altogether different from all others.[95] Denying that the bases on which the lions place their

---

[94] The hole presents an irregular, oval shape and it measures about 0.035 m. by about 0.02 m. at its opening and is only 0.016 m. in depth. Its bottom is not regular or even. It is doubtful that a clamp could be placed in it which could secure a heavy slab of stone. No traces or indications of attachment of such a clamp, no tearing of the side resulting from the falling off of the slab carrying the clamp with it, is preserved on the side or opening. The "hole" is on the one side of the top of the existing slab, on the other no corresponding hole exists,

but there the top is chipped and one could assume that originally a hole could have existed and that it disappeared when the chipping occurred. But then we shall have to admit that the assumed hole was very, very shallow, even shallower than the one on the other side. There is a trace of a vertical line which might be taken to have belonged to such a hole, but this is highly conjectural. Wace too maintains that the hole is a natural flaw. *BSA*, 24 (1919-1921), p. 206, n. 3; *contra* Åstrom, *loc.cit.*

[95] *Praktika of the Academy of Athens*, 31 (1956), pp. 400-415.

front paws are altars, he interprets them as symbolic of the sea separating two land masses. Based on Egyptian symbolism and iconography, he interprets the column as signifying the union of two kingdoms or domains, a union guarded by lions. There are a number of objections one could raise against this interpretation. The column is structural, it supports an entablature and as such it cannot stand for the aniconic essence of a deity; in the same manner it cannot stand for the abstract idea of union. The Egyptian examples are free-standing columns, thus differing from our relief. The symbolism of the sea in the frescoes of Amnissos is further indicated by wavy lines; perhaps these are the most important element of the symbolism. We would expect to find similar lines on the bases; they do not exist. The nature of the bases as altars is well established. If they symbolize two land masses separated by sea, how would we explain the identical object painted on the plaster plaque of Mycenae with the goddess of the figure-eight shield or its palladium? How would we explain the identical altar in front of the mountain sanctuary on the rhyton of Kato Zakro? The idea of union further would require the concept of a unified great kingdom with the ruler of Mycenae at its head, a coalition of two great domains, as was the case with Upper and Lower Egypt. This is a political system that seems not to have existed in the Mycenaean Age, as far as we can determine from the known evidence. And then the question of which land masses and which areas across the seas were brought under which ruler would arise. At the time of the construction of the Lion Gate the greatness of Minoan Crete was gone, and it will be impossible to prove that Crete came under the domain of the kings of Mycenae and not under that of the kings of Pylos, for example. The Ahhiyavā, mentioned in the Hittite documents, could be suggested; but again we shall have to prove that Ahhiyavā, now suggested to have been centered in Rhodes,[96] was under the domain of Mycenae. It seems to me that the problems raised by this interpretation are difficult to answer, and the fact remains that the column serves a structural end and cannot be conceived as standing for anything else but for a building.[97]

I maintain that the column with its entablature stands only for the royal palace, the royal house of Mycenae. In close connection with a royal house

stands, of course, the dynasty, the ruling family which abides in it. The column therefore could very well symbolize the palace and the dynasty, a palace and a dynasty guarded by lions, the guardians of the king. That lions and griffins were conceived as guardians of the ruler is indicated by the fresco paintings which stood on either side of the throne in the *domos* of the Palace of Nestor at Pylos. We may now note how the column is based on the altars and how it seems to grow from them like a tree growing from the earth. This, in my thinking, implies that the dynasty it symbolizes stands upon, is founded upon, the concept that its right to rule is based on and grows out of divine will, a concept also indicated by the title *wanax*. I believe that in the relief over the Lion Gate we have the artistic counterpart of the Homeric belief in the divine right of the kings, another close parallel between Homeric beliefs and Mycenaean practices. The relief over the main gate of Mycenae can be conceived as the emblem, the coat of arms, of the διογενεῖς βασιλεῖς, kings born of Zeus, the σκηπτοῦχοι, the scepter bearers whose "honor," as Homer states, "is from Zeus," and "whom Zeus, God of Council, loveth."[98] The lions guarding the column can be conceived, as Wace and Persson pointed out, as the badge of the ruling family of Mycenae. I maintain that the relief is contemporary with the gate, that both were made towards the middle of the LH III B period, or around 1250 B.C. If there is any kernel of truth in the traditions of Mycenae, around that date Atreus the Pelopid, the father of Agamemnon, ruled over the city. I should like to think that the lions were the particular emblem of the Pelopids who came to Greece from Asia Minor, a country where the use of lions as emblems of powerful rulers and citadels has a long history, and that the composition over the main gate of Mycenae is the coat of arms of Atreus and his descendants. However that may be, it is certain that the relief, representing the royal palace, was in position and that the lions had started their vigil over the entrance and the citadel when Agamemnon and his followers marched through the gate to start on their long and perilous expedition against Troy.

The survey of the relics found in the mainland of Greece proves that the Mycenaeans borrowed from Minoan Crete practically every article used in their ritual. Altars with incurved sides, tables of offerings,

---

[96] D. N. Page, *History and the Homeric Iliad*, pp. 15-17 and notes 53-55. Völkl, *Nouvelle Clio* 4 (1952), pp. 329 ff. *Contra* cf. Schachermeyr, *Hethiter und Achäer*, pp. 129 ff.

[97] Of course the interpretation of the column suggested by Colonel Mure (who thought that the lions were wolves and connected them with Apollo Lykeios, *Rhein. Mus.*, 6 [1838], p. 256), and then by Gerhard (*Mykenische Alterthümer, 10 Programm. Berliner Winckelmannsfest*, 1850, p. 10) and by Curtius (*Peloponnesos*, II, p. 405 and *Gr. Geschichte*, I, p. 116), stating that

the column is a "symbol" of Apollo Agyieus, or a herm as Göttling maintained (*N. Rhein. Museum*, I, 1842, p. 161) have long since been disproved by Adler (*Archäol. Zeitung*, Jan. 1865, p. 6), who remarked that the column of the relief has a structural significance since it had a capital-entablature, while all such monuments have plain tops.

[98] *Iliad*, II, 100 ff.; II, 197, 205-206, 547-549; IX, 98-99, for the revealing story of Agamemnon's scepter.

sacrificial tables, bull-shaped rhyta, beaked jugs, all find their prototypes in Crete. The heavy vestments worn by their priests seem to point to Syria, but it is not certain whether they were borrowed directly from the Near East or through Crete. There is one cult object which they do not seem to have borrowed: the votive double axe, the special symbol of the Minoan religion. Again it is not clear whether or not they adopted the device of the bird symbolizing the epiph-

any of a goddess. After LH I the only example of the divine epiphany is to be found on the sealing from the Rhyton Well of Mycenae; but even that example, dating from LH II times, could be considered an importation. However, the legends and the association of birds with Olympian deities, such as Athena, may indicate the adoption of the Minoan concept of divine epiphany by the Mycenaeans.

THE CULT OF THE DEAD

One of the most prevalent beliefs of modern scholarship regarding Mycenaean religious rites is the notion that a cult of the dead was practiced in the Mycenaean Age. It was advanced early in the history of Mycenaean research; it was adopted by later scholars, and it is repeated with certainty as an established fact which needs no verification. Even Nilsson, to whom we owe the first real, rational study of Minoan-Mycenaean religion, agrees that a cult of the dead was current in Mycenaean times, although he admits candidly "that such a cult existed can be assumed on general grounds because it exists everywhere, but from the actual evidence of the finds there are few archaeological traces of such a cult."[99] Now that a new assumption is being developed dealing with divine honors presumably bestowed upon the *wanax* of a Mycenaean state, the hypothesis of a cult of the dead will be strengthened. As a matter of fact, it is now stated that the divine honors that a *wanax* enjoyed in his lifetime had to be continued after his death; this is an assumption based on another unfounded assumption.[100] Furthermore, Palmer's proposition that a festival in honor of the dead may be attested by the Oil Tablets from Pylos will strengthen the prevailing view.[101] Consequently the discussion of the subject becomes both essential and timely. Before we review the evidence marshaled by Nilsson, we must rapidly examine a unique object which, although found in Crete and not in the mainland, is often linked with the Mycenaean world by eminent scholars.

The Sarcophagus of Aghia Triada

The remarkable object in question is the sarcophagus of Aghia Triada, first described fully by Roberto Paribeni.[102] It was found in 1903 near the Minoan

villa and since then it has been described and discussed a number of times by international scholars. We do not intend to add another description to those existing, but we propose to point out that it does not reflect Mycenaean practices and ideas. Perhaps the most realistic discussion of the representations on the sarcophagus and their meaning is that of Nilsson. After citing the explanations advanced by other scholars, he concludes that the best answer to a number of vexing questions would be to suppose first that "the paintings on the sarcophagus must refer to the deceased who was laid in it"; secondly, "to suppose that the dead was deified and consequently worshiped in the forms of the divine cult"; and, finally, to assume "that at this time," i.e., LM II to LM III, the calculated date of the sarcophagus, "a Mycenaean chieftain seized Aghia Triada, settled there for a while, and died there. His kin or his retinue wanted a great funeral display according to Mycenaean customs, and to continue the remembrance of it they charged Minoan artists with executing paintings of the funeral cult on his sarcophagus. . . . It seems that a mingling of Mycenaean veneration of the Mighty Dead and Egyptian divinization of the dead, covered with a garb of Minoan divine cult, accounts satisfactorily for these astonishing funeral paintings."[103]

I am in agreement with the parts of the conclusion which deal with the Minoan and Egyptian elements, but I would like to ask what elements there are in the representations on the sarcophagus to justify the assumption that in it was buried a Mycenaean chieftain whose kin or retinue "wanted a great funeral display according to Mycenaean custom," which they wished to make permanent through the paintings on the sarcophagus. The sarcophagus was found in an

---

[99] Μυκῆναι, pp. 150 and 170. Wace, *Mycenae*, p. 116. Nilsson, *op.cit.*, p. 428 and pp. 584-619.

[100] Webster, *op.cit.*, p. 100 states: "The divine or near divine king lived in his palace. . . . After death the king lived on in a royal tomb . . ." and p. 53, "when he died, he was buried in his sumptuous tomb to which divine honours were paid." But no evidence is brought forth to substantiate the statements. As for the divine or semi-divine status of the *wanax*, see *infra*,

p. 208.

[101] Palmer, *op.cit.*, pp. 252 ff. The equation of *dipsioi* and the Thirsty Dead is highly conjectural and as yet not proved. It is rather damaging to the conjecture that only oil was offered to or is connected with the Dipsioi.

[102] R. Paribeni, *MonAnt.*, 19 (1908), pp. 1 ff., "Il sarcofago dipinto di H. Triada."

[103] Nilsson, *op.cit.*, pp. 438 and 442.

un-Mycenaean rectangular built grave with a door but without a *dromos*. If the kin and retinue were trying to give their chieftain a magnificent Mycenaean burial they would have constructed for him a tholos tomb, or even a chamber tomb. This was not done. That chamber tombs were not unknown in the neighborhood of Aghia Triada is proved by the fact that a number of them were found just about a kilometer from the site.[104] The body of the "chieftain" was laid to rest in a rectangular stone sarcophagus. In the mainland, burial in sarcophagi is unknown in the transitional years from LM II to LM III or their equivalent of LH II to III. Only one verified burial in a bathtub was found in the cemetery of Prosymna (Tomb XVII), and that belongs to the closing years of the LH III period.[105] A fragment of a bathtub was found in a tomb in Thebes by Keramopoullos and another was found by Wace in Tomb 502 of Mycenae,[106] which, as pointed out, is not certainly identified as belonging to a tub; however, it belonged to the period of the granary style of pottery, that is, to the closing years of the Mycenaean Age. To the same closing years or at best to the late years of LH III B belong the fragments of tubs used for burial we found at the site of Aghios Kosmas.[107] Iacovides and Vermeule now report painted larnakes from the area between Attika and Boiotia.[108] These larnakes, however, as both authors state, belong to the very end of the Mycenaean period, to the closing years of LH III C. They are the result of the fusion of elements drawn from a variety of sources and of the confusion that resulted from the fall of the Mycenaean state. In contrast to the paucity and the late date of the material from the mainland, we find that sarcophagi were employed in Crete from Early Minoan times,[109] long before the days of the example from Aghia Triada. The Minoan receptacles are regular lidded sarcophagi made especially for the purpose. They were placed often enough in rectangular pits like the grave of Aghia Triada. The sides of the Minoan sarcophagi or larnakes and even their lids were elaborately painted, like the example from Aghia Triada. In the painting and even in the use of a sarcophagus for his burial, the kin of the deceased were following a well-established Minoan custom, not a Mycenaean practice.

The examination of the paintings themselves will lead to the same conclusion (Fig. 134). On the sar-

cophagus of Aghia Triada we find represented double axes and birds, and the scene of a sacrifice. The first two are stated to be symbols of the divine cult, and because of them it is concluded that the dead man was deified.[110] But on the sarcophagus from Episkopi we find the same symbols represented, the horns of consecration, the double axe, the bird, and the sacrificial bull.[111] Again on the sarcophagus from Palaikastro[112] we find "the symbols of the divine cult," the horns of consecration, the double axe, a winged creature. On a sarcophagus found not far from the palace at Mallia we have a large double axe with a bird perched on top of its shaft.[113] Were the people buried in these sarcophagi also deified and were they all mainlanders living all over the island? These examples, I believe, seem to indicate that the placing of these emblems on sarcophagi is a Minoan and not a Mycenaean practice and points to the fact that the "kin" of the deceased who wanted "a funeral display" according to their ancestral customs were Minoans, since in that display they used purely Minoan elements.

The bringing of gifts to the grave was both a Minoan and a Mycenaean custom. If a cult of the dead is depicted or reflected in the painting of the sarcophagus, we have to prove that this bringing of gifts did not occur at the time of burial but long afterwards, that, in other words, we do not have depicted funeral rites occurring at the time of burial. I think that this task will prove impossible. There is a small detail which may indicate that we are dealing with funeral rites and not with a cult. On the side of the sarcophagus where the appearance of the "deceased" before his grave is represented (Fig. 134), we find on either side of all the persons participating, with the exception of the "deceased" and the man holding the boat, a strange form of a three-line pattern, apparently attached to the people and directed towards the ground. This is not to be seen on the scene of the fruit and bull sacrifice on the other side of the sarcophagus, nor on the fragment of the wall painting from Aghia Triada illustrated by Nilsson and rightly interpreted as a scene of divine cult.[114] A similar three-lined, wavy pattern we find between the bull placed transversely and the bird on the sarcophagus of Episkopi. We find it also on the sarcophagus from Anoya

104 L. Savignoni, *MonAnt.*, 14 (1904), p. 500. Fourteen rock-cut chamber tombs were explored near the village Kalyvia; and pp. 627-666.

105 Blegen, *Prosymna*, p. 249.

106 *Deltion*, 3 (1917), p. 92 fig. 66. *Chamber Tombs*, pp. 9, 184.

107 Mylonas, *Aghios Kosmas*, pp. 61-62.

108 Iacovides 1, *AJA*, 70 (1966), pp. 43 ff. E. Vermeule, *Greece in the Bronze Age*, 1964, pp. 210-214.

109 Cf. Pendlebury, *The Archaeology of Crete*, p. 65.

110 Nilsson, *op.cit.*, p. 433.

111 *Deltion*, 6 (1921) *Parartema*, p. 158 fig. 5.

112 *BSA*, 8 (1901-1902), pl. XVIII.

113 *BCH*, 52 (1928), p. 150, pl. IX and p. 151 fig. 1. Other examples of sarcophagi with the one or the other of these "cult symbols" are to be seen in the museums of Crete.

114 Nilsson, *op.cit.*, p. 436. Also used in his argument.

and on that from Katsamba;[115] perhaps what Joly called "vrille" on the Mallia sarcophagus may stand for this element. Evidently it is an apparatus to be seen only on sarcophagi with scenes connected with burials, and since we do not have it in any representation of the divine cult it must belong to the ritual for the dead. The lines suggest long ribbons or even tresses of hair and bring to mind the custom of dedicating hair at the grave of the deceased at the time of burial. If this identification is correct, it may indicate that we are dealing with funeral rites held at the time of burial and not with a cult of the dead. At any rate this small detail is purely Minoan, used not only on the elaborate sarcophagus of Aghia Triada but also on the less exalted examples from Episkopi, Anoya, and Katsamba.

The structure in front of which the dead man stands, his grave, must correspond to the type of graves characteristic of or used in his homeland. It certainly is neither a tholos tomb nor a chamber tomb. The tree pictured in front of the "deceased" indicates that the grave-structure stands above ground. Its nearest parallel is the "temple-tomb" of Knossos and not the sepulchers of the mainland. All the elements which can be determined, the type of grave, the painted sarcophagus, the emblems of the divine cult, are to be found in a somewhat similar combination in Minoan Crete and not on the mainland. They represent customs well rooted in Crete and not in the Mycenaean world. The assumption that a Mycenaean chieftain was buried in the sarcophagus is unfounded. The sarcophagus of Aghia Triada cannot be used to indicate the existence of a cult of the dead in the Mycenaean territory. It indicates only that a Minoan artist under Egyptian influence painted a scene of funeral rites usual in the Minoan world and embellished them with notions current in Egypt; but for the benefit of a Cretan chieftain or wealthy man and his Cretan relatives and friends, not for a Mycenaean chieftain.

Cult and Funeral Rites

It is time now to examine the elements on which is based the assumption of the existence of a cult of the dead in the Mycenaean world. At the outset, we must clearly differentiate a cult from funeral rites held at burial. Nilsson in his monumental work on Minoan-Mycenaean religious beliefs and practices has pointed out that the burial rites are performed but once—on the occasion of a man's interment or cremation; the cult of the dead results from the "tendance" of the dead, from the "bringing of gifts, the offering of sacrifices, etc., to the dead man and to his tomb on certain days or on certain occasions" in the years that follow the burial.[116] A regular repetition of religious observances and acts over the years is the essential characteristic of the cult. What evidence would suggest, indicate, or prove the regular repetition of rites over the graves of the Mycenaean era?

Grave Circles

Grave Circle A, the circular wall enclosing it, the cave and the so-called altar over Grave IV, the fact that it was never encroached upon by later structures, and that the Cyclopean Wall was made to sweep around it, are usually taken to prove the cult of the dead in Mycenaean times. Under the influence of the general belief and the apparent evidence of Circle A, I maintained in my study of the Mycenaean burial customs, and even in later writings,[117] that the Mycenaeans could have believed that a few chosen individuals were fated not to end in the same way as common men, but that they were allowed to have an interest in and to influence the life of the living even after their bodies had decomposed; that these individuals, mighty chieftains on whom people depended during their lifetime, had to be honored and worshiped in a cult of the dead. The exploration of Circle B, the further investigation of Grave Circle A, and the study of the writings of Schliemann, Tsountas, and Wace proved to me that I was wrong in assuming the special role in the affairs of men fated to be kings and rulers and made me reexamine the evidence preserved in the grave circles. We have seen above (pp. 94, 96) that the "cave" and the "altar" of Grave Circle A were deeply buried under its floor level when it was rearranged and terraced in LH III B times; that they could not have been used for a cult or for any other purposes in the period when the west Cyclopean wall and the Lion Gate were constructed, when the monumental Treasury of Atreus was erected. No other tangible evidence was found in the fill of Grave Circle A to indicate that it was used for a cult or other religious rites after its reconstruction.

It is assumed that when the area of the shaft graves was surrounded by the circular parapet wall, it was transformed into a *temenos*; the parapet wall, it is maintained, made it into a *temenos*.[118] Now we know that the area of the shaft graves was from the very beginning surrounded by a circular wall, that the parapet of LH III B times was built merely to take the

[115] Evans, *Palace of Minos*, IV, part 1, p. 338 fig. 281. Orsi, "Urne funebri cretesi," *MonAnt.*, I (1889), pp. 202 ff. pls. 1-2. *Ergon*, 1963, fig. 192.

[116] Nilsson, *op.cit.*, pp. 585-586. Cf. also Tsountas and Manatt, *Mycenaean Age*, pp. 149-150.

[117] *AJA*, 52 (1948), pp. 77-78. "The Cult of the Dead," pp. 99-100.

[118] Wace, *Mycenae*, p. 116.

place of the older wall. If the mere building of a wall around the graves transformed their area into a *temenos* that had to remain inviolate, where a cult was to be held, then Grave Circle B must be another *temenos*, since the area of its graves was also enclosed by a circular wall. Grave Circle B, however, did not remain inviolate; the Mycenaeans did not respect its area in spite of its circular wall. The builders of the so-called Tomb of Klytemnestra cut into the circle and violated its territory; the stone cutters, who prepared the blocks used in the construction of its vault or its mound, worked the stone in the area of the circle and in its adjacent section. The mound piled over the tholos of the same tomb extended over the circle, perhaps covering more than half of its area. Certainly, the Mycenaeans who trespassed so much on the area of Grave Circle B could not have considered it a *temenos*. And if one circle was not considered a *temenos*, the other could not have been so considered just because of its form and its enclosing wall. We need more evidence before we can accept the notion. Such evidence does not exist. We may remark here that in excavating Grave Circle B, Papadimitriou and I, with the problem in mind, scrutinized exhaustively the fill of the area to obtain any possible evidence indicating a cult; we found not a trace of such a cult in Circle B.

Years ago Tsountas rejected the assumption that Grave Circle A was a *temenos* and, noting that its entrance was an open passage, remarked "now it is hardly conceivable that a consecrated place should be left open to all comers,—even to dogs, which we know were kept inside the Mycenaean akropolis."[119] That the area of Circle A was respected is, of course, definite. But it was respected as the burial place of the old kings who laid the foundations of the glory of Mycenae and its ruling family, as a historic landmark to be shown proudly to visitors at the great capital of the Mycenaean world. At any rate, neither Grave Circle A nor Grave Circle B has yielded evidence indicating the existence of a cult practiced in their areas.

Niches in Graves

Inferences were drawn from certain elements, structural and other, found in graves. Niches, for example, were projected as indicating the existence of a cult.[120] These do exist in a number of chamber tombs, and they are found cut on the sides of the *dromos* and in the chambers. The latter were used generally to accommodate bones that were swept from the floors and rarely for burials. Certainly their contents prove

that they could not have been used for cult purposes, and besides being in the chamber whose *stomion* was blocked, they were not accessible to the public for the periodic observances required by a cult. The evidence obtained from most of the graves at Prosymna, Mycenae, Nauplia, and Asine indicate that the niches on the lateral walls of the *dromoi* served for the burial of the dead.[121] In a number of them skeletal remains were found; in others walls or slabs blocked their openings, a feature characteristic of graves. Most of the niches were cut a little above the floor of the grave. This alone would indicate that they could not have been used for cult purposes, since the earth with which the *dromoi* were filled up after each burial would have made these niches inaccessible. How could they have been used for the "tendance" of the dead at prescribed intervals, as required by a cult, if they were inaccessible? Besides, no evidence whatever was found in any Mycenaean niche indicating that it served a cult purpose.

In the *dromos* of Chamber Tomb 5 at Asine, a niche was found cut in the rock only 60 cm. below the top of the edge of the side. Its opening was found closed by a packing of rubble wall. Within it were found three post-Mycenaean or proto-Geometric vases. One of these vases, a crater, was half filled with burnt earth and calcined animal bones, and this was taken to be clear evidence of a "sacrifice to persons buried in the chamber. . . . It is evident," concludes Nilsson, "that this find, which does not contain any human remains, is an offering made after the tomb was closed."[122]

A number of details, however, presented by this niche do indicate that its evidence does not prove the existence of a cult of the dead in Mycenaean times. At best, it would indicate the existence of a cult in *post-Mycenaean* times since the pot containing the remains of the so-called sacrifice is stated by the excavator to be a post-Mycenaean or Proto-Geometric pot. Again, why was the opening of the niche blocked by a wall if it served a cult? This was a characteristic feature of graves, so characteristic indeed that the wall blocking the door of Tomb 3 at Asine was brought forth by the excavators as a proof that the tomb was actually used. To the possible assertion that Tomb 3 had never been used as a tomb, Persson counters "that the stone packing of the door . . . would not have been put into position except in connection with a burial, that is to say, immediately after such had taken place."[123] This remark, valid for Tomb 3, is equally valid for the niche of Tomb 5. Its packing would

---

[119] *Mycenaean Age*, p. 107.
[120] Nilsson, *op.cit.*, pp. 587 ff.
[121] Mylonas, "The Cult of the Dead," pp. 84-88. Additional examples of niches in *dromoi* were found by Verdelis in 1962

and by me in 1964 at Mycenae. All had been used for burials.
[122] Nilsson, *op.cit.*, p. 588. Frödin-Persson, *Asine*, pp. 178-179 and 357.
[123] Frödin-Persson, *Asine*, p. 173.

indicate that it was used for a burial, perhaps of a child whose bones dissolved completely. That this is not unusual, in the case especially of children, is well-known to all excavators; we have seen that the skeleton of the Vapheio cist had completely dissolved. Now we find that in the Proto-Geometric cemetery of Asine, which yielded interments only, a number of what the excavators called tomb-altars were found on which "sacrificial gifts have been burnt."[124] The burnt earth and the calcined bones of the Proto-Geometric pot found in the niche seem to be the remnants of such an offering made at the time of the burial of the child, in accordance with a post-Mycenaean custom proved by the excavations of the site. Again, we have seen how in Proto-Geometric times a niche was cut on the wall of the tholos tomb of Dendra, high up above its floor, and used for the burial of an adult. It is evident that the niche of Tomb 5 of Asine was used for burial and did not serve a cult; that it was used in post-Mycenaean times and contained the remains of gifts burnt at the time of the burial of a child.

Cists

It is generally accepted now that pits and cists cut in the floor of the graves served usually for the storing of bones swept away from the floor. Occasionally, people—especially important people like kings who exercised great power in their lifetime—had pits cut in the floors of the chambers to be used for the burial of members of the family for whom they felt special affection. This was perhaps prompted by the desire to have their earthly remains and their cherished possessions left undisturbed, by the aversion they may have experienced in their lifetime when they viewed the sad fate of the bones of those buried before. Whatever reason may have prompted their action, the fact remains that the cists and pits which served for burial do not indicate the existence of a cult. The so-called sacrificial pits of the tholos tomb of Vapheio and of Dendra did not serve a cult, but only a rite held at the burial. They are within the grave, separated from the outside world by the blocking of the *stomion* and the fill of the *dromos*; they were not accessible for the regular observances required by a cult. The sacrificial pit of the cenotaph of Dendra served a special purpose, as we have seen, the purpose of inducing the wandering "spirits" of people who died abroad and remained without proper burial, to return to the grave built for them at home. It did not serve a cult.

Fires and Burnt Offerings

Traces and even extensive remains of fires have

been found in a good number of Mycenaean graves. Tsountas, who cleared more than one hundred chamber tombs at Mycenae, wrote long ago that charcoal was found in nearly all the tombs, and his testimony was confirmed by the explorations of Blegen, Wace, Persson, Verdelis, and others.[125] The notion that these fires proved the existence of the practice of cremation in the Mycenaean Age has been abandoned. It is now generally accepted that fires were used for the fumigation and the purification of the chambers before additional bodies were interred in them; that they were used in connection with the burial rites, not infrequently they seem to have been used to burn offerings. In our description of the tholos tombs of Vapheio and Midea-Dendra we noted even "ritualistic pits" which contained remnants of fires and burnt offerings. There we also noted that Tsountas as early as 1888 reported the discovery of burnt offerings—trinkets and toilet accessories—in some chamber tombs. These burnt offerings present us with a problem which I indicated in my study of the Mycenaean burial customs when I wrote: "if the burning of the belongings of the dead was customary, it will remain unexplained why some of the κτερίσματα were burned, while others, the majority indeed, were laid out around the corpse."[126] Nilsson agreed that these offerings were burned at the time of burial, in other words, that they do not indicate a cult, and suggested that this resulted from the survival of the custom of burning the furnishings together with the corpse. He further explained that "this implies that the Greeks, when they immigrated, used cremation, but having settled in Greece succumbed to Minoan culture in burial customs as well as in other habits of life and in art, though they sometimes kept the burning of gifts to the dead as a survival of their old custom."[127]

It is still generally believed that the first wave of the Greek-speaking Indo-European inhabitants of Greece invaded and settled in the mainland of Greece at the end of the Early Helladic period, around 1900 B.C. A great many graves of the Middle Helladic period belonging to the descendants of these invaders have been excavated, especially on the eastern section of the mainland. Not a single example of cremation has been found as yet, and inhumation is the only mode of burial practiced from after 1900 B.C. to the date of the tholos tomb of Dendra and even after it. If Nilsson's suggestion were true, cremation burials would have been found. To assume that the ancestors of the Dendra people for at least five centuries did not practice cremation and that all of a sudden after so

---

124 *Ibid.*, p. 426.
125 *Mycenaean Age*, p. 138. Cf. Nilsson, *op.cit.*, pp. 595 ff.
126 Tsountas, *Ephemeris*, 1888, p. 134. *Mycenaean Age*, p.

147. Mylonas, *AJA*, 52 (1948), p. 74.
127 Nilsson, *op.cit.*, p. 599.

many years they remembered a custom which did not exist in Greece and of which they could have no remembrance, is, I believe, altogether impossible. Some other explanation should be suggested.

We cannot, of course, be positive about explanations that deal with unrecorded customs and which are not clearly confirmed by the relics. But I would like to repeat an explanation I suggested in 1951 and which I still find valid.[128] I suggested that perhaps gifts were burned as offerings to those buried previously whose corpses had not decayed completely when the grave had to be opened again for a new burial. This was a means of placating them, of making amends for the disturbance. The partial decay of the body may have suggested the rite of burning these gifts; consumed by fire they may have been more acceptable offerings to the half-decayed dead who perhaps were conceived to be already nearing the domain of Hades, the end of their long trip. The burning of the gifts would have served also as a means to reassure the relatives who had to open and enter the chamber not so long after one of their kinsmen had been interred. In the tholos tomb of Midea-Dendra the grave had to be entered again after the burial of the mighty king for the burial of his queen. The fact that the weapons beyond the king's feet were piled up in a heap, instead of being swept aside along with the bones of his lowest extremities, may indicate that the body of the king had not decayed completely and so his "spirit" had to be placated by burning gifts. The same could be maintained for the evidence found in the tholos tomb of Vapheio. In this way perhaps the burning of some offerings could be explained.

Evidence of Cult in Geometric Times

The survey of the elements used in favor of a cult proves definitely, I believe, that they do not even indicate its existence in Mycenaean times. There is definite evidence proving the existence of a cult of the dead, but in post-Mycenaean times. At Mycenae itself in the *dromos* of the Tomb of Klytemnestra a mass of Geometric pottery was found, and above Tomb 520 Wace discovered a deposit of Geometric pottery indicating the existence of a cult.[129] On the southwest edge of Grave Circle B and over the collapsed roof of a chamber tomb Papadimitriou and I disclosed a circular structure where a cult was prac-

ticed in Geometric times.[130] Blegen recorded definite evidence found in the chamber tombs of Prosymna proving the existence of a cult, but again in Geometric times. Marinatos reports a sacrifice of a stag from the Mycenaean tomb at Akona of Geometric date.[131] Evidence for such a cult practiced in later times is known from Attika, the tholos tomb of Acharnai-Menidi, and from Western Triphylia, from the tombs cleared by Marinatos. In the last mentioned the remains of sacrificed animals are proved by pottery to belong to Hellenistic times.[132]

The Tholos Tomb of Acharnai-Menidi

It is usually assumed that in the *dromos* of the tholos tomb of Acharnai-Menidi evidence was unearthed which proves the existence of a cult in Mycenaean times. The reexamination of the evidence becomes imperative. That tholos tomb was accidentally discovered and was excavated by the German Institute of Archaeology in Athens in 1879, only three years after Schliemann's exploration of Grave Circle A. Its remains were described in a monograph in 1880 by its excavator, H. Lolling, and the vases found in and around it were published by Wolters in 1899.[133] Nilsson declares that in the tholos tomb of Acharnai-Menidi we have "the most obvious example of a cult at a tomb persisting through the ages," and gives what he considers the pertinent evidence favoring his conclusion.[134] The *stomion* of the tomb was found blocked by the usual stone wall, which, however, was not extended to the lintel, but left an opening about 30 cm. between its upper edge and the lintel of the doorway. The *dromos*, barred by a cross wall near its outer end, was filled with earth to the height of its cross wall. The opening left between the lintel of the doorway and the top of the wall which blocked the *stomion* "had later been blocked by stones fallen from the walls into the *dromos*." In the lowest layers of this mass of stones were found several sherds of Mycenaean vases, sherds No. 48-52 in Wolters' section (Fig. 135) and large fragments of coarse pottery and pithoi.[135] Because these sherds were blackened by smoke, even in their interior, they were assumed by Wolters and later by Nilsson to have belonged "to offerings burnt before the door of the tomb." Fragments of vases and terra cottas of the historic period—Early Attic, Corinthian, black-figure—were found in four other parts

---

[128] Mylonas, "The Cult of the Dead," pp. 91-92.
[129] Wace, *Chamber Tombs*, p. 23. Nilsson, *op.cit.*, p. 604.
[130] Papadimitriou, *Praktika*, 1953, p. 208.
[131] In 13 of the 50 graves he explored, Blegen found evidence of a "wide-spread cult of the dead carried on in the late Geometric period." *Prosymna*: Tomb III (p. 182), VIII, IX, X (p. 199), XIII (p. 195), XXV (p. 89), XXXIV (p. 113), XXXVII (p. 126), XLIII (p. 186), XL (p. 133), XLIX (p. 136). *Ephemeris*, 1937, pp. 377-390.

[132] For the Acharnai-Menidi tomb, see *infra*, p. 184. For the Marinatos report see *supra*, p. 116, the Peristeria tomb, and Κρητικὰ Χρονικά, 15-16 (1961-62), pp. 179 ff.; also *Praktika*, 1961, pl. 131a.
[133] H. G. Lolling *et al.*, *Das Kuppelgrab bei Menidi*, 1880. P. Wolters, "Vasen aus Menidi II," *Jahrbuch*, 14 (1899), pp. 103-105.
[134] Nilsson, *op.cit.*, p. 603.
[135] *Das Kuppelgrab*, pp. 8 ff.

of the *dromos* (53-54, 44-45, etc., 55 in Wolters' plan, Fig. 135). Besides, it was noticed by the excavators that "about five meters from the door and a meter beneath the surface a layer of earth mingled with ashes and some fragments of bones" were found. "Similar remains, though in a smaller quantity, were also found much deeper down."[136]

This is a summary of the evidence taken from Nilsson's description, whose conclusion is that these articles "were votive offerings, brought to this sacred place," that a cult of the dead was practiced here until the Peloponnesian War. However, all the articles on which the conclusion was based belong to the Historic Era, to years which followed the Proto-Geometric period; and there can be little doubt that a cult was practiced there beginning with the Geometric period and continuing to the Peloponnesian War. The evidence on which it was assumed that a cult was held in Mycenaean times is composed of a few sherds, blackened by smoke and found in the layer of stones in front of the lintel of the doorway of the tomb. Is this evidence sufficient to prove the existence of a cult of the dead in Mycenaean times, and what is the actual nature of the sherds?

Nilsson finds sufficient the evidence assumed to have been preserved by the few sherds blackened by smoke and concludes (p. 603): "This is the most obvious example of a cult at a tomb persisting through the ages from the Mycenaean downwards to classical times and there is no doubt that it must be called a hero cult, even if we do not know by what name the hero was called." That he believes that the cult was continuous throughout the periods he mentions is indicated by his statement, on page 601: "From the time when the tomb was closed somewhere before the end of the Mycenaean Age the cult went on uninterruptedly into the fifth century B.C., as is shown by the discovery of offerings in the *dromos*."

This *uninterrupted* cult of the dead is not proved by the evidence uncovered and summarized by Nilsson. The oldest specimens of the Historic Era which were found in the *dromos* could be placed at best towards the middle of the eighth century B.C. The prehistoric sherds found in front of the lintel date from the thirteenth or the twelfth century B.C. We have no specimen dating from the period between the twelfth and the eighth centuries. A gap of some three and a half centuries exists in the periods represented by the finds from the *dromos*. Consequently, the conclusion of an *uninterrupted* cult from Mycenaean to classical times is not justified by the evidence. Furthermore, that

conclusion was based on the assumption that the Mycenaean sherds found belong to offerings used in a cult for the dead. But are these sherds the remnants of offerings to the dead?

When Wolters reached his conclusion, which incidentally was not shared by the excavators,[137] our knowledge of the burial customs and practices of the Mycenaeans was very limited indeed, and his assumptions were justified. But since his time a great many graves have been explored and our knowledge has increased considerably so that his conclusion, viewed in the light of the present, will not stand. These sherds, it is assumed, were placed where they were found after the use of the tomb for burials had ended. We must assume that they were complete vases when they were burned and left in front of the lintel if they are offerings. However, not a single vase was put together from the sherds found, and all are but broken parts of vases. Since no traces of fire were found in the area of the stones among which and under which the sherds blackened by smoke were found, we shall have to assume that the offerings were burnt somewhere else, were broken there and only parts of them were carried to and placed before the lintel. This certainly does not seem to be reasonable. That the excavators were able to distinguish traces of fire is indicated by Nilsson's statement that layers of earth with ashes were noted in various parts and depths in the fill of the *dromos*, but not in the area of the sherds.

The level in which these sherds were found will prove that they could not have belonged to offerings. According to Wolters' conception, accepted by Nilsson, these sherds were placed in the position in which they were found after the *dromos* had been filled up. The assumed surface of that fill was indicated by Wolters in the section of the tholos tomb which he published (Fig. 135) not only by a broken line but also by the inscription "Bodenhöhe nach Verschluss des Grabes." The restoration of the line of that surface was apparently determined by the levels in which the Mycenaean sherds were found, the sherds of the later centuries, and the top of the wall which blocked the outer end of the *dromos*. If we study the line of that surface, as indicated in Wolters' section, we shall find that it slopes towards the façade of the grave. This would have been impossible in reality, because then the *dromos* would have formed a broad drain through which rain water would have been channeled into the grave. We have to remember that an opening of some 30 cm. existed between the lintel of the doorway and the top of the blocking wall of the *stomion*;

---

[136] Nilsson, *op.cit.*, pp. 601-603.
[137] Nilsson remarked that although the grave "has long been known, it was passed over in silence by those who did not believe in the connexion of the cult of the heroes with that of

the dead" (*op.cit.*, p. 600). On page 602 he states, regarding the Mycenaean sherds blackened by smoke, "We can only assume with Professor Wolters that they belong to offerings burned before the door of the tomb."

through that opening rain water would have been drained into the tholos. Nor could we assume that the opening would have been barred by earth, which would have prevented the passage of the water. In that case the water would have accumulated in front of the lintel and again would have drained into the tholos by means of the openings left in the superstructure. That superstructure over the lintel was not in the form of the usual relieving triangle, which could have been blocked by a slab, but it was made of four superposed horizontal, flat slabs which left between them openings ranging from 15 cm. to 20 cm. Through those openings the rain water would have found its way into the tholos. We know how anxious the Mycenaeans were to protect their tholoi from moisture. To assume that they would have filled the *dromos* in a way that would expose the vaulted construction and chamber to the destructive action of rain water is altogether untenable. Certainly they would have filled in the *dromos* in such a way that the natural drainage would have been away from the façade of the grave; that the surface created over the *dromos* would have been above the line of Wolters' "Bodenhöhe nach Verschluss der Grabes," and possibly even above the topmost empty space between the horizontal slabs of the façade. Consequently the Mycenaean sherds (Fig. 135, Nos. 48-52) found in front of the lintel were not left on the new surface as offerings but were buried under a deep layer of earth when the *dromos* was filled up after the last interment. We may now recall that "about five meters from the door and a meter beneath the surface" the excavators found "remnants of a fire and animal bones." The depth of one meter would exclude a modern date for the fire. Apparently it and the bones are the remnants of the funeral meal consumed after the filling up of the *dromos*, a custom attested to throughout the Mycenaean world. If this is true, then the remnants of the fire would indicate that the surface of the fill would have reached a line above the topmost horizontal slab of the façade. Again we must recall that a mound of earth was poured over the tholos. That mound certainly would have covered the façade of the grave so that the area immediately in front of the lintel could not have formed a place where a cult could have been practiced and burnt offerings could have been left.

It has been assumed that the stones found in front of the lintel "had fallen down from the walls into the *dromos*." To reach the depth in which the lowest course of this mass of stone was found, we must assume that an empty space existed before the superstructure of the façade reaching the opening left under the lintel, for Nilsson states that "the opening had later been blocked by stones fallen down from the walls into

the *dromos*." This presupposes the level of the filled-up *dromos* indicated by Wolters' "Bodenhöhe, etc." We have seen that this is impossible, since then the surface of the *dromos* would have formed a drain reaching the opening which only "later" was blocked by the assumed fallen stones. According to Wolters' section this mass of stones measures more than 2 m. in width at the base and some 3 m. in height. All this mass of stones could not have fallen down from the walls which, according to the drawing of the excavators, were pretty well preserved almost to their original height at the time of the exploration of the grave. The stones which might have fallen from the façade, and which, as we can see from those that are still standing, are rather flat and small, could not have rolled some 2 m. away from the façade thus to form a solid mass of the width indicated in the section. It has become evident, I believe, that the assumptions advanced regarding the remains of the tholos tomb create a number of almost insurmountable difficulties which point up the impossibility of adopting them.

We must now point out that the opening between the lintel and the blocking wall as well as the mass of stones in front of the superstructure of the façade are not unique elements found only in the tholos tomb of Acharnai-Menidi. Long ago Tsountas found other examples at Mycenae itself. His observations explain fully the details noted in the tholos tomb under discussion. In his study of the chamber tombs he excavated (*Ephemeris* for 1888, p. 129), he wrote: "The *stomia* of the graves were always blocked by walls of unworked stones, and once (Grave 24) of unbaked brick. The blocking wall, however, did not reach the lintel, but a small opening was left between it and the wall," exactly as is the case in the tholos tomb of Acharnai-Menidi. "Then," he continues, "the *dromos* was filled up with earth, and when the fill reached a little below the lintel, they placed before the opening left under it, big stones which prevented the earth from falling into the chamber." For the tholos tomb of Menidi Nilsson states "this opening had been blocked by stones." This much of his statement corresponds to the findings of the excavators, but when he adds to this "stones fallen down from the walls into the *dromos*" he is adding a subjective explanation which may or may not be correct. Tsountas goes on to state: "on top of the big stones they placed many others to the original surface of the slope so that the sections of the *dromos* in front of the triangle"— i.e., in front of the superstructure of the façade above the lintel—"was filled especially by stones, whose extraction from above was most difficult, if not impossible, since, as we said above, the walls of the *dromos* narrowed upwards. In consequence to open the grave it became necessary to begin to empty the *dromos* from its outer end, a process which would have required much time and work." Thus the graves were insured against tomb robbers. We must note that Tsountas is discussing chamber tombs cut in the rock, consequently there can be no assumption that the stones found in front of the superstructure of the façade fell down from the walls of the *dromos*. Tsountas' facts correspond absolutely with the facts revealed by the excavators of the tholos tomb of Acharnai-Menidi and his explanations are valid also for the tholos tomb. We can, therefore, conclude that the mass of stones was placed there at the time when the *dromos* was filled up after the last burial, and it was then that the Mycenaean sherds found their way to the positions in which they were discovered. Consequently they could not have belonged to offerings to the dead made periodically in pursuance of a cult in the years which followed the final closing of the tomb.

However, Mycenaean sherds covered with smoke were found in front of the lintel. These, we have seen, cannot be attributed to cult offerings. Can we find an explanation for them consistent with the proved customs of the mainlanders? Of a certainty, we can. We have seen above that the chamber tombs had to be purified and fumigated when numerous bodies were interred in them, and that for the purpose fires were lit in the chambers. Fire also seems to have been used sometimes in the burial rites; we have seen how some offerings even were purposely burned on occasion. It has been proved that the Mycenaeans were not careful as to where the fire in the chamber was lighted, and often enough it was started among skeletal remains and furnishings. This resulted in blackening of bones and pottery. "In the centre of Tomb 524," writes Wace, "a large fire seems to have been lighted which blackened but did not burn the bones and potsherds of previous interments."[138] Similar examples we have from Prosymna, Asine,[139] etc. In a similar manner the Mycenaean sherds of our tholos tomb could have been blackened. That fires were lighted in the chamber of the Menidi tholos tomb is proved by the fill which was found in the cist cut in the floor of its chamber. We must hasten to add that the cist could not have served cult purposes, since it was covered by a bench apparently constructed during the closing years of the use of the grave.

Another established custom of the Mycenaeans will account for the discovery of these blackened sherds outside the burial chamber. We have seen above that

often enough sherds belonging to the same vase were found in different parts of the chamber and outside of it in the *dromos*. Wace's statement on the matter is striking and conclusive. "In the *dromoi* of tombs 516, 517, 518, 529, 530 and 533," he writes, as well as in the *dromos* of tomb 515, "were found pieces of L.H. I-II ware which join on to other fragments found in the chambers," and he adds, "Tsountas in his excavations also noticed the comparative frequency with which sherds found in the *dromoi* joined on to others found in the chamber."[140] This has been the experience of other excavators also. The explanation of this established fact is well known. In the course of clearing the floor of a chamber to make room for later burials, the bones and belongings of those buried previously were swept to the sides; as a rule their vases were smashed and some were thrown out of the chamber into the *dromos*. It was then that fragments were scattered in various parts of the grave. In a similar manner the blackened sherds of the tholos tomb of Menidi found their way outside the tholos. There were at least six burials in the tholos tomb of Menidi. Consequently the earth filling the *dromos* was dug and redug a number of times. In the process of this repeated work the sherds in question remained on the upper levels and were thrown along with the stones in front of the lintel to block the superstructure of the grave as seems to have been customary with the Mycenaeans.

I believe that this rational explanation of the remains of the Menidi tholos tomb, based upon established facts relative to Mycenaean ways of construction and burial customs, excludes any attribution of a religious nature to the blackened sherds found in front of its façade. They do not indicate, let alone prove, that a cult of the dead was practiced in front of that grave in Mycenaean times. A cult of the dead was practiced there, but in late Geometric and Archaic times, not in Mycenaean times.

The Graves of Delos

The Sanctuary of Apollo at Delos is also counted as a place where a cult of the dead was practiced in Mycenaean times.[141] That the island was inhabited in the Mycenaean era has been definitely proved by its excavators, although only scanty remains of houses and a limited amount of pottery were found. That perhaps it possessed an important shrine seems to be indicated by the discovery of numerous fragments of Mycenaean ivory carvings, of gold and bronze objects, including a double axe, found and reported in 1947.[142]

[138] Wace, *Chamber Tombs*, p. 141. This case is also mentioned by Nilsson, *op.cit.*, p. 595.
[139] Blegen, *Prosymna*, pp. 250 ff. Frödin-Persson, *Asine*, pp. 159 ff.

[140] *Chamber Tombs*, p. 131.
[141] Nilsson, *op.cit.*, pp. 611-614.
[142] *BCH*, 71-72 (1947-1948), pp. 148 ff.

That it has yielded evidence of the existence of a cult of the dead in Mycenaean times, as is assumed, is not proved by the remains uncovered. The remains on which the assumption is based were discussed by F. Courby, by C. Picard and Replat, by Vallois, by Nilsson and most recently by H. Gallet de Santerre.[143] Let us see what this evidence is.

A grave composed of two built chambers at right angles to each other was excavated before the Hall of Antigonos. One of them could be considered the *dromos*, although it would have been a very unusual *dromos*, the other the burial chamber. At the time of the excavation scattered human bones were found in both. Courby, who was the first to describe the monument, suggested that the chamber was an ossuary and that in its *dromos* bones also were stored; his suggestion has been accepted. Two upright stones, some 70 cm. high, apparently were "the door jambs of the destroyed tomb." In Hellenistic times the grave was surrounded by a circular peribolos wall, and it was transformed into an *abaton* and an altar perhaps was constructed against its north wall. The ossuary was identified as the *Theke* of Opis and Arge mentioned by Herodotos (IV, 35). In the chamber of the tomb were found two Cycladic and three Mycenaean vases: one of these resembles a MM II shape, one is a beaked jug from LM II, and the third is a stirrup vase. No votive objects were found either in the chamber of the tomb or in the precinct. However, it was pointed out that although this tomb must have been visible, it was not removed in the course of the purification of the island either by Peisistratos or later by the Athenians when in 426 B.C. the contents of the graves of Delos were transferred to Rheneia. This, added to the fact that in Hellenistic times it was encircled with a peribolos, certainly proves that in the Classical age and later the area of the tomb was considered a holy place.

In 1923 Picard uncovered an interesting monument "in the precinct of the temple of Artemis." It consists of a platform cut in the rock found a meter below the slabs of tufa covering the floor. A wall, of which only one block survives, of a semicircular form seems to have surrounded a platform of water-worn stones. This is accepted as another sacred place, another *abaton*. It was suggested by Picard and Replat that this was another grave, the *sema* of the other two Hyperborean maidens, Hyperoche and Laodike, mentioned by Herodotos (IV, 34). Its funerary character is

defended by Gallet de Santerre, in spite of his admission that the monument presents a form less characteristic of a grave, and is characterized by the complete absence of any human remains.[144] This monument was transformed into an *abaton*. Among its foundations were found fragments only of pottery which were grouped in the following three classes by its discoverers: 1) Sherds belonging to types and styles of pottery current in MM II-III times. 2) Some 15 sherds called "mycéniens" and placed in LM I-II times. 3) Sherds belonging to the archaic period and among these are to be found some Corinthian fragments and parts of a bronze cauldron.

These are the actual finds as reported to date. One wonders whether they are sufficient to indicate a cult of the dead in Mycenaean times. That the grave known as the *Theke* was not removed in the days of Peisistratos and later certainly cannot indicate that it was considered in any way sacred in Mycenaean times. Furthermore, the scattered remnants of bones found even in the *dromos* prove that the contents of the grave were thoroughly disturbed perhaps even in Mycenaean times and sherds not belonging to it could have found their way into its chamber in the course of the disturbance, and even when its roof had collapsed. One is justified in asking what Mycenaean objects or other data were found to indicate that a cult of the dead was practiced in or around the grave. The sherds of various prehistoric periods may indicate simply that the grave was used for many many years, and nothing else. As far as we can see from the publications there is no evidence whatever even suggestive of a cult practiced in Mycenaean times. Perhaps it should be added that the type of grave and its contents is closer to Minoan ossuaries than to Mycenaean chamber tombs.

The case of the *sema* is equally dark. What actual finds do we have from it which would indicate a cult not in the Classical but in the Mycenaean age? I am afraid that there again the answer is none. Our earliest pointers are the Archaic Greek sherds. And we could maintain more cogently that the *Theke* and the *Sema* were accidentally discovered by the islanders in a period when the hero cults were current, when prehistoric graves accidently found were identified as those of local heroes featured in local traditions, that the Delian examples were equated with graves of the mythical Hyperborean Maidens, that this identifica-

[143] F. Courby, *Fouilles de Délos*, v, pp. 63-74 figs. 82-87, plan facing p. 64. C. Picard and Replat, *BCH*, 48 (1924), pp. 247 ff. Vallois, *Topographie délienne*, I, pp. 411 ff. H. Gallet de Santerre, *Délos primitive et archaïque*, 1958, pp. 89 ff. Nilsson, *op.cit.*, pp. 611-614.

[144] Gallet de Santerre, *op.cit.*, pp. 95-96. Perhaps it should be noted that the grave identified as the *Theke* is in form

nearer to some of the early graves of the Mavro Spelio cemetery near Knossos than to the Mycenaean chamber tombs; that also it may have served as an ossuary the way Minoan tombs of the Middle Minoan period were used. It would prove the existence of Minoan elements on the island, but nothing beyond that.

tion was followed with the celebration of rites which led to a cult. It is noteworthy that neither in the *Theke* nor in the *Sema* sherds of the Proto-Geometric and even of the Geometric period were found. The lack of such finds would indicate that the possible cult around these monuments began in early Archaic times. Whatever the explanation may be, the fact remains that no evidence whatever was found or exists to prove that these two monuments in the island of Delos were places where a cult for the dead was held in Mycenaean times.

The survey of the existing evidence, I believe, has proved that a cult of the dead, either in honor of the common man or of the mighty princes and kings, did not exist in Mycenaean times. It proved, however, that it did exist in the Greek mainland in Geometric and later times; it seems that in Geometric times Mycenaean graves accidently disclosed were associated with local legends and became the center of a cult. The cult of the dead, therefore, did not form part of the religious beliefs of the Mycenaeans.

CHAPTER VIII

SOME ASPECTS OF MYCENAEAN SOCIETY

"One chair of spring type, inlaid with kyanos and silver and gold on the back, (which is) inlaid with men's figures in gold, and with a pair of gold finials, and with golden griffins and with griffins of kyanos. One footstool inlaid with kyanos and silver and gold, and with golden bars."[1]

"The wise Penelope came forth from her chamber like unto Artemis or golden Aphrodite, and for her they set by the fire, where she was wont to sit, a chair inlaid with spirals of ivory and silver, which of old craftsman Ikmalios had made, and had set beneath it a footstool for the feet, that was part of the chair." (*Odyssey*, XIX, 53-58. Tr. A. T. Murray)

The Lions guarding the Citadel of Mycenae, the Cyclopean walls raised over the plain and over the brow of rugged ravines, the colorful frescoes of the stately palaces, the domed sepulchers, and especially the Treasury of Atreus with its soaring vault marvelously balanced on stone rings, the gems and the rings have given us a glimpse into the art developed and cultivated by the Mycenaean Greeks. This is a mature and vigorous art, an art that reveals an imaginative and gifted people who could absorb, master, develop, and create with such vigor and integrity that their influence has been unparalleled in the life history of primitive peoples. To study their art fully would require a separate volume. Here we may but note a few of its outstanding aspects.

The astonishment experienced when the contents of the royal graves of Mycenae were brought to light by Schliemann in 1876 has yielded to a thorough understanding of techniques and principles followed by the Mycenaean artists.[2] It is interesting to remark that in spite of the great discoveries of the last seventy-five years in the Hellenic area, little new and different artistic material has been added in late years to modify or even enhance our knowledge of Mycenaean art. The work of Tsountas, Wace, and Blegen on the mainland, and the achievement of Evans and the other specialists in the Minoan field, enable us to trace influences and even sources and they offer a complete picture of a culture excellently described in their fundamental books and articles. Their descriptions, discussions, and analyses we shall follow in this brief summary.

ART AND ARCHITECTURE

The Master Builders

There can be little doubt that in the realm of construction and architecture the Mycenaeans reached a high state of development, the progress of which we have already outlined. The builders of the Cyclopean walls, of the tholos tombs, of the palaces within the citadels proved their greatness with their ability to cut and shape hard stone, to transport, lift, and place in position immense blocks of conglomerate, to terrace, rearrange, and fit the natural terrain to their building schemes, as they did at Mycenae. Their daring ingenuity in engineering is illustrated by the underground cistern of Mycenae and by the astonishing fountain of the Akropolis of Athens. Their ability to incorporate into existing structures the lessons learned in the course of building is indicated by the inner gate of Tiryns, by the corridors and storerooms recently found in the north Cyclopean wall of Mycenae, by the underground passages to a water supply, discovered in December 1962 at Tiryns. Their sense of orderly design in construction is proved by the megara they built, oriented to the axis of a central court, to serve as the main units around which evolved not only the various apartments but also the very life and activity of the occupants. They were able to provide for those occupants whatever their needs and their sense of grandeur and authority demanded: impressive reception rooms brilliantly decorated with frescoes, guest rooms, bathrooms, stately stairways and propyla, wait-

[1] Michael Ventris and John Chadwick, *Documents in Mycenaean Greek*, p. 344.
[2] So incredible the achievement seemed that important scholars of the times expressed their disbelief by suggesting that the "so-called Mycenaean Art is nothing else than Phoenician art of the second millennium B.C." (Helbing in *Academy*, July 20, 1895, and *CR*, Oct. 1896) or that it is "nothing but Gothic art of the third century of our era . . . treasures buried at Mycenae by the Heruli about A.D. 267, containing partly the work of Gothic artists and partly plunder of Greek cities." (Stephani in *JHS*) 1[1880], pp. 94-106.

ing rooms with stone benches covered with stucco, and even painted pavements. We may again admire their ability in constructing roads over miles of mountainous terrain, roads of which sections have defied time and could be used even today. Viaducts over ravines they also attempted and, although our evidence is still limited, it seems that stone aqueducts bringing water to their cities from far away mountainous springs were not beyond their powers of achievement.

When we stand in the vaulted room of the Treasury of Atreus and face the tremendous lintel over its *stomion*, or in front of the Lion Gate, or at the precipitous edge of the Chavos ravine and look at the soaring south Cyclopean wall, or on the slopes of Zara and see the various levels on which "the Palace of Agamemnon" was built, almost in accordance with rules followed in what we call today split-level architecture, we cannot help but conclude that the Mycenaean architects reached a degree of excellence that is unparalleled in Bronze Age culture the world over. It is true that their work was influenced and inspired by that of the Minoan builders, that they borrowed many architectural elements from Crete: the Minoan column tapering downward, the many-storied arrangement of apartments other than the megaron, the fresco work with which walls were covered, the designs with which they decorated the façades of their imposing graves, perhaps even the art of building of roads and viaducts—but they used these elements to advance their own conceptions in an imaginative and functional way which resulted in filling the needs of the mainlanders, in some respects different from those of the inhabitants of the island. Witness, for example, their development of the citadel and the system of fortification, the placing of their gates to take advantage of weaknesses in the armor of an enemy, of forcing a reduction in the number of an army attacking the gates. Perhaps one could claim that the Mycenaean builders at the end surpassed their Minoan teachers in the art of construction. Certainly their work survived many more hazards and spoliations, to testify to their ability and excellence.

Sculpture

Comparatively little large-scale sculpture has survived from the Mycenaean Age. There can be little doubt that the mainlanders learnt the niceties of this art from the Minoans and perhaps a good many of the carved objects surviving from the early years of the age are the works of Minoan artists. These come from the shaft graves and include gems, rings, objects in gold foil, and others decorated in repoussé work. They are outstanding examples of miniature carving, and from the numerous examples found in the island we now know that the Minoan artist was a consummate miniaturist. Apparently, however, the Mycenaean disciples had a tendency towards monumental sculpturing, and so they produced the sculptured stelai that were erected over the royal shaft graves.

The custom of erecting such stone stelai over a grave seems to have developed in the Middle Helladic period, but the early stelai were mere stone slabs undecorated and even irregular in form.[3] At the very beginning of the Mycenaean Age we find the stone workers not only cutting their slabs in regular rectangular shapes, thus turning them into stelai of a conventional form, but also adding a carved decoration on one of their flat surfaces. Perhaps their tools and their stone technique were inadequate to handle hard limestone, and so at first we find them working in softer material, in shelly limestone, which yielded easily to their bronze tools but which was not so conducive to sculptural qualities.[4] Still under the influence of the miniature tradition and the realization of their inadequacies, in a number of cases they tried to reduce the area to be decorated with sculpture by dividing it into two registers separated by a broad band or fillet. The upper register was filled by connected spirals, the lower by figures, a narrative composition. Thus in the lower register of Stele 1428 from Grave Circle A we find a chariot scene; in the stele from Grave Gamma of Circle B, an attack of lions against animals defended by men (Fig. 104). Occasionally they tried to treat the surface of the stele as a single area to be decorated; in the stele found over Grave Alpha (Fig. 87) the composition was placed freely over the surface without the usual border of bands to frame the carved registers. But even in that example a feeling of inadequacy and reluctance for a large surface is indicated by the arrangement of the composition on the upper section, leaving underneath a considerable blank space.[5]

The technique followed in the decoration of the stele over Grave Alpha is rather primitive. The figures are actually outlined by incision, while the surface is not cut at all. The subject matter is a narrative; the attack of a bull against the pursuing hunters. Artisti-

[3] *Supra*, p. 93. The inspiration of decorating the stelai may have reached the Mycenaeans from Egypt. Perhaps the division of the face of the stele in two registers is also due to Egyptian conception.

[4] The provenience of this shelly limestone has given rise to many surmises, but apparently it could be quarried not far

from the citadel. Cf. G. E. Mylonas, *Ancient Mycenae*, pp. 114-115; S. Marinatos, *Geras*, pp. 78-79; J. Papadimitriou, *Praktika*, 1955, pp. 225 ff.

[5] For the stelai of Grave Circle A, see especially W. A. Heurtley, *BSA*, 25 (1921-1923), pp. 138 ff. Karo, *Schachtgräber*, pls. v-x and Mylonas, *AJA*, 55 (1951), pp. 134-147.

cally this stele is of little interest, but as a beginning towards large-scale sculpture it is noteworthy. A different, more developed technique, was followed in sculpturing the stele from Grave Gamma and the better stelai from Circle A, such as Stelai 1427-1429. The surface of the stone around the figures was cut away; a differentiation of figure and background was achieved, but the forms remain flat and neither rise above the rest of the surface of the stele nor sink into it. The figures, consequently, are without plasticity, their parts are not modeled, they are two-dimensional, but they exhibit clear contour lines. This technique is typical of wood work and one may be justified in suggesting that the stonecutters in their effort and desire to produce large scale sculpture in stone followed the work of the wood carvers since they lacked stone prototypes. Perhaps we should note that in their figure compositions there are abstracting tendencies typical of Middle Helladic decorative designs.

The stonecutters were indebted not only to the wood carvers, but also to the goldsmiths. The spirals with which they fill their registers are by nature foreign to wood carving but a familiar motif of the goldsmith, who can easily coil metal wire into spirals and similar decorative patterns. Among the finds from the shaft graves we have a good many examples of spiraliform ornaments so produced by the goldsmiths (Fig. 138), and in their figures we may also note the same abstracting tendencies evident on the stelai.

The work of the stone carvers, as illustrated by the stelai, seems so crude and uninspired that it was suggested that perhaps the carving served only as the ground for the application of colored stucco which would have formed the actual and finished artistic product. The work appears even more crude when it is compared to the contemporary products of the goldsmith and the lapidary who produced the magnificent rock crystal duck bowl found in Grave Omikron. We have, however, to bear in mind that the bowl as well as the gold articles found in the graves may have been imported from elsewhere, that they have a long tradition behind them going all the way back to the Early Minoan period, while the sculptured stelai are local productions, in an unprecedented scale and style.

Our next piece of Mycenaean monumental sculpture is of a much later time and of a vastly different type. This is the relief over the Lion Gate. If placing it about the middle of the thirteenth century B.C. is acceptable, and we maintain that the date is correct,

then we see that some three centuries separate it from the sculptured stelai of the shaft graves. Thus far we have no sculptured relics from the years between the end of the sixteenth and the middle of the thirteenth centuries B.C. Besides the relief over the Lion Gate we have the figured slabs now in the British Museum, the Elgin reliefs believed to have come from the Treasury of Atreus.[6] If they actually decorated that sepulcher, they too belong to the thirteenth century B.C. since the Treasury is usually accepted as contemporary with the Lion Gate. During the years for which we have no remains, the fifteenth and the fourteenth centuries, sculpture on a large scale must have made considerable progress, for the thirteenth century relief over the Lion Gate presents noticeable improvement (Fig. 16). The sculptors now attack harder stone, limestone of almost granite hardness; they use the entire surface and the elements emerge, not only differentiated from the original surface of the block but dominating it in bold and considerably high relief. The figures are now modeled in a vigorous style and the artist is capable of expressing the vitality and strength of animal forms in a definite and convincing way. The awkwardness of the early works, which at times left the artist's meaning in doubt, has disappeared. Relations and proportions of parts to the whole are understood and represented. Indeed, in the Lion Relief we have a mature art with developed technique and complete understanding of the possibilities and problems presented by the materials, of the role expected of the relief, of the qualities required by good design. The artist's understanding of materials is indicated by his use of a different kind of stone, perhaps of steatite, for the faces and heads of the lions which would have required more detail, difficult to render in harder stone. His sensitivity to the possibilities of the location of the relief is indicated by the excellent adaptation of his design to the architectural frame within which it was placed. It is no great exaggeration to maintain that the relief over the Lion Gate is one of the best examples of architectural sculpture in the history of that art in the Western World.

Unfortunately, little is preserved of the figure compositions on the Elgin slabs in the British Museum. The surviving fragment, however, with the neck and head of a charging bull with the tree (olive tree?) behind it is sufficient to prove the ability and excellence of the sculptors of the thirteenth century B.C. in representing wild nature with vigor and realism. In

---

[6] Evans, *Palace of Minos*, III, pp. 192 ff., p. 201 and fig. 138. *Catalogue of Greek and Roman Sculpture in the British Museum*, I, part I, pp. 14-31. The placing of the Elgin reliefs on the façade of the Treasury of Atreus is not justified by the remains. Perhaps they formed part of the decoration of its side chamber. It should be noted that Evans has pointed out that

the slabs are gypsum blocks perhaps imported from Knossos (*Palace of Minos*, III, pp. 192-193 and figs. 133, 136, 138). They should belong to the times when gypsum slabs were imported to be used in the Megaron of the Palace, i.e., to LH III B advanced times.

spite of the development, which seems to come late in Mycenaean activity, it must be admitted that very little sculpture in large scale was attempted. This perhaps was due to the fact that the Middle Helladic newcomers, the ancestors of the Mycenaeans, had no sculptural tradition and in Crete, from which their descendants drew inspiration, techniques, and models, monumental sculpture was not practiced. Yet they must have been familiar with the commemorative and decorative sculpture of Egypt especially, with the statues of the mighty and exalted rulers in the land of the Nile. Perhaps the immensity of the sculptured walls, the funereal character of most, and the beliefs and ideas which motivated their creation—ideas that were not attractive to the Mycenaeans—deterred them from following the Egyptian example. They were more successful in developing decorative reliefs used in architectural settings. We find friezes of spirals, roundels, the Mycenaean elongated rosettes and triglyphs, lozenges, spirals interspersed with plant motives, decorating the façades of tombs (cf. Fig. 114), propylaea, and the ceiling of the inner room of the "Treasury of Minyas" at Orchomenos.

Statues made of stone have not been discovered thus far and no evidence survives to indicate that perishable material, such as wood, was used. We have already noted the head of plaster found at Mycenae by Tsountas (Fig. 132). It is almost life-size. Whether or not it formed part of a statue the body of which was made of wood, the type of work known in later years as acrolithic, cannot be determined now. Perhaps the Mycenaeans did not feel the need of making statues in stone. In the early years of the Historic Greek era statues were made to represent gods and goddesses and their votaries. We have seen that the Mycenaeans did not represent their principal male gods in human form; the need therefore for cult statues may not have been felt and the impetus given by such statues to figure representations was lacking. In the shrine of Keos,[7] as we have seen, almost life-sized figures of terra cotta were found, comparable to figures, later in date, known from Gazi and Karphi in the island of Crete. The figures from Keos are now placed in the early years of the Late Bronze period and their main interest lies in their early appearance and in the technical quality of their manufacture. They have little aesthetic appeal. Their contribution to our knowledge of the art developed in the mainland in the Late Bronze Age will be determined after the final publication of the excavations at Keos. The similarity of the Keos figures to those from the sites of Crete suggests that they may belong to the Minoan rather than the Mycenaean orbit.

Gem Cutting

In contrast to large scale sculpture, miniature sculpture was very popular throughout the Mycenaean age. Most representative of that art are semiprecious stones known as gems, bearing superb designs carved as a rule in intaglio. There can be little doubt that the art of the gem carver and of the goldsmith, was introduced to the Mycenaean world from Minoan Crete, already well advanced and almost fully developed. Full credit for the beginnings and development of that art is due to the Minoan workers; but the Mycenaeans proved eager and gifted disciples, worthy of their masters. In technique and aesthetic principles they followed the Minoans, but from the very beginning they introduced their own inclinations, a tendency toward abstraction in figure composition inherited from Middle Helladic times and changes in the traditional subject matter of the compositions; and so we find on their small works of art, produced at the beginning of the period, scenes of war and the chase.[8] Again we find that hard, brittle stone was not avoided but ably used in the making of their gems; amethyst and carnelian were used for the gems found in Graves Gamma and Mu of Circle B, and rock crystal for the heads of pins and for the exquisite duck bowl from Grave Omikron. In the years that followed, agate, onyx, chalcedony, and jasper were added to the materials employed, and the range of subject matter increased immeasurably. Scenes of daily activity, of sacrifice and worship, of quiet pastoral life, of wild animal nature are carved on the small stones with a sensitiveness, vigor, and artistry that are remarkable (Figs. 124-126). When for example we stop to think that the small amethyst bead illustrated in Fig. 98, is only 9 mm. in extreme length, we may well wonder how its artist was able to carve on it such a vivid portrait of a Mycenaean without the help of a diamond point, and at the very beginning of the Mycenaean Age. Gem cutting became very popular in the fifteenth century, as is indicated by the numerous gems found by Tsountas at Vapheio and by Marinatos at Myrsinochorion-Routsi.

It would, of course, be an omission not to single out for special comment the rock-crystal bowl in the form of a duck found in Grave Omikron. We cannot prove whether or not this unique object of art is a native

---

[7] For the Keos examples see J. L. Caskey, *Archaeology*, 15 (1962) pp. 223-226 and *Hesperia*, 33 (1964), pp. 326-335 and fig. 2. For the examples from Gazi and Karphi see Marinatos-Hirmer, *op.cit.*, figs. 128-131 and 135-137. The idols from Karphi are really sub-Minoan in age.

[8] See for example the scene of chase carved on the ring from Shaft Grave IV, Karo, *Schachtgräber*, pl. XXIV no. 240, and the scenes of war on objects from the shaft graves, Karo, pl. XXIV nos. 35, 116, 241.

product or an importation. The best parallels to it are to be found beyond the Hellenic peninsula, in Egypt.[9] In that area, as well as in Babylonia, rock crystal was used for decorative purposes in years much earlier than the beginning of the Mycenaean age. Furthermore, the material is foreign to the mainland and although rock crystal is to be found in the island of Crete, its quality and size seem not to be conducive to the making of works of art of any size or excellence.[10] Rock crystal was highly valued and its brilliance and hardness much admired. Diodoros (II, 52, 2) tells us that the Greeks of the Historic period believed that rock crystals were "composed of pure water which has been hardened, not by the action of cold, but by the influence of a divine fire, and for this reason they are never subject to corruption and take on many hues when they are breathed upon."

In the mainland of Greece articles of rock crystal appear in the shaft graves, but it was used for inlays in Crete from at least the beginning of the Middle Minoan period.[11] In the early years of the Mycenaean era rock crystal was used for the making of heads of bronze and silver pins (Fig. 136). Some of these are plain, globular in form, others are carefully ribbed and still others are hemispherical and exhibit coloring applied in the hollowed-out interior so that their surface exhibits a most pleasant iridescence. At all times the work is precise and sensitive and in the boring of these solid heads, usually performed from both ends meeting at the center with a slight variation in direction, the lapidaries show exceptional ability. Small, circular, flat beads of rock crystal were produced in great number; flat bars used for the decoration of a gaming board were found in Grave IV[12] and a single cylindrical knob inserted at the end of the hilt of a dagger from Grave Iota recalls the hilt of the magnificent sword of Mallia.[13]

The pride of the lapidary's art, however, must have been the duck bowl (Fig. 99). The modeling of the head, the bulging details of forehead and bill, the air of alertness imparted by the incised eye, the almost intuitive way in which neck and head have been turned to form the handle, are the results not only of artistic sensitivity but also of technical excellence. The walls of the bowl reach a thickness of only 3-4 mm.,

although the rim to which the head is attached is 8 mm. thick. How did the lapidary of the end of the seventeenth century B.C. produce such a work of art in rock crystal, which is not an easy material to work? Of course, an abrasive process was employed to impart to the object its smooth and well-modulated surface and to the handle the form of a bird's head. But how was the piece of rock hollowed out? Among the articles found by Evans in the vat room deposit of Knossos there is a fragment of rock crystal that gives us the answer. It is in the form of a "tapering cylinder, of thimble-like shape" that was recognized as a "core produced by boring, and, as in other cases, broken off by the lapidary in the process of hollowing out a vessel of that material."[14] The rock-crystal piece, as was the case with other stones, was hollowed out by repeated adjacent borings made by a tubular drill, possibly even by a common reed, rotated rapidly on the surface of the stone covered with fine, wet sand. After each boring the piece of stone remaining in the hollow of the drill was broken off and the process was repeated until the required depth and width were obtained. Then the interior was smoothed by abrasives. The small core from Knossos proves that the Minoan artists knew how to produce objects of rock crystal of the type of our bowl, and indeed in later years of the Middle Minoan period they produced cups and even a marvelous rhyton of considerable size discovered by Platon in 1963 at the Palace of Kato Zakro.[15] From the Minoans the Mycenaeans learned the technique and the value of objects made of rock crystal. The heads of pins they produced indicate their ability. There can be, therefore, no doubt that the Mycenaean lapidaries or their Minoan teachers were capable of producing the duck bowl found in Grave Omikron. The precise and almost tender workmanship, the sensitivity of the design, the technical care shown for every detail, make me believe that the object was produced at Mycenae by a Mycenaean or even a Minoan lapidary, and is not an importation from Egypt. We may finally add that rock crystal in the form of round, bossed discs may have been used as magnifying glasses by the gem cutters. One disc of this kind, along with two others was found in Tomb III of the cemetery of

[9] Cf. *Syria*, 1932, pl. VIII, 2. Frödin-Persson, *Asine*, pp. 388, 391 fig. 254. Furtwängler-Loeschcke, *Mykenischen Vasen*, pp. 14 and 15 fig. 3. For examples from Egypt, cf. A. Hermann, "Das Motiv der Ente mit zurückgewendetem Kopfe in Ägypten. Kunstgewerbe," *Zeitschr. für Ägypt. Sprache und Altertumskunde*, 68 (1932), pp. 86-105 pls. VII-XI, especially pp. 91 ff. I owe the reference to Professor Mellink to whom go many thanks.

[10] S. Marinatos, *Ephemeris*, 1931, pp. 158-160. On p. 160 n. 3 Professor Marinatos mentions that rock crystal is reported to have been found in the Chalcidice and also in the island of Mytilene.

[11] Evans, *Palace of Knossos*, I, pp. 469 ff., 473 ff. etc. He also reports a flake of rock crystal from a Neolithic stratum, *op.cit.*, II, p. 14 see his *Index*, under rock crystal. For painted ornamentation of rock-crystal spherical heads see Schliemann, *Mycenae*, p. 200 no. 308.

[12] Evans, *Palace of Minos*, I, p. 484 and fig. 348. Karo, *op.cit.*, pls. CLII, CLIII.

[13] *Supra*, p. 103. *Monuments Piot*, 1926, pp. 4-5 and pl. I.

[14] Evans, *Palace of Minos*, I, p. 170 and fig. 119, b.

[15] *Ergon*, 1963, p. 169 fig. 181. Cf. Evans, *Palace of Minos*, III, fig. 272.

Mavro Spelio near Knossos, and has been estimated by H. C. Beck to have a power of ten diameters.[16]

The Work of the Goldsmith

A good deal of the work produced by the goldsmith was decorated by carving similar to that on gems. We have already noted scenes carved on the bezels of gold rings (Figs. 123-127), which allowed us a glimpse of Mycenaean religious practices. The earliest rings we have, from Grave Upsilon, Circle B, are without decoration, but those from Circle A bear elaborate secular compositions. Rings with religious subjects seem to appear towards the end of the sixteenth century B.C. and after that date they are met with frequently. Royal seals were, of course, carved, as we may surmise from the flattened cylindrical seal of gold found in a tholos tomb near the Palace of Nestor at Ano Englianos. Both sides of the seal are covered with design; on the one we find a grid pattern and on the other, in intaglio, a very handsome, crested griffin seated on a dais decorated by a frieze inspired by the Mycenaean half-rosette pattern (Fig. 137).[17] In the way the metal is carved, in the arrangement of the design, in the sensitivity and excellence of the workmanship, the goldsmiths prove themselves the peers of the gem carvers. As a matter of fact one wonders whether the same artist was not a gem carver as well as a goldsmith. We may recall the solid jasper ring found at Mycenae by Tsountas with the "Gilgamesh-like hero" holding at arm's length two lions (Fig. 125, No. 40), and another ring of white onyx found by Schliemann in its citadel.[18]

The artist knew perfectly well the possibilities and the qualities of his materials and obtained from them the best possible results. The fluting of the gold cups found in the shaft graves, even the pointed technique used to decorate the bottom of the cup from Grave Nu (Fig. 94) indicate his complete knowledge of the possibilities inherent in the metal. Gold was beaten out in sheets of marvelous delicacy to be used as applied decoration on articles of more solid and less precious material; it was drawn out into the finest possible wire to be used for the making of delicate chains; it was granulated and freely used in the making of jewelry. The ingenuity of the goldsmith and his expertness at a very early age can be surmised from one of the bracelets found in Grave Omikron. Gold with a small amount of silver in it was drawn into a heavy

wire and this was doubled to make two bands one longer than the other. The end of the shorter band was coiled into a series of spirals which were secured on the top of the longer strand. This was extended to some length, turned around and coiled to form another series of spirals, which were attached to the first group (Fig. 138). Thus, a graceful yet strong bracelet of spirals was made with consummate skill. Again their technical ability, increased by experience with the passing of time, can be seen in small figures of animals and birds—owls, frogs, heads of bulls, figure-eight shields and ewers made of gold and embellished with expert granulation.

In the articles of gold decorated in repoussé we have a chance to admire the firm hand, the true touch, and the great ability of the artist, who was not only a goldsmith but a miniaturist sculptor for the representations in repoussé presuppose the carving of the design on some hard material which serves as the core against which is pressed the foil of gold to which the design is to be transferred. That design has to be well and sharply cut and excellently balanced on the core to achieve satisfactory results. The small discs of gold covered with spiraliform patterns of great complexity and delicacy, the embossed patterns on diadems, armbands, and breastplates (Fig. 93), the marvelous representations of lions and other animals on gold beads to be used in necklaces, on gold plaques to be applied on wooden boxes, on gold foil for sword pommels and hilts, prove the high degree of perfection of the goldsmith's art.

These works of art have been described and illustrated so often since the days of Schliemann that they do not require special discussion.[19] However, it may prove profitable to note at least some early examples of the goldsmith's activity and to this end we choose the twelve gold plaques from Shaft Grave V which once covered the sides of a six-sided wooden box[20] (Fig. 139). All are decorated in repoussé technique, but with a variety of subjects; four are covered with connected spirals; on four others we find a lion in full pursuit of an antelope (?), while over the lion's leaping body we have the head of a bull, perhaps symbolic of other victims of the king of animals, and branches of trees; the last four plaques are covered with the representation of a fierce lion pursuing a stag in a wooded landscape filled with stylized palm trees. The scenes are framed by a marginal rope pattern.

[16] *BSA*, 28 (1926-1927), p. 288 and *Antiquaries Journal*, 8 (1928), p. 329. In Crete these same round discs occasionally were exquisitely painted in miniature style; Evans, *Palace of Minos*, III, pp. 108-111.

[17] Blegen, *AJA*, 58 (1954), pl. 9 no. 15.

[18] *Mycenaean Age*, fig. 54. Schliemann, *Mycenae*, p. 131 fig. 175.

[19] The objects from the shaft graves are discussed and illus-

trated in the monumental work of G. Karo, *Die Schachtgräber von Mykenai*, to which we have often referred. The most important objects are excellently illustrated in pls. 161-225 of Marinatos-Hirmer's *Crete and Mycenae*, which is more accessible to the general reader and in which are to be found most of the objects mentioned in this chapter.

[20] Karo, *op.cit.*, pls. CXLIII-CXLIV.

The work has an exceptional decorative appeal. The vigorous action is emphasized by the form of the lions in the typically Minoan-Mycenaean "flying gallop" position—while the pathos of the experience is stressed by the positions and turning heads of the doomed animals. Especially noteworthy is the stylization and the tendency towards generalization and abstraction, a feature, which perhaps stems from Middle Helladic traditions, characteristic of Mycenaean as compared to Minoan art.

Repoussé technique reached its apogee in Late Helladic II times, when the Vapheio cups were made. Whether these are the work of a Minoan or a Mycenaean artist under strong Minoan influence is in question but it is unanimously accepted that these cups represent the best that the goldsmith could produce. Schuchhardt, long ago, stated that "for originality of design and delicacy of execution (the Vapheio cups) are unrivaled except perhaps by the finest goldsmith's work of the Italian Renaissance";[21] and his statement summarizes the opinions and evaluation of scholars and students of the Minoan-Mycenaean achievement. Thin sheets of gold bearing the design are secured on the thicker gold plate that forms the body of the cup, turned over at the rim to hold the decorated sheets. Thus the cups show no seams, except at the joining of the ends of the decorated sheet, and this is almost covered by the handle. The designs are marvelously arranged on the limited surface. They present a vivid contrast in subject matter: violent action of wild life, of powerful bulls, on the one; and on the other quiet, almost pastoral animal life (tamed bulls) in a setting filled with olive trees exquisitely represented. In the center of the first cup a bull is caught in a net stretched from tree to tree, while a pair of bulls, grazing peacefully with heads almost touching, occupy the same position on the other. An infuriated bull is tossing a hunter on his horns on the first cup, while in the same section of the second cup we find a powerful bull hobbled to be driven to sacrifice or work (Fig. 120); the only protest the tame bull seems to make is to bellow mightily against the indignity, "as when a dragged bull roareth, that the young men drag to the altar" sings Homer (*Iliad*, xx, 403). The composition is vigorous, bold, and at the same time sensitive and most expressive of the wild force of nature which can be harnessed to the needs of man.

In the gold cup found by Persson in the royal tomb at Dendra[22] we can admire the ability of the goldsmith to impress a marvelously balanced design on thick gold plate and to convey the mystery as well as the charm and beauty of sea life (Fig. 121). It was an ability already in evidence in the days of the shaft graves, for in Grave IV a gold cup was found bearing a plant composition impressed on the thick plate used for the making of a fine cup.[23] It is evident that the gold plate was hammered to shape and this technique was followed in the making of practically all the cups known from the Mycenaean world. The technique finds its best expression in the well-known rhyton from Shaft Grave IV in the form of a lion head, a most impressive piece even by modern standards.[24]

One of the common articles of adornment produced by the goldsmiths in an astonishing variety are beads, found in great numbers in all the Mycenaean sites. Of these we shall mention only the so-called relief-beads, that appear in the seventeenth century B.C. and become most popular between 1450 and 1300 B.C. They were strung together to form necklaces or were attached to garments to embellish them. They were made up of two small sheets of gold soldered together, one of which was impressed with a design in regular repoussé technique and formed the front of the bead, while the other, the back was left flat and smooth. Between the two sheets was placed fine sand to give weight to the body. The designs include stylized representations of marine and plant life especially, and sometimes they are enlivened by granulation and blue paste. Such beads strung in necklaces are usually worn by women represented in fresco compositions.

Silver, whether mined in Greece—in Siphnos, Laurium, or the Pangaean mountains—or imported from Syria, was used by the goldsmith in his art from the very beginning of the Mycenaean Age. Among the furnishings and other gifts of the Shaft Graves are included a number of objects fashioned of silver. In the remains of the first interment revealed in Grave Iota, of Circle B, we found a grooved silver cup with its rim covered by a band of gold.[25] A magnificent silver jug, 34.5 cm. in height, with a decoration of spirals and horizontal flutings, lately found to have been covered by niello, is among the furnishings of Shaft Grave V.[26] The royal tomb at Dendra yielded a silver cup, lined with gold foil and decorated with heads of bulls inlaid with niello secured on the silver surface. A similar arrangement is to be seen on the outer surface of a silver cup from a chamber tomb at Mycenae; on that cup, however, we have a series of

---

21 *Schliemann's Excavations*, p. 350. For the original publication of the cups see Tsountas, *Ephemeris*, 1889, pp. 159-163 pl. 9.

22 Persson, *The Royal Tombs at Dendra*, frontispiece.

23 Karo, *op.cit.*, pl. cx no. 313.

24 *Ibid.*, pl. cxvii no. 273.

25 Mylonas, *Ancient Mycenae*, fig. 71. The rim was covered by a band of gold doubled over it to protect the lips of the user from the sharp edge of the silver plate used for the cup.

26 Karo, *op.cit.*, pl. cxxxiv no. 855. Sakellariou, *Ephemeris*, 1957, *Chronika*, pp. 7-8, pl. Γ, a.

heads of bearded men inlaid between two rows of gold leaves. From Pylos too we have similar heads of bearded men which once were inlaid perhaps on a silver cup.[27] The method of securing applied motifs on the silver face of the cups is interesting and can be easily detected. The figures, regular cut-outs made of thin strips of gold plate, were placed in deep grooves impressed on the silver. The projecting edges of the grooves were then pressed towards the inlaid figures to flatten their perimeters and thus enclose and hold them. Finally the figures and frame were smoothed and polished. This technique was already in practice in the period of the shaft graves and an example, a beautiful inlaid electrum goblet, was found in Grave IV.[28]

A most interesting vessel made of silver is the rhyton from Shaft Grave IV, on which was represented in repoussé a war scene, an attack by Mycenaeans of a town on a sea coast.[29] Apparently, however, silver was not as popular as gold; perhaps the goldsmiths realized that it tarnishes easily and thus loses the impressiveness conveyed by a bright surface. It may also be that a good many objects made of silver have not been preserved, since the metal deteriorates badly in moist ground. A number of times we found objects of silver, whose form and even nature could not be determined because they were transformed into a putty-like mass hard to extract and to handle. The Mycenaeans were very adept in using a natural alloy of gold and silver known as electrum. Outstanding examples of articles made of electrum are the mask found in Shaft Grave Gamma and the beautiful goblet from Shaft Grave IV, already mentioned.[30] The mask is one of six known from the Mycenaean world; the other five, made of gold, were found in Shaft Graves IV and V.[31] The goblet, reminiscent of the Minyan goblets of the Middle Helladic period, has a charming inlaid decoration of "lilies and sprays of dittany" rising gracefully above a richly decorated altar.[32] Perhaps in the plants we have the "sacred boughs" of the Mycenaeans.

Work in solid silver was not totally avoided. A silver rhyton in the form of a bull's head is an outstanding example of this technique. It was found in Shaft Grave IV and exhibits a massiveness and realism that can hardly be improved or surpassed. Its gold trimmings—a gold rosette on the forehead, inlaid bands around the mouth, gold covered wooden horns—add considerably to the majestic effect of the head.[33]

Inlay Work

Besides repoussé, granulation, wire-work, hammered plate work, and solid metal modeling, the goldsmith developed cut-work and inlays of great delicacy and beauty. The sheathing for the handle or hilt of a sword found in Shaft Grave IV, originally thought to have been the top of a scepter, illustrates this cut-work excellently.[34] Made of gold plate, it covered a wooden core which actually gave body to the handle. The plate was cut so as to form an open pattern made up of four-petalled flowers with petals touching at their tips, to enclose an area inlaid with rock crystal. The top of the sheathing was made in the form of two dragons with scales of rock crystal beautifully secured in their gold frames. In other examples opaque glass paste was used as inlay. The best examples of this use are apparently the two "earrings" found in Grave III, and one of the gold rings from the Vapheio Tomb.[35] The latter, in place of a bezel, was furnished with a rosette which is inlaid with blue and violet glass-paste in regular alternation; the hoop is enlivened with similar pastes.

The best known examples of inlay work, however, are to be seen on the bronze daggers found in Shaft Graves IV and V.[36] Their discoverer, Schliemann, never saw their colorful inlays, for a heavy coat of corrosion covered their blades when he turned them over to the Museum officials. A few years later the amazing compositions were disclosed by cleaning. Figures made of gold and silver were then disclosed with details in niello secured on a thick coat of black substance resembling niello, placed in a shallow bed along the flat midrib of the daggers. A color contrast was attained by using different grades of precious metals and niello. On one of the blades from Shaft Grave IV is represented a hunting scene in a most vivid manner (Fig. 140): a group of hunters with spears and shields, tower and figure-eight shields alternating, and one archer are attacking three lions. Two of the animals

---

[27] Persson, *The Royal Tombs at Dendra*, pls. XII-XV. Tsountas, *Ephemeris*, 1888, pl. 7, 2. Blegen, *AJA*, 59 (1955), pl. 23 fig. 3.

[28] Karo, *op.cit.*, pls. CXII-CXIII. Sakellariou, *op.cit.*, p. 6.

[29] Karo, *op.cit.*, pl. CXXII no. 481. Marinatos-Hirmer, *op.cit.*, p. 100.

[30] Our Fig. 97. Karo, *op.cit.*, pls. CXII and CXIII.

[31] Karo, *op.cit.*, pls. XLVII-LII nos. 253, 254, 259 and Grave IV; nos. 623, 624 from Grave V. No. 624 (Our Fig. 84) is usually referred to as the "mask of Agamemnon" because Schliemann stated that it belonged to that king. But the masks antedate the great king by at least three and a quarter centuries. For the technique followed in the making of these masks see Fischer in Karo's *Schachtgräber*, pp. 320 ff. For Mycenaean jewelry in

general see R. A. Higgins, *Greek and Roman Jewellery*, pp. 68-89.

[32] Marinatos-Hirmer, *op.cit.*, fig. 186. What we take to be an altar is often explained as a "flower-pot."

[33] Karo, *op.cit.*, pls. CXIX-CXXI no. 384.

[34] Schliemann, *Mycenae*, pp. 286-287 nos. 451, 452. See also *Mycenaean Age*, p. 168. Karo, *op.cit.*, pl. LXXXVII no. 294 and LXXXVIII.

[35] Karo, *op.cit.*, pl. XX no. 61. *Mycenaean Age*, p. 184, figs. 77-78.

[36] Karo, *op.cit.*, pls. XCII, XCIV. Marinatos-Hirmer, *op.cit.*, for excellent color reproductions of Mycenaean inlaid daggers.

are running away from the scene of action, the third has turned back and is attacking the hunters, one of whom is lying, perhaps dead, on the ground. Another hunting scene is represented on a blade from Shaft Grave V. This time, cats are chasing ducks alongside a stream whose banks are covered with papyrus and lotus plants. Small fish of gold are inlaid in the meandering silver band to make sure that it is identified as a river. There can be little doubt that at least the subject represented on this blade, if not the technique, was inspired by Egypt. On a third blade from Grave IV a simpler design was attempted: three lions represented in a flying gallop. Most pleasing is the fragment of a dagger with gold-plated hilt decorated with lilies in repoussé technique and a bronze blade on the flat midrib of which were inlaid detached lilies with petals in pale electrum and with red anthers. The lilies were inlaid in a hard niello band made of an alloy of silver and iron.

Scholars do not agree as to the origin of the technique. Some details in the hunting scene, such as the slim waists of the hunters and the shields, as well as the excellent workmanship and finish of the work, point to Crete. However, the niello work, very evident on the daggers, is foreign to Minoan art. The Nilotic scene may suggest Egypt, where we find a copper axe with an inlaid gold griffin and a dagger from the grave of Ahhotpe, the mother of Amosis, first Pharaoh of the Eighteenth Dynasty; these objects, however, indicate contact and commercial relations of the two areas and suggest indebtedness of Egypt to Mycenae. Syria has been suggested as the place from which the Mycenaeans borrowed the technique of inlaying, since niello work was practiced there from an early period. Whatever the origin, the fact remains that in these daggers we have a very remarkable achievement of the jeweler, perhaps a Minoan artist working for a Mycenaean master whose predilections he incorporated in his work.

The art of inlaying continued to be practiced after the years to which the shaft graves belong. Fragments of inlaid daggers were found in the Vapheio tholos tomb,[37] which belongs to the early years of the LH II period, shortly after 1500 B.C. Two inlaid daggers were found by Marinatos in the tholos tomb of Myrsinochorion-Routsi, which perhaps is a little later than the Vapheio tomb, but belongs to the fifteenth century B.C. A blade with a single dolphin on each side was found by Blegen in Tomb XIV of Prosymna dating

from the LH II period, the fifteenth century B.C. On a second blade from Tomb III of the Prosymna cemetery, birds, perhaps of a domesticated breed, since they wear collars, are represented again in gold, silver, and niello. Lately an inlaid dagger was found by the Ephor Dr. Zapheiropoulos at Pharai in Achaia, apparently belonging to the early fourteenth century B.C.[38] On either side of its bronze blade two dolphins sport, exhibiting their brilliance of gold, silver, and niello. Inlaying of ceremonial daggers, the property perhaps of beautiful princesses, seems to have remained a popular art throughout the prosperous years of the Mycenaean Age. In this medium the goldsmith tried to rival the fresco painter in the variety of color and in the brilliance of his materials. Indeed, his technique has been called "painting with metal."

Work in Ivory

Ivory was also used for inlaying and the earliest example comes from Shaft Grave V: a wooden box decorated with dogs of inlaid ivory. It is in the fifteenth and later centuries, however, that ivory carving becomes popular and ivory inlays are used to ornament furniture in a manner mentioned not only in epic poetry but also in the inventory tablets of Pylos. Besides, toilet articles were made of or embellished with ivory covered with relief; mirror handles, combs, and pyxides (cosmetic boxes) have been found in a number of sites, and small plaques bearing elaborate compositions are characteristic of late Mycenaean artistic endeavor.[39] Even small figures in the round in the precious material have been found, as we have seen, at Mycenae and Prosymna. The group of the two women and a boy found by Wace is the best example of the known figures in the round, while the woman seated on a rocky bench found by Tsountas is the best example of raised relief work on an ivory plaque. Comparable to the latter is the ivory plaque from Delos with the figure of a warrior carved in high relief; he is standing in front of a figure-eight shield, holding a spear in his right hand and wearing a typical Mycenaean plumed helmet decorated with boars' tusks.[40] But we must also note the helmeted heads of warriors from Mycenae and Spata, the mirror handles with the representations in relief of two ladies facing each other and standing or seated above the branches of a palm tree that is carved on the vertical stem of the handle, the ivory plaques found by Wace in the

---

[37] Tsountas, *Ephemeris*, 1889, pl. 7 nos. 1-2. Marinatos, in *Essays in Aegean Archaeology*, pp. 63-71 and Evans, *Palace of Minos*, III, pp. 126 ff. For the objects from the grave of queen Ahhotpe cf. Persson, *New Tombs at Dendra*, figs. 129-130.

[38] Marinatos-Hirmer, *op.cit.*, pl. XXXVIII. Blegen, *Prosymna*, p. 330, pl. II. N. Zapheiropoulos, *Praktika*, 1956, p. 194 pl. 88a.

[39] Karo, *op.cit.*, pl. CXLV. For some ivory carvings see also *Mycenaean Age*, figs. 82-84. Marinatos-Hirmer, *op.cit.*, figs. 214-223.

[40] H. Gallet de Santerre, *Délos primitive et archaïque*, pl. 23 fig. 54.

buildings on either side of the so-called "House of the Oil Merchant."

On one of the better preserved plaques from the House of Sphinxes a pair of sphinxes confronted in profile stand on a platform with their front paws resting on the capital of a fluted column. Three sets of horns of consecration are depicted below or beyond the platform. The sphinxes wear necklaces and lily crowns surmounted by lofty plumes; their outspread wings are elaborately incised and their bodies are well articulated and vigorously rendered. The details of the composition and the modeling reflect those present in the relief over the Lion Gate of Mycenae from which the plaque of the sphinxes does not seem to be much removed in date. Couchant sphinxes are represented on other fragmentary plaques from the same building and from graves explored by Tsountas. In the House of Sphinxes, the House of Shields, and in Delos were found models of columns, figure-eight shields, lions, ivy leaves, lilies, argonauts, cockle-shells, etc., which were undoubtedly inlaid upon furniture and other articles.[41]

Articles entirely of ivory are not so common, but important among these are pyxides. A section of the tusk was commonly used for the making of pyxides, which consequently have a cylindrical shape. Two splendid examples of the type were found by the late Professor T. L. Shear in a chamber tomb on the slopes of the Areopagos at Athens.[42] They belong to the early years of the fourteenth century B.C. (LH III A). The larger pyxis, measuring 16 cm. in height with a diameter of 11.2 cm. measured on the lid, presents an interior lined with thin strips of tin. The top of the lid and the outer face of the sides are closely covered with decorative scenes representing a most spirited attack made by winged griffins on a herd of deer (Fig. 141). The composition is skillfully adjusted to the circular area it has to decorate, and the mastery of the carver is shown by the way in which he gave handles to the pyxis. He left two projecting knobs on each side high up on the body in positions which would not interfere with the main scene. On one of the knobs a fawn was carved lying with twisted body, while on the other a crouching lion. The bodies of these animals are perforated with holes for the cord by which the pyxis could be carried. A nautilus pattern freely placed over the walls of the smaller pyxis, which is only 5 cm. high, results in a rich decorative effect. The handles are again placed high and are in the form of figure-eight shields. They were made separately and inserted into slits.

Earlier in date, from the first half of the fifteenth century, is a third pyxis, from the tholos Tomb 2 of Myrsinochorion-Routsi.[43] It measures some 14 cm. in height and its walls are divided in long vertical panels by means of astragals. The panels are decorated alternately by rows of spirals and spirals with leaves. Small figure-eight shields placed high on the cylindrical body serve as handles. In the same tomb Marinatos found an ivory comb decorated with a scene of cats hunting wild ducks in very low relief.

Ivory carving remained popular throughout the Mycenaean age from ca. 1600-1200 B.C. In the destruction level of the citadel we found in 1964 a fragment of an ivory plaque, and this indicates that clear to the end Mycenae was a most important center for ivory carving (Fig. 142). Workmanship improved with the passing of time until it reached the high degree of perfection exhibited by the ivory group from Mycenae. There can be little doubt that the material was imported in tusks, most probably from Syria, and was worked in Greece. Unworked tusks are known from the mainland and from Crete and one small tusk covered with decoration was found by Tsountas in one of the chamber tombs at Mycenae (Fig. 143).[44] What purpose it served cannot be definitely determined, but its elaborate relief decoration may indicate that it could not have been the handle of a tool or a weapon. It could have been used as an elaborate horn-vessel for perfumed oil. Its skillful carvings—plants and lotus blossoms, stems decorated by lozenges, similar to those on the half columns of the Treasury of Atreus, terminating in blossoms arranged in side scrolls reminiscent of the Aeolic capital, wild goats with their graceful, long curving horns—are executed with sensitivity and elegance. Light touches of color, even gilding, applied on the ivory may have enhanced its decorative effect. The motives employed, the love of detail, the skill of execution will indicate that this is the work of a gifted Mycenaean artist of the end of the fourteenth century B.C.

The crested griffin and the sphinx were two of the popular motives in which the ivory carvers excelled. Their decorative treatment, their placement in small rectangular areas, and their air of serenity and grandeur can hardly be surpassed; indeed they were royal emblems, both apparently imported from the Near East. The Syrian original, developed and perfected

---

41 *BSA*, 48 (1953), pls. 4, 5, 9; 49 (1954), pls. 33-35, 38-40; 50 (1955), pls. 25, 26; 52 (1957) pl. 40, b. *Ephemeris*, 1888, pl. 8 no. 6. *BCH*, 71-72 (1947-1948), pls. 25-35.

42 Shear, *Hesperia*, 9 (1940), pp. 274 ff. and especially pp. 283-287 and figs. 27-31.

43 Marinatos-Hirmer, *op.cit.*, fig. 223, p. 175.

44 For permission to mention and illustrate this tusk, which remains unpublished, I am indebted to Dr. C. Karouzos and Mrs. A. Sakellariou. It should be noted that a great quantity of ivory plaques decorated in relief, now exhibited in the National Museum, were found in chamber tombs by Tsountas, and a quantity comes from the graves at Spata.

at Mycenae, was sent back again as ivory plaques, which in turn may have influenced Syrian art. Miss H. Kantor has pointed out recently that the ivory plaques with couchant crested griffins from the treasury at Megiddo should be considered as Mycenaean imports.[45]

Glass and Faïence

Trinkets made of colored glass paste and of faïence were commonly used, especially in LH III times. That they were not unknown in an earlier age is proved by the faïence pendant found in Grave Xi. Its position at the center of a necklace made up of rock-crystal beads was clear. It has a rectangular shape, is bluish in color and on its face bears lozenge-shaped elements, reminiscent of the Masonic emblem, and parallel bars along its short edges. Similar pendants and beads of faïence were found in Grave Upsilon. In later years, to the end of the Mycenaean age, a variety of beads, of small rectangular plaques impressed with a design, of shields, shells, rosettes, etc., were made of faïence and used for necklaces or as decorative elements on garments and furnishings. Interesting and important, in spite of their artistic inadequacy, are the so-called segmented beads, because their distribution indicates wide commercial intercourse. These were found as far west as Wiltshire in England and as far north as Hungary.

Glass paste painted blue was used in decorating the spirals of the alabaster frieze in the Palace at Tiryns and perhaps this material was the *kyanos* mentioned by Homer. It is interesting to note that at Mycenae there seems to have been a special group of *kyanos* craftsmen.[46] Perhaps the Mycenaeans learned to manufacture faïence and painted glass paste from the Egyptians, although the introduction of blue color in the making of glass paste may have been inspired by the Mesopotamian use of lapis lazuli in the decoration of figures and buildings. As a rule, trinkets of paste were cast in stone molds, a number of which have been found in Mycenaean sites. Often these trinkets were covered with gold foil to imitate jewels of solid gold; in the majority of cases they bear elaborate engravings.

This brief and highly selective and arbitrary account of the work of the goldsmith and the miniaturist will serve to illustrate the demands and taste of a well-to-do Mycenaean lady and gentleman. Bracelets, earrings, pins, and elaborate head-pieces, combs, hairpins, bands and ringlets of gold to keep curls and braids in place, rosettes, gold petals, spirals, lilies, spiraliform motifs to be applied on garments, beautiful inlaid daggers, articles of gold, of silver, of ivory, of glass, of semiprecious stones and of rock crystal, the valued products of the goldsmith's art, were, it seems, indispensable to Mycenaean society. The glamour of the ladies can be glimpsed from the processional scenes painted in brilliant colors on the walls of the palaces of Tiryns, Thebes, and Pylos. The virility of the men can be adduced from the swords which accompanied them to the grave. All the objects are testimony of a highly sophisticated and wealthy society whose leaders lived in elaborate palaces in Cyclopean citadels.

Work in Bronze

The Mycenaean bronzesmith, the *ka-ke-u* of the tablets, produced numerous vessels and weapons. Large cauldrons, jugs, jars, and open bowls have been found in the shaft graves and in the Chamber Tomb 2 of Dendra. Fragments of similar vessels and of smaller pots were found among the ruins of houses and palaces of the Mycenaean Age. These prove that the bronzesmiths were able to roll the metal into all kinds of interesting forms. Their skill, however, is illustrated in a most striking way by the excellent swords, daggers, knives, and spearheads they produced. Some of the swords, veritable rapiers, with ribbed blades 90 to 95 cm. in length, even now are formidable weapons. Others bear delicate engravings that make them works of art (Fig. 95). In later times, especially in LH III, after 1350 B.C., a two-edged slashing sword was produced and became popular. Its square shoulders as well as its hilt was flanged, its blade had no midrib, and its length was reduced considerably. Towards the end of the period broad knives of the same general appearance were produced, and curving blades of a crescent shape (Fig. 144). Examples of the latter are known from the Akropolis of Athens and from Mycenae.[47] Spearheads of a leaf-shaped blade, with a strong rib and a socketed base strengthened by a rolled ring, and arrowheads, often barbed, were produced throughout the period. On the tablets from Pylos, Series Jn, we find substantial allocations of bronze to smiths established in various areas of the state, for the making of these weapons of offense, and on the Knossos tablets we have on two tablets the total of 8,640 arrowheads stored presumably in the palace magazines. On the totaling tablet of Series Jn, No. 149, are recorded allocations amounting to some

---

[45] *Archaeology*, 13 (1960), pp. 18-19 and fig. 9A. Her excellent article is a pioneer attempt in the study of this aspect of Mycenaean art that has been neglected so long. The forthcoming *Corpus* of A. Dessenne will serve a great need.

[46] Chadwick, *The Mycenae Tablets*, III. For a figure-eight shield in faïence from Mycenae, see Fig. 142.

[47] Cf. Mylonas, "Three Late Mycenaean Knives," *AJA*, 66 (1962), pp. 406-408, pl. 121.

1,010 kg. of bronze, sufficient for the making of one million arrowheads.[48] These large numbers may indicate one of the manufactured commodities exported by the Pylians and one of their sources of revenue.

The fortunate discovery of a complete corselet by Verdelis and Åstrom in a chamber tomb at Dendra has revealed an article known until now only through the tablet records (Fig. 145).[49] It is a veritable and formidable coat-of-mail. Standing before it in the Museum of Nauplia, where it has been mounted, we can visualize the tall Achaean chieftain, made taller by his plumed helmet, covered with bronze, equipped with a long rapier and a shorter broad sword, holding a sturdy spear with a bronze point and trimmings of gold, advancing against the enemy with fierce eyes shining between heavy bronze cheek pieces. Such an Achaean, a veritable χαλκοχίτων, must have presented an awe-inspiring sight.

The introductory formula "smiths having a talasion" (an amount allocated by weight for processing) seems to imply that the word *talanton* (in Latin *pensum*) was already in use in Mycenaean times. The ingots allotted were perhaps of the so-called "dried ox-hide" shape, examples of which are known from Crete, the mainland, and Cyprus.[50] Some forty samples have been recovered recently from a shipwreck off the coast of Asia Minor. From Mycenae itself we have a complete example, found by Tsountas, and fragments discovered by Wace and myself. Bass has lately pointed out that these ingots were not of a fixed standard weight but served as bulk material from which pieces could be cut and used as needed.[51]

Not only gold, silver, and bronze, but lead as well, was employed for both utilitarian and artistic purposes. Quantities of lead have been found among the ruins of Mycenae by Tsountas, Wace, and myself in the course of our excavations, and vessels of lead are reported from other sites. In 1963 in Building M on the northwest slope of the citadel of Mycenae and in 1964 in Buildings A and B of the northeast extension we found crushed, but in their original position, vessels of lead measuring some 45 cm. in maximum diameter (Fig. 146). That lead was occasionally used for artistic products is indicated by the statuette found by Tsountas in the tholos tomb of Kampos in Lakonia.[52] It stands 20 cm. in height and may represent an athlete, a boxer perhaps. He is holding his hands before his chest and stands with feet apart. He is wearing only a loin cloth girded at the waist and a close-fitting cap. It brings to mind the statuettes of bronze from Mycenae and Tiryns which, according to Evans, represent the Syrian lightning-god Resheph.[53] Their "better and more naturalistic fabric than most similar figurines from Syrian sites" will indicate their Mycenaean origin, while the overlapping kilt and the conical head-piece will suggest a Syrian prototype. Gold, silver, bronze, and lead, as we learn from the inscribed tablets, were controlled by the king of a Mycenaean state, who would allocate to the smiths of his domain the necessary supply for their needs. Some of these artists and smiths may have worked in royal workshops located in the palace itself; others may have had their smithies in different districts.[54]

The Art of the Vase-maker

We know much more about the achievement of another class of artisans, of the vase-makers of the Mycenaean world. Their products have survived in great numbers.[55] Vessels of clay were a real need of the community that the potters capably filled. In gen-

---

[48] For the tablets of the Jn series cf. Ventris-Chadwick, *op.cit.*, p. 352 ff. For the totaling tablet Ja 749 cf. Palmer, *op.cit.*, p. 286. Of course the bronze allotted could have been used for the making of articles other than arrowheads and spearheads except in cases where it is so specified, as for example on tablet Jn09 = Jn 829 where arrowheads and spearheads are specifically mentioned.

[49] Verdelis, *Ephemeris*, 1957, *Chronika*, pp. 15-18 fig. 1. A single pair of bronze greaves in metal is known from the Mycenaean area. It was found by Dr. N. Yalouris in the Patras area (Achaia) and dates from ca. 1200 B.C. (*Ath.Mitt.*, 75 [1960], Beil. 28). The soldiers on the Warrior Vase and the painted stele from Mycenae wear cloth-leggings. No remnants of chariots have been found thus far. That such were in use in LH III B times is indicated by the tablets of the S series (Ventris-Chadwick, *op.cit.*, pp. 361-391 and Palmer, *Interpretation*, pp. 314-329). Grooves cut in the rock surface of Mycenaean roads also prove the use of wheeled vehicles cf. Fig. 78.

[50] The fullest study of these ingots to 1960 is that of Hans-Günter Buchholz, *Minoica*, pp. 92-115. For painted representations of Keftiu bearing, among other gifts, ingots of the "ox-hide" type on the tomb of Rekh-mi-rē at Thebes cf. Bossert, *Art in Ancient Crete*, figs. 546-548.

[51] For the discovery off the coast of Asia Minor and a new excellent discussion of the commodity cf. G. F. Bass, "The Cape Gelidonya Wreck," *AJA*, 65 (1960), pp. 267 ff. His revised chronology is to be preferred over that suggested by Buchholz. For the examples from Mycenae cf. J. Svoronos, *JIAN*, 1906, pl. v; Seltman, *Athens Its History and Coinage*, pp. 4, 5, figs. 3, 4; Wace, *BSA*, 48 (1953), p. 8 and pl. 2,e; Mylonas in *Ergon*, 1959, pp. 98-99.

[52] *Mycenaean Age*, p. 160, pl. XVII.

[53] *Palace of Minos*, III, p. 477 fig. 331. *Mycenaean Age*, figs. 55-56.

[54] The late Professor Keramopoullos disclosed remains of a royal workshop in the palace of Thebes (*Ephemeris*, 1930, pp. 29 ff.) and evidence of its existence was found recently in the ruins of the same palace by Dr. Platon and Mrs. Touloupa. In 1965 we located the workshop of the artists in the Palace of Mycenae; *supra*, p. 73. The areas mentioned in the tablets of Pylos where smiths were located indicate a wide dispersion of their workshops.

[55] To attempt a bibliography on Mycenaean pottery would prove a very long task. For our purpose it is sufficient to note the early work of Furtwängler and Loeschcke, *Mykenische Vasen*, Berlin, 1886; the chapters on pottery of Wace, in *Chamber Tombs of Mycenae*, and of Blegen in *Prosymna*; the indispensable work of Furumark, *The Mycenaean Pottery*, 1941, and *The Chronology of Mycenaean Pottery*, 1941. Our brief account is based on these works. For easily accessible illustrations see

eral the Mycenaean vases are characterized by careful, excellent workmanship and pleasant, often elegant forms. They are turned on the wheel and as a rule are covered with a smooth and well-polished slip on which designs are painted in a lustrous color ranging from black to brown and red. Occasionally white color is used but only as an auxiliary. There can be little doubt that the Mycenaeans learned from the Minoans the use of lustrous colors in the decoration of their vases. Their ancestors, the Middle Helladic inhabitants of the mainland, produced a pottery with painted designs; but the colors employed were matt, lustreless, and often were applied on the walls of the vase without the intervention of the smoothed slip. The use of lustrous color, often erroneously called glaze, marks the beginning of the Mycenaean period. With it were painted a variety of designs in a freehand style which gives added charm to the composition. Popular elements during the first period of the Mycenaean Age (Late Helladic I) are the connected spirals. They are carefully drawn with a thicker outer volute, thinner inside convolutions and a thick dot (an eye) at the very center. Often enough, small dots in white are painted on top of the color of the "eye" and on tangents connecting the spirals. Again characteristic are large black dots placed above and below tangents connecting spirals. This element reflects the popular design found on the gold discs from the shaft graves, used for the decoration of garments. Plant elements are equally popular and we find that ivy is especially favored. We have already noted that the double axe is often employed in the decoration of the vases of the period (Fig. 147). Cups of the Vapheio shape and small jugs are typical of the period.

In LH II times, i.e. the second period of the Mycenaean Age, the potter continued to be active and to produce quantities of decorated pots (Fig. 148). The technique of shaping the pots, polishing and decorating them in lustrous color, presented the same high quality as before. But now certain changes are apparent. The spiral with the large eye not only lost its popularity but was seldom used. The double axe gradually disappeared, while plant motives predominated and elements taken from marine life became popular. The octopus, the nautilus, the argonaut were often used, while the ivy with a double stem rising out of a rocky ground, the papyrus plant, and the palm leaf were common plant elements. Now the amphora and a squat alabaster, shaped somewhat like a round

loaf of bread, became popular. This period saw also the appearance and the use of what is known as the palace style amphora: a tall jar with an oval elegant body, broad and tall neck, and a flat flaring rim. Three small vertical handles are, as a rule, placed on its shoulder. The neck and the base are usually covered with a solid black color; the body is covered with plant and marine elements painted with vigor and often with exuberance (Fig. 148). Sometimes an elaborate decoration that is known as the "necklace" pattern covers its face.

In contrast to this elaborately decorated jar were produced stemmed goblets with a very limited decoration which came to be known as Ephyrean goblets since they were first discovered by Blegen at the site of Korakou, in the territory of the Homeric Ephyra.[56] They are excellently made of well-sifted, yellow-buff clay and in form, color, and workmanship recall the Middle Helladic yellow Minyan goblets, whose descendants most probaby they are. The patterns painted in a black or red-brown lustrous paint are simple, and include rosettes, lilies, crocuses, and argonauts. A single unit as a rule is painted on each side of the goblet (Fig. 148, c). In their simplicity and elegance they strike a restraining and sober note in the exuberant trend of the art of the period.

In the third era of the Mycenaean Age, in Late Helladic III, were produced most of the vases exhibited in our museums (Figs. 73 and 149). They are usually divided into three groups or ceramic phases, LH III A, B, and C, the general features of each of which are usually agreed upon; but there is no unanimity of opinion regarding the chronological limits of these phases and of the elements which characterize their transitions especially.[57] During LH III A and B times pottery manufactured in the mainland was exported to all parts of the Mediterranean world. In LH III A, it was exported to Egypt where we find it in the fill of Tell-Amarna, the site of the new capital of Ikhnaton, thus establishing a firm chronological datum for the ceramic phase to which it belongs. The many vases found in chamber tombs prove that the Island of Rhodes was in LH III times firmly held by Mycenaeans and was flourishing to such an extent as to be counted a worthy state by the mighty Hittite emperors who seem to have called it Ahhiyava. The pottery again proves that mainlanders established themselves among the native population of Cyprus and there, as well as in Rhodes, local workshops pro-

Marinatos-Hirmer, *op.cit.*, figs. 227-236. See also Mackeprang, "Late Mycenaean Vases," *AJA*, 42 (1938), pp. 537-559.

[56] Blegen, *Korakou*, pp. 54 ff. For a jar with a "necklace" pattern and another with octopus from Grave Circle B, cf. Mylonas, *Ancient Mycenae*, fig. 86.

[57] General agreement also has not been reached in the exact

classification and chronology of the designs which usually, along with the shapes, are employed to determine the date of a pot. Often what is considered to belong to a given sub-period by some is placed in another period by other equally qualified scholars.

duced the only variety of pots that can be differentiated from the general types manufactured in the mainland especially in LH III B times.[58]

The popularity of plant and marine motives continues into the LH III A period but now a process of stylization has set in and the various elements, though still recognizable, tend gradually to reach a more or less abstract form. The same excellence of technique is noticeable, and popular shapes are the false-necked amphora, the kylix on a high stem, the jug, and the squat alabastron (Fig. 149).

Vast quantities of pottery produced during the LH III B period have been found in all the excavated sites proving that the potter's industry had reached the apex of its prosperity in the course of the thirteenth century B.C., to which this period is usually ascribed. Perhaps now the decoration of the vases produced is not as artistic and as successful as that of the previous years, but it exhibits good draftsmanship, orderliness, and a typical open style; the quality of the fabric, the shapes of the pots, and the general impression of the decoration are excellent. A definite uniformity of pottery produced in the various sections of the Mycenaean world is so apparent that the adjective "koine" is usually applied to it. It has been stated with reason that no variations of any significance are to be found within the mainland area; only in Rhodes and Cyprus, as we have seen, a local variety was produced. To the shapes which were usual before, was now added the deep two-handled bowl and the krater, but the false-necked amphora, the high stemmed kylix, and a variety of jars remain popular (Figs. 72 and 149). Decorative elements are borrowed from plant and marine life, but they are so highly stylized as to become unrecognizable towards the end of the period. Bands are now common, painted in broad lines or in repeated thin lines, and abstract geometric patterns, including the spiral, become common. Besides the zonal disposition of the patterns, usually between the rim, the handles and the base, we find in use a paneled arrangement known as metopic, because of its resemblance to the metopes of the Doric architectural order of the Historic period. Antithetically arranged motives on either side of vertical bands are common.

During this period a figure style known as pictorial was developed, especially in Cyprus and Rhodes. Its beginnings go back to LH III A times, but now it finds its fullest expression. The krater is the most favored shape and chariot scenes prevail. However, other motifs such as bulls, fish, octopi, and birds are used and painted in a broad continuous frieze around the body. Even a naval scene and an adoration rite of a goddess seated on a three-legged throne are among the subjects painted. Occasionally plants, palm trees, highly stylized and decorative, are scattered in the background to symbolize the setting in which the action occurs. The chariot scenes, represented with such individuality that workshops and artists are discernible, seem to be connected with the burial rites and to revive the custom started by the carvers of the stelai of Grave Circle A. The style spread to the mainland where we have examples from Tiryns, Berbati, Mycenae, Corinth, and Argos (Fig. 150).[59]

The pottery produced in the third and last subperiod of the Mycenaean Age, in LH III C, presents a diversity of local styles contrasting with the uniformity characterizing the LH III B ware. We naturally find that the last variety of painted vases produced in LH III B times continues into the next period. Thus, the best example of the pictorial style thus far found in the mainland, the well-known Warrior Vase, belongs to the early years of LH III C. But there are two groups of pottery which characterize this closing period of the Mycenaean age. By far the more attractive group is what came to be known as the "close style" ware (Fig. 151).[60] Its vases, mainly false-necked amphorae and deep bowls or kraters, are covered with well-designed friezes of birds, octopi, dolphins, geometric patterns, concentric semicircles and cross-hatched triangles; their fabrics are good, draftsmanship is often excellent, and the shapes are true and pleasant. The use of hatching and cross-hatching is very characteristic of the style. The beginnings of the "close style" seem to go back to the closing years of the LH III B period and thus provide a connecting link between the two last sub-periods of the Mycenaean Age. The second class is known as the granary style, since vases belonging to it were found by Wace for the first time on the floors of the granary at

[58] Furumark, "The settlement at Ialysos and Aegean History, c. 1500-1400 B.C.," *Opuscula*, 6 (1950), pp. 150-271. Stubbings, "The Expansion of Mycenaean Civilization," Rev. ed. *CAH*, I & II, pp. 18-20, Monaco, "Scavi nella zona micenea di Jaliso," *Clara Rhodos*, 10 (1941-1949), pp. 42-199. Dikaios, "The Context of the Enkomi Tablets," *Kadmos*, 2 (1963), pp. 39-52; Gjerstad, "The Colonization of Cyprus in Greek Legend," *Opuscula*, 3 (1947), pp. 107 ff.

[59] For the pictorial style cf. Furumark, *Mycenaean Pottery*, pp. 430-470. S. A. Immerwahr, "The Protome Painter and Some Contemporaries," *AJA*, 60 (1956), pp. 137-141, where good

bibliography to 1960; brought up to date in the forthcoming publication of V. Karageorghis, *The Mycenaean Vases of the Pictorial Style*. The drawings of our Fig. 150 were made from the photographs published by Wace in *BSA*, 48 (1953), pl. 16, and Weinberg in *Hesperia*, 18 (1949), pl. 23.

[60] The best examples of the "close style" come from the cemetery of Perati excavated by Iacovides. For an excellent study of LH III C pottery, besides his books given in note 50, see Furumark, "The Mycenaean III C Pottery and Its Relation to Cypriot Fabrics," *OpusArch*, III, pp. 194-265.

Mycenae. Cups are typical of the class and deep mono-chrome bowls, with dark ground and two reserved bands above the base or a reserved band with a wavy painted line on it between the handles. Of inferior artistic merit, they may illustrate the declining demand for export of the Mycenaean potters' products. Nevertheless, we find this class of pottery abroad, even in the settlement which was built over the ruins of Priam's Troy, and it seems that it influenced considerably the so-called Philistine pottery of Syria. The granary style, at least in Mycenae, seems to have continued in use for a short time, even after the end of the Mycenaean Age.

In this period becomes popular a deep bowl with a wide opening, two horizontal handles below its flattened rim and a body that below its waist narrows perceptibly towards a small flat base. Widely spaced bands are painted on the body. Sometimes to the rim is added a side spout; occasionally figurines of women with hands on their heads (mourning women) are attached to the rim (Fig. 152). Examples of bowls with figurines have been found thus far in the cemetery of Perati in Attika, where apparently they were made to be placed in graves; examples are also known from Naxos and Rhodes.

Stone was also used for the making of vessels, and sometimes these were inlaid with various materials.[61] However, clay was the standard material used by the potter. Whether the vases themselves were exported as articles of commerce or were merely the containers of commodities being exported cannot be decided with any degree of certainty. But there can be little doubt that their shapes and decoration influenced the art of the potters of many adjacent districts, especially in LH III B times.

Fresco Work

The lords of the Mycenaean area copied the Minoan practice of covering with colorful frescoes the walls of their dwellings.[62] Of these only small fragments have been recovered (cf. Fig. 24) and the brilliant restorations we often see in books and periodicals owe a good deal to the modern artists who painted them. Thebes, Mycenae, Tiryns, and Pylos have yielded the most important fragments found in the mainland. Especially numerous and instructive are the remains found by Blegen in the ruins of the palace at Pylos. They are now being cleaned, classified, and studied by Mabel Lang, whose forthcoming publication will place our knowledge of this artistic activity on a firm

and definite basis and will eliminate some current misconceptions. For example, it is stated and it is believed that the work of the Mycenaean fresco painters as compared to the Minoan was dull, provincial, and uninspired; some fragments of their work do present these shortcomings, but neither do all fragments from Crete present a uniform excellence. The remains of Pylos and some of the newly found fragments in Thebes exhibit a brilliance of color, excellence of execution, attention to detail, and variety worthy of a Minoan master painter. Certain generally accepted facts, however, will continue to be valid. There can be no doubt that fresco painting was introduced fully developed from Minoan Crete to the mainland. It is reasonable to believe that at the beginning imported Minoan painters were employed, who arrived with their stock of formulas developed in Crete. The brilliant composition of the "Flying Fish," from the palace of Phylakopi in the Island of Melos, may point the way those artists followed from their own island to the mainland. Or, we may understand that artists were loaned to the mainland lords by the Minoan rulers. Soon, however, mainland painters were at work following closely the examples and formulas of their Minoan masters. They used the same two-dimensional style, the same color schemes, mannerisms, and conventions; they painted human forms in silhouette style, using deep red color for the nude parts of men and creamish-white for the face and arms of women; they continued to draw the eye in full front on a face in profile; they avoided contrasts of light and shadow and painted in two planes. The range of their colors was limited—red and blue with white, yellow, pink, brown and black for details—and was used in flat tones without gradations. The Mycenaean artists, however, make their contours stronger and more definite.

The fragments of Pylos emphasize another fact established by Tsountas and Wace at Mycenae, by Rodenwaldt and Müller at Tiryns: that the frescoes on the walls were sometimes removed and thrown in piles outside the palace to be replaced by others, often of the same subject. Perhaps they had been dulled by the smoke from the open hearth and from the torches used for illumination or damaged by fire or accident. The discovery of piles containing discarded fragments may help establish criteria for a more objective classification of the mainland fresco work than is now available. The greater or smaller dependance on Minoan prototypes of composition and figures was

[61] Cf. Wace, in *Mycenae Tablet*, II, figs. 18-23.
[62] For a discussion of Mycenaean frescoes see Rodenwaldt, *Der Fries des Megarons von Mykenai*, and *Tiryns*, II, pp. 28 ff.; *AM* 36 (1911), pp. 198-206 and 221-250, pls. IX-XII. Lamb, *BSA*, 25 (1921-1923), pp. 162 ff. For the fragments from Thebes cf. Keramopoullos, *Ephemeris*, 1907, pp. 205 ff. and H. Reusch, *Die zeichnerische Rekonstrucktion des Frauenfries im böetischen Theben*, Berlin, 1956. Blegen-Lang, *AJA*, 60 (1956), pls. 40 and 41; 61 (1957), pl. 45.

used to divide the known examples from Thebes, Tiryns, and Mycenae into an earlier LH III A and to a later LH III B style. To the earlier period belongs the processional scene of women that originally covered the walls of an inner room on the first palace of Thebes found by Keramopoullos. Such processional scenes, known also from Tiryns and Pylos, were inspired by similar themes, popular in Crete. They may have found favor in the mainland because they corresponded to festivals held there at certain times. In Pylos fragments of processional scenes were found in the piles of discarded frescoes and in Tiryns, too, pieces were discovered in the debris thrown over the west Cyclopean wall. The figures in these processional scenes are over life-size, and the appearance of the ensemble is impressive. In contrast, scenes of hunting and war which seem to characterize the Mycenaean effort and taste, are lively, smaller in scale, and seem to have been used to decorate the walls of the *domos*. Along with them we find representations of griffins, sphinxes, birds, flowers, and trees. The decoration that once covered the walls of the propylon at Pylos is very striking: two white horses painted above a dado covered by argonauts, a decoration found also in Tsountas' house at Mycenae.

The better known and most often illustrated frescoes from the mainland, besides the details from processional scenes, are those from Tiryns (the wild boar hunt, including two women in a chariot and grooms holding dappled hounds on long leashes), from Mycenae (the façade of a house or palace and the horses, warriors, and grooms) and from Pylos (the lyre-player). To these must be added the abstract and geometric patterns used for the decoration of dadoes over which the figured compositions were placed. The fragments found in the *domos* of the Palace of Nestor throw considerable light on the arrangement of the subjects on the walls of that most important room of the palace. Apparently at least four or five different subjects were used in that room. On either side of the throne that occupied the center of the north wall of the *domos* were painted a series of crested griffins and lions. The well-known scene of the lyre player, another scene with long-robed people seated at a table,

and a fourth containing a number of men painted in small scale formed part of the decoration. It seems that the last was placed on the south wall right across from the area of the throne. Could we imagine that they formed part of an army, or a group of captives which the *wanax* could view as he sat on his throne in the interior of his megaron? The scenes appear unrelated and the decoration does not seem to possess a unity of subject.

The *domos* of the palace at Mycenae was decorated in the same grand way. Fragments of frescoes were found along its north and west walls; its south wall as well as a good part of the east wall rolled down the ravine and was destroyed. Against the south wall was set the throne of the king and perhaps on either side of it we should imagine a standing or couchant lion. On the wall across from the throne and the hearth we find depicted a war scene: the façade of a building rises in three irregular stories; in the window-apertures of the building women are watching a battle that seems to be raging in the mountainous terrain beyond. A soldier seems to be falling headlong from the top, while other soldiers, officers, and grooms are readying horses, red and white in color, or are harnessing them to chariots. We have in the composition preparations for a battle, an actual scene of battle, and the city before which the action takes place in disconnected tableaux. Observing the scene from his throne, the king would enjoy the action and perhaps recall similar scenes from his own experience in battle. It is of course impossible to say whether a historic event was represented in this fresco. Most probably it stood for the general conception of warfare of the period.

The problem of lighting the megaron is closely connected with its decoration. In the dim light of an afternoon and evening would these frescoes be visible and could they be enjoyed to the full? Torch light helped the spectator the way candles serve the modern visitor of a Byzantine chapel. As the flickering light of the torches touched the brilliant colors on the wall, resting here one moment, there the next, it imparted to the figures the illusion of living forms. The brilliance of the spectacle reflected the greater glory of the *wanax*, master of the palace.

SOCIAL AND POLITICAL ORGANIZATION

Within such a brilliant setting moved the palace lords and ladies, great war lords and charming beauties. We really do not know whether in their daily routine, even at their banquets, they dressed in the gorgeous dresses of the Minoans, as they appear in the processions. Perhaps they wore tunics with short

sleeves as we see them in the action scenes; and the clay figurines covered with color strengthen this conception. But from the surviving relics we can picture them decked with necklaces and earrings, with bracelets and pendants. From the records preserved on the tablets we can imagine the richly inlaid tables and chairs which filled their rooms, the bronze cauldrons which filled their workrooms, the pottery, painted and plain, the bronze weapons, perhaps set against walls and columns. Herds of animals must have provided for the great banquets held in the palaces, as well as fish, octopi, shellfish, olive oil, wine, and various fruits.

Mycenaean Script: Linear B

We have left to the last the brief consideration of one of the important cultural elements of the closing period of the Mycenaean Age, the discussion of the script the Mycenaeans used in LH III times. For that script they were indebted to the Minoans, who in Middle Minoan times developed from their hieroglyphic writing a linear syllabic script known as Linear A; the omission of some signs and the addition of others to stand for syllables and sounds nonexistent in the Minoan language but important in Indo-European Greek resulted in the creation of the syllabic Linear B Script.[63] The existence of that Script on the mainland was indicated by some inscribed pieces of pottery found at Mycenae and Orchomenos even before the great discoveries of Evans at Knossos. More inscribed vases, as a rule false-necked amphorae, found at widely separated areas at Tiryns, Mycenae, Eleusis, and especially at Thebes where Keramopoullos discovered a group of twenty-eight in the ruins of what is considered to be the Palace of Kadmos, strengthened the assumption that writing was not altogether unknown in Mycenaean times. There was, too, an inscription on the rim of a bowl from Asine. However, the great number of tablets in Linear B found by Evans at Knossos made it seem possible that the inscribed documents found on the mainland might have been imports from the island.

Then in 1939 came the discovery of hundreds of tablets by Blegen in the Palace of Nestor. More tablets were found in that palace in subsequent years and especially in 1952, when excavations were resumed after the Second World War. A stray tablet was found by Papadimi-

triou and the Ephor Photios Petsas at Mycenae in 1952 and some 52 tablets and sealings were found by Wace in the House of the Oil Merchant and the House of the Sphinxes (Fig. 153). In 1958 Verdelis discovered some twelve fragments and tablets in the West House of Mycenae and in 1961 Mrs. David French found an additional tablet in the House of the Sphinxes. In 1961 for the first time fragments of tablets were found within the citadel among the calcined debris of the so-called Citadel House by Taylour and his collaborators. In February 1964 tablets were found in the area of the Palace of Kadmos in Thebes. Besides, a number of pots bearing inscriptions were found both at Tiryns and Mycenae, the latest of which is the fragment of a deep bowl bearing a name of three signs, from one of the rooms we found by the north Cyclopean wall in August 1962. The enumeration of the finds suggest that Linear Script B was in somewhat frequent use at least in the Peloponnesos in Mycenaean times.[64]

The discovery of tablets inscribed in Linear B gave rise to a number of questions some of which remain unanswered. It was noted at the very beginning that a chronological difference and a gap of some two centuries existed between the Linear B inscribed tablets found by Evans at Knossos and those found by Blegen at Pylos, and yet there was no appreciable difference in the form of the signs, in spelling, in dialect, in phraseology, in the two sources.[65] Generally the tablets of Knossos were placed in the LM II period, from ca. 1450-1400 B.C., while those of Pylos date from the very end of the thirteenth century, from about 1200 B.C. Some scholars tried to bridge the gap by placing the inscribed amphoras of the mainland in the fourteenth century; but this seems to be contrary to the archaeological evidence which places them in the thirteenth. Blegen suggested recently that perhaps the tablets of Knossos should be dated later and that the context in which they were found should be re-examined; Palmer now maintains with reason that the Knossian tablets date from Late Minoan III times and thus he brings them in closer chronological association

[63] The first real study of the scripts of Crete was made by Evans in his *Scripta Minoa*, 1909. References and chapters on the script are to be found in his *Palace of Minos* and especially in Volume IV, part II, pp. 619 ff. Evans' article in *JHS*, 14 (1894), pp. 270-372, marks the first attempt towards a collection of examples. Tsountas, incorporated a chapter in his book, *Mycenae*, 1893, and this was augmented by Tsountas and Manatt, in the *Mycenaean Age*, 1897, ch. XI, pp. 268-293. For bibliography on scripts to 1959, see Ventris-Chadwick, *op.cit.*, pp. 428-433. For current bibliography see Palmer, *op.cit.*, pp. 381-402 and E. Bennett and his *Nestor* and *passim* in Mycenaean Bibliography.

[64] For the thrilling story of the discovery and decipherment of the script to 1959 see Ventris-Chadwick, *op.cit.*, ch. I, pp. 3-27 and Chadwick, *The Decipherment of Linear B*. For the more recent finds see Bennett: *The Mycenae Tablets*, I and II, *TAPS*,

48, part 1 (1958), and Chadwick, *The Mycenae Tablets*, III, of the *TAPS*, 52, part 7 (1962). M. Lang, *AJA*, 62 (1958), and following years to date. In numerical terms, we have some 3,000 tablets from Knossos, over 1,000 tablets from Pylos, 51 from Mycenae, 14 fragments from Thebes.

[65] Professor Page, is among the most recent to emphasize this by "noticing the astonishing fact that the sign-forms, spelling, dialect, phraseology, and tablet-shapes at Pylos on the mainland about 1200 B.C. are almost identical with those at Knossos overseas 200 years earlier,—this almost incredible uniformity is perhaps the most persuasive of several proofs 'that writing was the preserve of specialists trained in a rigidly conservative scribal school.'" *History and the Homeric Iliad*, p. 179. Dow, "Minoan Writing," *AJA*, 58 (1954), pp. 120-122 and Ventris-Chadwick, *op.cit.*, p. 110.

with the tablets from the mainland.[66] The last view naturally has created a great controversy which is still current and which, I believe, can be settled only if new material and evidence is revealed in Crete, preferably at Knossos. For the time being many scholars will continue to believe that the two sets of tablets belong to widely separated periods, but that the scribes using the script were so conservative that they did not initiate any changes in the forms of the signs and in spelling which remained the same over a long period of time.

The question of where and by whom the Linear B Script was invented and used for the first time also remains unanswered; was it invented in the mainland or in Crete and by the scribes themselves? And were these scribes Cretans or mainlanders? It has been suggested that the script was formulated by Minoan scribes for the benefit of Mycenaean lords who ruled over Knossos in LM times, ca. 1450-1400 B.C.[67] They had the experience, the training, and the ability to change and adapt the ancestral Linear A Script to the new syllabary which could express the language of the new lords of Knossos, the Greek-speaking Mycenaeans. This is a plausible suggestion, but it is based on the hypothesis that Knossos was conquered and was occupied by Mycenaeans in LM II times. This is not fully proven, though the elements indicative of such an event, the palace-style amphorae and Linear B script limited only to Knossos, lend it great probability. Then we have the legend, one of many, that Kadmos, the founder of Thebes, introduced into Greece the φοινικήια γράμματα. This legend was used by Herodotos to prove that the Phoenician followers of Kadmos brought from their homeland to Greece the art of writing. Most probably the legend indicates that the mythical Kadmos introduced letters which were painted in red color and so were called φοινικήια.[68] The date assigned to Kadmos, the very beginning of the fourteenth and the end of the fifteenth century B.C., may suggest that these painted letters introduced into Greece may have been the Linear B Script developed

outside the mainland, in Knossos. This hypothesis again rests on inferences drawn from a legend the value of which cannot be determined. Whether or not Linear B was developed in Crete by Minoan scribes, the fact remains that it is found in the mainland at the earliest in the course of the thirteenth century B.C.

Again we cannot prove whether or not Minoan scribes were established in the mainland where they and their descendants controlled the art of writing, or whether in time a class of mainland scribes was developed. The fact that a systematic division of labor existed in the Mycenaean world would suggest that there was a class of scribes, though it is never mentioned in the surviving documents. It is sometimes maintained that only these professional scribes could read and write, that though the Mycenaean age was literate "writing was the preserve of specialists trained in a rigidly conservative scribal school,"[69] that this will explain the disappearance of Linear B after the collapse of the Mycenaean power. We have to remember, however, that besides the tablets a good many false-necked amphorae and even some bowls which may have been the property of wealthy citizens bear painted inscriptions; that, as Wace has repeatedly remarked, "it would have been useless to inscribe stirrup-jars to indicate their contents or ownership unless the men who handled them could read the inscriptions";[70] it is highly doubtful that those men were scribes. The same argument could be used for the sealings which bear inscriptions on the reverse. Indeed, although there was no general literacy in the Mycenaean Age, it seems probable that it was not confined to the class of the trained scribes, that others could read and write. Its disappearance may be due also to the fact that it was too unwieldy to be used for other purposes than the keeping of precise records of assessments and inventories of the possessions of the ruler. With the passing of the political regime to whose service writing was devoted the need to record assessments and properties may have passed also; and this, along with the elimination of the class of trained

---

[66] In Ventris-Chadwick the inscribed amphorae were placed ca. 1360 B.C. (p. 38) and Evans (*Palace of Minos*, IV, p. 755) maintained that they "should not be brought down to a later date than the close of the Fourteenth Century." I believe that I have proved that the amphorae of Thebes belong to the thirteenth century and perhaps to its very end, *Ephemeris*, 1936, pp. 64-70 and *AJA*, 1936, pp. 426-427; and I note with pleasure that Blegen places the last destruction of the Palace of Thebes within which they were found around 1200 B.C. (*The Mycenaean Age*, p. 23). Palmer's views are fully explained in his recent book *Mycenaeans and Minoans*, Blegen's in *Minoica*, pp. 61-66.

[67] For Mycenaean lords of Knossos cf. Wace *apud* Pendlebury, *The Archaeology of Crete*, p. 229. S. Dow, "The Greeks in the Bronze Age," *XIe Congrès international des sciences historiques*, pp. 13-16.

[68] Cf. Mylonas, *Studies of the Academy of Athens*, 23, no. 5 (1959), pp. 1 ff. The discovery of thirty-two seal cylinders in the palace at Thebes revived the view of Kadmos' arrival from Syria. However, these seals belong to various years and their presence indicates the antiquarian tendencies of a *wanax* who could have accumulated them in the course of normal commercial enterprises.

[69] See for example, Page, *op.cit.*, p. 179; also Ventris-Chadwick *op.cit.*, p. 110.

[70] Wace, in *Companion to Homer*, p. 354, also introduction to Bennett's *Mycenae Tablets*, II, p. 5. Besides the painted bowl from Mycenae (Mylonas, *Kadmos*, 2 [1962], pp. 95-97) and the possible inscribed sherd from Asine, we have a painted sherd from Tiryns (Chadwick, *Mycenae Tablets*, III, Appendix, p. 73 no. 6).

scribes who were employed by the royal regime, may have contributed to the abandonment of the script.[71]

For the most important problem concerning Linear B the historic achievement of Michael Ventris has fortunately provided us with a definitive answer. As a result of his sustained and successful efforts we are able to read and interpret a good many of the preserved documents. Scholars who preceded him were able to prove that the language of the script was inflected on Indo-European lines[72] and that it differed from the language of Linear Script A; that although in both we have the same numeral system, the weights and measures recorded indicated a different system in each script.[73] But they were unable to devise a system capable of providing the key to the decipherment of the script; some were of the belief that the script would never be deciphered. Perhaps the partial publication of the documents found at Knossos and their inaccessibility to scholars, even to the specialists in the field, may have been responsible for the pessimistic belief that the task of deciphering the script was impossible. But then came the discovery of the Pylos tablets, immediately followed by Blegen's decision to have the texts of these tablets published without delay, thus making the rich material accessible to scholarship. The task of the study, copying, and publication of the texts was entrusted to Professor Emmett L. Bennett, Jr., who carried out the assignment with admirable success.[74] With the wealth of material from Pylos supplemented by that from Knossos before him, Ventris with ingenuity and inspired effort was able to determine the syllabic values of the signs of Linear B and to provide the scholar with the means of its decipherment.[75] The many, successful, and very exciting steps in the process of his work have been so often explained, especially by his collaborator, John Chadwick, that it will be unnecessary to repeat them here.

Ventris' achievement will remain a brilliant landmark in the path of scholarship. As a result of his work we can read and understand a number of the Linear B inscriptions. The number of the skeptics is diminishing constantly and their arguments based on the uncertainties and difficulties presented by the system are counterbalanced by the amount of definite information which is offered by the suggested readings. There can be no doubt that uncertainties and difficulties do exist,[76] and they are increased by the limited range of the texts and by the Greek language of the times, older by some four centuries than any written examples of that language known to date; but there is the encouraging fact that the difficulties are being reduced and the hope that they will be eliminated in the course of time.[77]

Even before Ventris' decipherment of the script it was accepted that a good many of the tablets were inventories. Now we learn that they are administrative documents; some are indeed inventories, others are accounts of flocks and lands, but the great majority are records of assessment, of distribution of materials for production, of commodities produced, and of deliveries. Thus far, no tablets have been found with texts which can be considered literary or judicial. There are not even references to law, to literature, or to historic events. The surviving texts are brief and as unimaginative and dry as entries in a modern ledger. And yet they are proving an important source of information, especially for the political and social structure of the Mycenaean world.

One definite fact emerging from the tablets is that the language of Linear B is Greek, and that consequently the Mycenaeans were Greek-speaking Indo-Europeans. Another is that the political regime, at Pylos and Knossos at least, was an autocratic monarchy with a centralized, bureaucratic, administrative system. The mighty citadels at Mycenae, Tiryns, and Athens certainly indicated that their rulers could command the people and the resources needed for the construction of such immense projects. But the architectural and artistic relics uncovered did not prepare us for the all-pervasive, bureaucratic activities revealed by the tablets.[78]

It is essential, however, to emphasize one fact: to

[71] It has been pointed out that the signs are more suited to writing with pen and ink than to scratching on tablets (Ventris-Chadwick, *op.cit.*, p. 109), and it can very well be assumed that documents were written on other perishable materials which have not survived. Therefore the surviving samples cannot be considered as the determining proof.
[72] This was the late Miss A. Kober's contribution; *AJA*, 48 (1944), pp. 64-75; 49 (1945), pp. 143-151; 50 (1946), pp. 268-276; 52 (1948), pp. 386-389.
[73] Cf. E. L. Bennett, Jr., *AJA*, 54 (1950), pp. 204-222.
[74] *The Pylos Tablets, a Preliminary Transcription*, 1951. *The Pylos Tablets, Texts of the Inscriptions* from 1939-1954, 1955.
[75] Ventris and Chadwick, "Evidence for Greek Dialect in the Mycenaean Archives," *JHS*, 73, 84-103; Ventris and Chadwick, *Documents in Mycenaean Greek*, 1956.

[76] The uncertainties presented can again be illustrated by the different readings suggested for the introductory phrase, or heading, of tablet TA 711 from Pylos. Ventris and Chadwick read: "Thus P. (*u-ke-qi-ri*) made inspection, on the occasion when the king appointed Sigewas (?) to be a *damokoros*" explained as an official. Professor Palmer reads: "What '*Pu-ke-qi-ri*' saw when the *Wanax* buried Sja-ke-wa son of Damocles." Among scholars who are still opposing or doubtful are Beattie, E. Grumach, W. Eilers, etc. Cf. however L. R. Palmer in *Orientalische Literaturzeitung*, 53 (1958), pp. 101-117; B. Rosenkranz in *Bibliotheca Orientalis*, 16 (1959), pp. 11-17.
[77] A large and dedicated group of scholars are devoting their time and abilities to the reading of the tablets and the perfecting of the system; but see Beattie in *Minoica*, pp. 6-34.
[78] See Page, *op.cit.*, pp. 180-182.

date tablets with information of the political and social system come only from Pylos and Knossos. It is generally believed that during the period of Linear B mainlanders were the rulers of Knossos; that is, foreigners imposed their authority on the native population. They would, naturally, exercise a tight control over the economy and people of the area they occupied. The tradition preserved by Pausanias recalls Neleus' arrival in Messenia from Iolkos. He and his companions ejected, by force, the ruling class of the district and established themselves as lords and masters. Again Pausanias states that the Messenians accepted the terms offered them by Kresphontes, the leader of the Dorians, and "they were induced to make concessions by the suspicion with which they regarded their own kings, because they were by descent Minyans from Iolkos." In Pylos, also, we seem to have had the rule of outsiders over a native population, and this may account for the strict control over the economy and activity of its people. This condition did not exist at Mycenae where a refugee prince was asked by its people to take over the office of king when the native ruler was killed in battle; nor did it happen in Athens where we have a long line of native kings. Perhaps in Mycenae and at Athens a tight control was not established, and this may explain the scarcity of tablets that characterize Mycenae.[79] But even in the documents from Pylos and Knossos we find but few explicit details bearing on the political and social structure; some are fragmentary and in many cases obscure.[80]

The Hierarchy of Leadership

There can be little doubt that both at Pylos and at Knossos, and probably at Thebes, there was a supreme monarch called the *wanax* without further qualification. There was but one *wanax* at the head of the political structure in those states and perhaps in all Mycenaean states. We know little about his prerogatives, powers, and duties. Page has succinctly summarized from the tablets what we can learn of his prerogatives: "He has a temenos, a slice of land; he appoints bureaucratic officials; he has 'royal servants'—the king's potter, the king's fuller, the king's *e-te-do-mo*; there are textiles 'belonging to the king'; his title is recorded in obscure connexions with the places Pa-ki-ja and Pi-ka-na; and we are told how much seed he had for condiments at Knossos."[81] There

is no mention of his acting as a high priest or as the official administering justice.[82] Since there seems to exist a class of priests and priestesses it is doubtful that the *wanax* was also in charge of religious matters, and we can only infer that he may have been the chief authority in the administration of justice since he was an all-powerful monarch.

Below the *wanax* we find a number of officials, major and minor. Among the most important of these was an official known as the *Lawagetas*. The very fact that he alone of all the other officials has a *temenos* and a title that may mean the "Leader of the People" or the "Leader of the Host" would place him next to the king. The tablets name, besides, a number of officials whose prerogatives, relative positions, and duties remain uncertain. Thus we have the *te-re-ta*, *e-qe-ta*, *ko-re-te*, *pro-ko-re-te*, *mo-ro-pa*, and *pa₂-si-re-u*. Chadwick suggested that the *te-re-tai* or *telestai* may have been religious functionaries, but Palmer correctly identifies them as "the men of telos—the men of burden," "fief-holders."[83] The *e-qe-tai* must have been of importance, since in the records they are given name and patronymic; perhaps they were "companions" of the king. Ventris and Chadwick suggested that they were attached to troops "in the capacity of staff officers; possibly as liaison officers" between the command post and the king. Palmer, noticing that the "*e-qe-ta* is bracketed with religious functionaries," concludes that he must be "a functionary of high rank with cult connexions."[84] The fact that *e-qe-tai* were attached to groups keeping watch over the coast could not be satisfactorily explained by religious functions which they may have performed. On the other hand, shrines and temples of the gods seem to have been rich establishments with quantities of precious metals, slaves, herds, etc., and they seem to have been administered by priests and priestesses. The case of the priestess *E-ri-ta*, who tried to avoid paying taxes by claiming that she held the land for the god, seems to indicate that abuses among the religious functionaries were not unknown. I would like to suggest that the *e-qe-tai* performed among religious personnel a function similar to that they performed among military groups; that they were the representatives of the king, his liaison officers, attached to temple and shrine.

Ruiperez has proposed that *ko-re-te* was a commander of the army, with a subaltern (the *pro-ko-re-te*), that the name is reflected in the Homeric

---

[79] Pausanias, IV, 3, 3-4; IV, 3, 6-7; IV, 36, 1. Having challenged the Fates, I hope that I will be punished by the discovery of tablets with information regarding the political and social systems at Mycenae.

[80] Ventris-Chadwick, *op.cit.*, pp. 119-125.

[81] Page, *op.cit.*, p. 183.

[82] *Supra*, p. 168.

[83] Palmer, *op.cit.*, p. 85.

[84] Ventris-Chadwick, *op.cit.*, p. 120. Chadwick, *The Decipherment of Linear B*, p. 113. Palmer, *op.cit.*, pp. 152-153, and glossary, and pp. 211-212 for priestess *E-ri-ta*. Cf. also Palmer's *Mycenaeans and Minoans*, pp. 93-97, 105.

κοίρανος.[85] The *mo-ro-pa* remains unidentified, but the title *pa₂-si-re-u* suggested the *basileus* of historic times and was taken to indicate a provincial official. Palmer explains him as "an official responsible for royal bronzesmiths and not basileus." Since the bronzesmiths were settled in various areas one could assume that the local governor would have been responsible for them. This would combine the duties of administration of the province and supervision of an important industry for which the *wanax* would hold him responsible. It has been assumed until recently that the *pa₂-si-re-u* had a Council of Elders, a *ke-ro-si-ja* equated with *gerousia*; but Palmer now explains that the word indicates "a unit organization of bronzesmiths." It is evident from this brief discussion that unanimity regarding the relative status and functions, even of the officials named, does not exist, but perhaps it will help convey the impression of the existence of an intricate system of administration.[86]

The *wanax*, exercising supreme authority, was represented everywhere by a number of officials, more or less important, whose duty it was to see that his orders were carried out, that the assessments were made, allocations of rations and commodities decided, and the dues imposed by the king faithfully complied with. Of considerable importance seems to have been the *damos*, the commune or village. We usually meet with it in the tablets as the owner and leaser of communal land, but the text of Tablet Ep 704 (=135) seems to indicate that it had power and a decisive voice in public affairs. The text includes a statement regarding the disputed land-tenure claim of the priestess *E-ri-ta* and the protest or decision of the *damos* against it. That decision seems to have been accepted by the *wanax*, since it is recorded in the palace register.

Many tablets deal with ownership and use of land, Series E;[87] but in spite of their number they do not provide sufficient information to enable us to construct a clear picture of the Mycenaean practices in the field of land tenure. It seems that land was held by the *damos*—by the village or community—by the *wanax*, by a sanctuary, and by individual land owners who allowed part of their land to be cultivated by "tenants"; but we do not know what the exact obligations and position of these "tenants" were. The land as a

rule is measured in terms of seed grain, and this gives rise to great confusion. It is clear, however, that there existed at Pylos a well-established and definite system of land tenure, whose workings and factual details are still obscure.

The tablets, as we have seen, provide important evidence as to the divinities worshiped at the time, since a number of them are records of offerings to gods who are mentioned in the capacity of recipients of these offerings. Interestingly enough, perfumed oil is sent to the shrines of the gods in quantities, while no reference to its use by the people is preserved. We also learn from the tablets that the occupations of the people were thoroughly organized and specialized; classes of artisans and workers are indicated by the occupational names recorded, which include: bronzesmiths, goldsmiths, potters, masons, carpenters, shipbuilders, flaxworkers, carders, spinners, weavers, fullers, unguent boilers, bakers, shepherds, bath-attendants, even a doctor. It is also evident from the tablets that slavery existed and we find slaves of the gods or goddesses, slaves in the service of officials, slaves of people, and even of a bronzesmith.[88] We may especially note that there is no reference to a class of scribes, although they must have been very useful to their rulers, nor are there on the tablets any signatures of scribes paralleling such found in Akkadian cuneiform documents. Yet Bennett has been able to prove that a number of scribes were responsible for the writing of contemporary tablets found in each site. At Mycenae alone, where a comparatively limited number of tablets has been found thus far, he was able to distinguish at least twelve different hands.[89] This seems to indicate that a class of scribes did exist, but that perhaps the "writing of a tablet was not a matter of pride to the scribe" and so he never affixed his name at the bottom of the record he compiled. It is interesting to note that, on sealings especially, we have the fingerprints of the scribe or handler and in a few cases we find that scribes were given to doodling.

The frequent mention of the *damos* in the Pylian tablets and the many *basileis* indicate perhaps that people lived in scattered villages, and not in the central area of Pylos which was the seat of the administration only; this seems to agree with the suggestion based on the excavated remains of Mycenaean sites

---

[85] Ruiperez, *Études mycéniennes*, pp. 105 ff. Palmer, *Interpretation*, glossary, p. 442, where references to *pa₂-si-re-u* and explanations, and p. 427 for the *ke-ro-si-ja*, its meaning and references.

[86] Perhaps there were other officials and nobles of similar stature and prerogatives for whom we have no information. We find for example on the tablets a man by the name of Echelawon who must have been a noble of great wealth and importance since his contribution recorded on tablet Un 718 (=171) is larger than that of a *damos* and immeasurably larger

than that of the *lawagetas*. That he was not a *wanax* is now generally accepted, but his exact social status remains unknown. Perhaps they were other nobles of similar stature whose existence we cannot confirm (Ventris-Chadwick, *op.cit.*, p. 267 and Page, *op.cit.*, p. 185).

[87] Ventris-Chadwick, *op.cit.*, pp. 232-274. Palmer, *Interpretation*, pp. 91-99.

[88] Ventris-Chadwick, *op.cit.*, p. 123.

[89] Bennett, *Mycenae Tablets*, III, pp. 68 ff.

that their people lived in small family groups or clans around the main citadel where the ruler had his palace. Again, this arrangement will demonstrate the supreme authority and power of the ruler who in the documents is called *wanax*.

The Divinity of the Wanax

It has been assumed that the Mycenaean king was considered divine, that he was the embodiment of the god.[90] His title *wanax*, upon which this concept is partially based was also used for a god or gods and, in many cases, it is not clear when the person referred to by title is a mortal king or a divinity. Palmer, for example, states that the *wanax* of Tablet Un 03 is "more likely to be divine than the earthly *wanax*" because he is the recipient of a "magnificent offering" and for no other objective reason. But he believes that the *wanax* of Tablet Un 219 is the earthly king and his association with the divinities mentioned there indicates his sacred character.[91] That tablet, however, seems to contain a list of divinities and their ministrant functionaries and we find the *wanax* mentioned before *po-ti-ni-ja*, e-[ra], and *em-ma-a*, that is, before Potnia, Hera, and Hermes. An earthly king would not have been placed at the head of a group of gods and it seems to us that in Tablet Un 219 the *wanax* mentioned is a god. Palmer in grouping the recipients of the tablet places the *wanax* in the group of the gods. Perhaps the title indicated only that the right to rule was granted the bearer by the god who was the real *wanax*.

The *wanax* possessed a *temenos* and this was conceived as strengthening the notion of his divine character. But it seems to us that in Mycenaean as well as in Homeric times the *temenos* did not have a religious connotation exclusively, as was the case in the classical period. The *temenos* was a cut or slice of land perhaps given to the *wanax* as a royal prerogative to enjoy, and to the *lawagetas* (the "leader of the host" or military commander), or may have been set aside for the benefit of a god so that its revenue could be used for his shrine. Even in Homeric times the secular meaning of the *temenos* was current. Then, too, we have *temenea* dedicated to the gods, but we have others belonging to mortals.

A *temenos* apparently was still the prerogative of kingship; thus the *temenos* placed by Hephaestos on the shield of Achilles is called βασιλήϊον (royal) (*Iliad*, XVIII, 550). Alkinoos, the King of Phaeacia, had a *temenos* (*Odyssey*, 6, 291 ff.); a *temenos* was allotted

to Bellerophontes, "to possess and enjoy it," when half of the kingdom was given to him (*Iliad*, VI, 194). The words spoken by Achilles over the body of Iphition (*Iliad*, XX, 389 ff.) seem to indicate that a *temenos* could be inherited, because he calls it the "demesne of thy father." And perhaps the *temenos* of Sarpedon was πατρώϊον (*Iliad*, XII, 313). A *temenos* was given by the people or was promised to valiant warriors not because they were divine but because of services rendered. Meleager was implored to "go forth and succour" his compatriots against the Kouretes; if he did so he would be given a mighty gift: "they bade him, where the plain of lovely Kalydon was fattest, there choose him out a fair tract (*temenos*) of fifty acres" (*Iliad*, IX, 577-578). He was to be given a *temenos* not because he was divine, but for services rendered; when he refused to render the service requested, he was not given the *temenos*. Achilles, apparently surprised by the stand of Aeneas, asks (*Iliad*, XX, 180 ff.): You take this hazardous stand because you hope to become the *wanax* of the Trojans, or because "the Trojans meted out for thee a *temenos* pre-eminent above all . . . that thou mayest possess it, if so be thou slayest me?" The Trojans would give a *temenos* to Aeneas not because they considered him divine, but because, by killing Achilles, he would have delivered them from a dangerous enemy. Thus, even in Homeric times the *temenos*, given by the people to a hero, was in return for services rendered and had a secular significance. It seems evident that we cannot conclude that the *wanax* of the Mycenaeans was considered divine or was given divine honors just because he had a *temenos*.

There is no evidence whatever to suggest that the royal title *wanax* implied a divine status. Even in Homeric times, when that title was predominantly given to the gods, it did not indicate divinity when given to mortals. Certainly Agamemnon was not considered the embodiment of a god because he was called ἄναξ ἀνδρῶν. It seems that even then the *wanax* was the superior and the *basileus* the inferior title and naturally enough to the god was given the superior title. Page points out that in Homeric poetry "the older distinction of the titles became confused, for the epic gives the title *basileus* to men who were clearly—in the Mycenaean sense—*wanaktes*." I do believe that the older distinction was carefully kept in the epic, although the importance of the inferior title *basileus* was increased.[92]

The Trojan expedition was a common undertaking

---

[90] See for example T. B. L. Webster, *From Mycenae to Homer*, pp. 11, 22, 53, 100, etc. Palmer, *Interpretation*, p. 267. Ventris-Chadwick, *op.cit.*, p. 266 Er. 01.

[91] Palmer, *op.cit.*, pp. 249, 258-259, 267. Unfortunately I was unable to find and read B. Hemberg's, ΑΝΑΞ, ΑΝΑΣΣΑ *und*

ΑΝΑΚΤΕΣ *als Götternamen*, Uppsala, Univ., Arsskript, 1955.

[92] Page, *op.cit.*, p. 188. As we have seen, in Mycenaean documents the title "basileus," or *pa-si-re-u*, was given to less important, perhaps provincial officials. The title and the office may have become very important after the breaking up of

placed under the command of one man. In a way this command was comparable to a state with one supreme ruler. Many chieftains participated in the expedition by contributing their armies, the way many officials in a state contributed their services to govern the various areas of the state. But the commander of the expedition was the supreme authority; he was the *wanax* of the expedition, while the others, so far as the expedition was concerned, and that is the theme of the epic, are of inferior rank. Agamemnon was the acknowledged leader of the expedition and he alone is called ἄναξ ἀνδρῶν; his usual title is *wanax*. Occasionally, indeed very sparingly, the title *wanax* is given to the one or the other of the chieftains under him in the expedition, and often when absolute authority over certain matters or their home states is to be indicated. Thus in the *Iliad* (XVI, 172) it is stated that over his 50 ships and men Achilles placed as leaders five ἡγεμόνας, but he kept the supreme authority over his own contingent; he was the *wanax* of his force: ἤνασσε. In the *Odyssey* (I, 392 ff.), Telemachos states that one of the basileis, who are many in Ithaka, may succeed Odysseus as the ruler of the state but, he says, "I will be the *wanax* of my own house." Only Agamemnon as a rule is generally given the title *wanax*. A preliminary account reveals the fact that at least 49 times this title is given to the supreme commander. The way Achilles talks to him, and even the young Diomedes, certainly does not imply that his title and his office conveyed to Agamemnon a divine status: "Folk-devouring king, seeing thou rulest over men of naught," storms Achilles,[93] while the youthful Diomedes in full assembly tells him "with the scepter hath [Zeus] granted thee to be honored above all, but valor he gave thee not." Certainly accusing a leader of lack of strength and of cowardice in the presence of his army, which applauds the statement ("and all the sons of Achaeans shouted aloud, applauding the words of Diomedes") is not an indication of divine honors or status awarded to the ἄναξ ἀνδρῶν, who only is honored more than the others.

It is furthermore assumed that a reminiscence of the divine status of the *wanax* survives in Homeric terminology.[94] The epithets δῖος, διοτρεφής, ἀντίθεος, διογενής, ἀθανάτοισιν ὁμοῖος, etc. and statements such as "men gaze upon him as upon a god," are taken to be surviving echoes of the Mycenaean attitude towards their rulers. However, they can be proved to be poetic exaggerations and merely indicate honors accorded not only to rulers but to other mortals. No one will take seriously epithets given today by the Greeks and found in their literature to beloved persons or capable leaders and even politicians of doubtful virtue: statements such as "I worshipped her as a goddess," "my holy virgin and my angel," "we followed him blindly as a god," etc. are common expressions of exaggerated devotion and loyalty. Similarly the term ἀντίθεος for example is not only given to Odysseus, but also to his fictitious followers "who yielding to wantonness," wasted the lands of the Egyptians, and carried off women and little children and slew the men.[95] Polyphemos the Cyclops is called ἀντίθεος (*Odyssey*, 1, 70) but later (*Odyssey*, 9, 428 and 494), he is characterized as "savage man—that monster, with his heart set on lawlessness."

Not only Agamemnon, Achilles, Odysseus, "were honored as gods" but also the fictitious Cretan father of Odysseus, whose only qualifications were that he was a rich man and not a ruler or in any way connected with gods or famous warriors; he was also "at that time honored as a god among the Cretans in the land for his good estate, and his wealth, and his glorious sons."[96] The expression indicates respect and honor, but in no sense can it be construed to indicate divinity or divine honors bestowed upon kings.

Neither the tablets nor Homeric terminology would indicate that divine honors were paid to the supreme ruler of a Mycenaean state, to the *wanax* or any other of his officials. He certainly enjoyed the prerogatives of his position, but he does not seem to have been considered divine, as far as we can find out to date either from the written documents or from the remains of his palaces and citadels. The possible existence of a shrine in the palace gave rise to the assumption that the Mycenaeans believed that their gods and goddesses, who occasionally dwelt in these shrines, lived with the king in the palace and this led to the further assumption that the king was therefore considered as divine. The shrine of Asine, found in a simple house, and the shrine of Berbati would indicate the fallacy of the assumption, since then we have to assume that the

---

the Mycenaean states in the course of the eleventh and tenth centuries B.C.; then the official of a small section, of a village even, became the only ruler and hence the most important man of the place, a real king.

93 *Iliad*, I, 231. Yet Achilles recognized that Agamemnon alone had the power to issue orders to the army at large when he asks the king to rouse the Achaeans to battle (*Iliad*, XIX, 68 ff.) and in XXIII, 156 he tells him "σοὶ γάρ τε μάλιστά γε λαὸς Ἀχαιῶν / πείσονται μύθοισι." See also Odysseus' statement to

Agamemnon in *Iliad*, XIV, 84 ff. where not a word of divine status for the *wanax* is added.

94 Webster, *Companion to Homer*, p. 455.

95 *Odyssey*, 14, 246 ff.

96 *Odyssey*, XIV, 205. Odysseus was to be honored as a God by the Phaeacians and yet Euryalos insults him (*Odyssey*, VIII, 159 ff.) and in answer Odysseus makes a most illuminating statement, *loc.cit.* 169 ff.

owners of these houses, too, who were not *wanaktes*, were considered divine, as hosts of gods and goddesses.

Commercial Activities

In spite of the existence of the *lawagetas*, the *wanax* must have been the supreme commander of the army, since in a state of warriors the command of the armed forces is its most important office. That the Mycenaeans were warriors is generally accepted. Their mighty citadels, their weapons, their delight in representing war and hunting scenes in works of art, their traditions filled with wars and expeditions prove definitely their military character.[97] But they were expert sailors and merchants as well. The texts of the tablets seem to indicate that the *wanax* was in control of the commercial and artistic activities of the state. He rationed metal to the smiths and spices to the unguent boilers; detailed accounts were kept for him of all activities. Beginning with the sixteenth century B.C. a great overseas commercial activity was initiated,[98] and its volume increased constantly until, in the fourteenth and thirteenth centuries, it encompassed the comparatively vast area from Sicily and the Aeolian island of Lipari to Troy and Miletos, to Syria and Egypt. It is possible to assume that commercial outposts were then established along the coasts of the central and eastern Mediterranean, a typical example of which we find at Minet-el-Beida, the port town of Ras Shamra. We even seem to have documentary evidence of their activity along the coast of Syria in the second half of the thirteenth century B.C. In a treaty between the Hittite Emperor Tuthalijas IV (ca. 1250-1220 B.C.) and a prince of Amurry, it is stipulated that "no ship may sail to him [the king of Assyria] from the land of Ahhiyavā."[99]

Commodities which they traded must have included pottery, perfumed oil, even olive oil, wine, objects of art such as sculptured ivory plaques, pottery, objects made of bronze, and trinkets of faïence.[100] In exchange, the Mycenaean merchant would bring home metal ore—gold, copper, and tin—spices, elephant tusks from Syria, textiles, and perhaps purple dyes extracted from murex shells. Canaanite jars found in Mycenaean sites would indicate importation of some liquid commodity requiring such vessels;[101] the names of spices, such as *sa-se-me* (=sesame), *ku-mi-no* (=cumin) etc., would prove their importation from Semitic lands; the name of the commonest Greek garment, *ki-to* (=chiton) linen garment, may indicate not only the importation of textiles, but also the means by which the motifs of the griffin, of the sphinx, and of the palm trees became known and were incorporated into the repertory of the Mycenaean artist. We cannot be as certain for the dye from murex shells, since remnants of shells proving the manufacture of dye found in Crete and at the site of Aghios Kosmas in Attika seem to indicate a local production. The name, however, *po-ni-ki*, crimson color, may indicate Semitic origin of the process.

Whether grain was also one of the commodities imported on a regular basis, as it has been assumed recently, cannot be proved.[102] There is absolutely no evidence corroborating the assumption, and the suggested grain imports seem to be imaginary. If such an activity did exist, we would expect to find a record or even a hint of some detail in the tablets that cover such a variety of activities. The supposition that importation of grain was indispensable for feeding the large population of the mainland in Mycenaean times is a mere speculation. The allocations of seed to a variety of people recorded on the tablets indicate that the land was under cultivation, and the areas of Pylos, Mycenae, and Thebes were sufficient to provide for the needs of a large population. Even in classical times these areas were self-supporting. So few sites have been excavated sufficiently to permit an approximate estimate of their people that we cannot know what the population of Greece was in the Heroic age. For over three-quarters of a century scholars have been digging the soil of Mycenae, but no one as yet has ventured to state what the population of that city was in the days of Agamemnon. We noted at the very beginning of our study that the Mycenaeans lived in small family groups surrounded by the graves of their ancestors; cities in the modern sense of the word, i.e. an agglomeration of houses of the entire population, did not

---

[97] For a concise account of war see now Taylour, *The Mycenaeans*, pp. 139-165.

[98] We may recall the vases of LH I in Egypt proved by Wace and Blegen to be Mycenaean (*Klio*, 1939, p. 147). Also the incised dagger on one of the menhirs of the outer circle of Stonehenge stated to be Mycenaean, but see O.G.S. Crawford, "The Symbols Carved on Stonehenge," *Antiquity*, 28 (1954), pp. 25-31.

[99] Sommer, *Die Ahhijava-Urkunden*, pp. 320-327, document XVII, iv, 23. For an excellent and concise account of Mycenaean commerce cf. S. Immerwahr, "Mycenaean Trade and Colonization," *Archaeology*, 13 (1960), pp. 4 ff. Also S. Marinatos, "The Minoan and Mycenaean Civilization and Its Influence on the Mediterranean and Europe," *VI Congresso dell Scienze Preist.*

Protoistoriche I, 1961, pp. 161 ff. H. Kantor, *The Aegean and the Near East in the Second Millennium B.C.*, 1948. M. Cavalier, "Les cultures préhistoriques des îles Éoliennes et leur rapport avec le monde Égéen," *BCH*, 84 (1960), pp. 319 ff.

[100] Most common are the segmented faïence beads found over a wide area. *Supra*, p. 197. Perhaps a good many of them are due to local middlemen rather than to actual visits of Mycenaean merchants. Similarly, the Baltic amber found in Mycenaean territory could have reached the area through a series of local middlemen.

[101] V. R. Grace, "The Canaanite Jar," *The Aegean and Near East*, pp. 80-109.

[102] E. Vermeule, *Archaeology*, 13 (1960), p. 66 and *Greece in the Bronze Age*, p. 257, where the suggestion is repeated.

exist then. The system followed by the Mycenaeans yields the impression of large areas occupied by a great number of people, but in actuality the total of people whose existence is usually surmised from a few sherds found in surface exploration or even from pots discovered in a trench or two or in widely scattered tombs, may have been very small. Our present knowledge of settlements derived from complete excavations is so small that it permits no conclusions on the matter. The evidence at hand would certainly indicate that the important Mycenaean areas of Messenia, Lakonia, Argolis, Corinthia, Boiotia, Thessaly-Magnesia, even if they were well populated, would not have felt the need of importing grain from abroad. Their own produce would have been sufficient to fill their needs.

Trading Posts

The commercial activity of the Mycenaeans resulted in the establishment of trading posts along the routes their sailors followed to reach the rich lands of Syria and Egypt. Some of these posts developed into veritable colonies and centers from which their culture and their people spread in ever-widening circles. In this they followed the example of the Minoans, who preceded them and whose trading posts and functions they took over, especially after the fall of Minoan Knossos.[103] Very instructive in this respect is Rhodes, an island strategically situated on the route to Syria and Egypt. There we find a Minoan settlement near the modern site of Trianda. In LH II times not far from the Minoan site a Mycenaean trading post was established, and its people lived for some time in peace and amity with the Cretan settlers. Then the Minoan village disappeared, while the Mycenaean flourished; its people, and others arriving from the mainland, spread all over the island and transformed it into a Mycenaean state of such importance that, as we have seen, it has been equated with the Ahhiyavā of the Hittite documents.

We find the same situation at Miletos on the southwest coast of Asia Minor, where a Cretan settlement was established in LM I times. Shortly afterwards it was destroyed, and its site was taken over by Mycenaeans, who controlled it to the end of the age. As a matter of fact, in LH III B times they surrounded their settlement with a Cyclopean *peribolos* wall. In Cyprus Mycenaean merchants lived among the people of the island, influencing their art, especially in LH III B times, and in LH III C the island was thickly inhabited by Mycenaeans. The island of Kos presents the same picture with an increase of relics in LH III C times. It was natural for the Mycenaeans to be preoccupied with the East, with Syria and Egypt, with areas rich and culturally advanced. But they did not neglect the West, and we find their products in Sicily, and especially in southern Italy; in the neighborhood of modern Taranto (at the Scoglio del Tonno), they established a colony which perhaps served as the focal point of their activity in the West.

The Question of Empire

Whether the state over which presided the *wanax* of Mycenae or of any other area could be called an empire, as is sometimes done, is a question which can be answered definitely. The tablets found at Pylos, and as a matter of fact those from Knossos, indicate that the archon of that state was not under the domination of a mightier ruler, as would have been the case if a Mycenaean empire did exist. The pottery of LH III B, on which the concept is based, presents a strong argument against the assumed view of the empire. The so-called pictorial style developed not only in Cyprus but also in Rhodes, and its export to lands as far west as southern Italy would indicate the independence of the workshops of the islands and of their commercial activity at a time when it is believed that art products and articles to be exported were completely controlled by the *wanax*. All surviving traditions that go back to the Mycenaean era speak of independent states with independent rulers: Thebes with its kings is independent of Athens and its reputed rulers, of Mycenae, and the mighty Atreides. Nowhere does the memory exist of a unified state with overseas dependencies which could be termed an empire. Even Knossos, which seemed to be in the hands of Mycenaeans in LM II times, had a ruler, a *wanax*, independent of the mainland monarchs. I believe that it is misleading to call the Mycenaean state an empire, its rulers emperors, and its capital an empire city. Instead we must conceive the mainland of Greece as composed of a number of independent states, corresponding to the city states of the Historic Era, ruled by a *wanax*.

The survey of the evidence contained in the tablets gives us a glimpse into the political, religious, and social system prevalent in Mycenaean times at least in Pylos and supplements the picture offered by the excavated archaeological remains. Indeed, many gaps exist in the picture, but even at its present stage it gives us a striking and clear conception of a vigorous and brilliant culture that can stand comparison with any known contemporary civilization. We can learn very little about the Mycenaean culture and people from the writings of their neighbors. The references

---

[103] Cf. Stubbings, "The Expansion of Mycenaean Civilization," rev. ed., *CAH*, I and II, fasc. 26, pp. 18-20.

detected in Egyptian inscriptions are vague and impossible to verify.[104] The hopes based on the Hittite documents have been reduced to the single fact of the existence of a state known as Ahhiyavā, the state of the Achaeans, in the closing centuries of the Hittite Empire.[105] Years ago, I suggested that these documents permit the assumption of the existence of two states under that name, one on the coast of Asia Minor and another beyond the coast of that land.[106] On the coast of Asia Minor a Mycenaean settlement, that of Miletos, has been definitely proved by excavations. Another is indicated by chamber tombs in the district of Halikarnassos.[107] The Ahhiyavā beyond the sea has been equated with the Island of Rhodes where late Mycenaean settlements flourished, or the mainland of Greece itself.[108] The name preserved on the Hittite documents and the uninterrupted progress of Mycenaean culture to the very end of the period will perhaps justify the attribution of the name Achaeans to the people who produced this Mycenaean culture although nowhere in their own written documents does the name appear. The question of the relation of the Mycenaean culture to that depicted in the epic poetry of Homer is a special study which cannot find a place here.[109]

[104] Breasted, *Ancient Records*, III, §306, §349, §576, §600 and IV, §64.

[105] The exciting suggestions made by E. Forrer, "Vorhomerische Griechen in dem Keilschrifttexben von Boghaz-Koï," *Mitt. der d. Orientges.*, 63 (1924), have been proved untenable: Sommer, "Ahhijava und kein Ende?," *IGForsch*, 55 (1937), pp. 169 ff. See also his *Die Ahhijava-Urkunden, Abhand., der Bayer. Akad. der Wiss., phil.-hist. Abt.*, 6 (1932), pp. 1-469.

[106] Mylonas, *Ephemeris*, 1930, p. 22.

[107] G. Bass, *AJA*, 67 (1963), pp. 353-361.

[108] See Page, *op.cit.*, pp. 8 ff. and 35 n. 53. Rhodes as Ahhiyavā was suggested by Hronzy, *AO.*, 1 (1929), pp. 323 ff., but the suggestion was rejected by F. Schachermeyr, *Hethiter und Achäer*, pp. 129 ff., although he admitted that the island fulfills most of the conditions required. It is championed now by Denys L. Page. Schachermeyr's conclusions that Ahhiyavā was a mainland kingdom with Mycenae as its capital were in turn rejected by Page.

[109] Books dealing with the subject are Denys L. Page, *History and the Homeric Iliad*, 1959; Wace and Stubbings, *A Companion to Homer*, 1962; and the definitive work of H. Lorimer, *Homer and the Monuments*, 1950. I hope to add to this list a book of my own in the future.

EPILOGUE: THE END OF AN AGE

"The day shall come when sacred Ilios shall be laid low and
Priam and the people of Priam with good spear of ash."
(*Iliad*, IV, 164-165. Tr. A. T. Murray)

As a glowing fire emits its last bright flame before it dies, so the brilliant achievement of the Mycenaeans, which we have outlined, gave its last spark in the course of the thirteenth century and then, gradually in some parts, abruptly in others, faded away. The remains of the Palace of Nestor at Pylos, the constructions carried out at Mycenae and Tiryns around the middle and in the latter half of that century, the amazing Treasury of Atreus and the so-called Tomb of Klytemnestra, the contents of buildings outside the walls, the construction of roads across valleys and mountains, the erection of the walls of the Akropolis of Athens and its underground fountain, all these testify to an activity and prosperity that has not been properly stressed. From the thirteenth century B.C. there is evidence of misfortune and destructions: parts of palaces destroyed or damaged by fire or other causes were rebuilt and renovated, entire buildings were burned down or were destroyed by earthquakes and some of them were never rebuilt; but the activity evident in parts as far removed as Pylos and Mycenae, Athens and Iolkos, does indicate that almost to the end of the thirteenth century prosperity flourished in the Mycenaean area.

Pottery discovered from Syria and Egypt to the northwest coast of Asia Minor, from Rhodes and Cyprus to South Italy and Sicily, indicates a continued and uninterrupted commercial activity to the end of the century. Conversely, ivory and gold objects found in the Mycenaean area or attested to by inscriptions, and the various oriental spices recorded on tablets which date from the latter half or the closing years of that century, prove the constant and presumably profitable commercial connections with the east. Recalling the numerous art objects of ivory found by Wace in the House of the Sphinxes and the House of Shields, by Stamatakes in the chamber tombs at Spata, by Blegen in the Palace of Nestor, by Tsountas in the grave of the dromos of the Tomb of Klytemnestra and in the chamber tombs he excavated at Mycenae, by us in the citadel of Mycenae, and conversely, imported objects from the Mycenaean world, the thirteenth cen-

tury ivory plaques with the magnificent couchant griffin in the treasury of Meggido,[1] we realize the close connections which continued to exist between that world and the ancient middle east to about 1200 B.C.

The Mycenaean area throughout the thirteenth century B.C. is a world of warriors, artisans, and merchants engaged in vast activity, enjoying great prosperity, carrying out a successful and widespread overseas enterprise. Whether or not this world was politically integrated cannot be definitely demonstrated; whether or not the Ahhiyava of the Hittite documents can be equated with an empire centered in the mainland or with a kingdom existing in the island of Rhodes cannot be decided with certainty; but the tablets from Pylos seem to indicate the existence of separate political entities on the mainland, independent of each other, each under its own king known as the *wanax*, with a definite hierarchy and an elaborate, centralized, bureaucratic government. The Argolid seems to us to have been the most important area, the one which exercised leadership in artistic, cultural, and commercial activities. Within its territory we find the awe-inspiring citadels of Mycenae and Tiryns, the most impressive group of tholos tombs, a road system without a parallel in the mainland, a good number of settlements exhibiting a high level of artistic activity, and great prosperity. Its potters apparently set the standards and styles followed closely by others. The capital of that section, Mycenae, is without doubt the most important and one of the most strategically located cities of the period. The ruler of Mycenae, its *wanax*, must have been preeminent among the other rulers of the times. It is, I believe, interesting and instructive to note that this preeminence is remembered in the traditions preserved by epic poetry. It is the king of Mycenae who in the *Iliad* is called "the most kingly of all" and "the *wanax* of men"; he is the leader of the expedition against Troy—the first expedition, according to Thucydides, undertaken in common by the Greeks. The same historian very cogently remarked, "It was, as I think, because Agamemnon surpassed in power the princes of his time that he was

[1] H. J. Kantor, *Archaeology*, 13 (1960), pp. 18-19 and fig. 9. In August 1965 we discovered hundreds of discarded chips of ivory proving that the ivory carvers were still at work when the

east wing of the palace was destroyed in the years of transition from LH III B to LH III C times.

able to assemble his fleet, and not so much because Helen's suitors whom he led, were bound by oath to Tyndareus" (I, 9. 1). The king of Mycenae contributed the most to the common military enterprise. Immediately after him Nestor should be ranged, since the king of Pylos contributed to the common cause the largest number of ships after Agamemnon. It is again interesting to remark that the territory included in Nestor's domain is now being proved by Blegen and Marinatos to be a most important center of Mycenaean art and activity, second only to the Argolid.

With the turn of the century the picture changed. As a result of many destructions apparently the old centers in the mainland fell on evil days. The great citadels of Mycenae and Tiryns still raised their defiant silhouettes against the Greek sky and behind their Cyclopean walls people continued to live, but their power and activities were reduced. A decline set in which gradually led to a final catastrophe that marks the end of the Mycenaean Age. In the twelfth century began the dying out that ended in the final eclipse of the Mycenaean civilization.

It has been stated with reason that the population of the Argolid and of other great centers of the Mycenaean world was reduced in that century of decline. Small settlements were abandoned, and perhaps a good many of the inhabitants migrated to other lands, to Achaia in the Peloponnesos, and especially to the islands beyond the east coast of the mainland. What brought about the destructions characterizing the end of the thirteenth century, the depopulation, the decline, and the final catastrophe? Some attribute these disasters to the successive incursions of northern people to which the general name of the Dorian Invasion has been given. Others believe that it was brought about by incursions of the people forming what has come to be known as the Illyrian migration. Others suggest that internal struggle and civil strife were responsible for the decline. Still others attribute it to the breaking down of the security of the seas and the consequent disruption of commercial activities brought about by the reputed movements of the mysterious Sea Peoples of the Egyptian inscriptions. To account for the end of the age and the dark centuries which followed an uprising of the people against their rulers has been suggested, and a great earthquake with tidal waves which inundated the shores, destroying cities and trees. We shall discuss all these suggestions later but may we emphasize that regardless of the cause Mycenaean power and civiliza-

tion began to decline with the opening of the twelfth century B.C. and came to an end before the close of that century.

The memory of events which preceded and followed the decline of Mycenaean power and civilization is preserved in a good many legends to be found in the writers of later ages. It is generally agreed that legends and myths should not be treated as historic facts, but that they contain some kernel of truth, that they may have originated in some unrecorded fact, is only occasionally and grudgingly admitted. There are those who would reject legends as a source of information and yet they use certain of these legends in their reconstruction of the early history of Greece. For example, the so-called Dorian invasion is generally treated if not as an established historic fact at least as a fixed starting point for the history of Greece. And yet our knowledge of that event is entirely based upon legends and tradition; I know of no contemporary inscription or written document specifically mentioning the event. Lately, it has been assumed that certain tablets from Pylos which refer to military and naval operations are sure indications of the Dorian menace. However, there is not a particle of evidence justifying the assumption. The records most probably indicate precautionary measures extant for some time, taken by a king whose palace rose on top of a hill unprotected by fortification walls; a palace that would have been an easy prey to an assaulting piratical expeditionary force if it was allowed to land undetected on the sandy shores of Pylos.[2] Every literary reference to the "Dorian Invasion" belongs to years removed by centuries from the event.

In spite of the fact that the scholar in using legends is open to attack from unsympathetic quarters, they have to be used, at least as pointers, since they are the only literary remnants we have from the Heroic Age of Greece. It would be difficult to maintain that they should be summarily rejected until their truth is proved by definite archaeological remains, although this may be preferable to the habit of rejecting some while adopting others with our temporary needs and predilections serving as the only guide. And let us also remember that it is still more objectionable to create myths of migrations and conquests which are not substantiated by definite archaeological evidence. But let us see what are the facts and the legendary evidence available in our search for the causes of the end of the Mycenaean preeminence and the identity of the people who brought about that end.

[2] See on these tablets now D. L. Page, *History and the Homeric Iliad*, pp. 193-196, and Palmer, *Interpretation*, pp. 105 ff.

THE TROY OF PRIAM

The decline of Mycenaean power and culture was ushered in by the Trojan War, an event with which ancient Greek history begins and in which the people of Mycenae and their rulers played an important part. Long considered a legendary exploit, it can now, in the opinion of the majority, be considered as historic fact. The definitive excavation of the site of Hissarlik by Blegen and the Cincinnati expeditions has made it possible to accept the settlement known as Troy VIIa as the city of Priam; its burned and destroyed buildings stand as an eloquent proof of the historicity of the event.[3] Schachermeyr has projected the view that Troy VIh and not VIIa was Priam's city. Some other scholars have followed his view.[4] In my study "Priam's Troy and the Date of its Fall," I have explained why I maintain that all the available evidence, archaeological and historical, proves that the city ruled over by Priam, the Homeric Troy (if ever such a city existed, and I believe that it did) can be no other than the citadel known as Troy VIIa.

Precisely when that citadel, Troy VIIa, was destroyed has not been established as yet to the satisfaction of all scholars, in spite of Blegen's systematic and successful excavations and exemplary publications. In their final report the excavators concluded that Troy VIIa, that is Priam's Troy, lasted from about 1275 (?) B.C. to about 1240 B.C.[5] In his article on Troy, included in the revised edition of Volume I and II of the *Cambridge Ancient History*, Blegen states that "the fall of Troy and the end of Settlement VIIa should be placed about 1250 B.C., coinciding with the estimate of Herodotus. In any event, the expedition against Troy must surely have been carried out about the middle of the ceramic phase III B." In the latest statement on the matter, included in his lecture "The Mycenaean Age," delivered in memory of Louise Taft Semple, Blegen expressed the view that Troy VIIa, "the Homeric Troy, if there ever was one . . . was sacked and burned before the middle stage of the ceramic style III B," that ". . . it came to its end by enemy action in the decade around 1270 or 1260."[6] This variety of dates, advanced within the last ten years, during which no new evidence related to the LH III B

ceramic phase has been found, seems to indicate that the absolute choronology of the Fall of Troy cannot be established with a degree of certainty on the basis of the remains unearthed on the hill of Hissarlik.[7] If, instead of adding upwards the two or three decades we placed them downwards we would reach the end of the thirteenth century, and it seems to us that nothing compels us to add them upwards only.

In my study of Priam's Troy, I have demonstrated, I believe, that the Homeric city is proved to have been destroyed at the end of the ceramic phase known as Late Helladic III B and before the beginning of Late Helladic III C, at the very end of the thirteenth century B.C., by the Mycenaean pottery found in settlements VIh, VIIa, and VIIb-1, and by the sequence in the stratigraphy of VIIa and VIIb-1. The remains of Mycenae will make improbable the placing of this destruction at an earlier date. Furthermore, the final destruction of Mycenaean Thebes, which, according to the established tradition, occurred in the generation that later saw the storming of Priam's city by the Achaeans, will also indicate the end of the century for that conquest. Then it was that, under pressure of the impending invasion of their land, the people of Troy VIIa who were living in the countryside flocked into their fortified citadel and hastily built temporary homes in the available free spaces. In the floors of these flimsy structures they placed capacious pithoi in which supplies could be stored in anticipation of a long siege.

The conditions revealed by the spades of the excavators seem to reflect in a surprising way the legends of the Achaean expedition against Troy. According to those legends preparations for that expedition lasted for a long time. The people of Troy VIIa would have learned of those preparations since, as the imported pottery found in their city proves, they had commercial relations with the Mycenaean world. Characteristically, the amount of imported pottery found in Troy VIIa is very much smaller than that discovered in Troy VI; this would be natural since no importations from the land of their enemies was possible when their citadel was besieged by the Achaeans. Troy VIIa

---

[3] C. W. Blegen *et al.*, *Troy, Settlements VIIa, VIIb and VIII*, IV, 1958, pp. 10-13.

[4] F. Schachermeyr, *Poseidon*, 1950, pp. 189 ff.; in *Minoica*, p. 368. C. Nylander, "The Fall of Troy," *Antiquity*, 37 (1963), pp. 6-11. G. E. Mylonas, *Hesperia*, 33 (1964), pp. 352-380.

[5] *Troy*, IV, p. 12. They added, however: "We feel that the exact equation of the successive styles of Mycenaean pottery with specific terms of years has not yet been definitely established, but is still subject to shifts of a decade or two. Any such change would impose a corresponding adjustment in our dates for Phase VIh and perhaps for the beginning of Troy

VIIa." Since the publication of the volume, 1958, no new evidence has been unearthed that would necessitate the change of the "specific terms of years" the succession of styles followed at the time of writing the above.

[6] *CAH*, I-II, rev. edn., Blegen, fasc. 1, "Troy," p. 14; Blegen, "The Mycenaean Age," pp. 15 and 27-28.

[7] It should be noted that the date is based completely on pottery imported from the Mycenaean territory and not on local evidence, or on data based on importations from areas whose products can be dated more accurately than the Mycenaean of the LH III A, B, and C periods.

was defended valiantly, but was finally captured and destroyed by fire. According to the legends, Agamemnon's army sailed for home after the destruction, leaving the charred ruins of Priam's city to the survivors. The excavators report that the destroyers of Troy VIIa did not establish themselves in the citadel they captured and in the land it controlled. "In VIIb-1," that is, in the settlement built over the ruins of Priam's city, they write, "we are dealing with an immediate reoccupation of the site by the survivors who somehow escaped the disaster that laid the citadel of Troy VIIa in smoldering ruins." According to its excavators the new settlement, built immediately after the destruction of Priam's city by the survivors of the Trojan War "comes in with, but does not outlast, the Granary Class of Mycenaean pottery."[8] In other words, the settlement which succeeded Troy VIIa belongs to the twelfth century B.C. to which the Granary ware also belongs. Consequently, Troy VIIa, which preceded Troy VIIb-1, has to come down to the end of the thirteenth century B.C.

THE HITTITES AND THE TROJAN WAR

Not only the date and the locality of the Homeric city, but also the cause of the war between the Achaeans and the Trojans has been the subject of many learned discussions. Page has recently maintained that the historical background of the Trojan War is to be found "in the conflict between rival forces, Achaeans and the League of Assuwa, over the territory at long last vacated by the Hittites."[9] The territory was vacated in the closing years of the reign of Tuthalijas IV (ca. 1250-1220) or in the course of the reign of his successor Arnuwandas IV (ca. 1220-ca. 1190 B.C.). This is indicated by the documents recording the conflicts of Emperor Tuthalijas IV with the League of Assuwa and with Kukkulis, the son of the King of Assuwa, whom he spared in his first successful campaign. Page points out that the territory of the League must be placed on the western coast of Asia Minor north of Miletos and somewhat south of Troy, "in the valley of Kaikos or Hermos or Kaÿster," and he concludes "that the Achaeans attacked Troy soon after the defeat of Assuwa by Tuthalijas, perhaps within a decade (either way) of 1230 B.C." Evidently he reached that conclusion under the influence of the date suggested for the fall of Priam's Troy by its excavator, since he admits the possibility that the final fall of Assuwa may have occurred in the days of Arnuwandas IV. If this was the case, then the territory was not vacated by the Hittites until after ca. 1220 B.C. and consequently the conflict between Achaeans and the members of the League over the territory which forms the historical background of the Trojan War could not have started until after that date.

Of course the weight and value of the information to be derived from the Hittite documents depends largely on the equation Truisa=Troja=Troy, which is possible to assume, and on the identification of the territory of the Assuwa League, which is, I believe, well defined by Page. But even without those equations we learn that after ca. 1250 B.C., the date Tuthalijas assumed office, he was still powerful enough to subdue a rebellion in Arzawa and to defeat twice the collected armies of the League of Assuwa, of some twenty-two places located to the north of the Arzawa territory.[10] And one is justified in wondering whether a powerful Hittite emperor would have allowed an incursion of Asia Minor in the decade around 1270 or 1260 or even 1240 and whether the Trojans, who, according to the tradition, sought and obtained help from so many territories, would not have appealed for help to the most powerful emperor in Asia Minor, an emperor who could have successfully faced the Achaean army. Kukkulis' rebellion, which must have occurred after the lapse of some time, and the successful second campaign of the Hittite king would indi-

---

[8] C. W. Blegen *et al.*, *Troy*, IV, pp. 142, 146.

[9] Page, *op.cit.*, pp. 102-110. Our details have been drawn from his discussion. See especially his footnotes on pp. 114-117. Also G. Huxley, *Achaeans and Hittites*, 1960, pp. 29 ff.

[10] Page maintains that Kukkulis was set as a vassal ruler over some territory other than that of Assuwa, since, as he writes, it would be "an incredible coincidence, if the numbers of his infantry and chariots were exactly the same as those captured by the Hittites in the previous campaign." But it would be unbelievable also to assume that Kukkulis, placed as a vassal ruler over some strange territory, was able to stir into rebellion all the 10,000 infantry taken as captives in the first campaign and to master every single one of the chariots the Assuwans lost in their first attempt against the Hittite emperor. It is logical to assume that those prisoners were dispersed and were not in the area over which Kukkulis ruled so as to "be stirred by him to rebellion"; that a good many may have even been kept at Hattusas and used for the needs of the emperor and his nobility and consequently beyond the reach of Kukkulis. Furthermore, it would be difficult to maintain that the captured chariots were not incorporated in the Hittite army and placed under the control of Hittite warriors and lords. The round numbers given would also indicate that they do not correspond strictly to the fact but are general and perhaps a favorite quotation. The numbers, however, do indicate that Kukkulis's army was much smaller than that used in the first campaign, and this would be a natural consequence of the devastation of Assuwa and the capture and death of so many of its people in the course of the disastrous first campaign. Even that smaller army Kukkulis could have mastered only after some years of recuperation and only in his ancestral lands where he and his family were known and where the people felt allegiance to him.

cate that the withdrawal of the Hittite power from the territory had not as yet taken place in the decades suggested and any Achaean invasion so soon after the rebellion of Assuwa would have caused Hittite intervention.[11]

It would also be inconceivable that Kukkulis would have attempted a revolt against the Hittite emperor, who still was powerful, if an Achaean army was on the northwest coast of Asia Minor besieging Troy or had just left after devastating the territory. Again, we could wonder whether after the fall of Troy, if placed in the decade around 1270 or 1260 or 1240, and the devastation of its territory as well as that of the lands to the south, the people of Assuwa could have mustered such an army to fight against the Hittites as that indicated by the number of prisoners. Besides, it seems very reasonable to assume that the Achaeans, taking advantage of the weakening of the possible allies of the Trojans through their repeated defeats and the devastation of the lands of Assuwa at the hands of the Hittites, attempted their expedition against Troy. In this connection it may be pointed out that in Book II of the *Iliad*, where Priam's allies are listed, the central part of West Asia Minor is represented only by the Maeonians, "whose birth was beneath Tmolos" (B, 864-866). Could this indicate the result of the repeated invasions and devastations of that central area by the Hittites in the course of their two campaigns against the League of Assuwa? It is also interesting to note that the Phrygians, listed among Priam's allies, are not mentioned in the Hittite documents. Perhaps their pressure had not begun in the days of Tuthalijas IV.

We must, of course, admit that final conclusions should not be based on evidence that is not altogether free of uncertainty, and if one is willing he can find such uncertainties in the Hittite documents; but we must also maintain that the indications to be adduced from that source should not be ignored, especially if the indications are not in conflict with the proven facts obtained from excavations. The indications from the Hittite documents seem to favor the conclusion that the Trojan War occurred after 1230 B.C., and possibly even after ca. 1220 B.C.

The fall and destruction of Thebes is another event that took place in the course of the Mycenaean Age. It is little remembered because any epic poetry that

may have been composed to celebrate its details has not been preserved. The story of its fall is known from tradition and is reflected in the work of the tragedians of the fifth century B.C. We hear that after the failure of a first attempt, Thebes was sacked by the sons of the leaders who had failed, by the *Epigonoi*. In the *Iliad* (IV, 404-408) we find that some of the *Epigonoi* took part in the Trojan War fighting with the Achaeans under the leadership of Agamemnon. It therefore seems justified to assume that according to the tradition Thebes was destroyed early in the generation that later saw the fall and destruction of Priam's city. It is interesting to note that Thebes is not to be found among the cities which contributed a contingent to the Achaean expeditionary force, although Hypothebai are mentioned, and that princes from the royal family of Kadmos and Oidipous are not mentioned among the warlords of Agamemnon. Thebes did not participate in that epic war because it could not, since shortly before the expedition it had been destroyed. Strabo (412) has preserved the tradition that after the final destruction the Palace of Kadmos was not rebuilt.

Years ago Keramopoullos excavated the akropolis of Thebes and brought to light what he maintained were the charred remains of the palace of its kings, the remains of the Palace of Kadmos as he called it. Based upon the facts then known, its excavator placed the destruction of that palace at the beginning of the fourteenth century B.C. The fragments of frescoes found were attributed to that century, and the sherds discovered in its ruins contain some that belong to the Amarna style of the LH III A period, but some, found in the destruction level, belong to the LH III B ceramic phase and the second and later half of that phase. Noticeable is the absence of sherds that could be identified as LH III C or even as heralding the approach of that style. Furthermore, the well-known 28 inscribed false-necked amphorai were found in one of its corridors (corridor Δ). These, too, belong to the closing years of LH III B. In 1964 a number of clay tablets were found bearing inscriptions in Linear B. The pottery found with them as well as with the 32 seal-cylinders bearing reliefs and the partially worked semiprecious stones duplicating the material found by Keramopoullos so long ago, belong to the second half of the LH III B period.[12] Based on this new discovery

---

[11] It seems that Tuthalijas was well aware of the Achaeans and that he did interfere with their activities when his interests demanded it. See, for example, the stipulation he incorporated in his treaty with a prince of Amurry quoted *supra*, p. 210.

[12] A. Keramopoullos, *Praktika*, 1921, pp. 32-34; and 1922-24, pp. 28-31. *Ephemeris*, 1930, p. 33. Evans, *Palace of Minos*, IV, pp. 739-744, figs. 724a and 724b. Mylonas, *Ephemeris*, 1936, pp. 61 ff. Vermeule, *Greece in the Bronze Age*, p. 189, seems to be-

lieve the suggestion created by the enthusiasm the discovery generated—that this latest find matches "the Greek legend that Kadmos the son of Agenor came from Phoenicia to found the city, bringing the art of letters with him." The seal-cylinders, however, range in date from a period antedating by centuries the legendary arrival of Kadmos, an event that according to "erratic Greek chronology" "happened in 1518 B.C.," to years long after his reputed founding of a city. There can be little doubt that the Oriental seal-cylinders resulted

N. Platon and Eve Stasinopoulou Touloupa postulate an initial destruction of the palace early in the LH III B period, and a later second destruction occurring in the course of that period.[13] Recently Blegen has maintained that "the House of Kadmos at Thebes came to its end in a similar disaster [to that which overtook the Palace of Nestor at Pylos] almost surely to be dated to the same fateful juncture," i.e. shortly before the end of LH III B, shortly before 1200 B.C.[14] If we place any credence on legends and if we accept the burned foundations of the structure in Thebes as the remnants of the palace finally destroyed by the *Epigonoi*, then we have to place the Fall of Troy after the date of the destruction of the palace at Thebes. The evidence to be derived from Thebes again seems to indicate a later date for the Fall of Troy than that projected by its excavators ca. 1240, or the latest suggested date, ca. 1270 to 1260 B.C.

The early date now suggested for the Fall of Troy, the decade around 1270 "before the middle stage of the ceramic style III B," does not seem to accord with the evidence obtained at Mycenae. We have seen above that the construction of the Lion Gate and the west Cyclopean wall and the rearrangement of Grave Circle A took place towards the middle stage of the ceramic style III B, since the pottery found in the foundations of the west Cyclopean wall, of the gate and in the retaining wall of Circle A belongs to that stage. If we assume an early date for the Fall of Troy, we shall be forced to maintain that all these monumental structures as well as the Treasury of Atreus, which is believed to be contemporary with the Lion Gate, and the Tomb of Klytemnestra were constructed after that fall. Can the established archaeological facts in that case be harmonized with the picture preserved in the legends? What happened at Mycenae after the Fall of Troy? The murders in the ruling family which followed the victorious return of Agamemnon, and the turbulent times which they of necessity brought about, certainly were not conducive to the undertaking and carrying out of the impressive works which survive. These works were erected before the Trojan expedition; they indicate the end of the thirteenth century as the only possible date for the fall of Priam's city. They indicate in addition that in the second half of that century conditions were conducive to the common expedition against Troy. The structures at Mycenae, the most important in the Mycenaean world, furthermore prove the preeminence of its ruler among the other *wanaktes* and justify both his traditional leadership and Thucydides' statement that Agamemnon was accepted as the leader because he surpassed in power the princes of his time.

THE DORIAN INVASION

We have insisted on the scrutiny of the evidence bearing upon the determination of the date of the Fall of Troy, because on that date depends the event which is usually recognized as fixing the end of the Mycenaean Age—the Descent of the Herakleidai, the so-called Dorian Invasion. Thucydides has recorded the tradition according to which the Descent of the Herakleidai occurred eighty years after the Fall of Troy. That information has been considered trustworthy thus far and it has been used consistently by scholars in their calculations. It has been generally believed that the Descent of the Herakleidai brought about the collapse of the Mycenaean power and the destruction of its great centers. In his publication of the Mycenaean fountain of the Akropolis of Athens, Broneer was the first to make the important observation that a number of Mycenaean sites in the Argolid and beyond it were either abandoned or destroyed in the second half of the thirteenth century B.C. and to suggest that the destruction was due to the Dorian Invasion. In 1956 he repeated this view, placed the destruction at the end of LH III B, and concluded that the incursions of the invaders lasted a long time; that though the lower city of Mycenae "was sacked sometime before the end of the 13th century, the citadel may have held out for many years against repeated attacks," and that the Trojan expedition could not have been launched in LH III C times.[15] The sites destroyed were Pylos, Mycenae, Tiryns, and Berbati, while those abandoned were Zygouries and Prosymna. In this important view he now has the weighty support of Blegen, who added the sites of Thebes and Gla to Broneer's list.[16] Nylander, in a recent study, reviewed this record of destruction and abandonment and cited Ålin's tabulation of 397 sites in the Mycenaean area thus abandoned or destroyed.[17] A brief survey of the palace sites and their dependencies will help us to determine whether or not the suggestions projected

---

from commercial activity and antiquarian interest of one of the rulers of Thebes of the thirteenth century B.C.

[13] To Dr. Platon I am grateful for permission to mention this tentative conclusion.

[14] "The Mycenaean Age," pp. 15, 22, 23.

[15] O. Broneer, *Hesperia*, 8 (1939), p. 426; *Antiquity*, 30 (1956), pp. 9-18 and especially pp. 16-17.

[16] Blegen, "The Mycenaean Age," pp. 22-24.

[17] C. Nylander, "The Fall of Troy," *Antiquity*, 37 (1963), p. 8. Ålin Per, *Das Ende der mykenischen Fundstätten auf dem griechischen Festland*, 1962.

agree with the evidence unearthed by excavators. We may begin with Thebes, where in 1964 more evidence was being unearthed.

Thebes

The charred remains of its palace, uncovered by Keramopoullos and Platon, would certainly indicate that the site was destroyed. As we have seen above, its excavator placed its destruction in LH III A times. The pottery which he published includes examples of an advanced stage of LH III B times. Perhaps the pottery indicates that we have an earlier and a later final destruction. The tablets, and the pottery found in 1964 in the destruction stratum belong also to those times. These latest discoveries as well as the evidence obtained earlier support Blegen's view that the final disaster occurred sometime before 1200 B.C. The destruction level of the Palace of Nestor yielded LH III C sherds; not a single LH III C potsherd has been found in the ruins of the palace at Thebes. This would indicate that the final destruction of the House of Kadmos occurred before that of the Palace of Nestor and certainly before that of the palace at Iolkos.

Gla

The pottery of its latest levels is reported in the publications of Threpsiades as being late LH III. Nowhere is it stated that by late LH III is meant the end of the LH III B phase. According to a personal communication the site is said to have been abandoned at the "close of the pottery phase III B." Was it abandoned about 1200 B.C., before, at the same time, or after the destruction of Thebes? We have to await the publication of the pottery found to be able to reach definite conclusions.

Iolkos

Again we have to await the complete excavation of the Palace of Iolkos and the publication of its finds for a definite conclusion regarding that site. In the statements made advocating a general destruction towards the end of LH III B the Palace of Iolkos is included. And yet Theochares, in his preliminary report published in the *Praktika* for 1956 (p. 128), categorically states that the palace was destroyed by a fierce fire in the course of LH III C-1.

Athens

A great deal has been made of the "humble houses" built along the northeastern ascent to the Akropolis.[18] In actuality these houses number only four. The fact that broken vases were found on the floor of one is taken to indicate that at the approach of an enemy they were abandoned in a hurry by the poor people who lived in them. That enemy is identified as the Dorians, or as the same enemy who destroyed Pylos, Mycenae, and Tiryns. We have seen above that the evidence indicating the nature of the structures is not clear; we may maintain with equal probability that they were shelters built under the shadow of the walls of the citadel for the temporary protection of people who, perhaps, came from the country to escape invaders. But even if we accept them as permanent homes of poor people, which were abandoned at the approach of an enemy, how can we prove who the enemy was? Could it have been the Dorians? According to the Athenian traditions, which in this respect are proved correct by archaeology, their territory was never conquered by an enemy, and the only time the Dorians threatened Athens was in the days of King Kodros, whose heroic sacrifice was an event that could well be remembered by ensuing generations. The reign of Kodros is universally placed after the Trojan War, even after the fleeing of the grandsons of Nestor from Pylos. Besides, the Athenian legends speak of repeated wars against Eleusis, which seem to have occurred in LH III B times in the days of Erechtheus; in one of these even warriors from Thrace took part. The memory of those wars was kept alive by a sculptured group erected on the Akropolis and standing there to the days of Pausanias.[19] How can we know that the abandonment of the shelters, even if we admitted that they were abandoned under the threat of war, was not the result of an Eleusinian attack, or of some other attack? And why did not the poor people, after the retreat of the enemy, go back to their "humble homes" to retrieve their vases and other valuables and to continue to live there? That they did not perish in the course of the enemy invasion is granted as indicated by the fact that the Akropolis, in which they sought refuge, was not captured.

The Peloponnesos

The Cyclopean wall "built across the Isthmus" has yet to be fully studied, and perhaps it will be wiser to wait for that study and the final publication before any conclusions are drawn dealing with invasions and threats of invasions at the end of the LH III B period. Our exploration of the Cyclopean walls of Mycenae, carried out in the course of three campaigns (1958, 1959, and 1963) proved that it is not easy to find dependable ceramic material to be used in dating fortifications. In his preliminary publication Broneer

---

[18] *Supra*, pp. 39-40.
[19] Mylonas, *Eleusis and the Eleusinian Mysteries*, 1961, pp. 24 ff. Pausanias, I, 27, 4.

states that the stirrup vase and the jug, usually accepted as dating the wall, are "from the Cyclopean wall in the village of Isthmia."[20] Does that mean that he found them in the village in some house with the information that they were found in the wall? In this case their value for dating purposes is rather dubious. Complete or almost complete vases from the interstices or foundations of even well-preserved Cyclopean walls are not only very rare but non-existent in the major sites of Mycenae and Tiryns. We may also note that the published plan of the area indicates that the Cyclopean wall does not go across the Isthmos but seems to enclose a circular area of the coast in the general direction of Kenchreai. In this respect its course differs considerably from that of the much later Justinian wall which does go across the Isthmos and which originates in the section in which the Cyclopean wall begins. This observation, when verified, will reduce the importance of the wall to our problem and to the history of the Mycenaean Age.

Pylos

At the other end of the Peloponnesos we have the Mycenaean palace at Ano Englianos. There can be no doubt that the palace was destroyed by fire while the LH III B style was still in existence and when LH III C began to be used. Blegen places the destruction about 1200 B.C.

Zygouries

Of paramount importance are the Mycenaean sites in Corinthia and Argolis, of which one of the better known is Zygouries. The site was abandoned towards the end of LH III B. However, we should note that Zygouries was not a major settlement, that it was not fortified, although it occupied the top of a flat hill rising gently to a height only a little above the plain, that "it continued to subsist as an *insignificant hamlet*" down to the time when it was abandoned. "As an unimportant community," writes Blegen, "it continued to exist into LH times attaining in the third stage (apparently LH III B times) . . . some measure of prosperity."[21]

Prosymna

Only one LH cemetery of the site has been explored thus far. Of the 50 chamber tombs cleared "more than 1,200 vases were recovered . . . , the bulk of them

belonging to the style of Mycenaean III B; but not one vessel, not even a potsherd, assignable to Mycenaean III C came to light."[22] However, its settlement has not been excavated as yet, and until it is we cannot be sure of the life story of the site. Desborough has recently noticed that from the settlement of Prosymna are known some vases which seem to belong to LH III C times.[23] In Waldstein's publication of the early excavations at the Heraeum we find illustrated an amphora of a type more commonly used in LH III C times and at least two sherds belonging to bowls evidently from those times. Other potsherds from a transitional stage of LH III B to III C are among those published by Caskey and Amandry.[24] One could assume that more evidence will be found when the Mycenaean settlement is excavated and that the LH III C graves may be grouped in some other part of the territory.[25] Even if we accepted as a fact that the site was abandoned, we shall have to ask the same question again: exactly when is the site supposed to have been abandoned and why? No definite answer to this question is forthcoming.

Berbati

We shall have to await the final publication of the site, but Åkerström's reported statement that the site was abandoned at the end of LH III B and that no habitations of LH III C times are to be found at the site is definite and must stand until the appearance of the publication.[26]

Tiryns

Its palace was wrecked and burned, but we do not know when. Blegen states that "Tiryns suffered a like fate at the same time" as Mycenae's citadel, the time being the end of the ceramic phase LH III B; "the palace was burned and wrecked and was later reconstructed only in modest scale." Unfortunately, there is no tangible evidence proving the time of the destruction. Its excavators, as we have seen above,[27] maintain that the palace stood intact until the middle of the eighth century B.C. when it was burned, that the building considered as a modest late Mycenaean reconstruction will best be explained as a temple of the late Geometric period. We have seen that the evidence unearthed by Verdelis is not adequate to prove the destruction of the entire palace; the burned fill could as easily be attributed to one of those partial and

[20] Broneer, *Hesperia*, 28 (1959), pp. 298 ff.; for the pottery see p. 334; *Antiquity*, 32 (1958), pp. 80-81 fig. 2.
[21] Blegen, *Zygouries*, pp. 222 and 216.
[22] Blegen, *Prosymna*, p. 422; "The Mycenaean Age," p. 24.
[23] V. R. d' A. Desborough, *The Last Mycenaeans and Their Successors*, 1964, pp. 77-78, and C. Waldstein, *Argive Heraeum*, 1902, II, p. 83 fig. 13 and pl. 54.
[24] *Hesperia*, 21 (1952), pp. 165 ff. and pl. 44, especially p.

173 nos. 52-53.
[25] It is interesting to note that the Geometric pottery found in the Mycenaean graves proves the existence of a settlement, but no Geometric cemetery has been found. Troy VIIa was inhabited, but no graves have been found belonging to it.
[26] Blegen, "The Mycenaean Age," pp. 23-24.
[27] *Supra*, p. 49.

periodic damages to which these buildings proved liable. Ålin has pointed out that a number of destructions occurred at Tiryns in the course of the LH III B period, but found no evidence to prove that the serious destruction indicated by Müller's and Verdelis' discoveries marked the end of the palace's life and the desertion of the citadel.[28] It seems that we are in too much of a hurry to abandon preeminent sites such as Tiryns and Mycenae. In his recent book Desborough concludes that "it seems clear that the citadel was virtually deserted after the disaster" at the end of LH III B. "The next sign of occupation is that of the very late LH III C or sub-Mycenaean graves."[29] Mrs. E. T. Vermeule repeats, "Tiryns also underwent extensive rebuilding and strengthening at the end of LH III B, as a natural guardpost of the Bay of Nauplia; it was burned and abandoned shortly afterwards."[30]

Verdelis' discovery and exploration of the underground passages leading to the water supply in 1963 proved that these statements and others of a similar nature do not correspond to historic facts. In those passages was found a large quantity of LH III C pottery, proving conclusively that the citadel continued to be well-inhabited in the twelfth century B.C. On the basis of the pottery found in the fountain of the Akropolis of Athens by Broneer, Desborough concluded that the site was inhabited in LH III C times.[31] In a similar manner from the much more numerous pottery found by Verdelis, we may conclude that the citadel of Tiryns was not abandoned at the end of LH III B but continued to be occupied in the period of the LH III C ware which followed, in the twelfth century B.C. One may wonder whether conquerors and destroyers of a mighty citadel would have allowed one of the assets to remain which made the citadel formidable and hard to take, namely its secure access to a water supply; whether they would not have eliminated an element which could have been used successfully by survivors prone to rebel against their conquerors. The palace at Tiryns was finally destroyed, but we do not know when. What is the tangible evidence which will place the destruction ca. 1200 B.C.?

Mycenae

We have left until last the capital city of Agamemnon because about it we now have more information than about any of the other destroyed or abandoned settlements in the Argolid. Evidence of destruction was brought to light by all contemporary excavators of the site. Wace proved that outside the citadel a number of buildings were destroyed by fire, most important of which are the structures known as the House of the Oil Merchant, the House of the Sphinxes, and the House of the Shields. He placed the destruction at the end of LH III B and his conclusions were accepted until recently.[32] To the north of this complex Verdelis cleared the West House, which was also destroyed by fire at the same time as the others but according to its excavator "before the end of the Late Helladic III B period."[33] Now, Mrs. David French states categorically that the destruction of the group of buildings to the south of Grave Circle B—i.e. the House of the Oil Merchant, the House of Sphinxes, the House of Shields and the West House—"cannot be later than the middle of LH III B."[34] If this is true, then these houses were destroyed at a different time than the so-called Citadel House, whose destruction is placed by Taylour at about 1200 B.C.

Some fifty m. to the south of the Treasury of Atreus in 1962 and 1963 Mrs. Shear cleared completely what survives of a Mycenaean house to be known as House I, and the foundations of parts of adjacent houses. House I was suddenly destroyed, but not by fire. The piles of stones found all over its area, the smashed vases with all their pieces in place under stones, the lack of burned remains, the discovery of a female skeleton in the doorway of its main room with skull broken by fallen stones, all seem to indicate that House I was destroyed by earthquake shortly before the Middle of LH III B. If the group of houses to the south of Grave Circle B were also destroyed before the middle of LH III B, their fateful end could be ascribed to the same earthquake. After destruction the houses thus far cleared outside the walls were not rebuilt and their areas were no longer used for habitations in the course of the Mycenaean Age at least. Other houses were constructed to the north of House I in the second half of LH III B.

Within the citadel itself it is assumed that the palace on top of the hill was destroyed by fire at the end of LH III B. That it was destroyed finally by fire is certain. That in the course of the LH III B period the palace suffered heavy damage by fire periodically to an extent which cannot be determined now is indicated by the Pillar Room and the burned floor of gypsum slabs revealed in 1963 by Shear, below that of the Pithos Room on the very summit of the hill. But precisely when the final destruction of the palace occurred cannot be established by concrete evidence that is available to date. A general destruction is indi-

---

[28] Ålin, *op.cit.*, pp. 25 ff.

[29] *Op.cit.*, p. 79.

[30] E. T. Vermeule, "The Fall of the Mycenaean Empire," *Archaeology*, 13 (1960), p. 70.

[31] Desborough, *op.cit.*, p. 113.

[32] *JHS*, 71 (1951), pp. 255 ff. and 74 (1954), pp. 170 ff.; *BSA*, 48 (1953), pp. 9 ff.; 50 (1955), pp. 177 ff.

[33] Verdelis, in *The Mycenae Tablets*, III, p. 27.

[34] *BSA*, 58 (1963), p. 50.

cated at the end of the Mycenaean Age, sometime in LH III C, by the remains of the granary at least. Most recently, Desborough has projected three destructions and catastrophes at Mycenae;[35] the first indicated by the first destruction by fire of the Citadel House, sometime in the course of LH III B; the second, proved by the second destruction of the same house by fire ca. 1200 B.C.,[36] and the third at the close of the Mycenaean Age. The destruction of some of the sites in the Argolid and the abandonment of others he equates with the second catastrophe.

We shall have to await the final and complete publication of the evidence obtained in the excavation of the Citadel House before we can determine objectively the validity and sequence of these destructions. The evidence on which the sequence is based seems to come from a section of which part of the floor had collapsed into a basement thus producing a definite change and special arrangement in the stratification. The sherds contained in the bricks of the walls add to the uncertainty of the date of the destruction. Meanwhile, however, we may ask what constitutes a dependable criterion for a destruction that can be accepted as indicative of a general catastrophe, caused by enemy action or internal upheaval. Does the destruction by fire of a single building, whose function even is not well established, constitute a dependable base for the conclusion that a general destruction overtook a site? The Citadel House, we are told, was destroyed by fire twice. What other buildings in its neighborhood were destroyed by fire at the same time that would make possible the acceptance of the conclusion? Some of the buildings surrounding it were brought to light at an early date of the excavation of Mycenae and consequently the data they may have preserved are not known. But parts of other buildings, such as the Ramp House, the South House, and the granary, were excavated by Wace in 1920. In his admirable report of the work he gave a detailed statement of the stratified deposits he found in these houses, a description of their floor levels and the sequence of the pottery he discovered in their fill.[37] In no instances does he mention indications of two or more destructions by fire; in all instances we find but a final destruction. The pottery found in the granary, the sherds belonging to a bowl decorated in the close style found in the East Room of the South House, would indicate that the final destruction occurred in LH III C times.

Tsountas, in his brief but lucid report of his excava-

tion of the building now known under his name and in his excavation diaries, does not mention earlier and later destructions by fire but only one final catastrophe. Before we can admit as a fact that the burning of the Citadel House indicates a general catastrophe we have to prove that it was not a misfortune which overtook that building alone. Perhaps this will prove possible when all the data from the structure are published, meanwhile it seems to me that the projection of three general destructions of Mycenae to which others in the mainland of Greece should be referred is premature. Equally unwarranted, I believe, is the attribution of these destructions to enemy incursions; some of them may have been caused by other agencies like an earthquake, or even a fire started by carelessness.

Our work at the citadel indicates definitely that to the end of the LH III B period Mycenae was flourishing; pottery of the closing years of that period is disclosed in abundance wherever a little unexcavated earth is to be found. The remnants of fires indicate that a destruction did occur at the very end of the LH III B period, perhaps even shortly afterwards, in the years when pottery was being produced of a type Furumark called "sub-III B." Our excavations of 1964 revealed more fully the structures which once stood in the area of the northeast extension. On the floor of some of their rooms pots were found as they were crushed by the caving-in of roofs and the tumbling of walls (Fig. 146). These vases constitute the largest group thus far found in a destruction level and chronologically belong together. They correspond to pottery found in the destroyed east wing of the great palace and indicate that at or shortly after the close of the LH III B period a disaster befell the citadel of Mycenae. This catastrophe, however, was not the final one; that the citadel continued to be held is proved by the numerous LH III C sherds which were found not only in the Granary but also in the east and in the northwest slopes of the hill. The sherds from the last named area do not come from stratified layers, because that area was thoroughly disturbed by Hellenistic constructions and by previous excavations. But their very existence proves that the site was still held in LH III C times.

These seem to be the facts about Mycenae. Before we try to see what they mean it may prove wise to discuss briefly another hypothesis which has lately assumed the proportions of an established fact. It is assumed that the expected attacks of enemies forced

---

[35] *Op.cit.*, p. 76.

[36] That date is given by Taylour in *The Mycenaean Tablets*, III, p. 46.

[37] Wace, *BSA*, 25 (1921-1923), pp. 38-60, 74-96. The excavation of the area to the southwest of the Citadel House in

1964, which I had the privilege to direct along with Taylour, did not disclose evidence of repeated destructions. For an excellent summary of the data from Mycenae to 1961 see Alin, *op.cit.*, pp. 10-25.

the Mycenaeans to fortify their citadels more strongly, that already "in the middle of the . . . period III B the Greek mainland is seen preparing itself against enemy attack which eventually comes and destroys the great palaces" that the "early part of the period Myc. III B was an age of great commercial and cultural expansion . . . but in the later part of this period the archaeological material points to a remarkable change in the living conditions and fortunes of the Mycenaean world."[38] Does the archaeological evidence revealed to date support these sweeping statements?

The evidence obtained at Pylos certainly does not indicate a change of fortune in the later part of LH III B. The tablets recording lists of objects existing in the last year of the life of the site speak of furniture covered with gold, ivory, and silver, characteristic of a prosperous age. The vast amount of pottery found in the various rooms, the numerous pithoi in the magazines, the many amphorae which were still filled with oil on the day of the destruction of the palace, the frescoes covering the walls, the designs on well-kept floors and hearths, the offerings to the sanctuaries and to the gods seem to prove that the same prosperous times experienced in the earlier years of the period continued to the day of the destruction of that palace. If the Mycenaean world was apprehensive in the later part of LH III B, why did not the *wanax* of the palace at Pylos attempt to fortify his hill top as the other rulers at Mycenae, Tiryns, and elsewhere are supposed to have done?

The latest discoveries in the Palace of Kadmos—the cylinders, the semiprecious stones imported to be worked in the place, the ivories found at a short distance from the palace—seem to indicate that peaceful and prosperous conditions existed in Thebes to the date of its destruction, that commerce was flourishing. Certainly no change of living conditions is indicated in the remains of Mycenaean Athens.

Our latest excavations, as we have seen, resulted in some very important disclosures regarding the citadel of Mycenae. They proved that the Lion Gate, the postern gate, and the west Cyclopean wall were added to the original *enceinte* around the middle of LH III B, that is, around the middle of the thirteenth century B.C. Certainly these were not the result of pressure and fear, but the result of confident strength and greatness. One does not build a gate as monumental as the Lion Gate, nor decorate it with a great relief if one is in fear of hostile incursions and invasions. People who live in constant fear would be satisfied with what they have in terms of fortifications such as the ones possessed by the original citadel; they would not build with such exactitude and excel-

lence the magnificent sweep of the west Cyclopean wall, which could not be built overnight and with forced labor. That the area so enclosed was not meant to accommodate people already established outside the citadel is indicated by the fact that the complex of buildings cleared by Wace and Verdelis remained beyond the walls. That an area was not enclosed to provide free space to the fearful citizens who were established by clans in the open country, is proved by the fact that a good deal of it was covered with houses evidently used by a few nobles.

Contemporary with the Lion Gate is the Treasury of Atreus and even later the so-called Tomb of Klytemnestra, which belongs to the second half of the thirteenth century. These, among the most important structures of the Mycenaean world, indicate neither decline, nor fear, nor strained circumstances. Other projects were undertaken and carried out around the middle and in the last half of the period: the grave circle was re-arranged; after a time the majestic ramp to the top of the hill was constructed; the later propylon of the northwest entrance to the palace and its impressive terracing were erected; the southwest grand staircase was added. The area of the citadel was augmented by the northeast extension almost at the very end of the thirteenth century B.C. In the general discussions about Mycenae this extension is ignored and only its subterranean cistern is described. Yet its walls are constructed in a manner that indicates leisure and patience; in many parts their thickness reaches the maximum of eight meters. People do not build so carefully and so massively when they are harassed by enemy pressures. One may recall the nature of the post-Persian Themistoklean wall of Athens to realize the immense difference, and the improbability of the inferences advanced about Mycenae of the late thirteenth century B.C. A mere survey of the northeastern extension will prove that it is impossible even to imagine that it was constructed in a hurry and under pressure. The works carried out at Mycenae around the middle and in the second half of the thirteenth century B.C. are not small projects produced by a declining and fearful community, but undertakings that testify to the pride and confident strength of their producers.

Beyond Mycenae we have the citadel of Tiryns. In the second half of the thirteenth century B.C. not only were the fortification walls augmented but a new gate, almost a duplicate of the Lion Gate, was constructed in conglomerate blocks carted from the area of Mycenae. People do not indulge in the luxury of building a massive gate in imitation of another in the capital city, when in the same area two other gates already exist, adequately filling the needs of the citadel, if they are fearful of enemy action and if they live in anxiety and under strenuous economic conditions.

In the second half of the thirteenth century B.C. a second and more elaborate road was constructed on the slopes of the hills and mountains to the east of Mycenae leading to the territory of Corinth. And yet another road running along the west slope of Mount Elias connected Mycenae with Corinth. The viaduct-bridge of St. George over the Chavos in the outskirts of the modern village of Mycenae was constructed at the end of the century if not later. The extent of the second road to Corinth, its very construction, the nature and massiveness of its retaining walls with culverts built in Cyclopean fashion, and its astonishing grading, prove that its construction was not undertaken in a hurry and in times of stress, especially since another road connected Mycenae and Corinth; and to harassed and anxious people a second road and a massive viaduct would have appeared a superfluous luxury.

The mere mention of works undertaken and carried out in the later part of the thirteenth century B.C. proves, we believe, that even to the close of that century the Mycenaean states were prosperous, strong, and free of anxiety. In late LH III B times in the territory of Mycenae we find in spite of local disasters, conditions that would have permitted the preparation and the carrying out of an expedition of the size and type of that launched against Priam's Troy. And in the works at Mycenae we find a reflection of the prestige and strength of its king and a justification for the choice of this ruler to lead that expedition. Thucydides wisely stated that "it was . . . because Agamemnon surpassed in power the princes of his time that he was able to assemble his fleet." The remains of Mycenae justify fully the statement.

THE DESTRUCTIONS AT THE END OF LH III B.

It remains a fact, of course, that buildings were destroyed by fire at Mycenae, that other sites were partially or totally destroyed or abandoned towards the end of the thirteenth century B.C. How can this fact be interpreted? Let us start with Mycenae. According to the prevailing opinion, the destruction of the group of buildings outside its walls occurred at the end of the LH III B period; that it was brought about by enemy action, either by the so-called Dorian Invasion or, according to the newest theory, by an incursion of the people who made up the "Illyrian migration," or by other marauding northerners. To that same invasion or migration are attributed the destruction and abandonment of the sites presumed to have been destroyed or abandoned at the end of LH III B. If this assumption is correct then it follows that the destruction both inside and outside the citadel of Mycenae brought about by enemy action occurred at one and the same time since the second so-called catastrophe indicated by the remains of the Citadel House is placed ca. 1200 B.C. Could that have been possible?

Wace drew attention to the fact that the destroyed buildings outside the walls yielded rich furnishings—a great quantity of ivory, for example. This certainly indicates that Mycenae was prosperous and flourishing at the time of the destruction, that it was enjoying peaceful conditions, since such structures were built and furnished beyond the protection of the walls. Whether we like to see in these structures an appendage to the palace, where perfumed oil was manufactured, or houses of rich merchants, we have to admit that the catastrophe which overtook them came suddenly and unexpectedly; otherwise their owners or their workers would have had a chance to carry their valuables within the walls some two hundred yards away. Is the assumption of such a sudden catastrophe justified if we held the Dorians or the members of the Illyrian migration responsible for it? Can we maintain that the enemy without being detected appeared suddenly before the Lion Gate and plundered and burned the dwellings outside the citadel? As we have seen, among the Pylos tablets are some which give us a glimpse into the system developed by the Mycenaeans to watch over vulnerable areas of their state, the sandy seacoast of the Pylian territory in that instance. Small groups of men, in multiples of ten, under a "commander" were stationed at certain command posts and with them was a "royal officer" known as *e-qe-ta*, a "follower," whose duty perhaps was to keep the command post in touch with headquarters.[39] Do we have any indications that the people of Mycenae had established comparable means for the detection of an approaching enemy? I believe that we do. We have to recall that at least three roads connected Mycenae with Corinth, with the area from which the Dorians or the Illyrian migrants would have descended to the Argolid.[40] It is reasonable to assume that in their southward movement the invaders would have used one or the other of these roads. It has been established

[39] M. Ventris and J. Chadwick, *op.cit.*, pp. 185-194. Page, *op.cit.*, pp. 193-195 and bibliography pp. 211-214 n. 69-84. H. Mühle-stein, *Die Oka - Tafeln von Pylos*, 1956.

[40] H. Steffen, *Karten von Mykenai*, 1884, pp. 8-10.

by actual remains that small lookout posts and guard-houses existed along the roads and it is natural to assume that contact was kept between the guards and the capital. On top of Mount Elias the remains of a large lookout post have been found. From that post fire signals could have been transmitted to the citadel at the approach of an enemy. The famous φρυκτωρίαι of Aeschylos' *Agamemnon*, by means of which the Fall of Troy was signaled to Mycenae, and the sentinel on the roof of the palace watching for the fire that would herald the return of Agamemnon, perhaps are reflections of a long-remembered tradition. Certainly the remains on top of Mount Elias are still to be seen.[41] It is reasonable to assume that the guards of one or the other of the posts would have signaled the approach of an enemy to the people in the capital. It is assumed that the Mycenaeans under fear and pressure of enemy attack improved and enlarged their fortifications. If indeed they anticipated such enemy action, then certainly they would have seen to the perfection of their warning system; they would have placed on the alert the guards controlling the roads thus making it impossible for an invading army or even a smaller group of marauders to reach Mycenae undetected and to take its people by surprise; they would not have left rich establishments fully equipped beyond the walls. It seems to me that a sudden, unheralded attack of Mycenae by an invading army is excluded by the conditions vouched for by the existing remains.

The site of Zygouries was abandoned at about the same time, presumably under pressure of enemy action or fear of impending action. This unpretentious settlement lies at an important junction of roads. An enemy coming from the north would have passed near the settlement, which they could easily have captured since it was unfortified and had a small population. If indeed the site was abandoned under pressure, its people would have sought refuge in the fortified citadel that was nearest to them—the citadel of Mycenae; and this they could have reached by two different roads, one more mountainous, and hence less dangerous and freer of enemy attack than the other. Their coming would have warned the Mycenaeans of the approach of the enemy; thus a surprise attack would have been impossible.

No matter how we look at things we find that the Mycenaeans would have had sufficient warning and time to transfer themselves and all their belongings to the citadel. But the houses beyond the walls were found still containing precious objects. The sudden destruction of the houses by enemy action seems difficult if not impossible to justify. But it may be sug-gested that not an organized army moving *en masse* but small bands of warriors, able to infiltrate undetected, were responsible for the destruction of the houses outside the citadel. The Dorian Invasion could be pictured as composed of such small bands roaming in the unprotected countryside moving always southward.

The sudden destruction of the houses beyond the walls of the citadel, according to the same scholars, however, was not the only misfortune experienced at ca. 1200 B.C. In the akropolis itself, the Citadel House, and even parts of the palace, if not all of it, were destroyed by fire at the same time. If the houses beyond the walls were destroyed by invaders, the houses within the citadel were destroyed in a similar fashion by the same invaders. This would have occurred only if the enemy had captured the citadel. The formidable Cyclopean walls, I believe, are adequate proof that the citadel could not have been stormed by the small bands which we have assumed, not even by a large organized army at a first attempt. Broneer voiced the general opinion that "the citadel may have held out for years against repeated attacks"; but according to the general assumption fires destroyed structures in and outside the citadel at the same time and if the latter were destroyed by the members of the Dorian invasion the former also were destroyed by those members, who are assumed to have attacked the citadel repeatedly over a long period of time. It seems to me that the difficulties raised by the assumption that the destructions at Mycenae of 1200 B.C. were caused by the Dorian Invasion or any other migrants or marauders, are many and perhaps unsurmountable.

We may recall that Mrs. David French now maintains that the destruction of the group of houses outside the walls did not occur at the end but towards the middle of the LH III B period, at a time some fifty years before 1200 B.C. when the destruction occurred within the walls. It is, however, stated that an earlier destruction overtook the Citadel House. Did that earlier destruction take place at the same time as that of the houses outside the walls; and if it did, does that mean that it occurred long before the stated destruction and abandonment of sites assumed to have occurred at ca. 1200 B.C.? And were they the same invaders, whether Dorians or Illyrian migrants, who meted out these destructions at Mycenae some fifty years apart? Could this destruction around the middle of LH III B be attributed to an earthquake? The destruction at Mycenae of the middle of LH III B does not seem to have amounted to a great catastrophe, since after it so many major works were undertaken.

---

41 Wace, *BSA*, 25 (1921-1923), pp. 429 ff. Tsountas and Manatt, *Mycenaean Age*, pp. 35-38.

The questions raised by Mrs. French's change in the date of the destruction of the houses outside the walls are equally numerous and impossible to answer until the final publication of all the material unearthed in this area. It is clear that to conjure up incursions of enemies to account for the destructions does not provide the answers needed.

The destructions, however, did occur. Is there any other more plausible explanation to be had? In the legends of Mycenae, I believe, we find an explanation that does seem to give an adequate answer. The stories of the quarrel between Atreus and Thyestes, of the murder of Agamemnon on his return, and the killing of Aigisthos and Klytemnestra by Orestes are too well known to repeat or elaborate. Wace, some time ago, attributed the destruction of the houses outside the walls to the upheaval caused by the quarrel of Atreus and Thyestes. The later destruction within the walls occurred almost at the same time as that of the Fall of Troy, at ca. 1200 B.C. It was then that Agamemnon was murdered. At the time he was a hero, the supreme commander of a victorious army, of which at least a contingent, the proud veteran conquerors of a famous adversary, returned home with him bringing the loot of a successful although long campaign. Only eight years later, Aigisthos and Klytemnestra were killed. They were then the rulers of the state presumably with a host of friends and supporters, with an army and dependents. If they had had no adequate support to begin with they would not have attempted the murder of the great king, and retinues and friends increase at least for a time for those in supreme authority. Is it possible to believe that such violent deeds could have been carried out against men in possession of power and friends without disturbance, conflict, and destruction? The almost simultaneous destruction within and without the citadel can be explained satisfactorily, I think, as the result of the tumultuous conflicts which must have followed the appalling deeds. The destruction could have resulted from internal struggles between the leaders and their followers. It may be objected that we base this explanation on legends; but legends, too, are the stories connected with the Dorian Invasion and the theories inspired by the Illyrian migrations. If it is

permissible to use the latter, it should be permissible to use the former.

Granted that the legends of Mycenae may account for the destructions revealed in that site by the spade of the archaeologist, how, then, can the other destructions and abandonments noted above and mentioned first by Broneer, and then added to by others, be explained? To begin with, we must emphasize the limitation of scientific data available from a number of sites included in the lists of destroyed or abandoned settlements which does not justify general conclusions.[42] Final reports on the excavations of many sites have not as yet been published, while a number of others have not been fully investigated. The problems they represent are more complex than assumed; they may require different and individual solutions; generalizations are inadequate. The destruction of some major sites, however, is well established and the comparison of the data they provide may prove of importance.

Thebes, the city of Kadmos and of Oidipous, is one of the sites which furnish a definite chronological base. We learn from the *Iliad* (IV, 404-408) that the city was finally destroyed by the *Epigonoi* before the Fall of Troy. If the destruction of Pylos occurred at the hands of the Dorians, then Thebes could not have been destroyed by the Herakleidai since, according to the tradition, the Dorian Invasion took place eighty years after the Fall of Troy and Thebes fell in the generation of the Trojan War. The tradition preserved in the *Iliad* seems to be in agreement with the archaeological indications, which, as we have seen, will place the final destruction of Thebes at an earlier date than that of Pylos and even of Troy VIIa. Again the literary indications are that Thebes was destroyed before the Trojan expedition since it is not mentioned in *Iliad* II; and it is not to be found in the Catalogue of Ships, which, according to Page, seems to have been composed by someone who "knew more and cared more about Boeotia than about Agamemnon or Achilles or the siege of Troy."[43] Thebes did not participate in the expedition, since it was already in ruins when preparations were started for the project. It seems clear that Thebes was not destroyed by the Dorians. Who then were its destroyers? In the legends

---

[42] Later more thorough investigations may bring to light evidence completely opposite to what was assumed on the basis of a preliminary statement. Nylander, for example, states definitely that the palace of Iolkos, one of the sites in the lists, was destroyed "leaving Myc. III B pottery as evidence of the date of the catastrophe." In the only report of the excavation published in the *Praktika* for 1956 p. 128, but circulated recently, D. Theochares, the excavator, specifically states that "on the floors of Rooms 1 and 2 are to be seen most evident remnants of a frightful fire, which reduced to

ashes the building in the course of the LH III C - 1 period." The large list of sites compiled by Alin and his statements of objects found and the number of destructions experienced make evident the fact that the problem is not as simple as has been assumed nor that its solution can be based on a single, general cause or fact. For years, I have been advocating that various causes may have been responsible for the catastrophes, a different cause for each or for a group of local destructions.
[43] *Op.cit.*, p. 125.

of Thebes we find an adequate explanation for the destruction of the city of Kadmos.

The legends of Athens will explain the abandonment of the shelters by the postern gate of its citadel. The Eleusinian wars, remembered to the days of Pausanias, are as well documented as the Dorian Invasion or the modern legend of the Illyrian migration.

In the Peloponnesos we have the Palace of Nestor at Ano Englianos, whose destruction is established chronologically by archaeological evidence. Concrete evidence proves that the destruction of the palace occurred shortly after the Fall of Troy. In its burned levels were found LH III C sherds, while, it is stressed, no pottery of that ceramic phase was found in the destruction levels of the city of Priam. In terms precisely of years the difference in the destruction dates of the two sites cannot now be determined because all the material unearthed at Pylos is not yet available for study; besides there is a difference of opinion as to the date of the appearance of LH III C pottery and perhaps divergences of opinion as to how long it takes for imported pottery to appear in places other than its center of production. One thing is definite. A chronological difference between the two events is archaeologically established, and this agrees with the tradition of Nestor's return from Troy to his palace where he entertained Telemachos, the son of Odysseus. But no evidence was found in the excavated ruins of that palace indicating the identity of its destroyers.

It is being assumed that the Dorians were responsible for the destruction, that the Palace of Nestor was another of the sites they devastated in their southward movement. In my study on Priam's Troy, I have pointed out that traditions recorded by Pausanias do not permit the attribution of the destruction of Pylos, which is proved to have occurred ca. 1200 B.C., to the Dorians.[44] If we use tradition to establish the identity of the destroyers, then the conclusion has to be that the Dorians were not responsible for the destruction of the palace of Ano Englianos. In that same study I maintained, and I wish to repeat myself now, that the destruction of Ano Englianos was brought about by a successful piratical attack by people who remain unknown, which occurred shortly after Nestor's return from Troy ca. 1200 B.C. We have to remember that the excavations proved that the palace was unfortified. It stood unprotected on the top of a hill whose two sides at least are abrupt and not easy to climb. This, however, would not have made unnecessary the construction of walls. The slopes of the citadel of Mycenae are even more abrupt, yet its palace is protected by mighty walls; the slopes of the Akropolis of Athens are more rocky and hard to climb, yet fortification walls crown its summit. The slopes of Ano Englianos would not have made it difficult for an enemy to approach the palace and attack it. That palace is at a comparatively short distance from the sea. A series of hills conceal it from that sea but they also block the view of the immediate coast line to the west and northwest. The coast nearest the palace is sandy and its waters deep to a few yards from the land. It offers easy approach and moorings to ships of those times. We can readily see that sudden, piratical attempts to land and attack the palace were possible.

That the ruler of Ano Englianos was aware of the exposed position of his palace is proved by the series of tablets found in its ruins dealing with military and naval operations which we have already mentioned. The destruction of the palace on the hill of Ano Englianos is assumed to have been but one in a chain of catastrophes which occurred all over the Mycenaean world and which were anticipated over a number of years by the Mycenaeans. If that were so, one wonders why the *wanax* of Pylos did not even attempt to build a wall around his palace to protect it. The naval and military tablets prove only that the ruler of Ano Englianos was aware of the dangers to which undetected, piratical attacks would expose the focal point of his domain, his unprotected palace, and took measures to guard against a surprise.

The destruction of the palace and the devastation of its territory was a blow from which the ruling class of Pylos did not recover. We may assume that the political and economic conditions following the disaster were such that they did not permit the erection of another palace in the period left until the conquest of the land by the Dorians. It is interesting to note Pausanias' story of the seizure of the territory by the Dorians of Kresphontes (IV, 3, 6-7, Trans. Frazer), based of course on tradition. "The old Messenian commonalty," he tells us, "were not driven out by the Dorians, but submitted to be ruled by Kresphontes, and to give the Dorians a share of the land. These concessions they were induced to make by the suspicion with which they regarded their own kings, because they were by descent Minyans from Iolkos." After the destruction of the palace and the looting of the wealth which followed, the people of Pylos perhaps were too poor and not eager to build palaces for the rulers whom they considered foreigners, who proved incapable of protecting them against piratical attacks and who perhaps were too weak to impose their will on the people. One wonders whether the elaborate control of every aspect of life indicated by the tablets from Pylos did not stem from a political regime established by a small group of foreign war-lords over a peaceful, agrarian population.

Our discussion thus far may have brought together sufficient reasons for doubting the attribution of the destructions placed at the end of the thirteenth century to the Dorians. Are there any reasons to believe that they are the results of the wanderings of northern people that came to be known as the Illyrian migration?[45] Before this theory is accepted it has first to be proved definitely and on the basis of scientific data that all the sites listed were destroyed or abandoned about the same time. At present this would prove an impossible task. The hypothesis of the Illyrian migrants' invasion of parts or of the whole of Greece is based on assumptions and generalizations which as yet have to be substantiated by evidence. We are called upon to see invaders seeking a territory to establish themselves because they were forced out of their homeland, coming down into Greece from the north, destroying the palace at Iolkos in LH III C-1 times, the palace of Thebes, which is farther south, in late but not the latest LH III B times, threatening Athens, at the end of LH III B, by-passing a "strong wall with towers" at the Isthmos (or did they storm it?), devastating the area of the Argolis forcing the abandonment of sites like Zygouries, Prosymna, and Berbati, storming the formidable citadel of Mycenae as well as that of Tiryns in the same general year, proceeding south to Sparta and destroying the Mene-laion site, then swinging westward and burning the palace at Pylos in the general years in which their exploit at Mycenae and Tiryns was performed, then marching northward and disappearing into Macedonia and farther east. Through all this march they passed by a number of plains and sites where they could settle; the impressive plain of Thessaly, the verdant area of Boiotia, the plain of Argos and Sparta, the admirable land of Messenia; and although their main purpose, we are told, was to find a good place to settle, they did not establish themselves anywhere nor did even one of their tribes find it advisable to stay in Greece. The migrants, furthermore, fought their way over distances long for the times, marched over rough terrain, and forced by the might of their arms mountain passes. Thermopylai, which only treachery subdued, may have been one. And yet they left behind not a trace, not an arrowhead, not a broken piece of pottery, not a jaded or broken weapon. Though they were not immortals, they seem not to have suffered casualties, since not a single grave of theirs has been found, a feat not even imagined by the mythographers

of old. Perhaps their traces will be found in the future; an archaeologist never excludes anything however unbelievable, but for the time being no concrete evidence of their existence, progress, and achievement has been found. Some of the scholars who advocate the Illyrian migrants' invasion of Greece tell us that legends must not be used in outlining the early history of Greece; to make any use of them is un-scientific. We have, however, to be careful not to sub-stitute for ancient legend a modern version of ancient mythology by picturing invaders looking for areas to settle and yet marching through Greece from north to south and from east to west, then making an exit without leaving any trace behind them save destroyed citadels which would outlast a long siege. It may have happened so. But before we accept it as a historic fact or even as a hypothesis, we need some tangible evidence revealed by excavations and proved archaeo-logically; the same kind of evidence which the pro-pounders of that view demand of the legends. The so-called Illyrian migration will not account for the destructions that mark the closing years of the LH III B period. Nor can the mysterious Sea Peoples of the Egyptian inscriptions, if they are conceived as dif-ferent from those of the Illyrian migrants and as operating from the sea, be projected as the destroyers since most of the sites that are assumed to have been destroyed or abandoned at the end of that period are located at a prohibitive distance from the sea.

It has become evident, I hope, from our discussion, that the available archaeological data are too few and our knowledge too limited to justify generalizations and final conclusions regarding the destructions which took place towards the end of the thirteenth century B.C., that the problem is too complex to be solved by a single assumption. Meanwhile, it seems to me that more satisfactory results will be obtained if each dis-trict and case is examined first by itself and a special effort made to determine whether individual, local causes may have been responsible for its destruction; then an attempt should be made to link one district with another and generalizations should be attempted. Thus, for example, before we attach the names of Iolkos, Pylos, Thebes, and Mycenae to the chain of assumed contemporary destructions we ought to find out whether their evidence excludes such a treatment and their fate is accounted for more fully by local conditions and established traditions. The case of the Argolid, for example, where a number of sites are said to have been simultaneously destroyed and aban-doned, should be scrutinized with the available evi-

---

[45] Milojcic, *AA*, 1948-1949, pp. 14-15. Bengston, *Griechische Geschichte*, 1960, pp. 44 ff. Heubeck, *Gnomon*, 33 (1961), p. 115. Starr, *The Origins of Greek Civilization*, pp. 66 ff. E. Town-send Vermeule, *Archaeology*, 13 (1960), pp. 66 ff. Nylander, *op.cit.*, p. 9.

dence as a guide. This evidence does not tell us who or what was responsible for the destructions and abandonments vouched for by archaeology. A good many scholars have found an answer in the traditions of the Greeks which tell us of the Descent of the Herakleidai, of the so-called Dorian Invasion. Others, who deny the value of tradition as a source of information and who maintain that legends should be avoided, nevertheless have created the modern myth of Illyrian migrants wandering up and down the Greek peninsula to account for events some of which do not seem to belong together chronologically.

We believe that the legends of Mycenae better than any other hypothesis explain the situation in Argolis revealed by archaeological research and excavation. The discord and killings in the royal family, in the circle of the *wanax*, perhaps standing for the genesis of opposing and quarreling factions, must have caused an internal upheaval. People and officials throughout the domain must have sided with one faction and thus brought upon themselves the revenge of the other. The killings in the royal family must have weakened the political system centered in the *wanax*, made necessary the use of force to impose the will of this or that faction that emerged a temporary victor in a continued contest, and broke down order and allegiance in the domain. Uncertain times and lack of safety must have resulted in the country. Such conditions bring about destruction, abandonment, and the desire of people in the country to emigrate to other lands where they can live in peace. Until more evidence is revealed by excavation that will establish beyond doubt a cause, I believe that it is reasonable to maintain that the events at the end of the thirteenth century B.C. are better accounted for by the local conditions which are reflected in the legends of the areas. These conditions in the Argolid appear after the Fall of Troy, according to the local tradition, and according to Thucydides they developed in other parts of Greece. For he wrote (I, 12, 1-2) "Indeed, even after the Trojan war Hellas was still subject to migrations and in process of settlement, and hence did not get rest and wax stronger. For not only the return of the Hellenes from Ilium, occurring as it did after a long time, caused many changes, but factions also began to spring up very generally in the cities, and, in consequence of these, men were driven into exile and founded new cities" (Trans. C. F. Smile). The disturbed conditions that existed then in the country perhaps gave rise to the tradition reflected in another statement of the great historian. "Indeed," he wrote, "all the Hellenes used to carry arms because the places where they dwelt were unprotected, and intercourse with each other was unsafe; and in their everyday life they regularly went armed just as the barbarians did." (I, 6, 1-2).

THE FINAL PERIOD

The period which followed the widespread misfortunes of the end of the thirteenth century B.C., the period known as LH III C, is one of decline. The Mycenaean domain did not recover from the blows it received in the years which followed the Fall of Troy. Exact and detailed knowledge of the twelfth-century Mycenaean states is not available. Statements are made but they are based on assumptions. We have seen, for example, that as recently as 1960 and 1963 it was stated that Tiryns was abandoned at the end of the thirteenth century B.C.; yet in 1962 and 1963 a mass of pottery was found in its underground passages to the water supply proving that the site was occupied and active in LH III C times. We seem to believe that our knowledge of Mycenae is most adequate if not complete and on this belief are based a good many assumptions. But exactly what do we know about Mycenae of the twelfth century? Unfortunately the area of its citadel has been denuded of so much of its original fill by resettlement and by early excavations that it is impossible even to block out a sketch of its structures. What is the exact evidence which will prove the date of the southwest grand staircase? If I maintained that it was built during the LH III C period, that during that period the Palace on the summit was still standing in splendor, how can I be proved wrong by strictly scientific criteria? That the people of the twelfth-century Mycenae were not as well off economically as before seems to be indicated by their graves. That some of the buildings which they erected to replace those destroyed ca. 1200 B.C. were flimsy and unimportant seems to be suggested by remains revealed in the area of the Citadel House. Substantial buildings, however, as indicated by the granary, seem to have existed in the citadel in the twelfth century. During that century was built the large structure above the northeast corner of the Lion Gate. The storerooms and corridors along the north Cyclopean wall were still in use, as is proved by LH III C pottery found on their floors. The recent excavations have brought to light LH III C pottery in every section explored, although not in stratified deposits. It is unfortunate, but it is true that our knowledge of the twelfth century B.C. is very inadequate to allow sweeping statements and generalizations.

What we know about this period can be summarized briefly. Mycenae and Tiryns were still occupied. Although some sites in the Argolid, such as Zygouries, may have been abandoned, others were still inhabited and active. Among them we find Asine, Nauplia, Midea, Argos, and perhaps Prosymna. In the territory of Corinth, Korakou continued to be inhabited and to the west the district of Achaia was thriving. The few graves found seem to prove that the population of the community at Mycenae was reduced in numbers and wealth. Attika seems to have been well inhabited and at least some of its parts were prosperous. The graves explored in the last eight years by Iacovides at Perati offer definite proof of prosperity. They offer also the proof of continued contact and relations with the eastern world. We may recall that the Athenians claimed that their land was never conquered by invaders, that the same people lived there for generations; archaeology proves that this tradition corresponds to the facts. Contacts with areas beyond the mainland were not broken off; this is proved by pottery of the LH III C style found in some quantity in Rhodes, Cyprus, Asia Minor—including Troy VIIb-1—in the Syrian and Palestinian coastal regions. As a matter of fact it was used as a prototype by the makers of the Philistine ware. Objects of gold, of semiprecious stones, seals, and scarabs found in the Mycenaean area also prove that relations with the Near East were not interrupted.

The total of the facts revealed by excavations shows that in the period no new elements of art or culture appeared that proved the establishment of intruding foreign peoples in the Mycenaean area.[46] The inhabitants of the twelfth century continued the arts of their predecessors, buried their dead in chamber tombs, following the old rites and burial customs, and produced the same kind of clay figurines some of which may represent the benevolent goddess known to their ancestors. In the area of Mycenae during the twelfth century great works were not produced, the building of tholos tombs for example was discontinued; the people of the area did not enjoy the prosperity of past generations—the grave furnishings are as a rule poor and unimpressive; their art products lack the strength and merit of the dynamic community of the fourteenth and thirteenth centuries. A decline had set in at the beginning of the century and continued in the years which followed.

The misfortunes at the beginning of the twelfth century which brought about the partial break in the established administrative system were certainly responsible for the beginning of the decline of the main centers of Mycenaean power and culture. In a recent study Professor Emily T. Vermeule projects another reason for the decline. "It was not the 'destructions,'" she maintains, "which hurt Mycenaean centers so much as economic deprivations which made it impossible for them to maintain and rebuild in the old manner"; this deprivation is attributed to the disruption of the overseas commercial activities of the Mycenaeans. "The disruption of commerce in the late thirteenth century," she states, "may have been more disastrous for Greece than direct invasions and this followed inevitably upon the coming of the Sea Peoples whose hunt for land and subsistence threw the Aegean into chaos."[47] These mysterious Sea Peoples, to whom it has become customary to attribute all evils, appear in Egyptian documents to have been active from the reign of Ramses II (ca. 1301-1234) through that of Merneptah (ca. 1234-1222) to the reign of Ramses III (ca. 1195-1164). The strength of the Mycenaean civilization, she maintained with reason, "depended greatly upon invigorating contact with Crete and the East from the time of the Shaft Graves onward. When contact was broken, Mycenaean culture drifted so far into sterility that it is hard to recognize."[48] The contact was broken apparently when the Aegean was thrown into chaos.

This explanation, formulated so imaginatively, cannot stand close scrutiny. There can be no doubt that the Mycenaeans owed a great deal to Crete and the East, that their commercial activities enhanced their intellectual horizons and invigorated their art efforts, that the termination of these activities was detrimental to their state. These facts were stressed long ago by a number of scholars, even by Tsountas. The question, however, is *when* these commercial activities and contacts were terminated. Finds from Thebes, Mycenae, and Pylos—such as ivories, semiprecious stones, records of unguents and condiments—prove that communications were open and commercial enterprises active to the end of the LH III B period. Pottery scattered over the Mediterranean coastal areas tells the same story. At the end of that period the expedition against Priam's Troy was undertaken.[49] If the

[46] This may be another reason for doubting the attribution of the destructions around 1200 B.C. to the Dorians, who moved southward to establish themselves in new lands and who actually did so.

[47] *Archaeology*, 13 (1960), p. 67.

[48] *Ibid.*, p. 74. This conception in a somewhat less concrete form and well modified is suggested in her *Greece in the Bronze Age*, pp. 208, 269 ff.

[49] For the event, Mrs. Vermeule accepts this date, *Greece in the Bronze Age*, p. 276, suggested by me in 1959 in a study published in the *Annual of the School of Philosophy of the University of Athens*, 1960, pp. 408 ff.

Sea Peoples had thrown the Aegean into chaos at that time, it is reasonable to maintain that the Mycenaeans would have devoted their efforts to the task of bringing order in the eastern Mediterranean so that their commerce could have continued its course;[50] and we must remember how important to the welfare of their state was commerce and a free sea. Instead they mounted an expedition against Troy to obtain uncertain wealth or to secure another foothold in Asia Minor that would have been useless to them if the sea had not been safe. The fact that they undertook an expedition across the Aegean would prove that the sea was safe at the end of the LH III B period.

It is a well-known fact that even today the people of the Cyclades import their food supplies; so they did in the past. They would have been the most logical candidates for suffering from a deterioration of sea communications. Yet we find that in LH III C-1 times they flourish. This certainly proves that the Aegean was not thrown into chaos by the activities of the "Sea Peoples," who are reported to have been restless in the days of Ramses III.

After a thorough survey of the existing evidence Desborough in his latest study maintains that in the early part of LH III C the "Central and South Aegean remained in contact with outside areas which produced gold and semiprecious stones, and one such area was certainly the East Mediterranean." In another conclusion based on facts he states: "In general, the sea remained a free highway to those who lived on the shores of the Central and South Aegean."[51] Certainly, Tiryns and Asine are by the sea and so is Argos, and not far from them are Mycenae, Prosymna, and other sites in the Argolid. If the sea remained a free high-

way, as Desborough proved, the Aegean had not been thrown into chaos, the contact with the East was not broken, commerce could not have been interrupted unless the centers from which it emanated were incapable of carrying out such activities because of local conditions. The sea, far from being in a chaotic condition which caused interruption of commercial activities and insecurity to the coast, "the sea protected . . . the coastal sites on the Greek Mainland remote from the route of invasion," and these coastal sites "felt no apprehension for the future . . . they pursued their way in security and prosperity." The Sea Peoples and the presumed chaotic condition of the Aegean cannot account for the destruction of LH III B or for the decline which followed.

The Theory of Social Revolution

It has been suggested by Andronikos that the destructions of Mycenaean sites and the end of the age were due to a widespread social revolution, to the general uprising of the people against their ruling and wealthy classes.[52] This view has not been considered seriously. We have, however, Blegen's opinion, and it is rather decisive.[53] "I could believe," he is quoted in rebuttal, "in one social revolution, or even in two social revolutions, at Mycenae and Tiryns. But it is not sensible, in my opinion, to assume that all the Bronze Age kingdoms except Athens could have been destroyed by revolutions which broke out almost simultaneously, from one end of Greece to the other." Furthermore, the theory of social revolution, he added, fails to account for the Greek dialect pattern of the Classical age. To his objection we may add that there is no trace of a social revolution in the islands where

[50] It may be helpful to note that very few of the people mentioned in the Egyptian records could be identified with certainty. In the record of the battle of Kadesh, 1288 B.C. we find people, the Derden (Dardanians?) among them, who seem to be located in Asia Minor and would have reached the battlefield by land. Again the date is too early and one around which a good deal of Mycenaean overseas activity is well established. In the inscription of Merneptah we find the names of people who assisted the Libyans in their invasion of the Delta about 1223 or 1215 B.C. Among the allies were the Ekwesh "from the land of the Sea" who have been equated with the Achaeans. Of course, the Achaeans could have taken part as mercenaries or for the loot, but would they have allowed their comrades in arms to throw the Aegean into chaos and thus disrupt their own profitable commercial enterprises? Furthermore, years ago Prentice pointed out that the Egyptian record states that these Ekwesh were circumcised and claimed that they were not Indo-Europeans (*AJA*, 33 [1929], pp. 206-218). Commenting on the same evidence Page states that the equation is "put beyond the bounds of probability by the fact, if it is a fact, that the Agiyawasa (= Ekwesh) practiced circumcision" (*op.cit.*, p. 21 n. 1, where pertinent discussion). The third instance of invasion, in which the Ekwesh do not participate, occurred in the fifth year of the reign of Ramses III, perhaps ca. 1193 or 1190. Again the Libyans and their allies invaded the Delta and again they were defeated. One

could maintain that the Ekwesh = Achaeans did not participate in the raid because they were too occupied with the Trojan War and its aftermath. The last and fourth encounter occurred after the fifth but before the eighth year of the reign of Ramses III, perhaps ca. 1187 B.C., but, as Page states, even as late as 1172 B.C. In connection with the last encounter, in which Ramses was victorious both on land and sea, the record contains the oft-repeated statement "the northern countries, which are in the isles, are restless in their limbs; they infest the ways of the harbor mouths. . . . Their main support was Peleset, Thekel, Shekelesh, Denyen, and Weshesh" (Breasted, *Records*, IV, §64 ff. and Page, *op.cit.*, p. 22). The Denyen have been equated with the Danaans; but this equation has been challenged (cf. discussion in Page, *loc.cit.*). The third and fourth encounters are too late to be considered responsible for the destruction of the LH III B period and for the lean years that followed. They do not indicate the existence of chaotic conditions in the Aegean, because as Desborough proves, the South Aegean was quiet and safe for commerce in the years they occurred.

[51] Desborough, *op.cit.*, pp. 228-229.

[52] *Hellenika*, 13 (1954), pp. 221-240.

[53] It is quoted in J. Alsop, *From the Silent Earth*, 1964, p. 132. The same view was maintained by the late John Papadimitriou, who expounded it to me in 1953, and over which we spent many a night arguing.

Mycenaean kingdoms flourished and where the same social conditions existed; also the curious fact that a number of small agricultural settlements were deserted and fortresses were similarly abandoned, such as those of Gla and Eutresis, presumably built to protect the possessions of the people of a number of rural communities against invading foes. People who rise against their masters do not leave their farms and homes, not even when they fail to succeed in their efforts, nor do they abandon fortresses built for their security. Pausanias has preserved the tradition according to which the people of Messenia remained in their homes and farms when the Dorians took over the territory and only the ruling class had to flee the country. In a similar manner the people of the rural districts would have remained in their settlements after the revolution. Nor do we find an influx of people in the capitals indicating that after a successful revolution they took over and settled where they would naturally expect to find more comfortable living; on the contrary we find evidence of reduced population in the greater centers of Mycenaean life. This was especially stressed by Desborough who finds unlikely the theory of an internal general upheaval.[54] The theory of social revolution does not seem to provide the answer to our quest.

Gradual Decline

The widespread destruction of the closing years of the thirteenth century B.C. resulted in an economic and cultural setback. After 1200 some attempt was made at recovery in the territory of Mycenae. The granary in its citadel was enlarged, good pottery, continuing the older forms and designs was produced, the new type of pottery known as the close style was further developed and became characteristic of the early part of the century, the group of plain wares (the granary style) was introduced and became the prototype followed as far away as Syria and Palestine. The recovery does not seem to have acquired great momentum and as time passed the art of the people declined further until it was brought to an end. These developments in the twelfth century can be explained if conditions in the Argolid, disrupted by internal dissension and fighting, deteriorated further under the progressive pressure of enemy action, and I maintain that the pressure was provided by the bands of people known as the Dorians, by the movement of clans known to the ancients as the Descent of the Herakleidai. Broneer recently has reiterated the view that these Dorians did not march south into the Peloponnesos

at one and the same time,[55] organized in a huge army corps; that they moved southward in small bands or clans over a number of years, periodically devastating the territory until finally they managed to overcome the harassed Mycenaean people and to establish themselves in the land. It seems to me that this view is correct. The constant menace of these periodic infiltrations did not allow the people to achieve a complete recovery from their setback and to develop their cultural activities; the *wanax* of the mighty citadel, after the breakdown of his power, no longer was able to protect them; the menace forced them off the land which was one of the main sources of their wealth and encouraged further emigration to territories beyond the route of incursions, to Achaia, to Kephallenia, to the islands of the Aegean, even to Cyprus where they introduced Chamber Tombs and where now they seem to have played an important part in the life of the island.

The end of the Mycenaean Age does not seem to have come about in the wake of a destructive holocaust, but gradually and almost imperceptibly it moved towards its fate. The end came when the once great and still formidable citadels of Mycenae and Tiryns were stormed or perhaps were taken through the treachery of a few, and their palaces and buildings once again were burned; but this time they were destined to remain in calcined ruins and not to rise again. Exactly when this finish to the drama occurred, we cannot be sure, but it is safe to suggest the third quarter of the twelfth century, the decade around 1120 B.C. People who establish themselves in a territory bring with them their own characteristic elements of culture, and evidence for some of these is apt to survive. Is there any evidence that at the time we postulate the establishment of the Dorians new cultural elements were introduced in the Mycenaean area? It seems that there is. In widespread territories there now appears a type of grave altogether different from the ancestral chamber tombs of the Mycenaeans; a cist grave consisting of a rectangular pit sometimes lined with slabs containing a single body.[56] It is probable that this type of sepulcher was brought by the new settlers, who forced the old inhabitants to flee from their ancestral land in all directions, to seek refuge in the mountainous terrain of Arkadia where the venerable Achaean dialect survived surrounded by Doric-speaking settlers, to islands and coasts beyond the Aegean, or to remain in small numbers among the ruins of their once renowned citadels.

Thus the Dorian invaders, bands of men gradually

---

[54] Desborough, "The End of the Mycenaean Civilization," rev. ed. *CAH*, I and II, p. 5.

[55] *Antiquity*, 30 (1956), pp. 16-17.

[56] This conclusion reached independently and explained in

my third Colver Lecture in November 1961, now finds a good advocate in Desborough, *The Last Mycenaeans*, pp. 231 ff. especially p. 252 and *CAH*, rev. ed. I and II, fasc. 13, pp. 8-11.

moving southwards over a period of years, finally became the masters of the greater part of the Peloponnesos and from their centers of control—Corinth, Argos, Sparta—dominated the conquered territory for centuries. However, the end of the Mycenaean Age and the Dorian Invasion could not have been expected to occur without bequeathing to the scholars problems and difficulties, and the question is still debated whether or not the destruction wrought by the Dorians was so great that it was followed by years of darkness, poverty, and ignorance, as was taught a few years ago. There are those, among whom we find Wace,[57] who now maintain that the destruction was neither so general nor so radical. Whatever the truth of the matter may be, certain cultural elements disappear with the end of the Mycenaean Age; among the most important of these is the bureaucratic monarchical system disclosed by the tablets of Pylos and Knossos, the system of officials and leaders. The system of keeping elaborate records of transactions to which writing was especially devoted was extinguished with the abandonment of the monarchic bureaucracy. As a result perhaps, the class of scribes was eliminated and the art of writing was abandoned. The craftsmanship developed in the construction of palaces and fortifications gradually waned, since the need for such structures was eliminated with the passing of the rulers who inspired and demanded them. The construction of tholos tombs became a forgotten art and so was forgotten the art of decorating with frescoes the interiors of palaces and dwellings. The final collapse of the centralized power of the *wanax* brought about unsettled conditions over the land and the task of preservation became the chief concern of the individual and the community. Apparently Greece, broken into segments, each of which was left to its own limited resources, gradually lapsed into the poverty and ignorance that is at the core of her legends. It was then that conditions were created which gave birth to the belief voiced by Herodotos so many centuries later that "Hellas hath ever had poverty for her companion" (VII, 102). Whether or not we believe that the Dorians destroyed the great Mycenaean centers around 1200 B.C. the fact remains that the culture developed in them persisted for almost a century more, to about 1125 B.C., in a scale of course unworthy of its past, until it gradually faded away into the mist of the proto-historic era.

The elation a scholar feels when he traces the beginnings and the development of a culture to its climax gives way to a mood of sadness when, following its decline step by step, he finally points to the inexorable end. But the scholar of Mycenaean culture is cheered by the knowledge that from the ashes of the Heroic Age there flowered another civilization deeply rooted in the Mycenaean achievement and that this, the Age of Perikles and Sokrates, was to provide the foundation for our western civilization.

57 *Viking*, 1954, p. 222.

CHRONOLOGY, ABBREVIATIONS, AND SELECTED BIBLIOGRAPHY

CHRONOLOGY

HELLADIC: The Bronze Age period of the mainland of Greece from ca. 2500 to ca. 1120 B.C., to be distinguished from the Bronze Age of the island of Crete known as the Minoan period. The Helladic is usually subdivided into the following sub-periods:

Early Helladic = EH = (I, II, III), from ca. 2500 to ca. 1900 B.C.
Middle Helladic = MH = (I and II), from ca. 1900 to ca. 1580 B.C.
Late Helladic = LH = (I, II, III), from ca. 1580 to 1120 B.C.
Late Helladic I = LH I = from ca. 1580 to ca. 1500 B.C.
Late Helladic II = LH II = from ca. 1500 to ca. 1400 B.C.
Late Helladic III A = LH III A = from ca. 1400 to ca. 1300 B.C.
Late Helladic III B = LH III B = from ca. 1300 to ca. 1190 B.C.
Late Helladic III C = LH III C = from ca. 1190 to ca. 1120 B.C.

MYCENAEAN HISTORY AND MYTHOLOGY

17th century B.C., end of	Beginning of the Mycenaean Period
ca. 1650- ca. 1550 B.C.	Grave Circle B. Excavated by the Greek Archaeological Society 1952-1953-1954; proves increasing prosperity.
ca. 1600- ca. 1510 B.C.	Grave Circle A. Excavated by H. Schliemann in 1876. Perhaps earliest primitive palace built on top of citadel.
ca. 1450 B.C.	Begins the great period of expansion and prosperity that lasts to 1200 B.C. Building of the early palaces at Mycenae, Tiryns and Thebes.
ca. 1375 B.C.	First Cyclopean citadel of Tiryns (Proitos?)
ca. 1350-1340 B.C.	First Cyclopean citadel of Mycenae (Perseus?)
ca. 1330 B.C.	Palace construction on large scale: Mycenae, Tiryns, Pylos, Thebes.
13th century B.C.	Expansion and prosperity continues.
ca. 1250 B.C.	Second Cyclopean citadel of Mycenae; the Lion Gate; the Treasury of Atreus. (Atreus rule?)
ca. 1240 B.C.	Second Cyclopean citadel of Tiryns in its last phase. Beginning Cyclopean fortifications of the Akropolis of Athens and of Gla. Palace construction of late phase: Mycenae, Tiryns, Pylos.
Towards end of 13th century B.C.	Northeast expansion of the citadel of Mycenae; building of lower citadel of Tiryns; completion of fortifications of the Akropolis of Athens (addition of tower); construction of underground fountains at Mycenae, Tiryns and Athens.
ca. 1200 B.C.	The Trojan War and the Fall of Troy (Agamemnon).
ca. 1200-1190 B.C.	Destruction of the palace of Nestor at Pylos. Abandonment of sites and widespread destruction of Mycenaean sites. Migrations of Mycenaeans. Prosperity in the islands of the Aegean and Dodekanese.
ca. 1120 B.C.	Final destruction of Mycenae and Tiryns. The Dorian Invasion. End of the Mycenaean era.
480 B.C.	The Mycenaeans take part in the defense of Thermopylai.
479 B.C.	The Mycenaeans and the Tirynthians take part in the battle of Plataia.
ca. 468 B.C.	Mycenae destroyed by the Argives.
ca. 300 B.C.	Mycenae becomes Argive township; repairing of Cyclopean walls.
A.D.	
ca. 150-160	Pausanias visits Orchomenos, Athens, Mycenae and Tiryns.
ca. 300	Mycenae, as a small village, survives still.
1700 on	Western travelers visit Mycenaean sites.
1800-1818	Mycenae's relics pilfered by art collectors and treasure hunters.
1841	The Greek Archaeological Society begins work at Mycenae.
1874	Schliemann tested the citadel of Mycenae by means of trenches.
1876	Schliemann's great discovery of the royal tombs of Mycenae; 5 shaft graves explored in Grave Circle A. Begins excavating Tiryns with the assistance of W. Dörpfeld.

Chronology

1876-1877	Stamatakes exploration of shaft grave VI and the dromos of the Treasury of Atreus.
1877-1902	The Greek Archaeological Society, through C. Tsountas, excavated a good part of the citadel of Mycenae and many of its graves. The "palace of Agamemnon" was then revealed.
1884-1885	Schliemann and Dörpfeld continue the excavation of Tiryns.
1885-1890	The Greek Archaeological Society, through P. Kavvadias and G. Kawerau, systematically excavated the Akropolis of Athens.
1906-1907	Keramopoullos revealed part of the palace of Thebes.
1910-1912	Müller, Dragendorff, and Karo continue the excavation of Tiryns.
1919-1923	A. J. B. Wace continued the exploration of the citadel of Mycenae and its graves.
1922-1930	Swedish excavations at Asine under O. Frödin and A. W. Persson.
1923	Kurt Müller resumed excavations at Tiryns.
1926-1963	Discovery and exploration of tholos and chamber tombs at Dendra.
1931-1938	O. Broneer explored the north side of the Akropolis of Athens.
1936-1939	N. Balanos discovered the Mycenaean tower of the Akropolis of Athens.
1939	Wace began the exploration of the houses of Mycenae.
	C. W. Blegen and K. Kourouniotes began the excavation of the palace of Ano Englianos (the palace of Pylos).
1940-1950	Interruption of the work by World War II.
1950	Wace resumed work at Mycenae.
	The Greek Archaeological Society, through J. Papadimitriou and F. Petsas, began the exploration of Mycenaean houses.
1950-1957	Wace continued his excavations of the houses and early cemetery of Mycenae.
1951-1959	The Greek Service for the Restoration and Preservation of Monuments, under the direction of A. Orlandos and E. Stikas, restored the Tomb of Klytemnestra, the Cyclopean walls and the palace of Mycenae.
Nov. 1951	Discovery of the Second Grave Circle of Mycenae.
1952-1954	Exploration of the Second Grave Circle by the Greek Archaeological Society by John Papadimitriou and an advisory committee of Keramopoullos, Marinatos and Mylonas.
1952	C. W. Blegen resumed his excavations of the Palace of Nestor at Pylos (Ano Englianos), which continue to date.
	S. Marinatos began his exploration of West Messenia and Triphylia, which continue to the present.
1955	S. Iacovides began his excavations of the Mycenaean cemetery of Perati; continued to 1963.
	Threpsiades began his excavations at Gla which continued until his death in 1962.
1956	D. Theocharis began the exploration of the palace of Iolkos.
1958	N. Verdelis began his excavations of the West House of Mycenae, continued to 1961.
1958	Mylonas proceeds with excavations at Mycenae, which continue to the present
1960-1963	Papadimitriou and Taylour continued Wace's excavation of the Citadel House.
1964	Mylonas and Taylour continued the excavation of the Citadel House.
1962	Verdelis explored the underground fountain of Tiryns.
1963	N. Platon and Mrs. Touloupa begin excavations at Thebes, which continue to the present
1965	Verdelis continues excavation of Tiryns

ABBREVIATIONS

AJA	*American Journal of Archaeology*
AO	*Archiv Orientální*
Ath.Mitt.	*Athenische Mitteilungen*
BCH	*Bulletin de correspondance hellénique*
BSA	*Annual of the British School of Archaeology at Athens*
CAH	*Cambridge Ancient History*
CR	*Classical Review*
Ephemeris	Ἀρχαιολογικὴ Ἐφημερίς and Ἐφημερὶς Ἀρχαιολογική
Hesperia	*Hesperia,* Journal of the American School of Classical Studies at Athens
IGForsch	*Indogermanische Forschungen*
Jahrbuch	*Jahrbuch des k. deutschen archäologischen Instituts*
JHS	*Journal of Hellenic Studies*
JIAN	*Journal international d'archéologie numismatique*
MonAnt	*Monumenti Antichi*
OpusArch	*Opuscula Archaeologica*
Praktika	Πρακτικὰ τῆς ἐν Ἀθήναις Ἀρχαιολογικῆς Ἑταιρείας
PAPS	*Proceedings of the American Philosophical Society*
TAPA	*Transactions of the American Philological Association*
TAPS	*Transactions of the American Philosophical Society*

SELECTED BIBLIOGRAPHY

Ålin, P., *Das Ende der mykenischen Fundstatten auf dem griechischen Festland*, Lund, 1962

Bennett, E. L., *The Pylos Tablets*, Princeton, 1951

——, "The Mycenae Tablets," *PAPS*, 97 (1953)

——, *A Minoan Linear B Index*, New Haven, 1953

——, *The Mycenae Tablets II*, Philadelphia, 1958

——, *Nestor*, ed., *Mycenaean Studies*, Madison, 1964

Blegen, C. W., *Korakou, a Prehistoric Settlement near Corinth*, Boston and New York, 1921

——, *Zygouries, a Prehistoric Settlement in the Valley of Cleonae*, Cambridge, Mass., 1928

——, *Prosymna, the Helladic Settlement Preceding the Argive Heraeum*, Cambridge, Mass., 1937

——, *Troy and the Trojans*, London, 1963

——, *The Mycenaean Age*, Cincinnati, 1962. See also Wace-Blegen

Blegen, C. W. *et al.*, *Troy*, I, II, III, IV, Princeton, 1950-58

Blegen, C. W. and Marion Rawson, *The Palace of Nestor at Pylos in Western Messenia, I. The Buildings and Their Contents*, Princeton, 1966

Bossert, H. T. *The Art of Ancient Crete*, London, 1937

Broneer, O., "Athens in the Late Bronze Age," *Antiquity*, 30 (1956)

Cambridge Ancient History, rev. ed., vols. I-II, fascs. 1, 2, 7, 12, 13, 15, 18, 24, 26

Caskey, J. L., "Excavations in Keos," *Hesperia* 31 (1962) to date

Chadwick, J., *The Decipherment of Linear B*, Cambridge, 1958

——, *The Mycenae Tablets III*, Philadelphia, 1963. See also Ventris-Chadwick

Desborough, V. R. d'A., *The Last Mycenaeans and Their Successors*, Oxford, 1964

Dörpfeld, W., "Kretische, mykenische, und homerische Paläste," *Ath.Mitt.*, 30 and 32 (1905 and 1907)

Dow, S., "Minoan Writing," *AJA*, 58 (1954)

——, "The Greeks in the Bronze Age," XIe Congrès international des sciences historiques

Dussaud, R., *Les Civilisations préhelléniques dans le bassin de la mer Égée*, 2nd ed., Paris, 1914

Evans, Sir Arthur, *The Palace of Minos at Knossos*, London, 1921-1935

——, *The Shaft Graves and Beehive Tombs of Mycenae and Their Interrelations*, London, 1929

Fimmen, D., *Die kretisch-mykenische Kultur*, 2nd ed., Leipzig, 1924

Forsdyke, Sir John, *Greece Before Homer*, London, 1956

French, E., "Pottery Groups from Mycenae," *BSA*, 58 (1963)

——, "Late Helladic III A-1 Pottery from Mycenae," *BSA*, 59 (1964)

Frödin, O. and A. W. Persson, *Asine, Results of the Swedish Excavations, 1922-1930*, Stockholm, 1938

Furtwängler, A. and G. Loeschcke, *Mykenische Vasen*, Berlin, 1886

Furumark, A., *Mycenaean Pottery, Analysis and Classification*, Stockholm, 1941

——, *The Chronology of Mycenaean Pottery*, Stockholm, 1941

Glotz, G., *La civilisation égéenne*, Paris, 1953

Heurtley, W. A., "The Grave Stelai of Mycenae," *BSA*, 25 (1921-1923)

Holland, L. B., "Architectural Commentary," (Mycenae), *BSA*, 25 (1921-1923)

Iacovides, S., Ἡ μυκηναϊκὴ ἀκρόπολις τῶν Ἀθηνῶν, Athens, 1962.

Karo, G., "Mykenische Kultur," *Pauly Wissowa*, Supplement VI (1935)

——, *Die Schachtgräber von Mykenai*, Munich, 1930-1933

Kavvadias, P., "Ἀνασκαφὴ ἐν τῇ Ἀκροπόλει," *Ephemeris*, 1886

——, Προϊστορικὴ ἀρχαιολογία, Athens, 1909

Kavvadias, P. and Kawerau, G., Ἡ ἀνασκαφὴ τῆς ἀκροπόλεως ἀπὸ τοῦ 1885 μέχρι τοῦ 1890, Athens, 1906

Keramopoullos, A. D., "Ἡ οἰκία τοῦ Κάδμου," *Ephemeris*, 1909

——, "Θηβαϊκά," *Deltion*, 3 (1917)

Lolling, H. G., *Das Kuppelgrab bei Menidi*, Athens, 1880

Lorimer, H. L., *Homer and the Monuments*, London, 1950

Marinatos, S., "Numerous Years of Joyful Life from Mycenae," *BSA*, 46 (1951)

——, "Περὶ τοὺς νέους βασιλικοὺς τάφους τῶν Μυκηνῶν," Γέρας Ἀντωνίου Κεραμοπούλλου

——, "Der 'Nestorbecher' aus dem IV. Schachtgrab von Mykenai," Festschrift Bernhard Schweitzer, Stuttgart, 1954

——, "Excavations Near Pylos," *Antiquity*, 31 (1957)

——, "Excavations in Messenia and Triphylia," *Praktika*, 1952 to date

Marinatos, S. and M. Hirmer, *Crete and Mycenae*, London, 1960

Matz, F., *Kreta, Mykene, Troja*, Stuttgart, 1956

——, *Crete and Early Greece*, London, 1962

Moon, B. E., *Mycenaean Civilization* (Bibliographical summaries), London, 1957, 1961

Müller, K., *Tiryns, III, Die Architektur der Burg und des Palastes*, Augsburg, 1930. Cf. also Vols. I, II, and IV

Mylonas, G. E., "Homeric and Mycenaean Burial Customs," *AJA*, 52 (1948)

——, "The Cult of the Dead in Helladic Times," *Studies Presented to David Moore Robinson*, I, St. Louis, 1951

——, "The Figured Mycenaean Stelai," *AJA*, 55 (1951)

——, "Μυκηναϊκὰ εἰδώλια," *Yearbook*, School of Philosophy University of Athens, 1954-1955

——, "Seated and Multiple Mycenaean Figurines in the National Museum of Athens," in *The Aegean and the Near East*, New York, 1956

——, *Ancient Mycenae: The Capital City of Agamemnon*, Princeton, 1957

——, *Eleusis and the Eleusinian Mysteries*, Princeton, 1961

——, "Luvian Invasions of Greece," *Hesperia* 31 (1962)

——, *The Walls and Gates of Mycenae*, Ephemeris, 1962 (1966)

——, *Grave Circle B of Mycenae*, Lund, 1964

——, "Excavations at Mycenae," *Praktika*, 1958 to date

——, "Priam's Troy and the Date of Its Fall," *Hesperia* 33 (1964)

——, "The East Wing of the Palace of Mycenae," *Hesperia* 35 (1966)

Mylonas, G. E. and J. Papadimitriou, "The New Shaft Graves of Mycenae," *Archaeology*, 5 (1952)

——, "The New Grave Circle of Mycenae," *Archaeology*, 8 (1955)

Nilsson, M. L., *The Minoan-Mycenaean Religion and Its Survival in Greek Religion*, 2nd ed., Lund, 1950

——, *Homer and Mycenae*, London, 1933

——, *The Mycenaean Origin of Greek Mythology*, Berkeley, 1932

Noack, F., *Homerische Paläste*, Leipzig, 1903

Oikonomos, G. P., *Volume in Memoriam G. P. Oikonomos, Ephemeris*, 1953-1954

Page, D. L., *History and the Homeric Iliad*, Berkeley, 1959

Palmer, L. R., *Achaeans and Indo-Europeans*, inaugural lecture, Oxford, 1955

——, *Mycenaeans and Minoans*, London, 1961

——, *The Interpretation of Mycenaean Greek Texts*, Oxford, 1963

Papadimitriou, J., "Excavations at Mycenae," *Praktika*, 1951-1954. See also Mylonas-Papadimitriou

Pendlebury, J. D. S., *Aegyptiaca*, Cambridge (England), 1930

Perrot, G. and C. Chipiez, *Histoire de l'art dans l'antiquité: VI. La Grèce primitive, l'art mycénien*, Paris, 1894

Persson, A. W., *Royal Tombs at Dendra Near Midea*, Lund, 1931

——, *New Tombs at Dendra Near Midea*, Lund, 1942. See also Frödin-Persson

——, *The Religion of Greece in Prehistoric Times*, Los Angeles, 1942

Pickard, C., *Les religions préhelléniques*, Paris, 1948

Pryce, F. N., *British Museum Catalogue of Greek and Roman Sculpture*, I, Part I, London, 1928

Reichel, W., *Homerische Waffen*, Vienna, 1901

——, "Die Schachtgräber-Terasse von Mykenai während Schliemanns Ausgrabung," *Antike Denkmäler*, II, pls. 46, 49

Robertson, D. S., "New Light on the Façade of the Treasury of Atreus," *JHS*, 61 (1941)

Rodenwaldt, G., "Mykenische Studien I. Die Fussböden des Megarons von Mykenai," *Jahrbuch*, 34 (1919)

——, "Die Wandgemälde von Tiryns," *Ath.Mitt.*, 36 (1911)

——, "Votivpinax aus Mykenai," *Ath.Mitt.*, 43 (1918)

——, *Der Fries des Megarons von Mykenai*, Halle, 1921

Schachermeyr, F., *Die ältesten Kulturen Griechenlands*, Stuttgart, 1955

Schliemann, H., *Mycenae: A Narrative of Researches and Discoveries at Mycenae and Tiryns*, New York, 1880

——, *Orchomenos*, Leipzig, 1881

——, *Tiryns. The Prehistoric Palace of the Kings of Tiryns*, New York, 1885

Schuchhardt, C., *Schliemann's Excavations*, London and New York, 1891

Stais, V., *Collection Mycénienne du Musée National*, Athens, 1911

——, "Περὶ τῆς χρήσεως Μυκηναϊκῶν τινων κοσμημάτων," *Ephemeris*, 1907

Steffen, Captain H., *Karten von Mykenai*, Berlin, 1884

Stubbings, F. H., *Mycenaean Pottery from the Levant*, Cambridge, 1951

Taylour, Lord W., *Mycenaean Pottery in Italy*, Cambridge, 1958

——, *The Mycenaeans*, Cambridge, 1964

Thiersch, F., "Die Tholos des Atreus zu Mykenai," *Ath.Mitt.*, 4 (1879)

Thomas, H. "The Acropolis Treasure from Mycenae," *BSA*, 39 (1938-1939)

Tiryns, *Die Ergebnisse der Ausgrabungen des Instituts*, Vols. I-IV

Tsountas, C., "'Ανασκαφαὶ Μυκηνῶν, *Praktika*, 1886

——, "'Αρχαιότητες ἐκ Μυκηνῶν," *Ephemeris*, 1887

——, "'Ανασκαφαὶ τάφων ἐν Μυκήναις," *Ephemeris*, 1888

———, " Ἐκ Μυκηνῶν," *Ephemeris*, 1891

———, "Γραπτὴ στήλη ἐκ Μυκηνῶν," *Ephemeris*, 1896

———, "Κεφαλὴ ἐκ Μυκηνῶν," *Ephemeris*, 1902

———, "Μυκῆναι καὶ Μυκηναῖος Πολιτισμός," Athens, 1893

———, "Zu einigen mykenischen Streitfragen," *Jahrbuch*, 1895

Tsountas, C. and J. I. Manatt, *The Mycenaean Age*, London, 1897

Valmin, M. N., *The Swedish Messenia Expedition*, Lund, 1938

Ventris, M. and J. Chadwick, "Evidence for Greek Dialect in the Mycenaean Archives," *JHS*, 73 (1953)

———, *Documents in Mycenaean Greek*, Cambridge, 1956

Vermeule, E. T., *Greece in the Bronze Age*, Chicago, 1964

Wace, A. J. B., "The Date of the Treasury of Atreus," *JHS*, 64 (1926)

———, *Chamber Tombs at Mycenae*, Oxford, 1932

———, "The Treasury of Atreus," *Antiquity*, 14 (1940)

———, *Mycenae. An Archaeological History and Guide*, Princeton, 1949

———, "Excavations at Mycenae, 1939," *BSA*, 45 (1950)

———, "Mycenae, 1939-1952," *BSA*, 48 (1953)

———, "Mycenae, Preliminary Report on the Excavations of 1953," *BSA*, 49 (1954)

———, "The Tholos Tombs at Mycenae: Structural Analysis," in A. Persson, *Royal Tombs at Dendra*

———, "The Last Days of Mycenae," in the *Aegean and the Near East*, New York, 1956

Wace, A. J. B. *et al.*, "Excavations at Mycenae," *BSA*, 24-25 (1919-21 and 1921-23), 49 (1954), 50 (1955), 51 (1956), and 52 (1957)

Wace, A. J. B. and C. W. Blegen, "The Pre-Mycenaean Pottery of the Mainland," *BSA*, 22 (1916-1918)

———, "Middle Helladic Tombs," *Symbolae Osloenses*, 9 (1930)

———, "Pottery as Evidence for Trade and Colonisation in the Aegean Bronze Age," *Klio*, 1939

Wace, A. J. B. and F. H. Stubbings, ed., *A Companion to Homer*, London, 1962

Webster, T. B. L., *From Mycenae to Homer*, London, 1958

Weinberg, S., "Aegean Chronology," *AJA*, 51 (1947)

INDEX

abstraction, in designs, 189; in gem carvings, 190

Achaeans, in Hittite documents, 4; expedition of, 4, 6, 45, 215ff; capital of, 5; return of, 90; long-haired, 102; name of, 212

Achaia, equated with Ahhiyavā, 4; greaves from, 92n; tholos tombs of, 120; inlaid dagger from, 195; Mycenaeans in, 232

Acharnai-Menidi, tholos tomb of, 168, 172; discussion of evidence from, 181-84; no cult of dead proved, 184

Achilles, promises to, 6; chariot of, 94; dominion of, 226

Addler, F., on additions to Cyclopean walls, 19f

administrative system, *see* political system

adyton, shrine of Keos, 146f

Aegaleon, Mt., 52

Aegean sea, conditions in, 230f; islands of, 232

Aegina, 45; pendant from, 152

Aeschylos, *Agamemnon*, 225

afterlife, conceptions of, 15, 113

Agamemnon, king of Mycenae, 6; domain of, 6, 7, 34n; grave of, 7, 90, 96, 124; expedition against Troy, 8, 213, 217f, 224ff; prophecy of, 45; mask of, 92; reign of, 175. *See also* palace of

agate, beads and gems of, 127, 138, 152, 164, 190; pommel of, 127

Aghia Triada, sealings from, 124; steatite vase, 163; sarcophagus of, 166, 168, 171, 176ff; frescoes, 177

Aghia Eirene, *see* Keos

Aghios Ioannes, tumulus of, 110

Aghios Kosmas, fortification wall, 44; houses of, 85; tub-burials, 177

Aglauros, cave of, 40f

agora, of Gla, 84f; of Athens, 9

Ahhiyavā, in Hittite documents, 4; domain, 175; Mycenaean state of, 199, 211f; location of, 213

Aigeus, king of Athens, 9

Aigisthos, rule and death of, 6, 7, 226. *See also* tholos tomb of Aigisthos

aithousa, of palaces, 46f, 53, 58, 60, 62, 67f, 78

Åkerstrom, A. B., on Berbati, 220

Akona, sacrifice at, 181

Akrisios, king of Argos, 5

alabaster, slabs from Tiryns, 47; pommels, 101; vessel of, 107

Alexiou, S., on goddess of blessing, 115n, 154n

Ålin, P., on destroyed sites, 218, 221

Alkinoos, palace of, 11, 47n, 173

almond stones, *see* conglomerate

Alpheios, 8

altars, of Tiryns, 46, 162, 163; square, 57, 140f, 146, 151, 162; built, from Mycenae, 62, 162; portable, 70; of Circle A, 94f, 163, 178; of Lykosoura, 144; of Berbati, 146; with incurved sides, 157, 162, 172-75

Amandry, P., 220

amber, beads of, 93, 104; from the Baltic, 104

amethyst, for beads and gems, 105, 126, 138, 152, 190

Amnisos, frescoes from, 175

Amphion, builder of Thebes, 9

amulets, of faïence, 104

amygdaloid gems, 152

Amyklai, sacred enclosure, 148; figurines, 155

ancestors of Mycenaeans, 190

Andronikos, M., theory of social revolution, 231

aniconic, indication of divine essence, 148, 161, 173, 175; tendencies in MH times, 157; in religion of mainland, 160

animals, bones of, 94, 99, 116; pelts of, 100, 109; mythical, 101, 124, 154, 172; sacrificial, 116f, 140, 158, 163ff; on rings and gems, 141, 149, 151; dogs, 116f, 128f; horses, 116; bulls, 140, 163f; goats, 149, 164, 166, 172n; sheep, 149, hornless heads of, 150; with severed heads, 158; boars, 164f; rams, 164, 166; hogs and sows, 166; ox, 166; ewes, 166

Ano Englianos, palace of, 8, 9, 46, 50, 52, 53f, 192, 220, 227; periodic destructions, 51; final destruction, 58. *See also*, palace of Nestor

antithetic groups, on rings, 172; common theme, 174

Aphrodite, peribolos of, 40; figurines of, 139; on rings, 150

Apollo, cave of, 40; sanctuary at Delphi, 148; *Paiawon*, 159; altar and sacred tree of, 163; Homeric hymn to, 170; at Delos, 184

Apollodoros on Perseus, 6

aqueducts, 31, 32, 86ff, 188

Archaic period, temple of at Mycenae, 72

archer, from Knossos, 102; on inlaid dagger, 194

Argive, plain, 5, 34; township at Mycenae, 7; history of, 33; destruction of Mycenae, 16, 33

Argolid, occupied by Indo-Europeans, 3; controlled, 6, 7; citadels in, 35, 231; importance of, 213, 220; destructions in, 218, 221, 228f, 239; roads in, 224; depopulation of, 214, 232; conditions in LH III C, 232

Argonautic expedition, 4, 84

Argos, leadership of, 4, 5; kings of, 5; controlled by Mycenae, 6, 34, 35; rivalry in, 7; road to, 28; horse in tomb of, 116; gem from, 165; in LH III C times, 230f

Arkadia, 5, 7; ships to, 6; refugees in, 232

Arkhanes, gem from, 164

army led by *lawagetas*, 210

Arne equated with Gla, 10, 43

arrowheads, 92, 94, 102, 106, 197f

Artemis, on tablets, 159; as Mistress of Animals, 160; temple of in Delos, 185

Artemision in Delos, 148, 170

artists, quarters at Mycenae, 73; Mycenaean, 187, 191, 193; Minoan, 188, 191, 193

Arzava, rebellion of, 216

ascent to summit of Mycenae, 27, 73f

ashes, in cave of Circle A, 94; in cist of Vapheio, 126

ashlar, masonry at Mycenae, 16f, 20, 24, 33, 64, 78; represented on gold foil, 138

Asia Minor, beginnings of Indo-Europeans in, 3; Mycenaean settlements in, 4; Neleids in, 8; as land of Cyclopes, 34; fortifications in, 45; lions from, 175; shipwrecks off coast of, 198; and the Hittites, 216f, 231. *See also* Ahhiyavā

Asine, citadel of, 44; finds from, 103, 116; shrine of, 146, 155, 160, 165f, 170, 209; niches in tombs, 179; cemetery, 180; inscribed bowl from, 203; in LH III C times, 230f

Askalon, relations with, 4

Aspis, walls of, 45

asprochoma, used in Cyclopean walls, 19, 21f. *See also* plesia

Assuwa, league of, 216f

Åstrom, P., on Lion Gate relief, 173n; finds of, 92n, 198

Athena, visits Athens, 4, 9; temples of, 59, 83; tree of, 150; named in tablets, 159f; palladium, 160; in association with birds, 176

Athens, Mycenaean, 4, 8, 170; escapes destruction, 4, 9, 43, 45; Neleids find refuge in, 8; legends of, 9; chamber tombs, 9, 111; demes of, 11; citadel of, 35-43; officials of, 168f; in LH III B times, 218-23, 227f

    Akropolis of, palace on, 9, 46, 83; stepped passage, 35ff, 39f; gates, 36-39, 40; west tower, 37, 39, 41; guard rooms, 39; temporary shelters, 39f; fountain on, 40ff, 187; date of fortifications, 41; bronze hoards, 77

Atreus, King of Mycenae, 4, 6, 7, 109, 175, 226

Attika, occupied by Indo-Europeans, 3; Eurystheus killed in, 6; graves from, 111, 120; finds, 154; in LH III C times, 230

Attis, grave of, 141

Aulis, in Boiotia, 4

Babylonian, conception of heavenly bodies, 158; origin of daemons, 168; use of rock crystal, 191

baetyls, representation on rings, 140f, 143, 145, 148f, 161

Balanos, N., tower of Akropolis, 9, 37, 39

balconies, in palaces, 53, 55

baldric, from Grave Lambda, 106

balustrades, of the court of Mycenae, 63

bands, gold band from shaft graves, 92, 93, 100, 103-9

banquets, held in the megaron, 47

base, of stelai, 94, 107f; pyramidal base from Mycenae, 171

basileus, on tablets, 168, 169, 206, 207

Bass, G. F., on shipwrecks, 4n, 198n

1. Mycenae. Restored northwest corner of citadel

2. Tiryns. Ramp to east entrance

3. Tiryns. West section of circuit walls with rounded bastions of postern gate (PG) after restoration

4. Tiryns. Postern gate after restoration

5. Gallery of Tiryns

6. Tiryns. Entrance below wall to south underground passage to water springs

7. Tiryns. Vaulted passage to water springs

retaining wall. (7) Postern gate

8b. Mycenae. General view of citadel after restoration

9. Mycenae. Air view of citadel from southwest

10. Mycenae. Cyclopean construction

11. Mycenae. Court in front of Lion Gate: (P) Polygonal construction

12. Mycenae. Vaulted room attached to north Cyclopean wall

13. Mycenae. Lion Gate

14. Mycenae. Threshold and west doorpost of Lion Gate

15. Mycenae. Threshold of Lion Gate

16. Mycenae. Relief over Lion Gate

17. Mycenae. Postern gate, exterior view after restoration

18. Mycenae. Postern gate, interior view

19. Mycenae. Sally port in northeast extension of citadel walls, exterior view

20. Mycenae. Sally port in north Cyclopean wall after restoration

21. Mycenae. Restoration in progress along north Cyclopean wall.
(PG) Postern gate

22. Mycenae. North Cyclopean wall founded on rock

23a. Mycenae. Sherds from north Cyclopean wall

23b. Mycenae. Sherds from west Cyclopean wall (fragments of
figurines in lower left corner)

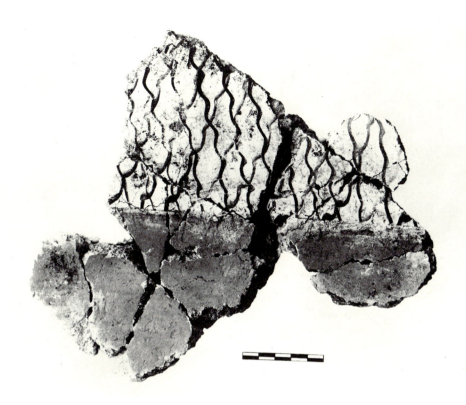

24. Mycenae 1965. Fragments of fresco and tables of offerings
from citadel

25. Mycenae 1958. Threshold of Lion Gate revealed

26. Mycenae. 1958. West end of threshold block of Lion Gate

27. Mycenae 1958. Threshold of Lion Gate with inner face on south side revealed

28. Mycenae. West Cyclopean wall, showing foundation stones set in clay

29. Mycenae 1958. Threshold of postern gate revealed

30. Mycenae 1958. Northeast turn of north Cyclopean wall (N) and later extension

31. Mycenae. Southeast corner of south Cyclopean wall, showing attachment of south wall of northeast extension

32. Mycenae 1962. Southwest section of citadel:
(A) West Cyclopean wall. (B) Cyclopean wall TW.
(C) Area of southwest staircase

33. Mycenae. The great ramp

34. Mycenae 1959. Foundation of ramp set on top of broken section of slabs of parapet in Circle A

35. Mycenae 1959. Trench of great ramp showing Ramps 1 to 4

36. Mycenae 1962. Doorways to Rooms 1 and 2 from Corridor B and Stairway B

38. Mycenae 1961. Handle in form of bull (?) on rim of painted phiale of L H III C style

37. Mycenae 1962. Corridors (C and D) and stairway (D) along north Cyclopean wall (NCW)

39. Mycenae. Passage cut obliquely through north Cyclopean wall to the underground cistern

40. Mycenae. Entrance to the passage to underground cistern as seen from inside

41. Mycenae. Lower staircase to underground cistern

42. Mycenae 1964. Entrance to underground cistern: (SP) North sally port. (R) Retaining wall

43. Mycenae 1964. Ramp leading to north sally port

44. Mycenae 1964. Remains of Building A in northeast extension. Upper left corner: pithos room

45. Mycenae 1964. Building B in northeast extension: (W) Entrance to underground cistern.
(R) Retaining wall of cistern

46. Athens. Fragment of west Cyclopean wall of Akropolis with Parthenon in background

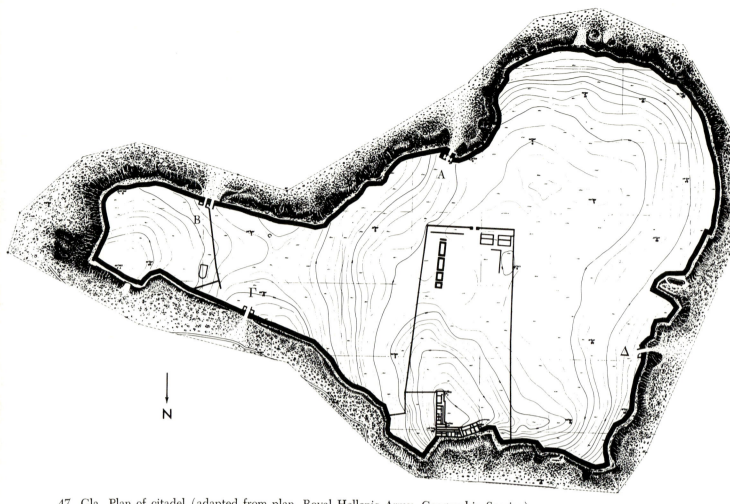

47. Gla. Plan of citadel (adapted from plan, Royal Hellenic Army, Geographic Service)

48. Gla. The citadel from the air

49. Gla. South circuit wall

50. Gla. North gate

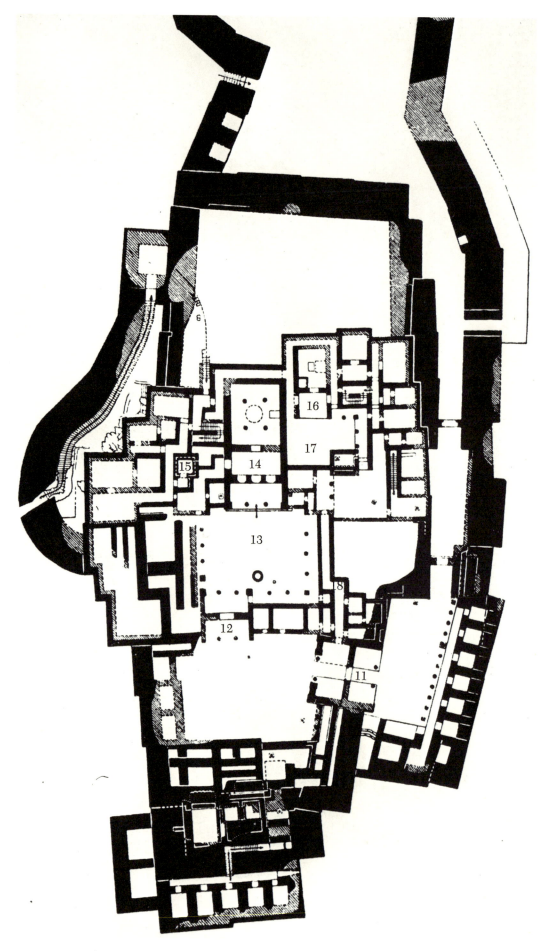

51. Tiryns. Ground plan of palace (after Müller)

52. Pylos. General view of main insula
53. Pylos. Northeast section of main insula seen from northwest

54. Pylos. Southeast section of main insula

55. Pylos. Bathroom

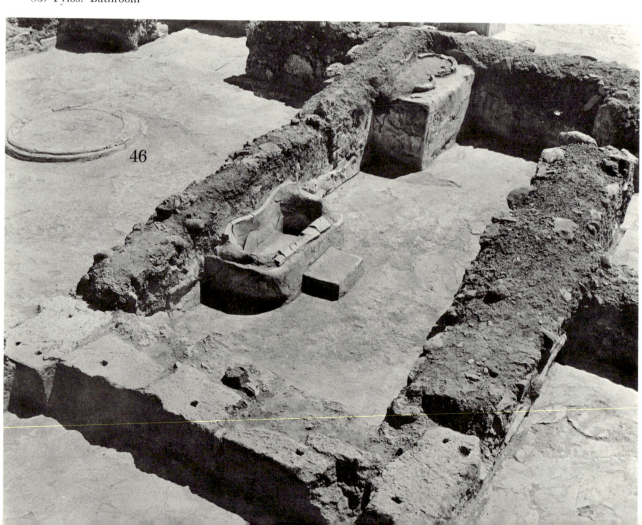

56. Mycenae 1963. General view of palace from Mt. Zara after restoration:
(53) Court. (57) Megaron. (14) Remains of the summit.

57. Mycenae. General view of megaron and court (53) from southwest

58. Mycenae. *Aithousa* from south

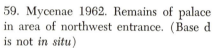

59. Mycenae 1962. Remains of palace in area of northwest entrance. (Base d is not *in situ*)

60. Mycenae 1962. Two conglomerate bases in south portico of propylon

61. Mycenae 1962. Stairway S with fragment of threshold in position

62. Mycenae 1959. Preserved steps of north staircase with cuttings on rock for terrace walls (C)

63. Mycenae 1959. Cyclopean retaining wall (C) of Ramp E to northwest entrance

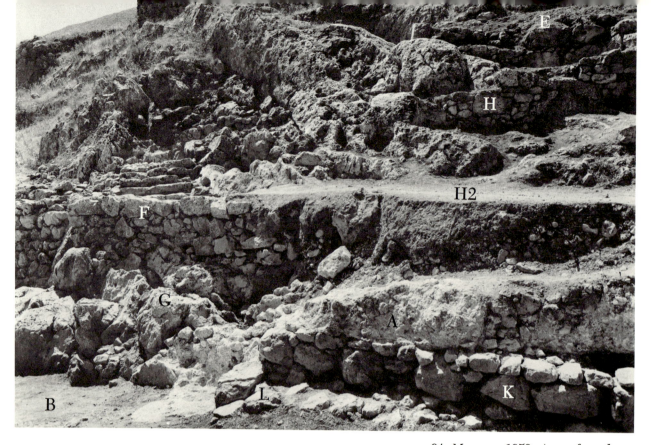

64. Mycenae 1959. Area of north staircase: (A) The end of Main Road A from Lion Gate. (B) The end of Road B from postern gate. (F) Wall built across width of north staircase. (G) Rock foundation of lower section of staircase after demolition. (H) Hellenistic structures. (H2) Hellenistic path. (K) Retaining wall of Main Road A. (L) Foundation of retaining wall

65. Mycenae 1961. Main Road A

66. Mycenae 1961. North (N) and south (S) retaining walls of Main Road A, with Hellenistic structure (H) above

67. Mycenae 1959. Hoard of bronzes in retaining wall of Main Road A

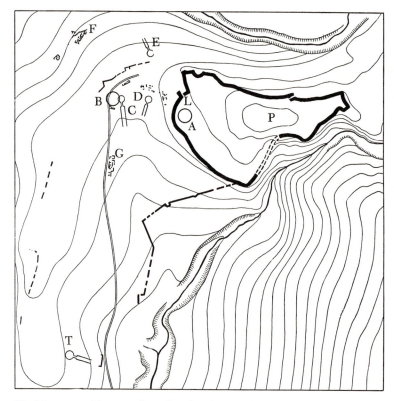

68. Mycenae. Topographic sketch of citadel and its environs:
(A) Grave Circle A. (B) Grave Circle B. (C) Tomb of Klytemnestra.
(D) Tomb of Aigisthos. (E) Tomb of the Lions. (F) House of the
Wine Merchant. (G) House of Oil Merchant, etc. (L) Lion Gate.
(P) Palace. (T) Treasury of Atreus

69. Mycenae. Air view of the citadel and area west of Lion Gate:
(E) Tomb of Lions. (G) House of Oil Merchant, etc. (P) Palace.
(T) Treasury of Atreus. (Z) Parking Lot

70. Mycenae 1962. Panaghitsa Hill showing Treasury of Atreus (left) and House I (behind pines)

71. Mycenae 1962. House I: Broken vessels and remains of flue around hearth. Skeleton of woman on threshold

72. Mycenae 1962. House I. Characteristic vases

73. Mycenae 1962. House I: Central room with hearth

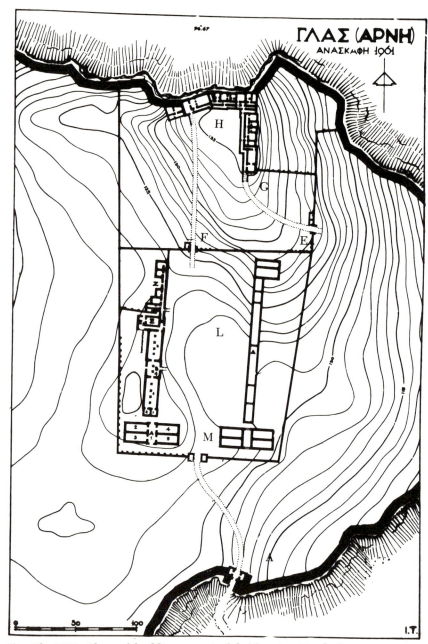

74. Gla 1961. Plans of buildings on citadel (drawing Travlos)

75. Gla. Columnar hall of so-called agora

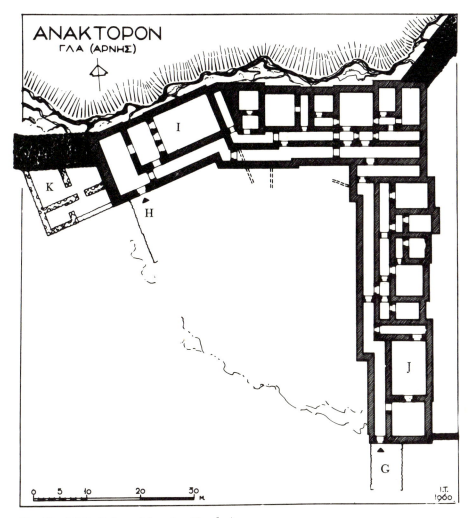

ΑΝΑΚΤΟΡΟΝ
ΓΛΑ (ΑΡΝΗΣ)

76. Gla 1960. Palace (drawing Travlos)

77. Gla. General view of ruins of palace

78. Mycenae. Roadway below north wall showing marks of chariot wheels

79. Mycenae 1962. Retaining wall and culvert, known today as *lykotroupi*, of Road 1.

80. Mycenae 1962. Retaining wall of Road 1

81. Mycenae. Grave Circle A, with view of Argive plain

82. Mycenae. Detail of Grave Circle A: Retaining wall
(B) of parapet of slabs (A) and below original circular
wall (C) with west Cyclopean wall (D) beyond

83. Mycenae. Grave Circle A: Grave found by
Papadimitriou, cut in rock

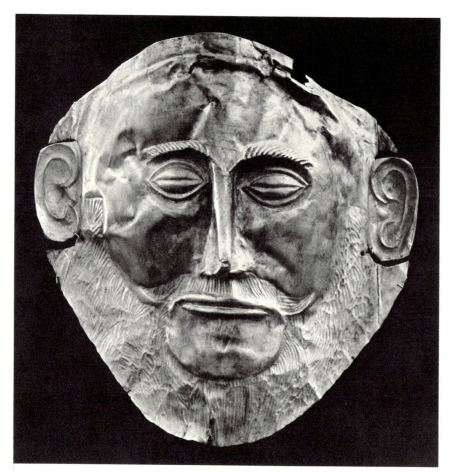

84. Mycenae. Grave Circle A: Gold mask from Grave v

85. Mycenae. Grave Circle A: Gold goblet from Grave IV

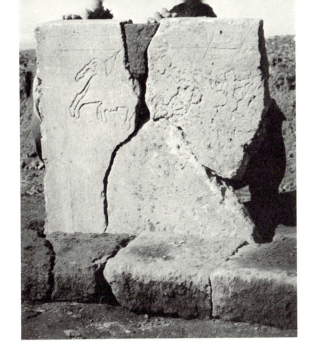

86. Mycenae. Grave Circle B: Segment of parapet wall

87. Mycenae. Stele over Grave Alpha

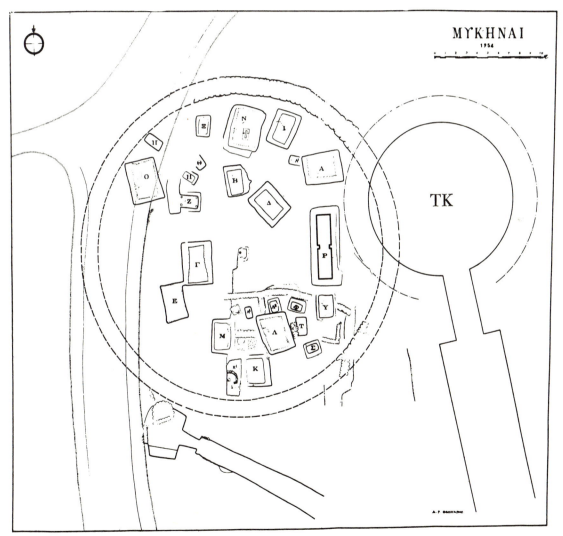

88. Mycenae. Plan of Grave Circle B: Tomb of Klytemnestra (TK) (drawn by D. Theochares)

89. Mycenae. Contents of Grave Eta

90. Mycenae. Contents of Grave Gamma

92. Mycenae. Grave Circle B:
Contents of Grave Iota

91. Mycenae. Contents of Grave Nu

93. Mycenae. Grave Circle B: Detail of gold band decorated in repoussé from Grave Omikron

94. Mycenae. Grave Circle B: Two views of gold cup from Grave Nu

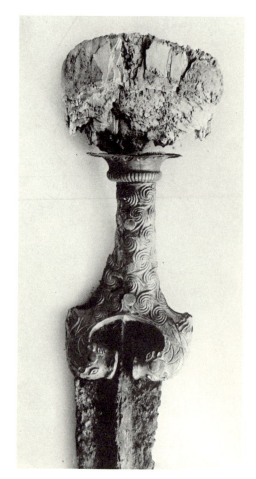

95. Butterfly design on sword blade, possibly covered originally with gold foil

96. Sword from Grave Delta

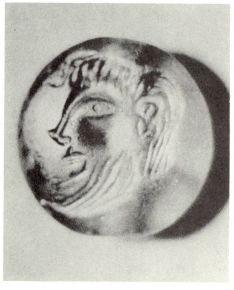

98. Amethyst bead with portrait of Mycenaean

97. Electrum mask from Grave Gamma

95-99. MYCENAE. GRAVE CIRCLE B

99. Rock crystal bowl from Grave Omicron

100. Contents of Grave Upsilon

101. Gold rosette from Grave Omikron

100-103. MYCENAE. GRAVE CIRCLE B

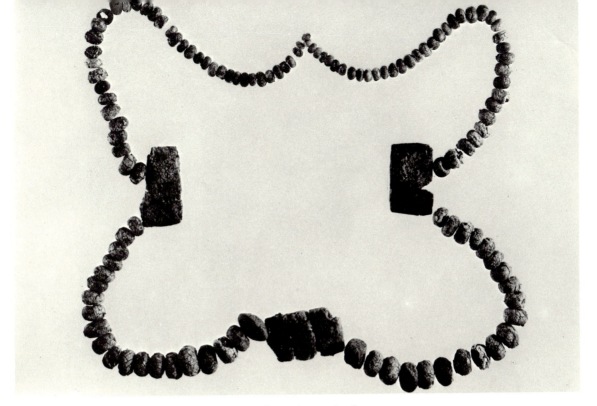

102. Amber necklace from Grave Omikron

103. Grave Rho

104. Mycenae. Grave Circle B: Stele over Grave Gamma as found and as reassembled

105. Mycenae. Grave Circle B: Fragments of stele over Grave Nu

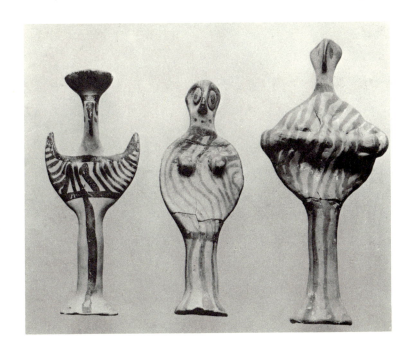

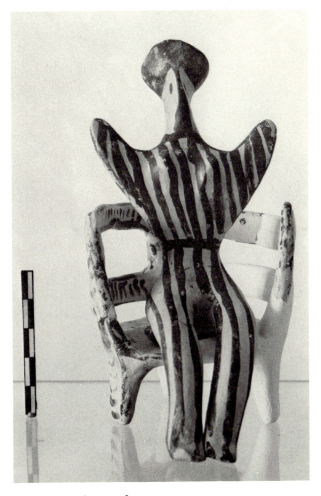

106-109. Mycenae. Terra-cotta figurines from chamber tombs

110. Eleusis. West cemetery: Burial of mother and child, with figurines of ϕ type by child

111. Marathon. Skeletons of horses found by Papadimitriou in *dromos* of tholos tomb

112. Mycenae. Treasury of Atreus

113. Mycenae. Vault of Treasury of Atreus with door to side chamber

114. Mycenae. Façade of Treasury of Atreus: Restoration of the decoration after
Wace, Marinatos, and Mylonas (drawing Roudebush)

115. Mycenae. Tomb of Klytemnestra

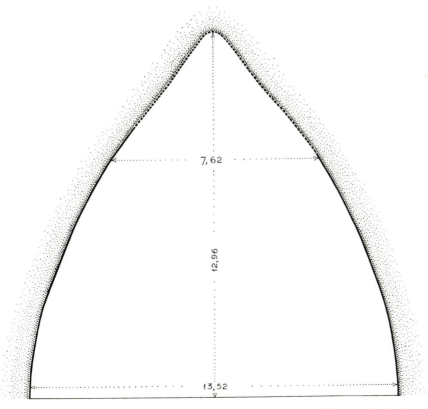

7,62

12,96

13,52

116. Mycenae. Tomb of Klytemnestra, section of tholos (drawing Stikas)

117. Mycenae. Gem with Goddess of Blessing

118-119. Attika. Clay figurine in collection of Mme. Stathatou

120. Vapheio. Gold cup

121. Midea-Dendra. Gold cup from grave of king

122. Mycenae. Grave Circle A: Articles in gold foil

Ring 2

Ring 16

Ring 10

Ring 15

Ring 12

Ring 18

123. Representations on gold rings

Ring 3

43

Ring 9

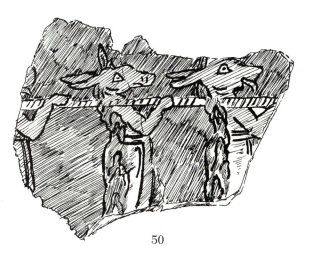

50

42

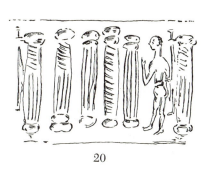

20

21

44

124. Representations on rings and gems. No. 50 fragment of fresco

34

32

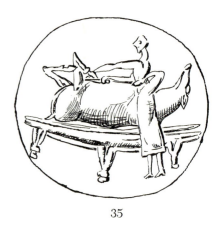

35

40

31

Ring 1

Ring 8

41

125. Representations on rings and gems

25

26

27

22

23

24

28

29

30

126. Representations on gems and glass plaques

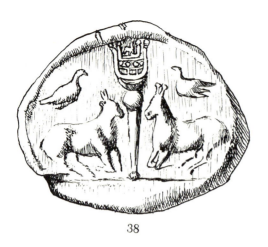

Ring 13

38

Ring 4

Ring 6

37

36

127. Representations on rings and gems

128. Mycenae 1962. Figurine from the citadel

130. Mycenae. Ivory group, showing hole for attachment on base

129. Mycenae. Ivory group

131. Mycenae. Painted plaster tablet

132. Mycenae. Plaster head

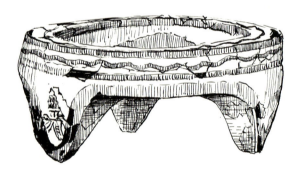

133. Mycenae. Clay altar (after Wace)

134. Crete. Sarcophagus of Aghia Triada

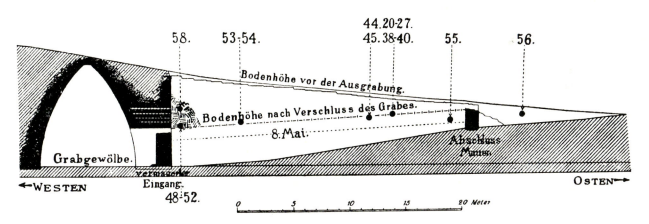

135. Tholos tomb of Acharnai-Menidi, cross section (after Wolters)

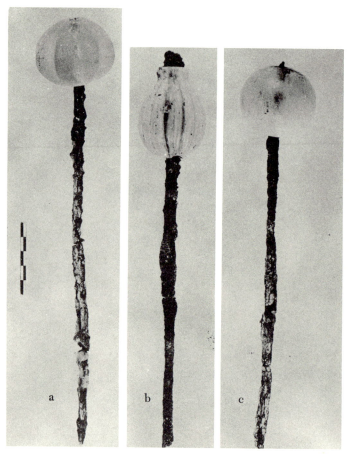

136. Mycenae. Grave Omikron: Pins with
rock crystal heads

137. Pylos. Crested griffin on royal seal of gold

138. Mycenae. Grave Circle B:
Part of bracelet from Grave
Omikron

139. Mycenae. Grave Circle A: Restored wooden box from Grave v with repoussé decoration

140. Mycenae. Grave Circle A: Inlaid dagger
blade from Grave IV

141. Athens. Agora excavations: Ivory pyxis

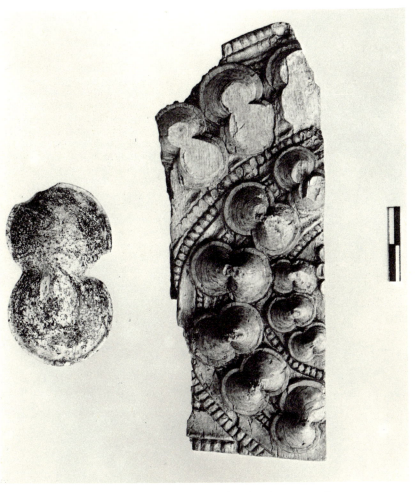

142. Mycenae 1964. Destruction level: Fragment of carved ivory plaque and shield of faïence

143. Mycenae. Ivory tusk covered with relief decoration, found by Tsountas

144. Mycenae 1959. Bronze knives from the hoard of Main Road A

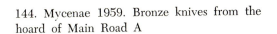

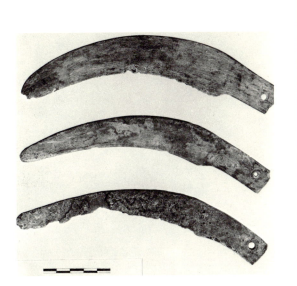

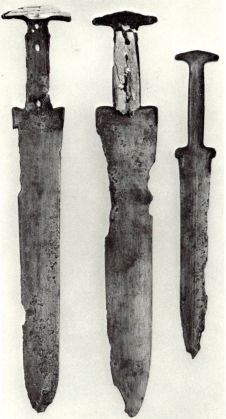

145. Dendra. Bronze corselet

146. Mycenae. Crushed vessels of lead and clay from northeast extension

147. Late Helladic I pottery (drawing by Papaeliopoulos after Wace and Blegen)

148. Late Helladic II pottery. Amphora of palace style (a); squat alabastron (b); Ephyrean goblet (c) (drawing by Papaeliopoulos after Wace and Blegen)

149. Late Helladic III A (a, b, c), III B (d), and III C (e) pottery (drawing by Papaeliopoulos after Wace and Blegen)

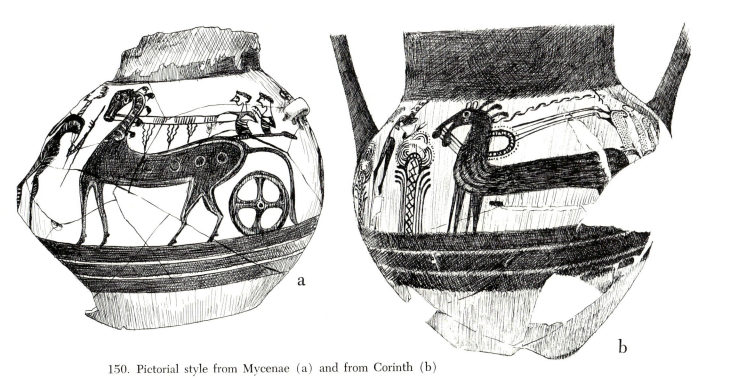

150. Pictorial style from Mycenae (a) and from Corinth (b)

151. Perati. Vases of the close style, L H III C, from the cemetery (after Iacovides)

152. Perati. Bowl from Grave 5

153. Mycenae. Tablet